REDESCRIBING CHRISTIAN ORIGINS

Society of Biblical Literature

Symposium Series

Christopher R. Matthews,
Editor

Number 28

REDESCRIBING CHRISTIAN ORIGINS

REDESCRIBING CHRISTIAN ORIGINS

Edited by
Ron Cameron and Merrill P. Miller

Society of Biblical Literature
Atlanta

REDESCRIBING CHRISTIAN ORIGINS

Copyright © 2004 by the Society of Biblical Literature

All rights reserved. No part of this work may be reproduced or transmitted in any form or by any means, electronic or mechanical, including photocopying and recording, or by means of any information storage or retrieval system, except as may be expressly permitted by the 1976 Copyright Act or in writing from the publisher. Requests for permission should be addressed in writing to the Rights and Permissions Office, Society of Biblical Literature, 825 Houston Mill Road, Atlanta, GA 30329 USA.

Cover photo of the leaf of Papyrus 46 containing 2 Cor. 11:33–12:9 courtesy of the Papyrology Collection, Graduate Library, University of Michigan.

Library of Congress Cataloging-in-Publication Data

Redescribing Christian origins / edited by Ron Cameron and Merrill P. Miller.
    p. cm. — (Society of Biblical Literature symposium series ; no. 28)
  Includes bibliographical references and indexes.
  ISBN 1-58983-088-1 (alk. paper)
    1. Christianity—Origin—Congresses. I. Cameron, Ron. II. Miller, Merrill P. III. Symposium series (Society of Biblical Literature) ; no. 28.
  BR129.R43 2004
  270.1—dc22   2004004747

12 11 10 09 08 07 06 05 04   5 4 3 2 1

Printed in the United States of America on acid-free, recycled paper conforming to ANSI/NISO Z39.48-1992 (R1997) and ISO 9706:1994 standards for paper permanence.

In memory of Andy and Lena Cameron

and

To my mother, Ruth Miller,
and in memory of my father, Arthur Miller,
and my brother, Kerry Miller

Contents

Abbreviations xi

Introduction: Ancient Myths and Modern Theories of
    Christian Origins
    Ron Cameron and Merrill P. Miller 1

Part 1: Alternate Beginnings: The Sayings Gospel Q and the *Gospel of Thomas*

Introduction to the Papers from the Third Year of
    the Consultation
    Merrill P. Miller 33

The Schooling of a Galilean Jesus Association
    (The Sayings Gospel Q)
    Willi Braun 43

Why Q Failed: From Ideological Project to Group Formation
    William E. Arnal 67

Ancient Myths and Modern Theories of the *Gospel of Thomas*
    and Christian Origins
    Ron Cameron 89

"Keep Speaking until You Find...": *Thomas* and the
    School of Oral Mimesis
    Arthur J. Dewey 109

Discussion and Reflections
    Merrill P. Miller 133

Part 2: A Jesus School in Jerusalem?

Proposal for the First Year of the Seminar
    Ron Cameron 141

Introduction to the Papers from the First Year of the Seminar
    Ron Cameron 151

Acts and the History of the Earliest Jerusalem Church
    Christopher R. Matthews 159

Antioch, Paul, and Jerusalem: Diaspora Myths of Origins
    in the Homeland
    Merrill P. Miller 177

What Do We Really Know about the Jerusalem Church?
    Christian Origins in Jerusalem according to Acts and Paul
    Dennis E. Smith 237

A Jewish Jesus School in Jerusalem?
    Burton L. Mack 253

History, Historiography, and Christian Origins: The Jerusalem
    Community
    Luther H. Martin 263

Agenda for the Annual Meeting, Discussion, and Reflections
    Ron Cameron 275

PART 3: A PRE-PAULINE *CHRISTOS* ASSOCIATION

Proposal for the Second Year of the Seminar
    Ron Cameron 285

Introduction to the Papers from the Second Year of the Seminar
    Ron Cameron 293

The Problem of the Origins of a Messianic Conception of Jesus
    Merrill P. Miller 301

Christos as Nickname
    Barry S. Crawford 337

From Messiahs to Christ: The Pre-Pauline Christ Cult in Scholarship
    Christopher R. Matthews 349

Why *Christos*? The Social Reasons
    Burton L. Mack 365

The Anointed Jesus
    Merrill P. Miller 375

Agenda for the Annual Meeting, Discussion, and Reflections
    Ron Cameron..417

Backbay Jazz and Blues
    Burton L. Mack 421

Smoke Signals from the North: A Reply to Burton Mack's
"Backbay Jazz and Blues"
    Willi Braun 433

Issues and Commentary
    Ron Cameron and Merrill P. Miller 443

PART 4: METAREFLECTIONS

Social Formation and Mythmaking: Theses on Key Terms
    William E. Arnal and Willi Braun..459

Remarkable
    Burton L. Mack 469

Redescribing Christian Origins: Historiography or Exegesis?
    Luther H. Martin 475

Dayyeinu
    Jonathan Z. Smith 483

Mythmaking, Social Formation, and Varieties of Social Theory
    Stanley K. Stowers 489

Conclusion: Redescribing Christian Origins
    Ron Cameron and Merrill P. Miller 497

Select Bibliography..517

Index of Ancient Texts..521

Select Index of Modern Authors 535

Index of Subjects 537

Contributors 539

Abbreviations

Primary Sources

1 En.	*1 Enoch* (*Ethiopic Apocalypse*)
1QM	*Milḥamah* or *War Scroll*
1QS	*Serek Hayaḥad* or *Rule of the Community*
1QSa	*Rule of the Congregation* (Appendix a to 1QS)
1QSb	*Rule of the Blessings* (Appendix b to 1QS)
2 Bar.	*2 Baruch* (*Syriac Apocalypse*)
4QCommGen A	*Commentary on Genesis A,* formerly *Patriarchal Blessings* or *Pesher Genesis*
4QFlor	*Florilegium*
4QMessAp	*Messianic Apocalypse*
11QMelch	*Melchizedek*
Ap. Jas.	*Apocryphon of James*
Apuleius	
Metam.	*Metamorphoses* / *The Golden Ass*
Aristotle	
Mem. rem.	*De memoria et reminiscentia* / *Memory and Reminiscence*
Poet.	*Poetica* / *Poetics*
As. Mos.	*Assumption of Moses*
CD	Cairo Genizah copy of the *Damascus Document*
Crates	
Ep.	*Epistula* / *Epistle*
Did.	*Didache*
Epictetus	
Diss.	*Dissertationes* / *Dissertations*
Eusebius	
Hist. eccl.	*Historia ecclesiastica* / *Ecclesiastical History*
Exeg. Soul	*Exegesis of the Soul*
Gen. Rab.	*Genesis Rabbah*
Gos. Heb.	*Gospel of the Hebrews*
Gos. Thom.	*Gospel of Thomas*
Gos. Truth	*Gospel of Truth*

Irenaeus
    Haer.   *Adversus haereses* / *Against Heresies*
Josephus
    Ant.   *Jewish Antiquities*
    War   *Jewish War*
Jub.   *Jubilees*
L.A.B.   *Liber antiquitatum biblicarum* (Pseudo-Philo)
Libanius
    Orat.   *Orationes* / *Orations*
m.   Mishnah
Midr.   Midrash
Philo
    Flacc.   *In Flaccum* / *Against Flaccus*
    Legat.   *Legatio ad Gaium* / *On the Embassy to Gaius*
    Praem.   *De praemiis et poenis* / *On Rewards and Punishments*
Plutarch
    Conj. praec.   *Conjugalia Praecepta* / *Advice to the Bride and Groom and a Consolation to His Wife*
P.Oxy.   Oxyrhynchus papyri
Pss. Sol.   *Psalms of Solomon*
Quintilian
    Inst.   *Institutio oratoria* / *The Orator's Education*
Shepherd of Hermas
    Herm. *Sim.*   Shepherd of Hermas, *Similitudes*
Sib. Or.   *Sibylline Oracles*
T. Jud.   *Testament of Judah*
T. Levi   *Testament of Levi*
T. Reu.   *Testament of Reuben*
Taʿan.   *Taʿanit*
Tg. Neof.   *Targum Neofiti*
y.   Jerusalem Talmud

SECONDARY SOURCES

AB	Anchor Bible
ABD	*Anchor Bible Dictionary.* Edited by D. N. Freedman. 6 vols. New York: Doubleday, 1992.
ABRL	Anchor Bible Reference Library
AGJU	Arbeiten zur Geschichte des antiken Judentums und des Urchristentums
ANRW	*Aufstieg und Niedergang der römischen Welt: Geschichte und Kultur Roms im Spiegel der neueren*

	Forschung. Edited by H. Temporini and W. Haase. Berlin: de Gruyter, 1972–.
ATDan	Acta theologica danica
BCSSR	*Bulletin: Council of Societies for the Study of Religion*
BDAG	Bauer, W., F. W. Danker, W. F. Arndt, and F. W. Gingrich. *Greek-English Lexicon of the New Testament and Other Early Christian Literature*. 3rd ed. Chicago: University of Chicago Press, 2000.
BETL	Bibliotheca ephemeridum theologicarum lovaniensium
Bib	*Biblica*
BibInt	Biblical Interpretation
BJS	Brown Judaic Studies
BTB	*Biblical Theology Bulletin*
BZAW	Beihefte zur Zeitschrift für die alttestamentliche Wissenschaft
BZNW	Beihefte zur Zeitschrift für die neutestamentliche Wissenschaft
CBQ	*Catholic Biblical Quarterly*
Cont	*Continuum*
CRINT	Compendia rerum iudaicarum ad Novum Testamentum
CSHJ	Chicago Studies in the History of Judaism
CurBS	*Currents in Research: Biblical Studies*
DJD	Discoveries in the Judaean Desert
DSD	*Dead Sea Discoveries*
ER	*The Encyclopedia of Religion*. Edited by M. Eliade. 16 vols. New York: Macmillan, 1987.
ETL	*Ephemerides theologicae lovanienses*
FF	Foundations and Facets
FRLANT	Forschungen zur Religion und Literatur des Alten und Neuen Testaments
FZPhTh	*Freiburger Zeitschrift für Philosophie und Theologie*
GBS	Guides to Biblical Scholarship
GCS	Die griechische christliche Schriftsteller der ersten [drei] Jahrhunderte
HDR	Harvard Dissertations in Religion
HR	*History of Religions*
HTR	*Harvard Theological Review*
HTS	Harvard Theological Studies
HUCA	*Hebrew Union College Annual*
ICC	International Critical Commentary
Int	*Interpretation*

JAAR	*Journal of the American Academy of Religion*
JBL	*Journal of Biblical Literature*
JECS	*Journal of Early Christian Studies*
JJS	*Journal of Jewish Studies*
JRH	*Journal of Religious History*
JSNT	*Journal for the Study of the New Testament*
JSNTSup	Journal for the Study of the New Testament Supplement Series
JSOTSup	Journal for the Study of the Old Testament Supplement Series
JSPSup	Journal for the Study of the Pseudepigrapha Supplement Series
JSS	*Journal of Semitic Studies*
JTS	*Journal of Theological Studies*
LCL	Loeb Classical Library
LSJ	Liddell, H. G., R. Scott, H. S. Jones. *A Greek-English Lexicon*. 9th ed. with revised supplement. Oxford: Oxford University Press, 1996.
MTSR	*Method and Theory in the Study of Religion*
NHC	Nag Hammadi Codices
NHMS	Nag Hammadi and Manichaean Studies
NHS	Nag Hammadi Studies
NovT	*Novum Testamentum*
NovTSup	Novum Testamentum Supplements
NTAbh	Neutestamentliche Abhandlungen
NTS	*New Testament Studies*
NTTS	New Testament Tools and Studies
PTSDSSP	The Princeton Theological Seminary Dead Sea Scrolls Project
PVTG	Pseudepigrapha Veteris Testamenti Graece
QD	Quaestiones disputatae
RechBib	Recherches bibliques
RelSRev	*Religious Studies Review*
RevQ	*Revue de Qumran*
RevScRel	*Revue des sciences religieuses*
RHPR	*Revue d'histoire et de philosophie religieuses*
RHR	*Revue de l'histoire des religions*
SAC	Studies in Antiquity and Christianity
SBLBMI	Society of Biblical Literature The Bible and Its Modern Interpreters
SBLBSNA	Society of Biblical Literature Biblical Scholarship in North America
SBLDS	Society of Biblical Literature Dissertation Series

SBLEJL	Society of Biblical Literature Early Judaism and Its Literature
SBLMS	Society of Biblical Literature Monograph Series
SBLSBS	Society of Biblical Literature Sources for Biblical Study
SBLSCS	Society of Biblical Literature Septuagint and Cognate Studies
SBLSP	Society of Biblical Literature Seminar Papers
SBLTT	Society of Biblical Literature Texts and Translations
SBS	Stuttgarter Bibelstudien
SBT	Studies in Biblical Theology
SEÅ	*Svensk exegetisk årsbok*
SemeiaSt	Semeia Studies
SHANE	Studies in the History of the Ancient Near East
SHR	Studies in the History of Religions (supplement to *Numen*)
SJLA	Studies in Judaism in Late Antiquity
SJT	*Scottish Journal of Theology*
SNT	Studien zum Neuen Testament
SNTSMS	Society for New Testament Studies Monograph Series
SPhilo	*Studia philonica*
SR	*Studies in Religion*
ST	*Studia theologica*
STDJ	Studies on the Texts of the Desert of Judah
StOR	Studies in Oriental Religions
SUNT	Studien zur Umwelt des Neuen Testaments
SVTP	Studia in Veteris Testamenti pseudepigrapha
SWBA	Social World of Biblical Antiquity
TB	Theologische Bücherei: Neudrucke und Berichte aus dem 20. Jahrhundert
TDNT	*Theological Dictionary of the New Testament*. Edited by G. Kittel and G. Friedrich. Translated by G. W. Bromiley. 10 vols. Grand Rapids: Eerdmans, 1964–76.
TDOT	*Theological Dictionary of the Old Testament*. Edited by G. J. Botterweck and H. Ringgren. Translated by J. T. Willis, G. W. Bromiley, and D. E. Green. 8 vols. Grand Rapids: Eerdmans, 1974–.
TJT	*Toronto Journal of Theology*
TLZ	*Theologische Literaturzeitung*
TQ	*Theologische Quartalschrift*
TRu	*Theologische Rundschau*
TU	Texte und Untersuchungen
TZ	*Theologische Zeitschrift*
VC	*Vigiliae christianae*

VTSup	Supplements to Vetus Testamentum
WMANT	Wissenschaftliche Monographien zum Alten und Neuen Testament
WUNT	Wissenschaftliche Untersuchungen zum Neuen Testament
ZNW	*Zeitschrift für die neutestamentliche Wissenschaft und die Kunde der älteren Kirche*
ZTK	*Zeitschrift für Theologie und Kirche*

Introduction: Ancient Myths and Modern Theories of Christian Origins

Ron Cameron and Merrill P. Miller

Prompted by the conversations of a number of persons interested in reassessing the beginnings of Christianity, a group of scholars began to meet at the annual meetings of the Society of Biblical Literature, starting in San Francisco in 1992, to explore the prospects and lay the groundwork for a new, collaborative project devoted to the task of redescribing Christian origins. We proposed a two-year SBL Consultation on Ancient Myths and Modern Theories of Christian Origins, to be followed by a six-year Seminar, that would focus both on the diverse myths of origin found in the writings of the earliest Christians and on competing scholarly theories of explanation and interpretation. Such a bifocal approach was deemed necessary in order to explain how and why certain myths got into place as well as to clarify alternatives and points of consensus among the different methods and models that are currently being used to describe the beginnings of the Christian religion.

Scholars have, of course, been aware for some time now of the diversity of early Christianities. Nevertheless, little effort has been made to compare ancient mythmaking with modern theorizing or to understand mythmaking as a correlate to social formation. Accordingly, even though scholars recognize that the beginnings of Christianity were pluriform, most constructions of Christian origins remain the same. They presuppose at the inauguration of the Christian era a dramatic event, a kerygmatic conviction, and a linear development, based primarily on the narrative construct of the book of Acts.[1] Three strategies have been employed in the construction of the traditional scenario of Christian origins: (1) beginning with the historical Jesus as the only—and ultimate—point of origination, (2) trajectories

---

[1] See Ron Cameron, "Alternate Beginnings—Different Ends: Eusebius, Thomas, and the Construction of Christian Origins," in *Religious Propaganda and Missionary Competition in the New Testament World: Essays Honoring Dieter Georgi* (ed. Lukas Bormann et al.; NovTSup 74; Leiden: Brill, 1994), 501–25, esp. 512–15 nn. 55–63.

have been traced from that singular genesis in the form of free-floating traditions, (3) which are understood eschatologically: set in motion by Jesus' death, which necessitated the resurrection, that gave rise to the church established in Jerusalem, which served as the center for two great missions, first to the Jews and then to the Gentiles. With such a scenario and strategies in place, the central problems in each case—notwithstanding many differences in detail—remain the same. On the one hand, the frame of reference for the historical description of Christian origins continues to be the New Testament picture itself. On the other, the New Testament provides a synthetic account of the myth of origins of a religion which is understood to be unique, and that fosters such an understanding because biblical scholarship continues to be correlated with theories of religion that are focused on personal experience, transforming events, and dramatic breakthroughs. The reason these problems make for such a deadly combination is that:

> For almost two thousand years, the Christian imagination of Christian origins has echoed the gospel stories contained in the New Testament. That is not surprising. The gospel accounts erased the pre-gospel histories; their inclusion within the church's New Testament consigned other accounts to oblivion; and during the long reach of Christian history, from the formation of the New Testament in the fourth century to the Enlightenment in the eighteenth, there was no other story.... According to Christian imagination, Christianity began when Jesus entered the world, performed miracles, called disciples, taught them about the kingdom of God, challenged the Jewish establishment, was crucified as the Christ and Son of God, appeared after his resurrection, overwhelmed his disciples with his holy spirit, established the first church in Jerusalem, and sent the apostles out on a mission to tell the world what they had seen and heard. Telling what they had seen was enough to convince the Jews and convert the gentiles into thinking that God had planned the whole thing in order to start a new religion. The new religion was about sin and redemption. What it took to start the new religion was all there as a kind of divine implantation in the life of Jesus, needing only to germinate and develop as early Christians heard about it, believed it, and came to understand its import. We might call this scenario the big bang concept of Christian origins.... Allowing the gospel paradigm to define Christian origins is quite understandable. It is the only scenario that everyone automatically shares, thus providing a comprehensive frame of reference for scholarly research and discourse. It serves as a kind of map within which we try to place our various, detailed labours. It also protects a set of assumptions about the way Christianity began, forming as it does the basis for what has been imagined as an otherwise inexplicable emergence of a brand new religion of unique conviction and singular faith. Something overwhelming must have possessed those early Christians, so the thinking has been, or they would not have converted to the new religion with its extraordinary

claims. It is the gospel story that feeds that suspicion of an overwhelming something at the very beginning of the Christian time.[2]

The problems with this scenario are not simply historical. The fundamental issues are imaginative and theoretical: the New Testament serves as the sole framework for the scholarly imagination of Christian origins, even when scholars recognize that picture as tendentious, overly simplified, or legendary. This problem persists despite the recognition of the diversity of early Christianities and despite the application of new methods and the contributions of new voices in the field of biblical studies. Accordingly, we must break the spell of the gospel paradigm; otherwise, all texts—canonical and noncanonical alike—will "have no [adequate] frame of reference to give them any significance"[3] and, thus, no adequate framework for a genuinely critical history of Christian beginnings.

To reposition the terms of the debate and redescribe the beginnings of Christianity are quite a challenge. Although we remain undaunted, we should be mindful of the demands involved in rewriting the history of early Christianities. One of the least obvious—and potentially most fatal—pitfalls is illustrated by the following remarks of Philip R. Davies, provoked by a quotation from *Time* magazine, in an article in its annual Christmas issue entitled "Are the Bible's Stories True?":

> "To suggest that many things in the Bible are not historical is not too serious. But to lose biblical history altogether is to lose our tradition." With these words, Frank Cross ... implies that the biblical story loses its value

---

[2] Burton L. Mack, "On Redescribing Christian Origins," *MTSR* 8 (1996): 247, 250, adding: "However, since the Enlightenment, the effort to understand Christian origins has been pursued by scholars as a matter of historical and literary criticism, and the New Testament account has slowly been dismantled. The New Testament is no longer seen by critical scholars as a coherent set of apostolic texts that document a single set of dramatic events and their monolinear history of subsequent influence and theological development. Instead of one gospel story, we have four different accounts within the New Testament and several other gospels that were not included. Instead of one picture of the historical Jesus that all early Christians must have had in view, we now have several competing views. We now know that there were many groups from the beginning, creating disparate traditions, responding to other groups differently, and developing various rituals and patterns of social congregation. Plural theologies and conflicting ideologies, as well as competing authorities and leaders, were the order of the day. So factors other than the marvels portrayed in the gospel account must have been at work. And yet, the older picture of Christian origins according to the gospel story, largely Lukan, is still in everyone's mind. It is as if the emergence of Christianity cannot be accounted for any other way. It is as if the accumulation of critical information within the discipline of New Testament studies cannot compete with the gospel's mystique" (ibid., 247–48; repr., with revisions, in *The Christian Myth: Origins, Logic, and Legacy* [New York: Continuum, 2001], 59–60, 63).

[3] Mack, "Redescribing Christian Origins," 248; repr. in *Christian Myth*, 60.

if too much of it turns out to be unhistorical. Here he illuminates, in fact, an important aspect of modern biblical history writing. Biblical scholarship wants to hold onto its received story (because that is the theological value it has acquired) but also wants its received story to be validated as a critically reconstructed history. What Cross (and others) dream of is *a history that has critically-secured data but the old biblical framework.*[4]

What we need to do now is change the subject and engage in a redescription of Christian origins from a religious-studies perspective, in terms of anthropology, social history, and the human sciences, in disciplined ways that do not simply reproduce, by continuing to paraphrase, the dominant (essentially Lukan) paradigm of Christian origins. The alternative of a scholarship that continues to paraphrase, refine, adjust, and defend a religious community's canonical account of itself is problematic. Therefore, another way will have to be found to make sense of the data we have taken for granted, another means discovered to determine their significance, another theory of religion proposed that can render intelligible the beginnings of Christianity in terms of the social interests, investments, and attractions that define the human enterprise.

The Consultation on Ancient Myths and Modern Theories of Christian Origins arose out of the conviction that the beginnings of Christianity could and must be accounted for some other way. We are persuaded that modern constructions of Christian origins have overlooked the actual processes of social formation and mythmaking that provide the rationale for the emergence of the Christian religion. Accordingly, our project is predicated upon the critical tasks of locating significant moments in the textual landscape of ancient Christianities that bear the marks of a lived social history, and of reconsidering their place—as junctures of mythmaking and social formation—within biblical scholarship. Our first Consultation, held in Philadelphia in 1995, addressed in a single session the theme "Assessing the Categories of New Testament Scholarship." The program was designed to gauge the prospects for undertaking a collaborative project of redescription. As such, the papers and responses were intended to be indicative of the bifocal approach of the Consultation: (1) to reexamine the categories that have held a privileged place in the scholarly imagination of Christian origins, and (2) to develop constructive proposals for reimagining the frame of reference, remapping the earliest

---

[4] Philip R. Davies, "Whose History? Whose Israel? Whose Bible? Biblical Histories, Ancient and Modern," in *Can A 'History of Israel' Be Written?* (ed. Lester L. Grabbe; JSOTSup 245; Sheffield: Sheffield Academic Press, 1997), 114–15, emphasis original. The citation from Frank Moore Cross is quoted in Marlin Levin et al., "Are the Bible's Stories True?" *Time*, 18 December 1995, 69.

history, and rethinking the methods and models of understanding the beginnings of Christianity.

In addressing the need and possibilities for such a project, Burton L. Mack's paper "On Redescribing Christian Origins" took note of a host of aporiae, clichés, unexamined assumptions, and unresolved issues currently under debate in New Testament studies and still in need of explanation, items such as:

- The notion that Jesus was a reformer of Judaism.
- Messianic expectations as definitive of the Jewish mentality at the time.
- The notion of a first church in Jerusalem.
- The original impulse for using the designation *Christ*.
- The attraction of the concept "Israel."

None of these, Mack observed, is accounted for by the traditional scenario of Christian origins, which "the gospel paradigm presents but cannot explain"; all can "be understood as items that became issues because their study threatened" that paradigm. In addition, Mack suggested how dozens of recent studies could be regarded as "building block[s] to be used in the construction of another history of Christian beginnings." If there were "a project, seminar, or discourse" where such studies were framed in social theories of religion and tested by more adequate methods of comparison, then they could all be taken seriously and would count as "contributions to a redescription of Christian origins."[5] Calling for a reassessment of the New Testament from the perspective of a social history of religion, Ron Cameron's paper focused on the problem of category formation. In tracing "The Anatomy of a Discourse: On 'Eschatology' as a Category for Explaining Christian Origins," Cameron showed how eschatology has been deployed as a privileged ontological category, rather than a descriptive one, in the history of New Testament scholarship. By circumventing both historical placement and comparative perspective in specific instances of apocalyptic thinking, the particular rationales of an apocalyptic imagination are obscured and apocalyptic eschatology is made to appear as the all-pervasive matrix of early Christianities:

> Dislodged from real apocalyptic settings in the Greco-Roman world, eschatology is now applied so indiscriminately to virtually anything and everything that the term works solely as a "magic wand," to signal the uniqueness of the New Testament and the incomparability of Christian

---

[5] Mack, "Redescribing Christian Origins," 249, 250, 261, 263; repr. in *Christian Myth*, 61, 62, 63, 76, 78.

origins.... Accordingly, if eschatology is to have any utility at all, if the term is to be retained as a category, it must be subjected to a thoroughgoing process of rectification. In the process, early Christian texts and traditions will have to be critically reimagined, placed at the intersection of complex literary and social histories, and subjected to a detailed redescription. Comparison with other texts and movements from the cultures of context will highlight similarities and differences that can be used to clarify how and why some Christians entertained an apocalyptic eschatological imagination. Recognizing that some—but not all—early Christian groups sought a rationale for their activities by invoking the language and imagery of eschatology means that eschatological argumentation was an ordinary feature of mythmaking and social formation, used for strategic reasons at certain moments or junctures of a group's history.[6]

The papers by Mack and Cameron were both reviewed at the Consultation by Jonathan Z. Smith and John S. Kloppenborg, who called attention to a particular strength of biblical studies for students of religion: the fact that biblical scholars "take as part of their normal activities so keen a sense of their own history of scholarship." By providing "an unusually thick dossier of the history of its enterprise," New Testament scholarship "offers the potential of providing an arsenal of test cases, of e.g.s," in Smith's words, "provocative of thought."[7] However, whereas Smith underscored the cognitive problems underlying many of the studies that Mack regarded as potential examples of contributions to a redescription project, Kloppenborg emphasized the range and complexity of the scholarly enterprise and the need to examine, not parochially but with care, the changing circumstances, social locations, and larger "discursive formations that have been at work in earlier scholarly hypotheses" of Christian origins.[8]

Mack's proposal for redescribing Christian origins situates the study of Christian beginnings, and their social processes of mythmaking, within the context of the human sciences:

> If we want to account for the emergence of Christianity, including the formation of groups and congregations, the development of their various practices and rituals, the production of their mythologies, and the writing

---

[6] Ron Cameron, "The Anatomy of a Discourse: On 'Eschatology' as a Category for Explaining Christian Origins," *MTSR* 8 (1996): 240–41, citing Dieter Georgi, "Rudolf Bultmann's *Theology of the New Testament* Revisited," in *Bultmann, Retrospect and Prospect: The Centenary Symposium at Wellesley* (ed. Edward C. Hobbs; HTS 35; Philadelphia: Fortress, 1985), 82.

[7] Jonathan Z. Smith, "Social Formations of Early Christianities: A Response to Ron Cameron and Burton Mack," *MTSR* 8 (1996): 271.

[8] John S. Kloppenborg, "Critical Histories and Theories of Religion: A Response to Burton Mack and Ron Cameron," *MTSR* 8 (1996): 283.

of their literature ... if we want to discover the reasons for and the motivations involved in their many investments in their new associations ... [indeed,] if we want to account for Christian origins as a thoughtful human construction ... we need a theory of religion that gives the people their due. We need a theory of religion firmly anchored in a social and cultural anthropology, capable of sustaining a conversation with the humanities.[9]

Arguing for a comparative method and an intellectualist approach to matters of theory, Mack suggests that a different perspective needs to be entertained as "a kind of lens ... working hypothesis ... [or] framework" to guide the task of redescription, a theory of religion that he presents in the form of five propositions:

1. Religion is a social construct.... The myths, rituals, symbols, beliefs and patterns of thinking that are *shared* by a people ... [are] cultural constructs [that] can be experienced and manipulated in a variety of ways by individuals, but it is their self-evident status as common cultural coin that marks them as the religion of a people.

2. Social formation defines the human enterprise. Constructing societies large and small is what people do. It is a fragile, collective craft requiring enormous amounts of negotiation, experimentation, living together, and talking ... result[ing] in very complex arrangements of relationships, agreements reached on better and less better ways to do things, and practices established to pass on the knowledge and skills accumulated in the process.... [If] ask[ed] about the reasons for and the processes whereby early Christian myths and rituals were first conceived and agreed upon ... [the answer would be that] the Jesus movements and the congregations of the Christ were attractive as intentional experiments in social formation and mythmaking.

3. Myths acknowledge the collective gifts and constraints of the past and create a foil or gap for thinking critically about the present state of a group's life together.... Early Christians entertained fantastic mythologies, not because they were overwhelmed by encounters with a god or a son of God, but because they wanted to comprehend and justify their investments in a movement that made social sense to them.

4. Rituals are the way humans have of concentrating attention on some activity or event of some significance to a group, and observing its performance apart from normal practice. ... Rituals are social occasions, require roles, invite attendance, display skills, confirm loyalties, trigger

---

[9] Mack, "Redescribing Christian Origins," 254; repr. in *Christian Myth*, 67–68.

commitments, evoke thoughtfulness, and reconstitute the structure of a group without having to engineer it any other way.

5. Mythmaking and social formation go together.... Experimentation and bricolage mark the ways in which myths get rearranged and groups reform.... Even the most daring social experiments and the most fantastic mythic constructs turn out to be thoughtful and constructive attempts to regain sanity in a social situation that threatens human well-being. In the case of early Christians ... the making of their myths and the processes of forming social groups were constructive and thoughtful human activities. And [so,] whenever we have the chance to catch sight of both mythmaking and social formation happening at the same time in the same place, we need to explore the relationship of the one to the other.[10]

In seeking to situate New Testament studies within the discourses of the social and human sciences, Mack draws heavily on Smith's scholarship in the history of religions, both in embracing a comparative method and in endeavoring to construct a cultural (and for Smith, a cognitive) theory of religion. In particular, Mack proposes the way in which Smith works as a model for our project of redescription. For Smith's essays are always constructive and programmatic, "exploring crucial junctures in the history of the discipline ... in quest of methodological clarity and sound theoretical foundations":

The typical essay is organized around four components: (1) a text is placed in view to provide an exegetical challenge; (2) a commonly accepted interpretation of the text is reviewed; (3) an alternative reading is given, based on strictly historical methods of textual reconstruction and placement; and (4) conclusions are drawn for questions of method and theory in the study of religion.... The texts selected for analysis turn out to be programmatic in and of themselves ... the very texts that have served earlier scholars as points of departure for constructing theories of religion. They are thus the "canonical" texts of the discipline, and their reinterpretation will prove to be critical.... In every case, [then,] theories are confronted with texts, the texts are placed in their own historical contexts, and the theories are reassessed as to their adequacy and plausibility.[11]

---

[10] Mack, "Redescribing Christian Origins," 254, 255–56, emphasis original; repr. in *Christian Myth,* 68–70.

[11] Burton Mack, "Introduction: Religion and Ritual," in *Violent Origins: Walter Burkert, René Girard, and Jonathan Z. Smith on Ritual Killing and Cultural Formation* (ed. Robert G. Hamerton-Kelly; Stanford, Calif.: Stanford University Press, 1987), 32–33.

Mack describes these procedures, methodologically, as "the performance of four operations, not necessarily in separate, sequential stages: description, comparison, redescription, and the rectification of categories."[12] Elaborating on this description of his own work, Smith distinguishes "four moments in the comparative enterprise":

> [1] Description is a double process which comprises the historical or anthropological dimensions of the work: First, the requirement that we locate a given example within the rich texture of its social, historical, and cultural environments that invest it with its local significance. The second task of description is that of reception-history, a careful account of how *our* second-order scholarly tradition has intersected with the exemplum. That is to say, we need to describe how the datum has become accepted as significant for the purpose of argument. Only when such a double contextualization is completed does one move on to the description of a second example undertaken in the same double fashion. With at least two exempla in view, we are prepared to undertake their [2] comparison both in terms of aspects and relations held to be significant, and with respect to some category, question, theory, or model of interest to us [as students of religion]. The aim of such a comparison is the [3] redescription of the exempla (each in light of the other) and a [4] rectification of the academic categories in relation to which they have been imagined.[13]

Starting with the historical-critical method, Smith's program gives prominence to the careful placement of texts in their social-historical contexts, their accurate and exhaustive description, the particular occasion in which a text or topic was first noticed as significant in the discourse of scholarship, and the recognition of difference—rather than similarity—as the point of entrée and critical leverage for explanation and interpretation. The comparative enterprise thus entails thick descriptions, permitting their comparison to be undertaken in terms of stipulated "similarities and differences, understood as aspects and relations, rather than as 'things,'" and displayed in the service of some theory, method, category, or question of importance to the student of religion.[14] This "necessary procedure of double

---

[12] Mack, "Redescribing Christian Origins," 256; cf. 256–59; repr. in *Christian Myth*, 70; cf. 70–74.

[13] Jonathan Z. Smith, "The 'End' of Comparison: Redescription and Rectification," in *A Magic Still Dwells: Comparative Religion in the Postmodern Age* (ed. Kimberley C. Patton and Benjamin C. Ray; Berkeley and Los Angeles: University of California Press, 2000), 239, emphasis original.

[14] Ibid. This is why Smith has argued that, "for the self-conscious student of religion, no datum possesses intrinsic interest. It is of value only insofar as it can serve as exempli gratia of some fundamental issue in the [scholarly] imagination of religion.... It is this act of second order, reflective imagination which must be the central preoccupation of any student of

archaeology," of accounting descriptively not only for the situation of a given text or topic in historical or ethnographic terms, but also for the placement of the example in question in our own scholarly discourse, is an urgent task, enabling redescriptions to be framed in such a way as to sustain "argumentation, the process that converts facts into data."[15]

The process of comparison is, for Smith, not only "a fundamental characteristic of human intelligence"; comparison "remains *the* method of scholarship ... beyond question."[16] However, though scholars have employed various methods—ethnographic, encyclopedic, morphological, or evolutionary—for making (anthropological) comparisons, when applied to the study of (comparative) religions, comparison has been conceived primarily in terms of similarity and contiguity. "The perception of similarity has been construed as the chief purpose of comparison; contiguity, expressed as historical [borrowing, diffusion,] 'influence' or filiation, has provided the explanation."[17] For the historian of religion, then, the problem has been to find a way to combine comparative methods with historical disciplines: to discover how to "develop a complex model of tradition and the mechanisms for its transmission" and reinterpretation, and how to "ground comparison and patterns in a historical process" that accounts for the role of continuity and change.[18]

Starting with the observation that every scholar of religion is concerned with "phenomena that are historical in the simple, grammatical sense of the term, that is to say, with events and expressions from the

---

religion.... For this reason, the student of religion ... must be relentlessly self-conscious ... able to articulate clearly why 'this' rather than 'that' was chosen as an exemplum. His primary skill is concentrated [strategically] in this choice. This effort at articulate choice is all the more difficult, and hence all the more necessary, for the historian of religion who accepts neither the boundaries of canon nor of community in constituting his intellectual domain, in providing his range of exempla. Implicit in this effort at articulate choice are three conditions. First, that the exemplum has been well and fully understood. This requires a mastery of both the relevant primary material and the history and tradition of its interpretation. Second, that the exemplum be displayed in the service of some important theory, some paradigm, some fundamental question, some central element in the academic imagination of religion. Third, that there be some method for explicitly relating the exemplum to the theory, paradigm, or question and some method for evaluating each in terms of the other" (idem, "Introduction," in *Imagining Religion: From Babylon to Jonestown* [CSHJ; Chicago: University of Chicago Press, 1982], xi–xii).

[15] Smith, "Social Formations of Early Christianities," 271.

[16] Jonathan Z. Smith, "*Adde Parvum Parvo Magnus Acervus Erit*," *HR* 11 (1971): 67, 68, emphasis original; repr. in *Map Is Not Territory: Studies in the History of Religions* (SJLA 23; Leiden: Brill, 1978; repr., Chicago: University of Chicago Press, 1993), 240, 241.

[17] Smith, "The 'End' of Comparison," 237.

[18] Jonathan Z. Smith, "In Comparison a Magic Dwells," in *Imagining Religion*, 29; repr. in *Magic Still Dwells*, 34.

[remote or recent] past, reconceived vividly," Smith concludes that "the scholar of religion is, therefore, concerned with dimensions of memory and remembrance—whether they be the collective labor of society or the work of the individual historian's craft." Elaborating on "the earliest full theory of memory" developed by Aristotle, who introduced terms of difference alongside notions of similarity and contiguity in discussing the relationship of comparison to memory (*Mem. rem.* 451b19–20),[19] Smith argues that "it is the category of the different that marks [a theoretical] advance."[20] This means that comparison, as both a cognitive process and a theoretical discipline, may be described as an intellectual act of invention, "occasioned by surprise." Comparison, "the negotiation of difference to some intellectual end, is [therefore] not an enterprise confined to odd surviving adherents of some *religionsgeschichtliche Schule*—it is the absolute requirement of responsible thought."[21] This means that "we need to think about the enterprise of comparison under the aspect of difference":[22]

> It is axiomatic that comparison is never a matter of identity. Comparison requires the acceptance of difference as the grounds of its being interesting, and a methodical manipulation of that difference to achieve some stated cognitive end. The questions of comparison are questions of judgment with respect to difference: What differences are to be maintained in the interests of comparative inquiry? What differences can be defensibly relaxed and relativized in light of the intellectual tasks at hand?[23]

As such, comparison "does not necessarily tell us how things 'are'" but "how they might be 'redescribed'":

> A comparison is a disciplined exaggeration in the service of knowledge. It lifts out and strongly marks certain features within difference as being of possible intellectual significance, expressed in the rhetoric of their being

---

[19] Smith, "In Comparison a Magic Dwells," 20; repr. in *Magic Still Dwells*, 24–25.

[20] Smith, "The 'End' of Comparison," 240 n. 3. The roles that similarity and contiguity play in memory had already been identified by Plato (*Phaedo* 73D–74A). Aristotle's contribution was to describe how, in memory, we start "from something similar [ὅμοιος], or different [ἐναντίος], or contiguous [σύνεγγυς]" (*Mem. rem.* 451b19–20). See Richard Sorabji, *Aristotle on Memory* (London: Duckworth, 1972), 42–46, 54, 96–97.

[21] Smith, "Social Formations of Early Christianities," 273, 274.

[22] Jonathan Z. Smith, *Drudgery Divine: On the Comparison of Early Christianities and the Religions of Late Antiquity* (Jordan Lectures in Comparative Religion 14; London: School of Oriental and African Studies, University of London; Chicago: University of Chicago Press, 1990), 46–47.

[23] Jonathan Z. Smith, *To Take Place: Toward Theory in Ritual* (CSHJ; Chicago: University of Chicago Press, 1987), 13–14; idem, *Drudgery Divine*, 47.

"like" in some stipulated fashion. Comparison provides the means by which *we* "re-vision" phenomena as *our* data in order to solve *our* theoretical problems.... [Accordingly,] it is the scholar's intellectual purpose—whether explanatory or interpretative, whether generic or specific—which highlights that principled postulation of similarity which is the ground of the methodical comparison of difference being interesting.[24]

Smith seeks "to situate the comparative enterprise," including biblical studies, "within the overall project of the study of religion, a project entailing definition, classification, comparison, and explanation." What these processes have in common is that each is a varying mode of redescription.[25] Moreover, since Smith "always does his work as a contribution to the discussion of theory in the study of religion," all of his work "can be understood as a rectification of categories common to the history of religions":[26]

> The truly ingenious feature of Smith's program for the application of the scientific model of investigation to social and cultural phenomena lies in his proposal for what he has called the *rectification* of categories. That is because, for Smith, a category in our field takes the place of a theorem, proposition or hypothesis in the natural sciences model.... A category should not cease to be descriptive, derived as it must be from observations on the surface of social behavior ... but it must be general enough to designate a set of phenomena thought to be similar in some respect while differing in their specific cultural articulations. A category should be capable of handling both similarities and differences in cross-cultural comparisons. The category as a descriptive generalization has tremendous theoretical significance for the humanities [and social sciences], because it allows for the construction and testing of general theories without the need of making universal claims. According to Smith, rectified categories (or descriptive generalizations) are the building blocks for the pursuit of a general theory that explains religion as part and parcel of the intellectual labor humans invest in making their worlds work and in finding their working societies interesting. Because there are many ways to make a society work, a given category ... need not claim universal status. But it

---

[24] Smith, *Drudgery Divine*, 52, 53, emphasis original. See Max Black, "Models and Archetypes," in *Models and Metaphors: Studies in Language and Philosophy* (Ithaca, N.Y.: Cornell University Press, 1962), 219–43, esp. 236–38; Fitz John Porter Poole, "Metaphors and Maps: Towards Comparison in the Anthropology of Religion," *JAAR* 54 (1986): 411–57. The term "redescription" appears to be borrowed from Mary B. Hesse, "The Explanatory Function of Metaphor," in *Models and Analogies in Science* (Notre Dame, Ind.: University of Notre Dame Press, 1966), 157–77. See Jonathan Z. Smith, "Sacred Persistence: Towards a Redescription of Canon," in *Approaches to Ancient Judaism: Theory and Practice* (ed. William Scott Green; BJS 1; Missoula, Mont.: Scholars Press, 1978), 11, 27 n. 2; repr. in *Imagining Religion*, 36, 141 n. 2.

[25] Jonathan Z. Smith, "Bible and Religion," *BCSSR* 29/4 (2000): 87.

[26] Mack, "Redescribing Christian Origins," 256, 259; repr. in *Christian Myth*, 70, 74.

does need to be explained as making a contribution to the human enterprise of social construction.[27]

Since all texts are "texts in context, specific acts of communication between specified individuals, at specific points in time and space, about specifiable subjects," the task "for the historian of religion ... becomes one of imagining the 'situation,' of constructing the context, insofar as it is relevant to his [or her] interpretative goals."[28] Categories that have been rectified and phenomena redescribed by means of thick description, social-historical placement, and cross-cultural comparison make it possible for us to place our texts at some intersection of social and intellectual history. Establishing adequate situations as the contexts within which a particular discursive formation or social practice makes sense—the social, historical, cultural, and rhetorical factors of significance for analyzing a text or topic, myth or ritual, and for testing the adequacy of the categories used to describe it—is essential if we are to understand the moment or occasion in which a given text was produced and intended to be understood. For this reason, "the 'end' of comparison cannot be the act of comparison itself" but a redescription of the exempla and a rectification of the categories of scholarship.[29] "A new designation for a recognizable phenomenon can become a building block for constructing a descriptive system.... [And] because the new designations are won by comparing examples cross-culturally, they have already been raised to a level of generalization without losing their descriptive power."[30] Accordingly, the task of redescribing Christian origins and rectifying the categories of New Testament scholarship means that a project of redescription is, at once, an effort in critical historiography and in theory of religion.

The purpose of a Seminar devoted to Ancient Myths and Modern Theories of Christian Origins is thus to contribute both historiographically to a redescription of Christian beginnings and imaginatively to the construction of a general theory of religion. In response to Mack's proposal to situate the study of Christian beginnings within the context of the human sciences, Smith raises cognitive issues of the "costs, consequences, or entailments" of such a project, "the acceptance of which is the price of admission to the practice."[31] In particular, Smith focuses on translation as an intellectual operation that necessarily entails difference and discrepancy and, therefore, that constitutes the horizon of both scientific explanation and humanistic

---

[27] Burton L. Mack, "After *Drudgery Divine*," *Numen* 39 (1992): 227–28, emphasis original.
[28] Smith, "Introduction," in *Imagining Religion*, xiii.
[29] Smith, "The 'End' of Comparison," 239.
[30] Mack, "Redescribing Christian Origins," 259; repr. in *Christian Myth*, 74.
[31] Smith, "Social Formations of Early Christianities," 275, 272.

interpretation. Translation—"itself the most urgent current intellectual issue within the human sciences"[32]—is a "proposal that the [second-order] language that is appropriate to one domain (the known/the familiar) may translate the language characteristic of another domain (the unknown/the unfamiliar)."[33] "Central to any proposal of translation are questions as to appropriateness or 'fit,' expressed through the double methodological requirement of comparison and criticism."[34] Smith raises this issue in order to focus on its implications and their consequences. First, "translation, as an affair of language, is a relentlessly social activity, a matter of public meaning rather than one of individual significance."[35] Indeed, "the use of terminology such as 'translation' reminds us that the human sciences have as their preeminent intellectual domain matters of language and of language-like systems and, therefore, study 'eminently social things.'" It follows, necessarily, that "rather than experience preexisting language which then expresses it, we cannot experience the world independently of the conventional, and therefore social, ways in which it is represented.... There is [thus] no post-Easter experience which then is 'given voice' in Christian discourse; the experience is contained in and by that discourse."[36] Second, "translation is never fully adequate; there is always discrepancy." Indeed, "the cognitive power of any translation or model," map or redescription, "is a result of its difference from the phenomena in question and not from its congruence.... A map which precisely reproduces the territory is useless; a paraphrase," the most common sort of weak translation, most notably in biblical studies, "will usually be insufficiently different for

---

[32] Jonathan Z. Smith, "Teaching the Bible in the Context of General Education," *Teaching Theology and Religion* 1 (1998): 77.

[33] Smith, "Social Formations of Early Christianities," 273.

[34] Jonathan Z. Smith, "Close Encounters of Diverse Kinds," in *Religion and Cultural Studies* (ed. Susan L. Mizruchi; Princeton: Princeton University Press, 2001), 15. Commenting on the observation of Isaiah Berlin that, "in a sense, the mere existence of an extraordinary variety of very dissimilar languages ... is itself an index or, one might say, a model of the irreducible variety of human self-expression, such that even in the case of cognate languages, complete translation of one into any other is in principle impossible; and the gap—indicative of differences in ways of perceiving and acting—is at times very wide indeed," Smith notes that "in culture as in language, it is difference which generates meaning" (ibid., citing Isaiah Berlin, "Giambattista Vico and Cultural History," in *The Crooked Timber of Humanity: Chapters in the History of Ideas* [ed. Henry Hardy; London: Murray, 1990; repr., Princeton: Princeton University Press, 1997], 61).

[35] Smith, "Bible and Religion," 91.

[36] Smith, "Social Formations of Early Christianities," 274, alluding to Emile Durkheim, *The Elementary Forms of Religious Life* (trans. Karen E. Fields; New York: Free Press, 1995). "Language," accordingly, "is not posterior to experience, rather, it is the very way in which we think and experience" (Jonathan Z. Smith, "A Twice-Told Tale: The History of the History of Religions' History," *Numen* 48 [2001]: 137).

purposes of thought."³⁷ Therefore, since "a theory, a model, a conceptual category, *cannot be simply the data writ large*,"³⁸ our critique is that theories of Christian origination that reproduce, by continuing to paraphrase, the dominant (canonical) paradigm of Christian origins pay insufficient attention to difference, lacking an adequate theory of translation.

This problem may be illustrated by Jorge Luis Borges's parable "On Exactitude in Science," which imagines a nation of geographers whose map reproduces exactly the territory it is designed to represent, and which we quote in its entirety:

> ... In that Empire, the Art of Cartography attained such Perfection that the map of a single Province occupied the entirety of a City, and the map of the Empire, the entirety of a Province. In time, those Unconscionable Maps no longer satisfied, and the Cartographers Guilds struck a Map of the Empire whose size was that of the Empire, and which coincided point for point with it. The following Generations, who were not so fond of the Study of Cartography as their Forebears had been, saw that that vast Map was Useless, and not without some Pitilessness was it, that they delivered it up to the Inclemencies of Sun and Winters. In the Deserts of the West, still today, there are Tattered Ruins of that Map, inhabited by Animals and Beggars; in all the Land there is no other Relic of the Disciplines of Geography.³⁹

For Borges, "a map without distortion, a map with absolute congruency to its subject matter," is "absolutely useless to second-order intellection.... When map is the territory, it lacks both utility and any cognitive advantage with the result that the discipline which produced it, deprived of its warrants, disappears."⁴⁰

The generative problem for a project of redescription is the necessity to establish an alternative frame of reference to the canonical paradigm or normative religious account that holds sway in Christian imagination, in order to be able to formulate a genuinely critical, historical account of the beginnings of Christianity as religion. Accordingly, our Seminar has been established on the premise that the controlling position of the canonical paradigm in standard descriptions of Christian origins must be challenged

---

³⁷ Smith, "Social Formations of Early Christianities," 273.

³⁸ Smith, "Bible and Religion," 91, emphasis original.

³⁹ Jorge Luis Borges, "On Exactitude in Science," in *Collected Fictions* (trans. Andrew Hurley; New York: Viking, 1998), 325. As Claude Lévi-Strauss has argued, "the intrinsic value of a small-scale model is that it compensates for the renunciation of sensible dimensions by the acquisition of intelligible dimensions" (*The Savage Mind* [Chicago: University of Chicago Press, 1966], 24).

⁴⁰ Smith, "Bible and Religion," 91.

directly, and set aside, if a plausible account of how that paradigm got into place is to be written and any new framework constructed or accounts proposed. A Seminar devoted to redescribing Christian origins must do more than repeat the slogan about the diversity of early Christianities. It must seek to change the picture. For this reason, a new map of Christian beginnings entails making a complete break with any attempt to rescue the notion of singular origins, whether that be by appeals to the historical Jesus as the ultimate source of the variety of early Christian groups and texts, or by attempts to link the variety of mythologies of Jesus and the Christ to a singular moment of religious experience that remains impenetrable to ordinary human understanding. The alternative, a scholarship that continues to paraphrase a religious community's canonical narrative account of itself, has been recognized as a crucial problem for critical scholarship in cognate fields of study as well—including ancient Israel, early Judaism, the rabbis, and Islam—which represent, in conjunction with Christian origins, the Western tradition.[41] As such, other new

---

[41] On ancient Israel, see Robert B. Coote and Keith W. Whitelam, *The Emergence of Early Israel in Historical Perspective* (SWBA 5; Sheffield: Almond, 1987); Philip R. Davies, *In Search of 'Ancient Israel'* (2nd ed.; JSOTSup 148; Sheffield: Sheffield Academic Press, 1995); Grabbe, *Can A 'History of Israel' Be Written?*; Niels Peter Lemche, *Ancient Israel: A New History of Israelite Society* (Biblical Seminar 5; Sheffield: JSOT Press, 1988); idem, *The Israelites in History and Tradition* (Library of Ancient Israel; London: SPCK; Louisville: Westminster John Knox, 1998); idem, *Prelude to Israel's Past: Background and Beginnings of Israelite History and Identity* (trans. E. F. Maniscalco; Peabody, Mass.: Hendrickson, 1998); Thomas L. Thompson, *The Origin Tradition of Ancient Israel: I. The Literary Formation of Genesis and Exodus 1–23* (JSOTSup 55; Sheffield: JSOT Press, 1987); idem, *Early History of the Israelite People: From the Written and Archaeological Sources* (SHANE 4; Leiden: Brill, 1992); idem, *The Mythic Past: Biblical Archaeology and the Myth of Israel* (New York: Basic Books, 1999); Keith W. Whitelam, *The Invention of Ancient Israel: The Silencing of Palestinian History* (London: Routledge, 1996); and Jeremy Zwelling, "The Fictions of Biblical History" (review of Thomas L. Thompson, *The Mythic Past: Biblical Archaeology and the Myth of Israel*), *History and Theory* 39 (2000): 117–41. On early Judaism, see James S. McLaren, *Turbulent Times? Josephus and Scholarship on Judaea in the First Century CE* (JSPSup 29; Sheffield: Sheffield Academic Press, 1998). On the rabbis, see Jack N. Lightstone, "Whence the Rabbis? From Coherent Description to Fragmented Reconstructions," *SR* 26 (1997): 275–95; idem, *Mishnah and the Social Formation of the Early Rabbinic Guild: A Socio-rhetorical Approach* (Studies in Christianity and Judaism 11; Waterloo, Ont.: Wilfrid Laurier University Press, 2002). On Islam, see John Wansbrough, *Quranic Studies: Sources and Methods of Scriptural Interpretation* (London Oriental Series 31; Oxford: Oxford University Press, 1977); idem, *The Sectarian Milieu: Content and Composition of Islamic Salvation History* (London Oriental Series 34; Oxford: Oxford University Press, 1978); the essays on "Islamic Origins Reconsidered: John Wansbrough and the Study of Early Islam" by Herbert Berg, "Foreword," *MTSR* 9 (1997): 1–2; idem, "The Implications of, and Opposition to, the Methods and Theories of John Wansbrough," *MTSR* 9 (1997): 3–22; G. R. Hawting, "John Wansbrough, Islam, and Monotheism," *MTSR* 9 (1997): 23–38; Andrew Rippin, "*Quranic Studies*, part IV: Some Methodological Notes," *MTSR* 9 (1997): 39–46; Norman Calder, "History and Nostalgia: Reflections on John

maps of the beginnings of Western religious traditions are starting to be drawn. In all of these instances and efforts of redescription, what is shared is the critical issue of perspective: the growing impact among scholars of the implications of recognizing that a religious community's narrative of its origins and (mythic) past cannot serve as the framework for a critical historiography, since the narrative has been constructed to serve as a source of divine legitimation and authorization for that very community, and not as an account of ordinary human interests and doings. Nor can the categories intended to account for the literature serve as analytical categories, since they are derived from that very literature. Establishing an alternative frame of reference and critical imagination is, however, no easy matter. In fact, the effort to avoid it is one of the distinguishing features of modern scholarship in religious studies—not least in the quest for the origins of Christianity, which is characterized by the circularity of a scholarly quest that is driven by the very imagination that produced the gospel account of Christian origination.[42]

The working hypothesis being tested by the Seminar stipulates that the pluriformity of the Jesus groups and the variety of mythologies they produced are better explained as reflexive social experiments than as responses to the historical Jesus or as generative forces set in motion by singular events and personal revelations. These experiments were concerned to shape meaningful collective identities in the face of the constraints and challenges of the times and can be compared to similar sorts of social experimentation occasioned by the times. The data of Christian beginnings can be recontextualized by viewing the variety of pictures not as evidence of variant traditions traced to a unique origination, but as evidence of the variety of social experiments and their mythic rationalizations that opens on to a vista of analogous social experiments and stands as a commonplace, rather than an extraordinary feature, of an age of "transplanted peoples and conflicting cultures."[43] The primary strategy for the choice of data to be submitted for redescription is to notice the way a text, or set of texts, might be relocated at a juncture of discursive activities such as epic revision, the formulation of codes, or rhetorical elaboration

---

Wansbrough's *The Sectarian Milieu*," *MTSR* 9 (1997): 47–73; Charles J. Adams, "Reflections on the Work of John Wansbrough," *MTSR* 9 (1997): 75–90; and G. R. Hawting, *The Idea of Idolatry and the Emergence of Islam: From Polemic to History* (Cambridge Studies in Islamic Civilization; Cambridge: Cambridge University Press, 1999).

[42] See Burton L. Mack, *A Myth of Innocence: Mark and Christian Origins* (Philadelphia: Fortress, 1988), 3–9; idem, "Redescribing Christian Origins," 247–48; repr. in *Christian Myth*, 59–61.

[43] Burton L. Mack, "Explaining Christian Mythmaking: A Theory of Social Logic," in *Christian Myth*, 105.

and be related plausibly to a locus of social interests and attractions. In this way, an intersection of mythmaking and social formation can be identified, situated, and redescribed. The general working procedure of the Seminar is (1) to provide a critical assessment of scholarship that continues to locate the New Testament and other early Christian literature within a paradigm of singular origins; (2) to recontextualize the materials by a calculated selection of analogies leading to redescription; and (3) to explain the interests and attractions of a particular social-textual site by appeal to an anthropology grounded in social theory.

Our second Consultation, held in New Orleans in 1996, addressed the theme "Meals, Mythmaking, and Social Formation." Papers were presented by Stanley K. Stowers ("On Construing Meals, Myths and Power in the World of Paul") and Hal Taussig ("Gathering Together the Bread Scattered upon the Mountains: Early Christian Meals as Occasions for Mythmaking and Rituals of Perfection"), with responses by Mack and Dennis E. Smith. We chose this theme because the social setting of meals provides an especially important locus for testing a project concerned with redescribing Christian origins. As such, our program was designed to apply to a particular topic, and test on a selection of texts, the programmatic concerns set out in our initial Consultation in Philadelphia. And so, having become persuaded that the time had come to account for the emergence of Christianities in terms of anthropology, religious studies, and the human sciences; having gauged the prospects for undertaking a project aimed at redescribing the beginnings of Christianity; and having applied comparative methods and models to a particular topic and set of texts, we proposed a third and final year of our Consultation, to be held in San Francisco in 1997, in which we would address the theme "Mythmaking and Social Formation in the Jesus Schools." The Sayings Gospel Q and the *Gospel of Thomas* were chosen because these texts, arguably, provide the best examples of early Jesus groups whose patterns of mythmaking and social formation do not fit the dominant paradigm of Christian origins. As such, they provide a perfect opportunity to rethink imaginatively the beginnings of Christianity as religion. To accomplish such a redescription, however, we will have to change the way we approach our work, keeping in mind that "anthropology is the science of culture as seen from the outside" and, thus, that "anthropology, whenever it is practiced by members of the culture it endeavors to study, loses its specific nature [as anthropology] and becomes rather akin to archaeology, history, and philology."[44] The "same

---

[44] Claude Lévi-Strauss, "The Work of the Bureau of American Ethnology and Its Lessons," in *Structural Anthropology*, vol. 2 (trans. Monique Layton; New York: Basic Books, 1963–76), 55. Citing this passage from Lévi-Strauss, Jonathan Z. Smith argues that "anthropology may be described as the science of the 'other.' ... That is to say, anthropology holds that there is

principle" should guide our understanding of religious studies.[45] Like anthropologists, biblical scholars can gain insight from the study of texts and cultures that appear to be strange, uncommon, or remote. "For there is extraordinary cognitive power in ... 'defamiliarization'—[in] making the familiar seem strange *in order to enhance our perception of the familiar.*" Since the origins of Christianity seem so self-evident to most students and scholars of the New Testament, what is needed is another point of departure, some other text or topic that will enable us to retest the discoveries of the past and see old truths in a new light. A different starting point gives us an enormous cognitive advantage in the way we imagine the emergence of Christianities. And the choice of "other gospels" as the focal point for redescription—texts which are similar, yet different; near, yet far—can only enhance our perception of difference and help make the familiar seem fresh again. Q and *Thomas* are both "foreign enough for comparison and interpretation to be necessary," and "close enough for comparison and interpretation to be possible."[46] By subjecting these mythic moments to a thick redescription, and comparing our findings with the results of other scholars, we anticipated discovering many pieces that do not fit the prevailing picture of Christian origins. As a result, we sought to continue our work in a more disciplined, concentrated format as a Seminar, not only to build on our findings and see how these and other pieces might be reassembled and repositioned, nor simply to suggest how the beginnings of Christianity might be reconceived, but in fact, to demonstrate how a single shift in perspective enables us to redescribe Christian origins: by bringing to the familiar data of biblical scholarship the discourses of anthropology, social history, and religious studies.

The results of our Consultation's deliberations about the necessity of a project of redescription and of our initial analyses of the processes of mythmaking and social formation prepared us to launch into a Seminar. Starting

---

cognitive power in 'otherness,' a power that is removed by studying the 'same.' The issue ... is not the sheer [temporal or spatial] distance of the object of study, but rather the mode of relationship of the scholar to the object. In anthropology, the distance is not to be overcome, but becomes, in itself, the prime focus and instrument of disciplinary meditation.... [Accordingly,] anthropology is essentially a project of language with respect to an 'other,' which concedes both the presence of meaning and the possibility of translation at the outset" ("What a Difference a Difference Makes," in *"To See Ourselves as Others See Us": Christians, Jews, "Others" in Late Antiquity* [ed. Jacob Neusner and Ernest S. Frerichs; Scholars Press Studies in the Humanities; Chico, Calif.: Scholars Press, 1985], 17, 18, 19).

[45] Smith, preface in *Map Is Not Territory*, ix.

[46] Smith, "Introduction," in *Imagining Religion*, xiii, xii, emphasis original, citing Victor Shklovsky, "Art as Technique," in *Russian Formalist Criticism: Four Essays* (ed. and trans. Lee T. Lemon and Marion J. Reis; Regents Critics Series; Lincoln: University of Nebraska Press, 1965), 13; cf. 13–22.

with what we know, we proposed a general, working hypothesis to be used and tested in the context of a Seminar. We know that throughout the first century, and from the earliest evidence we have in Q, *Thomas,* and Paul, there were many different groups that claimed Jesus as their founder. These groups thought of themselves variously on the models of schools, movements, associations, clubs, congregations, cults, and kingdoms. They took themselves seriously and were fascinated with the exploration of social notions that appear to have been novel combinations of older existing anthropologies. And they imagined Jesus' role and authority as the founder of these groups differently from group to group, but always in some correspondence to the anthropology or social configuration with which a particular group was working.[47] Therefore, if the importance of these two common features for social formation and mythmaking is understood—founder figure and social notion—and the two are held in balance, then a locus for the generation of early Christian interest and energy can be imagined that is not only different from the traditional scenario but also more interesting and historically plausible. Indeed, a shift in focus—away from Jesus and toward the group—locates the reasons for the generation of such energy in mythmaking activity and identifies the various profiles of Jesus as products of the mythmaking activity generated by the reflexive interests of the group.

The pluriformity of the Jesus groups, together with the variety of mythologies they produced, is a very important recognition in recent scholarship. It is no longer possible to posit a monolinear trajectory of development, true to a single, original impulse from which these many different groups must be thought of as divergent. Pluriformity signifies social experimentation as well as thoughtful rationalization. The conjunction of founder-figure mythologies with mythologies about and in support of novel social notions lets us mark their center of interest. These groups were interested in experimenting with social anthropologies in both theory and practice. The combination of social experimentation with interest in the mythology and conceptualization of a social anthropology clues us in to the fact that all of these groups were aware of what they were doing.

---

[47] For a discussion of the ways in which early Jewish and Christian groups used ideal figures, anthropologically, to represent ways of thinking through an entire social structure, compressing in the characterization of a single figure collective notions of how working societies were (to be) constructed, see Burton L. Mack, *Wisdom and the Hebrew Epic: Ben Sira's Hymn in Praise of the Fathers* (CSHJ; Chicago: University of Chicago Press, 1985); idem, "Wisdom Makes a Difference: Alternatives to 'Messianic' Configurations," in *Judaisms and Their Messiahs at the Turn of the Christian Era* (ed. Jacob Neusner et al.; Cambridge: Cambridge University Press, 1987), 15–48; idem, "The Christ and Jewish Wisdom," in *The Messiah: Developments in Earliest Judaism and Christianity* (ed. James H. Charlesworth; The First Princeton Symposium on Judaism and Christian Origins; Minneapolis: Fortress, 1992), 192–221.

Their awareness of the import of their social experiments and intellectual labors defines them as reflexive movements or social units.

> These groups were *experimental* in that the marks of novelty, discussion, debate, and changing configurations of both social formation and mythology are features shared by all.... They were *reflexive* in ... that they positioned themselves within and over against the larger social and cultural worlds by rendering critical judgments about their cultures of context and their relationships to them, and by seeking liaison with other groups and social institutions ... result[ing] in the critique, borrowing, rearrangement, and resignification of various practices and ideas from that larger world context.[48]

As such, these social experiments exhibit familiar processes of social formation and display typical responses to the broader constraints and challenges of their time and place. Accordingly, we propose the following description as a working hypothesis to be used and tested in the Seminar:

> Early Jesus groups were reflexive social experiments fascinated with the exploration of novel anthropologies in response to the challenges and opportunities presented by the social histories and diversities of cultures in the Greco-Roman world, many of which participated in similar sorts of social experimentation.

Building upon what we know, then, this hypothesis provides a different starting point for the critical, constructive task of redescribing the beginnings of Christianity. It does not simply recognize the diversity of early Christianities but seeks to account for that fact. It does not simply reproduce, by continuing to paraphrase, the canonical paradigm of Christian origins but suggests a different framework in terms of theory. Acknowledging the pluriformity, social experimentation, social anthropologies, and reflexivity of the early Jesus groups identifies them as thoughtful constructions exemplary of the human enterprise. By noting the way in which a particular group had formed and the role it saw itself playing in the larger scheme of things, we can place our texts at a particular moment in the history of early Christian groups and see how each was responding to its times. Our categories for these activities are *social formation* and *mythmaking*.

The plan for the Seminar is to identify critical moments or junctures of mythmaking and social formation that make a difference in our understanding of the emergence of Christianities, and to subject them to a thick

---

[48] Burton L. Mack, "The Christian Origins Project," in *Christian Myth,* 211, emphasis original.

description. Since these junctures are not given (according to a preconceived map, geographical region, set of texts, or privileged account of Christian origins), they must be constructed. As such, they will become specific examples or loci in a *redescription* of the history of early Christianities. Our category for such moments or junctures of mythmaking and social formation is *social location*. We can identify these junctures through our texts, for a social location is a discourse, constituted by a text (or set of texts), that both presupposes and takes up other discourses and that responds to social opportunities and cultural challenges in such a way that a significant intersection of social formation and mythmaking can be identified. By recognizing the constructive character of historical knowledge, what is learned from positioning a given discourse at the intersections of mythmaking and social history will provide the basis for a social construction of the beginnings of Christianity as religion.

Like the term *social formation* itself, the reflexive notion of creating a discourse refers to a process. We have wanted to see if members of the Seminar can engage each other, take positions, present analyses, and make responses on matters of substance, without assuming that there was an essential bond that existed and a continuous development that led from the historical Jesus to the gospel story of his appearance, death, and resurrection, and from there to the Jerusalem church in Acts and the apostle Paul and his mission. It is a discourse being constructed, in the first place, by showing why it is necessary to make a complete break with the foregoing assumption, which is what we are referring to when we speak of the dominant paradigm or the canonical narrative framework of Christian origins, a frame of reference in which almost all New Testament scholarship—notwithstanding many differences in detail—still continues to situate itself. Similarly, we are endeavoring to forge a discourse about religious origins that neither imagines the "religious" as a sui generis category, and thus, in the final analysis, as an unfathomable mystery, nor regards "origins" as a cipher for dramatic encounters with supernatural agents or forces. In fashioning our own discourse, we have chosen a different scholarly construct. We are disposed to translate the insider language of a religious community into the ordinary constraints and imaginative horizons of human thought, into the human social interests to which the labor of the creation and maintenance, contestation and change of human societies might be reduced. Thereby, we are highlighting what all members of the Seminar will recognize as fundamental: how the scholarship of Jonathan Z. Smith and Burton Mack is foundational for the conception of our project. Smith's constructive program, with its methodological precision and theoretical rationale, is a "rigorously controlled, comparative exercise in the description and classification of religious practices." As such, it is "fully appropriate for a quest for a social theory of religion," since it is "unabashedly empirical with regard to data, historical with regard to description, and rational with regard to the sense of a given religious practice."[49]

Select Publications by Jonathan Z. Smith

- "Native Cults in the Hellenistic Period," *HR* 11 (1971): 236–49.
- "The Social Description of Early Christianity," *RelSRev* 1 (1975): 19–25.
- "Too Much Kingdom, Too Little Community," *Zygon* 13 (1978): 123–30.
- "Towards Interpreting Demonic Powers in Hellenistic and Roman Antiquity," *ANRW* 16.1:425–39.
- *Map Is Not Territory: Studies in the History of Religions* (SJLA 23; Leiden: Brill, 1978; repr., Chicago: University of Chicago Press, 1993).
- *Imagining Religion: From Babylon to Jonestown* (CSHJ; Chicago: University of Chicago Press, 1982).
- "Mythos und Geschichte," in *Alcheringa oder die beginnende Zeit: Studien zu Mythologie, Schamanismus und Religion* (ed. Hans Peter Duerr; Frankfurt am Main: Qumran, 1983), 27–48.
- "No Need to Travel to the Indies: Judaism and the Study of Religion," in *Take Judaism, for Example: Studies toward the Comparison of Religions* (ed. Jacob Neusner; CSHJ; Chicago: University of Chicago Press, 1983), 215–26.
- "What a Difference a Difference Makes," in *"To See Ourselves as Others See Us": Christians, Jews, "Others" in Late Antiquity* (ed. Jacob Neusner and Ernest S. Frerichs; Scholars Press Studies in the Humanities; Chico, Calif.: Scholars Press, 1985), 3–48.
- "Prayer of Joseph," in *The Old Testament Pseudepigrapha* (ed. James H. Charlesworth; 2 vols.; Garden City, N.Y.: Doubleday, 1985), 2:699–714.
- "Hellenistic Religions," *The New Encyclopaedia Britannica*, 15th ed. (1986), 18:925–27, 929.
- "Jerusalem: The City as Place," in *Civitas: Religious Interpretations of the City* (ed. Peter S. Hawkins; Scholars Press Studies in the Humanities; Atlanta: Scholars Press, 1986), 25–38.
- "Dying and Rising Gods," *ER* 4:521–27.

---

[49] Burton L. Mack, "A Radically Social Theory of Religion," in *Secular Theories on Religion: Current Perspectives* (ed. Tim Jensen and Mikael Rothstein; Copenhagen: Museum Tusculanum Press, 2000), 130, 131.

- "The Domestication of Sacrifice," in *Violent Origins: Walter Burkert, René Girard, and Jonathan Z. Smith on Ritual Killing and Cultural Formation* (ed. Robert G. Hamerton-Kelly; Stanford, Calif.: Stanford University Press, 1987), 191–205.
- *To Take Place: Toward Theory in Ritual* (CSHJ; Chicago: University of Chicago Press, 1987).
- "'Religion' and 'Religious Studies': No Difference at All," *Soundings* 71 (1988): 231–44.
- "'Narratives into Problems': The College Introductory Course and the Study of Religion," *JAAR* 56 (1988): 727–39.
- "Connections," *JAAR* 58 (1990): 1–15.
- *Drudgery Divine: On the Comparison of Early Christianities and the Religions of Late Antiquity* (Jordan Lectures in Comparative Religion 14; London: School of Oriental and African Studies, University of London; Chicago: University of Chicago Press, 1990).
- "A Slip in Time Saves Nine: Prestigious Origins Again," in *Chronotypes: The Construction of Time* (ed. John Bender and David E. Wellbery; Stanford, Calif.: Stanford University Press, 1991), 67–76, 232–33.
- "Differential Equations: On Constructing the 'Other'" (The University Lecture in Religion 13, Arizona State University, Tempe, Arizona, 5 March 1992).
- "Scriptures and Histories," *MTSR* 4 (1992): 97–105.
- "Trading Places," in *Ancient Magic and Ritual Power* (ed. Marvin Meyer and Paul Mirecki; Religions in the Graeco-Roman World 129; Leiden: Brill, 1995), 13–27.
- "Introduction," in *The HarperCollins Dictionary of Religion* (ed. Jonathan Z. Smith; San Francisco: HarperSanFrancisco, 1995), xix–xxiv.
- "Wisdom's Place," in *Death, Ecstasy, and Other Worldly Journeys* (ed. John J. Collins and Michael Fishbane; Albany, N.Y.: State University of New York Press, 1995), 3–13.
- "A Matter of Class: Taxonomies of Religion," *HTR* 89 (1996): 387–403.
- "Social Formations of Early Christianities: A Response to Ron Cameron and Burton Mack," *MTSR* 8 (1996): 271–78.
- "Teaching the Bible in the Context of General Education," *Teaching Theology and Religion* 1 (1998): 73–78.
- "Constructing a Small Place," in *Sacred Space: Shrine, City, Land* (ed. Benjamin Z. Kedar and R. J. Zwi Werblowsky; New York: New York University Press, 1998), 18–31.
- "Religion, Religions, Religious," in *Critical Terms for Religious Studies* (ed. Mark C. Taylor; Chicago: University of Chicago Press, 1998), 269–84.

- "Cross-Cultural Reflections on Apocalypticism," in *Ancient and Modern Perspectives on the Bible and Culture: Essays in Honor of Hans Dieter Betz* (ed. Adela Yarbro Collins; Scholars Press Homage Series 22; Atlanta: Scholars Press, 1998), 281–85.
- "Canons, Catalogues and Classics," in *Canonization and Decanonization: Papers Presented to the International Conference of the Leiden Institute for the Study of Religions (LISOR), Held at Leiden 9–10 January 1997* (ed. A. van der Kooij and K. van der Toorn; SHR 82; Leiden: Brill, 1998), 295–311.
- "Classification," in *Guide to the Study of Religion* (ed. Willi Braun and Russell T. McCutcheon; London: Cassell, 2000), 35–44.
- "The 'End' of Comparison: Redescription and Rectification," in *A Magic Still Dwells: Comparative Religion in the Postmodern Age* (ed. Kimberley C. Patton and Benjamin C. Ray; Berkeley and Los Angeles: University of California Press, 2000), 237–41.
- "Bible and Religion," *BCSSR* 29/4 (2000): 87–93.
- "Acknowledgments: Morphology and History in Mircea Eliade's *Patterns in Comparative Religion* (1949–1999), Part 1: The Work and Its Contexts," *HR* 39 (2000): 315–31.
- "Acknowledgments: Morphology and History in Mircea Eliade's *Patterns in Comparative Religion* (1949–1999), Part 2: The Texture of the Work," *HR* 39 (2000): 332–51.
- "A Twice-Told Tale: The History of the History of Religions' History," *Numen* 48 (2001): 131–46.
- "Close Encounters of Diverse Kinds," in *Religion and Cultural Studies* (ed. Susan L. Mizruchi; Princeton: Princeton University Press, 2001), 3–21.
- "Religion Up and Down, Out and In," in *Sacred Time, Sacred Place: Archaeology and the Religion of Israel* (ed. Barry M. Gittlen; Winona Lake, Ind.: Eisenbrauns, 2002), 3–10.
- "Great Scott! Thought and Action One More Time," in *Magic and Ritual in the Ancient World* (ed. Paul Mirecki and Marvin Meyer; Religions in the Graeco-Roman World 141; Leiden: Brill, 2002), 73–91.
- "Manna, Mana Everywhere and /ᴗ/ᴗ/ᴗ," in *Radical Interpretation in Religion* (ed. Nancy K. Frankenberry; Cambridge: Cambridge University Press, 2002), 188–212.
- "Here, There, and Anywhere," in *Prayer, Magic, and the Stars in the Ancient and Late Antique World* (ed. Scott Noegel et al.; Magic in History Series; University Park: Pennsylvania State University Press, 2003), 21–36.

Mack's scholarship, for its part, constitutes a forthright attempt to apply Smith's program of research to the study of Christian beginnings, concerned, in particular, with how "to position a given myth, ritual, text, rhetoric, or social practice at its own intersection of ... *social formation* and *mythmaking*." As such, Mack's interests lie in investigating the social logic or "relationship of a [given] myth to the process[es] of social formation," highlighting "the ideological strategies for legitimizing social experiments" and illustrating "the social and intellectual production of ... religion *as* a human construction *within* a social history," without recourse to mystification, "mythic origins," or special pleading.[50]

SELECT PUBLICATIONS BY BURTON L. MACK

- "Imitatio Mosis: Patterns of Cosmology and Soteriology in the Hellenistic Synagogue," *SPhilo* 1 (1972): 27–55.
- *Logos und Sophia: Untersuchungen zur Weisheitstheologie im hellenistischen Judentum* (SUNT 10; Göttingen: Vandenhoeck & Ruprecht, 1973).
- "Exegetical Traditions in Alexandrian Judaism: A Program for the Analysis of the Philonic Corpus," *SPhilo* 3 (1974–75): 71–112.
- "Weisheit und Allegorie bei Philo von Alexandrien: Untersuchungen zum Traktat *De congressu eruditionis*," *SPhilo* 5 (1978): 57–105.
- "Under the Shadow of Moses: Authorship and Authority in Hellenistic Judaism," in *Society of Biblical Literature 1982 Seminar Papers* (SBLSP 21; Chico, Calif.: Scholars Press, 1982), 299–318.
- "Philo Judaeus and Exegetical Traditions in Alexandria," *ANRW* 21.1:227–71.
- "Decoding the Scripture: Philo and the Rules of Rhetoric," in *Nourished with Peace: Studies in Hellenistic Judaism in Memory of Samuel Sandmel* (ed. Frederick E. Greenspahn et al.; Scholars Press Homage Series 9; Chico, Calif.: Scholars Press, 1984), 81–115.
- *Wisdom and the Hebrew Epic: Ben Sira's Hymn in Praise of the Fathers* (CSHJ; Chicago: University of Chicago Press, 1985).
- "Gilgamesh and the Wizard of Oz: The Scholar as Hero," *Foundations and Facets Forum* 1/2 (1985): 3–29.
- "The Innocent Transgressor: Jesus in Early Christian Myth and History," *Semeia* 33 (1985): 135–65.

---

[50] Ibid., 131, emphasis original. For the programmatic application of Smith's constructive method and theory in Mack's own work, see idem, *Myth of Innocence*, esp. 19–20 with nn. 8–9, 22–23 n. 10, 27–28 n. 1, 40 n. 10, 50 n. 17. Note that Smith has described *A Myth of Innocence* as "the first study of 'Christian origins' which may be taken up, with profit, by the general student of *religion*" (*Drudgery Divine*, 110 n. 43, emphasis original).

- With Roland E. Murphy. "Wisdom Literature," in *Early Judaism and Its Modern Interpreters* (ed. Robert A. Kraft and George W. E. Nickelsburg; SBLBMI 2; Atlanta: Scholars Press, 1986), 371–410.
- With Edward N. O'Neil. "The Chreia Discussion of Hermogenes of Tarsus: Introduction, Translation and Comments," in *The Progymnasmata* (vol. 1 of *The Chreia in Ancient Rhetoric*; ed. Ronald F. Hock and Edward N. O'Neil; SBLTT 27; Atlanta: Scholars Press, 1986), 153–81.
- "Anecdotes and Arguments: The Chreia in Antiquity and Early Christianity" (The Institute for Antiquity and Christianity Occasional Papers 10; Claremont, Calif.: Institute for Antiquity and Christianity, 1987).
- "Wisdom Makes a Difference: Alternatives to 'Messianic' Configurations," in *Judaisms and Their Messiahs at the Turn of the Christian Era* (ed. Jacob Neusner et al.; Cambridge: Cambridge University Press, 1987), 15–48.
- "Introduction: Religion and Ritual," in *Violent Origins: Walter Burkert, René Girard, and Jonathan Z. Smith on Ritual Killing and Cultural Formation* (ed. Robert G. Hamerton-Kelly; Stanford, Calif.: Stanford University Press, 1987), 1–70.
- "The Kingdom Sayings in Mark," *Foundations and Facets Forum* 3/1 (1987): 3–47.
- "The Kingdom That Didn't Come: A Social History of the Q Tradents," in *Society of Biblical Literature 1988 Seminar Papers* (SBLSP 27; Atlanta: Scholars Press, 1988), 608–35.
- *A Myth of Innocence: Mark and Christian Origins* (Philadelphia: Fortress, 1988).
- "Sirach (Ecclesiasticus)," in *The Apocrypha and the New Testament* (vol. 2 of *The Books of the Bible;* ed. Bernhard W. Anderson; New York: Scribner's, 1989), 65–86.
- With Vernon K. Robbins. *Patterns of Persuasion in the Gospels* (FF; Sonoma, Calif.: Polebridge, 1989).
- Review of Gary R. Habermas and Antony G. N. Flew, ed. Terry L. Miethe, *Did Jesus Rise from the Dead? The Resurrection Debate, History and Theory* 28 (1989): 215–24.
- "Lord of the Logia: Savior or Sage?" in *Gospel Origins and Christian Beginnings: In Honor of James M. Robinson* (ed. James E. Goehring et al.; Forum Fascicles; Sonoma, Calif.: Polebridge, 1990), 3–18.
- "All the Extra Jesuses: Christian Origins in the Light of the Extra-Canonical Gospels," *Semeia* 49 (1990): 169–76.
- *Rhetoric and the New Testament* (GBS; Minneapolis: Fortress, 1990).

- "A Myth of Innocence at Sea," *Cont* 1/2 (1991): 140–57.
- "Q and the Gospel of Mark: Revising Christian Origins," *Semeia* 55 (1991): 15–39.
- "Staal's Gauntlet and the Queen," *Religion* 21 (1991): 213–18.
- "Wisdom and Apocalyptic in Philo," in *Heirs of the Septuagint: Philo, Hellenistic Judaism and Early Christianity. Festschrift for Earle Hilgert* (ed. David T. Runia et al.; Studia Philonica Annual 3; Atlanta: Scholars Press, 1991), 21–39.
- "The Christ and Jewish Wisdom," in *The Messiah: Developments in Earliest Judaism and Christianity* (ed. James H. Charlesworth; The First Princeton Symposium on Judaism and Christian Origins; Minneapolis: Fortress, 1992), 192–221.
- "After *Drudgery Divine*," *Numen* 39 (1992): 225–33.
- *The Lost Gospel: The Book of Q and Christian Origins* (San Francisco: HarperSanFrancisco, 1993).
- "Persuasive Pronouncements: An Evaluation of Recent Studies on the Chreia," *Semeia* 64 (1993): 283–87.
- *Who Wrote the New Testament? The Making of the Christian Myth* (San Francisco: HarperSanFrancisco, 1995).
- "On Redescribing Christian Origins," *MTSR* 8 (1996): 247–69.
- "Q and a Cynic-like Jesus," in *Whose Historical Jesus?* (ed. William E. Arnal and Michel Desjardins; Studies in Christianity and Judaism 7; Waterloo, Ont.: Wilfrid Laurier University Press, 1997), 25–36.
- "Power, Purity, and Innocence: The Christian Imagination of the Gospel," in *Power, Powerlessness, and the Divine: New Inquiries in Bible and Theology* (ed. Cynthia L. Rigby; Scholars Press Studies in Theological Education; Atlanta: Scholars Press, 1997), 241–61.
- "Many Movements, Many Myths: Redescribing the Attractions of Early Christianities. Toward a Conversation with Rodney Stark," *RelSRev* 25 (1999): 132–36.
- "Social Formation," in *Guide to the Study of Religion* (ed. Willi Braun and Russell T. McCutcheon; London: Cassell, 2000), 283–96.
- "A Radically Social Theory of Religion," in *Secular Theories on Religion: Current Perspectives* (ed. Tim Jensen and Mikael Rothstein; Copenhagen: Museum Tusculanum Press, 2000), 123–36.
- "Caretakers and Critics: On the Social Role of Scholars Who Study Religion," *BCSSR* 30/2 (2001): 32–38.
- *The Christian Myth: Origins, Logic, and Legacy* (New York: Continuum, 2001).

By adopting the standards, perspectives, and questions of a thoroughgoing social anthropology, this volume endeavors to launch a critical discourse-in-the-making about the beginnings of Christianity. It represents an attempt to present in published form three years of intense, in-house discussion and debate carried on by members of the SBL Seminar on Ancient Myths and Modern Theories of Christian Origins through working papers, e-mail responses, annual meetings, and retrospective reflections focused on a series of carefully selected social-textual sites. Instead of constructing yet another portrait of the historical Jesus as the sole—and unique—point of origination, the Seminar is testing the thesis that the historical beginnings of Christianity are best understood as diverse social experiments.[51] Instead of assuming that the gospel story has its foundation in a human encounter with transcendence or in the dramatic religious experience of individuals, the Seminar is examining the textual data of early Christianities for indices of mythmaking as social practice. The editors have sought to render each year's work by placing working papers for the annual meetings in the context of an introduction, summary, commentary, and reflection. This volume also features a set of metareflections by members of the Seminar on issues that attend the making of a discourse as well as that pertain to the definitions and strategies for achieving further goals. The conclusion to the volume offers the editors' judgments about the difference that our scholarship has made toward the redescribing of Christian origins.

The publication of this volume will demonstrate how we have expanded and distributed the creative moments of beginnings for the writing of a critical history of early Christianities. All students of the New Testament will recognize the ambitious and controversial nature of this undertaking. The Seminar's work does not merely add new wrinkles to an already established consensus about the diversity of early Christianities. We intend nothing less than to change the traditional picture of Christian origins. Nevertheless, the methods employed are common to the field, and

---

[51] For a critique of the entire quest of the historical Jesus, see Burton L. Mack, who observes that "the quest has not produced any agreement about a textual data base from which to work. The textual units used for this or that profile change from scholar to scholar without any agreed-upon theoretical framework to adjudicate the differences among them. This is a serious indictment of the guild of New Testament scholarship ... [which] resists the pursuit of a theoretical framework and the accompanying rules of argumentation necessary for coming to agreements about matters of data, method, explanation, and replication of experiments or research projects. These are foundational matters for an academic discipline.... If there is no agreement about what texts count and how to turn them into data for historical reconstructions, it means that the quest [of the historical Jesus] cannot be thought of as an academic discourse within a scholarly discipline.... This means that we need to start over with the quest for Christian origins. And the place to start is with the observation that the New Testament texts are not only inadequate for a Jesus quest, they are data for an entirely different phenomenon. They are ... the myths of origin imagined by early Christians seriously engaged in their social experiments. They are data for early Christian mythmaking" ("The Historical Jesus Hoopla," in *Christian Myth*, 34, 35, 40).

the problematizing of standard categories and assumptions points to aporiae well known to biblical scholars. Those who work in cognate fields will find in this volume an engagement with familiar issues regarding the relationship of religious narratives to critical historiography. Those who follow the debates on the Bible and history in the popular media will find here an alternative way of formulating the issues of that debate. The making of a discourse about the beginnings of Christianity is intended as a contribution to the wider field of the academic study of religion. By drawing on cognitive and social approaches to the study of religion, the Seminar is in the process of defining the subject of Christian origins in such a way as to provide a particular example of theory in religion.

PART 1

ALTERNATE BEGINNINGS: THE SAYINGS GOSPEL Q
AND THE *GOSPEL OF THOMAS*

Introduction to the Papers from the Third Year of the Consultation

Merrill P. Miller

The papers published below are four of those that were presented, received written responses, and were discussed at our third Consultation, held in San Francisco in 1997. Although we were not yet operating according to the SBL format as a Seminar, but read and then discussed the papers and responses, all of the contributions were solicited from individuals who had declared their interest in joining as full members of the proposed Seminar, and the papers were intended to address the first locus selected for a project of redescription: the Jesus schools of the Sayings Gospel Q and the *Gospel of Thomas*.[1]

When Q and *Thomas* are taken seriously as texts capable of sustaining ideological interests and group formations among the earliest followers of Jesus, they constitute as a set of texts alternative points of departure to the typical assumption of the apocalyptic and kerygmatic orientation of the first followers of Jesus. Our intention was to build on the potential cognitive advantage to be gained by starting with texts that did not support the dominant (canonical) paradigm of Christian origins and to explore three areas that seemed fundamental to the task of redescription: (1) the problematizing of the dominant paradigm; (2) the selection of analogies in the interest of redescription; and (3) the social

---

[1] Two of these papers were originally published in *MTSR*, as were the two papers and responses from our first Consultation. See Merrill P. Miller, "Introduction to the Consultation on Christian Origins," *MTSR* 8 (1996): 229–30; Ron Cameron, "The Anatomy of a Discourse: On 'Eschatology' as a Category for Explaining Christian Origins," *MTSR* 8 (1996): 231–45; Burton L. Mack, "On Redescribing Christian Origins," *MTSR* 8 (1996): 247–69; Jonathan Z. Smith, "Social Formations of Early Christianities: A Response to Ron Cameron and Burton Mack," *MTSR* 8 (1996): 271–78; John S. Kloppenborg, "Critical Histories and Theories of Religion: A Response to Burton Mack and Ron Cameron," *MTSR* 8 (1996): 279–89; Merrill P. Miller, "Introduction to Selected Papers from the Third Consultation on Christian Origins," *MTSR* 11 (1999): 207–9; Willi Braun, "Socio-Mythic Invention, Graeco-Roman Schools, and the Sayings Gospel Q," *MTSR* 11 (1999): 210–35; Ron Cameron, "Ancient Myths and Modern Theories of the Gospel of Thomas and Christian Origins," *MTSR* 11 (1999): 236–57.

attractions that can be inferred from an account of several stages of a social history or that render an explanation of the rhetorical and mythic features of the texts.

Willi Braun positions his paper on "The Schooling of a Galilean Jesus Association (The Sayings Gospel Q)" in the stream of recent scholarly studies which have shown that Q, both as a text and a social entity, is the product of "deliberate, thoughtful sociomythic invention."[2] The expression "sociomythic invention" is Braun's shorthand tag for "the dynamic and dialectical process of collective identity construction highlighted by 'myth-making' and 'social formation,'" the redescriptive categories introduced by Burton L. Mack for analysis, explanation, and theoretical reflection on the intellectual and behavioral activities of persons constructing a shared, social identity.[3] Braun alerts us at the outset to a particular methodological issue. If the categories are to sustain a project of redescription, they must retain sufficient generality to be able to fit local sites within the larger cultural arena; but they must become neither so vague nor so reified that they provide no focus for comparison or occlude differences among local sites. Accordingly, Braun begins the task of "stalking" the school analogy to see how it might help us understand Q as a particular sociomythic invention and how it might serve "to qualify the categories of mythmaking and social formation themselves."[4]

Although "school" can refer to a great variety of venues, Braun argues for the descriptive and strategic usefulness of the "school" label for Q: descriptive of the evidence of scribal abilities and mentality, and strategically posed against "theories of origin that obscure, diminish, or erase intellectual efforts and means in the highly complex process of producing group identities in the larger cultural arena." The production of Q as a scholastic effort characteristic of "a scribal mythmaking intelligence and competence"[5] is especially compelling when features of Q's "textuality," "composition," "genre," and "school technologies" are given sustained consideration and when the relation of erudition to power and authority in the Greco-Roman world is taken into account.

Braun proceeds to link these scribal indicators to the social identity of Q's producers as uprooted (or deracinated) urban scribes of "middling" status, a hypothesis first suggested by John S. Kloppenborg[6] and

---

[2] Willi Braun, "The Schooling of a Galilean Jesus Association (The Sayings Gospel Q)," 43 (in this volume).

[3] Ibid., 43 n. 1.

[4] Ibid., 44.

[5] Ibid., 47.

[6] John S. Kloppenborg, "Literary Convention, Self-Evidence and the Social History of the Q People," *Semeia* 55 (1991): 85–89.

now argued at length by William E. Arnal.[7] This suggests to Braun where we might look for a wider field of analogies to Q as a group and as a document that, together, "display an evident bent on investing in the power of text production ... as locus and means of social formation in response to the experience of displacement."[8] Braun discusses three recent scholarly projects of redescription as especially instructive: (1) the work on the Greek magical papyri and Jonathan Z. Smith's suggestion that the papyri represent "a displacement of ritual practice into writing";[9] (2) Bernard Frischer's work on Epicurean fraternities;[10] and (3) Jack N. Lightstone's redescription of the emergence of the rabbinic guilds.[11] The discussion can be highlighted by reference to four observations that Braun makes. First, each of these analogies shows how the perception or experience of uprootedness leads to "imagining reemplacement in a reconfigured social space" and "causes seguing toward alternate social visions."[12] Second, the strategies for responding to analogous social conditions go in *"different directions"*[13] and cannot be predicted from these conditions themselves; nor does the evidence of intentional responses predict the consequences for social formation or the direction of further discursive activity. Third, drawing on Lightstone's observation that the chief interest of a defunct temple scribal class following the destruction of the temple was the reemplacement of scribal skills for group survival, Braun suggests that the trajectory from Q^1 to Q^2 and Q^3 is "moved in part by the centripetal force of the group's increasing attachment to itself,"[14] rather than by the constancy of a myth or by an ideal social design. Fourth, none of the analogies to which Braun points is self-evident, but each is a product of recent scholarly redescription. Nor are the closest analogies to the Q "research group" necessarily to be found in other early Jesus groups.

While Braun makes cautionary remarks regarding an intellectualist approach to social formation, calls attention to the tendency to reify analytic

---

[7] William E. Arnal, *Jesus and the Village Scribes: Galilean Conflicts and the Setting of Q* (Minneapolis: Fortress, 2001).

[8] Braun, "Schooling of a Galilean Jesus Association," 59.

[9] Ibid., 59 n. 71, citing Jonathan Z. Smith, "Trading Places," in *Ancient Magic and Ritual Power* (ed. Marvin Meyer and Paul Mirecki; Religions in the Graeco-Roman World 129; Leiden: Brill, 1995), 26.

[10] Bernard Frischer, *The Sculpted Word: Epicureanism and Philosophical Recruitment in Ancient Greece* (Berkeley and Los Angeles: University of California Press, 1982).

[11] Jack N. Lightstone, "Whence the Rabbis? From Coherent Description to Fragmented Reconstructions," *SR* 26 (1997): 275–95.

[12] Braun, "Schooling of a Galilean Jesus Association," 60.

[13] Ibid., 61, emphasis original.

[14] Ibid., 65 n. 96.

categories, and underscores the explanatory challenges that confront a historiographical project of redescription, he carries out a quest for appropriate analogies to Q not only by focusing on scholastic activities and communities but also by stressing the discursive side of social formation. That point of emphasis is clearly different in Arnal's paper on "Why Q Failed: From Ideological Project to Group Formation," which challenges the view that discursive practices are determinative of social history. Consequently, they do not play a constitutive role in the social processes that account for the failure of the Q project.

Arnal begins his paper with a summary analysis of Mack's account of the preliterary and compositional layers of Q and their relationship to the social history of the Q group,[15] drawing from that discussion some critical conclusions about social formation in general. Arnal maintains that social formation is conceived in too narrow a way when it is identified with a sense of belonging to a group self-consciously detached from a larger social-cultural environment. Mythmaking as a discursive practice is also too simply equated with the activity of a "group defined by its own ideological self-referentiality." For Arnal, group emergence does not begin with critical ideas that take on social shape as a way of life, giving rise to a social vision and subsequently to social formation; rather, "ideology, social discourse, and (voluntary) social grouping are always relational: they take place within some form of larger social totality and quite self-consciously refer to that totality."[16] Arnal agrees that the school analogy for Q has a particular fit with Mack's account of the social history of Q, but he maintains that this is the case only because Mack's account is "idealist: critical ideas ... lead to a 'social program,' which, when it cannot be implemented in general, comes to be implemented for and among its proponents only, which generates further parochial sensibilities."[17] In contrast, Arnal views the rhetoric of Q^1 beatitudes "in light of a social agenda that does not imply 'group formation,' that is, that does not imply a social discourse that emanates at every stage of its development from itself ... but rather from the efforts of those individuals to engage the social body around them and to modify aspects of its broader social discourse (mythology?) as it is already given."[18]

---

[15] Burton L. Mack, "The Kingdom That Didn't Come: A Social History of the Q Tradents," in *Society of Biblical Literature 1988 Seminar Papers* (SBLSP 27; Atlanta: Scholars Press, 1988), 608–35; idem, *The Lost Gospel: The Book of Q and Christian Origins* (San Francisco: HarperSanFrancisco, 1993).

[16] William E. Arnal, "Why Q Failed: From Ideological Project to Group Formation," 74 (in this volume).

[17] Ibid., 73.

[18] Ibid., 74.

Since the beatitudes are not prescriptive, they should not be construed as indicating a way of life that is isomorphic with the conditions described; rather, on Arnal's view, they reflect in their Q^1 setting a change of interest from engaging a general condition of economic deracination to responding to a specific situation of the social deracination of village scribes. Arnal argues that the composition of Q^1 does not represent the crystallization into group formation of an earlier social vision but should be seen as the response to the failure of an earlier social agenda. The failure of Q is not the consequence of a failed rhetoric or social program, but simply the inability of these scribes to restore their status, despite an impressive inversionary rhetoric and social program.[19] Thus, the social processes that determined the failure of the Q project are all extradiscursive. Arnal concludes that what needs to be mapped and understood are the social processes that are determinative of social history, and that these processes are always extradiscursive.[20]

Ron Cameron's paper on "Ancient Myths and Modern Theories of the *Gospel of Thomas* and Christian Origins" addresses directly the issue of how *Thomas* problematizes the canonical picture of Christian origins and its continuing impact as the operative framework for most scholarship at the levels of historical description and theoretical imagination. When Cameron imagines the *Gospel of Thomas* in a school space of disciples gathered around a master, he finds that this entails much more than merely the recognition of the diversity of early Christianities. It challenges the very assumption of a singular point of origination (from which diverse groups are thought to have emerged); it questions the adequacy of a theory of comparison that serves to protect the assumption of the uniqueness of the Christian religion; and it shows why an anthropology rooted in social interests and cultural investments, rather than in personal experiences of transcendence, requires a different way of accounting for the emergence of Christianities.

In Cameron's account, most scholarship on the *Gospel of Thomas* has served, all too often, not the interests of the creation of new knowledge but the wistful confirmation of what is already known, or what is taken for granted. "From the beginning," he observes, "scholars have been concerned chiefly with three basic questions: the authenticity of the sayings attributed to Jesus in the text, the relation of the *Gospel of Thomas* to the New Testament, and whether or not this Gospel is 'gnostic.'"[21] Confining the discussion to "questions of authenticity, textual dependence, and

---

[19] Ibid., 82–84.
[20] Ibid., 84.
[21] Ron Cameron, "Ancient Myths and Modern Theories of the *Gospel of Thomas* and Christian Origins," 89–90 (in this volume).

gnostic influence ironically truncates the analysis, serving—whether intentionally or not—to marginalize the text and its import for the scholarly imagination of Christian origins."[22] Cameron raises this issue in order to focus on two matters of consequence for the Seminar. First, "we have yet to pay sufficient methodological attention to the fundamental issue of difference." Second, "we need to devote ourselves to more sustained theoretical discourse, specifically about the intellectual process of translation: the necessity to engage in explanation and interpretation from a human-sciences perspective, in disciplined ways that do not simply reproduce, by continuing to paraphrase, the dominant (essentially Lukan) paradigm of Christian origins."[23]

The potential impact of *Thomas* for reimagining the beginnings of Christianity is neutralized by presupposing "the Bible ... as the privileged point of comparison,"[24] by subordinating the *Gospel of Thomas* to the canonical Gospels, such that "*Thomas* is not taken seriously ... but is reduced to the status of a textual variant in the history of the Synoptic tradition,"[25] and by ignoring the differences between the *Gospel of Thomas* and the New Testament, viewing *Thomas*'s sayings as variants of the canonical myth of the resurrection. Cameron takes note of and elaborates on each of these tendencies and characterizes them all as inadequate to bring into relief the difference between the *Gospel of Thomas* and the canonical imagination of Christian origins. In particular, Cameron criticizes the recent efforts of Gregory J. Riley to interpret *Thomas* in terms of a theological debate with, and polemic against, a doctrine of the resurrection said to be held by the Gospel of John.[26] Such efforts illustrate the problem of shoehorning our evidence into conventional categories of interpretation, of accumulating more data and then reducing it all to variations of habituated patterns of thought. "By privileging the resurrection as the historical starting point, foundational event, transformative experience, ubiquitous persuasion, distinguishing criterion, and decisive category for explaining the beginnings of Christianity," Cameron argues, "biblical scholarship persists in perpetuating in its discourse a widely

---

[22] Ibid., 91.

[23] Ibid., 91, 92.

[24] Ibid., 91, adding: "any differences between the *Gospel of Thomas* and the canonical Gospels are ignored, and all discourse of a social, historical, literary, or theological character is said to be the same. Every distinguishing feature of *Thomas* has thus been erased in the interests of maintaining the reliability of the words, traditions, accounts, and authority of the New Testament" (ibid.).

[25] Ibid.

[26] Gregory J. Riley, *Resurrection Reconsidered: Thomas and John in Controversy* (Minneapolis: Fortress, 1995).

assumed—but totally unwarranted—conservative theological theory that has caused untold mischief in the scholarly imagination of the New Testament and Christian origins."[27] The notion of "resurrection is absent from *Thomas* not because *Thomas* presupposes it as a central symbol or narratable experience, but because the metaphor of resurrection is fundamentally incompatible with ... this Gospel."[28] Accordingly, "the *Gospel of Thomas* cannot be explained as a variation of the myth of origins constructed by Luke and canonized in the New Testament, because *Thomas*'s genre, designs, logic, and theology are incompatible with the dominant paradigm of Christian origins."[29]

We should not be surprised that attempts to take *Thomas* seriously as a witness to Christian origins by enfolding its differences into the familiar picture never manage to change the picture. Cameron demonstrates that these strategies do not adequately explain the text of *Thomas*, precisely because the *Gospel of Thomas* is not a window that opens on to a more intricate and nuanced sighting of a familiar picture. Instead, it opens on to the wider vista of responses to the conditions and challenges of the Greco-Roman world and shows us another point of departure for imagining the emergence of Christianities, one that will also require different ways of reading the strong texts of the canonical (gospel) paradigm and, thus, that will lead to revising the conventional view of Christian beginnings. This should not be construed as a matter of which data to privilege. It is, rather, to see that *Thomas* provides another point of departure because it requires a different "frame of reference" and "mode of comparison" for its understanding, a frame of reference and mode of comparison that no paraphrase of the canonical picture, however critical, could ever accommodate. It is to say that "*Thomas* demands a different discourse, series of scholarly assumptions, and theory of religion ... a different social anthropology, set of interpretative categories, and critical imagination to map out the characteristics and contours of a social history" of early Christianities.[30]

Arthur J. Dewey's paper, "'Keep Speaking until You Find ...': *Thomas* and the School of Oral Mimesis," presents his own version of a different discourse and set of scholarly assumptions required to account for the *Gospel of Thomas*. Like Cameron, he draws principally on the rhetorical schools for his model and tradition. He also takes the collection of sayings to presuppose a circle of disciples gathered around the master, and, like Cameron, he regards the sorites of *Gos. Thom.* 2 as the hermeneutical key

---

[27] Cameron, "Ancient Myths and Modern Theories," 98–99.
[28] Ibid., 100.
[29] Ibid., 107.
[30] Ibid., 107, 108.

of the document.[31] With Braun and Arnal, Dewey identifies the document's tradents with the social level and professional skills of the *grammatikos*. But whereas Cameron imagines an intertextual process productive of a written document and characteristic of the intellectual labor of a literate culture, Dewey's emphasis is on the manner in which the written document contributes to the practice of oral mimesis and makes the labor of "seeking and finding" a reflection of the processes of an oral pedagogy, "the 'toil' ... of coming to speech."[32] Moreover, while Arnal and Braun have called attention to the *grammatikos* and other lower-level scribes as a social type and have emphasized their literate competencies and investment in the power of text production, Dewey is thinking specifically of the elementary pedagogical tools and recitation skills of the *grammatikos*. Much more than the literate skills of a scribal intelligence, it is the improvisational skills of an oral intelligence that are discerned and woven into a thesis in Dewey's paper.

The thesis is wide ranging. The sayings in the *Gospel of Thomas* are viewed as the product of an oral pedagogy. *Gospel of Thomas* 2, the hermeneutical key of the text, is said to reflect the oral procedure of hearing, recitation, and improvisation. Dewey takes the various sayings within the document as evidence of this oral strategy, which also provides a clue to the structure of the document. The authority of the written document is understood to rest entirely on its facilitating oral communication. The meaning of many of the sayings, especially those often thought to be most esoteric and gnosticizing, is the experience of oral communication itself. Accordingly, Dewey urges us to consider how sayings about "origin" and "rest" may be understood to reflect the nature of the speech act itself and do not require metaphysical interpretation. "Protology" and "eschatology" are not matters of a time chart but the "creative process of coming to speech."[33] Similarly, the notion of "two becoming one" is not a metaphysical statement of identity but describes the "real solidarity of the community brought about by the recitation and improvisation of the sayings of Jesus."[34]

Oral mimesis is also the way in which identity and authority are challenged and constructed in *Gos. Thom.* 12 and 13. "What the 'likening' really is ... is not a matter of labeling.... Rather, the 'likening' is essentially a mimesis, an activity whereby the disciple learns how to speak like Jesus.... Identity is achieved not through some metaphysical or mystical sleight of

---

[31] Arthur J. Dewey, "'Keep Speaking until You Find ...': *Thomas* and the School of Oral Mimesis," 117–18 (in this volume).
[32] Ibid., 123.
[33] Ibid., 126.
[34] Ibid., 129.

hand, or conceptual tour de force, but through the actual learning how to speak the words of Jesus."[35] The riddle language of "two becoming one" is thus, in essence, "the art of impersonation."[36] The school of *Thomas* mimics the voices of other school traditions, not only those of the Pharisees but also those of other Jesus schools (e.g., the Judeans in their false distinctions, Q² and Mark in their apocalypticizing tendencies), distinguishing itself from them by virtue of its insistence on the oral medium and pedagogical process for transmitting the tradition, for keeping the memory of Jesus alive, and for making the kingdom present in the sayings of Jesus. It is this same medium and same process that, according to Dewey, convey the image of Jesus the riddler and that have "best preserved the 'feel' of the oral tradition of Jesus."[37]

---

[35] Ibid., 123.
[36] Ibid., with 124 nn. 33–34.
[37] Ibid., 131.

THE SCHOOLING OF A GALILEAN JESUS ASSOCIATION (THE SAYINGS GOSPEL Q)

Willi Braun

1. INTRODUCTION

The recent record of scholarship on the early Christian Sayings Gospel Q has brought us to the point where the view of Q as both product of as well as reflective and productive of deliberate, thoughtful sociomythic invention by a particular group no longer needs to be argued.[1] What E. P. Thompson said of the making of the English working class applies to Q—and any other early Christian group—as well: It "did not rise like the sun at an appointed time. It was present at its own making."[2] Burton L. Mack rightly speaks of Q (both as text and social entity) as a "precious" exemplar of "an entire history of an early 'Christian' community-in-the-making."[3] This view, amply warranted by recent literary and social studies of Q, stands as a reasonable presupposition that not only permits but also requires a move toward a new set of questions that would enable us to qualify and differentiate sociomythic inventions and processes in antiquity at "local" (*Gospel of Thomas*, Q, etc.) sites by a necessarily complex toggling procedure: (1) fitting specific sociomythic formations into a broader picture in order to save our "local" analysis from thin conclusions by acts of analogy and comparison, and (2) relying on local, particular sociomythic formations to keep generalizations and typologies based on surveys of the

---

[1] I use "sociomythic invention" not to coin a neologism but as my shorthand tag for the dynamic and dialectical process of collective identity construction highlighted by "mythmaking" and "social formation" that Burton Mack has persuasively introduced as analytic and explanatory categories. See Burton L. Mack, "On Redescribing Christian Origins," *MTSR* 8 (1996): 247–69; repr., with revisions, in *The Christian Myth: Origins, Logic, and Legacy* (New York: Continuum, 2001), 59–80; idem, "Social Formation," in *Guide to the Study of Religion* (ed. Willi Braun and Russell T. McCutcheon; London: Cassell, 2000), 283–96.

[2] E. P. Thompson, *The Making of the English Working Class* (London: Gollancz, 1963), 9.

[3] Burton L. Mack, *Who Wrote the New Testament? The Making of the Christian Myth* (San Francisco: HarperSanFrancisco, 1995), 49.

larger cultural basin pliable and subject to adjustment. The second part of the toggle is linked to a concern for the categories "mythmaking" and "social formation" themselves as theoretical constructs and as tools for social description and classification.[4] If they are going to sustain a prolonged and plausible redescription project, we will have to be on guard against our categories exhausting themselves in their own vagueness, on one side, and against reification of either of its two prongs as abstract, formulaic tools that merely redecorate the "old, old story" with a new vocabulary veneer, on the other.

With this notice of an "alert" of the methodological thicket that surrounds the project of redescribing early Christianities, I begin the task of stalking—and this essay represents no more than a stalking exercise that, in the end, hardly gets beyond desultory reaches for toeholds of a conceptual and methodological kind—the assignment given to me: an initial exploration of the Greco-Roman "schools" as arenas of sociomythic formation to see if we find there some help with the question of how Q was actively present at its own making and, presumably, how the focus on "school" might help us to qualify the categories of mythmaking and social formation themselves.

At the beginning of this task, however, stands a desideratum: there are no self-evident, clear paths or unbroken lines between the contextual analogue of the Greco-Roman "school" and the sociomythic project signified by Q. Analogizing clarification requires first a definition of "school" that will allow us to make discriminating selections of our analogues. We know well that as a bare term "school" is a tag on a bag of unsorted things. It is a label that encompasses a spectrum of possible referents, ranging from geographically and temporally diffused generalities, such as the philosophical schools of thought (αἱρέσεις) subsumed under φιλοσοφία as an omnibus of polymorphous theory-praxis systems and variegated sets of cultural stances, to the concrete (spatial and social) locations, curricula, and tutoring methods of the educational system during the Hellenistic era. In the in-between of "schools of thought" and the formal schools as instruments of training in letters and rhetoric were countless venues and modes of social discourse in which scholastic dimensions were integral in more or less disciplined ways: both φιλοσοφία as well as its technicalization and spectacle in sophistry, rhetoric, and "handbook" production spilled from

---

[4] As Erik Olin Wright's "biography" of the concept of "class" shows: "Concepts are produced. The categories that are used in social theories, whether they be the relatively simple descriptive categories employed in making observations, or the very complex and abstract concepts used in the construction of 'grand theory,' are all produced by human beings. . . . They are never simply given by the real world as such but are always produced through some sort of intellectual process of concept formation" (*Classes* [London: Verso, 1985], 20).

Academy, Garden, Stoa, or classroom into public spaces in town and city, into controlled-access spaces such as the many philosophical study circles (διδασκαλεῖα) that gathered around gurulike guides[5] and other voluntary associations of various kinds,[6] and into domestic locales of formal as well as everyday discourse.[7] Merely tallying the venues and practices that might be contained in the "school" bag is, however, hardly anything more than an exercise in list-production, a kind of sociography Clifford Geertz once lampooned as going "round the world to count the cats in Zanzibar."[8] Some initial calculation of our interest by which we could select particular "cats" for further inspection seems unavoidable.

These obstacles notwithstanding, the "school" label which Mack[9] has attached to Q has commended itself not only as a descriptive term that reflects the Q-purveyors' scribal abilities, values, "wisdom" mode of research, and choice of the instructional genre as a means of textualizing that research,[10] but also as a term of strategic usefulness. What it does do

---

[5] See Peter Brown (*The Body and Society: Men, Women and Sexual Renunciation in Early Christianity* [Lectures on the History of Religions NS 13; New York: Columbia University Press, 1988], 104) on the later Christian attraction to the older model of the διδασκαλεῖον: "Small study-circles were the powerhouses of the Christian culture of the second and third centuries. The extraordinary intellectual ferment of the period is unthinkable without them."

[6] Recent work on Greco-Roman voluntary associations demonstrates how "school" and "voluntary association" converge as venues of scholastic activities. See, in general, John S. Kloppenborg and Stephen G. Wilson, eds., *Voluntary Associations in the Graeco-Roman World* (London: Routledge, 1996), esp. Steve Mason's argument for considering the *philosophiai* as voluntary associations in idem, "*Philosophiai*: Graeco-Roman, Judean and Christian," in Kloppenborg and Wilson, *Voluntary Associations*, 31–58. On "wissenschaftliche Vereine," see Erich Ziebarth, *Das griechische Vereinswesen* (Leipzig: Hirzel, 1896; repr., Wiesbaden: Sändig, 1969), 69–74; on early Christian groups as a hybrid of "philosophical school" and "association," see Robert L. Wilken, "Collegia, Philosophical Schools, and Theology," in *The Catacombs and the Colosseum: The Roman Empire as the Setting of Primitive Christianity* (ed. Stephen Benko and John J. O'Rourke; Valley Forge, Pa.: Judson, 1971), 287; for a good survey of scholarly discussions of school and voluntary association, see Richard S. Ascough, *What Are They Saying about the Formation of Pauline Churches?* (New York: Paulist, 1998), 29–49, 71–94.

[7] See, e.g., Jan N. Bremmer, "The Family and Other Centers of Religious Learning in Antiquity," in *Centers of Learning: Learning and Location in Pre-modern Europe and the Near East* (ed. Jan Willem Drijvers and Alasdair A. MacDonald; Leiden: Brill, 1995), 29–38; Stanley K. Stowers, "Social Status, Public Speaking and Private Teaching: The Circumstances of Paul's Preaching Activity," *NovT* 26 (1984): 59–82; John Patrick Lynch, *Aristotle's School: A Study of a Greek Educational Institution* (Berkeley and Los Angeles: University of California Press, 1972); John T. Townsend, "Ancient Education in the Time of the Early Roman Empire," in Benko and O'Rourke, *The Catacombs and the Colosseum*, 139–63.

[8] Clifford Geertz, "Thick Description: Toward an Interpretive Theory of Culture," in *The Interpretation of Cultures: Selected Essays* (New York: Basic Books, 1973), 16.

[9] Mack, *Who Wrote the New Testament*, 45.

[10] See John S. Kloppenborg, "Literary Convention, Self-Evidence and the Social History of the Q People," *Semeia* 55 (1991): 77–102.

is direct attention to the immanent as well as contextual dimensions of social emergence and formation that have to do with imaginative concept formation, diagnostic and prognostic self-reflection, the "heady" (to use a Mackianism) handling of the cultural repertoire to articulate both an emerging group's initial groans and then to develop a rhetoric to clarify and mobilize motive and initial shape of action. The "school" concept brings into analytic focus the role of the intellectual in social formation.[11]

The impulse to look to Greco-Roman "schools" in processes of social and ideological formation for purposes of clarifying comparison is of course not new. E. A. Judge's argument, now four decades old, for early Christian communities to be viewed as "scholastic communities" in which "distinctly intellectual" operations of a "scholarly kind" were the "methods" and "means" of forging social organization and group identities is an example worth noting. Thus Judge states in the concluding paragraph of his article:

> [A]t each stage of the [Christian] movement[s] *the initiative lay with persons whose work was in important respects of a scholarly kind,* and ... they [the scholars] accepted the status in the community that this required, and employed the *conventional methods of instructing and organizing their followers....* [T]he means to this end are *distinctly intellectual....* Thus although the movement[s] may have drawn in persons of all social ranks, and though [their] principles may have been socially revolutionary or, as the case may be, conformist, it will not be these [social] aspects ... that determined necessarily [their] role in society at the time.[12]

Judge's stress on the elevated status and functional importance of "persons of a scholarly kind" may strike us as an objectionable privileging of intellectual over social aspects in measuring the "initiative" and the "means" in

---

[11] I trust that my use of the words "strategic" and "analytic" make it clear that I am not trying to slip in some notion of "intellectual" that is itself not fundamentally social, that is, recursively dependent on the contextuality of common (shared) motivations, interests, and the various means of articulating these interests that makes thought and communication among people possible in the first place. Nor am I suggesting sympathy for a "top down" conception of social structuration dynamics that renders the common person as a passive, ineffectual "inarticulate dolt" (ἰδιώτης τῷ λόγῳ, 2 Cor 11:6) who is dependent on the intellectual specialist as an external provider of discursive goods, on the assumption that the common person has neither the cognitive diagnostic wherewithal to be a "sociologist" nor the ability to be an intentional actor in the social arena. Nor, finally, am I representing an idealist/intellectualist theory of social emergence and formation, in contrast to a materialist theory. Neither the term "intellectual" nor so-called intellectual competencies and modes of communication and influence need entail an idealist or intellectualist theoretical stance; rather, "intellectual" is a category subject to materialist conditions and analysis.

[12] E. A. Judge, "The Early Christians as a Scholastic Community," *JRH* 1 (1960–61): 136, emphasis added.

early Christian groups' social formation, but that is not what he was up to. Rather, he wanted to set straight the "methods of social description"[13] of the then still-prevalent view of the proletarian beginnings of Christian associations and, by implication, that early Christian groups were *Lumpengesellschaften* who, though short in academic skills, contested the learned élites and the system, over which they presided to their disproportionate benefit, with the superiority of (self-evident) proletarian virtue that needed no great deal of thought or skilled articulation. One might bring in Karl Kautsky, though it pains me to do so, to testify to the conception that Judge criticizes as "misconceived":

> It is generally recognized that the Christian congregation originally embraced proletarian elements almost exclusively, and was a proletarian organization. . . . There is not a single Christian thought that requires the assumption of a sublime prophet and superman to explain its origin.[14]

It is a view, Judge argues, that obscures what the Christian writings should lead us to conclude, namely, that this representation of a contest of humble virtue against mighty (cultured élite) depravity is itself a rather sophisticated Christian self-representation behind which stands perhaps not an intellectual "superman" but a scribal mythmaking intelligence and competence nonetheless.

It is precisely in this strategic respect—criticizing theories of origin that obscure, diminish, or erase intellectual efforts and means in the highly complex process of producing group identities in the larger cultural arena—that Judge's argument for thinking of early Christian groups as "scholastic communities" who made themselves in part by disciplined (learned) instrumentalities of oral and textual discourse represents a significant regauging of the track for social description and for theorizing early Christian social formations.[15] The train of redescription along this track leads, by way of major outfitting pauses—redaction criticism, rhetorical analyses, cultural context studies, and, more recently, general social theories—to the point where we are required to posit literate, literary, studied hermeneutical agency and rhetorical know-how at the earliest visible

---

[13] Ibid., 4.

[14] Karl Kautsky, *Foundations of Christianity* (trans. Jacob W. Hartmann; New York: Monthly Review Press, 1925), 323, 326. Judge's criticism is in "Early Christians as a Scholastic Community," 4, 5.

[15] Although Judge himself does not do so, he could just as well have directed his criticism of the "proletarian origins" theory also against the Bultmannian form-critical view of the history of the Synoptic tradition and its mysterious "law" of *Kleinliteratur*, in which a folk process, itself notoriously conceived as a process without intentionally active folk contesting real social and material interests, displaced the role of a schooled intelligence.

stages of the production of the Jesus traditions generally,[16] and the Q instantiation of this production in particular.

2. The Schooling of Q

With respect to Q, its production as a scholastic effort from its visible beginning to the point where we lose sight of it has been demonstrated well enough. Indeed, the history of recent Q scholarship is the history of the discovery of Q as a literary document and the Q community as an increasingly self-conscious and fairly sophisticated research collective. A schematic summary of the main and mutually supporting levels on which this demonstration rests should be sufficient here.[17]

Textuality

Q must be regarded as a written text rather than as a "source" consisting of oral traditions.[18] By itself the written nature of Q does not require us to assume it as a school project, however we define school; a written text merely presupposes an author of a certain level of literateness. But it is nonetheless a significant starting point for appreciating the literary competency and instrumentality that was at work in the production of Q, especially when its "writtenness" is conjoined with the recognition that it was written in Greek[19] and in a locale where competence in Greek can hardly be assumed for just anyone and where especially literary competence in Greek must be regarded as the property of a small "scholarly" sector.

Composition

Redactional and stratigraphical studies have shown that literary Q did not happen all at once but emerged in a series of at least three chronologically successive compositional "phases," as John S. Kloppenborg has shown,[20] where each phase (now conventionally designated Q^1, Q^2, and Q^3) consists of material that was congealed with the material of the previous phase in a manner that cannot be regarded as some uncontrolled activity of

---

[16] See the demonstrations in Burton L. Mack and Vernon K. Robbins, *Patterns of Persuasion in the Gospels* (FF; Sonoma, Calif.: Polebridge, 1989).

[17] Readers should now consult the magisterial fruition of scholarship on Q in John S. Kloppenborg Verbin, *Excavating Q: The History and Setting of the Sayings Gospel* (Edinburgh: T&T Clark, 2000).

[18] John S. Kloppenborg, *The Formation of Q: Trajectories in Ancient Wisdom Collections* (SAC; Philadelphia: Fortress, 1987; repr., Harrisburg, Pa.: Trinity Press International, 1999), 42–51.

[19] Ibid., 51–64.

[20] See Kloppenborg's argument concerning Q's literary history in *Formation of Q*.

quantitative expansion. That is, the literary techniques in Q's manner of phased composition is such that Q is neither mere list nor catalogue. This not only adds robustness to the requirement of learned authorship (contra the anemic authorial role in the form-critical model)[21] but also introduces the temporal dimension that bespeaks some perdurance of interest in returning to the same text again and again. While prolonged tinkering with a single text does not perforce lead us to suppose "school production," it would seem to be prerequisite to a school hypothesis, for time is surely an important "environmental" element in forming a school entity.[22]

GENRE

What James M. Robinson suggestively argued in his famous "*LOGOI SOPHON*" article,[23] Kloppenborg decisively demonstrated in his *Formation of Q,* namely, that Q belongs to the ancient instructional genre. Although Kloppenborg has not used Q's generic affiliation to argue a "school" hypothesis,[24] he does see it as an important clue concerning Q's purveyors and audience, an audience that has an identifiable research orientation dominated by scribal values documented in analogous wisdom texts:

> [T]he instructional genre itself is most frequently associated with palace and scribal schools, although occasionally more general audiences seem

---

[21] See my criticism of the form critics' "author" in Willi Braun, *Feasting and Social Rhetoric in Luke 14* (SNTSMS 85; Cambridge: Cambridge University Press, 1995), 134–36.

[22] Although studies on Q have not been inattentive to the topic of time in Q itself (see, e.g., Mack's comments in *Who Wrote the New Testament,* 53, on Q's effort to place itself within a cosmic *Urzeit-Endzeit* teleology by means of combining in its Jesus the retrospective knowledge of wisdom and the prospective knowledge of the apocalyptic prophet) or to the issue of Q's real time span in the first century, a school hypothesis might require additional consideration of Q and time, both in terms of duration (how long does it require to set up the disciplinary apparatus?) and use of time (how was "study" time designated and located, that is, temporally, physically, and socially emplaced?) to promote and make possible scholarly *askesis*. See Anthony Giddens, *The Constitution of Society: Outline of the Theory of Structuration* (Cambridge: Polity, 1984), 110–61, for a discussion of "time" as both environment and instrument of social formation—a discussion culminating in a conversation with Michel Foucault's argument (in *Discipline and Punish*) that time is a mechanism of confinement that makes discipline possible.

[23] James M. Robinson, "ΛΟΓΟΙ ΣΟΦΩΝ: Zur Gattung der Spruchquelle Q," in *Zeit und Geschichte: Dankesgabe an Rudolf Bultmann zum 80. Geburtstag* (ed. Erich Dinkler; Tübingen: Mohr Siebeck, 1964), 77–96; ET: "*LOGOI SOPHON:* On the Gattung of Q," in *Trajectories through Early Christianity* (ed. James M. Robinson and Helmut Koester; Philadelphia: Fortress, 1971), 71–113.

[24] While Kloppenborg's observation of scribal values and techniques in Q allows him to bring Q into a school orbit, he also notes that "Q does not show the same sort of self-conscious and studied composition expected in the products of the elite scribal establishments" ("Literary Convention," 84–85).

to be envisaged. The genre typically reflects the values of the scribal sector: a celebration of human learning, positive valuation of the process of tradition ... and concern for both the content of wisdom ... and the *origin, nature and means* by which wisdom is acquired.... [T]he scribal penchant [is] to view both transmitted texts and contemporary reality, both physical and social, as fundamentally enigmatic and therefore the object of research. But whatever the means of acquisition, wisdom—both as a particular mode of conduct and as a vision of the divine—is for the scribe the redemptive medium itself.[25]

Kloppenborg then takes the generic clue a step further and examines the contents of Q itself. What he found is coherent with what the instructional form itself suggests: the contents of both major strata of Q display scribal values, topics, and techniques, despite the shifts in predominant forms, mood, and social posture from one stratum to the next.

SCHOOL TECHNOLOGIES

When one turns from larger literary clues (textuality, compositional/redactional sophistication, genre) to examine the techniques of arrangement and manipulation of Q's constituent clusters and speech complexes, an older form-critical view of Q's inner creation by what Kloppenborg describes as a "relatively complex [block] process, with complex blocks of sayings being created by quasi-organic forces, by 'growth' from individual sayings to small clusters to larger speeches,"[26] can no longer be held with any ease. Rather, the general Greco-Roman literary culture's value placed on "invention" (εὕρεσις; *inventio*) and the school-taught rhetorical techniques associated with that value seem to have been at work at both major strata of Q, though there are differences in Q's argumentation from one stratum to the next.

"Invention" should be regarded in two senses that combine to give the term some leverage in arguing for a school scenario. At one level it refers simply to use of Hellenistic school technologies for arranging sayings in suasive, argumentative patterns and for elaborating chreiai into arguments, and the like, many of which are present in Q with notable sophistication[27]

---

[25] Ibid., 82–83, emphasis original.

[26] John S. Kloppenborg, "Conflict and Invention: Recent Studies on Q," in *Conflict and Invention: Literary, Rhetorical, and Social Studies on the Sayings Gospel Q* (ed. John S. Kloppenborg; Valley Forge, Pa.: Trinity Press International, 1995), 7.

[27] See, e.g., Ronald A. Piper, "Matthew 7, 7–11 par. Lk 11, 9–13: Evidence of Design and Argument in the Collection of Jesus' Sayings," in *Logia: Les paroles de Jésus—The Sayings of Jesus: Mémorial Joseph Coppens* (ed. Joël Delobel; BETL 59; Leuven: Peeters and Leuven University Press, 1982), 411–18; repr. in *The Shape of Q: Signal Essays on the Sayings Gospel* (ed. John S. Kloppenborg; Minneapolis: Fortress, 1994), 131–37; Ron Cameron, "'What Have You

and authorizing intent.²⁸ These are fairly advanced text-handling operations that would require of its practitioners "scribal literacy" rather than bare "craftsman's literacy."²⁹ In terms of training, one might think of the expertise of the *grammaticus,* someone with many of the skills and erudition of the rhetor, though not of the latter's status and access to élite social strata.³⁰

On another level, invention concerns the question of whom to credit with the complex speech and argument construction one finds in Q: Q authors themselves or some pre-Q ghost composers (whether speakers or writers)? A conclusive answer is subject to further study, but Leif E. Vaage's argument, sharply stating earlier suggestions, that Q's inaugural sermon (Q 6:20–49) was likely not known prior to its appearance in Q¹,³¹ and William Arnal's contention for similar *de novo* "fabrication" of John the Baptist's speech in Q² (3:7–9, 16–17),³² provide grounds for supposing a tradition/invention ratio in Q that is overbalanced in the direction of invention in all literary strata of the document.³³ Q's time frame itself favors the supposition of literary entrepreneurship, of the Q tradents

---

Come Out to See?' Characterizations of John and Jesus in the Gospels," *Semeia* 49 (1990): 35–69; R. Conrad Douglas, "'Love Your Enemies': Rhetoric, Tradents, and Ethos," in Kloppenborg, *Conflict and Invention,* 116–31.

²⁸ Shawn Carruth, "Strategies of Authority: A Rhetorical Study of the Character of the Speaker in Q 6:20–49," in Kloppenborg, *Conflict and Invention,* 98–115.

²⁹ For more on the distinction, see William V. Harris, *Ancient Literacy* (Cambridge: Harvard University Press, 1989), 7–8.

³⁰ Issues of training, function, and status pertaining to the *grammaticus* are analyzed by Robert A. Kaster, *Guardians of Language: The Grammarian and Society in Late Antiquity* (The Transformation of the Classical Heritage 11; Berkeley and Los Angeles: University of California Press, 1988).

³¹ Leif E. Vaage, "Composite Texts and Oral Mythology: The Case of the 'Sermon' in Q (6:20–49)," in Kloppenborg, *Conflict and Invention,* 75–97.

³² William Arnal, "Redactional Fabrication and Group Legitimation: The Baptist's Preaching in Q 3:7–9, 16–17," in Kloppenborg, *Conflict and Invention,* 165–80.

³³ Burton L. Mack makes an additional move that is relevant. Informed by his expertise in ancient rhetoric he observes that the blocks of material in Q¹ are built upon an "aphoristic core" (*The Lost Gospel: The Book of Q and Christian Origins* [San Francisco: HarperSanFrancisco, 1993], 110). On the logic that aphorism precedes both clustering and argumentative elaboration, he suggests that Q¹ had its origins in "aphoristic discourse," which then allows him to get "in touch" with the earliest stage of Q's social history (ibid.). Supposing Mack is right in his demarcation of an aphoristic beginning as the "documentary" foundation for literary Q (at least Q¹), the tradition/invention distinction is about collapsed. Earliest Q invents the "tradition" that later Q will comment on, elaborate, and revise for years to come. This is possible, perhaps even likely. On the oxymoron of the "invention of tradition" and discussion of modern examples, see Eric Hobsbawm and Terence Ranger, eds., *The Invention of Tradition* (Past and Present Publications; Cambridge: Cambridge University Press, 1983).

composing their text largely from material they themselves generated in their history of research.[34]

ERUDITION, POWER, AND AUTHORIZATION

Whatever else they may be, societies are also "organized power networks" in which the ability to impose or to resist authority depends in part on abilities to manipulate the recognized cultural canon by means that are equally recognized as authoritative.[35] Relevant to our period generally: despite very uneven distributions and unbalanced levels of literacy and the higher scholastic competencies that presupposed literacy, even despite (and perhaps partly because of) widespread illiteracy over against which text-skills were valued as a scarce "golden gift,"[36] the high social regard for intellectuals as displayed in the iconographic record[37] shows that Greco-Roman societies were scholastically oriented societies, if only in the recognition that a kit bag of competencies derived from literacy was an important way to get one's hands on instruments of power in social discourse generally,[38] but also in dealing with the civic and imperial bureaucratic structures—and this whether deployed for conservation or for corrosion of the dominant cultural "facts." Q seems to recognize the power of letters in its apparently paradoxical insistence (remarkably accentuated in Q²) on reassuring its "knowledge," obtained outside of and in "putschy" opposition to the media associated with the sage and scholar (Q 10:21–22),

---

[34] On the dating of Q strata, see William E. Arnal, *Jesus and the Village Scribes: Galilean Conflicts and the Setting of Q* (Minneapolis: Fortress, 2001), 172: Q¹ in the 30s or 40s; Q² in the 40s or 50s. Arnal's estimates are based on his analysis of Q's knowledge of and reaction to "the long-term and structural effects of Galilee's gradual incorporation into the Roman-Herodian orbit—increased trade and monetization, more effective extraction of taxes and other dues, increasing debt, incrementally increasing tenancy and land consolidation, and the restructuring (and revaluing) of village and town administrations and social organization—[which] were beginning to be felt with a vengeance" at this time.

[35] Michael Mann, *A History of Power from the Beginning to A.D. 1760* (vol. 1 of *The Sources of Social Power*; Cambridge: Cambridge University Press, 1986–93), 1–33. On the relationship of authority, power, class-emplacement, and the discursive instruments for establishing or corroding authority, see also Bruce Lincoln, *Discourse and the Construction of Society: Comparative Studies of Myth, Ritual, and Classification* (New York: Oxford University Press, 1987); idem, *Authority: Construction and Erosion* (Chicago: University of Chicago Press, 1994).

[36] Harris, *Ancient Literacy*, 337.

[37] Paul Zanker, *The Mask of Socrates: The Image of the Intellectual in Antiquity* (trans. Alan Shapiro; Sather Classical Lectures 59; Berkeley and Los Angeles: University of California Press, 1995).

[38] Note the ritualized recognition of this in a child's prayer: "Lord, give me the grace of good understanding, that I might learn letters and gain the upper hand over my fellows" (*Vita Eutychii* 8; cited by Kaster, *Guardians of Language*, 11).

by those very same repudiated media. An epistemology of revelation that stresses the immediacy of (superior) knowledge, self-evident modes of persuasion, and spontaneous articulation in situations that demand judiciousness of speech (Q 12:10–12) apparently needs to be sustained and legitimated by textualized, learned rationales and, pronouncedly in Q² and Q³, with measured and competent recourse to Judaism's "canonical" repository, the so-called Great Tradition.[39] Q is not terribly unique in making a scribal return to an apparently repudiated scribal modality of discourse in order to empower its own self-evidences. Rough analogies abound: in other Christian circles;[40] in the massive production of more or less technical religious handbooks and compendia of specialized knowledge as a kind of replacement ritual activity where text replaces temple as the site of religious research;[41] generally, in the late Hellenistic "rhetoric of dissent" exemplified by, say, Philostratus's literary (i.e., argued) doxography of Apollonius's self-authorized "display of truth" (ἐπίδειξις τῆς ἀληθείας),[42] or by the textualization of Cynic rhetoric of demonstrative action[43] as serialized aphoristic wit such as we find it Diogenes Laertius or other gnomologia.

Along an adjunct vein, although early Q is evidently animated about standing at the brink of its own metaphoric and social "novelty" (the kingdom of God),[44] social novelties don't just happen "on the third day," as it

---

[39] See Kloppenborg, "Literary Convention," 91–96 (on Q²); idem, "City and Wasteland: Narrative World and the Beginning of the Sayings Gospel (Q)," *Semeia* 52 (1990): 145–60 (on Q³).

[40] E.g., Paul or the *Gospel of Thomas;* see Mason, *"Philosophiai,"* 48.

[41] See Jonathan Z. Smith, "Trading Places," in *Ancient Magic and Ritual Power* (ed. Marvin Meyer and Paul Mirecki; Religions in the Graeco-Roman World 129; Leiden: Brill, 1995), 13–27; idem, "The Temple and the Magician," in *God's Christ and His People: Studies in Honour of Nils Alstrup Dahl* (ed. Jacob Jervell and Wayne A. Meeks; Oslo: Universitetsforlaget, 1977), 233–47; repr. in *Map Is Not Territory: Studies in the History of Religions* (SJLA 23; Leiden: Brill, 1978; repr., Chicago: University of Chicago Press, 1993), 172–89. Cf. Jack N. Lightstone, "Whence the Rabbis? From Coherent Description to Fragmented Reconstructions," *SR* 26 (1997): 275–95.

[42] See Willi Braun, "Argumentation and the Problem of Authority: Synoptic Rhetoric of Pronouncement in Cultural Context," in *The Rhetorical Analysis of Scripture: Essays from the 1995 London Conference* (ed. Thomas H. Olbricht and Stanley E. Porter; JSNTSup 146; Sheffield: Sheffield Academic Press, 1997), 185–99. Cf. A. Billault, "The Rhetoric of a 'Divine Man': Apollonius of Tyana as Critic of Oratory and as Orator According to Philostratus," *Philosophy and Rhetoric* 26 (1993): 231, who characterizes Apollonius's discourse as a "rhetoric of sovereign speech."

[43] E.g., Antisthenes: "Excellence is a matter of actions, not of discoursing or learning" (Diogenes Laertius 6.11). Cf. Crates, *Ep.* 21.

[44] The notion of "novelty" in relation to "new" social movements is a slippery and contested concept among social theorists; see Alberto Melucci, "The New Social Movements Revisited: Reflections on a Sociological Misunderstanding," in *Social Movements and Social Class: The Future of Collective Action* (ed. Louis Maheu; London: Sage, 1995), 107–22. How easily some notion of "novelty" can be converted into a mystified and inscrutable "origin,"

were; they are "something con-structed, put together"[45] in a process of recursive reproduction of available cultural givens.[46] Recursive reproduction happens in Q in various ways and is well enough charted in Q scholarship. Q's excitement about the new thus is tempered by the strategy of submitting the novel to some quick-aging activity so as to be able to construct the "new" as really something "old" and thus to claim for the "new" the power and sanctity of "tradition," a phenomenon Eric Hobsbawm and Terence Ranger try to evoke with the oxymoron "the invention of tradition."[47] The past is convertible to social power in the present—

---

effected by a *deus ex machina,* is exemplified in the historiography determined by the Lukan-Eusebian myth of Christian beginnings; see Ron Cameron, "Alternate Beginnings—Different Ends: Eusebius, Thomas, and the Construction of Christian Origins," in *Religious Propaganda and Missionary Competition in the New Testament World: Essays Honoring Dieter Georgi* (ed. Lukas Bormann et al.; NovTSup 74; Leiden: Brill, 1994), 501–25; cf. Robert L. Wilken, *The Myth of Christian Beginnings: History's Impact on Belief* (Garden City, N.Y.: Doubleday, 1971). On the fascination for absolute origins even among modern historians of religion, see Tomoko Masuzawa, "Origin," in Braun and McCutcheon, *Guide to the Study of Religion,* 209–24. If, however, "novelty" is revalued, as Mack, Cameron, and others have begun to do, as a term that focalizes attention on the social and intellectual moves in the emergent moment of social formation, a redescribed use of novelty may help us alight on disciplined (learnt and learned) Hellenistic-Roman means of "track laying" to enable "switches" in social-religious formations. (The metaphor of "track laying, and converting to a new gauge" is used by Mann [*History of Power,* 28], adjusting Max Weber's image of "switchmen," to talk about the importance of manipulating ideas to potentialize, especially in times of socioeconomic and political instability, the emergence of new arrangements out of social interstices.) For helpful conceptualizing by social historians and theorists on emergent moments of social formations and practices, see Hobsbawm and Ranger, *Invention of Tradition;* Benedict Anderson, *Imagined Communities: Reflections on the Origin and Spread of Nationalism* (London: Verso, 1983); and, on comparative studies of working-class formations, Ira Katznelson, "Working-Class Formations: Constructing Cases and Comparisons," in *Working-Class Formation: Nineteenth-Century Patterns in Western Europe and the United States* (ed. Ira Katznelson and Aristide R. Zolberg; Princeton: Princeton University Press, 1986), 3–41; Michelle Perrot, "On the Formation of the French Working Class," in Katznelson and Zolberg, *Working-Class Formation,* 71–110.

[45] Lincoln, *Discourse and the Construction of Society,* 10–11.

[46] The idea of "recursive reproduction" is argued complexly by Giddens in *The Constitution of Society.* Its key point is that social action, even in times of high degrees of social change, is bounded by and dependent on the structures (material, economic, political, etc.) and resources (means of communication, mythmaking, etc.). The full package of a society's constitution thus is both means and outcome of social actions and practices. Analogy: even a "novel" sentence is a reproduction of the rules of grammar and the bounded vocabulary of the language in which the sentence is uttered. For an instructive application of Giddens's structuration theory to the formation of theological ideologies in a post-Pauline Christian circle, see David G. Horrell, "The Development of Theological Ideology in Pauline Christianity: A Structuration Theory Perspective," in *Modelling Early Christianity: Social-Scientific Studies of the New Testament in Its Context* (ed. Philip F. Esler; London: Routledge, 1995), 224–36.

[47] Hobsbawm and Ranger, *Invention of Tradition.*

hence the variety of "instant-aging" maneuvers familiar to us from the early Christian groups we study.⁴⁸ "Strategic tinkering with the past"⁴⁹ is a ubiquitous cross-cultural social rationalizing and formation device, as Bruce Lincoln demonstrates, and not restricted to times of social de- and rearranging out of which new groupings emerge. But moments of emergence demand it with accentuated urgency and provide exciting opportunity for tinkering, precisely because these are moments when the social world as it is experienced is exposed as fabricated (rather than self-evidently natural) and therefore also as "fabricatable."⁵⁰

Persuasive tinkering with the past, however, is hardly imaginable as an easy activity that just anyone can do with equally forceful effect. It is a scholarly craft, for, once again, it demands not only familiarity with the contents of the cultural archives (myths, epics, wisdom collections, etc.) but equal familiarity with exegetical skills and hermeneutic specialties with which to correlate the old and the new. Q's ability, at its literary beginning (3:7b–9, 16b–17; from the Q² stratum), to appropriate and evoke the Lot/Sodom narrative to map its own experience onto a reinterpreted story as a paradigmatic tale of divine protection in a scorched wasteland is, as Kloppenborg has demonstrated,⁵¹ a masterful trick of metaphoric cartography, effective not only for displacing the regnant Holy Place but also for re-placing the sacred center in the Q circle itself. Appropriation of "Israel" in Q², by successionist linkages in relation to the myth of Wisdom (*Sophia*) as a divine intermediary, or the Hebrew patriarchs, or the line of abused prophets, and then by placing Jesus in these successions so as also to establish him as fountainhead of Q-to-come, does not quite add up to the philosophical schools' self-understanding as venerable "successions,"⁵² but the difference is not a difference of kind as much as of degree of explicitness and local particularity. To speak of Q as a διαδοχή may be a useful distortion for bringing into view Q's scribal-discursive bent in authorizing its novel discoveries in relation to a (revised) honored past and

---

⁴⁸ See Wilken, *Myth of Christian Beginnings;* cf. Willi Braun, "Amnesia in the Production of (Christian) History," *BCSSR* 28/1 (1999): 3–8.

⁴⁹ Lincoln, *Discourse and the Construction of Society,* 21.

⁵⁰ See esp. Pierre Bourdieu (*Outline of a Theory of Practice* [trans. Richard Nice; Cambridge Studies in Social and Cultural Anthropology 16; Cambridge: Cambridge University Press, 1977], 168) for a reflection on how the "natural" truth of a society is exposed as artificial when "objective crises" (such as class divisions) generate the practical destruction of the self-evidence of a society's social facts. Once these facts are no longer factual, either by rationale of law (*nomos*) or nature (*physis*), the possibility of refabrication is in place.

⁵¹ Kloppenborg, "City and Wasteland."

⁵² On this see especially Walter von Kienle, *Die Berichte über die Sukzessionen der Philosophen in der hellenistischen und spätantiken Literatur* (Berlin: Reuter, 1961); cf. Mason, "*Philosophiai,*" 31–37.

by means of treating its own text as an emerging literary διαδοχή that was both medium and product—and, as Q² and Q³ show by their refractive study of Q¹, also the source—of its meditations. That is, it seems possible to see in Q's collusive operations of social experience/formation and myth-making all the interlinked "moments" of its own historical production, both social and literary: (1) fact making (social experience and experiment), (2) fact assembly (an archive of remembered actions, rationales, etc.), (3) fact retrieval (crafting the narrative), and (4) signifying and valuing the narrative (the creation of history "in full," giving it its authoritative character of myth of origins, social charter, and myth of destination).[53] The competencies required to pull this off are hardly doltish!

SOCIAL LOCATION AND STATUS OF THE Q SCRIBES

The range of intellectual/scribal indicators in Q naturally has raised among Q scholars the question of the identity of Q's producers. Several issues are entangled in this question: the ethos of social radicalism articulated especially in Q¹; the correspondence of this ethos to a real social stance and location (Galilean urban versus rural); the social status (vagabonding beggarly types versus settled, urban intellectual-professional types) of those who assumed the ethos of Q¹ as a way of life; a postulation of motivations for the countercultural sociomythic "world" imagined in Q; the range of competencies that the Q document requires us to assume of its producers. It is neither possible nor necessary here to recall and referee the options on all these issues, especially as they are crystallizing themselves in the options of "itinerant radicalism,"[54] given its fullest expression with help of the analogue of Cynic subversive virtue by Vaage,[55] and what we might now call the "deracination" argument first suggested by Kloppenborg,[56] now worked out in great detail by Arnal.[57] If the "itinerancy" option is not too insistently tied to a view of the Q¹ purveyors/audience as peasants, itinerant laborers, and tradespeople, nor overly committed to homologizing an "itinerant intelligence" (so Vaage) and actual, physical roving of shoeless vagabonds, but understands "itinerancy" as a tropic imagination responding to perceived or real experiences of

---

[53] On these interlinked moments of historical production, see Michel-Rolph Trouillot, *Silencing the Past: Power and the Production of History* (Boston: Beacon, 1995), 1–30, esp. 26.

[54] See Gerd Theissen, "Wanderradikalismus: Literatursoziologische Aspekte der Überlieferung von Worten Jesu im Urchristentum," *ZTK* 70 (1973): 245–71.

[55] Leif E. Vaage, *Galilean Upstarts: Jesus' First Followers according to Q* (Valley Forge, Pa.: Trinity Press International, 1994).

[56] Kloppenborg, "Literary Convention," 85–89.

[57] Arnal, *Jesus and the Village Scribes*.

socioeconomic, religious, and intellectual *atopia*,[58] it does not need to stand in opposition to the virtually unavoidable conclusion that Q¹ and certainly Q as a whole represent the intellectual/scribal labors of people who had both competence and means for such labors.

The literary achievements evident in Q itself, along with close attention to indicators of social location in the document,[59] suggest a "clear homology"[60] between literary Q¹ and a social group from the ranks of an urban retainer class of "middling" status.[61] Indeed, Robert A. Kaster's description of the social status of the grammarian[62] is perhaps of a general utility for trying to imagine the Galilean small-town scribal intelligentsia who had the combination of social affiliations, intellectual and literary competencies, and status ambiguities and disaffections for us to think of them as the conceptual, rhetorical, and textual framers of Q.[63] The grammarian/scribe was one

---

[58] On *atopia* (or deracination), see Bernard Frischer, *The Sculpted Word: Epicureanism and Philosophical Recruitment in Ancient Greece* (Berkeley and Los Angeles: University of California Press, 1982), 54. One might note that Vaage makes this metaphoric move in a note where he acknowledges the criticisms of Theissen's "itinerants," then decides to "pick up and play off" Theissen's idea in such a way that itinerancy is now a trope for "an alternate 'type' of 'intelligence' characterized by its 'itinerant' (or in postmodern speak, disseminating) logic, comparable, e.g., to the account of *metis* or *Cunning Intelligence in Greek Culture and Society* by Détienne and Vernant" (*Galilean Upstarts*, 185 n. 4).

[59] See Kloppenborg, "Literary Convention"; R. A. Piper, "The Language of Violence and the Aphoristic Sayings in Q: A Study of Q 6:27–36," in Kloppenborg, *Conflict and Invention*, 53–72; Jonathan L. Reed, "The Social Map of Q," in Kloppenborg, *Conflict and Invention*, 17–36; Arnal, *Jesus and the Village Scribes*.

[60] See esp. Arnal, *Jesus and the Village Scribes*.

[61] "Middling" is Kaster's term (*Guardians of Language*, 106). Kloppenborg's suggestion of "'petit bourgeois' in the lower administrative sector in the cities and villages" ("Literary Convention," 85) in the upper Galilee, suggested by Q's "mapping" of its geographical location, of course begged the question if one could postulate a sufficient number of people in the mid- to lower-level administrative and scribal class in the region. His own initial positive answer, based on examination of evidence concerning administrative infrastructures, receives further support from Arnal (*Jesus and the Village Scribes*), though with a view toward describing their circumstances that could support plausible theorizing of real deracination as the motive for responding to those circumstances in the manner that Q does.

[62] See Kaster, *Guardians of Language*, 106–34.

[63] Several of the usual cautions against analogizing apply here: Kaster's evidence is drawn from Late Antiquity (his prosopographical survey covers 250 to 565 C.E.), though he reaches into earlier data when he can find it. His focus is specifically on the *grammaticus* and thus may not offer a reliable typical profile of other lower-level functionaries in the civic or provincial apparatus. Nevertheless, as a social type (rather than a narrowly defined professional type) the grammarian perhaps may help us to think about the scribal mediators who are imagined as the authorial figures behind Q. The type thus allows for a metaphorical analogizing. On the difference between metaphoric and metonymic comparison, see Jonathan Z. Smith, "Social Formations of Early Christianities: A Response to Ron Cameron and Burton Mack," *MTSR* 8 (1996): 275.

of antiquity's ubiquitous, yet largely anonymous (as far as the documented historical record goes) and unsung "middling" figures, ranking well below other public intellectuals, such as the rhetorician, the sophist, and the philosopher, on scales of public recognition, honor, income, and opportunities of upward advancement, even though the grammarian/scribe shared some of the competencies for which the latter are known, competencies that, as I have noted, must be presupposed in relation to Q.

When Kaster characterizes the grammarian/scribe as occupying a level of "middling respectability" in the civic system he means several things.

(1) *Social origins* were of a spectrum on the ladder of social rank and respectability, ranging from people of "low birth" to people of curial status,[64] though generally coming from the *mediocritas* level, people of at least enough resources and points of access to acquire the skills to qualify them for their professional demands.[65]

(2) Kaster adduces evidence that suggests that grammarians enjoyed only a *modest social status;* their ascribed respectability derived chiefly from their professional competencies.

(3) The grammarian's *class commitments* were ambiguous. On the one hand, he was dependent on the élite and circulated among their ranks in limited and controlled ways, but this controlled access indicated only that he was not one of them. On the other hand, in the course of his professional activity, contact with the lower-strata people required this middling type to be the interface between the urban élite class and the lower-strata clients dependent on the civic/imperial system but without the (literate) means to negotiate it. Kaster's notice that the grammarian thus was of torn loyalty, suffering from a double *atopia* owing to the double-surface-ness of his brokerage function, makes a great deal of sense.[66]

(4) In terms of *wealth,* although the range of imperial evidence suggests "at least a modest surplus of wealth and comfortable standard of living" that allowed for "touches of civilized life,"[67] complaints about irregular income or unsatisfactory substitution of kind (alimentary goods) for cash (*salarium;* σύνταξις) were not unheard of.[68]

---

[64] Representation from both extreme ends of the social hierarchy is exceptional. Kaster found few people from among the *humiliori* and only one example of a grammarian of equestrian background (*Guardians of Language,* 108).

[65] Ibid., 107–11.

[66] Kaster describes the grammarian as "the man whose function set him amid many vital spheres of activity [but who] most often was without a place at the center of any of them" (ibid., 7).

[67] Ibid., 112; cf. 114–23.

[68] Ibid., 115–16; see the analysis of a particular case from Oxyrhynchus by P. J. Parsons, "Petitions and a Letter: The Grammarian's Complaint, 250–60 A.D.," in *Collectanea Papyrologica:*

(5) One is not surprised to see that grammarians were remarkably *mobile figures,* both geographically and in terms of the versatility of professional or scribal activities derived from their mastery of literate instrumentalities. A grammarian's move from the classroom to an assessor's post, advocacy, or other administrative portfolios is a matter of record;[69] a move from village administration to an urban tax-collection job, such as one might suppose for some Q scribes, is likely. Kaster's prosopographic data indicates that a quarter of the grammarians moved from their homelands or changed their place of practice.[70] Presumably, mobility of both kinds is related to demographic and other socioeconomic factors associated with urbanization and centralizations (or decline of centers) of administrative infrastructures that created a surplus of middling bureaucrats here while generating shortages elsewhere. For the scribe/grammarian whose mobility was encumbered by force of sentiment or by familial and social ties to native region or hometown, these same factors would contribute both to a real and a perceived sense of professional and personal devaluation and out-of-place-ness.

3. Looking For a Field of Analogies

It thus seems fitting to envisage both the social and the literary formation of Q in a school "space." That is, both the group and its document display an evident bent on investing in the power of text production (perhaps to be understood as ritual practice, though concerning Q this latter needs further thought)[71] as locus and means of social formation in response to the experience of displacement. Where to go from here? Does this provide any direction for contextualizing Q in a field of analogies? A few unconcluding thoughts suggest themselves.

Texts Published in Honor of H. C. Youtie (ed. Ann Ellis Hanson; Papyrologische Texte und Abhandlungen 20/2; Bonn: Habelt, 1976), 409–46.

[69] Kaster, *Guardians of Language,* 124–25.

[70] Ibid., 126–28, 463–77.

[71] I am uncertain about how one locates Q's research and writing beyond pointing out that Q is a product of such activity. In part the question is one of physical placement and one of time allocation. In part, however, it concerns valuation of both place and time and the intersection of textual and communal formation in ritual practice. I am here mindful of Smith's comment on the Greek magical papyri as representing "a displacement of ritual practice into writing, analogous, in important respects, to the displacement of sacrifice into speech in the emergent Judaisms and Christianities" ("Trading Places," 26–27). On the intersection of texts, group formation, and ritual, see the collection of essays in Jonathan Boyarin, ed., *The Ethnography of Reading* (Berkeley and Los Angeles: University of California Press, 1992), esp. the articles by Boyarin ("Voices around the Text: The Ethnography of Reading at Mesivta Tifereth Jerusalem," 212–37) and Elizabeth Long ("Textual Interpretation as Collective Action," 180–211).

Assuming that the representation of the schooling of Q I have drawn above is plausible, the initial frustration about how to reflect on the formation of Q with reference to "school" analogies may be eased to some extent in that the representation may delimit and focus the analogical scope. Most generally, if one thinks of Q as a project that exemplifies what Jonathan Z. Smith has called "trading places,"[72] of responding to the experience of *atopia* by imagining reemplacement in a reconfigured social space and enacted in scribal and discursive ways, one might look in the first place for comparisons with other instances where "the major sociological burden" of "alienation and deracination"[73]—however real or perceived and however severe either the reality or the perception—by a scribal/intellectual sector causes seguing toward alternate social visions, roles, and arrangements in conjunction with literary activity and canon-making. Several examples may be enough to indicate directions in which to look for such comparative data.

First, Smith's own long and sustained effort both to document and to reflect on such instances in Hellenistic-Roman antiquity may bring some previously unseen comparative possibilities into view. Who else would have thought, for example, that Q might have something to do with the creation of collections such as the Greek magical papyri[74] or with Thessalos of Tralles' re-placement of defunct temple media and medical wisdom by an astro-herbal text that is both product and reproductive site of an alternate wisdom, wisdom that, much as in Q, is offered as unmediated goods, the result of meeting the god "one on one" (μόνῳ μοι πρὸς μόνον)?[75]

Second, Bernard Frischer's work on the Epicurean fraternities, although largely concerned with explaining their paradoxical recruitment practices, is cast within a sociological historiographical frame that permits him to eke out a redescription of the philosophical schools as sociomythic formations in response to literal or perceived deracination of the philosopher as public intellectual.[76] The emergence of Epicureans, Cynics, Pythagoreans, and possibly other philosophical-social associations should

---

[72] Smith, "Trading Places," 13–27.

[73] Frischer, *Sculpted Word*, 53.

[74] Smith, "Trading Places."

[75] *Thessalos* 1.proem.22; text in Hans-Veit Friedrich, ed., *Thessalos von Tralles: Griechisch und lateinisch* (Beiträge zur klassischen Philologie 28; Meisenheim am Glan: Hain, 1968), 53. On the importance of Thessalos of Tralles, see Smith, "The Temple and the Magician," 233–47; repr. in *Map Is Not Territory*, 172–89.

[76] Frischer, *Sculpted Word*, esp. 52–66; cf. 1–6; see also Joseph M. Bryant, *Moral Codes and Social Structure in Ancient Greece: A Sociology of Greek Ethics from Homer to the Epicureans and Stoics* (SUNY Series in the Sociology of Culture; New York: State University of New York Press, 1996).

be good places to think about the formation of Q and, more generally, about the phenomenon of scribal/intellectual reemplacement strategies itself, and especially for noting and theorizing about the *different directions* these strategies can go concerning options on whether to secede from the "world" or to engage it a number of different ways, and on whether to embody the response to deracination in alternate community formation (Epicureans) or to shrink the sense of alienation and, hence, one's difference, to the level of pursuing individual cunning (μῆτις)[77] and virtue in a world perceived to be misguided and rotten (Cynics).

The point about difference as a theoretical challenge may be illustrated by noting an endemic problem in social-historical work that relies on comparison and typology-construction, namely, the tendency toward assuming a predictable commensurability between cultural conditions and social-formational reactions to it: if conditions X are in place, reaction Y will follow; if reaction Y is observed, conditions X must be supposed.[78] It is on this methodological issue alone that Arnal, in his essay on "the rhetoric of marginality" in Q and the *Gospel of Thomas,* contributes a critical insight that should to be taken seriously, for there he demonstrates that a "shared critical stance toward [similar] distressing socioeconomic changes perceived to be taking place" generates diverging reactions, Q moving toward sectarian community formation rationalized with an apocalyptic rhetoric, the *Gospel of Thomas* taking a route toward "individualistic gnostic theology."[79] In view of their evident similarities at one stage of their respective histories, the difference in their final destinations—in Smith's categories,[80] Q remaining locative to the end, the *Gospel of Thomas* apparently preferring the utopia of its own deep head-space where it is able to "pass by" (*Gos. Thom.* 42) the world perceived to be a carcass (if this point can be drawn from saying 56; cf. sayings 60, 80)—is all the more interesting and in need of explanation. If *Thomas* shows that it is possible to get from something like Q^1 to a utopian hermeneutical school, Q^2 stands as a puzzling difference, as the way not taken by *Thomas,* and therefore the

---

[77] On μῆτις in Greek traditions, see Marcel Detienne and Jean-Pierre Vernant, *Cunning Intelligence in Greek Culture and Society* (trans. Janet Lloyd; Chicago: University of Chicago Press, 1991); see also Mack, "Elaboration of the Chreia in the Hellenistic School," in *Patterns of Persuasion in the Gospels,* 47–50.

[78] See, e.g., Katznelson, "Working-Class Formations," for criticism of this tendency in comparisons of working-class formations in France, Germany, and the United States.

[79] William E. Arnal, "The Rhetoric of Marginality: Apocalypticism, Gnosticism, and Sayings Gospels," *HTR* 88 (1995): 492, 494.

[80] See Jonathan Z. Smith, *Drudgery Divine: On the Comparison of Early Christianities and the Religions of Late Antiquity* (Jordan Lectures in Comparative Religion 14; London: School of Oriental and African Studies, University of London; Chicago: University of Chicago Press, 1990), esp. 106–7, 110, 120–42.

evolution from Q^1 to Q^2-Q^3 shows itself as not self-evidently in accordance with some inevitability, some "law" within the social formation and/or mythmaking process itself.

Although I do not wish here to belabor the Q^1-Q^2 problem too much, I do have some interest in pointing out that Q^2 is not the *necessary* flowering of a seed germinating in Q^1, even if Q^2 appears, as it does, as a sensible and masterfully refracted appropriation of Q^1. The point of the pointing is a social-theoretical one: it asks for an understanding of social formation that is perhaps best formulated in Anthony Giddens's proposition that:

> [t]he flow of [social] action continually produces consequences which are unintended by actors, and these unintended consequences also may form unacknowledged conditions of action in a feedback fashion. Human history is created by intentional activities but is not an intended project; it persistently eludes efforts to bring it under conscious direction.[81]

Speaking of Q, "it was present at its own making" (so Thompson) with intentional action, but its final outcome is nonetheless an unintended project, a surprise, from the vantage point of earliest Q. Q's formational "teleology" is evident only in retrospect, from the vantage point of Q^2 and Q^3, and then it shows itself as imagined by Q's own "narrativization" of itself, where narrativization should be understood as a "moment" in the historical production of social and literary Q.[82] Comparisons of Q's differences from analogous forms of emergent social/school formations likely will set before us in the first place the "fluidity of social formation,"[83] driven at once by human intention to activate apparent interests

---

[81] Giddens, *Constitution of Society*, 27.

[82] Cf. Trouillot, *Silencing the Past*, 1–30. Charting the evolution of Q as a recursive process of intended action and unintended consequences undoubtedly needs more thought that should also include factors of power exercised within the group itself and the possibility of sectoral ideological moves within the group to "take over" the group's interest and motivations. Note, e.g., Kloppenborg's suggestion that at its later stages "the group succeeded in attracting scholars, perhaps only a handful, for whom the institutions of Torah and Temple had essential and positive meaning" ("Literary Convention," 100). This infusion of Pharisaic talent and interest seems as unthinkable for earliest Q as it was consequential for later Q, perhaps effecting a shift from broader social movement to a more circumscribed Pharisaic-like club or διδασκαλεῖον. Arnal's observation (in *Jesus and the Village Scribes*, 153–54) on the "gradual transformation" of the prewar synagogues from local political assemblies into institutions with "a more explicitly religious" purpose whose revised primary function was "the affirmation of communal identity made in religious worship" may also be significant, if, speculatively speaking, this allows us to envision Q's decision at some point to locate (move?) its contest for itself as "Israel" within the Galilean synagogue(s).

[83] Lincoln, *Discourse and the Construction of Society*, 18.

and unintended consequences of those actions that then become junctures of renewed decision making, as an unavoidable explanatory challenge that will hardly be met with formulaic invocations of group-formation models.[84]

Third, we do know that the end of the Jerusalem temple in 70 C.E. meant that a large priestly-scribal sector lost not only jobs but its fundamental social, intellectual, and ritual raison d'être. This sector's "burden of alienation and deracination" can hardly be overestimated. We know the imaginative remaking of this group of itself as the formation of the rabbinic colleges that reconstituted a Judaism in which "temple" and the judiciary values based on temple were relocated in text and where textual talk about sacrifice and temple ritual became replacement ritual.[85] The description of this re-formation, however, is hampered by a similar historiographical "catch-22" that Mack has exposed as a problem for reconstructions of early Christianities.[86] Thus Jack N. Lightstone: "Almost everything Mack says of the scholarly study of the New Testament and of related reconstructions of early Christianities holds true for the study of early rabbinic literature and the social reconstruction of early Rabbinisms."[87] Commenting on modern scholarly accounts of the history of rabbinism, Lightstone contends that:

> in the main what one has is a scholarly refinement of rabbinic literature's own account of its own literary history. This [the rabbis' own] account, distilled and refined, becomes the [modern scholarly] description of the early rabbinic and proto-rabbinic social formation, in terms

---

[84] Bruce Malina's attempt to use "small group formation theory to explain Christian organizations" may be cited as an example. Apart from the fact that his model, characterized by stages of "forming, storming, norming, performing, adjourning," is frustrated by its application to poorly described early Christian groups, its weakness is its disinterest in the question of difference and how to account for it (see "Early Christian Groups: Using Small Group Formation Theory to Explain Christian Organizations," in Esler, *Modelling Early Christianity*, 103–6). A similar demurring arises against Victor Turner's well-known liminality-communitas-structure cycle, which Kloppenborg (in "Literary Convention") uses to elucidate stages in the social history of Q. The problem is not that Turner's categories do not fit Q, for they do; rather, the problem is that the categories tend to homogenize rather than differentiate social formations in that they would also fit the *Gospel of Thomas* and, as Frischer points out (*Sculpted Word*, 69), the formation of the Epicurean fraternities or any other group whose emergence is driven by antistructural sentiments.

[85] Smith, "Trading Places," 22. See also Lightstone, "Whence the Rabbis?" 286: "Through this exercise [Mishnaic textual and rhetorical practices] an ordered, fictive and ideal world is defined, in which (in the text) the Jerusalem Temple yet stands, and Temple-based judiciary and legislative institutions still operate."

[86] Mack, "Redescribing Christian Origins," 250–53; repr. in *Christian Myth*, 63–67.

[87] Lightstone, "Whence the Rabbis?" 277.

of which the literary history and character of the early rabbinic documents are explained, and in which framework their meaning is elucidated. "Catch-22!"[88]

The circular consensus of the rabbis' self-account and scholarly accounts of rabbinisms has produced a "historical narrative" in which literary history and corpus, embracing pre-70 "oral Torah," Mishnah, and the later canons of the Babylonian and Palestinian academies, are "a largely self-consistent whole."[89] Similarly, argues Lightstone, in this narrative the rabbis are a "synthesis" marked by a genealogical continuity between generations of predestruction Judean and Galilean sages, the Yavneh academy, and the school that produced the Mishnah under the direction of Judah ben Simeon ben Gamaliel at the end of the second century C.E. It is, as Lightstone points out, a picture of the social formation of rabbinism that lacks "almost any resolution or acuity."[90] By means of a reimagined historiography and sociorhetorical procedures he had already developed earlier,[91] Lightstone attempts to work himself out of the confines "of what rabbinic literature says about itself, its own history and the history and social formations of those whom the literature claims as its progenitors."[92] Here we need to note only the results of Lightstone's kind of thinking. The literary and rhetorical analysis suggests that Mishnah displays in (the selection of legal) substance and scribal-rhetorical technique "a priestly-scribal virtuosity of comprehensively mapping 'the world'" as a means of laying "claim to priestly-scribal authority for the College of Sages."[93] At the social level, Mishnah "bespeaks finally managing to create or to find at the end of the second century a new institutional home for the exercise and perpetuation of that guild expertise"[94] once institutionalized in the temple. When Lightstone turns to the question of the origin of the scribal/social formation documented in Mishnah, he notes that we must presuppose a portfolio of professional skills that "usually come from an institutionalized, social setting, where expertise is 'bought and paid for,'" and he suggests "that those persons who are at the largely veiled origin of Rabbinism are 'refugees' from the Temple-state's national bureaucracy and administration, who, having lost their institutional base, first tried to preserve and

---

[88] Ibid., 278.
[89] Ibid., 277, 279.
[90] Ibid., 279.
[91] Jack N. Lightstone, *The Rhetoric of the Babylonian Talmud: Its Social Meaning and Context* (Studies in Christianity and Judaism 6; Waterloo, Ont.: Wilfrid Laurier University Press, 1994).
[92] Lightstone, "Whence the Rabbis?" 281.
[93] Ibid., 289.
[94] Ibid., 291.

pass on their professional guild expertise."[95] In a note he makes clear what he means by "first":

> What I suggest is that preservation of the guild, through preservation of its characteristic virtuosity, "drove" the development of the earliest rabbinic movement—this more so than any motivation to define a Judaism without a functioning Temple and Temple-state, or to preserve the legal traditions of that Temple-state.[96]

Lightstone's argument is remarkable—for what it portends for a redescription of the emergence of rabbinic Judaism itself, of course, but also because it opens up an analogy for Q's sociomythic reemplacement project by scribal-textual instrumentalities, an analogy, moreover, that is within the very Jewish scribal history in which Q contends its own claims, a history in which neither the post-70 temple scribal "refugees" nor the Q "research group" is the only example of scribal deracination.

It may be worth pointing out, finally, that the three contextualizing directions I have suggested with reference to the work of Smith, Frischer, and Lightstone share a common feature: none are self-evident analogies; all are themselves products of recent scholarly invention (εὕρεσις) by redescription. The discovery or creation of yet other analogies is surely possible and not a little dependent on exactly what it is that we want to know about social formation and mythmaking in Q—or elsewhere.[97]

---

[95] Ibid., 290.

[96] Ibid., 290 n. 36. Lightstone's point that group survival, including the preservation of relatively high-status expertise and social authority associated with it, may be a primary force behind a group's mythic inventions, can perhaps be dragged over to Q. Its trajectory from the aphoristic stage (if one is permitted to speak of that as a real stage in Q's literary *and* social history), certainly from Q^1 to Q^2 and unto Q^3, appears to be moved in part by the centripetal force of the group's increasing attachment to itself. Put crudely, the constant in Q is not some bright star in the sky (myth; "kingdom of God") nor the unflickering beacon of an ideal social design—Q, after all, is ready to adjust its early views on both of these things—but the experience of alienation from those outside and increasingly deliberate and noisier efforts in Q^2 to arouse and articulate grounds for a compensating attachment to the group that feels that way. Thus, the "treasure" (Q 12:34) is the group itself and its survival in *some form,* and the campaign of Q is to win "hearts"—the "sentiment" of "affinity," in Lincoln's terms (*Discourse and the Construction of Society,* 8–11)—to this treasure (the group, rather than a fixed vision of the group) and to keep them devoted to it at all costs (see Q 9:57–60, which in the context of final Q works as a trope for pleading: "Stick with us, folks!").

[97] This is a slightly revised version of a paper originally published as "Socio-Mythic Invention, Graeco-Roman Schools, and the Sayings Gospel Q," *MTSR* 11 (1999): 210–35.

Why Q Failed: From Ideological Project to Group Formation*

William E. Arnal

Burton Mack, on the Social History of Q

Using the literary stratification of Q proposed by John S. Kloppenborg as his starting point,[1] Burton L. Mack has argued that the preliterary social history of Q might also be imagined to have taken place in a series of stages. Just as the literary stratification of Q attests to a background involving stages in social development,[2] so also does the form-critical or tradition-historical progress of the material incorporated into these discrete stages

---

* I wish to thank Willi Braun, Ron Cameron, Merrill P. Miller, and especially Burton L. Mack for their helpful engagement with the issues communicated in this essay and their various discussions with me about those issues. I hope it will be clear to all readers that the criticisms of Mack's ideas and methods offered herein are offered from the perspective of one who thinks that Mack's work is among the best and most promising current work in the field. It is from this perspective and out of a desire to see his insights and general approach taken even further that I offer the criticisms I do.

[1] John S. Kloppenborg, *The Formation of Q: Trajectories in Ancient Wisdom Collections* (SAC; Philadelphia: Fortress, 1987; repr., Harrisburg, Pa.: Trinity Press International, 1999). According to Kloppenborg, Q developed in three discrete written stages, as follows (Q texts are cited by Lukan versification, without prejudice to their original wording or location): (1) formative stratum (Q^1): 6:20b–23b, 27–49; 9:57–62; 10:2–11, 16; 11:2–4, 9–13; 12:2–7, 11–12, 21b–31, 33–34; 13:24; 14:26–27; 17:33; 14:34–35; (2) redactional stratum (Q^2): 3:7–9, 16–17; 6:23c; 7:1–10, 18–23, 24–28, 31–35; 10:12–15, 21–24; 11:14–26, 29–36, 39–52; 12:8–10, 39–40, 42–46, 49, 51–53, 54–56, 57–59; 13:25–30, 34–35; 14:16–24; 17:23, 24, 26–30, 34–35, 37b; 19:12–27; 22:28–30; (3) late additions and glosses (Q^3): 4:1–13; 11:42c; 16:17. Mack modifies this breakdown somewhat. Most notably, he assigns the entirety of Q 6:22–23 to Q^2 and is much more generous (and, one might argue, less rigorous) than Kloppenborg in assigning material to the tertiary stage of Q. In addition to the handful of texts so designated by Kloppenborg, Mack includes in the tertiary stage: Q 10:21–22; Q/Luke 11:27–28; 12:5; 13:34–35; 16:16, 18; 22:28–30. See the stratified reconstruction of Q in Burton L. Mack, *The Lost Gospel: The Book of Q and Christian Origins* (San Francisco: HarperSanFrancisco, 1993), 81–102.

[2] On which see, in general, John S. Kloppenborg, "Literary Convention, Self-Evidence and the Social History of the Q People," *Semeia* 55 (1991): 77–102.

allow us to discern the finer features of the social development that predates the literary codification of the layers in question. Thus may a series of fairly detailed stages in social history be sketched on the basis of the literary evidence available to us.

According to Mack, in general the followers of Jesus pursued a kind of common sociality, expressed most characteristically at meal times.[3] For Q in particular, however, the first stage in its social development—which involved little change from the message of Jesus himself[4]—is characterized in terms of the invention, circulation, and collection of aphorisms.[5] The grounds for such a conclusion derive from the literary formation of the clusters that comprise Q[1]:

> Every smaller unit of composition has at least one terse saying. Some are formulated as maxims, others as imperatives, but all have the quality of aphoristic speech. Most of these aphorisms function within their units as core sayings around which the unit clusters, or on which supporting considerations build. When viewed together, moreover, these sayings make a comprehensive set of sage observations and unorthodox instructions. They delight in critical comment upon the everyday world and they recommend

---

[3] See Burton L. Mack, *A Myth of Innocence: Mark and Christian Origins* (Philadelphia: Fortress, 1988), 80–83.

[4] Although Mack characterizes the message of the historical Jesus as not having extensive social implications, he appears to concede in places that the group formation represented by earliest Christianity was in fact set in motion by Jesus. Thus, on the one hand, he argues that: "The social critique was general; the invitation was specific in its address to individuals. The invitation would have been to something like the Cynic's 'kingdom,' that is, to assume the Cynic's stance of confidence in the midst of confused and contrary social circumstances. Simply translated, Jesus' 'message' seems to have been, 'See how it's done? You can do it also'" (ibid., 73). But on the other hand, some of his other descriptions of Jesus imply significant social consequences, and even embryonic group formation, such that the aphorism-collecting stage, one may hint, need not be far removed in social intention from the "designs" of Jesus himself: "Rather remarkable changes in conditions, status, and behavior are the points emphasized in most of the [miracle] stories, exaggerated to be sure in keeping with the miracle genre.... [A]ll of the miracle stories betray signs of the social circumstance that gave significance to the transformation. That circumstance was the crossing of a social boundary. The perspective on the crossing of social boundaries is oblique, but present nonetheless around the edges of the graphic depictions of physical changes in the lives and circumstances of individuals.... What Jesus set in motion was, then, a social experiment. Crossing a social boundary into an arrangement of social relationships sensed as novel may well have been experienced as transformation" (ibid., 76–77).

[5] See esp. Mack, *Lost Gospel*, 105–12. This book is an expansion of the basic ideas expressed earlier in idem, "The Kingdom That Didn't Come: A Social History of the Q Tradents," in *Society of Biblical Literature 1988 Seminar Papers* (SBLSP 27; Atlanta: Scholars Press, 1988), 608–35. For a further explication of these views, see idem, "Q and a Cynic-like Jesus," in *Whose Historical Jesus?* (ed. William E. Arnal and Michel Desjardins; Studies in Christianity and Judaism 7; Waterloo, Ont.: Wilfrid Laurier University Press, 1997), 25–36.

unconventional behavior. These sayings put us in touch with the earliest stage of the Jesus movement when aphoristic discourse was the norm. I shall refer to this period in the social history of the movement as stage 1.[6]

This stage is characterized, ideologically, by a general inquisition—humorous and pungent—of ordinary social norms, combined with the "assumption that there must be a better way to live."[7] However, the aphorisms in question do not specify what that "better way" might be; instead, they subject the current order to inquisition, and they do so hopefully, but not programmatically.[8]

While Jesus may have restricted himself to such open-ended critique, the Q people, even at this first stage, go just a little further. The "alternative" implied by the piquant maxims around which the Q^1 clusters were organized is spelled out rather more exactly by a series of imperatives that also function as core sayings for these clusters. "This means that the better way of life was actually enjoined as livable."[9] This better way of life, Mack thinks, as attested in the various recurrent themes of these imperatives, is Cynic or Cynic-like.[10] As such, there is not really a conscious social program behind it but rather a call to individuals to exercise a kind of critical acumen:

> The way society worked in general was taken for granted, in the sense of "What more can one expect?" Instead, the imperatives were addressed to individuals as if they could live by other rules if they chose to do so. It is important to see that there was no sense of external, institutional threat to motivate this change in life-style. It is especially important to see that the purpose of the change was not a social reform.[11]

Yet even at this first stage there are signs of incipient "social formation" above and beyond the pure vision and critique of the message of Jesus himself: (1) a shift has taken place from aphoristic observations to generalizing

---

[6] Mack, *Lost Gospel*, 109–10. It is worth noting that similar—although hardly identical—conclusions about the development of Q^1 speech clusters have been proffered by Ronald A. Piper, "Matthew 7, 7–11 par. Lk 11, 9–13: Evidence of Design and Argument in the Collection of Jesus' Sayings," in *Logia: Les paroles de Jésus—The Sayings of Jesus: Mémorial Joseph Coppens* (ed. Joël Delobel; BETL 59; Leuven: Peeters and Leuven University Press, 1982), 411–18; repr. in *The Shape of Q: Signal Essays on the Sayings Gospel* (ed. John S. Kloppenborg; Minneapolis: Fortress, 1994), 131–37; idem, *Wisdom in the Q-Tradition: The Aphoristic Teaching of Jesus* (SNTSMS 61; Cambridge: Cambridge University Press, 1989).
[7] Mack, *Lost Gospel*, 111.
[8] Ibid., 111–12.
[9] Ibid., 112.
[10] Ibid., 112–20.
[11] Ibid., 120.

maxims; (2) exhortations have been multiplied and occur with greater frequency; (3) readers are addressed using the second-person plural; (4) there is increased focus on the transformative effect of novel interpersonal relationships; and (5) there is an increased interest in egalitarian social experiments.[12]

Mack thus pushes us forward through Q's prehistoric chronology to the next stage by observing that "a movement based on such a personal challenge was nevertheless capable of generating a social vision,"[13] as the tendencies enumerated above demonstrate. This vision is manifested more completely in the collection and organization into argumentative blocks of the various aphorisms and imperatives that floated around (orally?) during the earliest stage. At this point, the nascent tendencies toward group formation found in the generation and preservation of the earlier sapiential sayings come to fruition within patterns of argumentation, based on earlier sayings, in which community rules and ethical principles for the group are laid down.[14] Group identity is signified in the language of the "kingdom of God,"[15] and Cynic-like injunctions become principles around which group regulation and identity can crystallize.[16] The process of crystallization is of course reflected in the literary movement from aphorisms to aphoristic speeches—as the group crystallizes, so also does its charter document; genre reflects ideology. Q¹ is thus a product of this tendency toward codification, a tendency that more or less directly reflects the shift of the Jesus people from an outward-directed and individualistic critical movement to an inward-directed social program enacted at the group level:

> [A]s groups formed in different places and the teachings of Jesus became a topic of conversation, recognition of kindred spirits became an issue, and the arena of activity shifted from the public sphere to the house group. The earlier Cynic-like life-style, geared as it was for a critical encounter with the world, would have become inappropriate. What it meant to live in accordance with the rule of God would now have to be worked out in relation to persons and problems within the group. *Thus*

---

[12] Ibid., 121.
[13] Ibid., 120.
[14] Ibid., 121–22.
[15] Ibid., 123–27.
[16] Ibid., 121. Mack seems to think that such a process is rather unusual: "This is most curious, for an aphoristic view of the social world, and a challenge to live against its codes, are hardly an adequate foundation for constructing positive community rules and ethical principles" (ibid.). This surprise is rather misplaced, however; it is by no means odd that relatively unorganized countercultural impulses would result in alternative positive options. And in fact Mack's qualifications here contradict his earlier observations that germinal social formation is already present in the first stage itself.

the codification of Cynic-like injunctions as community rules in Q^1 can be understood as a response to the problems of social formation.[17]

As a final set of developments prior to $Q^{(2)}$'s movement in a polemical and apocalyptic direction, the concern with measuring loyalty to Jesus' words has resulted in his being cast as the founder of a movement (e.g., Q 6:46–49; 10:3; Q/Luke 12:13–14)[18] and even in understanding allegiance to the group's ethos as being for the sake of Jesus (e.g., Q 6:22–23a; 14:26–27).[19]

Although later stages in this process are not directly pertinent, it is worth outlining them in basic form. The community reflected already in the composition of Q^1 becomes even more defined by the time Q^2 is produced.[20] This sharper definition—one might say (although Mack does not),[21] sectarianism—is a function of, and natural development from, concerns already hinted at in the Q^1 material, in particular concerns about loyalty to the group and concern with the social stresses associated with divided families (presumably divided as a result of allegiance to the group).[22] By the time Q^2 is composed, these concerns and stresses have resulted in a raising of the ante, so that the rhetoric of Q^2 serves "to put muscle into their judgments upon the present state of their world."[23] The process here, as with earlier stages, is somewhat dialectical: not merely do social circumstances generate or define certain types of rhetoric, but the rhetoric itself appears also to have certain social consequences, as opposition to the Q agenda "triggered a spate of countercharges that determined the emerging self-identification of the Jesus movement."[24] Q's opponents, (understandably) using Jewish epic narrative and common cultural values to refute Q's countercultural agenda, set the stage for the Q people to respond by appeal to that same set of traditions, caused them selectively to cite stories, events, and texts from within the canon by which they had come to be refuted, in order to refute the refuters.[25] The conversation now has developed a broad, even universal frame of reference. Mack's own words are worth quoting at some length, as they best describe the final steps Q takes toward developing its own "myth of broad horizon":

---

[17] Ibid., 130, emphasis added.
[18] Ibid., 137–38.
[19] Ibid., 138–39.
[20] Ibid., 141.
[21] Ibid., 134.
[22] Ibid., 134–36.
[23] Ibid., 134.
[24] Ibid., 142; cf. 146.
[25] Ibid., 145–47.

[T]here is more than a hint of delight in seeing the Jesus people on the right side of things as the epic history was reviewed and the apocalyptic finale imagined. . . . But mythmaking demands much more. Connections need to be made among many historical moments, including the present time, and a place must be secured for the new community in relation to other peoples and their cultures. The sweep of history needs to have its rhyme and reason coursing through the present situation. And the Archimedean point of vantage for comprehending the whole has to be located. The authors of Q^2 were not quite there, but they had laid some firm foundations. In order to make the connection with all that had gone before they appropriated the mythological figure of the wisdom of God. In order to make the connection with what was to come they cleverly manipulated the description of the son of man. And in order to join these two mythological figures exactly where they had to be joined, the people of Q reimagined Jesus as the child of wisdom and as the seer who knew what the son of man would say at the end of time.[26]

Social Formation, in General

That there is a general schematization of social formation behind Mack's reconstruction is quite clear.[27] His whole account opposes a "way of life" to "a conscious social program." As a result, a progression is envisioned for group development from (1) individual critique arising out of a personal vision, to (2) an alternative way of living, to (3) a "social vision." One should additionally posit potential further stages in the process of group development: social formation (as distinct from social vision), and later, conceivably, sectarian development with some attendant mythologizing tendencies. Each new stage seems to flow logically out of its precursor. And, it seems, each new stage represents a failing of sorts. This, I think, is very important for understanding Mack's work: group development appears in the guise of—as the equivalent of—a kind of parochial institutionalization, in which thought and behavior become increasingly inward-directed. Essentially disconnected thoughts and insights—themselves the mythic origination-point for Mack's thought, his own "myth of innocence"—turn into agenda, which in turn solidify into groups, which in turn generate defensiveness and prejudice, rationalized through mythic charters. A group is evidently, for Mack, something at odds with the social totality in which it appears.

---

[26] Ibid., 146–47. Cf., similarly, Kloppenborg, "Literary Convention," 94–96.

[27] For an explicit articulation of the self-conscious theorization behind Mack's work on Q, see now Burton L. Mack, "Social Formation," in *Guide to the Study of Religion* (ed. Willi Braun and Russell T. McCutcheon; London: Cassell, 2000), 283–96.

Group formation and attendant mythmaking thus acquire a recognizable pattern, a pattern predicated on failure. The comparative or modeling focus of this year's Seminar session poses the question whether the workings and dynamics of ancient "schools" provide a useful, intelligible, or edifying analogue to the formational processes, the social history, of the Christian movement as attested in documents such as Q or the *Gospel of Thomas*. The response to the question, as framed, can only be affirmative. But in my view this affirmation is necessary only because the question has been formulated from within a perspective dominated by the kinds of assumptions we see at work in Mack's social history of the Q people. To put it perhaps more clearly: working within schools ourselves, and working primarily with and in terms of ideas, we imagine social formation in much the same specific terms, intuitively, in which we ourselves experience it. And these are the terms in which we encounter social formation in Mack's description of the social history behind Q. Schools might thus, appropriately enough, be understood as loci of ideas, which ideas, disconnected from social context imagined in a strong sense, may, under just the wrong circumstances, generate a sufficient sense of embattlement to trigger a detached "group identity." That is, the school model works well with Mack's reconstruction of Q's social history insofar as it is idealist: critical ideas (unfortunately?) lead to a "social program," which, when it cannot be implemented in general, comes to be implemented for and among its proponents only, which generates further parochial sensibilities.

On the other hand, there is also a strange tension between Mack's views and some of the implications of comparison of Q's social history with "schools." This tension pertains to the question of the social precursors to the group formation in question. Mack, for reasons I entirely sympathize with, wants the social formation behind Q to be largely *ex nihilo:* that is to say, it "just happens," rather than being a function of the deliberate carrying forward of some precious cultural "deposit" such as belief in the resurrection.[28] Rather, the whole social evolution takes place from individual ideas to group identity, instead of in the passing of an idea from group to group. The "school" model appears to imply, by contrast, that there is or may be an already-extant group, with its own sense of ideological identity, that undergoes evolution. However, in either case the

---

[28] This, of course, is one of the great contributions Q has made—with its successively more mythological stages and with its general lack of interest in kerygmatic understandings of the crucifixion and resurrection—to the re-visioning of earliest Christian history. Mack has been considerably active in drawing these implications to our attention. See also John S. Kloppenborg, "'Easter Faith' and the Sayings Gospel Q," *Semeia* 49 (1990): 71–99; David Seeley, "Blessings and Boundaries: Interpretations of Jesus' Death in Q," *Semeia* 55 (1991): 131–46; idem, "Jesus' Death in Q," *NTS* 38 (1992): 222–34.

common presumption is that like calls to like: that any logical precursor for self-bounded and self-conscious social item X must either be an X-like social item bounded and conscious in similar ways (i.e., more traditional models, which see the social character of Christianity as the vehicle that carries forward a set cultural deposit) or not exist at all (i.e., Mack's apparent view that the social entity generates itself in and through discourse). Precursors, in other words, if they exist, must be isomorphic with rhetorical rationalizing and defining strategies. Thus where Q fails to describe itself, in its various acts of rhetoric, as a group, it does not represent a group; and where it engages in mythmaking, that is, the generation of cosmically grounded social charters, it does represent a group, and moreover a group defined by its own ideological self-referentiality.

This is an assumption that I find rather difficult to accept. Ideology, social discourse, and (voluntary) social grouping are always relational: they take place within some form of larger social totality and quite self-consciously refer to that totality. Q^2's invocation of the epic of Israel's compact with God, for instance, indicates that the Q people understand themselves in terms of a broader social unit that extends beyond their own geographical limits as well as stretches forward and backward in time. The more forceful and sharp the sectarian self-understanding becomes, the more obviously and energetically it refers itself to the larger social entity to which it "belongs." But in the traditional understanding of Christian origins, or in Mack's reconstruction of Q's history, or in the various potentialities associated with a model of "mythmaking and social formation," social or group belonging is conceived in a relatively detached way, as though one can speak of social history only to the extent that a group self-consciously detaches itself from the sociocultural soup from which it "emerges." Again, to clarify: no one ever *makes* a myth, just as no one ever *forms* a social body. Society and its discourses are always experienced as given and, moreover, are insufficiently understood as signs (i.e., as veritably discursive) if their character as references to the larger social matrix in which they have their only genuine referentiality is ignored. Hence from both emic and etic perspectives, the detachment, sufficiency, and monothetic agency of "group" implied in our discussion of "mythmaking and social formation" are potentially misleading and do not sufficiently add to our understanding. In the analysis of the $Q^{(1)}$ beatitudes that follows, I attempt to consider $Q^{(1)}$'s rhetoric in light of a social agenda that does not imply "group formation," that is, that does not imply a social discourse that emanates at every stage of its development from itself (sui generis) or from the collective esprit de corps of the individuals responsible for it, but rather from the efforts of those individuals to engage the social body around them and to modify aspects of its broader social discourse (mythology?) as it is already given.

The Q Beatitudes and Social Development

The Q[(1)] beatitudes (Q 6:20b–23b)[29] offer a salient example of a rhetorical and social process that finds analogues elsewhere in Q[1].[30] As the opening teaching of the first recension of Q, they serve a programmatic function for what follows: they are more an *assertion* of Q[1]'s overall viewpoint than an *argument* for it, but they influence the tone of all that follows.[31] This programmatic function, as well as the bare content, of the Q version of the beatitudes encourages the view that Q is addressed to, if not actually written by, the destitute and miserable and dominated overall by an interest in them.[32] This view is further bolstered by the wording of the first beatitude, which blesses not simply "the poor" but the πτωχοί. The distinction between πένης and πτωχός is made much of by some commentators, as denoting a distinction between the merely poor (i.e., those who have to work for a living) and the utterly destitute.[33] Thus,

---

[29] I.e., excluding v. 23c as a Q[2] gloss. See Kloppenborg, *Formation of Q*, 173, 187, 190, 243; Christopher M. Tuckett, *Q and the History of Early Christianity: Studies on Q* (Edinburgh: T&T Clark; Peabody, Mass.: Hendrickson, 1996), 179–80.

[30] Esp. within the argumentative clusters identified by Piper ("Matthew 7, 7–11"; idem, *Wisdom in the Q-Tradition*) but also in the redactional development of the Q[1] "mission charge" (Q 10:2–11, 16) and its even later (Q[1] redaction) juxtaposition with Q 9:57–62.

[31] On the introductory function of the beatitudes, at least for the initial Q sermon, see, among others, Shawn Carruth, "Strategies of Authority: A Rhetorical Study of the Character of the Speaker in Q 6:20–49," in *Conflict and Invention: Literary, Rhetorical, and Social Studies on the Sayings Gospel Q* (ed. John S. Kloppenborg; Valley Forge, Pa.: Trinity Press International, 1995), 108–9; David R. Catchpole, *The Quest for Q* (Edinburgh: T&T Clark, 1993), 80; R. Conrad Douglas, "'Love Your Enemies': Rhetoric, Tradents, and Ethos," in Kloppenborg, *Conflict and Invention*, 125; Kloppenborg, *Formation of Q*, 188–89 with n. 77; idem, "Literary Convention," 81; Tuckett, *Q and the History of Early Christianity*, 226: "They form the start of the Great Sermon which inaugurates Q's account of Jesus' teaching. They can therefore justifiably be seen as outlining the terms in which the whole of what follows is to be seen."

[32] See, e.g., John Dominic Crossan, *The Historical Jesus: The Life of a Mediterranean Jewish Peasant* (San Francisco: HarperSanFrancisco, 1991), 273–74; Robert W. Funk and Roy W. Hoover, eds., and the Jesus Seminar, *The Five Gospels: The Search for the Authentic Words of Jesus* (New York: Macmillan; San Francisco: HarperSanFrancisco, 1993), 138–39; Kloppenborg, *Formation of Q*, 188: "they pronounce blessing upon a group defined by social and economic circumstances: poverty, hunger, sorrow and persecution. In Q they pronounce blessing upon the community"; Risto Uro, "Apocalyptic Symbolism and Social Identity in Q," in *Symbols and Strata: Essays on the Sayings Gospel Q* (ed. Risto Uro; Publications of the Finnish Exegetical Society 65; Helsinki: Finnish Exegetical Society; Göttingen: Vandenhoeck & Ruprecht, 1996), 87–88. Tuckett, *Q and the History of Early Christianity*, 226, sees them as allusions to Isa 61:1–2, thereby symbolically indicating that Jesus is the eschatological prophet.

[33] Most emphatically, Crossan, *Historical Jesus*, 270–73. Crossan quotes (270–71) as the *locus classicus* for this distinction Aristophanes, *Plutus* 535–54, esp. the words of personified "Poverty":

in blessing the πτωχοί, Q 6:20b is doing more than simply blessing those who are not wealthy; it is blessing the destitute, the beggars, the "Unclean, Degraded, and Expendable classes."[34]

This reasoning does not entirely stand up to scrutiny, in part because the structural role of the beatitudes for the entirety of Q¹ is not given sufficient consideration, nor is the process by which they came to fill this role. The first point that must be stressed is that this cluster of beatitudes, even in its Q¹ form, is composite and went through several stages of development. Classically, Rudolf Bultmann pointed to the distinction in both form and content of the fourth of the Q beatitudes from the first three:

> [I]t is essential to see that Lk. 6:22 or Matt. 5:11f. is a new element of the tradition which is clearly distinguished from the older element Lk. 6:20f. or Matt. 5:3–9 in form (second person and detailed grounds of blessedness) and content, arising *ex eventu* and for that reason created by the Church. It is in this second set that we first have a direct reference to the person of Jesus.[35]

It is clear that the first three Q beatitudes constitute a set marked by similarity in form (μακάριοι οἱ + plural substantive, followed by a single-part

---

'Tis the beggar [*ptôchou*] alone who has nought of his own,
  nor even an obol possesses.
My poor [*penêtos*] man, 'tis true, has to scrape and to screw
  and his work he must never be slack in;
There'll be no superfluity found in his cot;
  but then there will nothing be lacking.

L. Gregory Bloomquist ("The Rhetoric of the Historical Jesus," in Arnal and Desjardins, *Whose Historical Jesus*, 98–117) has rightly observed that the distinction offered here cannot be taken at face value: it serves the (rhetorical) interests of the figure of Poverty, defending herself against the accusations of Chremylus.

[34] Crossan, *Historical Jesus*, 273, citing Gerhard E. Lenski, *Power and Privilege: A Theory of Social Stratification* (McGraw-Hill Series in Sociology; New York: McGraw-Hill, 1966; repr., Chapel Hill: University of North Carolina Press, 1984).

[35] Rudolf Bultmann, *The History of the Synoptic Tradition* (trans. John Marsh; rev. ed.; New York: Harper & Row, 1963), 110. See also Crossan, *Historical Jesus*, 273–74; Funk, Hoover, and the Jesus Seminar, *Five Gospels*, 138–39, 290–91; Kloppenborg, *Formation of Q*, 172–73; Heinz Schürmann, "Beobachtungen zum Menschensohn-Titel in der Redequelle: Sein Vorkommen in Abschluss- und Einleitungswendungen," in *Jesus und der Menschensohn: Für Anton Vögtle* (ed. Rudolf Pesch and Rudolf Schnackenburg; Freiburg: Herder, 1975), 130–31; repr. in *Gottes Reich—Jesu Geschick: Jesu ureigener Tod im Licht seiner Basileia-Verkündigung* (Freiburg: Herder, 1983), 160–61; ET: "Observations on the Son of Man Title in the Speech Source: Its Occurrence in Closing and Introductory Expressions," in Kloppenborg, *Shape of Q*, 80–81; Tuckett, *Q and the History of Early Christianity*, 226. I am here excluding from consideration v. 23c as an even later (i.e., Q²) gloss.

ὅτι-clause)[36] and in focus (i.e., apparently on socioeconomic categories). Even these three beatitudes were not originally a series[37] but were collected together on the basis of their similar form and because they all make the same basic point.[38] The fourth beatitude does not fit this original set, not only in its focus on reputation, its connection of this concern to "in-group" membership (ἕνεκεν ...), its address to "you," and its use of "Son of Man" as a title apparently in reference to Jesus, but also in its extended form and multiple rationalizations.[39] This fourth beatitude is composite in its own right, not only by virtue of the Q² gloss at verse 23c, but also, as the independent parallel in *Gos. Thom.* 69a (cf. saying 68) demonstrates, in the addition of the ἕνεκα/ἕνεκεν clause (v. 22c) and the imperative clause (v. 23a: χαίρετε καὶ ἀγαλλιᾶσθε).[40] Q 6:23b, ὅτι ὁ μισθὸς ὑμῶν πολὺς ἐν τῷ οὐρανῷ, or some version of it, on the other hand, is probably original to the makarism, as it is attested in both of *Thomas*'s versions of the saying.[41] We do not need to trace the process by which these elaborations were added; it is sufficient to note that all of the additions (excluding v. 23c) were probably made subsequent to this saying's association with the other three beatitudes but prior to their attachment to the following instructions on love of enemies and forgiveness.[42]

---

[36] Kloppenborg, *Formation of Q,* 172.

[37] See Funk, Hoover, and the Jesus Seminar, *Five Gospels,* 290; Leif E. Vaage, "Composite Texts and Oral Mythology: The Case of the 'Sermon' in Q (6:20–49)," in Kloppenborg, *Conflict and Invention,* 81.

[38] They are not collected together in *Gospel of Thomas* or, in some instances, are collected in a slightly different way (e.g., the association of the persecution beatitude with the hunger beatitude in *Gos. Thom.* 69).

[39] Thus the fourth beatitude stands apart even if one rejects Bultmann's schematization (as do Crossan, *Historical Jesus,* 273–74; Funk, Hoover, and the Jesus Seminar, *Five Gospels,* 290; but cf. Kloppenborg, *Formation of Q,* 173; Schürmann, "Beobachtungen zum Menschensohn-Titel," 131; repr. in *Gottes Reich—Jesu Geschick,* 161; ET: "Observations on the Son of Man Title," 81), which characterizes it as *ex eventu* and "Church"-related.

[40] Neither one of which appears in either of the two *Thomas* parallels, indicating that the saying circulated as a bipartite unit: a blessing on the persecuted followed by a motive clause describing the rewards or results of the persecution. The amplification of the description of persecution in Q 6:22a,b is probably also secondary.

[41] That is, some kind of result or reward is described as the second half of the saying. In *Gos. Thom.* 68 the result is that "no place will be found, wherever you have been persecuted," while in *Gos. Thom.* 69a the reward is that they "have truly come to know the Father." Both formulations in *Thomas* are almost certainly secondary: they evince the redactional characteristics of the document as a whole, including the terminology of "place" (ⲠⲘⲀ or ⲠⲦⲞⲠⲞⲤ) and "Father" (ⲠⲈⲒⲰⲦ). But they indicate, as noted, that the saying circulated independently in a bipartite form with some type of result clause, the original wording of which is unknown. Even in this bipartite form, however, the saying was structurally distinct from the first three beatitudes.

[42] The basis for the association of the fourth beatitude with the first three is its rough formal similarity to them as well as its thematic similarity ("blessed are those who weep, for...;

What this indicates, among other things, is that already prior to their incorporation into Q⁽¹⁾, the beatitudes, as a single unit, had come to refer to something other than literal poverty or destitution: they were used, rather, to enunciate a set of paradigmatic inversions of basic social positions in support of a final conclusion to the effect that adherence to X program (that is, ἕνεκεν X) would be beneficial in spite of apparent disadvantages. As a result, the "kingdom of God" in the first beatitude also comes to have this self-referential sense: it too becomes denotative of the specific program (X) marked by ἕνεκα/ἕνεκεν.[43] Even the juncture of the first three beatitudes indicates that something other than a voluntarily chosen lifestyle or ethos is directly at issue. Regardless of the *Sitz* of the blessings on the poor or on the hungry, their association with the blessing on those who weep is certainly indicative of a general and principled inversion (the world turned upside down) rather than of a specific and practicable one accomplished by choice, such as voluntary itinerancy or Cynic-like *askesis*. A group defined largely or exclusively in terms of its ideological program may choose to be poor and even perhaps hungry, but they do not choose weeping as a definitional feature of their lifestyle! Indeed, strictly speaking, "weeping" (κλαίοντες) is not a socioeconomic index at all; thus even the

---

blessed are you when they revile you, and..."): both of these features are clearly apparent only in the persecution beatitude's original, bipartite, form. Once it has been added to the end of this list, however, it serves as an interpretive key for the foregoing three beatitudes, so that by clarifying its referent (those persecuted on behalf of the Son of Man), the referent of the entire list is clarified. Thus, in its final position, this beatitude has suffered considerable modification, while the others have been left relatively intact. Note also that the expansion in v. 23a, χαίρετε καὶ ἀγαλλιᾶσθε, may have been inspired by the prior association with v. 21, ὅτι γελάσετε. On the other hand, once an association has been made between the beatitudes and the speech on love of enemies, there is little reason to add such amplifications as we find in vv. 22–23 because (1) they redirect the beatitudes toward a rather different thematic focus than the association with 6:27–36 would suggest, and (2) vv. 22–23 no longer occupy as rhetorically significant a position once the set of beatitudes is associated with the following material.

[43] On the "kingdom (of God)" as a self-referential cipher, see, somewhat obscurely, Burton L. Mack, "Teaching in Parables: Elaboration in Mark 4:1–34," in *Patterns of Persuasion in the Gospels* (ed. Burton L. Mack and Vernon K. Robbins; FF; Sonoma, Calif.: Polebridge, 1989), 159–60, describing the "kingdom of God" as a cipher for the content of early Christian paideia; and, much more clearly, idem, *Myth of Innocence*, 69–74; and, most clearly of all and with explicit reference to Q, idem, *Lost Gospel*, 123–27: "the link between the notion of the rule of God and the pattern of Q's countercultural practices is very, very strong" (124), but "[t]he thought had not yet occurred at the Q^1 level, as it did later at the Q^2 stage, that the location of God's kingdom was to be found precisely in the social formation of the movement" (127). See also Leif E. Vaage, *Galilean Upstarts: Jesus' First Followers according to Q* (Valley Forge, Pa.: Trinity Press International, 1994), 55–65. Mack in particular is one of the only commentators to make sense of the phrase in any clear and convincing way; most accounts of its referent are (unsurprisingly) obscurantist.

very early clustering of the first three beatitudes represents a shift away from the strictly socioeconomic force of the first and second beatitudes taken in isolation.[44] The point has become general and (relatively) abstract. The addition of a fourth (persecution) beatitude, attracted by the influence of the third (weeping) beatitude, further shifts attention away from the strictly economic character of the first two blessings and sharpens and elaborates the apparent reference to weeping: "those who weep" are weeping because they are reviled, cast out, or reproached. On the influence of this motif, then, the last beatitude is elaborated and amplified to express this theme more clearly and to specify the motivations behind the reproaches, influencing, as a result, the tenor of the entire list of blessings.

Thus the thematic progress of the beatitudes in the course of their development was: (1) economic inversion → (2) general or abstract inversion → (3) a specific social inversion (involving esteem or repute) → (4) social inversion as a result or consequence of adherence to a specific program.[45] Such a progression of course already matches to some degree the rhetorical pattern imputed by Ronald A. Piper to the aphoristic blocks that constitute Q^1. The composition of Piper's pre-Q^1 argumentative clusters follows the same course rhetorically (synchronically) as the beatitudes follow tradition-historically (diachronically): that is, they are (1) based on radical sayings that are (2) used to express inversion in the abstract, in the service of (3) some specific type of social exhortation (often involving esteem or repute). The fourth step, on the other hand, not present at the stage in which the pre-Q^1 clusters developed, is however paralleled in the Q^1 redactional juxtaposition of the "mission charge" ([3] a specific set of social behaviors, concerned with welcome, i.e., esteem or repute) with the discipleship sayings of Q 9:57–62 ([4] the idea that social destabilization occurs as a result of adherence to the program).[46]

---

[44] See, in this vein, Vaage, *Galilean Upstarts*, 57: "It is clear in 6:20b that a share in God's kingdom means not going along with the customary understanding of misery and bliss, if only because one is convinced that present tears and hunger will soon give way." Note the logical connection in Vaage's reading of the first beatitude between its meaning and the presence of the two following beatitudes. Even the juxtaposition of the first with the second beatitude mitigates the force of the former somewhat: poverty is a status and is restricted to only some people, while hunger is a state and is experienced in greater or lesser degrees by everyone; poverty is imagined to be a permanent feature of the people blessed, while hunger will be mitigated.

[45] If there is any general pattern to be seen here at all, it is the movement from a specific (indeterminable?) setting to a generalized one, from which subsequent and increasingly specific applications may be made. The stage of generalization is what allows for the new applications.

[46] Of course the fifth step, visible at the level of Q^2 redaction, but not undertaken (much) in Q^1, is to use authoritative and conventional *topoi* (such as apocalyptic judgment, or biblical

And within the overall context of Q¹, as its programmatic introduction, the beatitudes serve a similar literary and rhetorical (synchronic) function to that served by the opening lines of Piper's argumentative clusters: they establish a general or abstract inversionary tone (stage 2, above) that is used as a basis upon which to develop further arguments. Thematically, however, this incorporation into the totality of Q⁽¹⁾ means that they function in terms of diachronic stage 4, that is, as denotative of social inversion that stems from advocacy of a certain program. This is natural enough: it corresponds to the final stage in the development of these beatitudes in their Q¹ form. This is all to say, in other words, that although the beatitudes as a unit already show in their aggregational development an orientation toward the theme of social uprooting as a consequence of certain choices, they function rhetorically within Q¹ as generalizations promoting the principle of inversion and as identifications of that comprehensive inversion-in-principle with the "kingdom of God" or "the Son of Man." Thus all of what follows has the character of specific applications of Q⁽¹⁾ 6:21–23, just as many of Piper's constituent clusters attempt specific applications of the general principles with which they open. Shawn Carruth is at least partly correct when she argues that the authority of Jesus as the speaker is presumed here, not developed:

> Enunciating a number of beatitudes does not prove a case, but it does intensify the sense of the speaker's authority by showing that he or she can illuminate the situation of the hearers in a comprehensive way. Here in the exordium of the sermon, where rhetorical principle emphasizes the establishment of the speaker's character, Jesus is shown to be one who overturns common wisdom and lays down a different way of perceiving one's situation. The acceptance of this new wisdom will depend in large measure on the authority attributed to Jesus by the audience.[47]

Apparently Jesus was a sufficiently authoritative character for the people responsible for Q¹ (or for their fictive/putative audience) that an effort was made to assimilate or subsume material already circulating under his name. Carruth may, however, be reversing cause and effect. The association of Jesus with such inversionary sayings may have been part of the reason he was selected as a speaker in the first place. These inversionary sayings have a powerful suasive force of their own, and to the extent that Q¹'s agenda was in fact subversive, and to the extent that its tradents identified themselves as uprooted and/or their audience as responsive to this rhetoric,

---

proof texts, or the Deuteronomistic schema of Israel's history) to rationalize that destabilization: "for so their fathers did to the prophets."

[47] Carruth, "Strategies of Authority," 108–9.

such material—if it could be successfully integrated into the program at hand—must have been extraordinarily attractive in its own right, Jesus himself notwithstanding.

This logic is the logic of the categorical opening statements of Piper's clusters and is partly attractive simply because of its categorical, black-and-white, and arresting view of reality.[48] The sayings are memorable and powerful precisely because they are not subtle, not casuistic. But even more so, they are powerful because of the way they force the hearers to imagine for themselves the circumstances under which they might be true. It is for that reason that one should describe these opening sayings above as enthymeme-like in their rhetorical effect. What the beatitudes do, as the opening for Q¹ as an entire document, is invoke that speculation in the most general, explicitly inversionary, and comprehensive way possible. Appropriately enough, the beatitudes are enthymemes, in their formal characteristics, and not simply in terms of the logic they depend upon.[49] As such, the readers/hearers are left to supply the premises that will make the main assertions of these sayings come true. They are warned (or promised) that the arguments to follow will be inversionary but not how they will be inversionary; they are warned that the arguments that follow will depend on and articulate a condition known as "the kingdom of God" but are not told the terms and prerequisites of this condition. Transformation is promised but not described. Not only is the serialization of the blessings attendant upon hearkening to wisdom a known introductory strategy within the genre of wisdom instructions,[50] but their formulation as enthymemes[51] is perfectly appropriate to Q¹'s subsequent rhetoric and tone. Moreover, it serves to "hook" the reader or hearer, inviting not simply (1) speculation and consideration about the character of this future inversion, but also (2) curiosity about the remainder of the document ("how will these promises be fulfilled?"), (3) the assumption that the arguments that follow do indeed fulfill the agenda of general inversion ("these ideas are what it is that will make the poor, the hungry, and so on

---

[48] In this sense they are not, formally speaking, much unlike conventional wisdom. A view of the world in which categories are sharply drawn is not eschewed; it is simply inverted.

[49] Carruth, "Strategies of Authority," 107–8.

[50] Kloppenborg, *Formation of Q*, 188.

[51] In contrast to most of the examples cited by Kloppenborg (ibid., 188 n. 77), which (1) tend to be prescriptive and (2) have fully articulated premises. See, e.g., Tob 13:14b: "Blessed are those who grieved over all of your afflictions; for they will rejoice for you upon seeing your glory." The framing of beatitudes with dropped premises—presumably in order to foster consideration and reflection about wisdom and the good life, to invite assent—is not unique to Q, however. See, e.g., Sir 26:1: "Happy is the husband of a good wife; the number of his days will be doubled." Here the premise "an unhappy home life will kill you" (or the like) is left unstated. It is, however, very easily inferred.

happy"), and possibly also (4) assent in advance (by forcing the audience to imagine the topsy-turvy world in which such sayings would be true, the audience creates that world mentally, making what follows all the more plausible).[52]

In sum, then, within the context of Q^1 as a document, the beatitudes are not indicative of beggary among the audience or speakers, nor are they even indicative of a principled interest in beggary. There is no germinal "Idea" here driving forward various social developments. The use of πτωχοί in the first of these blessings is not as significant as it has been made out to be. In Hellenistic literature, πένης and πτωχός are used interchangeably, and for the New Testament πτωχός is the usual term for poverty.[53] The kind of conditions these sayings outline is decidedly not prescriptive,[54] and hence their inversionary rhetoric is only imperfectly accounted for by hypotheses of group behavior or group ethos isomorphic with the conditions in question. In the form in which they appear in Q, the beatitudes have already been considerably "domesticated" and now serve rhetorically to promote an abstract sense of inversion that both thematically situates or reinforces the material that follows and actively attempts to engage the audience prior to the commencement of what promises to be an unconventional project. By the time we arrive at the redaction of Q^1, this project, invoking the Jesus traditions and (apparently) Jesus himself, is already being viewed retrospectively. The composition of Q^1, in time with and (thematically) of a piece with the evolution of the individual traditions harbored by the group, may have been in part a response to the failure of an earlier agenda[55] represented by (1) the initial formulation of Piper's argumentative clusters, (2) the mission speech (as a unit and in its Q^1 form), and (3) the initial serialization of the first three beatitudes and especially their juncture with (the original form of) the fourth beatitude. But for the persons represented by $Q^{(1)}$'s development, the alienation expressed in the beatitudes has come some considerable distance from the economic deracination that served as the apparent *Sitz* of their original formulation;

---

[52] Any audience might be resistant to simple description of such an outlandish world; it is difficult to imagine how such a description could be, or even appear to be, realistic. But by forcing the audience to create the image for themselves, not only is assent to its reality compelled, but its characteristics will match the desires and resonances of each person's imagination. This basic technique (the compulsion of assent) is the way Sir 26:1 works: the imagination constructs a happy man living well at home, or a haggard man unhappy at home, and one's own mind has already—in the course of merely trying to follow the argument—supplied an image that confirms the author's conclusions and thus convinces one that those conclusions are agreeable and, indeed, self-evident.

[53] Ernst Bammel, "πτωχός, κτλ.," *TDNT* 6:894 with n. 79; 902 with n. 155. Cf. BDAG 896.

[54] So also Kloppenborg, *Formation of Q*, 188.

[55] And hence a desire to collect such traditions in lieu of the mission to disseminate them.

the alienation expressed is metaphoric, rhetorical, and deliberately vague. It is invoked only in the service of more specific points that are considerably less "radical" (and less mysterious) and that focus on social esteem to a considerable degree. Thus the economic deracination evoked by some of the Q¹ material appears, rhetorically, to be yoked to the service of a redactional and preredactional Q^(1) interest in social deracination. That interest, in turn, seems to center on—or to have once centered on—a specific social vision in which esteem, honor, and local standing are of paramount importance.

Conclusions?

The implications of this jaunt into detailed textual analysis are fairly important, I think, for how we conceive of "the Q group's" social development. What is notable in the literary reconstruction suggested above is that the social *Sitz* for each stage in the literary use (a better term than "development," at least for my purposes here) of the beatitudes is different from and independent of that which goes before it. Moreover, each new *Sitz* appears to relate to a "group" defined by and within a larger social totality—that is, a group already-given, and already-given in terms of external social structures and functions that have little to do with the discursive identity applied by the group in question to itself.

The very earliest identifiable stage of the beatitudes—their formulation—implies a concern with deprivation in terms of the given indices of economic well-being, including "poverty" in general and hunger more specifically. The collection of the beatitudes, by contrast, shows a generalizing interest in the question of economic inversion, which is then applied to a very specific interest in refuting differential indices of status within villages and small towns. If, as some have suggested,[56] the persons primarily responsible for Q¹ were village scribes, we might associate this stage of use of the Q traditions with a *Sitz* involving relative loss of status among individuals who are certainly not destitute. These individuals, addressing an entirely different question than poverty at large, but still a question that involves at the very least the whole of social relationships at the village level, have appropriated an already-extant discourse and applied it to a new problem, a problem already-given, and not given by or as a result of the discourse in question, but by the social forces and conditions exterior to that discourse.

---

[56] See esp. Kloppenborg, "Literary Convention"; William E. Arnal, "The Rhetoric of Marginality: Apocalypticism, Gnosticism, and Sayings Gospels," *HTR* 88 (1995): 471–94; idem, *Jesus and the Village Scribes: Galilean Conflicts and the Setting of Q* (Minneapolis: Fortress, 2001).

The same kind of process might even be imagined for the development from Q^1 to Q^2, even if the same individuals responsible for the first stage were also responsible for the second. If the Q^1 agenda was indeed intended to address relative loss of status among village scribes, and if a broader social program was indeed envisioned by them, we can and should understand the failure of that program as simply a failure to restore their social status. The polemic of Q^2, and its redefinition of Israel, the first steps toward appropriating a broad cosmic mythology to locate the group, all might be seen as indications of progressive loss of status among the group, that is, of the same processes that led to Q^1 in the first place, and not as indications of the suasive failure of the specific rhetorical project or social program that was articulated in Q^1.

The Q^1 project failed not because its argumentative strategies were flawed, or unconvincing, or because "members" of the group fled. Rather, it failed because the persons in question had already lost sufficient power by the time they formulated these speeches that they were unable to exercise sufficient influence to halt further loss. So the situation simply got worse. It did not get worse because of the mythologizing or internal social steps taken by the individuals (as a "group") responsible for Q, but rather in spite of these steps. Persuasion comes, as it were, from the barrel of a gun, and the Q people had no guns. The processes we need to analyze, if it is indeed social processes that we wish to map and genuinely understand, are all extradiscursive. Mack wants the process to be discursive in its origination and wants the discourse to follow an internally determined course, as do most other scholars of earliest Christianity. But why does Q jump the rails from critique to group formation? Why launch the critique in the first place? Because, in every instance, of a desultory lack or loss of power, a lack or loss prescribed from without, and from without discourse.

It is precisely in emphasizing the extradiscursive—that is, the conceiving of Q as operating primarily within and with a view to the social totality of which its tradents are a part, rather than in terms of a self-conscious "group" constituted, per se, by the document's tradents—that my theoretical differences with Mack, as well as divergences in application, come to a point and hence, also, where my conception of earliest Christian history differs from what appears to be the guiding vision of this Seminar. Mack views religion, here drawing from Louis Althusser, as a "semiautonomous instance" of human sociality[57] and so quite explicitly denies either the sufficiency of "religious" explanations for groups that define themselves in terms of religious ideology or the autonomy of religious expressions from human social formation in general. On these points Mack and I agree, as

---

[57] Mack, "Social Formation," esp. 283.

we do, apparently, in our predilection for Marxian (and even Althusserian) theoretical formulations of human society. But we diverge sharply in two respects, one essentially practical and the other more clearly theoretical.

First, in his treatment of the "semiautonomous" character of religion, Mack seems to emphasize the "autonomous" more than the "semi-." The point of Althusser's formulation can only be grasped from within Marxist discourse[58] and should be seen as an effort to reject deterministic or mechanistic understandings of the base-superstructure relationship, but by no means to dispense with that formulation altogether. What Althusser is providing is simply a more sophisticated model of how it is that social forms relate to, depend on, and reflect an economic causal nexus formulated as a "mode of production," just as Marx suggested; it is not an alternative to Marxian reduction. And the "autonomy" in question refers to the relative freedom of the social to develop its own forms within the constraints established by the organization and forces of production; it does not refer to a tendency of social groupings to form into sectarian enclaves or subunits. What all of this means, to my mind, is that an Althusserian reading of "religious" groups, or of early Christianity, or of Q, should precisely emphasize, and attempt to explicate, the ways in which specific social configurations do relate to broader economic forces (in spite of the relative freedom with which they creatively rationalize or configure these relations). In other words, and in short, it strikes me as more likely to lead to real understanding of the phenomena in question if we use Althusser's conception of "semiautonomy" precisely as a tool for *linking* subgroup phenomena to their social totality, rather than one for separating them.

Second, and at a more explicitly theoretical level, it appears to me that in Mack's formulation of the theoretical underpinnings of his work, he allows for an interesting—but very problematic—slippage between social interests and the interest in sociality, which are in fact entirely different things.[59] Althusser's typically Marxian emphasis on social interest signifies the particular and differential goals of various social groupings in ways ultimately ("in the last instance") relative to economic class. It does not signify the proliferation of subgroupings on the grounds of a basic human attraction to communal interaction.[60] This latter observation has little

---

[58] One might go further and say it can only be grasped within communist discourse—the formulation is in fact a strategic move from within the PCF, offering a cloaked challenge to the Party's continued Stalinism in the form of a repudiation of mechanistic economism. See, briefly, Gregory Elliott, preface in *Althusser: A Critical Reader* (ed. Gregory Elliott; Oxford: Blackwell, 1994), viii.

[59] See esp. Mack, "Social Formation," 284–85.

[60] As does Mack (ibid., 288). The assertion that humans naturally gravitate to each other is, no doubt, valid enough, although it strikes me as more Durkheimian than Althusserian.

explanatory force or theoretical utility, serving only to reiterate that humans are social beings but failing to offer any grounds for the specific and often conflictual forms that their sociality takes. Mack's corollary term, "mythmaking," likewise seems to depend on a generalized tendency to rationalization of social coherence, but again without appearing to have much potential to explain the positional and conflictual interests that drive various groupings and agenda.

A result of these differences in emphasis and in conceptualization is a tendency on Mack's part to idealism (elaborated at some length above), toward the reification of intellectual work, and hence to his treating concepts as having an independence and autonomy from overarching social structures and social agenda. "Religious" conceptions are, quite properly, accorded no special standing or unique autonomy among other intellectual expressions of "social projects," but intellection in general and its tendencies toward "group formation" are treated as if they were self-explanatory, stood on their own, or existed in some sort of social vacuum that made their larger (political, economic) context unimportant. The only way to avoid this tendency—a tendency I see to be predominant in the traditional approaches to Christian origins that Mack has contributed so much to call into question—is to deconstruct the notion of linearity, or the assumption of linearity, in the development and progression of ideas. This is not some sort of postmodern call to reject causality or linearity as such but represents rather an interest in moving ideas away from the center of our historical discourse. In my opinion, this goal—which best serves our genuine and reductive understanding of the phenomena in question—requires that we view the ideological artifacts of ancient Christianity as effects, not as causes, and attempt to understand them in terms of the complex external web of circumstances rather than in terms of the endless reference of ideas to earlier ideas.

These are more than merely strategic differences, I think. While both Mack and I are equally interested in offering a sketch or even explanation for developments in ancient Christian history, in my opinion, the linear and idealist character of the scenarios offered by Mack so far only serve to perpetuate, almost inevitably, the same old Lukan "story" of the "rise of Christianity." Individual episodes may be reconfigured; characters and events may be evaluated slightly differently. But our "redescription," if we are not careful, may in the end become just that: a redescription of the essentially straight line of development—from Jesus the teacher (schools) to the Jerusalem apostles (the pillars) to the Hellenist and Gentile-positive Antioch-based mission (pre-Pauline Christ cults) to Paul and thence to the ends of the earth—initially described by Luke and redescribed ever since. Indeed, to the extent that we view the various moments in which the scattered and desultory earliest Christians poke their heads above the historical horizon as linked to each other, we will be beholden to the Lukan myth. To the extent that we conceptualize them as, precisely, moments, rather than stages or steps, and as moments in which groups, already given and constituted by the larger social order, opportunistically use (or redefine, or deploy, or take advantage of) concepts, identity tags, "religious" language, and the like, in support of their own, very distinctive and positionally determined agenda, we will be on our way to a genuinely reductive understanding of the earliest Christians and their literature.

Ancient Myths and Modern Theories of the *Gospel of Thomas* and Christian Origins

Ron Cameron

I don't need any more data.
What I need is a theory to explain it all.
— David Lodge, *Small World*

I

The discovery of any manuscript is always a joyous occasion, not least when the manuscript is a venerable document that makes a difference in our understanding of religion and culture. In the past century two such discoveries, each fifty years apart, have provided us with the opportunity to pause, take stock of our studies, and reassess what we know about the beginnings of Christianity. I am referring, of course, to two separate discoveries of the same early Christian text: the *Gospel according to Thomas*.

The *Gospel of Thomas* is an anthology of 114 sayings preserved in the name, and under the authority, of Jesus. Fragments of three different manuscripts of the Greek text of *Thomas* (P.Oxy. 1, 654, 655) were discovered nearly one hundred years ago in a garbage dump in the ancient town of Oxyrhynchus, Egypt, and published at the turn of the century. Fifty years later, a Coptic translation of the entire Gospel was discovered at Nag Hammadi, Egypt, where it was buried (in a large storage jar) in the fourth century, unearthed in 1945 (by Muhammad Ali), and published the next decade. *Thomas* quickly became the subject of intense scholarly debate. Since no fewer than 68 of the 114 sayings in the text have biblical parallels, establishing a connection between *Thomas* and the New Testament was thought to have far-reaching consequences. The outcome is not restricted to the narrow confines of biblical source criticism. Broader issues are at stake as well, including the significance of the *Gospel of Thomas* for the history of the Jesus traditions, the place of *Thomas* in the intersection of cultures symbolized by the term "Christian beginnings," and the designs of the Gospel itself.

From the beginning, scholars have been concerned chiefly with three basic questions: the authenticity of the sayings attributed to Jesus in the text, the relation of the *Gospel of Thomas* to the New Testament, and whether or not this Gospel is "gnostic."[1] In fact, the debates started two years before the Coptic text was established and a first edition even published. In 1957, in one of the first two studies of the Coptic *Gospel of Thomas* to appear in print, Gilles Quispel addressed these issues and concluded with the following assessment of the parable of the tenants (*Gos. Thom.* 65 // Mark 12:1-8 par.):

> [*Thomas*] transmits essentially the same message as our Bible.... The importance of the ... discovery [of the *Gospel of Thomas*] ... could [therefore] be ... that we may have now an independent Gospel-tradition, which if not verbally, at least in the broad outlines both of style and of theology agrees to a large extent with the text of our canonical Gospels.... In this sense the Gospel of Thomas confirms the trustworthiness of the Bible.[2]

---

[1] The history of scholarship on the *Gospel of Thomas* may be traced through the surveys of Pierre Prigent, "L'Évangile selon Thomas: État de la question," *RHPR* 39 (1959): 39-45; Ernst Haenchen, "Literatur zum Thomasevangelium," *TRu* 27 (1961-62): 147-78, 306-38; H. Quecke, "L'Évangile de Thomas: État des recherches," in *La venue du messie: Messianisme et eschatologie* (ed. É. Massaux; RechBib 6; Brussels: Desclée de Brouwer, 1962), 217-41; Kurt Rudolph, "Gnosis und Gnostizismus, ein Forschungsbericht," *TRu* 34 (1969): 181-94; Francis T. Fallon and Ron Cameron, "The Gospel of Thomas: A Forschungsbericht and Analysis," *ANRW* 25.6:4195-4251; Stephen J. Patterson, "The Gospel of Thomas and the Synoptic Tradition: A Forschungsbericht and Critique," *Foundations and Facets Forum* 8 (1992): 45-97; G. J. Riley, "The *Gospel of Thomas* in Recent Scholarship," *CurBS* 2 (1994): 227-52; Klaus-Gunther Wesseling, "Thomas," *Biographisch-Bibliographisches Kirchenlexikon* 11 (1996): 1292-1323, esp. 1292-98, 1303-15. Recent comprehensive discussions include those of Ron Cameron, "Thomas, Gospel of," *ABD* 6:535-40; Philip Sellew, "The *Gospel of Thomas*: Prospects for Future Research," in *The Nag Hammadi Library after Fifty Years: Proceedings of the 1995 Society of Biblical Literature Commemoration* (ed. John D. Turner and Anne McGuire; NHMS 44; Leiden: Brill, 1997), 327-46; Richard Valantasis, *The Gospel of Thomas* (New Testament Readings; London: Routledge, 1997); Ramón Trevijano Etcheverría, *Estudios sobre el Evangelio de Tómas* (Fuentes Patrísticas, Estudios 2; Madrid: Editorial Ciudad Nueva, 1997); Risto Uro, ed., *Thomas at the Crossroads: Essays on the Gospel of Thomas* (Studies of the New Testament and Its World; Edinburgh: T&T Clark, 1998); Thomas Zöckler, *Jesu Lehren im Thomasevangelium* (NHMS 47; Leiden: Brill, 1999). A complete listing of the publications on the *Gospel of Thomas* (through 2000) may be found in David M. Scholer, *Nag Hammadi Bibliography 1948-1969* (NHS 1; Leiden: Brill, 1971), 136-65; idem, *Nag Hammadi Bibliography 1970-1994* (NHMS 32; Leiden: Brill, 1997), 309-47; idem, "Bibliographia Gnostica: Supplementum II/1," *NovT* 40 (1998): 88-89; idem, "Bibliographia Gnostica: Supplementum II/2," *NovT* 41 (1999): 80-81; idem, "Bibliographia Gnostica: Supplementum II/3," *NovT* 42 (2000): 64-70; idem, "Bibliographia Gnostica: Supplementum II/4," *NovT* 43 (2001): 65-70; idem, "Bibliographia Gnostica: Supplementum II/5," *NovT* 44 (2002): 79-82; idem, "Bibliographia Gnostica: Supplementum II/6," *NovT* 45 (2003): 89-91.

[2] G. Quispel, "The Gospel of Thomas and the New Testament," *VC* 11 (1957): 206, 207; repr. in *Gnostic Studies II* (Uitgaven van het Nederlands Historisch-Archaeologisch Instituut te Istanbul 34/2; Istanbul: Nederlands Historisch-Archaeologisch Instituut te Istanbul, 1975), 15,

Although much can be learned by comparing the *Gospel of Thomas* with the New Testament, a serious problem remains: "The frame of reference for the historical description of Christian origins continues to be the New Testament picture itself."³ The conclusion drawn by Quispel illustrates the problem. With the Bible presupposed as the privileged point of comparison, any differences between the *Gospel of Thomas* and the canonical Gospels are ignored, and all discourse of a social, historical, literary, or theological character is said to be the same. Every distinguishing feature of *Thomas* has thus been erased in the interests of maintaining the reliability of the words, traditions, accounts, and authority of the New Testament.

Confining the discussion of the *Gospel of Thomas* to questions of authenticity, textual dependence, and gnostic influence ironically truncates the analysis, serving—whether intentionally or not—to marginalize the text and its import for the scholarly imagination of Christian origins. I raise this issue in order to focus on two matters of consequence for our purposes. First, we have yet to pay sufficient methodological attention to the fundamental issue of difference. Construing connections with the New Testament solely as a matter of dependence means that the numerous parallels between *Thomas* and the canonical Gospels are examined, not as analogies to foster interpretation, but exclusively for purposes of "establishing direct relations ([of] borrowing and dependency)" and "prestigious origins ([a biblical] pedigree)."⁴ The effects of subordinating the *Gospel of Thomas* to the canonical Gospels are especially pernicious, in that *Thomas* is not taken seriously as a Gospel worthy of study in its own right, but is reduced to the status of a textual variant in the history of the Synoptic tradition. Assigning a late dating to *Thomas,* moreover, typically serves to "render implausible the notion of [a contaminating, gnostic] 'influence' on first century Christianit[ies]."⁵ Such genealogical strategies betray, in Jonathan Z. Smith's words, "an overwhelming concern for assigning value, rather than intellectual significance, to the [enterprise and] results of comparison."⁶

---

16. Note that Quispel never modified his analysis or varied this conclusion, as his "last word on the *Gospel of Thomas*" makes clear: "The *Gospel of Thomas* confirms the trustworthiness of our Bible" (idem, review of Bentley Layton, ed., *Nag Hammadi Codex II,2–7 Together with XIII,2*, Brit. Lib. Or.4926[1], and P. Oxy. 1, 654, 655, VC* 45 [1991]: 87, 83).

³ Merrill P. Miller, "Introduction to the Consultation on Christian Origins," *MTSR* 8 (1996): 229.

⁴ Jonathan Z. Smith, *Drudgery Divine: On the Comparison of Early Christianities and the Religions of Late Antiquity* (Jordan Lectures in Comparative Religion 14; London: School of Oriental and African Studies, University of London; Chicago: University of Chicago Press, 1990), 47.

⁵ Ibid., 69.

⁶ Ibid., 46.

Second, we need to devote ourselves to more sustained theoretical discourse, specifically about the intellectual process of translation: the necessity to engage in explanation and interpretation from a human-sciences perspective, in disciplined ways that do not simply reproduce, by continuing to paraphrase, the dominant (essentially Lukan) paradigm of Christian origins.[7] This is not an issue that can be evaded or ignored, for both "the understanding of religion implicit in our discipline" and the imaginative means used to map the contours of a social history of the earliest Christians are "inadequate for the task of redescribing" the making of early Christianity as religion.[8] Even though scholars recognize that the beginnings of Christianity were pluriform, most constructions of Christian origins remain the same. They presuppose at the inauguration of the Christian era a dramatic event, a kerygmatic conviction, and a linear development, based primarily on the narrative construct of the book of Acts.[9] The problem with this scenario is not simply historical. The fundamental issues are imaginative and theoretical: the New Testament serves as the sole framework for the scholarly imagination of Christian origins, even when scholars recognize that picture as tendentious, overly simplified, or legendary. This problem persists "despite [the] recognition" of the "diversity of early Christianit[ies]" and "despite the application of new method[s] and the contributions of new voices in the field" of biblical studies.[10] Accordingly, we must break the spell of the gospel paradigm; otherwise, all texts—canonical and noncanonical alike—will "have no [adequate] frame of reference to give them any significance"[11] and, thus, no adequate framework for a genuinely critical history of Christian beginnings.

---

[7] See Jonathan Z. Smith, "Social Formations of Early Christianities: A Response to Ron Cameron and Burton Mack," *MTSR* 8 (1996): 271–78. On the centrality of theory to argumentation, Smith notes that "contestation arises over competing claims to comprehend the *same* data, an argument that, therefore, can never be settled at the level of data" (idem, "Connections," *JAAR* 58 [1990]: 10, emphasis original).

[8] Burton L. Mack, "On Redescribing Christian Origins," *MTSR* 8 (1996): 252; repr., with revisions, in *The Christian Myth: Origins, Logic, and Legacy* (New York: Continuum, 2001), 65.

[9] See Ron Cameron, "Alternate Beginnings—Different Ends: Eusebius, Thomas, and the Construction of Christian Origins," in *Religious Propaganda and Missionary Competition in the New Testament World: Essays Honoring Dieter Georgi* (ed. Lukas Bormann et al.; NovTSup 74; Leiden: Brill, 1994), 501–25, esp. 512–15 nn. 55–63.

[10] Miller, "Consultation on Christian Origins," 229.

[11] Mack, "On Redescribing Christian Origins," 248, adding: "A redescription of Christian origins [will] ultimately have to account for the emergence of the [canonical] gospels themselves, turning them into interesting products of early Christian thinking instead of letting them determine the parameters within which all of our data must find a place to rest" (ibid.; repr. in *Christian Myth*, 60–61).

II

Although most discussions of the *Gospel of Thomas* and the New Testament have sought to relate *Thomas* to the Synoptic Gospels, scholars have given more consideration of late to possible connections between *Thomas* and John. In particular, Gregory J. Riley has proposed that *Thomas* and John are best understood as texts reflecting communities in conflict, whose reciprocal relations of theological debate may be seen most clearly in the paradigmatic portrayal of the figure of Thomas at the end of the Gospel of John (John 20:24–29).[12] The "communities [of Thomas and John] differed fundamentally" on several matters, Riley has argued, including "the central [doctrinal] issues of the [so-called] Doubting Thomas pericope: physical resurrection, faith, and the deity of Christ."[13] Of the issues in dispute in this pericope, "the demonstration of the fleshly resurrection of Jesus is the central theme in [John's] debate with the Thomas community."[14] Therefore, John constructed the story of Jesus' appearance to Thomas to dispel doubt by demonstrating the physical reality of the resurrection through the touching of Jesus' body. In doing so, John sought to correct "the 'original,' that is culturally prior," position of the Thomas community, which denigrated the body, denied the physical resurrection, and insisted rather on a "'spiritual,' non-fleshly resurrection of Jesus."[15]

The *Gospel of Thomas,* for its part, interpreted the "free"-floating "temple saying,"[16] which it shares with the Synoptics and John (*Gos. Thom.* 71 // Mark 14:58 par. // John 2:19), to refer not to the destruction of the temple—which was the saying's "original point"[17]—but metaphorically to "the 'temple' of Jesus' body":[18]

> Jesus said, "I will destroy [this] house, and no one will be able to build it [...]." (*Gos. Thom.* 71)[19]

---

[12] Gregory J. Riley, "Doubting Thomas: Controversy between the Communities of Thomas and John" (Ph.D. diss., Harvard University, 1990); idem, "Thomas Tradition and the *Acts of Thomas*," in *Society of Biblical Literature 1991 Seminar Papers* (SBLSP 30; Atlanta: Scholars Press, 1991), 533–42; idem, "*Gospel of Thomas* in Recent Scholarship," 239–40; idem, *Resurrection Reconsidered: Thomas and John in Controversy* (Minneapolis: Fortress, 1995).

[13] Riley, *Resurrection Reconsidered*, 5.

[14] Ibid., 125 n. 68; cf. 105.

[15] Ibid., 178, 177; cf. 97, 107, 128–29, 155.

[16] Ibid., 155, 142.

[17] Ibid., 142.

[18] Ibid., 134; cf. 145–47, 153.

[19] Note that the ending of *Gos. Thom.* 71 is uncertain, since there is a lacuna (of ca. six to eight letters) in the papyrus at the bottom of the extant page (NHC 2,2:45.35) of the Coptic text. See *The Facsimile Edition of the Nag Hammadi Codices: Codex II* (Leiden: Brill, 1974),

In Riley's view, "the major reason for the inclusion of [this] saying in the *Gospel of Thomas* is clearly the final line: 'no one will be able to [re-]build it.'"[20] Indeed, of the "four separate elements" that make up a composite version of the saying (the temple's destruction, its rebuilding, a reference to three days, and its application to the resurrection of Jesus), only *Thomas*'s version "has no [reference to] 'rebuilding' at all"—and that, Riley maintains, "for polemical theological reasons; it was composed to contradict the promise of rebuilding interpreted as bodily resurrection" (cf. John 2:21, 22).[21] *Thomas* was "not in the least concerned with an eschatological destruction or rebuilding of the temple." However, since "early in the Church the [temple] saying was applied to the resurrection of Jesus," it was "at this stage that the Thomas community inherited and adjusted" the tradition,[22] appropriating "a version of the saying which [had come to be] applied to the body of Jesus, but chang[ing] it to deny his physical resurrection."[23] Whereas the Gospel of John employed the temple saying in its "defense of the physical nature of Jesus,"[24] the *Gospel of Thomas* has preserved an earlier version of the saying, to assert that this "'house' would *not* be rebuilt,"[25] that Jesus' body would not be raised.[26]

While an intertextual conversation between *Thomas* and John is certainly not implausible, there are serious problems with the reconstruction which Riley has presented of the controversy that engaged these two texts. First, Riley has not yet established that the story of Jesus' appearance to Thomas (John 20:24-29) was designed to correct a theological position actually held by the *Gospel of Thomas*. Moreover, Riley has not demonstrated that *Thomas* has invoked the metaphor of "resurrection" at all, to say nothing of a "spiritual" resurrection that regarded the body as "*real* ... [albeit] a mere dwelling of the soul which [would] not survive death."[27] The suggestion that John's Doubting Thomas pericope was created literarily, in part, by "a recasting of the character of an historical disciple" to represent

---

55; Bentley Layton, ed., *Nag Hammadi Codex II,2–7 Together with XIII,2*, Brit. Lib. Or.4926(1), and P. Oxy. 1, 654, 655* (2 vols.; NHS 20–21; Leiden: Brill, 1989), 1:80. For the restoration of "to build it [again]," see A. Guillaumont, H.-Ch. Puech, G. Quispel, W. Till, and Yassah 'Abd al Masîḥ, eds., *The Gospel according to Thomas* (Leiden: Brill; New York: Harper & Brothers, 1959), 40.

[20] Riley, *Resurrection Reconsidered*, 149, brackets his, adding: "This is the point and the issue of import. It is here that the Thomas community corrects the tradition, and debates with other Christians" (ibid.).

[21] Ibid., 142 with n. 39; cf. 147, 155–56.

[22] Ibid., 153.

[23] Ibid., 155.

[24] Ibid., 156.

[25] Ibid., 145, emphasis original; cf. 155.

[26] Ibid., 68, 142, 148, 149, 154.

"a community in the [author's own] 'present' ... [that] was in competition with his own"[28] is interesting and worthy of serious consideration. Nevertheless, Thomas is not presented as an innocent witness in a simple drama about touching the resurrected body of Jesus, but as the leading player in a dubious role that is never endorsed by the Gospel of John. For the demand of Thomas for a tangible demonstration of the risen Jesus is not simply doubt but a refusal to believe, tantamount to faith based merely on "signs" (cf. John 2:23–25; 4:48). And even though John does not state that Thomas actually did touch Jesus (the inference being that he did not), and does report that Thomas made a (Johannine) confession of faith, Thomas is still one who must see in order to believe. He therefore does not receive a blessing (John 20:29). For the Gospel of John, therefore, the story of Jesus' appearance to Thomas is not designed to "secure faith" and convince "the community of Thomas" of the physical reality of the resurrection.[29] Rather, the entire story has been revised to bring the Gospel to a conclusion with a saying that is addressed to future generations of Johannine Christians, to assure those persons who were not eyewitnesses that they are the ones to be blessed with faith.[30]

Second, Riley's interpretation of the history of the "temple saying" in the *Gospel of Thomas* is also problematic. Scholars have generally construed this saying in one of two ways: some have understood it to allude to the destruction of the Jewish temple,[31] and others have considered it to be a critique of the material world.[32] *Gospel of Thomas* 71 is, admittedly,

---

[27] Ibid., 155, emphasis original; cf. 154.
[28] Ibid., 99, 78; cf. 81–82, 102, 107.
[29] Against Riley (ibid., 126), who adds that "the conclusion of the Thomas pericope is *not* for the Thomas community *alone,* but for all who would read or hear th[e] Gospel [of John]" (ibid., 125, emphasis added).
[30] See Ron Cameron, *Sayings Traditions in the Apocryphon of James* (HTS 34; Philadelphia: Fortress, 1984), 44–54; idem, "Seeing Is Not Believing: The History of a Beatitude in the Jesus Tradition," *Foundations and Facets Forum* 4/1 (1988): 47–57.
[31] R. McL. Wilson, *Studies in the Gospel of Thomas* (London: Mowbray, 1960), 114–15; Bertil Gärtner, *The Theology of the Gospel according to Thomas* (New York: Harper & Brothers, 1961), 172–74; John Dominic Crossan, *In Fragments: The Aphorisms of Jesus* (San Francisco: Harper & Row, 1983), 307–12; Gilles Quispel, "The Gospel of Thomas and the Trial of Jesus," in *Text and Testimony: Essays on New Testament and Apocryphal Literature in Honour of A. F. J. Klijn* (ed. T. Baarda et al.; Kampen: Kok, 1988), 193–99, esp. 197–99. See also Stephen J. Patterson, *The Gospel of Thomas and Jesus* (FF; Sonoma, Calif.: Polebridge, 1993), 53, 149–50, 236–37; Ismo Dunderberg, "*Thomas'* I-sayings and the Gospel of John," in Uro, *Thomas at the Crossroads,* 56–58.
[32] Ernst Haenchen, *Die Botschaft des Thomas-Evangeliums* (Theologische Bibliothek Töpelmann 6; Berlin: Töpelmann, 1961), 64, 66; Rodolphe Kasser, *L'Évangile selon Thomas: Présentation et commentaire théologique* (Bibliothèque théologique; Neuchâtel: Delachaux et Niestlé, 1961), 95; Johannes Leipoldt, *Das Evangelium nach Thomas: Koptisch und Deutsch*

an obscure and difficult saying which presents Jesus in the role of a prophet announcing (in the first-person singular) the destruction of "this house" and declaring that no one will be able to "build" it. Therefore, determining the precise range and likely meanings of the symbolism of the "house" which Jesus says (in *Thomas*) he will destroy remains a pressing issue. For this term is ambiguous yet highly significant and can refer to several different human habitations and social relations, including the heavenly dwelling place of the soul (e.g., *Exeg. Soul* 128.36; 129.5; 132.21; 137.11), the created world (e.g., Bar 3:24), the abode of wisdom (e.g., Prov 9:1; Sir 14:24), the body (e.g., 2 Cor 5:1), the self (e.g., *Gos. Truth* 25.23), a people (e.g., Matt 10:6; 15:24), the structure of the family (e.g., *Gos. Thom.* 16, 48), one's household goods (e.g., Josephus, *War* 6.5.2 §282), a building (e.g., *Cologne Mani Codex* 92.15), a royal palace (e.g., Matt 11:8), one's ancestral lineage (e.g., Luke 1:27, 69), a scribal school (e.g., Sir 51:23), the church (e.g., Herm. *Sim.* 9.14.1), the city of Jerusalem (e.g., Q 13:35), or the temple in Jerusalem (e.g., John 2:16). For an understanding of this saying, establishing the identity of the "house" is indeed an urgent task. But it is the reader of the *Gospel of Thomas* who has to supply the context in which this enigmatic saying has meaning. If the text is intended as a polemic against the canonical Gospels' connection of the destruction of the temple with Jesus' death, it is remarkably subtle, much more than other sayings in *Thomas* which treat issues of self-definition and social difference when addressing Jesus' identity, parrying questions about the future, discussing group membership, or presenting a critical assessment of traditional codes of religious etiquette (cf. *Gos. Thom.* 3, 6, 39, 43, 52, 53, 89, 91, 102, 113, 114). However, if one reads the text in light of other sayings in the *Gospel of Thomas,* then the house in this saying may well signify "the social arrangements that dominate in the mundane world." As Richard Valantasis has argued, "houses (whether of religious institutions or of social) provide families (or members) with protection." The statement that Jesus "will destroy [this] house" thus points to the "conflict between the houses of the world and the people who enter the new world posited in these sayings." To declare that "no one will be able to build it" serves, in addition, to render "irreversible" the destruction of this old "house" and, thus, affirms the victory of the people who inhabit the social world of the text of *Thomas*.[33]

(TU 101; Berlin: Akademie-Verlag, 1967), 69; Jacques-É. Ménard, *L'Évangile selon Thomas* (NHS 5; Leiden; Brill, 1975), 172–73; Michael Fieger, *Das Thomasevangelium: Einleitung, Kommentar und Systematik* (NTAbh NS 22; Münster: Aschendorff, 1991), 202–3; Raymond Kuntzmann, "Le Temple dans le corpus copte de Nag Hammadi," *RevScRel* 67 (1993): 15–37, esp. 28–29.

[33] Valantasis, *Gospel of Thomas,* 150; cf. xiii, 25.

Most of all, Riley's interpretation of the *Gospel of Thomas* and Christian origins is based on a category mistake: the notion of "resurrection" itself. From the opening sentence of his book[34] to its final paragraph,[35] Riley invokes the "resurrection" indiscriminately to describe all manner of post-mortem existence (including the immortality of the soul, the resurrection of the body, and the reconstitution of the flesh), to refer to a myth that is assumed to be the foundational "event" at the origin of the Christian religion, to characterize the diversity of early Christianities, and to provide the basis for tracing the history and development of early Christian social formations, including those "groups which did not accept the doctrine of physical resurrection" at all.[36] But since Riley does not say why resurrection would be appealed to in all of these instances, he never clarifies what is at issue, and what at stake, in his use of resurrection language. Moreover, since resurrection, for Riley, is both the principal characteristic of Christianity and the sole means for conceptualizing its beginnings, the *Gospel of Thomas* is presented as just "another early witness to a Christianity which did not accept physical resurrection."[37] Ironically, therefore, though his aim is to take *Thomas* seriously, Riley has the same starting point and shares the same perspective as other scholars for whom the *Gospel of Thomas* has made no difference in their reconstruction of Christian origins.

Two examples will have to suffice. In 1948, prior to the publication of the Coptic *Gospel of Thomas,* Johannes Leipoldt introduced his discussion of the literary and history of religions features of the New Testament accounts of the resurrection of Jesus with the claim:

> To prevent any misunderstanding, let me say at the outset that the disciples must have been convinced that they had seen the resurrected Jesus. Otherwise the birth of the Jerusalem congregation and thus the Christian church becomes a mystery. Jesus died on the cross, contrary to the messianic hopes of Judaism. He died in a way that was regarded in the ancient world as particularly despicable. Furthermore, in the earliest of the four gospels, Jesus, in the throes of death, seems to utter a public confession of error or at least a cry of desperation to the effect that his whole life's work has been in vain (Mk 15:34). However, within a very short space of time we once again find a group of believers rallying to the name of Jesus,

---

[34] Riley, *Resurrection Reconsidered,* 1: "Early Christian missionaries proclaimed the resurrection of Jesus throughout the Roman world not only as the founding event of their own faith but also as the central event in human history."

[35] Ibid., 179: "Early Christianity proclaimed the resurrection of Jesus, yet it inherited a variety of conceptions of the afterlife, few of which included the doctrine of the resurrection of the flesh."

[36] Ibid., 59; cf. 58–68.

[37] Ibid., 154; cf. 116, 155, 179.

and indeed in the very city where his terrible death took place. Something must have happened between the crucifixion and this revival to renew the disciples' courage. This could only have been the emergence of belief in the resurrection of Jesus.[38]

Forty-eight years later, after the discovery and publication of the Coptic text of *Thomas,* Luke Timothy Johnson would conclude:

> Some sort of powerful, transformative experience is required to generate the sort of movement earliest Christianity was, and to necessitate the sort of literature the New Testament is.... [To argue] that the resurrection experience was found only among some early Christians but not all—[this view] suffers from a lack of positive evidence. Certainly, the canonical New Testament writings as we now have them all assume the resurrection.... [Moreover,] the Gnostic writings from Nag Hammadi that are demonstrably Christian (such as the *Gospel of Thomas* and [the] *Treatise on the Resurrection*) seem to have an understanding of the resurrection of Jesus that is distinctive, viewing it as a quality of his existence rather than a postmortem event, but they still assume that the resurrection is a central symbol that requires negotiation.... The effort to reduce the resurrection experience to just another historical event runs the risk of failing to account for the rise of the historical movement. The *denial* of the resurrection experience poses an even greater problem of origination: if some such experience was not at the root of the movement, what accounted for its unlikely birth, amazing growth, and peculiarly tension-filled literature?[39]

III

By privileging the resurrection as the historical starting point, foundational event, transformative experience, ubiquitous persuasion, distinguishing

---

[38] Johannes Leipoldt, "Zu den Auferstehungs-Geschichten," *TLZ* 73 (1948): 737; ET: "The Resurrection Stories," *Journal of Higher Criticism* 4/1 (1997): 138. Note that, once the photographic plates of the Coptic text of *Thomas* appeared in print (Pahor Labib, ed., *Coptic Gnostic Papyri in the Coptic Museum at Old Cairo,* vol. 1 [Cairo: Government Press, 1956]), Leipoldt published the first complete translation of the *Gospel of Thomas* (Johannes Leipoldt, "Ein neues Evangelium? Das koptische Thomasevangelium übersetzt und besprochen," *TLZ* 83 [1958]: 481–96). This translation was later revised and published posthumously in 1967 (idem, *Das Evangelium nach Thomas,* 26–53).

[39] Luke Timothy Johnson, *The Real Jesus: The Misguided Quest for the Historical Jesus and the Truth of the Traditional Gospels* (San Francisco: HarperSanFrancisco, 1996), 136, 138, 139, emphasis original; cf. 103, 134–36, 146. Note that the apologetic motivations that guide Johnson's scholarship, while fully disclosed in this polemical book, are also clearly present in the experiential-hermeneutical model proposed in his earlier, more scholarly work (idem, *The Writings of the New Testament: An Interpretation* [Philadelphia: Fortress, 1986], 1–20, 87–141, esp. 98, 101, 106).

criterion, and decisive category for explaining the beginnings of Christianity, biblical scholarship persists in perpetuating in its discourse a widely assumed—but totally unwarranted—conservative theological theory that has caused untold mischief in the scholarly imagination of the New Testament and Christian origins. By assuming that we already know what Christianity is, and how and why it began, scholars have concentrated on tracing the history of the tradition in terms of a diverse series of developments from a singular point of origination.[40] The centrality of the cross and a belief in the resurrection have been thought to be required to account for the emergence of the Christian religion. However, the fact that "the canonical New Testament writings ... [may] all assume the resurrection"[41] does not mean that an experience of Jesus' vindication is what produced the beliefs and behavior of the earliest Christians. Rather, it means that the New Testament reflects the kind of Christianity that is operative in the conceptual frame of reference that has produced the discipline of biblical studies. Accordingly, the crucial problem is not simply that the New Testament serves as the sole framework for the scholarly imagination of Christian beginnings. It is that the New Testament provides a synthetic account of the myth of origins of a religion which is understood to be unique, and that fosters such an understanding because biblical scholarship "continues to be correlated with theories of religion that are focused on personal experience, transforming events, and dramatic breakthroughs."[42]

This problem is compounded because the texts of the New Testament document the history that accounts for those texts. But to overcome the problem of circularity—to account for ancient Christian history, explain its beginnings, and explicate its texts—one cannot simply appeal to the

---

[40] Note that, in this paragraph and throughout this essay, I am distinguishing between "beginnings" and "origins," based in part on a critical distinction proposed by Edward W. Said. When he argued that "beginnings" are "humanly produced" and "ceaselessly re-examined," Said did not simply observe that a beginning provides "an inaugural direction" or "provisional orientation in method and intention." He meant that, by definition, beginnings require historical and intentional acts of imagination. Beginnings therefore entail interpretative judgments. Such conscious, creative beginnings are what authorize the *"making ... [of] difference"* and thus, in Said's words, enable the *"production of meaning"* (Edward W. Said, *Beginnings: Intention and Method* [New York: Basic Books, 1975; repr., New York: Columbia University Press, 1985], xiii, 316, xvii, 5, emphasis original). Following the pioneering historiography of Giambattista Vico (*The New Science of Giambattista Vico* [3rd ed. 1744; trans. Thomas Goddard Bergin and Max Harold Fisch; Ithaca, N.Y.: Cornell University Press, 1948]), Said contrasts such a "secular," intertextual understanding of "beginnings" with a "theological" conception of "origins" (*Beginnings*, 13, 42, 280, 349–50, 357, 372–73).

[41] Johnson, *Real Jesus*, 138.

[42] Miller, "Consultation on Christian Origins," 229.

diversity of early Christianities. That is because a redescription of Christian origins cannot be undertaken or concluded solely at the level of the texts, but must be addressed in terms of critical theory, with a reassessment of the assumptions of singularity and incomparability that have allowed the New Testament to be "examined rigorously without threatening the notion of originary uniqueness."[43] Therefore, another way will have to be found to make sense of the data we have taken for granted, another means discovered to determine their significance, another theory of religion proposed that can render intelligible the beginnings of Christianity in terms of the social interests, investments, and attractions that define the human enterprise.

Take the *Gospel of Thomas,* for example. The notion of resurrection is absent from *Thomas* not because *Thomas* presupposes it as a central symbol or narratable experience, but because the metaphor of resurrection is fundamentally incompatible with the genre, designs, logic, and theology of this Gospel. As John S. Kloppenborg has demonstrated, in Sayings Gospels such as Q and *Thomas,* Jesus' death was "not considered to be an insuperable [theological] obstacle, requiring a special moment of divine vindication."[44] Furthermore, the lack of concern for resurrection imagery is more than an exegetical inconvenience created by the fact that the *Gospel of Thomas* nowhere refers to the resurrection of Jesus.[45] For *Thomas* evidently knows of Jesus' death and seems to preserve two sayings that refer

---

[43] Burton L. Mack, *A Myth of Innocence: Mark and Christian Origins* (Philadelphia: Fortress, 1988), 7–8 n. 3, whose remark is part of a critique of "appeal[s] to 'the resurrection' [that constitute] the most mystifying of all the ciphers used to protect the myth of Christian origins from critical investigation. The notion is used regularly ... as if the resurrection were a datable piece of evidence. By allowing the mystery of Easter and the [resurrection] appearances to mark the point from which the Spirit effected the new age of Christian experience and mission, everything else can be examined rigorously without threatening the notion of originary uniqueness.... A point of origin has [thus] been established that is fundamentally inaccessible to further probing or clarification. [This] guarantees the uniqueness of early Christianity by locating its novelty beyond data and debate" (ibid.; cf. xi–xii, 3–4, 7).

[44] John S. Kloppenborg, "'Easter Faith' and the Sayings Gospel Q," *Semeia* 49 (1990): 92.

[45] This is so notwithstanding the standard reconstruction of the last line of the Greek text of *Gos. Thom.* 5, which deviates from the Coptic in adding: "nor buried that [will not be raised]" (P.Oxy. 654.31). The picturesque reading of ο[ὐκ ἐγερθήσεται ("will not be raised") was first suggested by the original editors of the Oxyrhynchus papyrus (Bernard P. Grenfell and Arthur S. Hunt, eds., *New Sayings of Jesus and Fragment of a Lost Gospel from Oxyrhynchus* [London: Frowde, 1904], 17–18, with a plate; repr. in *The Oxyrhynchus Papyri: Part IV* [London: Egypt Exploration Fund, 1904], 8–9, with plate I) and seems to be supported by a fifth- or sixth-century Christian burial shroud from Oxyrhynchus, which states: "Jesus said, 'Nothing is buried that will not be raised'" (see Henri-Charles Puech, "Un logion de Jésus sur bandelette funéraire," *RHR* 147 [1955]: 126–29; repr. in *Sur l'Évangile selon Thomas: Esquisse d'une interprétation systématique* [vol. 2 of *En quête de la Gnose*; Bibliothèque des Sciences Humaines; Paris: Gallimard, 1978], 59–63, with a plate).

Ancient Myths and Modern Theories

to it. In the first saying, when Jesus' followers are aware that he would pass away, they reflect upon the implications of his departure in terms of group leadership:

> The disciples said to Jesus, "We are aware that you will pass away from us [ⲕⲛⲁⲃⲱⲕ ⲛ̄ⲧⲟⲟⲧⲛ̄]. Who will be our leader?" Jesus said to them, "Wherever you are, you are to go to James the righteous, for whose sake heaven and earth came into being." (*Gos. Thom.* 12)[46]

The irony of the fact that James was regarded as a witness to the resurrection in other early Christian traditions should not go unnoticed.[47] This suggests that the *Gospel of Thomas* was familiar with other Christian groups and was distinguishing itself from them by means of leading questions broached by the "disciples."

In the second saying, "rather than invok[e] the apocalyptic metaphor of resurrection"[48] to affirm that Jesus and his followers are justified by God, the *Gospel of Thomas* links Jesus' cross conceptually to the lives of his followers, who bear their own crosses in imitation of his stance of endurance:

> Jesus said, "Whoever does not show disregard for his father and his mother cannot be my disciple. And whoever does not show disregard for his brothers and his sisters, and take up his cross like me [ⲛ̄ϥϥⲓ ⲙ̄ⲡⲉϥⲥⲧ[ⲁⲩ]ⲣⲟⲥ ⲛ̄ⲧⲁϩⲉ], will not become worthy of me." (*Gos. Thom.* 55)

The original significance of the cross in this saying is a matter of considerable debate. However, since one might expect a reference to "the cross"—rather than "one's (own) cross"—if *stauros* presupposed a martyr's death for Jesus, the image seems to have been proverbial, "a traditional symbol for suffering and sacrifice."[49] As "a metaphor for the ultimate test of a philosopher's integrity," to accept one's "cross" meant to "bear up under condemnation" when "having one's mettle tested" (cf. Epictetus, *Diss.* 2.2.20).[50]

For our purposes, there are five principal differences between *Thomas*'s version of this saying and its parallels in the Sayings Gospel (Q 14:26–27)

---

[46] For the use of ⲃⲱⲕ ("to go, depart") as a metaphor for dying ("to pass away"), cf. Mark 4:38; and see W. E. Crum, *A Coptic Dictionary* (Oxford: Clarendon, 1939), s.v. ⲃⲱⲕ (29a).

[47] Cf. 1 Cor 15:7; *Gos. Heb.* frg. 7; *Ap. Jas.* 2.7–39; Eusebius, *Hist. eccl.* 1.12.4–5; 2.1.2–5.

[48] Kloppenborg, "'Easter Faith' and the Sayings Gospel Q," 90.

[49] Rudolf Bultmann, *Die Geschichte der synoptischen Tradition* (9th ed.; FRLANT 29; Göttingen: Vandenhoeck & Ruprecht, 1979), 173.

[50] Burton L. Mack, *The Lost Gospel: The Book of Q and Christian Origins* (San Francisco: HarperSanFrancisco, 1993), 139, 138.

and the Gospel of Mark (Mark 8:34 par.). First, though Q and Mark speak of both carrying the cross and following after Jesus, the *Gospel of Thomas* refers only to the cross. This means that *Thomas* is not chiefly concerned here with the identity of Jesus and his followers' relationship with him. Second, whereas both Q and Mark speak of the disciple's bearing his or her cross, the *Gospel of Thomas* uses Jesus' own cross as an example to be imitated, to be "take[n] up ... like me." In the Synoptic Gospels, it is only Mark's context (Mark 8:31–9:1) which makes it clear that Jesus' death is presupposed or regarded as paradigmatic. Third, comparing a disciple with Jesus in terms of bearing the cross "like" him indicates that the cross retains its metaphorical character in *Thomas*'s version of this saying. Accordingly, accepting the cross is not literally required to be a worthy follower of Jesus. Fourth, while all versions of this saying imply that the "lifestyle of Jesus provides the pattern for community members,"[51] only *Thomas* makes this explicit by stating that a disciple is to take up his cross "like me." To be like Jesus thus specifies what it means to carry the cross: to imitate the exemplary activity of Jesus by putting one's convictions into practice as Jesus did. Fifth, the *Gospel of Thomas* identifies what it means to be like Jesus in terms of the renunciation of traditional family ties, expressed in the context of a saying about the family, not about the cross. And so, by imagining Jesus' activities as a model for mimesis, and by presenting his teachings as instructions to be assimilated, *Thomas* portrays the reader assembled in a circle of disciples around the master. Group membership is thereby depicted as belonging to a new fictive family, as illustrated in a subsequent version of this saying in the text:

> "Whoever does not show disregard for his [father] and his mother, as I do [N̄ΤΑϨΕ], cannot be my [disciple]. And whoever does [not] show regard for [his father and] his mother, as I do [N̄ΤΑϨΕ], cannot be my [disciple]. For my mother [...], but [my] true [mother] gave me life." (*Gos. Thom.* 101)

As David Seeley has shown, these discipleship sayings closely resemble contemporaneous Greco-Roman philosophical notions, particularly as formulated in Cynic and Stoic popular school traditions, which valued the virtue of endurance and emphasized the willingness of a student or disciple to follow properly—if metaphorically—the exemplary, noble death of a teacher. In one's readiness to face death with integrity, one qualified

---

[51] John S. Kloppenborg, *The Formation of Q: Trajectories in Ancient Wisdom Collections* (SAC; Philadelphia: Fortress, 1987; repr., Harrisburg, Pa.: Trinity Press International, 1999), 232.

as a true philosopher. And so, in presenting the cross in such terms, these sayings suggest that Jesus came to be remembered as a martyr because people were convinced he had lived his life as a philosopher.[52]

To allude to the cross but not mention resurrection indicates that "reference to Jesus' resurrection was not a common persuasion" in early Christianities, but "only one among many ways in which early Jesus movements and Christian groups imagined their beginnings."[53] The language of resurrection took shape in pre-Pauline and Pauline congregations of the Christ as an elaboration of the myth that Jesus' death—not his resurrection—was the founding event for the community. The resurrection, when invoked, thus belonged to the martyr myth, to claim that it was God who raised Jesus from the dead, who regarded his death as noble and right, and who thereby acknowledged that the cause for which Jesus had died—an ethnically mixed group of Jews and Gentiles—was justified. Therefore, "the earliest imagination of the resurrection of Jesus was a mythic imagination, worked out in the process of rationalizing a new social experiment," that initially treated the resurrection "as a sign of Jesus' own destiny, vindication, and continuing authority." Only later, "once the [martyr] myth was in place," was it "possible to think ... that, not only had Jesus 'died for' the community's justification, he had been 'raised for' the community's vindication" as well.[54] The kerygmatic formulation of the martyr myth, then, notwithstanding the appended list of resurrection appearances (1 Cor 15:3–5a, 5b–8), is not concerned with apostleship and authority,[55] but with mythmaking and social formation.[56] For in the Pauline corpus, the kerygma

---

[52] David Seeley, "Was Jesus Like a Philosopher? The Evidence of Martyrological and Wisdom Motifs in Q, Pre-Pauline Traditions, and Mark," in *Society of Biblical Literature 1989 Seminar Papers* (SBLSP 28; Atlanta: Scholars Press, 1989), 540–49; idem, "Blessings and Boundaries: Interpretations of Jesus' Death in Q," *Semeia* 55 (1991): 131–46; idem, "Jesus' Death in Q," *NTS* 38 (1992): 222–34; idem, *Deconstructing the New Testament* (BibInt 5; Leiden: Brill, 1994), 163, 173. Seeley's investigation of the death of Jesus in light of contemporaneous treatments of the noble death of philosophers and martyrs has convincingly demonstrated that the martyr myth's language and motivation are not cultic or sacrificial, but are based on honor and obedience to a cause (idem, *The Noble Death: Graeco-Roman Martyrology and Paul's Concept of Salvation* [JSNTSup 28; Sheffield: Sheffield Academic Press, 1990]).

[53] Burton L. Mack, review of Gary R. Habermas and Antony G. N. Flew, ed. Terry L. Miethe, *Did Jesus Rise from the Dead? The Resurrection Debate, History and Theory* 28 (1989): 219. See also Smith, *Drudgery Divine*, 109–10, 120–21, 134–42, esp. 138 (citing Mack, *Myth of Innocence*, 86).

[54] Mack, review of Habermas and Flew, 221.

[55] Against Riley (*Resurrection Reconsidered*, 89; cf. 65, 90), who states that "the kerygma is concerned with authority and apostleship, in addition to proof of [the] resurrection."

[56] See esp. Mack, *Myth of Innocence*, 98–123; idem, *Who Wrote the New Testament? The Making of the Christian Myth* (San Francisco: HarperSanFrancisco, 1995), 75–96.

functions as a rationale for sustaining the fabric of a stable society, which required a prior investment in social formation based on other commitments and concerns.

IV

The problem with appealing to a resurrection appearance or visionary experience to explain the origins of the Christian religion is, in the final analysis, its individualistic orientation: such a theory cannot sustain a social anthropology and, thus, cannot account for the interests, investments, and attractions that define the human enterprise. The *Gospel of Thomas* may refer to Jesus' departure, but it is not really interested in Jesus' death. For though *Thomas* includes sayings that comment indirectly on Jesus' passing, no saving function is ever assigned to his death, nor is vindication accomplished by means of a resurrection. Instead, as an anthology of attributed sayings, the *Gospel of Thomas* imparts its own distinctive claim of authority. In such a genre, the teacher is regarded as present in the words that are selected for inclusion in written form. As such, the teacher's wisdom may be legitimated by appeal to his own reputation, authorized by invoking the transcendent authority of God, or justified by claims to be an envoy or chief emissary of Wisdom.

In Late Antiquity, collecting the sayings of a sage became an authoritative vehicle for characterizing distinguished individuals, cultivating distinctive lifestyles, transmitting traditional cultures, exploring religious alternatives, and marking social differences.[57] The *Gospel of Thomas* is such a collection, fundamentally concerned with issues of social self-definition. In *Thomas,* "Jesus appears as a teacher of wisdom" and as one who "speaks with the authority of the heavenly figure of Wisdom."[58] Ascribing this Gospel to Jesus, therefore, who is characterized as a sage with a distinguished reputation, presupposes that his counsel is endowed with special wisdom. By identifying him as "the living Jesus," moreover, the claim is made that his wisdom is invested with divine authority. His authority resides not in the mythology of the risen Christ, but is localized in sayings that offer contemporizing wisdom, made available through the Gospel, for those who have ears to hear.

---

[57] See Mack, *Lost Gospel,* 194–201.

[58] Helmut Koester, *History and Literature of Early Christianity* (vol. 2 of *Introduction to the New Testament*; Hermeneia: Foundations and Facets; Philadelphia: Fortress; Berlin: de Gruyter, 1982), 150. For an assessment of Koester's contributions to scholarship on *Thomas,* see the tribute in Ron Cameron, "The *Gospel of Thomas* and Christian Origins," in *The Future of Early Christianity: Essays in Honor of Helmut Koester* (ed. Birger A. Pearson et al.; Minneapolis: Fortress, 1991), 381–92.

The profile of Jesus' wisdom and authority is enhanced in *Thomas* in relation to the efforts to make sense of the ethos proposed at the outset of the Gospel. The text opens with a prologue claiming formal authorship and an initial saying that introduces the theme of the Gospel:

> These are the hidden sayings that the living Jesus spoke and Judas Thomas "the Twin" wrote down. And he said, "Whoever discovers the meaning of these sayings will not taste death." (*Gos. Thom.* prologue, saying 1)

The designation of the *Gospel of Thomas* as "hidden sayings," whose "meaning," once ascertained, provides the elixir of life, indicates that these sayings have been "formulated so that they require interpretation in order to become efficacious." There is thus a direct correlation between the production of this text and the skills needed to interpret it correctly. According to the prologue, the hidden sayings that the living Jesus spoke are recorded in writing by his twin brother Thomas. Correspondingly, in saying 1, "the reader is to penetrate the opacity of the written word by means of a hermeneutical key which would unlock the secret of life."[59] That key is proposed programmatically in saying 2:

Gos. Thom. 2	P.Oxy. 654.5–9
Jesus said,	[Jesus said],
"Whoever seeks should persist	"Whoever seeks should persist
in seeking until he finds.	[in seeking until] he finds.
When he finds,	When he finds,
he will be disturbed.	
When he becomes disturbed,	
he will be astounded.	[he will be astounded].
	When he becomes [astounded],
And he will rule	he will rule.
over everything."	
	And [when he has ruled],
	he will [rest]."

In this saying *Thomas* employs a sorites, a four-part rhetorical chain syllogism that (notwithstanding the differences between the Greek and Coptic texts) proceeds, step by step, from persistence in seeking and finding, through becoming disturbed and astounded, to culminate in one's ruling or rest. By means of this sorites, the claim is made that if one begins the searching task of probing and perseveres unto the end, then intelligibility is possible, discovery promised, steadfastness rewarded, progress certified,

---

[59] Kloppenborg, *Formation of Q*, 301, 305; cf. 36, 296.

surprise expected, and victory assured. As an elaboration of the prologue and opening saying of the Gospel, this pericope announces an interpretative program that underscores the vital importance of effort in the production of meaning. The very beginning of the *Gospel of Thomas,* therefore, describes nothing less than a "process of 'sapiential research,'" in which "interpretation and salvation coincide."[60]

The theme of labor that is announced at the beginning of the text permeates the discourse of the entire Gospel. In its simplest form, it is expressed as a quest to seek and find (*Gos. Thom.* 92, 94). This quest can be depicted as a desire for wisdom (*Gos. Thom.* 69), as a granting of honor (*Gos. Thom.* 58), as a proverb guaranteeing that what is sought will be found (*Gos. Thom.* 5), or it can be elaborated in the form of an admonition for failing to continue to seek (*Gos. Thom.* 92). Most of all, the theme of labor is developed in the *Gospel of Thomas* through a series of parables: "comparisons" that, by definition, were taken from the "world of human observation and experience."[61] By means of parables *Thomas* cultivated a set of pedagogical metaphors to characterize the ethos of effort and discovery displayed by the teacher and offered in the text. One example, of the many parables that could be cited, will illustrate the point:[62]

> Jesus said, "What the kingdom resembles is a shepherd who had one hundred sheep. One of them, a large one, wandered off. He left the ninety-nine and sought that one out until he found it. Having accomplished his labors [**ⲚⲦⲀⲢⲈϤϨⲒⲤⲈ**], he said to the sheep, 'I desire you more than the ninety-nine.'" (*Gos. Thom.* 107)

Here, the theme of seeking and finding is combined with a concern for preferring the one to the many, with acknowledging a desire for the large sheep above all else. Whereas the version of this parable in the Sayings Gospel (Q 15:4-5, 7) emphasizes joy in recovering what was lost, the *Gospel of Thomas* proclaims the shepherd's "labors" to be laudable, announcing their significance explicitly when the shepherd speaks tenderly to the sheep. In describing the task of discovery as a special labor of

---

[60] Ibid., 305.

[61] Burton L. Mack, "Teaching in Parables: Elaboration in Mark 4:1–34," in *Patterns of Persuasion in the Gospels* (ed. Burton L. Mack and Vernon K. Robbins; FF; Sonoma, Calif.: Polebridge, 1989), 148; cf. 145–49.

[62] See Ron Cameron, "Mythmaking and Intertextuality in Early Christianity," in *Reimagining Christian Origins: A Colloquium Honoring Burton L. Mack* (ed. Elizabeth A. Castelli and Hal Taussig; Valley Forge, Pa.: Trinity Press International, 1996), 37–50; idem, "Myth and History in the Gospel of Thomas," *Apocrypha* 8 (1997): 193–205.

love, *Thomas* affirms the importance of striving passionately for the one thing that makes a difference, the most cherished possession of all.

The labor required to seek and find creates a culture of dedication and discovery that is fostered through parables in the *Gospel of Thomas*. The parables thus function self-referentially to illustrate the creative efforts of a culture. *Thomas* depicts those efforts through a series of meditations, expressed as parables:

- on the expertise of a fisherman, who chose the fine large fish without any effort (*Gos. Thom.* 8)
- on the resourcefulness of a merchant, who shrewdly bought the one pearl that he found (*Gos. Thom.* 76)
- on the skill of a woman, who took leaven and made it into large loaves of bread (*Gos. Thom.* 96)
- on the determination of an assassin, who practiced the execution of the task he wanted to accomplish (*Gos. Thom.* 98)
- on the accomplishment of a shepherd, whose labors made it possible to find the one large sheep he desired the most (*Gos. Thom.* 107).

Accordingly, the persons who crafted the roles represented by the characters in the *Gospel of Thomas* were actively involved in a distinctive kind of toil, in the task of creating and nurturing a group ethos. In cultivating these parables, *Thomas* was engaging in a critical assessment of the meaning of culture, construed as excellence undertaken in pursuit of wisdom.[63]

The *Gospel of Thomas* is a venerable document. If taken seriously, it makes a difference in redescribing the beginnings of Christianity as religion. To take this Gospel seriously, however, compels us to address forthrightly the fundamental issue of difference. The *Gospel of Thomas* cannot be explained as a variation of the myth of origins constructed by Luke and canonized in the New Testament, because *Thomas*'s genre, designs, logic, and theology are incompatible with the dominant paradigm of Christian origins. Therefore, in place of a singular point of origination, *Thomas* necessitates a different starting point, frame of reference, and mode of comparison. Instead of appeals to incomparability and uniqueness, *Thomas* demands a different discourse, series of scholarly assumptions, and theory of religion. Rather than invoke the mystifying

---

[63] See the fine descriptive definition of "wisdom" in Burton L. Mack, "The Christ and Jewish Wisdom," in *The Messiah: Developments in Earliest Judaism and Christianity* (ed. James H. Charlesworth; The First Princeton Symposium on Judaism and Christian Origins; Minneapolis: Fortress, 1992), 192–221, esp. 195–96.

aura of resurrection, *Thomas* requires a different social anthropology, set of interpretative categories, and critical imagination to map out the characteristics and contours of a social history of the earliest Christians. The *Gospel of Thomas* forces the issue of revising the dominant paradigm of biblical studies. Its challenge to the conventional view of Christian origins is therefore clear. To render the *Gospel of Thomas*—and other early Christian literature—intelligible, we will need to conceive of another way to describe the texts, determine their significance, and make sense of our data in terms of human interests, social attractions, cultural investments, and intellectual labor.[64]

---

[64] This is a slightly revised version of a paper that was first published in *MTSR* 11 (1999): 236–57. I am grateful to Merrill P. Miller for his helpful comments on an earlier draft of the paper.

"Keep Speaking until You Find ...":
Thomas and the School of Oral Mimesis
Arthur J. Dewey

Improvisation is one of the canonical exercises of universal teaching. But it is first of all the exercise of our intelligence's leading virtue: the poetic virtue. The impossibility of our *saying* the truth, even when we *feel* it, makes us speak as poets, makes us tell the story of our mind's adventures and verify that they are understood by other adventurers, makes us communicate our feelings and see them shared by other feeling beings. Improvisation is the exercise by which the human being knows himself and is confirmed in his nature as a reasonable man, that is to say, as an animal "who makes words, figures, and comparisons, to tell the story of what he thinks to those like him." ... In the act of speaking, man doesn't transmit his knowledge, he makes poetry; he translates and invites others to do the same. He communicates as an *artisan*: as a person who handles words like tools. Man communicates with man through the works of his hands just as through the words of his speech.
— Jacques Rancière, *The Ignorant Schoolmaster*[1]

Stories and sayings are authenticated not by virtue of their historical reliability, but on the authority of the speaker and by the reception of hearers.
— Werner H. Kelber, *The Oral and the Written Gospel*[2]

1. Introduction

The *Gospel of Thomas* has proven resistant to various attempts to understand its structure and function. Although there have been gross

---

[1] Jacques Rancière, *The Ignorant Schoolmaster: Five Lessons in Intellectual Emancipation* (trans. Kristin Ross; Stanford, Calif.: Stanford University Press, 1991), 64–65, emphasis original, citing Jean-Joseph Jacotot, *Enseignement universel: Musique* (3rd ed.; Paris: privately printed, 1830), 163.

[2] Werner H. Kelber, *The Oral and the Written Gospel: The Hermeneutics of Speaking and Writing in the Synoptic Tradition, Mark, Paul, and Q* (Philadelphia: Fortress, 1983), 71.

descriptions of the document, the attempt to determine the nature of the beast that is *Thomas* breaks down primarily because of its apparent lack of any coherent structure or narrative.[3]

My task in this paper is to inquire into the possibility of a school of *Thomas*. My angle of approach comes precisely from the intractability of the *Gospel of Thomas*. I shall attempt to interrogate the evidence rather closely. My principal line of attack will be to bring an appreciation of orality to the analysis of this text. The ancient schools, from the most elementary to the most advanced, were places of sound and declaration. Thus I contend that a close reading of *Thomas* demands not just a keen, analytical eye but also an attentive ear. What might well seem only as static to some interpreters of *Thomas* may prove intelligible on another wavelength. The very refractory nature of *Thomas* may provide a basic clue to its function.[4]

I begin with the apt remark of Bernard Brandon Scott, who notes that in the ancient world "one writes that others may hear,"[5] that is to say, writing in that era was not a silent phenomenon. Indeed, writing was intrinsically tied to the auditory experience.[6] Thus, for example, from the

---

[3] Francis T. Fallon and Ron Cameron, "The Gospel of Thomas: A Forschungsbericht and Analysis," *ANRW* 25.6:4206.

[4] This is a text in the tradition of the Wisdom of Solomon: it wants to give hermeneutical clues from the very structure of the piece. But this can only be realized by moving off the page to the possible educational process itself. The sayings are meant to be spoken aloud and then pondered. The fact that there are other sayings that echo throughout suggests that there might be the possibility of echoes influencing one another to bring about a change in consciousness. The Jesus they believe they know is preserved; the succession can go on. The transmission of sayings of Jesus which can be recorded deep within the heart, from which one can build community, is at stake. It might be correct to say that this is how they saw Jesus continuing. The lines of succession come about in the give and take of the learning process itself. (I want to thank the graduate students of my class, "The Oral, Written, and Electronic Gospel," for demonstrating this oral base in our engaged consideration of the *Gospel of Thomas*.)

[5] Bernard Brandon Scott, "Why and How of Sound Mapping" (paper presented at the Annual Meeting of the Society of Biblical Literature, New Orleans, La., 26 November 1996).

[6] Who is the "recorder" of the secret sayings of Jesus? Obviously one thinks it is Thomas because that is what is said. But consider: Thomas is a "twin." In *Gos. Thom.* 108 ("Jesus said, 'Whoever drinks from my mouth will become like me; I myself shall become that person, and the hidden things will be revealed to him'") Jesus becomes "that person." The true recorder of *Thomas* is the one who sought, found, was disturbed, and, marveling, rules. But that is the person who truly understands the traditions—the sayings. Just as in the ancient world, one finds the true tablets on the heart, so here, too, it is the case. The true recording comes in the repeating and searching for meaning in each saying. How? Through a constant echo-chamber effect. One saying elicits those who remember and speak out. One learns, comes to insight by connecting the dots, by interweaving the sayings. This can be done most efficiently through a group of students and a teacher, sharing their specific ways through *Thomas*.

outset of *Thomas* one must become aware that the opening words were inscribed to be heard.[7]

2. An Aphorism Revived

Let us begin our investigation with some observations regarding *Thomas*'s use of Q 11:9. *Gospel of Thomas* 94, 92.1, 38.2, 2.1 would appear to be either performantial variations or elaborations of the Q^1 saying. Saying 94 appears to be a variant of Q 11:9:

> Q 11:9: "Ask—it'll be given to you; seek—you'll find; knock—it'll be opened for you."[8]

> *Gos. Thom.* 94: (1) Jesus [said], "One who seeks will find, (2) and for [one who knocks] it will be opened."

Such a variation would be understandable within an oral climate. Of course, one must not overlook the simple introduction, "Jesus [said]." The oral saying has been quietly embedded in a Jesus tradition.

It is with sayings 92 and 38 that we find a further layering of this tradition. Saying 92.1 is a variant of saying 94.1:

> *Gos. Thom.* 92: (1) Jesus said, "Seek and you will find. (2) In the past, however, I did not tell you the things about which you asked me then. Now I am willing to tell them, but you are not seeking them."

However, there has been added an elaboration that seems reminiscent of John 16:12–15, 25–28:

> John 16:12–15: "I still have a lot to tell you, but you can't stand it just now. When <the advocate> comes, the spirit of truth, it will guide you to the

---

[7] Walter J. Ong describes the oral situation: "An interlocutor is virtually essential: it is hard to talk to yourself for hours on end. Sustained thought in an oral culture is tied to communication.... In a primary oral culture, to solve effectively the problem of retaining and retrieving carefully articulated thought, you have to do your thinking in mnemonic patterns, shaped for ready oral recurrence. Your thought must come into being in heavily rhythmic, balanced patterns, in repetitions or antitheses, in alliterations and assonances, in epithetic or other formulary expressions, in standard thematic settings, in proverbs which are constantly heard by everyone so that they come to mind readily and which themselves are patterned for retention and ready recall or in other mnemonic form. Serious thought is intertwined with memory systems" (*Orality and Literacy: The Technologizing of the Word* [London: Methuen, 1982], 34).

[8] Except where noted, all translations of texts from the *Gospel of Thomas* and the New Testament are from the Scholars Version, found in *The Complete Gospels: Annotated Scholars Version* (ed. Robert J. Miller; rev. ed.; Sonoma, Calif.: Polebridge, 1994).

complete truth. It will not speak on its own authority, but will tell only what it hears and will disclose to you what is to happen. It will honor me because it will disclose to you what it gets from me. Everything the Father has belongs to me; that's why I told you, 'It will disclose to you what it gets from me.'"

John 16:25–28: "I have been talking to you in figures of speech. The time is coming when I'll no longer speak to you in figures but will tell you about the Father in plain language. When that time comes, you will make requests using my name; I'm not telling you that I will make requests on your behalf, since the Father himself loves you because you have befriended me and believe that I came from God. I came from the Father and entered the world. Once again I'm going to leave the world and return to the Father."

A past is imagined where Jesus did not answer what the disciples had asked about. The stress is now placed upon the present, when Jesus is "willing to tell" but the disciples "are not seeking." In *Gos. Thom.* 38 we have a similar situation. The disciples had often "desired to hear these sayings," and Jesus is presently "speaking" them to the disciples. To this is added the warning that the days will come when they "will seek" and "not find" him:

Gos. Thom. 38: (1) Jesus said, "Often you have desired to hear these sayings that I am speaking to you, and you have no one else from whom to hear them. (2) There will be days when you will seek me and you will not find me."

In both sayings 92.2 and 38.1 there is a decided stress upon the present "speaking/telling" by Jesus. The past is brought up short by the present. The future (*Gos. Thom.* 38) is not where Jesus is to be found. Indeed, in saying 38 we have possible echo of Q 10:24:

Q 10:24: "I tell you, many prophets and kings wanted to see what you see, and didn't see it, and to hear what you hear, and didn't hear it."

Where "prophets and kings wanted ... to hear what you hear" (Q 10:24), it is now the disciples who have the opportunity "to hear these sayings" (*Gos. Thom.* 38.1). Any eschatological edge that the Q^2 saying might have conveyed is rendered null by the downplaying of the future in *Gos. Thom.* 38.2. The difference between *Gos. Thom.* 38 and Q 10:24 is that the emphasis is squarely on the speaker Jesus, the source of the sayings.[9]

---

[9] In Q 10:23–24 there is a balance upon sight and sound, with the "eyes" possibly having the advantage (cf. v. 23b): "Turning to the disciples he said privately, 'How privileged are the

Gospel of Thomas 38.2 ("There will be days when you will seek me and you will not find me") would suggest a time after the death of Jesus. Questions regarding succession and authority would appear to be at the heart of this saying. Saying 24 is related to this level of material. In response to a request similar to that in John 14:5

> John 14:5: Thomas says to him, "Master, we don't know where you're going. How can we possibly know the way?"

there is a major reversal in the direction of the conversation. We can notice that the response (*Gos. Thom.* 24.2) to the request (24.1) reverses the eschatological direction:

> *Gos. Thom.* 24: (1) His disciples said, "Show us the place where you are, for we must seek it." (2) He said to them, "Anyone here with two ears had better listen! (3) There is light within a person of light, and it shines on the whole world. If it does not shine, it is dark."

The response in *Gos. Thom.* 24.2–3 is a curious amalgam of the wisdom directional ("Anyone here with two ears had better listen!"), emphasizing once again an oral performance and insight derived from experience.[10] *Gospel of Thomas* 24.2 underscores the oral emphasis in which the tradition is moving. Moreover, *Gos. Thom.* 24.3 would suggest that the response to the disciples' demand to be shown "the place [**ΠΤΟΠΟC**] where Jesus is" depends upon enlightened experience of the listener. The listeners are challenged to "seek it." A percussive effect of sound and experience can be detected here.

A related sense of this present enunciation of Jesus is found in the complex of sayings 42–43:

> *Gos. Thom.* 42: Jesus said, "Get going!"[11]
> 43: (1) His disciples said to him, "Who are you to say these things to us?" (2) "You don't understand who I am from what I say to you. (3) Rather, you have become like the Judeans, for they love the tree but hate its fruit, or they love the fruit but hate the tree."

---

eyes that see what you see! I tell you, many prophets and kings wanted to see what you see, and didn't see it, and to hear what you hear, and didn't hear it.'" In the *Gospel of Thomas* the emphasis is solely on the oral transmission.

[10] Notice that the "light/dark" dualism becomes embedded in personal insight. Moreover, this saying assumes the ancient understanding of eye containing light. *Gospel of Thomas* 25.2 continues this association explicitly with "pupil of your eye."

[11] The more traditional translation ("Be passersby") leaves much in question. Cf. Arthur J. Dewey, "A Passing Remark: Thomas 42," *Foundations and Facets Forum* 10 (1994): 69–85.

Here we come to a most interesting chreia.[12] The brevity of *Gos. Thom.* 42 has not led to a paucity of possible translations and interpretations.[13] Whatever was the original meaning of saying 42, we can see that it functions at this point in *Thomas* as a point of "disturbance." The disciples immediately respond to the ambiguous saying with a direct questioning of authority (*Gos. Thom.* 43.1: "Who are you to say these things to us?"). A crucial doubt has entered into this secondary scribal material. What is capital for our investigation is that Jesus' response continues to underline the oral authority and tradition (43.2: "You don't understand who I am from what I say to you").[14] In *Gos. Thom.* 43.2 understanding comes as Jesus speaks. The sayings deliver understanding of his identity or at least the possibility to those who would listen and understand. Not to understand "from what Jesus says" is to place oneself among "the Judeans."[15] In *Gos. Thom.* 43.3 we have disciples labeled as "Judeans" because they do not derive their understanding from the oral performance of Jesus. Could this be a critique of some particular Jesus tradition?

---

[12] We can detect the following structure: (1) *Gos. Thom.* 42: provocative utterance; (2) 43.1: reaction/challenge, indicating lack of understanding; (3) 43.2: basic countercharge: understanding through what is said/oral utterance; (4) 43.3: retort: you have become (ⲰⲰⲠⲈ) like Judeans, dividers.

[13] See Dewey, "Passing Remark." The usual translation ("Be passersby") is rendered usually on an assumption that either the later community or Jesus espoused an itinerant movement. There have been more "gnostic" interpretations, stressing the "passing away" of either the world, the body, or the material part of the disciple ("Become as you pass away"). However, such gnostic or pregnostic interpretations also rest on manifest assumptions. Another, less wooden translation ("Be on the go!" or "Get going!") might suggest the boundary crossing and experimental nature of the early Jesus groups and, perhaps, Jesus himself. I would add another possibility. What if it reflects the words themselves or, better, the act of speech? This is the essence of oral utterances: words exist even as they fade away. Cf. *Gos. Thom.* 43.2, where understanding is derived from what/how Jesus speaks to the disciples (cf. sayings 28, 86).

[14] Ong (*Orality and Literacy*, 98) notes well: "in functionally oral cultures the past is not felt as an itemized terrain, peppered with verifiable and disputed 'facts' or bits of information. It is the domain of the ancestors, a resonant source for renewing awareness of present existence, which itself is not an itemized terrain either. Orality knows no lists or charts or figures." If in *Thomas* each saying in the mouth of the teacher becomes a resonant source, a way of discerning one's present awareness, then the challenging call (for the two to become one) is a discovery of one's true relationship.

[15] Cf. Q 6:43–45: "A choice tree does not produce rotten fruit, any more than a rotten tree produces choice fruit; for each tree is known by its fruit. Figs are not gathered from thorns, nor are grapes picked from brambles. The good person produces good from the fund of good in the heart, and the evil person produces evil from the evil within. As you know, the mouth gives voice to what the heart is full of." In *Gos. Thom.* 43.3 we have people who do not derive their understanding from the oral performance of Jesus. A wisdom saying pointing out how one can detect the origin from its effects is now turned into a caricature of those who oppose appearances to reality.

"Keep Speaking until You Find ..." 115

This focus upon the present experience can be also found in saying 59:

> *Gos. Thom.* 59: Jesus said, "Look to the living one as long as you live, otherwise you might die and then try to see the living one, and you will be unable to see."

One is challenged to "study" (ϭⲱϣⲧ) the "living one as long as you live." It is not simply a "looking" at the living one but a fixed "gaze."[16] Such a "studied" attention would be directed not to any vision or extended narrative but to the words that are handed on. This would be exactly the kind of work one would expect from a student of an early level of rhetoric, that of the grammarian, where there is a concern to learn the words of tradition and their proper enunciation.[17] There is also the possible hint of mimetic activity, where the learner "studies" the living one.[18]

A further instance of this educational initiation is found in saying 90 (cf. Matt 11:28–30; Sir 51:26–27):

> *Gos. Thom.* 90: (1) Jesus said, "Come to me, for my yoke is comfortable and my lordship is gentle, (2) and you will find rest for yourselves."

> Matt 11:28–30: "All you who labor and are overburdened come to me, and I will refresh you. Take my yoke upon you and learn from me, because I am meek and modest and your lives will find repose. For my yoke is comfortable and my load is light."

> Sir 51:26–27 (NRSV): Put your neck under her yoke, and let your souls receive instruction; it is to be found close by. See with your own eyes that I have labored but little and found for myself much serenity.

Although in line with the wisdom school tradition, *Thomas* nevertheless differs from Matthew in the following. Not only is the *Thomas* saying much shorter, but also it has not taken or does not know "I will refresh you." Still, *Thomas* does use "you will find rest for yourselves." This is in keeping with *Gos. Thom.* 2 (see below), with the sense that the listeners can

---

[16] See W. E. Crum, *A Coptic Dictionary* (Oxford: Clarendon, 1939), s.v. ϭⲱϣⲧ (837).

[17] Quintilian, *Inst.* 1.4.2 describes the grammarian's task as "recte loquendi scientiam et poetarum enarrationem." Indeed, *Gos. Thom.* 58 (Jesus said, "Congratulations to the person who has toiled and has found life"), congratulating "the one who toils," not only can play to the Cynic images of Hercules but also connects with the "toil" of those who are in the process of learning the basics of rhetoric. An initiation into a literary tradition was an introduction into the "gymnasium of wisdom." One achieved this through "the sweat of the Muses." See also Libanius, *Orat.* 1.12.

[18] See my remarks on *Gos. Thom.* 13 in the following section.

actively discover the point. *Gospel of Thomas* 90.1 would then suggest a wisdom teacher orally inviting students to enter his tutorship. They are to be taught by the *Thomas* Jesus. As we are beginning to see in *Thomas*, this means through the reception and discernment of the sayings.

If we turn to the following complex of sayings (*Gos. Thom.* 91–94), we can see a further indication of the oral performance underway in this material:

> *Gos. Thom.* 91: (1) They said to him, "Tell us who you are so that we may believe in you." (2) He said to them, "You examine the face of heaven and earth, but you have not come to know the one who is in your presence, and you do not know how to examine the present moment."
> 92: (1) Jesus said, "Seek and you will find. (2) In the past, however, I did not tell you the things about which you asked me then. Now I am willing to tell them, but you are not seeking them."
> 93: (1) "Don't give what is sacred to dogs, for they might throw them upon the manure pile. (2) Don't throw pearls [to] pigs, or they might ... it [...]."
> 94: (1) Jesus [said], "One who seeks will find, (2) and for [one who knocks] it will be opened."

The complex of *Gos. Thom.* 91–94 addresses the question of identity of Jesus (91.1: "Tell us who you are"). This challenging request is followed by a double retort (91.2a, b). It would seem that *Thomas* was aware of the saying also used by Q² (Q 12:56):

> Q 12:56: "You phonies! You know the lay of the land and can read the face of the sky, so why don't you know how to interpret the present time?"

In Q² the saying has a decidedly apocalyptic texture, but in *Gos. Thom.* 91.2 the apocalyptic fury is replaced by a present emphasis. As we have already noted, *Gos. Thom.* 92 gives some fresh hermeneutical advice. *Gospel of Thomas* 92.1 reiterates the oral process, and 92.2 places the stress upon the Jesus who speaks (cf. John 16:5, 12–15, 25–28). If one wants to know the identity of Jesus, one must construct that understanding not just from what comes through the tradition but from how the tradition is brought forward. It would seem that the tradition is being conveyed by the voice of Jesus. It is not just his sayings but it is Jesus who performs the role of *grammatikos*, practicing some sort of guidance. The Jesus of *Thomas* redirects the apocalyptic tendency into a present focus.

This emphasis on the oral tradition is underscored dramatically in *Gos. Thom.* 111.3, where there is a self-conscious use of the Jesus tradition:

> *Gos. Thom.* 111: (1) Jesus said, "The heavens and the earth will roll up in your presence, (2) and whoever is living from the living one will not see

death." (3) Does not Jesus say, "Those who have found themselves, of them the world is not worthy"?

Gospel of Thomas 111.3 actually begins by "quoting" Jesus: "Does not Jesus say...?" What starts off in an apparent apocalyptic voice (111.1) is redirected and tempered by the second part (111.2) and confirmed by the citation from Jesus (111.3). Moreover, although *Gos. Thom.* 111.3 sounds much like saying 80, it is not mere repetition:

> *Gos. Thom.* 80: (1) Jesus said, "Whoever has come to know the world has discovered the body, (2) and whoever has discovered the body, of that one the world is not worthy."

As we have seen already in our investigation, *Thomas* never simply repeats. I would contend that what we find is improvisation.

With the above in mind, if we return to our initial thread of investigation, the aphorism of "seeking and finding," we can begin to unravel the fascinating sorites of *Gos. Thom.* 2.[19] In contrast to the series of three aphorisms in Q 11:9, saying 2 turns an aphorism into intensive advice:

> Q 11:9–10: "Ask—it'll be given to you; seek—you'll find; knock—it'll be opened for you. Rest assured: everyone who asks receives; everyone who seeks finds; and for the one who knocks it is opened."

> *Gos. Thom.* 2: (1) Jesus said, "Those who seek should not stop seeking until they find. (2) When they find, they will be disturbed. (3) When they are disturbed, they will marvel, (4) and will rule over all."

Thomas knows the simpler version of this saying (*Gos. Thom.* 92.1; 94 *supra*). So here we have a conscious reworking with rhetorical effect. *Gospel of Thomas* 2.1 already puts a condition on the wisdom saying ("Don't stop seeking until you find"). Then *Gos. Thom.* 2.2 introduces the puzzlement as part of the search/discovery pattern. One will be "disturbed" upon "finding." This, in turn, will lead to "marveling," and that to "ruling over all." The ancient ideal of the philosopher-king can become a reality for those who enter into this toil.

If we consider the oral performance of this saying we could imagine how each part of the sorites could be dictated/recited line by line in the process of memorization. One would be driven by both the content and

---

[19] Cf. P.Oxy. 654.5–9: "[Jesus says], 'Those who [seek] should not stop [seeking until] they find. When they find, [they will be disturbed. When they are] disturbed, they will rule, and [when they rule], they will [rest].'" P.Oxy. 654 has added "rest" to the sorites.

the structure of the rhetoric to search out the meaning of the saying. Indeed, I would contend that one is enjoined to search out precisely through the sayings, as they are being uttered and reworked.

I would see in *Gos. Thom.* 2 the rugged initiation into understanding, the closest one will get to a general hermeneutic in *Thomas*. Here we can see the oral strategy of the *Thomas* school. Already in the incipit of *Thomas* we can detect the oral tension of this developing tradition:

> *Gos. Thom.* Prologue: These are the secret sayings that the living Jesus spoke and Didymos Judas Thomas recorded.
> 1: And he said, "Whoever discovers the interpretation of these sayings will not taste death."

The mythicized tradition comes from the living Jesus to Thomas to the audience of *Thomas*. A recitation ("the secret sayings that the living Jesus spoke") is put to writing, which, in turn, is done with an ear to further recitation (that is, the sayings of Jesus which follow). This is followed by what the ancients would call an internal writing as one embodied the oral tradition.[20] Further, the description of the sayings as "secret" becomes a provocative tool for teaching. Indeed, *Gos. Thom.* 1 intensifies this search by declaring openly that the one who interprets these "sayings" will not experience death. While *Gos. Thom.* 1 gives the basic challenge, *Gos. Thom.* 2 provides the hermeneutical structure to follow throughout. This saying mirrors the experience of the one who listens intently and understands insightfully. The listener would identify with "the one who" since *Gos. Thom.* 1 sets up the challenge to find (ϩⲉ). This sets up enormous expectations. The "seeking" enjoined in *Gos. Thom.* 2 becomes an existential challenge.

This strategy is concretized immediately in saying 3:[21]

---

[20] Arthur J. Dewey, *Spirit and Letter in Paul* (Studies in the Bible and Early Christianity 33; Lewiston, N.Y.: Mellen, 1996), 64–66.

[21] Cf. P.Oxy. 654.9–21: "Jesus says, '[If] your leaders [say to you, "Look,] the <Father's> imperial rule is in the sky," then the birds of the sky [will precede you. If they say] that it is under the earth, then the fish of the sea [will precede] you. And [the <Father's> imperial rule] is inside you [and outside <you>. You who] know [yourselves] will find this. [And when you] know yourselves, [you will understand that] you are [children] of the [living] Father. [But if] you do [not] know yourselves, [you live] in [poverty], and you are [poverty].'" We can detect in the Greek that there is a decided rhetorical cast to the kingdom portion. Then the saying "[you who] know [yourselves]" is a proverbial insertion, which functions as a hermeneutical clue. This allows for the inclusion of the final double saying. Emphasis is on ὑμεῖς in that final saying. This connects with ὑμῶν at the end of the kingdom saying. Additionally, the end of the kingdom saying (cf. Luke 17:21) has "inside you [and outside…"—this may well be a variant on Luke, not simply an addition.

Gos. Thom. 3: (1) Jesus said, "If your leaders say to you, 'Look, the <Father's> imperial rule is in the sky,' then the birds of the sky will precede you. (2) If they say to you, 'It is in the sea,' then the fish will precede you. (3) Rather, the <Father's> imperial rule is inside you and outside you. (4) When you know yourselves, then you will be known, and you will understand that you are children of the living Father. (5) But if you do not know yourselves, then you live in poverty, and you are the poverty."

Gospel of Thomas 3 plays to the best instincts of Deuteronomy as it enfolds the question of the coming of the kingdom.[22] *Gospel of Thomas* 3.3 takes an earlier saying (Luke 17:21: "People are not going to be able to say, 'Look, here it is!' or 'Over there!' On the contrary, God's imperial rule is right there in your presence") and redirects the question, just as the parody deflects the concern. Notice that *Gos. Thom.* 1 and 2 are future directed but not eschatological. *Gospel of Thomas* 3 parodies such apocalyptic castings.

We need also to consider that, by detecting the use of quotations in this saying, we can hear *Thomas*'s Jesus impersonating a variety of voices. First, there are the apocalyptic alarmists (*Gos. Thom.* 3.1–2: "If your leaders say to you...").[23] In fact, the scribe adds birds and fish as a stinging parody.[24] Then we have a voice for the early Jesus tradition (Luke 17:21). Now, there are no quotations for the third part of the saying in *Gos. Thom.*

---

[22] Particularly *Gos. Thom.* 3.1–2. See Deut 30:12–14; 5:8; Bar 3:29–30; and Rom 10:6–8:

Deut 30:12–14 (NRSV): "It is not in heaven, that you should say, 'Who will go up to heaven for us, and get it for us so that we may hear it and observe it?' Neither is it beyond the sea, that you should say, 'Who will cross to the other side of the sea for us, and get it for us so that we may hear it and observe it?' No, the word is very near to you; it is in your mouth and in your heart for you to observe."

Deut 5:8 (NRSV): "You shall not make for yourself an idol, whether in the form of anything that is in heaven above, or that is on the earth beneath, or that is in the water under the earth."

Bar 3:29–30 (NRSV): "Who has gone up into heaven, and taken her, and brought her down from the clouds? Who has gone over the sea, and found her, and will buy her for pure gold?"

Rom 10:6–8 (my trans.): "But the relationship of trust says, 'Do not say in your heart, "Who will climb up to the sky?"'—which is to say, to bring God's Anointed down. 'Or, "Who will plunge into the abyss?"'—which is, to bring God's Anointed back from the dead. But what does she say? 'Near you is the word—in your mouth—in your heart'—that is, the word of trust that we announce."

[23] In Rom 10 Paul has δικαιοσύνη speaking in personification. So here, in *Thomas*, the "leaders" are personified as speaking in apocalyptic tones. This may well be a critique of "leaders" who would place the kingdom at a distance—in effect, a critique of apocalyptic speculators, such as those messianists Mark 13:21 alludes to in his own warning: "And then if someone says to you, 'Look, here is the Anointed,' or 'Look, there he is!' don't count on it!"

[24] Vernon K. Robbins ("Oral, Rhetorical, and Literary Cultures: A Response," *Semeia* 65 [1995]: 82) would call all of this an oral-scribal culture reconfiguration.

3, since Jesus is already the source. The tradition itself emerges full-bodied. Next comes an anonymous wisdom saying that echoes "Know thyself," the famous maxim of Thales.[25] It becomes a guiding voice for those who would listen, as well as an elaboration of *Gos. Thom.* 3.3.[26] Finally, a more prophetic caution comes in *Gos. Thom.* 3.5. Poverty becomes an existential reality, not a condition, but the very basis of existence, the lack of self-knowledge.

If we are to hear *Gos. Thom.* 3 with *Gos. Thom.* 2 echoing within, we must be alert to the note of disturbance. It would seem that 3.3 would force the listener to reevaluate the storm and fury implied in the apocalyptic voices of 3.1–2. Causing some aporia, to say the least, 3.3 would function as a surprise,[27] with 3.4 and 3.5 serving as additional insights and provocative statements. *Gospel of Thomas* 3.4 is to be contrasted with 3.5:

> *Gos. Thom.* 3: (4) "When you know yourselves, then you will be known, and you will understand that you are children of the living Father. (5) But if you do not know yourselves, then you live in poverty, and you are the poverty."

3. Communal Murmurs

We have already begun to detect a movement of social formation in the sayings under consideration. *Gospel of Thomas* 38–43 would suggest not only that this situation comes after the death of Jesus (38.2) but also that there is some definite discrimination of social boundaries (39.1–2 versus 39.3):

> *Gos. Thom.* 38: (1) Jesus said, "Often you have desired to hear these sayings that I am speaking to you, and you have no one else from whom to hear them. (2) There will be days when you will seek me and you will not find me."
> 39: (1) Jesus said, "The Pharisees and the scholars have taken the keys of knowledge and have hidden them. (2) They have not entered, nor have they allowed those who want to enter to do so. (3) As for you, be as sly as snakes and as simple as doves."

---

[25] Cf. Diogenes Laertius 1.40.

[26] The words of Rancière are timely: "'Know yourself' no longer means, in the Platonic manner, know where your good lies. It means come back to yourself, to what you know to be unmistakably in you" (*Ignorant Schoolmaster*, 57). *Thomas* very much anticipates this modern development.

[27] One can use the recent terms of the debate on "light" in modern physics to begin to achieve new metaphors for the kingdom. The kingdom would be a "field," not particles, nor waves. The kingdom is a field encompassing and including those who would listen.

40: (1) Jesus said, "A grapevine has been planted apart from the Father. (2) Since it is not strong, it will be pulled up by its root and will perish."
41: (1) Jesus said, "Those who have something in hand will be given more, (2) and those who have nothing will be deprived of even the little they have."
42: Jesus said, "Get going!"
43: (1) His disciples said to him, "Who are you to say these things to us?" (2) "You don't understand who I am from what I say to you. (3) Rather, you have become like the Judeans, for they love the tree but hate its fruit, or they love the fruit but hate the tree."

The debate for the "reciter" of *Thomas* is grounded on the tradition of the "sayings" of Jesus (*Gos. Thom.* 38.1). This tradition is contrasted with the attempted control of "knowledge" by the "Pharisees and scholars" (39.1). The existence of *Gos. Thom.* 102 ("Jesus said, 'Damn the Pharisees! They are like a dog sleeping in the cattle manger: the dog neither eats nor [lets] the cattle eat'") would indicate that *Thomas* knows of the name-calling typical of competing school traditions. It is important also to note that *Gos. Thom.* 38–43 is artfully constructed from earlier traditions, coming from Q and Matthew.[28]

It is interesting to recall that Q 10:24; 11:52; 19:26 come, in John S. Kloppenborg's estimation,[29] from Q². Moreover, the Matthean material seems to come from developments within the growing community of Matthew. Matthew 10:16 (cf. *Gos. Thom.* 39.3) is tied into the earlier mission material, while Matt 15:13 (cf. *Gos. Thom.* 40) also is connected with disputes with Pharisaic competitors. In other words, the language game that *Thomas* shares is that of a developing community, engaged in defining itself against another school tradition. It is crucial to see that for *Thomas* the basis of the "proper schooling" rests in reciting the "sayings" of Jesus, thereby being able to understand who Jesus is "from what he

---

[28] Compare *Gos. Thom.* 38.1 with Q 10:24: "I tell you, many prophets and kings wanted to see what you see, and didn't see it, and to hear what you hear, and didn't hear it"; *Gos. Thom.* 39.1–2 with Q 11:52: "You legal experts, damn you! You have taken away the key of knowledge. You yourselves haven't entered and you have blocked the way of those trying to enter"; *Gos. Thom.* 39.3 with Matt 10:16: "Look, I'm sending you out like sheep to a pack of wolves. Therefore you must be as sly as a snake and as simple as a dove"; *Gos. Thom.* 40 with Matt 15:13: "He responded: 'Every plant which my heavenly Father does not plant will be rooted out'"; *Gos. Thom.* 41 with Q 19:26: "He replied, 'I tell you, to everyone who has, more will be given; and from those who don't have, even what they do have will be taken away'"; and *Gos. Thom.* 43.3 with Q 6:43–44a: "A choice tree does not produce rotten fruit, any more than a rotten tree produces choice fruit; for each tree is known by its fruit."

[29] John S. Kloppenborg, *The Formation of Q: Trajectories in Ancient Wisdom Collections* (SAC; Philadelphia: Fortress, 1987; repr., Harrisburg, Pa.: Trinity Press International, 1999), 203, 121, 139–48, 164–65.

says" (*Gos. Thom.* 43.2) to the disciple. Indeed, the very use of sayings within the Jesus tradition (from Q and pre-Matthew) would suggest that the voice of Jesus is conveyed not only through the recitation of these sayings but "in the way" these sayings are transmitted.

We can see how this "sayings" tradition is conveyed quite dramatically in sayings 12–13:

> *Gos. Thom.* 12: (1) The disciples said to Jesus, "We know that you are going to leave us. Who will be our leader?" (2) Jesus said to them, "No matter where you are, you are to go to James the Just, for whose sake heaven and earth came into being."
> 13: (1) Jesus said to his disciples, "Compare me to something and tell me what I am like."
> (2) Simon Peter said to him, "You are like a just angel."
> (3) Matthew said to him, "You are like a wise philosopher."
> (4) Thomas said to him, "Teacher, my mouth is utterly unable to say what you are like."
> (5) Jesus said, "I am not your teacher. Because you have drunk, you have become intoxicated from the bubbling spring that I have tended."
> (6) And he took him, and withdrew, and spoke three sayings to him.
> (7) When Thomas came back to his friends, they asked him, "What did Jesus say to you?"
> (8) Thomas said to them, "If I tell you one of the sayings he spoke to me, you will pick up rocks and stone me, and fire will come from the rocks and devour you."

From what we can gather we are eavesdropping on a debate over authority in the period after the death of Jesus. *Gospel of Thomas* 12.2 would seem to settle the question of authority in favor of James the Just. However, if we continue to listen, we soon become puzzled by the succeeding *Gos. Thom.* 13. Jesus challenges his disciples to "liken him, to say what he is like." What is very important is to see how the responses to the challenge are to be understood. Both Simon Peter and Matthew, authoritative figures in the Jesus tradition, compare Jesus to an expected figure in a school tradition. Peter labels Jesus as an ⲀⲄⲄⲈⲖⲞⲤ. While one could see in this title an inchoate angelology, it could also refer to the Cynic teacher (see *Gos. Thom.* 88).[30] Matthew obviously labels Jesus as a teacher of wisdom.

The response of Thomas is unexpected. He declares his inability "to say what Jesus is like." However, this declaration is precisely the correct

---

[30] *Gos. Thom.* 88: (1) "Jesus said, 'The messengers and the prophets will come to you and give you what belongs to you. (2) You, in turn, give them what you have, and say to yourselves, "When will they come and take what belongs to them?"'" For the angelic possibilities, see Heb 1; for the Cynic as ἄγγελος, see Epictetus, *Diss.* 3.22.38.

understanding, since Jesus responds in *Gos. Thom.* 13.5 that he is not Thomas's teacher. Thomas has drunk from the "bubbling spring," that is, genuine wisdom. What I would like to underscore is this: Thomas's reply as nonresponse brings to light what the "likening" really is. It is not a matter of labeling, of externalizing the image of Jesus in any form, albeit honorable. Rather, the "likening" is essentially a mimesis, an activity whereby the disciple learns how to speak like Jesus. This comes home in saying 108.1:

> *Gos. Thom.* 108: (1) Jesus said, "Whoever drinks from my mouth will become like me; (2) I myself shall become that person, (3) and the hidden things will be revealed to him."

I would contend that this is not simply an allusion to the experience of the getting of wisdom but a description of how the process comes about. It is an oral process, mouth to mouth, from reciter to reciter, each learning how to speak in the way Jesus "speaks." Identity is achieved not through some metaphysical or mystical sleight of hand, or conceptual tour de force, but through the actual learning how to speak the words of Jesus, that is, through the "toil" (see *Gos. Thom.* 58)[31] of coming to speech, of learning the words of Jesus and the way in which Jesus speaks. In essence, it is the art of impersonation.[32]

Thus we can say that Thomas's response is that he cannot label or classify Jesus, owing to the experience that underlies his speech. We can even

---

[31] *Gos. Thom.* 58: "Jesus said, 'Congratulations to the person who has toiled and has found life.'"

[32] Epictetus (*Diss.* 3.22.26), in describing the "task" of the Cynic, points out that the Cynic must be able to "mount the stage" and "come to speak like Socrates." This is not unusual since the Cynic is adept at personification. See Dewey, *Spirit and Letter in Paul,* 174–77. There is a danger in assuming that the sayings which allow the interpreter to discover one's true connection to the "Living One" are a simple metaphysical assertion or claim. The sayings reflect the social reality of those engaged in the pedagogical progress/process. *Gos. Thom.* 108 can be understood to mean a metaphysical identification of the interpreter with Jesus ("[1] ... will become like me; [2] I myself shall become that person"), but that is to miss the way in which these sayings may have been used. If this is an oral performance, then there is one person delivering the saying and another not only hearing but trying to understand. This possibility is compounded with the possibility of others who, on hearing other sayings, would help work through to the meaning of the sayings. In effect, the way of discovering the meaning becomes the social glue or process whereby the community is formed. *Gos. Thom.* 108 is not a simple metaphysical identification but a way in which the tradition issue has been solved. In Plutarch's *Coniugalia praecepta* (145b–46) we see that the husband should gather whatever is useful and teach his wife, who will, in turn, become conversant with the "sayings of the wise." Here is an instance of a "home school" where wisdom is passed from mouth to mouth.

see in *Gos. Thom.* 13.5 the language of oracular inspiration. Because Thomas is aware of how not to speak, he can receive three sayings (13.6). His subsequent response to the other disciples is "disturbing." It leaves the listener to seek until one finds the significance signaled by the disturbing saying.[33] Thomas, in short, can imitate Jesus' speech. Jesus is thus remembered by being imitated in his speech pattern. Here we have the school of Thomas the mimic or impersonator.[34] One can see, moreover, why *Gos. Thom.* 13 follows 12. One would think that authority would flow from what is suggested in saying 12, but that is not the way authority or the tradition flows for *Thomas*. It is through oral mimesis. *Gospel of Thomas* 13 becomes a teaching lesson in hearing the tradition/sayings.[35]

We can then begin to make sense of saying 50:

> *Gos. Thom.* 50: (1) Jesus said, "If they say to you, 'Where have you come from?' say to them, 'We have come from the light, from the place where the light came into being by itself, established [itself], and appeared in their image.' (2) If they say to you, 'Is it you?' say, 'We are its children, and we are the chosen of the living Father.' (3) If they ask you, 'What is the evidence of your Father in you?' say to them, 'It is motion and rest.'"

I would contend that we find here the three sayings that Thomas "heard" (*Gos. Thom.* 13.6). *Gospel of Thomas* 50 seems to be a commentary or elucidation of saying 49:

---

[33] The "two become one"—this is a dance in words, where there is a synchronicity of meaning, of understanding. In *Gos. Thom.* 13.8 to those who understand, they could find amusement here. But it frustrates the people who want plain speaking, that is, no nuance, no accent, no inflection. But this material works totally through inflection and deflection. Think of the mimic imitating the actions of another so that they are side by side, the same. Lucille Ball and Harpo Marx! See my remarks in the following footnote regarding *Gos. Thom.* 22.4–7.

[34] In light of this mimetic possibility *Gos. Thom.* 22.4–7 takes on a new sense: 22: (4) "... Jesus said to them, 'When you make the two into one, and when you make the inner like the outer and the outer like the inner, and the upper like the lower, (5) and when you make male and female into a single one, so that the male will not be male nor the female be female, (6) when you make eyes in place of an eye, a hand in place of a hand, a foot in place of a foot, an image in place of an image, (7) then you will enter [the <Father's> domain].'" I would contend that the riddle language (the "two becoming one," the "inner like the outer," etc.) actually comes from the experience of mimesis. The mimic does make the male and female one; that is, the mimic can imitate the other, thus becoming one in the activity of mimesis. The language of "an eye in place of an eye, etc." works well within this sense of mimetic activity. In fact, this "imaging" brings one "into the kingdom," that is, the sphere of such mimetic action.

[35] The political force of such impersonation or improvisation is well understood by Rancière: "Learning to improvise was first of all *learning to overcome oneself* . . . [a] refusal to submit oneself to [another's] judgment" (*Ignorant Schoolmaster,* 42, emphasis original).

Gos. Thom. 49: Jesus said, "Congratulations to those who are alone and chosen, for you will find the <Father's> domain. For you have come from it, and you will return there again."

There are three challenges presented those in the community: the question of origin (50.1), identity (50.2), and evidence of transcendence (50.3). Some have argued that this verse assumes the mythology of the heavenly worlds and the examination by the powers. But it is not at all clear from the text that there is some hostile or adversarial tone to the questions. Others have suggested that this is actually a confessional or liturgical response.[36] I would say that there may be a twofold function: (1) a response to the objections of other Jesus groups (cf. Gos. Thom. 13),[37] and (2) a confessional statement. Both functions support the self-understanding (use of "we") of the community. The *Thomas* community is under construction.

Finally, it would be helpful to dwell on the "evidence" of the third response (50.3). Evidence—**MAEIN**, "sign, wonder"—is "motion and rest." Such a "sign" is hardly an objective demonstration. Nor is it a metaphysical or mystical intuition. Rather, I would argue that the term "rest" hearkens back to *Gos. Thom.* 2, where "rest" comes about through searching. The imaginative search itself in *Gos. Thom.* 2 is both motion and rest. Indeed, this search is carried out through the act of recitation and improvisation. In oral experience words are set in motion, but every speech act is simultaneously a return to the origin, to silence, to rest.

4. A Nonapocalyptic Accent

It is because *Thomas* has an understanding of how to continue to speak "like" Jesus that a decidedly apocalyptic critique can be mounted. We have already seen the frontal attack on apocalyptic speculation in *Gos. Thom.* 3. This is accomplished by *Thomas*'s Jesus impersonating not only the voices of the apocalyptic speculators but also the earlier Jesus tradition.

---

[36] See Fallon and Cameron, "Gospel of Thomas," 4230–36.

[37] In *Gos. Thom.* 50, we have the speaking Jesus coaching what to say to those who would question the origin, identity, and authenticity of the community. Hints of the opposition might be found in *Gos. Thom.* 3. I have argued above that the "leaders" may well represent an apocalyptic faction. *Gos. Thom.* 18 would also seem to oppose an apocalyptic strategy, while *Gos. Thom.* 88 ("messengers" [**NAΓΓΕΛΟC**] and "prophets") may be a further indicator of the people responsible for such speculation. However, *Gos. Thom.* 46.1–2 also suggests possible opposition from the followers of the Baptizer: (1) "Jesus said, 'From Adam to John the Baptist, among those born of women, no one is so much greater than John the Baptist that his eyes should not be averted. (2) But I have said that whoever among you becomes a child will recognize the <Father's> imperial rule and will become greater than John.'"

This impersonation is spoken for the self-understanding of the listeners (3.4). The understanding of the present reality of the kingdom undercuts such future obsessions.[38]

Sayings 18–19 continue to work against the apocalyptic grain:

> *Gos. Thom.* 18: (1) The disciples said to Jesus, "Tell us, how will our end come?" (2) Jesus said, "Have you found the beginning, then, that you are looking for the end? You see, the end will be where the beginning is. (3) Congratulations to the one who stands at the beginning: that one will know the end and will not taste death."
> 19: (1) Jesus said, "Congratulations to the one who came into being before coming into being. (2) If you become my disciples and pay attention to my sayings, these stones will serve you. (3) For there are five trees in Paradise for you; they do not change, summer or winter, and their leaves do not fall. (4) Whoever knows them will not taste death."

The question of the disciples is typical of apocalyptic timetable speculation. The response by *Thomas*'s Jesus is a challenge to discover not the end but the beginning. Some will immediately point out the emergence of a "protology" over against an "eschatology." But it is not simply a time chart at stake. *Gospel of Thomas* 18.2 delivers a gnomic parry to the apocalyptic thrust. A macarism is thereupon created (18.3), which plays on the puzzlement desired by *Thomas*'s strategy of searching until one finds. *Gospel of Thomas* 19.1 delivers another macarism that sounds much like the previous and yet differs to extend the riddling. *Gospel of Thomas* 19.2 puts the oral reality of this strategy directly in front of us. If one "listens to his sayings," the disturbing (*Gos. Thom.* 2), "unnatural" breakthrough will occur (cf. *Gos. Thom.* 13). One finds oneself in Paradise, among "five trees," by catching the accent of the words. It is not simply a return to the origin, to the source, but a stance in the original creative process of coming to speech.

The search for an apocalyptic *topos,* a place to project all one's hopes and fears, is countered in saying 24:

> *Gos. Thom.* 24: (1) His disciples said, "Show us the place where you are, for we must seek it." (2) He said to them, "Anyone here with two ears had better listen! (3) There is light within a person of light, and it shines on the whole world. If it does not shine, it is dark."

---

[38] One can put it another way: the apocalyptic movement cuts off the experience of present speech. It places the locus of hope in the future, taking the living word of Deuteronomy right out of one's mouth. Thus, it is not a matter of different tastes but a question whether the Jesus tradition is a present reality.

Just as the disciples in John 14:5 seek a place of meaning, so do the disciples in *Gos. Thom.* 24.1. This request is met with advice "to hear." This is followed by an allusion to the inner "light" (the ocular assumption of the ancient world). The sacred *topos* is no longer projected out but is discovered in the common inner experience.[39]

Similarly, saying 37, while beginning with an apocalyptic concern for the time of the second coming, turns the issue right back into the experience of the community:

> *Gos. Thom.* 37: (1) His disciples said, "When will you appear to us, and when will we see you?" (2) Jesus said, "When you strip without being ashamed, and you take your clothes and put them under your feet like little children and trample them, (3) then [you] will see the son of the living one and you will not be afraid."

There may well be some allusion to the baptismal experience of the early Jesus tradition. Certainly a reversal of the Genesis fall story is indicated. But here we must recall what we have found out about what follows in *Gos. Thom.* 38–43. The sayings of Jesus and the way the sayings are handled allow the listener to see how "the son of the living one" (37.3) can appear in the present in his "sayings." A further instance is found in saying 51:

> *Gos. Thom.* 51: (1) His disciples said to him, "When will the rest for the dead take place, and when will the new world come?" (2) He said to them, "What you are looking forward to has come, but you don't know it."

The timetable question is set on its heels by the saying that what is sought has come already but was not recognized. This is also the brunt of sayings 97 and 113:

> *Gos. Thom.* 97: (1) Jesus said, "The [Father's] imperial rule is like a woman who was carrying a [jar] full of meal. (2) While she was walking along [a] distant road, the handle of the jar broke and the meal spilled behind her [along] the road. (3) She didn't know it; she hadn't noticed a problem. (4)

---

[39] *Gos. Thom.* 25 follows up the allusion to the eye with an explicit use of the term: (1) "Jesus said, 'Love your friends like your own soul, (2) protect them like the pupil of your eye.'" This is then continued forward in saying 26: (1) "Jesus said, 'You see the sliver in your friend's eye, but you don't see the timber in your own eye. (2) When you take the timber out of your own eye, then you will see well enough to remove the sliver from your friend's eye.'" It is important to see that the "inner experience" of 24.3 is not a simple isolated reality. It has a connection to "the whole world." Moreover, this inner life is the basis for relationships with the "brother." Thus, we are not necessarily talking about injunction to an isolated individual, despite the use throughout of **MONαXOC**.

When she reached her house, she put the jar down and discovered that it was empty."

Gos. Thom. 113: (1) His disciples said to him, "When will the <Father's> imperial rule come?" (2) "It will not come by watching for it. (3) It will not be said, 'Look, here!' or 'Look, there!' (4) Rather, the Father's imperial rule is spread out upon the earth, and people don't see it."

Finally, saying 61.1–4 is a brief dialogue illustrating how an apocalyptic saying (cf. Q 17:34) can be turned into a riddling scene:

Q 17:34: "I tell you, on that night there will be two on one couch: one will be taken and the other left."

Gos. Thom. 61: (1) Jesus said, "Two will recline on a couch; one will die, one will live."
(2) Salome said, "Who are you, mister? You have climbed onto my couch and eaten from my table as if you are from someone."
(3) Jesus said to her, "I am the one who comes from what is whole. I was granted from the things of my Father."
(4) "I am your disciple."
(5) "For this reason I say, if one is <whole>, one will be filled with light, but if one is divided, one will be filled with darkness."

The future image of anxiety is replaced by the present identity of the one speaking. Salome indicates her understanding by declaring her discipleship.

In short, one can say that there is evidence that *Thomas* knows the trend toward apocalyptic speculation and strenuously speaks in counter-terms. *Thomas* knows of apocalyptic voices and redirects those voices by refining them through other sayings in the tradition or by creating new ones that attempt to uproot any attempt to move the sayings of Jesus away from the present experience of the community.

5. An Embodied Voice

There is a tendency to imagine the *Thomas* community as an isolated, ascetic group.[40] They are understood as separate, heroic individuals of self-knowledge. Their only connection is attained through a metaphysical

---

[40] One can also note that the Salome and Mary material (sayings 21, 61, 114) would seem to argue that women might have been as prominent as men in the *Thomas* community. Certainly Salome "got it" as did Thomas. Mary has access to transformation, despite the ignorance and prejudice of Peter: *Gos. Thom.* 21: (1) "Mary said to Jesus, 'What are your disciples like?'";

conceptuality or mystique. Thus, the following appear to substantiate such a position:

> *Gos. Thom.* 16: (4) "and they will stand alone."

> *Gos. Thom.* 11: (4) "On the day when you were one, you became two. But when you become two, what will you do?"

> *Gos. Thom.* 22: (5) "and when you make male and female into a single one, so that the male will not be male nor the female be female...."

> *Gos. Thom.* 23: (1) Jesus said, "I shall choose you, one from a thousand and two from ten thousand, (2) and they will stand as a single one."

> *Gos. Thom.* 48: Jesus said, "If two make peace with each other in a single house, they will say to the mountain, 'Move from here!' and it will move."

> *Gos. Thom.* 106: (1) Jesus said, "When you make the two into one, you will become children of Adam, (2) and when you say, 'Mountain, move from here!' it will move."

However, *Gos. Thom.* 16.4 assumes that there is more than one standing "alone." Likewise 23.2 puts it, "They will stand as a single one." In *Gos. Thom.* 48 "two make peace ... in a single house," and in 106.1, when the "two become one," "you" (plural) become the children of humanity. In effect, the notion of "becoming one" does not remove the plurality of those in the community. I would argue that, instead of a metaphysical solution, one should look at the attempt to describe social formation by these terms. The "one" is the body of the community (the "single house," *Gos. Thom.* 48). This is *Thomas*'s way of speaking of the real solidarity of the community brought about by the recitation and improvisation of the sayings of Jesus.

The return to "an original unity" or origins is a reflection or a clue to the speech event of *Thomas*. As one repeats the saying one literally returns to the origins and "becomes one" with the teacher who has pronounced the saying. It is a description of the speech event when one is always

---

61: (2) ... "Salome said, 'Who are you, mister? You have climbed onto my couch and eaten from my table as if you are from someone.' (3) Jesus said to her, 'I am the one who comes from what is whole. I was granted from the things of my Father.' (4) 'I am your disciple'"; 114: (1) "Simon Peter said to them, 'Make Mary leave us, for females don't deserve life.' (2) Jesus said, 'Look, I will guide her to make her male, so that she too may become a living spirit resembling you males. (3) For every female who makes herself male will enter the domain of Heaven.'"

brought back to the beginning, one always has to speak anew, even in repetition. At the same time, the student is encouraged to say the saying "like Jesus." If the student moves from simply hearing the saying to becoming startled, then a change occurs. The student internalizes not just the words but also the meaning. This allows the student to recite the saying in an improvised fashion. This means that the saying will be uttered differently in improvisation. There is an educational mime going on, but hardly a static affair. The student learns how to improvise, that is, continue the game of handing over the tradition.

Although there is a decided tendency to read sayings that seem to elicit a return to origins in a conceptual model, one can say that there is another paradigm for reading the material. The language might be reflective of the speech pattern itself. One is asked to return to the oral beginning, to become one with the speaking Jesus, just as one becomes one with the teacher who enunciates the saying of Jesus. Thomas stands for the disciple who understands the speech pattern of Wisdom, indeed, the imagined speech pattern of Jesus. This is the way Wisdom/Jesus sounds. By writing these words down, "Thomas" furnishes the community with the pedagogical means to continue to learn wisdom through imitating the "voice" of Jesus.

The Jesus tradition is thus passed down but in a nonnarrative fashion. Elementary pedagogical tools are used in advancing this "handing over." This is not the finished training of a rhetorician. It is more the recitation level of a *grammatikos*.[41] The *grammatikos* is concerned with the tradition and with the proper way to convey it.[42] Here we have a text that recalls the oral traditions of Jesus. It is most likely aware of the earlier level of Q as well as the growing apocalyptic speculation that issued on one front with the second level of Q and on another with the Gospel of Mark. But *Thomas* has chosen to maintain a nonnarrative manner of continuing the tradition. I would suggest that this follows more closely the language strategy of the historical Jesus. There is an interesting modern

---

[41] As Robert A. Kaster points out (*Guardians of Language: The Grammarian and Society in Late Antiquity* [The Transformation of the Classical Heritage 11; Berkeley and Los Angeles: University of California Press, 1988], 443), there were various entitlings for the "primary level" teacher. *Magister ludi* is appropriate for what is happening in *Thomas*.

[42] Here the words of William E. Arnal are quite pertinent ("The Rhetoric of Marginality: Apocalypticism, Gnosticism, and Sayings Gospels," *HTR* 88 [1995]: 489–90): "Although the evidence is far from unambiguous, the *Gospel of Thomas* seems to reflect a lower-level scribal group, moderately educated but with little literary sophistication. As with Q_1, the *Gospel of Thomas* likewise shows an overriding and repetitive concern with, and awareness of, debt and legal issues (particularly involving land). These concerns more clearly link the document's tradents with the village scribes and public clerks who were responsible for recording precisely such matters."

analogy. With television there is a decided construction and freezing of images, especially of the given narrative; in radio, where only sound is found, one is free to improvise as one remembers the words. Likewise there is a decided difference between *Thomas* and the narrative Gospels. The narrative to a great degree congeals the sound in a frieze of images—although it is still freer than television or painting. *Thomas* lives on through improvisation.

6. Logia upon Logia

- The *Gospel of Thomas* contains the seeds of its own pedagogy.

- The *Thomas* Jesus continues talking, but in a certain accent.

- The *Thomas* Jesus continues to invite the elect in and to lead them into his way of talking, his way of understanding.

- The key for the person entering is to follow the way Jesus talks, that is, to go through the aporiae, to ride the waves of riddling, to begin to mediate the puzzling with one's own understanding.

- The image of Jesus the riddler comes through. He teases the listener to seek out the meaning, to be discomforted by what is spoken, to be provoked, to be at a loss, and then to let the insight come ("marvel") and to recognize the new condition ("rule over all").

- The Jesus of *Thomas* may be the "closest" Gospel image whereby one can get to the historical Jesus. *Thomas* may have best preserved the "feel" of the oral tradition of Jesus; moreover, it may have better kept alive the historical Jesus' vision and challenge of the kingdom, which is a present and effective reality in people's lives.

- The figure of Thomas epitomizes the one who understands the accent, breaks the code. He thus is the one who has the right to write, the authority to set the tradition down so it can go forward.

- The result is the continuance of the recitation and writing down.

- There is no end to the way Jesus speaks, no final chapter, since that would presuppose a narrative journey, a beginning, middle, and end. But in the getting of Wisdom, it is a constant returning to the source (to "the bubbling spring"), and then more words come. In that sense it is oracular.

- In *Thomas* one can verify coming into the presence, the kingdom, by speaking the words to others in Jesus' inflection.

DISCUSSION AND REFLECTIONS
Merrill P. Miller

Although the papers from the third year of the Consultation had received written responses, the discussion of the papers was limited by the format required for an SBL Consultation. This would change as we moved to the status of a Seminar, as would the way in which each year's work was to be planned. By the end of the first two years of the Seminar, it would also be possible to review the papers of this Consultation and to realize, in retrospect, that they had raised several issues of importance for our discourse-in-the-making and for ways of thinking about the project that were not sufficiently clarified or discussed at the time, and that perhaps had not fully registered. Here we can only try to anticipate these issues.

In the case of the Sayings Gospel Q, one might ask whether the difference between a Cynic hypothesis for imagining social formation and the hypothesis of the deracination of a scribal sector[1] is largely a methodological

---

[1] On the social situation and location of Q's mythmaking and social formation, see William E. Arnal, "The Rhetoric of Marginality: Apocalypticism, Gnosticism, and Sayings Gospels," *HTR* 88 (1995): 471–94; idem, *Jesus and the Village Scribes: Galilean Conflicts and the Setting of Q* (Minneapolis: Fortress, 2001); Ron Cameron, "'What Have You Come Out to See?' Characterizations of John and Jesus in the Gospels," *Semeia* 49 (1990), 35–69; Michael L. Humphries, *Christian Origins and the Language of the Kingdom of God* (Carbondale: Southern Illinois University Press, 1999); John S. Kloppenborg, "Literary Convention, Self-Evidence and the Social History of the Q People," *Semeia* 55 (1991): 77–102; John S. Kloppenborg Verbin, *Excavating Q: The History and Setting of the Sayings Gospel* (Edinburgh: T&T Clark, 2000), 166–261, 409–44; Burton L. Mack, "The Kingdom That Didn't Come: A Social History of the Q Tradents," in *Society of Biblical Literature 1988 Seminar Papers* (SBLSP 27; Atlanta: Scholars Press, 1988), 608–35; idem, *The Lost Gospel: The Book of Q and Christian Origins* (San Francisco: HarperSanFrancisco, 1993); Jonathan L. Reed, "The Social Map of Q," in *Conflict and Invention: Literary, Rhetorical, and Social Studies on the Sayings Gospel Q* (ed. John S. Kloppenborg; Valley Forge, Pa.: Trinity Press International, 1995), 17–36; Leif E. Vaage, *Galilean Upstarts: Jesus' First Followers according to Q* (Valley Forge, Pa.: Trinity Press International, 1994). On the Cynic hypothesis, see most recently John S. Kloppenborg Verbin, "A Dog among the Pigeons: The 'Cynic Hypothesis' as a Theological Problem," in *From Quest to Q: Festschrift James M. Robinson* (ed. Jon Ma. Asgeirsson et al.; BETL 146; Leuven: Peeters and Leuven University Press, 2000), 73–117; idem, *Excavating Q*, 420–32; cf. 436–44.

difference of priority in sequencing, in an effort to locate a point of departure for social formation as a process. Mack's understanding of the composition of Q^1 as reflecting the ethos of a particular group formation is, in large part, the consequence of his focus on attribution as a mythmaking strategy[2] and of the priority he gives to mythmaking as the social practice most accessible in our texts. The deracination hypothesis begins with what is now a careful and detailed analysis of the effects of economic changes in first-century Galilee.[3] To ask if the difference is methodological is not to say that it is minimal. Arnal's position that the composition of Q^1 does not represent crystallization into group formation, but a response to the failure of an earlier social agenda, presents a significantly different reading of the data. Still, the difference might be viewed as methodological. For Mack is not likely to disagree with Arnal that ideology, social discourse, and group formation always relate to, and take place within, a larger social totality, and Arnal is not likely to disagree with Mack that attribution is a mythmaking strategy.

But what if Mack were saying that the deracination hypothesis does not explain the mythmaking or the social formation, because mythmaking cannot be reduced to an ideological formation within a base-superstructure model and social formation cannot be reduced to class interests? And what if Arnal were saying the same thing about the Cynic hypothesis, because it focuses mythmaking on self-referentiality and assumes that discursive formations are constitutive of social processes? In that case, the difference would not be methodological or a question of the sort of data to be given priority; it would not be chiefly an issue of adjudicating two different hypotheses about Q. Rather, it would be a question of the definition of our categories and of their relationship. Indeed, the enormous implications for explaining historical change are obvious in Arnal's concluding statement that the "social processes" we need to understand, analyze, and map "are all extradiscursive"[4]—especially if one considers the opposite and argues that the constitutive practices and processes determinative of social history are never completely extradiscursive. This difference has emerged as a genuine theoretical issue, as the metareflection on "Social Formation and Mythmaking: Theses on Key Terms" by Arnal and Braun indicates.[5]

The deracination hypothesis also figures in the paper by Braun, but here with a particular connection to the search for helpful analogues to the

---

[2] Mack, *Lost Gospel*, 6–7, 191–205.

[3] Arnal, *Jesus and the Village Scribes*, 97–155, 221–44.

[4] William E. Arnal, "Why Q Failed: From Ideological Project to Group Formation," 84 (in this volume).

[5] William E. Arnal and Willi Braun, "Social Formation and Mythmaking: Theses on Key Terms" (in this volume).

social vision and scholastic features of Q. While Braun may accept the view that economic change is a basic cause of the uprootedness to which the Q tradents respond, economic factors would not appear to be a major consideration in the choice of analogues discussed in the paper. The notion of reemplacement in a reconfigured social space also appears to move in a different direction from Arnal, especially when Braun suggests that the compositional strata of Q are "moved in part by the centripetal force of the group's increasing attachment to itself."[6] However, it is not so much the differences between Braun and Arnal that need to be highlighted, but the questions that both of their essays pose for an understanding of the categories of mythmaking and social formation and of their relationship. Braun's paper raises the question whether social formation as a category necessarily tells us anything about an intrinsic historical relationship between, or among, the Jesus groups, for he shows that there may be more illuminating non-Christian analogues to both Q and *Thomas* (than to other Jesus groups) and that there is no mythic trajectory that can be plotted for Q or *Thomas* (only discontinuity in discursive formations). Braun notes, for example, that scribal strategies for responding to analogous social conditions go in *"different directions"* that cannot be predicted from the conditions themselves. This point "may be illustrated by noting an endemic problem in social-historical work," namely, "the tendency toward assuming a predictable commensurability between cultural conditions and social-formational reactions to it."[7] Taking his cue from an insight of Arnal, who "demonstrates that a 'shared critical stance toward [similar] distressing socioeconomic changes perceived to be taking place' generates diverging reactions" on the part of Q and *Thomas,* Braun argues that "in view of their evident similarities at one stage of their respective histories, the difference in their final destinations ... is all the more interesting and in need of explanation." Indeed, Q^2 stands "as a puzzling difference, as the way not taken by *Thomas*," indicating that Q^2 itself is not inevitably or self-evidently "the *necessary* flowering of a seed germinating in Q^1"[8] but is "a surprise, from the vantage point of earliest Q."[9]

The papers by Cameron and Dewey broach the issue of language in relation to experience. When Dewey proposes that the *Gospel of Thomas* is the text of a school of oral mimesis, he is thinking of an oral pedagogy that gives access to a privileged knowledge in a face-to-face encounter between a master and disciples. Dewey's concern is to express

---

[6] Willi Braun, "The Schooling of a Galilean Jesus Association (The Sayings Gospel Q)," 65 n. 96 (in this volume).
[7] Ibid., 61, emphasis original.
[8] Ibid., 61, 62, emphasis original, citing Arnal, "Rhetoric of Marginality," 492.
[9] Braun, "Schooling of a Galilean Jesus Association," 62.

the experiential dimension of an oral pedagogy. So when Dewey states that the meaning of *Thomas*'s sayings is indicative of the experience of oral communication itself, it is clear that his view of language takes experience to have priority, theoretically, over language: orality provides a purer sense of experience by encapsulating language into experience. Cameron's concern with language in his paper is to emphasize that language is prior, in a theoretical sense, to experience. Indeed, he has discussed the *Gospel of Thomas* in order to clarify the language strategies that are used to express social interests and investments. The whole thrust of Cameron's paper is to move scholars away from thinking that *Thomas* is a text that is, somehow, supportive of the experience of resurrection. For Cameron's approach to redescribing the *Gospel of Thomas* and Christian origins presupposes that "language . . . is not posterior to experience . . . [but] is the very way in which we think and experience."[10] It follows, necessarily, that "there is no post-Easter experience which then is 'given voice' in Christian discourse; the experience is contained in and by that discourse."[11] Cameron's efforts to rethink the importance of the *Gospel of Thomas* for reimagining the beginnings of Christianity are not concerned with a way to participate in a master-disciple relationship, but are designed to find out how we can account for *Thomas* in other terms and then use the text to understand and explain Christian origins differently.[12] What is surprising about Dewey's concluding appeal to the historical Jesus

---

[10] Jonathan Z. Smith, "A Twice-Told Tale: The History of the History of Religions' History," *Numen* 48 (2001): 137, adding: "For those of us who study religion . . . as is characteristic of the human sciences in general, the little prefix *re-* is perhaps the most important signal we can deploy. It guarantees that we understand both the second-order nature of our enterprise as well as the relentlessly social character of the objects of our study. We re-present those re-peated re-presentations embedded in the cultures and cultural formations that comprise our subject matter. . . . The history of the history of religions is not best conceived as a liberation from the hegemony of theology. . . . A more fundamental issue that yet divides us . . . is the debate between an understanding of religion based on *presence,* and one based on *representation.* . . . The human sciences become conceptually possible largely through the acceptance of the . . . argument that [one's] objects of study are holistic linguistic and language-like systems, and that, therefore, they are the study of 'eminently social' human projects. . . . The central debates within the study of religion [thus] revolve around the relations of language and experience" (ibid., 131, 132, 137–38, emphasis original, alluding to Emile Durkheim, *The Elementary Forms of Religious Life* [trans. Karen E. Fields; New York: Free Press, 1995]).

[11] Jonathan Z. Smith, "Social Formations of Early Christianities: A Response to Ron Cameron and Burton Mack," *MTSR* 8 (1996): 274.

[12] Russell T. McCutcheon asks: "Must participants and their meaning systems be understood on their own terms?" and answers: "This is *the* methodological issue that remains at the very heart of our field [of religious studies]: it is the old insider/outsider problem" ("Our 'Special Promise' as Teachers: Scholars of Religion and the Politics of Tolerance," in *Critics Not Caretakers: Redescribing the Public Study of Religion* [SUNY series, Issues in the Study of Religion; Albany: State University of New York Press, 2001], 171, emphasis original).

is that it does not contribute to the thesis he is arguing. Although it appears that the bottom line in Dewey's paper is how close *Thomas* is to the "language strategy [and voice] of the historical Jesus,"[13] appealing historically to Jesus does not follow from the discussion (about a difference between sayings and narrative Gospels in carrying on the Jesus tradition) or explain the nature of oral pedagogy.

For those of us in the process of formulating a proposal for the Seminar and laying plans for the first two years, what could be seen was the importance of the Sayings Gospels site and the school analogue we were testing for the analysis of data we hoped to redescribe at the sites of Jerusalem and the Hellenistic Christ cults. All of the papers from the Consultation acknowledge, in different ways, the strategic importance of the Sayings Gospel Q and the *Gospel of Thomas* for a project of redescribing Christian origins. Thus, in the strategy of thinking of Q as a scholastic community, Braun sees "a significant regauging of the track for social description and for theorizing early Christian social formations."[14] Despite finding the school analogy perhaps too convenient for academics, Arnal also refers to research on Q that calls into question the assumption of some originary moment or the assumption of social formation as the means of "carrying forward ... some precious cultural 'deposit' such as belief in the resurrection."[15] For Cameron, the *Gospel of Thomas* cannot be accommodated to the way we have thought about comparison or to the implicit theories of religion that bear directly on the scholarly imagination of Christian origins. And with his thesis of oral pedagogy, Dewey also provides an angle from which to reconsider the "voice" of the narrative Gospels. In short, we maintain that our work on the Jesus schools of Q and *Thomas* already sets us at a distance from the canonical framework of Christian origins. In planning the Seminar, our intention was precisely to use these alternate beginnings to defamiliarize data that are central to the construction of the canonical story, in the interest of a more plausible account of beginnings.

The Sayings Gospel Q and the *Gospel of Thomas* demonstrate that we do not have to start with the historical Jesus, the crucified Christ, an eschatological event, or apocalyptic expectations to account for the beginnings of Christianity. The advantage of alternate beginnings is not in having an alternative point of absolute origination, but in having a cognitive advantage and, thus, the possibility of new knowledge. Whether we actually

---

[13] Arthur J. Dewey, "'Keep Speaking until You Find ...': *Thomas* and the School of Oral Mimesis," 130 (in this volume).

[14] Braun, "Schooling of a Galilean Jesus Association," 47.

[15] Arnal, "Why Q Failed," 73.

gain new knowledge about Christian origins, however, depends on whether different points of departure encourage and contribute to a rethinking of other data, especially of data that have been crucial for maintaining scholarship in the grip of the dominant paradigm. The only way to test our contention about the advantage of beginning with the Jesus schools of Q and *Thomas* is to find out if such alternate beginnings help us to redescribe that other sort of data. This was the key strategic observation in choosing Jerusalem and a pre-Pauline locus as the initial sites to reconsider in the first two years of the Seminar. The first church of the apostles in Jerusalem and the pre-Pauline congregations of northern Syria are important, for our purposes, because of the paramount significance that the textual data associated with these settings have enjoyed, in scholarly imagination no less than in the canonical narrative of Christian origins. And since the book of Acts locates the origins of Christianity in Jerusalem, as have biblical scholars and church historians ever since,[16] we thought it best to begin our Seminar by devoting the first year to a redescription of the "Jerusalem church."

---

[16] See Ron Cameron, "Alternate Beginnings—Different Ends: Eusebius, Thomas, and the Construction of Christian Origins," in *Religious Propaganda and Missionary Competition in the New Testament World: Essays Honoring Dieter Georgi* (ed. Lukas Bormann et al.; NovTSup 74; Leiden: Brill, 1994), 501–25, esp. 512–15 nn. 55–63.

PART 2

A JESUS SCHOOL IN JERUSALEM?

Proposal for the First Year of the Seminar
Ron Cameron

The traditional map of Christian origins begins in Jerusalem, not only because scholarship has tried to locate most of the data of beginnings in terms of the Lukan picture, on or in close proximity to the mythic map portrayed in Luke's Gospel and Acts, but also because "Jerusalem" is "a category and root metaphor of the [Christian] imagination of Christian origins. Thus, it has occupied and continues to possess a privileged place among the data that bear on the beginnings of Christianity," serving in antiquity as well as today "as the locus of what Christianity is [all] about and how it got started."[1] The initial challenge facing the Seminar was to see whether we would agree that the data in Acts, in its entirety, had to be reassessed as evidence of a later myth of origins, and whether it would then be possible to construct a profile of a Jerusalem group without falling back on the usual stratagem of some critical paraphrase of the monolinear development presented in the book of Acts. A recently published paper by Merrill P. Miller, calling for just such a reassessment, was sent to members of the Seminar for critical evaluation and response. Miller argued that scholarship has failed to provide a critical history that could identify plausible connections between the teaching and activity of Jesus in Galilee, his execution as a messianic pretender in Jerusalem, and the immediate formation of a messianic community in Jerusalem, which survived relatively unmolested for more than a generation:

> The question of a critical historiography cannot come to rest merely on whether historians can plausibly account for the execution of Jesus, or on whether the writer of Acts has drawn on traditions that in some cases may put at our disposal isolated facts. The historian must determine whether it is possible to identify historical connections between the teaching and activity of Jesus, the death of Jesus, and the movement that continued after his death. [Accordingly,] the major task of this paper is to expose the

---

[1] Merrill P. Miller, "'Beginning from Jerusalem...': Re-examining Canon and Consensus," *Journal of Higher Criticism* 2/1 (1995): 3.

problem of making a connection between the death of Jesus and the existence of the Jerusalem church once these data are imagined in the canonical form of the execution of Jesus as a messianic pretender followed by the formation of a community announcing its identity and mission in terms of the vindication and exaltation of Jesus as Messiah. [For] despite the flood of research on matters pertaining to the death of Jesus and the beginnings of Christianity, the problem of how to reconcile the execution of Jesus and the establishment and survival for more than a generation of a Jerusalem church as a messianic movement in that same city has hardly ever surfaced let alone been adequately addressed.[2]

The most remarkable feature of Miller's paper is the persistence with which he engages in detail the argument of E. P. Sanders, whose *Jesus and Judaism* is virtually the only study of Christian origins concerned with the issue of connecting Jesus' teaching, the reasons for his crucifixion, and the movement that continued after his death. To his credit, Sanders recognizes that making a connection between what Jesus is reported to have said in Galilee and his death in Jerusalem is not at all clear, and saying why the authorities would have wanted to kill Jesus on the basis of anything he is said to have done is equally problematic. Moreover, Sanders is one of the few scholars who has thought it necessary to raise the question of why the leadership of a messianic community in Jerusalem remained essentially unmolested after Jesus' execution as a would-be Messiah. Since the sayings of Jesus can account neither for his execution nor for a messianic movement of Jewish restoration after his death, Sanders harnesses the "teachings" of Jesus to "the almost indisputable facts" of Jesus' life, culled from a synthetic reading of the Synoptic Gospels, in order to explain the connections between Jesus' "intention," deeds, and "relationship to his contemporaries in Judaism," including "the reason for his death ... and the motivating force behind the rise of Christianity."[3] In so doing, what Sanders has produced is a paraphrase of the Gospel story—very little of which has been left out—that he uses to provide both the analytical and the historical frame of reference for understanding Jesus' activity and his fate. By starting with the alleged "facts" of "Jesus' career *and its aftermath*,"[4] Sanders has, in fact, simply "begun his historical investigation by adopting as history the narrative framework of the canonical gospel story and the interpretive framework found especially in the preaching of Peter in [speeches Luke composed for] the early chapters of Acts."[5]

---

[2] Ibid., 7.

[3] E. P. Sanders, *Jesus and Judaism* (Philadelphia: Fortress, 1985), 11, 1; cf. 4, 11–12, 17, 21–22, 57–58, 222–24, 227, 231, 294, 301, 307, 326–27.

[4] Ibid., 11, emphasis original.

[5] Miller, "Beginning from Jerusalem," 10.

Miller's achievement is to have called into question the logic of the set of assumptions that gave rise to the problems that Sanders posed in the first place, as well as to have demonstrated by means of a sustained argument that Sanders's solution cannot be sustained. Appealing (by means of paraphrase) to the Gospel accounts of Jesus' death and the narrative construct of the book of Acts, which present Jesus as a crucified Messiah who somehow "did something [symbolic] in the temple and said something [intentional] about its destruction"[6] and then present the first Christians in Jerusalem as proclaiming a messianic status for him after he was gone, does not explain either "the difficulty" Sanders seeks to address or "the problem" with his own position: "that the [Christian] movement survived, presumably because it posed no political or military threat, while Jesus was executed as 'king of the Jews,' despite the fact that he also posed no serious threat to Roman and Jewish establishments." For Sanders, "this poses the problem of how to account for the death of Jesus." For Miller, on the other hand, "the problem should be posed from the opposite direction, i.e., from the consequences, or rather, the non-consequences of the execution of Jesus. How is it possible to explain why the execution of Jesus did not have serious effects on the establishment and survival of a movement of Jesus' followers in the city where he was executed?"[7] Sanders's efforts to establish connections between Jesus in Galilee, his crucifixion as a messianic pretender, and the formation of a Jerusalem messianic movement of Jewish restoration eschatology are not convincing. The existence in Jerusalem of the sort of community he imagines cannot be reconciled with the reasons for the execution of Jesus that Sanders himself offers. Consequently, "his methodological point of departure"—that "we should begin our study [of the death of Jesus] with two firm facts before us: Jesus was executed by the Romans as [a] would-be 'king of the Jews,' and his disciples subsequently formed a messianic movement"—also "loses conviction." Attempts to harmonize the "passion narratives" in the canonical Gospels with Luke's apologetic program in the book of Acts and, indeed, to suppose that the former "constitute sources from which one can extract and reconstruct the historical circumstances and reasons for the death of Jesus," do not work.[8] To understand the emergence and attractions of the early Jesus groups and their constructions of Jesus and his fate, we need to place our texts in their social-historical contexts and examine the "connections" they were making, not what Jesus

---

[6] Sanders, *Jesus and Judaism*, 61; cf. 11–12, 61–76, 294–308.
[7] Miller, "Beginning from Jerusalem," 10–11, citing Sanders, *Jesus and Judaism*, 294; cf. 231.
[8] So Miller, "Beginning from Jerusalem," 21, 20; cf. 24, citing Sanders, *Jesus and Judaism*, 294. On the construction of the passion narrative, see Burton L. Mack, *A Myth of Innocence: Mark and Christian Origins* (Philadelphia: Fortress, 1988), 247–312, 315–49.

was (said to be) about. For example, since "the crucifixion of Jesus by the Roman and Jewish authorit[ies] in Judea has, in the perspective of Acts, theological and historical consequences for the Jews, but no social and political consequences for the apostles," and since "the only time in Acts that the authorities make reference to the execution of Jesus is in response to accusations concerning their own guilt,"[9] to make sense of "Jerusalem" according to this privileged account of origination we will have to redescribe the making of Luke's myth of origins, not simply reproduce as history the theological perspective of Acts. The quest for Christian origins should thus be turned around: "not the mythic events at the beginning, but the social and intellectual occasions of their being imagined would be the thing to understand."[10]

In addition to this demonstration and its consequences, Miller has "raise[d] as matters for an agenda several other reasons why the scholarly consensus on the unitary origins of Christianity needs to be re-examined." First, since "there existed different ways in which the characterization, authority, and status of Jesus were enhanced," with "different myths of Jesus emerg[ing] in different locales and communities and [a] partial merger of myths t[aking] place in the course of a continuing social history ... neither the sayings tradition nor the kerygma can easily be said to account for the messianic identity of earliest Christianity and the community in Jerusalem." Therefore, "it is unlikely that either the death of Jesus or the identity of the group of followers in Jerusalem revolved around messianic confrontations, claims, or titles."[11]

Second, rather than imagine that "conceptions of Jerusalem that serve the agenda of the writer of Acts around the turn of the century or that represent Paul's conception of his apostolate in the late forties and the decade of the fifties are actually rooted in the history of Christian origins in Jerusalem," Miller suggests that "conceptions of the messianic orientation of the Jerusalem church based on the foundational revelation of Jesus' resurrection, as well as conceptions of the role, authority and positions of its leading members are likely to reflect the internal disputes and competing claims for legitimation of individuals and communities engaged in a mission to Gentiles beginning in the late forties and the decade of the fifties." By arguing that "the actualization of such a mission, its conceptualization, contestation and legitimation in mixed communities outside Palestine [are] surely the context of our 'knowledge' of the Jerusalem church, as far as our canonical sources are concerned," what Miller has identified is nothing less

---

[9] Miller, "Beginning from Jerusalem," 14.
[10] Mack, *Myth of Innocence*, 8.
[11] Miller, "Beginning from Jerusalem," 25, 30.

than "a particular juncture of mythmaking and social history," namely, "a diaspora version of beginnings in the homeland designed to support a mission to Gentiles among different factions of Jewish and Gentile Christians in the Hellenistic cities of the diaspora."[12]

Third, since "alternative picture[s] of Christian origins" have begun to emerge, which "cannot be accommodated" to the dominant paradigm and which demonstrate that "the resurrection of Jesus is not the common center of all expressions of early Christianity," it is "now possible to pursue the question of community formation in Jerusalem by followers of Jesus without assuming the model of the kerygma-oriented Christ congregations as the only possible model."[13]

By demonstrating the implausibility of imagining historically a connection between the death of Jesus and the emergence of a Jerusalem group (as portrayed in the New Testament and accepted by nearly all biblical scholars), Miller is proposing that we take a fresh look at the problem of Jerusalem and do so by getting rid of the problematic category of messianic sect for Jerusalem. Inasmuch as the kind of picture we have in Acts is not usable as the basis of a critical historiography, even if there is some tradition in Acts, it will not help us much with constructing a picture of an early Jerusalem group, though it may make sense in Luke's own day, as mythmaking activity in the late first or early second century. In response, members of the Seminar were asked to evaluate Miller's argument and its implications for imagining the beginnings of Christianity.

The responses showed that it is easier to expose the serious aporiae in various scholarly attempts to work within an essentially Lukan framework of Christian origins than it is to imagine a Jerusalem group without some sort of messianic orientation. Nevertheless, there was wide agreement that Miller problematized the canonical presentation in the Gospels and Acts to such an extent that his paper "has stripped the canonical picture of its powerful center of gravity," as Christopher R. Matthews put it (in his e-mail of 18 May 1998). Some Seminar members suggested that messianic beliefs about Jesus in Jerusalem could be construed on the basis of other sources or considerations. While consideration was given to casting a wide net to assess sources of potential value as data for "Jerusalem," a rationale for the selection and ranking of sources was considered urgent. The letters of Paul, in general, and what can be reconstructed from the evidence of his statements in Gal 1–2, in particular, were seen as crucial. As William E. Arnal remarked (in his letter of 26 February 1998), "the real problem for Miller's suggestions is Paul," since Paul's references to the

---

[12] Ibid., 27–28.
[13] Ibid., 25, 26.

"pillars" "seem to fit with the standard scholarly conceptions" and suggest that they shared "a similarity of perspective" with him, "support[ing] the notion" that there was a group in Jerusalem which "had a messianic and resurrection-oriented understanding of Jesus." Arnal went on to observe that Miller's proposed reading of the evidence, that "Paul is himself mythologizing this group," presents a plausible and attractive alternative but needs to be buttressed with additional, close textual analysis to be convincing.[14]

Scholarship on Christian origins has typically taken recourse to some notion of Jesus' death and resurrection to account for the beginnings of Christianity in Jerusalem. In a forceful, penetrating critique of this privileged point of origination, Burton L. Mack has argued:

> Some event, it is thought, or moment, or impulse, needs to be discovered as the source for the novelty Christianity introduced into the world.... The fundamental persuasion is that Christianity appeared unexpectedly in human history, that it was (is) at core a brand new vision of human existence, and that, since this is so, only a startling moment could account for its emergence.... All scholars seem to agree ... on the importance of the resurrection. Three terms are frequently used, each encoded by custom within the discourse of the discipline, to refer euphemistically to the resurrection of Jesus from the dead: Easter, appearance, and spirit.... These coded signs, usually capitalized, do not enlighten because they mark the point beyond which the scholar chooses not to proceed with investigation, indeed, the point beyond which reasoned argument must cease [if Christianity is to retain its position of privilege in the guild]. They serve as ciphers to hold the space for the unimaginable miracle that must have happened prior to any and all interpretation. They have become an all too convenient rhetorical device for evoking the myth of Christian origins without [ever] having to explain it.... Appeal to "the resurrection" is the most mystifying of all ciphers used to protect the myth of Christian origins from critical investigation. The notion is used regularly to distinguish "pre-Easter" from "post-Easter" performances of Jesus' sayings, for instance, as if the resurrection were a datable piece of evidence. By allowing the mystery of Easter and the [resurrection] appearances to mark the point from which the Spirit effected the new age of Christian experience and mission, everything else can be examined rigorously without threatening the notion of originary uniqueness.... A point of origin has been established that is fundamentally inaccessible to further probing or clarification. [This] guarantees the uniqueness of early Christianity by locating

---

[14] For Arnal's own critique of Sanders's method of study, beginning with the "indisputable facts" of Jesus' life taken from the framework stories of the Synoptic Gospels—Jesus' baptism, the cleansing of the temple, and the passion narrative—see William Arnal, "Major Episodes in the Biography of Jesus: An Assessment of the Historicity of the Narrative Tradition," *TJT* 13 (1997): 201–26.

its novelty beyond data and debate.... In order to avoid the conclusion that the notion of the resurrection was a product of mythmaking in the Hellenistic congregations, scholars have frequently taken recourse to the "early" evidence for the "appearances" of the resurrected one. This persuasion is doubly convenient, for it traces the beginnings to an "experience" that cannot be questioned further, and it locates the first such experience in Jerusalem in agreement with the Christian myth of origins. It should be emphasized that this "evidence" finally reduces to (1) Paul's claims to have received a revelation of God's Son (Gal 1:12, 16; cf. 2 Cor 12:2–7), and (2) the appearances tacked on to the Christ myth in 1 Cor 15:5–8. It is on these verses attached to the kerygma that the entire edifice of the origins of Christianity (as a Christ cult) in Jerusalem ultimately must rest.... If one suspects that Paul was the one to add the list of appearances to the kerygmatic formula, it can be seen that he resolved the question of his authority and linkage to the first pillar [Peter] in a most interesting way. The chain of "tradition" in which Paul himself stands is not a passing on of the kerygma as teaching or preaching, but of a series of revelations that now include Paul's own visitation. Thus his claim to private revelation was preserved.... And the gospel? Note that the kerygma set forth as "tradition" is exactly Paul's own, the content of his preaching learned in the Christ cult. Thus Peter's "appearance" serves to validate Paul's own gospel.... Therefore, both Paul's own revelations, and his attribution of a kerygmatic appearance to Peter, presuppose the Christ myth.... All references to the resurrection presuppose "exaltation," that is, the mythic datum of vindication. None should be used to argue for a private vision at the beginning instead of a social experience in need of rationalization.[15]

Mack's alternative profile (in his letter of 12 March 1998) indicates the ways he would go about the task of redescribing the Jerusalem group: (1) start with the texts thought to support the dominant paradigm of Christian origins; (2) analyze "the degree to which they can be understood as constructions upon the past in the interest of claims specific to their own situations"; (3) see if their "references to a Jerusalem group allow us to extract any features that may still be attributed to it"; (4) make "a preliminary list of [those] features for consideration"; (5) bracket those that are "better explained as rhetorical fabrications in the interest of later mythmaking"; (6) assess that mythmaking rhetorically; (7) construct a profile from the remaining indicators of social practices; (8) ask pointedly about what sense it all would make; (9) propose analogies from the cultures of context with which the Jerusalem group may be profitably compared; and (10) theorize about the attractions and investments of such a group in

---

[15] Mack, *Myth of Innocence*, 3, 4, 7, 7–8 n. 3, 113–14 n. 11.

terms of human interest in social formation. By doing all of this, a place on the map of an experimental group of early Jesus people can be imagined, because an important locus of mythmaking and social formation will have been described.

Luther H. Martin (in his response of 31 March 1998) reviewed Miller's paper in light of recent discussion of theoretical issues in historiography, observing that "every social group produces narratives of its own origins," that Miller has shown that unitary origins (including Christian origins in Jerusalem) are mythological, and noting, in the words of Eric Hobsbawm, that "it is the professional business of historians to dismantle such mythologies."[16] Dennis E. Smith (in his e-mail of 10 April 1998) responded with the beginnings of a profile of Jerusalem, based primarily on data from the letters of Paul. Smith's profile, like Mack's, was not beholden in any way to apocalyptic, messianic, or kerygmatic persuasions, and both highlighted family resemblances with the Pharisees. We thought it important to see if these preliminary profiles were plausible and especially whether they could be sustained by taking careful account of Pauline data as well as recent scholarship on the early chapters of Acts. To begin to address these issues, working papers were solicited and assignments undertaken to carry further the work of redescription.

In addition, a letter was sent out (on 22 June 1998) to members of the Seminar, reviewing a few critical textual loci and identifying some perennial exegetical problems that would need to be addressed in a redescription of "Jerusalem":

- In Gal 1:16–17, were there already persons who thought of themselves as "apostles before [Paul]" in Jerusalem (to whom Paul did "not go up") in the 30s? Or are we to understand that Paul expresses himself this way because there were apostles (like him?) in the 50s?
- In Gal 1:19, though we may know what Paul means by *kyrios*, would James have called himself "the Lord's brother"?
- In Gal 1:22, with reference to the "churches of Judea that are in Christ," is this the Roman province of Judea (which, in the 50s, covered more territory than the area south of Samaria)? And how are we to understand the locative expression "in Christ"?
- In Gal 2:2, when Paul says he went up to Jerusalem "in response to a revelation," why does he say "to make sure that

---

[16] Eric Hobsbawm, "What Can History Tell Us about Contemporary Society?" in idem, *On History* (New York: New Press, 1997), 26, adding: "unless they are content ... to be the servants of ideologists" (ibid.).

I was not running, or had not run, in vain," if he had earlier argued for his independence from Jerusalem? Did Paul and Barnabas go up to Jerusalem as representatives of the church in Antioch (cf. Acts 15), or did they go on their own?

✦ In Gal 2:6, what exactly is meant by the expression "those leaders contributed nothing to me"? In both the private meeting that Paul had and in the larger group, is the argument really that Gentiles did not have to be circumcised? Is this supported by what is described in 2:11–14? But why, then, is Titus mentioned in 2:1? Isn't the major argument about the so-called division (of labor? of territory?) betweeen Paul and others?

✦ In Gal 2:7–8, why is the name "Peter" used (instead of "Cephas")? Is a contrast being made between Peter and Paul alone (though otherwise Paul uses the plural "we" and "they")? And do the terms "circumcised" and "Gentiles" refer to an ethnic division? to a territorial division? Did anyone know what anyone else was talking about? Did anyone abide by it? Did Jerusalem never make an agreement with Paul that Gentiles didn't have to be circumcised?[17] Were there really two different "messages"? What would they have been?

✦ In Gal 2:9–10, with whom was this "fellowship"? And what exactly is meant by "remember[ing] the poor"? Is "the poor" a technical term? Does it mean "especially pious"? Does it refer to the "impoverished"? Or does the text refer to a kind of tax that Gentiles were paying to Jerusalem? Should we think here of the collection in 1 Cor 16? Why does Paul never mention the Galatians' remembrance of the poor when he writes to the Romans? Does this mean that the Galatians did not come up with the money? Or does it mean that the collection wasn't for "Eastern" churches? Does the present tense ("we remember [the poor]") suggest that this remembrance was not a one-time issue but was to take place regularly? Then was the particular "collection" in Galatians an issue only between Antioch and Jerusalem? Does the collection have anything to do with what Jerusalem was asking for? Why, in Romans, is Paul afraid that Jerusalem will not accept it?

---

[17] In his letter of 12 March 1998, responding to Miller's paper that was sent out to the Seminar for critical evaluation, Mack states that "Paul's claim is only that they recognized him as a leader in a common movement despite their differences with regard to the circumcision of gentiles."

- In Gal 2:11–14, Paul's version of the incident at Antioch, what does Paul's facing Peter down mean? Are the "people from James" official representatives of Jerusalem? Exactly what did they come to Antioch for? Did they (not) have to know something about what was at issue there?
- In Gal 5:11, what does it mean for Paul to say "if I am still preaching circumcision"?
- In Gal 6:13, in thinking about "the circumcised [who] do not themselves obey the law," what are the options for relations between circumcised and uncircumcised? Didn't synagogues have many different connections with persons who didn't simply "convert"?
- In 1 Cor 9:20, when Paul refers both to his ministerial activity and his conception of it, why does he say "to the Jews I became as a Jew" if he is an apostle to Gentiles?
- In 1 Cor 15:11, does the reference to "I or they" refer to Peter, Paul, and/or Apollos, as if they all had the same theology?
- In 2 Cor 11:24, why does Paul apparently submit to Jewish (synagogal) jurisdiction if he wasn't active in synagogues? Did this happen before he became a "Christian"? Did he preach circumcision at that time?
- In Rom 11:13–14, when Paul refers to "glorify[ing his] ministry," it still seems that his view of Jerusalem remains highly ambivalent and that his view in Romans differs from that in Galatians. What were the different pressures in Rome that might have caused a different mythic construction of Jerusalem?
- In Rom 15:27, when Paul describes the reasons for the collection, he refers to the Gentiles' sharing in "spiritual blessings." Isn't this idea unimaginable in terms of what is described in Galatians?

We realized, of course, that we would not necessarily resolve all of these exegetical problems, but we did want to indicate some of the issues that needed to be addressed, as well as to suggest why it is important to change our perspectives on the social history and imaginative labor documented by the texts, in order to redescribe "Jerusalem" as a datum of "Christian origins."

Introduction to the Papers from the First Year of the Seminar

Ron Cameron

Matthews's paper on "Acts and the History of the Earliest Jerusalem Church" reviews recent scholarship on Acts for evidence of features from the dominant paradigm that might still be regarded as data for some Jerusalem group in the 30s and 40s. He takes note of the recent output and energy of scholars advocating the historical verisimilitude of Luke's second volume but finds the more disciplined redaction- and tradition-critical approach of Gerd Lüdemann a better test of "the historical value of the traditions in Acts."[1] On the one hand, Matthews notes, "the possibility of reconstructing putative underlying written sources for Acts has been foreclosed by the thoroughly Lukan nature of the existing narrative."[2] On the other, he concludes that, in almost every instance, the bits of "historical" data that have been identified as "traditions" are isolated and best interpreted as data of mythmaking, not history. While hardly serviceable for the historicistic purposes of much recent scholarship, the early chapters of Acts are far from disappointing as an ideological negotiation of Luke's own time. As Matthews puts it, "Luke's understanding of Jerusalem participates in an intertexture of other symbolic cartographies that place Jerusalem at the center of the world.... [Nevertheless,] when Luke wants to illustrate a 'breakthrough moment' in the spread of Christianity, he ends up using stories that have no necessary association with Jerusalem."[3] This is indeed a telling judgment. Matthews demonstrates that when Luke forges "Jerusalem" as the center, he does so not by preserving and transmitting "traditions" but by constructing myth as an invented tradition. And so, "while Luke's 'sense-making interests' in combination with

---

[1] Gerd Lüdemann, *Early Christianity according to the Traditions in Acts: A Commentary* (trans. John Bowden; Minneapolis: Fortress, 1989), 9.

[2] Christopher R. Matthews, "Acts and the History of the Earliest Jerusalem Church," 162 (in this volume), adding: "[This is] the critical consensus on this issue that has stood for decades" (ibid.).

[3] Ibid., 172, 174.

the practice of historiography as 'truthful fiction'" may be "a disappointment for those seeking the 'facts,' the myth of origins that Acts presents can only be admired in terms of the ideological negotiation it represents for Luke's time."[4]

Taking up Arnal's challenge to buttress the argument with additional, close textual analysis, Miller's paper on "Antioch, Paul, and Jerusalem: Diaspora Myths of Origins in the Homeland" addresses data from the Pauline corpus by shifting from models drawn from the study of Christian origins, in particular, to models based on locative factors of homeland and diaspora, which Jonathan Z. Smith, among others, has shown to be characteristic of Mediterranean religions in their Hellenistic and Late Antique phases.[5] By making this shift, Miller seeks to demonstrate from a close reading of passages in the Pauline corpus that what is usually taken as historical data of the beliefs, interests, and position of authority of the

---

[4] Ibid., 174.

[5] For an elaboration of the taxonomy of "locative/utopian" and its application to specific texts and traditions, including religions in both their homeland and the diaspora, see Jonathan Z. Smith, "Native Cults in the Hellenistic Period," *HR* 11 (1971): 236–49; idem, "Towards Interpreting Demonic Powers in Hellenistic and Roman Antiquity," *ANRW* 16.1:425–39; idem, *Map Is Not Territory: Studies in the History of Religions* (SJLA 23; Leiden: Brill, 1978; repr., Chicago: University of Chicago Press, 1993), xi–xv, 67–207; idem, "Hellenistic Religions," *The New Encyclopedia Britannica*, 15th ed. (1986), 18:925–27, 929; idem, *Drudgery Divine: On the Comparison of Early Christianities and the Religions of Late Antiquity* (Jordan Lectures in Comparative Religion 14; London: School of Oriental and African Studies, University of London; Chicago: University of Chicago Press, 1990), 106–7, 110, 120–42; idem, "Here, There, and Anywhere," in *Prayer, Magic, and the Stars in the Ancient and Late Antique World* (ed. Scott Noegel et al.; Magic in History Series; University Park: Pennsylvania State University Press, 2003), 21–36. Smith argues that "it is not sufficient to merely name a text; rather, it is necessary both to locate a text within a history of tradition and to provide some sort of explanation for the processes of continuity and change" (preface in *Map Is Not Territory*, xi). To accept this insight is "to insist on an important element of method and theory with regard to comparison: *the recognition and role of historical development and change*. This is a necessary principle of parity. The work of comparison ... requires acceptance of the notion that, regardless of whether we are studying [texts or] myths from literate or non-literate cultures, we are dealing with *historical processes of reinterpretation*, with tradition. That [is], for a given group at a given time to choose this or that mode of interpreting their tradition is to opt for a particular way of relating themselves to their historical past and social present. This is most especially the case in the study of the religions of Late Antiquity.... In almost no case, when treating ... the religions of Late Antiquity, do we investigate a new religion. Rather, almost every religious tradition that forms the focus of our research has had a centuries-old history. We study archaic Mediterranean religions in their Late Antique phases.... [As such,] the interrelationship between these two, archaic and Late Antique, under rubrics such as persistence and change forms the primary object of our study." In all of these studies, "concerned with [comparative questions of] persistence and change in Mediterranean religions," Smith has "argued for the presence (there, and elsewhere) of two world-views, the 'locative' and the 'utopian'" (*Drudgery Divine*, 106–7, 120–21, emphasis original).

Introduction to the Papers from the First Year of the Seminar 153

"Jerusalem church" is better understood as data of diaspora mythmaking concerned with origins in the homeland. In developing his thesis, Miller argues that "any historical reconstruction of the Jerusalem group and its leaders to be won from the data of Paul's letters, in particular from Gal 1–2, must be wrested from competing mythic imaginations of 'Jerusalem' of diaspora Jews engaged in projects of teaching, recruitment, and community formation among Jews and Gentiles in Hellenistic cities outside Palestine."[6] The inference to be made is that any interests of the "pillars" in Jerusalem in the 30s and 40s would not be those of a worldwide mission, messianism, resurrection appearances, or the kerygma, but those of a Jesus legacy and its application for establishing the markers of an appropriate Jewish identity in the shadow of the temple.

The shift in perspective to a locative model and employment of a distinction between homeland and diaspora make it possible for Miller to mark different perspectives on Jerusalem and, thus, to redescribe four different sites—Jerusalem, Antioch, Galatia, and Paul's own situation itself—in terms of diaspora myths of origins in the homeland. In order to achieve a more plausible reading of the relations between Pauline, Antiochene, and Galatian circles, on the one hand, and Jerusalem and Judean circles, on the other, Miller insists that we must be as explicit about our criteria and as rigorous in our selection and reading of the data from the Pauline corpus as we are with the book of Acts. By being precise and particular in our readings, we may distinguish discursive formations of the "Jerusalem church" that operate within the mythic horizons of Christian origins from readings of the data that aim to construct a profile of a possible Jerusalem group within the historical horizons of early Jesus and Christ groups. Since most of what we know about Jerusalem from the letters of Paul is influenced not only by Paul's own interests but also by his awareness that others are also constructing an image of Jerusalem that confirms their own leadership, strategies, and particular "gospel" message, Miller proposes a reading of Paul that does justice to Paul's own rhetorical strategies and practical agenda with respect to Jerusalem. This means that information used as data to construct a profile of a Jerusalem group must be correlated, in the final analysis, with alternative readings of Paul (and Acts) that do not merely paraphrase what the sources have to say about Jerusalem. Therefore, in addition to gaining insights from a mirror-reading of Paul's letters (particularly Gal 1–2), taking at least some of the polemical statements and emphases to reflect or rebut the counterstatements of Paul's opponents, Miller proposes to do a second reading of Galatians, with questions of

---

[6] Merrill P. Miller, "Antioch, Paul, and Jerusalem: Diaspora Myths of Origins in the Homeland," 181, emphasis omitted (in this volume).

mutual recognition, forms of relationship, and common or competing social interests in view.[7]

The role generally attributed to Jerusalem in the study of Christian origins not only misconstrues discursive formations of mythmaking for social reality but also presupposes, from the beginning, an international movement and universal mission to convert the world to Christ. The thesis of Miller's paper depends on a different perspective:

> The status and authority of Jerusalem and its leadership, the conceptions of their role and the representations of their views, are largely constructions fabricated in the interest of making sense of and promoting behaviors and relations in groups such as those in and around Antioch that have become independent of synagogues.... The Jerusalem "church," as they thought of it, serves as a link to a past and thus to identities that are in the process of change.... In other words, the Jerusalem "church" is not the presupposition, or the precursor, or the final court of appeal concerning situations and issues arising in Damascus and in Antioch.... Rather, the Jerusalem reflected in our sources is in large part the result of these developments.[8]

By making such an argument, Miller intends a shift from a notion of the historical precedence of a Jerusalem church based on an eschatological myth, to an understanding of "Jerusalem" as the source of mythic precedents in the interests of debates about how to relate current diaspora social experiments to a sanctified past. The distinction between homeland and diaspora suggests that "the so-called Jerusalem church ... functioned ideologically as a substitute homeland for diaspora circles of Hellenistic Jews engaged in innovative social and cultic experiments."[9] Accordingly, the homeland/diaspora model enables us to resolve the anomaly of Jerusalem, by indicating the context of our knowledge of "Jerusalem" and in whose interests it was to forge such myths. Rather than assume or appeal to the notion of a common kerygma between Antioch, or Galatia, or Paul and Jerusalem, we need another way to account for different and competing interests, patterns of conflict, and mutual recognition in the social formations of early Christianities. To come to terms with the problem of relating these various interests, contexts, and projects to issues of mutual recognition in early Christianities, without being "trapped in the myth of origins we wish to explain,"[10] is in fact the purpose of Miller's paper: "to

---

[7] Ibid., 200 n. 77, 203–4, citing John M. G. Barclay, "Mirror-Reading a Polemical Letter: Galatians as a Test Case," *JSNT* 31 (1987): 73–93.

[8] Miller, "Antioch, Paul, and Jerusalem," 203.

[9] Ibid., 181.

[10] Ibid., 235.

Introduction to the Papers from the First Year of the Seminar 155

demonstrate ... why we have to imagine the interests that were served in establishing relationships between individuals and between local groups without assuming that these individuals and groups must have shared some 'essential' elements of the gospel of Jesus Christ."[11]

Although Miller did not call into question the fact of group formation in Jerusalem at an early date, that is contested by Dennis Smith. In his paper on "What Do We Really Know about the Jerusalem Church? Christian Origins in Jerusalem according to Acts and Paul," Smith maintains that "the Jerusalem 'church' as a power broker in Christian origins was a mythological construct from the outset, first appearing among Paul's opponents in Galatia, then picked up and elaborated on by Luke in Acts.... The Jerusalem of myth was utilized to buttress a mythological Jerusalem 'church' in order to gain advantage in the early debates among the Jesus movements."[12] Smith suggests that "the 'opponents' of Paul in Galatia" were "a group of Jewish Christian missionaries who promote[d] their authority via their credentials as representatives of Jerusalem" and, thus, were the "first clear promoters of the myth of the primacy of Jerusalem."[13] More important, he argues that, since "the generally accepted version of Christian origins in Jerusalem derives almost entirely from Acts and, furthermore, depends on a historical reading of Acts," and since "a historical reading of Acts can no longer be taken for granted," then "given the weight attached to the Jerusalem church in Luke's overall theological scheme, it is appropriate that we question the entire hypothesis of Christian origins in Jerusalem."[14]

Building on his initial profiles,[15] but now in response to both of Miller's essays, Mack's paper on "A Jewish Jesus School in Jerusalem?" offers "a reconstruction of the Jesus people in Jerusalem," controlled by "reflection on the methods proposed" for the work of the Seminar and supported by a consideration of "social theory," a theory of religion as social interest that can explain Christian origins. Acknowledging that since "the dominant paradigm has been problematized by means of a critical analysis of its logic and its underlying assumptions," and since "the critical analyses of texts, assumptions, and argumentations traditionally used to support the dominant paradigm have made it impossible to continue thinking of Christian

---

[11] Ibid., 234.

[12] Dennis E. Smith, "What Do We Really Know about the Jerusalem Church? Christian Origins in Jerusalem according to Acts and Paul," 243 (in this volume).

[13] Ibid., 249.

[14] Ibid., 250–51.

[15] See Burton L. Mack, *A Myth of Innocence: Mark and Christian Origins* (Philadelphia: Fortress, 1988), 88–91; idem, *Who Wrote the New Testament? The Making of the Christian Myth* (San Francisco: HarperSanFrancisco, 1995), 67–70.

beginnings" according to "the traditional model"—a "combination of the Lukan story and Paul's pictures of the congregations of the Christ"—the challenge in reconstructing a group of Jesus people in Jerusalem is "to imagine a Jerusalem group with some connection to the Jesus movements (rather than assuming connections only to the congregations of the Christ, as has been customary)."[16] Since a number of assumptions about Christian origins belonging to the traditional model can no longer be used as a matter of course in reconstructing a Jerusalem group,[17] to suggest a different, more historically plausible reconstruction will require an "anthropological perspective that differs fundamentally from that assumed by the dominant paradigm of Christian origins," an "anthropology based on a conception of human interests" and investments in social formation and maintenance.[18]

Mack shows how we might imagine "mutual recognition ... based on some common interests with regard to social issues" in a "range of locations ... from Jerusalem and Judea to Antioch and Galatia."[19] The profile he draws of Jerusalem, based on the group that gathered to talk to Paul on his second visit there (Gal 2:1–10), includes features concerned with "the implication of Jewish practices for Jewish self-definition and Jewish-Gentile relations," specifically issues involving "questions of ethnic identity" and "etiquettes of cross-ethnic association."[20] What we have, then, is a mutual interest in debate about the practices appropriate to a Jesus legacy where, when, and as it overlapped with issues of Jewish identity and relations with Gentiles in the interest of group formation. "The interests in common that made mutual recognitions possible among the Jerusalem group, Paul, and the diaspora congregations must have been those we now associate with the Jesus movements, not those traditionally associated with Paul's depiction of the Christ cults."[21] So, "having set aside the Lukan-Pauline scenario, the picture of Christian origins changes markedly in the direction of ad hoc social formations and

---

[16] Burton L. Mack, "A Jewish Jesus School in Jerusalem?" 253, 254 (in this volume).

[17] "These include," Mack says, "the belief in Jesus as Messiah, the cult of presence based on appearances of the resurrected Jesus, the notion of (starting) 'missions' to both Jews and Gentiles in the interest of a global program of conversions to the Christian 'church,' eschatological ideology, anti-Jewish identity markers and/or reformist programs (whether the target be 'law,' 'temple,' 'Pharisees,' 'Judaizers,' or whatever), [and] claims to authority based on the notion of (twelve) 'disciples' or 'apostles'" (ibid., 254).

[18] Ibid., 255, 256, adding: "We are exploring the possibility that the Jesus people and early Christians were engaged in making sense of their social and cultural worlds just as others were doing during the Greco-Roman age, and just as all other peoples have been doing since the dawn of human history" (ibid., 255).

[19] Ibid., 257.

[20] Ibid.

[21] Ibid., 261.

wide-open ideological debate where and when people interjected the Jesus legacy into the situation of Jewish response to the Roman world." It could even be said that "the issues raised for Jews by the Jesus legacy had much to do with Jewish identity ... little with loyalties or markers pertinent to self-definition as a Jesus school or Christ cult."[22] Accordingly, in discussing "the interest on the part of the Jerusalem group in talking to Paul," Mack insists that "the important question is whether the Jerusalem group saw themselves as part of a movement that included the Christ congregations and got exercised about the acceptance of Gentiles within that movement, or whether their interest in Paul's question was more academic, that is, a question of importance for Jews and Jewish institutions in general."[23] Mack argues that the better analogies for understanding these common interests and social concerns are those situations and issues generally being addressed by Jewish intellectuals in synagogues of the time, not the Pauline congregations or Luke's Jerusalem church. And so, he introduces a theory of social interests in order to compare data from ethnography and cultural anthropology with data from the subcultural associations of the Greco-Roman world, thereby illustrating the distinctively Jewish variants of the basic interest, "common to all peoples," that "humans take in creating social structures and maintaining social existence."[24]

In his paper on "History, Historiography, and Christian Origins: The Jerusalem Community," Martin calls attention to some of the implications of the theoretical orientations of the Seminar: "If the sources for the early Christianities are understood to be myths produced as a consequence of social formation, then we must clearly stipulate not only our historiographical theory (or theories) but also our theory (or theories) of social groups and their formation.... We must, in other words, clearly state our

---

[22] Ibid., 257–58, 257.

[23] Ibid., 261, adding: "It is possible that [the Jerusalem group's] discussion of the question was more a matter of interest in the constituency and identity of the Antioch *synagogue* than in the definition of the new social formation Paul was calling the *church*" (ibid., emphasis original).

[24] Ibid., 259. For several recent papers by Mack in which he has elaborated in more detail his theory of social interests and its bearing on the redescription project of the Seminar, see Burton L. Mack, "Many Movements, Many Myths: Redescribing the Attractions of Early Christianities. Toward a Conversation with Rodney Stark" (review of Rodney Stark, *The Rise of Christianity: A Sociologist Reconsiders History*), *RelSRev* 25 (1999): 132–36; idem, "Social Formation," in *Guide to the Study of Religion* (ed. Willi Braun and Russell T. McCutcheon; London: Cassell, 2000), 283–96; idem, "A Radically Social Theory of Religion," in *Secular Theories on Religion: Current Perspectives* (ed. Tim Jensen and Mikael Rothstein; Copenhagen: Museum Tusculanum Press, 2000), 123–36, esp. 131–32; idem, *The Christian Myth: Origins, Logic, and Legacy* (New York: Continuum, 2001), 81–99, 101–25, 201–16.

view of the theoretical connection between mythmaking and social formation in historiographical research."[25] Martin criticizes, in particular, a reliance upon any "implicitly held or privately employed theory (or theories) ... about data alone as the public arbiter of historiographical validity," or any "models of historical positivism ... which tacitly assume that historical (textual) evidence, carefully gathered and accurately presented, speaks convincingly for itself."[26] In addition, he argues that "if the texts produced by early Christians are to be understood as the products of their mythmaking, they cannot then count as historiographical documentation in support of events portrayed in their production.... If, for example, references to 'Jerusalem' in Acts and Galatians belong to instances of Christian mythmaking ... [then] we must question the extent to which it is possible to use this mythographic data for any historiographical description of a 'Christian' group in Jerusalem."[27] Finally, Martin observes that "although there seems no good reason to doubt the existence of an early Jerusalem community of 'Jesus people,' the historical 'fact' remains that this community 'made no myths' of its own (or, at least, none that survived). Rather, the 'Jerusalem community' survives solely as a datum in the 'mythmaking' formations of others."[28]

---

[25] Luther H. Martin, "History, Historiography, and Christian Origins: The Jerusalem Community," 271 (in this volume).
[26] Ibid.
[27] Ibid., 269–70.
[28] Ibid., 270.

ACTS AND THE HISTORY OF THE EARLIEST JERUSALEM CHURCH

Christopher R. Matthews

The picture of the early Church presented by the opening chapters of Acts is that of a society of Galilean followers of Jesus who had lived together in Jerusalem from the day of the crucifixion and held peculiar views of their own. The Twelve, and especially Peter, were the leaders of this society. The historical difficulty of this presentation is largely concealed from the general reader of the New Testament, because either he unconsciously harmonises the Gospels and Acts together, until he becomes almost incapable of recognising any differences, or he reads Luke and Acts together and ignores Mark. Nevertheless Mark and Acts, not Luke and Acts, are our primary sources, and the historian ought undoubtedly to regard Luke as in the main a secondary source, and to take this fact into account in considering Acts. If this be done it becomes clear that the account in Acts is defective, because, by a kind of historical homoioteleuton, it leaves out a complete episode beginning and ending in Jerusalem. Of this episode there is no extant account, but Mark enables us to supply its outlines.[1]

HISTORICISTIC VENTURES

Merrill P. Miller's argument from "nonconsequences" in his reexamination of the place of the Jerusalem church in conceptualizations of Christian origins effectively exposes the problematic connection between the death of Jesus and the formation of the Jerusalem church as portrayed by Luke in the early chapters of Acts.[2] Yet Miller's voice echoes in a

---

[1] F. J. Foakes Jackson and Kirsopp Lake, eds., *The Beginnings of Christianity*, Part 1: *The Acts of the Apostles* (5 vols.; London: Macmillan, 1920–33; repr., Grand Rapids: Baker, 1979), 1:301–2. Of course, if Mark is "the origin for the Christian view of Christian origins" (Burton L. Mack, *A Myth of Innocence: Mark and Christian Origins* [Philadelphia: Fortress, 1988], 357), it will hardly serve as a historical corrective to Luke's picture.

[2] Merrill P. Miller, "'Beginning from Jerusalem...': Re-examining Canon and Consensus," *Journal of Higher Criticism* 2/1 (1995): 3–30.

scholarly wilderness in a period that has witnessed a strong surge of publications by modern advocates of the verisimilitude of Luke's second work, as if to guarantee the first Christian historian's credibility by sheer volume of printed pages.[3] Of course, we should be clear at the outset that it is a misnomer to suppose that Luke's modern "supporters" are in fact his heirs.

The recent commentary on Acts by Ben Witherington may briefly serve to typify current historicistic ventures.[4] Here the reality of the Jerusalem church is affirmed in exactly the terms laid out by Luke's narrative. The troublesome issue raised by Miller is never broached.[5] Witherington operates under the assumption that in Acts we confront the work of a "careful editor," who is limited by his source material just as he was in the Gospel:[6] "On the whole, Luke is not a very intrusive author, by which I mean he is not given to including a lot of his own comments, by way of parenthetical aside, in the text of Acts."[7] Thus both the narrative framework of the account of the birth of the Jerusalem church in Acts 2 and the speech delivered by Peter depend on source material.[8] Witherington presents a rather odd rationale for approaching the text in these terms: "Only the book of Acts records this story that we find in Acts 2, and this has seemed historically problematic to some scholars, even though Acts is the only Christian historical narrative we have from this period. For Luke, it is

---

[3] Chief among such works is Colin J. Hemer's *The Book of Acts in the Setting of Hellenistic History* (WUNT 49; Tübingen: Mohr Siebeck, 1989), which "seeks to build a compelling case for the historicity of the book of Acts on the basis of Luke's accuracy in matters of inconsequential detail as corroborated by external historical evidence" (to cite my review in *JBL* 109 [1990]: 726–29). Many following in Hemer's footsteps have contributed to the multivolume *The Book of Acts in Its First Century Setting* (ed. Bruce W. Winter; 6 vols.; Grand Rapids: Eerdmans; Carlisle: Paternoster, 1993–). Yet another recent collection of essays edited by I. Howard Marshall and David Peterson (*Witness to the Gospel: The Theology of Acts* [Grand Rapids: Eerdmans, 1998]) brings more of the same.

[4] Ben Witherington, *The Acts of the Apostles: A Socio-Rhetorical Commentary* (Grand Rapids: Eerdmans; Carlisle: Paternoster, 1998).

[5] The 875-page main text of the commentary makes no reference to Miller.

[6] Witherington, *Acts of the Apostles*, 111. That such a characterization for the author of Luke's Gospel is woefully inadequate should be the conclusion of any moderately careful reader's perusal of a Gospel synopsis. E.g., check the other columns for Luke 20:1 ("One day, as he was teaching the people in the temple...") and 21:37–38 ("Every day he was teaching in the temple...").

[7] Ibid., 120. This assessment, of course, ignores the fact that some one third of Luke's composition in Acts consists of speeches, in which we must presume that we find the formulations and opinions of the author. See Marion L. Soards, *The Speeches in Acts: Their Content, Context, and Concerns* (Louisville: Westminster John Knox, 1994).

[8] Witherington, *Acts of the Apostles*, 130 n. 5. Later even the summaries (2:42–47; 4:32–35; 5:12–16), though Lukan creations (ibid., 157), are taken as accurate representations of the Jerusalem church's communal life. On these summaries, see below.

clearly a critical event which sets in motion all that follows."[9] In fact, "it is quite clear that in crucial ways this event is *unique*."[10] The ways in which Witherington imagines his commentary to illuminate the sociorhetorical texture[11] of Acts may be illustrated by his observation on Peter's speech at Pentecost (Acts 2:14–41):

> Thus, here and in several similar speeches ... Luke follows [a] sort of archaizing practice by Septuagintalizing his source material. In doing this Luke shows himself concerned with the matter of suitability (προσω-ποποιία). Because he is presenting a Greek summary of a Jewish speech, perhaps even a speech originally in Aramaic spoken with a Galilean accent, he will nonetheless suit his presentation to the speaker and occasion by Septuagintalizing the summary.[12]

Before leaving Witherington in what he imagines to be the 30s of the Common Era, I must mention his take on Luke's fantastic claim that Peter's Pentecost speech resulted in three thousand converts (Acts 2:41). After suggesting that this figure may simply serve to indicate that a large number of Peter's listeners responded to his message, Witherington nevertheless argues with reference to the population of Jerusalem, the size of the temple precincts, and the ample water supply in Jerusalem (for the baptisms!) that the number is within the realm of possibility. Consequently, "it is wise not to dismiss such claims when hard evidence to the contrary does not exist."[13] It is instructive to reflect on Luke's numbers in conjunction with recent population-growth estimates for early Christianity. In his discussion of "the arithmetic of growth" in *The Rise of Christianity,* Rodney Stark projects that, based on an estimated Christian population between 5 and 7.5 million in the year 300, we may assume "that there were 1,000 Christians

---

[9] Ibid., 129–30.

[10] Ibid., 132, emphasis added.

[11] His method will not be confused with Vernon K. Robbins's sociorhetorical criticism as presented in *The Tapestry of Early Christian Discourse: Rhetoric, Society and Ideology* (London: Routledge, 1996); idem, *Exploring the Texture of Texts: A Guide to Socio-rhetorical Interpretation* (Valley Forge, Pa.: Trinity Press International, 1996).

[12] Witherington, *Acts of the Apostles,* 138. Compare Witherington's comment (ibid., 156) on Acts 2:40: "Whether Luke actually knew more of this speech, or whether, more likely, his source simply informed him there was a good deal more along the same lines, is not made clear."

[13] Ibid., 156. Similarly, Wolfgang Reinhardt ("The Population Size of Jerusalem and the Numerical Growth of the Jerusalem Church," in *The Book of Acts in Its Palestinian Setting* [ed. Richard Bauckham; vol. 4 of *The Book of Acts in Its First Century Setting;* Grand Rapids: Eerdmans; Carlisle: Paternoster, 1995], 265) concludes that "since there is ... no convincing theological interpretation of the figures 'about 3,000' and '(about) 5,000,' one will ... have to accept that Luke was dependent on a reliable transmission of these figures."

in the year 40" and "7,530 Christians in the year 100."[14] Thus Christians accounted for 0.0017 percent of the general population in the year 40 (based on a projected population for the Roman Empire of 60 million), and increased only to 0.0126 percent of the general population by the year 100.[15] It was only around the year 180, when "the total Christian population first passed the 100,000 mark, [that] there would finally have been enough Christians so that it is probable that traces of their existence would survive."[16] Keith Hopkins, who offers further observations based upon Stark's numbers, draws the obvious conclusion that "the statistical insignificance of Christians, in relation to the rest of the empire's population, allows us to complement and correct the perspective of surviving Christian writers."[17] While Hopkins focuses primarily upon Christian apologists after Luke, this numerical corrective highlights Luke's hyperbole in Acts with regard to the three thousand converts on the day of Pentecost, the five thousand believers by the time of Peter's first arrest (Acts 4:4), and the many thousands of Jewish believers in Jerusalem under James (21:20). While all such reconstructions of the early Christian population must remain speculative, and methodological questions may be raised with respect to Stark's procedures,[18] failure to err on the low side (e.g., the figures Stark suggests) in estimates of the number of early Christians would be yet one more way in which Lukan assumptions might continue to exercise control over reconstructions of early Christianity.[19]

Witherington's apologetic solution to the problem of sources in Acts, which assumes their ubiquitous presence,[20] blithely ignores the critical consensus on this issue that has stood for decades. Simply put, the possibility of reconstructing putative underlying written sources for Acts has been foreclosed by the thoroughly Lukan nature of the existing narrative.[21]

---

[14] Rodney Stark, *The Rise of Christianity: A Sociologist Reconsiders History* (Princeton: Princeton University Press, 1996), 5–6.

[15] See table 1.1: "Christian Growth Projected at 40 Percent per Decade," in ibid., 7.

[16] Ibid., 9.

[17] Keith Hopkins, "Christian Number and Its Implications," *JECS* 6 (1998): 195.

[18] E.g., Burton Mack, "Many Movements, Many Myths: Redescribing the Attractions of Early Christianities. Toward a Conversation with Rodney Stark" (review of Rodney Stark, *The Rise of Christianity: A Sociologist Reconsiders History*), *RelSRev* 25 (1999): 132–36. A brief "uncontrite" response from Stark appears within his "rejoinder" ("E Contrario," 259–67, esp. 260–61) to the essays on "Rodney Stark's *The Rise of Christianity*: A Discussion," *JECS* 6 (1998): 161–267.

[19] See Burton L. Mack, "A Jewish Jesus School in Jerusalem?" 254–55 (in this volume); Christopher R. Matthews, "Luke the Hellenist," in *Early Christian Voices: In Texts, Traditions, and Symbols. Essays in Honor of François Bovon* (ed. David H. Warren et al.; BibInt 66; Boston: Brill, 2003), 99–107.

[20] See Witherington, *Acts of the Apostles*, 165–73; cf. 480–86.

[21] See the classic presentation by Jacques Dupont, *The Sources of Acts: The Present Position* (trans. Kathleen Pond; London: Darton, Longman & Todd, 1964); see also Ernst Haenchen,

Yet as will become clear in the next section, even to approach Acts with this sober understanding of the source problem well in hand hardly guarantees that a more realistic assessment of the utility of Acts for historical reconstruction will ensue. As Miller has indicated, the Jerusalem church has remained "a category and root metaphor of the imagination of Christian origins"[22] even for those critical scholars who would eschew the accommodating commentary of Witherington. Rather than add a series of additional examples in this regard to the documentation that Miller has already provided, I will focus upon one critic who has already sought to identify what is historical in Acts. Then together we may deliberate on whether anything from the resulting catalogue has potential for clarifying our reimagination of the Jerusalem church.

ASSESSING THE HISTORICAL VALUE OF ACTS 1–8

Although the Acts account of the earliest beginnings of Christianity in Jerusalem is certainly incorrect, there can be no doubt that not long after the crucifixion of Jesus a considerable number of his followers, after having left the capital temporarily, established a church in Jerusalem which was of decisive importance for Christianity in and outside Palestine up to the time of the Jewish War.[23]

In 1987 Gerd Lüdemann presented a sustained critical attempt to assess the historical value of Acts.[24] In his introductory essay to this work,[25] after a brief overview of the history of scholarship on the question of the historical worth of Acts, he reformulates this issue in terms of the "historical value of the traditions in Acts."[26] Thus his aim "is to look at each individual

---

The Acts of the Apostles: A Commentary (trans. ed. R. McL. Wilson; Philadelphia: Westminster, 1971), 81–90, 117–21.

[22] Miller, "Beginning from Jerusalem," 3.

[23] Gerd Lüdemann, *Opposition to Paul in Jewish Christianity* (trans. M. Eugene Boring; Minneapolis: Fortress, 1989), 40.

[24] Gerd Lüdemann, *Das frühe Christentum nach den Traditionen der Apostelgeschichte: Ein Kommentar* (Göttingen: Vandenhoeck & Ruprecht, 1987); ET: *Early Christianity according to the Traditions in Acts: A Commentary* (trans. John Bowden; Minneapolis: Fortress, 1989).

[25] Another version of this introduction appears in Gerd Lüdemann, "Acts of the Apostles as a Historical Source," in *The Social World of Formative Christianity and Judaism: Essays in Tribute to Howard Clark Kee* (ed. Jacob Neusner et al.; Philadelphia: Fortress, 1988), 109–25.

[26] "We may not ask primarily about the historical value of Acts itself, but about the historical value of the traditions in Acts. If Luke has no personal idea of the events he describes, it would hardly be sensible ... to look for the historical value of Acts on the level of his narrative. Rather, Luke's activity as a writer consists in linking traditions together, i.e. of composing a consecutive narrative on the basis of traditions. It follows from this that the *first*

section to see the tradition which may possibly be contained in it and then if possible to give a reasoned judgment on its historical value."[27] Lüdemann understands his efforts to be a resumption of Foakes Jackson and Lake's five-volume project *The Beginnings of Christianity* inasmuch as his objective is to "investigate what historical facts can be gained from Acts which could be the basis for assured knowledge about earliest Christianity."[28] His preliminary conclusion that "Acts remains an important source for the history of early Christianity"[29] primarily reflects his investigations of the "Pauline" sections of Luke's work. Although he assumes that "in Acts 1–5 Luke relied on individual oral traditions from the early period of the Jerusalem community,"[30] he acknowledges that those sections of Acts that cannot be corroborated by Paul's letters "pose a special problem." It may be "possible only to reconstruct individual traditions, and in many cases judgments as to their historicity have a lesser degree of probability because our possibilities of controlling them are less."[31]

Lüdemann's procedure is to analyze the text of Acts, section by section, according to a four-part schema: (1) structure and outline of content, (2) redactional-critical analysis, (3) identification of traditional elements, and (4) indication of the historical worth of the isolated traditions. So let's cut to the chase: What does Lüdemann place under the rubric "historical" in Acts 1:1–8:3?

Acts 1:1–14

Oddly enough, first among the items to emerge as historical are the Jerusalem appearances of the risen Jesus.[32] Of course, for Lüdemann such "visions" are accounted for by "psychological processes" leading to "mass psychoses," so that "the assumption of a resurrection of Jesus is completely unnecessary as a presupposition to explain these phenomena."[33] While we might ask how the tradition of appearances of Jesus is to be dealt with in a redescription of Christian origins (in anthropological terms)

---

task is to separate redaction and tradition. The *second* task is to discover the historical value of the tradition" (Lüdemann, *Early Christianity*, 9, emphasis original).

[27] Ibid., 19.
[28] Ibid.
[29] Ibid., 17.
[30] Ibid., 22.
[31] Ibid., 17–18.
[32] "There were in fact appearances of the heavenly Jesus in Jerusalem (after those in Galilee)" (ibid., 29–30).
[33] Gerd Lüdemann with Alf Özen, *What Really Happened to Jesus: A Historical Approach to the Resurrection* (trans. John Bowden; Louisville: Westminster John Knox, 1995), 130. Of course, appeal to the notion of "mass psychoses" again shows the influence of Acts in terms of the numbers involved.

if Lüdemann's solution is not adopted, this issue principally concerns texts other than Acts.

Also judged historical is "the expectation of the imminent restoration of the kingdom to Israel through the parousia of Jesus,"[34] which, in Lüdemann's estimation, both accounts for the continued presence of Jewish Christianity in Jerusalem as well as its reluctant acceptance of the Gentile mission. But just as alternative explanations can be advanced to explain these last two phenomena, it must be acknowledged that factors arising in a period after the 30s and 40s may also account for the interest here in "kingdom expectation."

Finally in this opening section, the names of the disciples and the presence of women in "the earliest Jerusalem community" are taken to be facts.[35] Here we simply encounter a repetition of information from the Synoptic Gospels, and, as Lüdemann readily admits, the presence of women cannot be ascertained on the basis of 1:13–14. Already it is clear that Lüdemann simply assumes the existence of an "earliest Jerusalem community," which seems to subsist as the singular collective heir of Jesus; no other Jesus/Christ groups provide competition for this Jerusalem church.

Acts 1:15–26

In this section, after an affirmation of the historicity of Judas,[36] we encounter the key claim underlying the establishment of the Jerusalem church, namely, that "Peter ... reorganized the group of twelve founded by Jesus in Galilee and ... brought them with him to Jerusalem. In due course it was replaced by the group of apostles, which was constituted by a christophany (I Cor.15.7: the Jerusalem apostolate)."[37] There is no elaboration on the reasons motivating Peter's move to Jerusalem. Still, the notion that a group of Galilean Jesus people took up residence in Jerusalem is one that we need to talk about,[38] even though there is barely a shred of data in Acts 1 to assist us in our deliberations. Although we do not depend on

---

[34] Lüdemann, *Early Christianity*, 30.

[35] "The names of the disciples of Jesus are for the most part certainly historical.... The existence of women disciples as members of the earliest Jerusalem community is also a historical fact" (ibid., 31).

[36] "The disciple Iscariot is without doubt a historical person ... [who] made a decisive contribution to delivering Jesus into the hands of the Jewish authorities" (ibid., 35–36). Acts reprises the role of Judas in the death of Jesus as found in the Gospel tradition and reports the "fate of the traitor" also in dependence upon that tradition, which seemingly continues to undergo embellishment. Haenchen (*Acts of the Apostles*, 163) suggests that Luke here echoes "Palestinian traditions."

[37] Lüdemann, *Early Christianity*, 36.

[38] See Mack, *Myth of Innocence*, 89, quoted below at the head of the third section of this essay.

Acts for knowledge of the Twelve, we still must decide where this group comes from and what its significance is for the earliest period.[39] While the portrayal of the completion of the number of the Twelve (1:20–26) does not inspire historical confidence,[40] it clearly plays into Luke's program (a reconstitution of Israel in Jerusalem).[41]

ACTS 2:1–13

Although doubting that the specification "Pentecost" belongs to the tradition, Lüdemann supposes, on the basis of references to glossolalia in Paul's letters and the ecstatic prophecy of Philip's daughters (Acts 21:9), that "we may certainly regard a happening of the kind described by the tradition behind vv.1–4 as very possible." He connects the five hundred of 1 Cor 15:6 with this tradition, even while noting that there is a problem between "the large number 500 and the scene of the phenomenon 'in the house,' which allows only a far smaller number."[42]

ACTS 2:14–47

While the present form of the events portrayed in this section is judged to be "certainly unhistorical," four components of the scene are advanced as possibly preserving valuable information: (1) Peter's leadership role in the Jerusalem community; (2) the use of Joel 2:32 (3:5 LXX) as a proof text "at a very early stage"; (3) the employment of Ps 110 (109 LXX) "in christological discussions at a very early stage"; and (4) the gathering of the Jerusalem community "in common breaking of the bread" and for "instruction by the apostles."[43] With respect to this last item, however, "we cannot

---

[39] Lüdemann (*Early Christianity*, 36) contends that unless the Twelve go back to Jesus, problems with chronology arise, since "the group would have had to have lost its significance not long after it was formed."

[40] "One is ... inclined to challenge the historicity of the election of Matthias.... This does not mean, though, that the Jerusalem Christians Matthias and Joseph were not historical figures" (ibid., 37). As Haenchen (*Acts of the Apostles*, 164) notes: "It is striking that Jesus himself should not have appointed the new Apostle during the forty days."

[41] Haenchen (*Acts of the Apostles*, 164) situates Luke's understanding of the Twelve upon an even larger canvas when he observes that "when Luke presents the 'twelve Apostles' as the leaders of the congregation in the earliest times, he is reproducing the picture of the primitive Church which he himself—and most probably the rest of the Christian community—had before his eyes about the year 80.... What Luke offers is the late form of the tradition about 'the Apostles.'"

[42] Lüdemann, *Early Christianity*, 43.

[43] Ibid., 48–49, adding: "The instruction by the apostles is also to be accepted as historical, since in the early period of the Jerusalem community the apostles had a leading role. So Paul can speak of those who were apostles before him (in Jerusalem!, Gal.1.17)" (49). Of course, to avoid confusion one must distinguish between Paul's reference to these apostles and Luke's twelve apostles.

completely exclude the other possibility, that Luke, like Paul (Rom.12.12f.), is using paraenetic traditions from the Pauline mission sphere and prematurely transferring them to the Jerusalem community."[44] In this last scenario Lüdemann is forced to admit that there would be no grounds for seeking historical information concerning the assembled activities of the Jerusalem church in Acts 2:42–47.

Lüdemann locates the use of Joel 2:32 (3:5 LXX) as a proof text "at a very early stage" on the basis of its employment by Paul in Rom 10:13 and 1 Cor 1:2. While such use obviously antedates Luke, its origin in the first years of the Jerusalem group is by no means assured. Similarly, the use of Ps 110 at a "very early stage" still may not be early enough for our purposes. In fact, whenever we encounter the citation of scriptural passages in the speeches of Acts, it is more likely that we are coming into contact with Luke's concerns rather than uncovering the building blocks of early Christian thought in some unmediated form.[45]

Although the notion that one might find concrete data on the earliest Jerusalem church in Luke's summary statements (Acts 2:42–47; 4:32–35; 5:12–16) is difficult to sustain, this has not stopped proponents of such a view. For example, S. Scott Bartchy seeks to overturn Hans Conzelmann's assessment of the "idealized" character of the sharing of property in the Jerusalem church with an exegesis of Acts 2, 4, and 5 based on a "fictive-kinship understanding of interpersonal relationships" that makes it clear that "the texts describe recognizable social realities."[46] For Bartchy, it follows that once one recognizes that the "Jewish Christian community in Jerusalem" was a fictive kin group characterized by "radical inclusiveness," Luke's entire outline of the development of the early church up through the inclusion of "some hellenized Jews into the new kin group" makes

---

[44] Ibid., 48.

[45] E.g., Giuseppe Betori ("Luke 24:47: Jerusalem and the Beginning of the Preaching to the Pagans in the Acts of the Apostles," in *Luke and Acts* [ed. Gerald O'Collins and Gilberto Marconi; New York: Paulist, 1991], 103–20) suggests that Luke takes advantage of the "universalism" in Joel 2:28–32 (3:1–5 LXX) to provide an "interpretative key" for the Pentecost event. "The result is a salvation extended not to the members of a particular people but to 'everyone who (*pas hos*) calls upon the name of the Lord' (J[oe]l 3:5a = Acts 2:21).... And it is perhaps in this text, Joel 3:5b, which locates the saving event *en tô orei Siôn kai en Ierousalêm*, that we have the Old Testament text to which Luke 24:47 is referring when it says that the preaching of salvation to all nations begins in Jerusalem" (116). In all of this, Betori still assumes that Luke remained "faithful to the historical data" in the first chapters of Acts (119).

[46] S. Scott Bartchy, "Community of Goods in Acts: Idealization or Social Reality?" in *The Future of Early Christianity: Essays in Honor of Helmut Koester* (ed. Birger A. Pearson et al.; Minneapolis: Fortress, 1991), 315. Conzelmann's excursus on "the sharing of property" is found in idem, *Acts of the Apostles: A Commentary on the Acts of the Apostles* (Hermeneia; Philadelphia: Fortress, 1987), 24.

sense: "Thus I conclude that in Acts 2:42–47 and 4:32–5:11, Luke uses language that echoes Greek utopian hopes to describe the actual meeting of individual needs among the Jewish Christians in the Jerusalem housechurches by means of their pervasive acts of sharing, which Luke believed had indeed happened."[47] Ernst Haenchen's earlier judgment, however, that "the summaries appear to flow entirely from the pen of Luke" has, not surprisingly, been confirmed by more recent studies.[48] Gregory E. Sterling concludes that Luke used well-known literary descriptions of religious and philosophical groups as a model for presenting the Jerusalem community.[49] Thus the summaries will not contribute anything to a database of dependable historical information about the earliest Christians in Jerusalem.

ACTS 3:1–26

For the possible historical material here, Lüdemann offers both early and late scenarios. (One wonders whether there is anything in the early chapters of Acts that would not be amenable to such equivocation.) Nothing appears to be "assured." The miracle story in 3:1–10 "reflects the existence of a Christian community which reported great things of Peter's activity in Jerusalem and/or miracles performed by him."[50] Lüdemann suggests that the "development of the tradition will have to be imagined as having taken place in the first ten years after the crucifixion of Jesus, when Peter took over the leadership of the community in Jerusalem and probably also did 'wonders' there ... or even at a later time, when Peter was regarded as one of the leading figures of early Christianity." Verses 19–21 can either "be connected with the earliest Christianity in Jerusalem" or be seen "as a reflection on the delay of the *parousia* which would have led to an intensified call upon Israel for repentance," in which case its origin would be later.[51]

ACTS 4:1–31

> Despite what is in other respects the negative result of the historical analysis of the traditions in Acts 3–4.31, the question remains whether Luke's general knowledge of this period of the earliest community is of historical value. We should probably answer this in the affirmative,

---

[47] Bartchy, "Community of Goods," 315, 317, 318.
[48] Haenchen, *Acts of the Apostles*, 195. On Luke's composition of the summaries, see Maria Anicia Co, "The Major Summaries in Acts: Acts 2,42–47; 4,32–35; 5,12–16. Linguistic and Literary Relationship," *ETL* 68 (1992): 49–85; Gregory E. Sterling, "'Athletes of Virtue': An Analysis of the Summaries in Acts (2:41–47; 4:32–35; 5:12–16)," *JBL* 113 (1994): 679–96.
[49] Sterling, "Athletes of Virtue," 688–96.
[50] Lüdemann, *Early Christianity*, 54.
[51] Ibid., 54–55.

because his depiction of the conflict between the earliest community and the priestly nobility rests on correct historical assumptions. For the missionary activity of the earliest community in Jerusalem not long after the crucifixion of Jesus may have alarmed Sadducaean circles ... so that they might at least have prompted considerations about action against the Jesus community.[52]

Lüdemann then refers to the action against James in 62 C.E. At this point we can advert to Miller's argument from nonconsequences to deal with the gap that Lüdemann has collapsed between the crucifixion and the year 62; perhaps we should also invoke some corollary of the "Karl May rule" here to deal with the argument from "correct historical assumptions" (including assumptions about "missionary activity").[53] On the one hand, Lüdemann sees the narrative framework of 3:1–4:31 as "based on some accurate historical foundations, i.e. on facts." On the other hand, he asks whether Luke himself has not constructed his narrative framework "on the basis of the Gospel of Mark."[54]

ACTS 4:32–37

Lüdemann asserts that "there can hardly be any doubt about the historicity of Barnabas' sale of a field in favour of the Jerusalem community.... However, it is impossible to decide when the sale of the field for the community was made."[55]

ACTS 5:1–11

Lüdemann suggests that the Ananias and Sapphira "tradition probably came into being in the Jerusalem community, at its earliest period, when Peter was its leader," and that an event analogous to 1 Cor 5:1–13 "seems to underlie this as a historical nucleus."[56] He does not suppose that it is certain that anyone died as a result of the cursing. It is surprising that here

---

[52] Ibid., 60.

[53] Karl May (1842–1912) was a German novelist of American Indian culture (see further at http://karlmay.leo.org/ and http://german.about.com/library/blkmaylinks.htm). Hans Conzelmann observes (idem and Andreas Lindemann, *Interpreting the New Testament: An Introduction to the Principles and Methods of N.T. Exegesis* [trans. Siegfried S. Schatzmann; Peabody, Mass.: Hendrickson, 1988], 36), with reference to those who find Luke's version of Jesus in Nazareth (Luke 4:16–30) historically more reliable than the accounts of Matthew or Mark, that "it is good to remember an observation known as the 'Karl May rule' ... i.e., that an accurate description of the milieu and/or the broad rendition of verbatim speech proves nothing at all relative to the historicity or 'exactness' of the events told." Lüdemann (*Early Christianity*, 11) refers to this "rule" as Conzelmann applied it to Acts.

[54] Lüdemann, *Early Christianity*, 60.

[55] Ibid., 63.

[56] Ibid., 66.

in particular no alternative to the notion of a historical nucleus is offered, as is the case elsewhere.

ACTS 5:12–16
All redaction.

ACTS 5:17–42
"The Jewish reference to Deut.21.22f. was a counter-argument to the Christian thesis of the messiahship of Jesus."[57] But at what date?

ACTS 6:1–7

> There is almost universal consensus among scholars that the Hellenists are Greek-speaking Jews and the Hebrews Aramaic-speaking Jews of Jerusalem.... There was some controversy ... between the two parties in Jerusalem in the early period of the primitive community, although no further information about the nature of the conflict is available on the basis of the tradition contained in vv.1–6.[58]

Lüdemann thinks that, if the tradition in this section is genetically related to the tradition in 6:8–7:1, then we can conclude that the conflict was over the law. "This dispute took place in the early period of the primitive community in Jerusalem, since Paul was already persecuting members of this group of Hellenists outside Jerusalem and no longer found them in Jerusalem during his first visit."[59]

It has certainly been a scholarly commonplace to suppose that Luke has disguised a serious controversy between two segments of the early Christian community in Acts 6:1–7 for the sake of his portrayal of the essential unity of the early Jerusalem church.[60] Craig C. Hill has challenged this widely held view, holding that "the church of Jerusalem was not divided into ideological groups corresponding to the designations 'Hellenist' and 'Hebrew.'"[61] The terms are taken to indicate linguistic differences.[62] Hill argues that the "evidence we possess points to an ongoing

---

[57] Ibid., 72.
[58] Ibid., 78.
[59] Ibid., 79.
[60] See, e.g., Haenchen, *Acts of the Apostles*, 266; Conzelmann, *Acts of the Apostles*, 44.
[61] Craig C. Hill, *Hellenists and Hebrews: Reappraising Division within the Earliest Church* (Minneapolis: Fortress, 1992), 191.
[62] Hill (ibid., 22–24) follows Martin Hengel ("Between Jesus and Paul: The 'Hellenists,' the 'Seven' and Stephen [Acts 6.1–15; 7.54–8.3]," in *Between Jesus and Paul: Studies in the Earliest History of Christianity* [trans. John Bowden; Philadelphia: Fortress, 1983], 4–11) in the assumption that the point of the terminology is to distinguish Greek speakers from Hebrew/

diversity of opinion within the church of Jerusalem."[63] Yet his presentation continues to assume a "mother church" in Jerusalem[64] as well as the existence of "Hellenists." Martin Bodinger, on the other hand, argues that the names "Hebrews" and "Hellenists" have nothing to do with the languages spoken by members of the earliest Christian communities but stem from the terminology of Luke's day. Thus the Hellenists do represent a Hellenist ideology, and their presence in Acts functions to legitimate the Gentile mission. They promote Luke's notion of the development of Christianity by serving as examples for the presence of nonorthodox Jews among the followers of Jesus, thus preparing the way for the introduction of Stephen, Philip, and Paul, and so finally accounting for the conversion of the Gentiles. Consequently, in historical terms, they are neither a bridge between the Jewish Christianity of Jerusalem and the Gentile converts of the diaspora nor a bridge between Jesus and Paul but rather an example of the universalism of the church, conformed to Pauline theology, inserted into the narrative to prefigure later disputes.[65] Whatever we decide about the "Hellenists," it does seem reasonable to assume that Stephen and especially Philip in some way were prominent figures among early followers of Jesus who did not fit into Luke's understanding of a Jerusalem church.

ACTS 6:8–15

> The tradition of the presence in Jerusalem of the groups named in v.9 has a good deal to be said for it historically.... [But] the dispute will have arisen in one Hellenistic synagogue community to which Stephen belonged.... The issue was Stephen's critical view of the law, to which his opponents took offence.... [T]he tradition about Stephen which is twice presented by Luke as false witness has a historical basis ... [so] we must cautiously conclude that Stephen criticized the law and the temple.[66]

In fact, "we do not know where Stephen himself came from."[67] Along with most scholarship on Acts 6–7, Lüdemann assumes that one consequence of the dispute with Stephen "was a partial separation of Judaism and Christianity in Jerusalem, as the Hellenists were expelled from the capital."[68] Yet

---

Aramaic speakers. Hill does not, however, understand the Hellenists as a "bridge" to Paul (see *Hellenists and Hebrews*, 193–94).

[63] Hill, *Hellenists and Hebrews*, 194.
[64] Ibid., 144.
[65] Martin Bodinger, "Les 'Hébreux' et les 'Hellénistes' dans le livre des *Actes des Apôtres*," *Hen* 19 (1997): 39–58.
[66] Lüdemann, *Early Christianity*, 84–85.
[67] Haenchen, *Acts of the Apostles*, 271.
[68] Lüdemann, *Early Christianity*, 85.

172   Christopher R. Matthews

it is more likely that this expulsion should be recognized as a narrative device to forward Luke's plot (see below).

ACTS 7:1–53
All redaction.

ACTS 7:54–8:3
"Stephen's criticism of law and cult are to be regarded as historical. The expulsion of those of like mind from Jerusalem is the best reason for such an assumption."[69]

LUKE'S TRUE FICTION

> Some of his followers apparently saw a connection between Jesus' activity in Galilee and his fate in Jerusalem.... Attention could have shifted from the kingdom of God as it sounded in Galilee to very big thoughts about what it might mean for Jerusalem.... The very fact that the pillars took up residence in Jerusalem does indicate designs upon the religious history of Palestine.[70]

> Paul, prone to extremes, wanted to think that the (Gentile) Christianity, to which he had been converted (as a conservative Jew), started in the capital city of Pharisaic religion. Luke picked up on this idea even though by his time the pillars in Jerusalem were no longer there.[71]

Luke's understanding of Jerusalem participates in an intertexture of other symbolic cartographies that place Jerusalem at the center of the world on the basis of: (1) the table-of-nations tradition in Gen 10 (see *Jub.* 8–10); (2) its status as "mother city" to the diaspora (Philo, *Legatio ad Gaium*); and (3) its eschatological destiny (Ezek 38:10–12; *Ps. Sol.* 11.1–3, 7; *1 En.* 26.1; *Sib. Or.* 5.249–50).[72] But ultimately for Luke, Jerusalem

---

[69] Ibid., 93.
[70] Mack, *Myth of Innocence*, 89.
[71] Ibid., 88.
[72] Here I summarize the presentation of Mikeal C. Parsons, "The Place of Jerusalem on the Lukan Landscape: An Exercise in Symbolic Cartography," in *Literary Studies in Luke-Acts: Essays in Honor of Joseph B. Tyson* (ed. Richard P. Thompson and Thomas E. Phillips; Macon, Ga.: Mercer University Press, 1998), 155–71; see pp. 164–67 for his discussion of the implied reader's familiarity with the above-listed "options for 'locating' Jerusalem." Note also Peder Borgen's observations on "Philo, Luke and Geography," in *Philo, John and Paul: New Perspectives on Judaism and Early Christianity* (BJS 131; Atlanta: Scholars Press, 1987), 273–85, and his comment that "the central and universal role played by Jerusalem in Luke and Philo is due, of course, to the fact that both represent the geographical outlook of Diaspora Judaism" (280).

served a vital purpose unrelated to modern historical concerns with precisely documenting origins. Luke needed to document the consistent action of God in history:

> Luke was concerned to show that Christianity had its roots in the people of God, the children of Israel.... By showing that in the nascent period the gospel was closely related to the most important physical symbols of Judaism [Jerusalem and the temple], his description of Christianity as emerging from Jewish roots is enhanced. The reader of Luke-Acts cannot conclude that the group of people who came to be called Christians had no ties with the historic people of God.[73]

It would appear that Luke's aims in writing have little to do with our desires to reconstruct what happened in the earliest years of the Christian movements. Nevertheless, there are a few indications that some of the traditional materials that Luke has inserted into his narrative of the earliest church reflect "origins" apart from Jerusalem.

We may briefly note Stephen's reference in Acts 7:4 to Abraham's move "to this country in which you are now living," which distinguishes Stephen from his audience, suggesting that Stephen was not a resident of Jerusalem. Daniel R. Schwartz uses this observation to propose that Stephen "is portrayed as a Diasporan Jew in Jerusalem.... Thus, Stephen's audience was composed of *residents* of Judaea, while he was only visiting."[74] For Schwartz this raises the question "whether [the] Hellenists were residents or visitors in Jerusalem."[75] Allow me to forgo further discussion of "the Hellenists" at this point (see above) and simply note that our question is whether Luke betrays any use of traditional information in 7:4.

We know of Stephen on account of his violent death, which it is reasonable to assume was a part of early Christian tradition. Luke chose to identify this death as the precipitating event that first pushed the "witnesses" (Acts 1:8) outside Jerusalem. Luke thus exploits the irony that a "severe persecution" (8:1) fanned the flames of the spreading movement. Only the ideological/theological necessity that the apostles remain in Jerusalem (8:1) spoils the realism of Luke's literary device. The presence

---

[73] J. Bradley Chance, *Jerusalem, the Temple, and the New Age in Luke-Acts* (Macon, Ga.: Mercer University Press, 1988), 150. The five chapters of Chance's monograph serve to highlight Luke's strategy of portraying "a literal Jerusalem and a literal temple as important centers of God's eschatological salvation" in order "to show that the Jewish and Old Testament hope centering upon Jerusalem and the temple was not a vain one" (ibid.).

[74] Daniel R. Schwartz, "Residents and Exiles, Jerusalemites and Judaeans (Acts 7:4; 2:5, 14): On Stephen, Pentecost and the Structure of Acts," in idem, *Studies in the Jewish Background of Christianity* (WUNT 60; Tübingen: Mohr Siebeck, 1992), 119–20, emphasis original.

[75] Ibid., 121.

of Saul at Stephen's death (7:58) and his subsequent embodiment of the persecution (8:3; a narrative depiction of the information in Gal 1:13) obviously sets up the further ironic reversal in Acts 9:1–30. What is fascinating for our purposes are the traditional examples Luke turns to in the interim in order to illustrate the "proclamation of the word" (8:4) initiated by the persecution. All the weight falls on two traditional pieces about Philip, erstwhile member of the Seven (6:5). Luke first employs a traditional report about Philip's activities in Samaria (8:5–13).[76] Then he composes a fresh scene in 8:14–25 in order to demonstrate the involvement of Jerusalem and the apostles in this initial expansion of the Christian congregation beyond Jerusalem (this motif recurs in 11:1–18 and 11:22–24). Next Luke incorporates a traditional story (8:26–39) that portrays in legendary form Philip's encounter with a cultic misfit (owing to castration) from Ethiopia ("the ends of the earth").[77] Leaving the details of these Philip traditions aside, what is notable with respect to our current project is that when Luke wants to illustrate a "breakthrough moment" in the spread of Christianity, he ends up using stories that have no necessary association with Jerusalem. The latter connection depends upon Luke's obviously redactional framework. Thus by adopting these Philip traditions, Luke has preserved some evidence that there were other "Jesus people" out and about who were not following a program from Jerusalem. Luke's notes on Philip's further itinerary (Acts 8:40; Azotus and up the coast to Caesarea) and his eventual residence in Caesarea (21:8) suggest nothing to the contrary.

* * * * *

Luke's reconstruction of the Jerusalem church was a historical exercise methodologically unencumbered by modern standards of documentation. The challenge was to produce an account of Christian origins that would show how those beginnings clarified and confirmed the social and cultural situation of Christians in Luke's time. While Luke's "sense-making interests" in combination with the practice of historiography as "truthful fiction" is a disappointment for those seeking the "facts," the myth of origins that Acts presents can only be admired in terms of the ideological negotiation it represents for Luke's time. That later readers, divorced from the various

---

[76] In its pre-Lukan form this report seems to have functioned as a propagandistic trump over a local semidivine wonderworker named Simon, who later graduates to the head of his gnostic class. For my understanding of tradition and redaction in Acts 8:4–25, see Christopher R. Matthews, *Philip: Apostle and Evangelist. Configurations of a Tradition* (NovTSup 105; Leiden: Brill, 2002), 35–70.

[77] The details are treated in ibid., 71–94.

intertextualities that conspired in the composition of the Lukan corpus, adopted Luke's work for novel purposes should hardly be a cause for reproach toward the author of Acts.

Antioch, Paul, and Jerusalem:
Diaspora Myths of Origins in the Homeland

Merrill P. Miller

In 1984 a collection of essays was published honoring Francis Wright Beare and devoted to raising again the problem of the relation between Jesus and Paul.[1] In his contribution to that volume, Lloyd Gaston explored the different theologies of Paul and the Jerusalem church.[2] Following is a summary of those differences as Gaston sees them. (1) The Jerusalem church understood the death of Jesus to be "for our sins" (1 Cor 15:3; Gal 1:4a; Rom 4:25; 3:25). Paul, on the other hand, speaks of Christ being given up, crucified, made sin, made a curse "for us, for you, for persons, and never for our sins" (cf. Rom 8:3). Atonement means for Paul "not a way of dealing with sins but a one-time act of incorporating Gentiles into the body of Christ" at baptism. "We know little of the significance of baptism for the Jerusalem church; it may even have consisted in repeated lustrations." (2) The Jerusalem church conceived of the significance of Christ in terms of covenant or of renewed covenant, while "Paul never uses this concept." (3) "The righteousness of God effects the forgiveness of sins" for the Jerusalem church, while for Paul "it refers to the incorporation of Gentiles into the people of God." (4) The Jerusalem church spoke of Jesus as the Messiah, but Paul does not. His basic confession is that Jesus is Lord. "For Paul, Jesus relates neither to David nor to Moses

---

[1] Peter Richardson and John C. Hurd, eds., *From Jesus to Paul: Studies in Honour of Francis Wright Beare* (Waterloo, Ont.: Wilfrid Laurier University Press, 1984).

[2] Lloyd Gaston, "Paul and Jerusalem," in Richardson and Hurd, *From Jesus to Paul*, 61–72. Note that in this essay I do not use the term *church* to refer to the Jesus people in Jerusalem except when I am citing or discussing the work and views of others who do use the term. I do not think there are good grounds to suppose that followers of Jesus in Jerusalem applied the term ἐκκλησία to their own community. Moreover, I do not consider the use of the term to be in the interests of a redescription of the Jerusalem group, since it has the unfortunate effect of taking as matters already settled the very issues that need to be raised concerning mutual interests, shared assumptions, and common message among groups that related themselves to Jesus in some way.

but to Adam and to Abraham. Jesus is not the climax of the history of Israel nor the fulfillment of the covenant [as he is for the Jerusalem church] but the one who overcomes the powers which enslave the creation by fulfilling the promises of God concerning Gentiles." (5) "For Paul, Jesus is not only the revelation of God's eschatological activity [as he is for the Jerusalem church] but of God himself."[3]

These differences are clearly significant to Gaston. He even refers to them as different "patterns of religion," making use of a conception E. P. Sanders applied to distinguish Pauline Christianity from what Sanders conceived to be the normative religious pattern of Palestinian Judaism.[4] Would it be too much, then, to conclude that Gaston conceives the different theologies of the Jerusalem church and Paul as expressions of different religions? His conclusion is in fact interesting both for what it notes as well as for its extreme ambivalence: "The theology of Paul and the theology of Jerusalem are completely different, and yet Paul can say they are the same (1 Cor. 15:11) and that each acknowledged the position of the other (Gal. 2:1–10)."[5] How shall we take the notion of Gaston in light of the notion of Paul? Gaston remarks:

> Yet there was such a common core of conviction that many of the differences we have outlined may not have been seen by the first-century participants.... Perhaps we should speak of transmutations rather than differences. Paul pays tribute to the gospel of the Jerusalem church and is grateful to it for "spiritual blessings" which flow to the Gentiles (Rom. 15:27). At the same time, the common kerygma spoken in a different situation takes on a greatly transformed significance.[6]

Finally, Gaston notes, "If Paul can have such a different 'pattern of religion' from that of the Jerusalem church, how much more different would his 'pattern' be from the teaching of Jesus."[7]

Which way should we go? If the different theologies of the Jerusalem church and Paul amount to different patterns of religion, then surely from

---

[3] Ibid., 71.

[4] Ibid., 70. See E. P. Sanders, "Patterns of Religion in Paul and Rabbinic Judaism: A Holistic Method of Comparison," *HTR* 66 (1973): 455–78; idem, *Paul and Palestinian Judaism: A Comparison of Patterns of Religion* (Philadelphia: Fortress, 1977). Gaston is not concerned to describe more closely Sanders's concept *pattern of religion*, but in fact the way he draws on it raises the problem of what the concept means and its usefulness for the enterprise of comparison. In this connection, see Jonathan Z. Smith, "In Comparison a Magic Dwells," in idem, *Imagining Religion: From Babylon to Jonestown* (CSHJ; Chicago: University of Chicago Press, 1982), 33–34, 141.

[5] Gaston, "Paul and Jerusalem," 71.

[6] Ibid., 72.

[7] Ibid.

the scholar's vantage point and distance we must be prepared to speak of different Christianities, or of something that is Christianity and something that is not, or of different Judaisms. We might go even further down this road. If there was a considerable degree of mutual recognition despite these differences, what sort of theological differences would have prevented mutual recognition? If Gaston had concluded that their theologies were even more completely different than what he has outlined, would we then need to conclude that there would have been no basis for mutual recognition? Perhaps what we should conclude from Gaston's distinction between what we see and what they saw is that different "theologies" had no determinative bearing on relations between individuals or groups. But the other way to go is surely more common. Their "completely different" theologies are not really completely different at all. The initial description is phased out and replaced with the term "transmutations," or what are usually thought of as hermeneutical variations on a common kerygma. The shared features of the kerygma are standard fare in discussions of Christian origins: an eschatological orientation confirmed by the resurrection of Jesus, the saving death of Jesus, and the confession of Jesus as the Messiah, a conviction that must have been presupposed, if not articulated and argued for, in Paul's use of the term *christos*. But if these are the grounds of mutual recognition, how can Gaston's list of theological transmutations be thought of as different patterns of religion? Gaston wants to retain a sense of distinctive theologies appropriate to different missions but not without appeal to a common kerygma.

The potential of Gaston's essay for coming to terms with the difficult problem of relating different and conflicting interests, contexts, and projects to issues of mutual recognition in earliest Christianity is vitiated by the notion of a common kerygma.[8] The set of issues that come to expression under the rubric *Paul and Jerusalem* have been taken up with the concerns of contemporary Jewish-Christian relations in view, seen as expressions of the unity and diversity of early Christianity, or treated with the expansion of Christianity in mind. None of these perspectives has provided an appropriate context from which to gain some comparative leverage in accounting for both conflict and mutual recognition in the social formations of earliest Christianity.

I

Comparative leverage may be gained by shifting Paul's autobiographical statements in Gal 1–2 and other Pauline texts bearing on the identity

---

[8] See the essays in Lloyd Gaston, *Paul and the Torah* (Vancouver: University of British Columbia Press, 1987).

of a Jerusalem group from the narrower context of Christian origins to the larger context of Mediterranean religions in their Hellenistic and Late Antique phases. To cite Jonathan Z. Smith's review essay on native cults in the Hellenistic period:

> The study of Hellenistic religions is, properly conceived, a study of the dynamics of religious persistence and change. Almost every religion in this period occurred in both its homeland and in diasporic centers.... With few exceptions each of these religions, originally tied to a specific geographical area and people, had traditions extending back centuries before the Hellenistic period.[9]

To view Christian origins as an instance of religious persistence and change is already to disqualify the claim of a foundational event or the appeal to an overwhelming personal experience in order to account for religious innovations. For our purposes, what is most important to note in Smith's essay is the typological distinction between three groups. Those belonging to the homeland remain tied to local loyalties and national temples, exhibit conscious archaism in the copying of old texts and in the revival of mythic images, and engage in a variety of responses to cultural and political domination. Diasporic centers tended to feature two circles typical of immigrant groups: a first circle of more recent immigrants whose membership was drawn largely from the ethnic group and who retained the traditional language, and a second circle composed mostly of second- or third-generation immigrants and converts speaking Greek.[10] Smith summarizes the distinctiveness of each group in the following way:

> To the native religionist, homeplace, the place to which one belongs, was an important religious category.... To the new immigrant in the diaspora, nostalgia for homeplace and cultic substitutes for the sacred center became the important religious categories.... To the thoroughly diasporic member, who may not even have belonged to the deity's ethnic group, freedom from place became a major religious category.[11]

---

[9] Jonathan Z. Smith, "Native Cults in the Hellenistic Period," *HR* 11 (1971): 236–37.
[10] Ibid., 237.
[11] Ibid., 238. Smith acknowledges his debt to Morton Smith for the typology summarized at the beginning of the essay; see Morton Smith, "Religions in Hellenistic Times," in *Dartmouth College Comparative Studies Center: Report of the 1965–1966 Seminar on Religions in Antiquity* (ed. Jacob Neusner; Hanover, N.H.: privately printed, 1966), esp. 158–63. Jonathan Z. Smith's model for the study of religions of Late Antiquity was initially developed as a way of testing the description of sacred space represented (especially in the work of Mircea Eliade) in the general history of religions. For a fuller statement, see the preface to Smith's book, *Map Is Not Territory: Studies in the History of Religions* (SJLA 23; Leiden: Brill, 1978; repr., Chicago: University of Chicago Press, 1993), xi–xv.

This threefold typology has a heuristic value for the thesis that I want to argue, first, because it suggests that we ought to expect that the homeland group, whatever the degree of Hellenization it may itself have undergone, will retain a distinctiveness vis-à-vis the two diaspora circles, and, second, because it suggests that the so-called Jerusalem church could have functioned ideologically as a substitute homeland for diaspora circles of Hellenistic Jews engaged in innovative social and cultic experiments and, therefore, from whom we might expect expressions of nostalgia and attachment but also of disdain and alienation. The thesis to be argued in this essay is that *any historical reconstruction of the Jerusalem group and its leaders to be won from the data of Paul's letters, in particular from Gal 1–2, must be wrested from competing mythic imaginations of "Jerusalem" of diaspora Jews engaged in projects of teaching, recruitment, and community formation among Jews and Gentiles in Hellenistic cities outside Palestine.*

A similar typology for Hellenistic religions has been presented by Luther H. Martin, who distinguishes the discourses and practices of piety, mystery, and gnosis.[12] In a recent paper Martin applies to Hellenistic religions the model of kinship and kingship forms of social organization developed by William Robertson Smith for Semitic societies and relates the categories of piety, mystery, and gnosis to differing forms of kinship societies.[13] *Piety* designates a system of right relationships, "conventional practices concerning home and family ... part of being at home in one's world under the rule of a family of gods ... [practices] ... articulated in terms of a particular locale or place and ... transmitted through local tradition." *Gnosis* is a discourse rooted in kinship claims of descent from a divine ancestor or deity.[14]

Martin focuses in particular on *mystery* cults and distinguishes two types of fictive kinship. First, there are groups of ethnic brothers banded together in a foreign land. Separated from traditional kin, they acquire kin identity by initiation. In the increasingly cosmopolitan atmosphere of successive empires these social groups gradually lost their character as ethnic brotherhoods, recruiting a wider membership.[15] The second type establishes kinship by means of adoption by a deity. "To the extent that

---

[12] Luther H. Martin, *Hellenistic Religions: An Introduction* (New York: Oxford University Press, 1987).

[13] Luther H. Martin, "Akin to the Gods or Simply One to Another? Comparison with Respect to Religions in Antiquity," in *Vergleichen und Verstehen in der Religionswissenschaft: Vorträge der Jahrestagung der DVRG vom 4. bis 6. Oktober 1995 in Bonn* (ed. Hans-Joachim Klimkeit; StOR 41; Wiesbaden: Harrassowitz, 1997), 146–60.

[14] Ibid., 153, citing idem, *Hellenistic Religions,* 11–12.

[15] Martin, "Akin to the Gods," 154.

the mysteries were in some sense fictive kinship groups, adoption, the juridical category of kinship recruitment, provided a natural model for the rites of initiation."[16] In Galatians, part of Paul's argument with opponents who have entered the community revolves around modes of establishing kinship. Paul seems to want to counter the notion of adoption of a foreigner into the ancestral group through a ritual that replicates the act of the ancestor by drawing on the notion of adoption by the deity. In Paul's argument, Christ is both the descendant to whom the promise applies (Gal 3:16) and the divine agent or divine ancestor whose redemptive death brings about the condition and status of υἱοθεσία (Gal 4:5).[17]

In his book *The Commerce of the Sacred,* Jack N. Lightstone compares the structural relations of taxonomies characteristic of the restoration temple of the early Second Commonwealth with those of Greco-Roman Judaism of the diaspora to show that they exhibit quite disparate structures of homologies.[18] Lightstone cites Philo for a diaspora perspective on Jerusalem: "While she [Jerusalem] ... is my native city [πατρίς] she is also the mother city [μητρόπολις] not of one country Judaea but of most of the others in virtue of the colonies sent out at divers times to the neighbouring lands" (*Legat.* 281 [Colson, LCL]).[19] While the focus of Philo's demography is on Jerusalem, his social universe does not cohere with the temple model of concentric circles of humanity ordered around the temple. As Lightstone notes:

> Philo views the demography of the Judaic world not as one in which most Jews inhabit a chaotic exile [which it would be in the perspective of the temple's cosmic and social space], but a world studded with "colonies" of that mother of all sacred space, Jerusalem. Here each community is in itself a locus of sacred order, given birth by the home city, to be sure, but also with independent access to order in the midst of chaos.[20]

However, we should also note that the passage cited above from Philo's *Legatio ad Gaium* is contained in a letter of petition purported to be written by King Herod Agrippa I to the emperor (*Legat.* 276–329). It is thus not surprising that the idealization of Jerusalem is modeled on the empire, for whatever the actual loyalties of diaspora Jews toward Jerusalem, temple,

---

[16] Ibid., 155.
[17] See ibid., 156.
[18] Jack N. Lightstone, *The Commerce of the Sacred: Mediation of the Divine among Jews in the Graeco-Roman Diaspora* (BJS 59; Chico, Calif.: Scholars Press, 1984).
[19] Ibid., 11.
[20] Ibid., 12.

and Torah, the synagogue communities were of course not in fact created or sustained as colonies of Jerusalem.[21]

Lightstone's thesis that the appropriate Judaic background of early Christianity is at least more directly diasporic than Palestinian, specifically, than rabbinic Judaism, focuses especially on evidence from the area of Syrian Antioch. The evidence of dispute concerning dietary observance in Galatians and Acts is attributed by Lightstone more to "the attraction of Jewish practices visible across the street in the local Jewish populous than ... [to] the sensibilities of Peter and James in Jerusalem."[22] The explanation for the close interaction of Christians and Jews for centuries in that area is "that Early Gentile Christianity and Graeco-Roman Judaism shared common structures ... each formed a significant part of the religio-cultural milieu of the other for an extended period of time."[23]

It is significant that this symbiosis should exist in the place that has a better claim to be the locus of the origins of Christianity than Jerusalem.[24] "We face then a situation in which the birthplace of Gentile Christianity and indeed Christianity as something distinct from Judaism remains at the same time the locus at which for centuries the sociology of the two 'distinct' groups remains most blurred." This is seen, however, as an understandable state of affairs: "For that place where a distinct Christian identity first emerged might well remain less secure in that distinctive self-definition

---

[21] Cf. Philo's statement in *Flacc*. 46 (Colson, LCL): "For so populous are the Jews that no one country can hold them ... and while they hold the Holy City where stands the sacred Temple of the most high God to be their mother city [μητρόπολιν], yet those which are theirs by inheritance from their fathers, grandfathers, and ancestors even farther back, are in each case accounted by them to be their fatherland [πατρίδας] in which they were born and reared, while to some of them they have come at the time of their foundation as immigrants to the satisfaction of the founders."

[22] Lightstone, *Commerce of the Sacred*, 98. Note that this is a quite different reading of the situation in Antioch than the usual inferences drawn from Galatians and Acts. See, for example, Wayne A. Meeks and Robert L. Wilken, *Jews and Christians in Antioch in the First Four Centuries of the Common Era* (SBLSBS 13; Missoula, Mont.: Scholars Press, 1978), 18: "Antioch at this earliest point in the church's history looks then like a place of compromise, a bridge between Jewish and gentile Christianity. Neither in Acts nor in Paul do we learn of any locally bred division between Jewish and gentile Christians; division occurs only at the instigation of certain people from Jerusalem."

[23] Lightstone, *Commerce of the Sacred*, 136–37. On the Jews of Antioch attracting Gentiles to their cult practices and incorporating them in some way into their community, see Josephus, *War* 7.3.3 §45. For different evaluations of this passage, see Shaye J. D. Cohen, "Respect for Judaism by Gentiles according to Josephus," *HTR* 80 (1987): 417; idem, "Crossing the Boundary and Becoming a Jew," *HTR* 82 (1989): 27; and Martin Goodman, *Mission and Conversion: Proselytizing in the Religious History of the Roman Empire* (Oxford: Clarendon, 1994), 87.

[24] Lightstone, *Commerce of the Sacred*, 138. On this point, Lightstone is following Meeks, among others; see Meeks and Wilken, *Jews and Christians in Antioch*, 13–18.

than places into which Gentile Christianity was imported ready made as it were."[25]

The recent renewal of interest in the private or voluntary associations of the Greco-Roman world carried on in the work of the Canadian Society of Biblical Studies seminar has succeeded in demonstrating the broad overlap of characteristics marking communal institutions outside those of state, city, and family.[26] Casting the net as widely as possible under a single category helps us to see the many ways in which Jewish and Christian social formations fit the normal range of constraints and opportunities in the wider Greco-Roman society. The breadth of the materials considered also raises in important and helpful ways issues of classification and differentiation.[27] A number of characteristics typically seen to differentiate early Christian groups from voluntary associations have been called into question, such as the exclusivity toward other deities, the degree of inclusivity of membership, and the translocal character of early Christianity. It is the latter characteristic in particular that has a bearing on relations between Paul, the church of Antioch, and the Jerusalem group.

The common notion that Christianity from its inception constituted a translocal movement in contrast to the strictly local character of private associations has recently been called into question by Richard S. Ascough. To the contrary, he argues that Christian congregations were essentially local groups with limited translocal connections, a characterization that he wants to show fits voluntary associations in general quite well.[28] Translocal links among voluntary associations can be assumed to have existed to some degree wherever trade unions or cult associations were established by foreigners.[29] Among recent immigrant populations the desire to

---

[25] Lightstone, *Commerce of the Sacred*, 138, 139.

[26] A collection of essays from that seminar is found in John S. Kloppenborg and Stephen G. Wilson, eds., *Voluntary Associations in the Graeco-Roman World* (London: Routledge, 1996). See also John S. Kloppenborg, "Edwin Hatch, Churches and *Collegia*," in *Origins and Method: Towards a New Understanding of Judaism and Christianity. Essays in Honour of John C. Hurd* (ed. Bradley H. McLean; JSNTSup 86; Sheffield: JSOT Press, 1993), 212–38; and the earlier study by Robert L. Wilken, "Collegia, Philosophical Schools, and Theology," in *The Catacombs and the Colosseum: The Roman Empire as the Setting of Primitive Christianity* (ed. Stephen Benko and John J. O'Rourke; Valley Forge, Pa.: Judson, 1971), 268–91.

[27] See the opening essay by Stephen G. Wilson, "Voluntary Associations: An Overview," in Kloppenborg and Wilson, *Voluntary Associations*, 1–15; for a useful taxonomy, see the essay by John S. Kloppenborg, "Collegia and *Thiasoi*: Issues in Function, Taxonomy and Membership," in Kloppenborg and Wilson, *Voluntary Associations*, 16–30.

[28] Richard S. Ascough, "Translocal Relationships among Voluntary Associations and Early Christianity," *JECS* 5 (1997): 223–41.

[29] Ibid., 228–30.

maintain in some manner the forms of worship of the homeland can be assumed, and there is in fact considerable evidence of this. Even at the height of its greatest expansion, the cult of Isis and Sarapis was in control of Egyptians in Rome and Athens.[30] But this should not necessarily be taken to mean that these cults in their foreign locales were essentially controlled from the native country of the cult rather than locally. Even in the case of Jews there is no evidence to suggest that loyalty to the Jerusalem temple and the voluntary paying of a tax for its maintenance made it possible for Jerusalem to regulate most of the activities of diaspora synagogues. Ascough himself may give a somewhat misleading impression when he says, "More significantly, an adherent of the cult of Isis and Sarapis was able to travel throughout the Empire and be received by the local Isiac group wherever he or she happened to be."[31] He refers to Lucius's move from Africa to Rome in Apuleius's *Metamorphoses* and notes that, while Lucius is initiated again in Rome, this was not a condition of his membership. According to George La Piana, whom Ascough cites for this reference in Apuleius,[32] "The autonomous character of each Isiac congregation is manifest from the fact that in order to be aggregated to the Roman Isiac group Lucius had to receive a double and higher initiation, though he had already been initiated in the province."[33] In a more definitive sense La Piana avers, "But whatever the feeling of kinship among the faithful, each city-group or congregation remained isolated and independent. This was true of all cults, both in Rome and in the provinces. They were never more than scattered groups ... each living its own life in a separate environment ... but all under the strict control of the law which kept them from becoming political associations."[34]

A translocal or federative structure of private associations in different cities would have transformed those associations into political organizations. Sandra Walker-Ramisch has written:

> In Graeco-Roman political organization, the autonomous nature of the city-states precluded the formation of an inter-city federative structure among the collegia.... While they may have offered *isopoliteia* (reciprocity of rights) between similar organizations (as between city-states), membership, like citizenship, was not transferable. Any groups which begin to develop a trans-city organization would have been perceived as

---

[30] Ascough refers in particular on these matters to George La Piana, "Foreign Groups in Rome during the First Centuries of the Empire," *HTR* 20 (1927): 183–403, esp. 304–5, 308.
[31] Ascough, "Translocal Relationships," 231–32.
[32] Ibid., 232 n. 43.
[33] La Piana, "Foreign Groups," 337–38 n. 15.
[34] Ibid., 338.

a threat to the sovereignty of the imperial government, and such were often brutally suppressed.³⁵

Walker-Ramisch does not deny that intracity federations existed among *collegia* and cites the synagogues of Alexandria and those of Syrian Antioch as examples. She further argues that the *Damascus Document* with its reference to rural "camps" also reflects a federation of communities under a central executive body.³⁶

The limited translocal connections that Ascough documents in his paper do not constitute federative organizations that would have centralized authority over similar *collegia* in different cities, though by the first or second century C.E. the guild of Dionysiac artists may be an exception.³⁷ In my judgment, Ascough is correct that the picture does not differ significantly in earliest Christianity. There are some translocal connections, but the Pauline churches constitute a variety of locally based groups. The support Paul receives from the Philippian church seems to be based on a reciprocal patron-client relationship rather than on mutual obligation between the churches of different provinces (Phil 4:14–16; 2 Cor 11:9).³⁸ While the collection for Jerusalem is usually taken as one of the clearest signs of the translocal nature of early Christianity, Ascough thinks it points in the opposite direction: "Paul's troubles with raising the money promised, and his rhetorical strategies in his letters to the Corinthians (2 Cor 8:1–15; 9:1–5), suggest that they, at least, remained unconvinced that they

---

³⁵ Sandra Walker-Ramisch, "Graeco-Roman Voluntary Associations and the Damascus Document: A Sociological Analysis," in Kloppenborg and Wilson, *Voluntary Associations*, 135–36; see also 144 nn. 19–21, 23.

³⁶ Ibid., 138: "The clearest evidence for this type of Jewish federative organization is to be found in the literary and epigraphical sources for the large Jewish populations of Alexandria and Syrian Antioch. In these cities, an executive council (*gerousia*) performed some kind of administrative function over the city's Jewish *politeumata*, including all its synagogues and professional guilds. It would appear too, that the jurisdiction of the *gerousia* extended also to surrounding rural communities." Walker-Ramisch's description is drawn largely from S. Applebaum, "The Organization of the Jewish Communities in the Diaspora," in *The Jewish People in the First Century: Historical Geography, Political History, Social, Cultural and Religious Life and Institutions* (ed. S. Safrai and M. Stern; CRINT 1/1; Assen: Van Gorcum; Philadelphia: Fortress, 1974), 464–503.

³⁷ See Ascough, "Translocal Relationships," 233–34.

³⁸ Ibid., 237. Ascough acknowledges that Paul himself wants to think his congregations are connected: "Paul's use of the word [ἐκκλησία] in the plural shows that in his mind there were connections among Christian groups within one or more provinces rather than simply within a town" (238). However, as Ascough also notes, Paul never assumes his own communities are in contact with one another, nor does he encourage local leaders to meet with leaders from other locales. Paul is himself of course a translocal figure, but it is obvious that his authority thereby to correct the practices of his congregations was hardly undisputed (239 nn. 77, 82).

had a social and religious obligation to an otherwise unknown group."[39] Paul's rhetorical strategies in 2 Corinthians suggest that the Corinthians at least have a quite different perspective on funds for Jerusalem than what appears to be the case in the synagogue communities of the diaspora.[40] When Paul says in Rom 15:26–27 that Macedonia and Achaia were pleased to contribute and that they are spiritually in debt to the Jerusalem saints, one wonders what Paul might have responded if asked directly, Why? It is certainly not what he thought in writing to the Galatians. In any case, what Paul says in Rom 15 about spiritual obligation is certainly what most diaspora Jews would have assumed to be the case about their relation to the temple in Jerusalem. One might therefore suppose that, in writing to the church in Rome, Paul has his own reasons at that point for thinking of the matter from the perspective of a diaspora Jew.

Finally, the expressions in Paul's letters of the worldwide spread of the gospel do not in fact constitute evidence of a truly translocal movement: "It is unlikely that Paul's words that others 'invoke the name of our Lord Jesus Christ in every place' (I Cor 1.2 [cf. Rom 1:8]) would have been any different than a similar claim of a priest of Isis or of Asclepius, the worship of whom was spread throughout the empire."[41] Paul's mythic imagination is at once utopian and theocratic, responding to a cosmopolitan society

---

[39] Ibid., 237.

[40] Ibid., 237 n. 67. However, Ascough's attempt to play down the significance of the collection needs to be qualified; see below, pp. 218–27.

[41] Ibid., 240. Cf. Luther H. Martin, "The Anti-individualistic Ideology of Hellenistic Culture," *Numen* 41 (1994): 130–31: "The subcultural religious groups adapted to the claims of Hellenistic cosmopolitanism in varying ways. Most of these formerly native cults adopted Greek language and culture as a technique of international communication and acceptance. In addition, some, like that of Lucius' savior goddess, became universalized by elevating their deities from native soil to celestial enthronement where they might preside over their cult sites now redistributed throughout the terrestrial realm.... However, the catholicity of these internationalized native cults was, in actuality, a cosmopolitan fiction, as the local determinations of cult-practices, variations in iconographic and ideological interpretation, and flexibility in the indices of membership indicate. These cults were, in other words, neither charismatic nor episcopal, but congregational.... Only the early Christians had the increasing audacity to aspire to a political realization of the Hellenistic ideal of utopian universalism—an aspiration that eventually won them imperial sanctions." Cf. Walker-Ramisch, "Graeco-Roman Voluntary Associations," 144 n. 21: "and perhaps it was just this type of 'political' organization which transformed Christianity from a diverse group of *collegia licita* (synagogues?) within the constitution of the city to a political movement with a centralized leadership." Cf. Ascough, "Translocal Relationships," 240: "We see perhaps in the Dionysus artists' association an analogy to what may have occurred in Christianity. Over a period of three or four centuries this association grew from local groups with very loose translocal connections to the 'world-wide' guild of artists.... Likewise Christianity did become a strong, well-defined global movement, but not until a few centuries beyond the foundations of the original groups."

and to imperial propaganda.[42] He is not unique in this respect; Hellenistic religions in general were responding to this. But the mythic imagination of a Paul is hardly to be taken as a simple reflection of the actual situation of early Jesus and Christ social formations.[43]

If there is no established and fully recognized translocal authority even for the itinerant apostle in his own churches, and if the creation of any sort of intercity federative structure between communities is very unlikely and problematical, it would seem to me unwarranted to imagine that the meeting in Jerusalem and the mutual recognition between Paul and Barnabas and the "pillars," or between the Antioch and Jerusalem associations (as some would identify the major parties), entailed recognition of the legitimate jurisdiction and authority of Jerusalem leaders and community to intervene legally in the affairs of other leaders or communities. Thus, I find altogether unlikely a recent tendency to explain the appeal to Jerusalem, the "agreements" reached, and their consequences on the basis of a recognized and established subordination of Antioch to Jerusalem, with Paul's relationship to Jerusalem seen as mediated by his relationship to Antioch and therefore subject to the same subordination. For example, according to Bengt Holmberg:

> The Antiochene Christians saw in Jerusalem the salvation-historical centre of the Church, which obviously had certain legal consequences. This seems to have been the common opinion among the first Christians, that Jerusalem was the centre of the rapidly growing Church. This was owing to its role as the Holy City and theologico-juridical centre of Judaism, and to the fact that this was the place where Christ had died and risen, where the Spirit had been effused, and where the Apostles of Christ resided, they being the guardians of the divine Word, that tradition of and from Jesus which had gone out from Jerusalem.[44]

---

[42] See Dieter Georgi, *Theocracy in Paul's Praxis and Theology* (trans. David E. Green; Minneapolis: Fortress, 1991); Arthur J. Dewey, "Εἰς τὴν Σπανίαν: The Future and Paul," in *Religious Propaganda and Missionary Competition in the New Testament World: Essays Honoring Dieter Georgi* (ed. Lukas Bormann et al.; NovTSup 74; Leiden: Brill, 1994), 321–50; David Seeley, "The Background of the Philippians Hymn (2:6–11)," *Journal of Higher Criticism* 1 (1994): 49–72; and Martin, "Akin to the Gods."

[43] On the gap between the socially ideal and the socially real, see Jonathan Z. Smith, *To Take Place: Toward Theory in Ritual* (CSHJ; Chicago: University of Chicago Press, 1987), 40–46, 141–46; see also idem, "The Bare Facts of Ritual," in *Imagining Religion*, 53–65, 143–45; idem, "A Pearl of Great Price and a Cargo of Yams: A Study in Situational Incongruity," in *Imagining Religion*, 90–101, 156–62.

[44] Bengt Holmberg, *Paul and Power: The Structure of Authority in the Primitive Church as Reflected in the Pauline Epistles* (Philadelphia: Fortress, 1978), 20.

When Holmberg also states that Paul operates from this same salvation-historical view of Jerusalem,[45] we have what amounts to a rather straightforward presentation of the book of Acts.

It might not be worth rehearsing this were it not for the fact that, beginning with the work of John Howard Schütz,[46] a number of sociological studies concerned with the conception and context of apostolic authority, among them Holmberg's, have sought to gain some critical distance on Paul's anachronistic interpretation of events in Gal 1:11–2:14. While they are correct to call attention to the potential impact of Paul's subsequent break with the Antioch church on his conception of apostolic authority, these critical readings of Paul's account tend to lean much too uncritically on the programmatic perspective of Acts. Nicholas Taylor, building on work of Holmberg, James D. G. Dunn, Raymond E. Brown and John P. Meier, and Paul J. Achtemeier concerning the importance of the Antioch church in the Paul-Jerusalem scenario, has taken the consequences of this approach further.[47] According to Taylor, "Paul's break with the Antiochene church ... required a complete reorientation. He lost not merely the base and structural support of his missionary work, but also the very basis of his human and Christian identity. Both his self-understanding and his missionary work came to be expressed in terms of a personalized notion of apostleship, derived directly from God."[48] Taylor also thinks that the break with Antioch ended in practical terms Paul's relationship with Jerusalem until the delivery of the collection.[49] For Taylor, a relationship of κοινωνία already existed between the churches of Antioch and Jerusalem prior to the meeting in Jerusalem. Jerusalem was the senior partner, in a position of considerable authority to decide the issue.[50] "The primacy of the Jerusalem church, as the more ancient and eschatologically more significant, and led by the principal witnesses to the gospel events, could not be ignored, and was not ignored by the Antiochene

---

[45] Ibid., 28, following Peter Stuhlmacher, *Das paulinische Evangelium: I. Vorgeschichte* (FRLANT 95; Göttingen: Vandenhoeck & Ruprecht, 1968), 87–88.

[46] John Howard Schütz, *Paul and the Anatomy of Apostolic Authority* (SNTSMS 26; Cambridge: Cambridge University Press, 1975).

[47] See James D. G. Dunn, "The Relationship between Paul and Jerusalem according to Galatians 1 and 2," *NTS* 28 (1982): 461–78; idem, "The Incident at Antioch (Gal. 2:11–18)," *JSNT* 18 (1983): 3–57; Raymond E. Brown and John P. Meier, *Antioch and Rome: New Testament Cradles of Catholic Christianity* (New York: Paulist, 1983); and Paul J. Achtemeier, *The Quest for Unity in the New Testament Church: A Study in Paul and Acts* (Philadelphia: Fortress, 1987).

[48] Nicholas Taylor, *Paul, Antioch and Jerusalem: A Study in Relationships and Authority in Earliest Christianity* (JSNTSup 66; Sheffield: JSOT Press, 1992), 24–25.

[49] Ibid., 21, 146–52.

[50] Ibid., 102–3.

Christians."⁵¹ Fortunately for the Antioch church and their representatives Barnabas and Paul, the Jerusalem leadership decided in their favor. But it was they who decided the issue. Thus Taylor concludes, "The conference strengthened the authority of the Jerusalem church in its relationship with the Antiochene church. It also strengthened the authority of the leadership of the Jerusalem church. The fact that the ruling they gave was the one sought by the Antiochene delegation does not alter this."⁵² Again, we see that a critical reading of Gal 2 is achieved by essentially adopting the perspective and account of the book of Acts. It is not surprising, then, that remembering the poor is seen by Taylor as an obligation expressing "the right of the Jerusalem church to regulate Christian life in Antioch."⁵³

What is at stake is not just dependence on Acts 15. As can be seen in these descriptions, the account of Christian origins in Acts is presupposed. In some respects, the greater attention given to Antioch in these studies has the appearance of continuing to exorcize the ghost of Ferdinand Christian Baur, while assuring us at the same time that his ghost has not been spotted for decades. Thus, instead of Tübingen's dialectical opposition at the beginning to be mediated only later, a third term appears at the beginning. Baur assumed the resurrection of Christ to be common ground between the two factions, but on the vital issue of universalism and particularism the church was not united from the beginning but divided to the core. Moreover, while Jerusalem's particularism had gotten Jesus wrong, Paul's universalism had gotten him right.⁵⁴ Apart from the ideological cause represented in this position, and the genuine historical problems, it just would not do to have the church utterly divided at the beginning on this crucial issue. That later Jewish Christianity was wrong was no problem, but this ought not to have been the case for "the apostles" in Jerusalem. The task, then, has been to present a critical and plausible account of differences between Paul and Jerusalem in which Antioch provides the mediation and the proper perspective on both, but in such a way that the common ground of Christian origins as presented in Acts also remains unchallenged, and along with it, the notion of the primacy of the Jerusalem church in Christian origins.

---

⁵¹ Ibid., 99.

⁵² Ibid., 109.

⁵³ Ibid., 120. For challenges to the chronology on which the work of Taylor and his predecessors depends, see John Knox, *Chapters in a Life of Paul* (New York: Abingdon, 1950); Robert Jewett, *A Chronology of Paul's Life* (Philadelphia: Fortress, 1979); Gerd Lüdemann, *Paul, Apostle to the Gentiles: Studies in Chronology* (trans. F. Stanley Jones; Philadelphia: Fortress, 1984); and Niels Hyldahl, *Die paulinische Chronologie* (ATDan 19; Leiden: Brill, 1986).

⁵⁴ Ferdinand Christian Baur, *The Church History of the First Three Centuries* (ed. and trans. Allan Menzies; 2 vols.; 3rd ed.; Theological Translation Fund Library; London: Williams & Norgate, 1878–79), 1:41–55.

Just how entrenched this position is in scholarship on Christian origins can be seen by noting that Wilhelm Heitmüller, the earliest scholar to utilize Paul's letters and Acts to create distance between Jesus and Paul by hypothesizing a Hellenistic Christianity that he argued was the source of Paul's knowledge of the gospel (and not traditions directly stemming from the Jerusalem church), continued to posit a common kerygma, even though he did not think this common kerygma had the same context or filled the same role in the primitive Jerusalem church as it did in Hellenistic Christianity. It is worth citing at length exactly how he put the matter:

> Hier [in 1 Cor 15] gibt Paulus den Hauptinhalt seines Evangeliums an, und zwar bezeichnet er ihn als überkommen, als überliefert ... hat er das Evangelium nicht in Jerusalem kennen gelernt, sondern ausserhalb Palästinas, etwa in Damaskus, so gibt er eben hier genau genommen nicht, wie man immer annimmt, das an, was er von der Urgemeinde im strengen Sinn überkommen hat, sondern das, was er in dem *hellenistischen* Christentum ... als Überlieferung vorgefunden und empfangen hat.... Freilich weist Paulus ausdrücklich auf die älteren Apostel hin 15, 11: sie predigen gerade so. Aber wenn das auch sicher richtig ist, dass sie von dem Sühnetod Jesu für die Sünde und von der Auferstehung predigten, so haben wir doch allen Anlass, daran zu zweifeln, dass die Führer der ältesten jerusalemischen Urgemeinde sich mit dem was Paulus 15, 1ff. als Hauptstücke des Evangeliums nennt, als Kern des Evangeliums begnügt haben sollten. Es kommt doch nicht bloss auf die einzelnen Stücke an, sondern vor allem auch auf die Stellung, die sie einnahmen, und auf das, was sonst noch mit ihnen verbunden oder nicht verbunden war.... Die Beschränkung auf das dürftige Schema Tod, Begräbnis, Auferstehung als Hauptinhalt des Evangeliums ist nicht verständlich für die Gemeinde, der wir die Spruchquelle und den Grundstock des Markusevangeliums verdanken. Sie ist nur erklärlich in einem Kreise, der von der geschichtlichen Wirklichkeit des Lebens Jesu mit ihrem Reichtum weiter entfernt war als die jerusalemische Gemeinde.[55]

Since it has become evident in more recent scholarship that it was not necessary for the kerygma to be preached or presupposed in every group that cultivated teachings of Jesus, it seems hardly possible to sustain the notion of a common kerygma, however differently contextualized, on the basis of a text such as 1 Cor 15:11 without also assuming the critical historical value of the "Jerusalem church" and the "apostolic preaching" as recorded in the book of Acts.[56]

---

[55] W. Heitmüller, "Zum Problem Paulus und Jesus," *ZNW* 13 (1912): 331, emphasis original.

[56] The scholarly proclivity to follow the example of Eusebius in using Acts as the main source for the history of early Christianity, even when scholars are engaged in quite different

While acknowledging the value of recent emphasis on Syrian Antioch for the reading of Gal 2, I view its importance in a quite different way. I will try to show later in this essay why we not only should think of the project of "mission" and the issues associated with it as arising in Antioch but should also suppose that the different positions, factions, and proposals are oriented to Antioch and its environs as well. I will also propose that for its part the Jerusalem association of Jesus-followers and its leadership could do little directly to determine the behavior or practices of the Antioch church or to intervene in its projects, nor am I convinced they had any inclination to do so. On the other hand, "Jerusalem" as the "mother church" and origin of "apostolic mission" could provide an ideological anchor for different positions taking shape in diaspora groups among those directly engaged in the issues.

Given the situation Paul addresses in his letter to the Galatians, we should expect that the formulation of an effective response is likely to result in a variety of anachronisms in his account of the past. But should we suppose that the manner in which Paul represents the origin of his gospel was occasioned by a specific turning point in the course of his preaching and travels or by a crisis in his relations with Antioch? The Antioch and Jerusalem groups probably engaged their own representatives in establishing local satellite communities.[57] On the other hand, the impulse to establish the cult of a god somewhere else is regularly represented as coming through a revelation, often received in a dream.[58] Should we see Paul's "call" to preach Christ among the Gentiles as in some important sense parallel to the notion of divine initiative in introducing the worship of a deity to a new area? Is early Christian "mission" simply one example of the general spread of foreign cults in the Greco-Roman world?

These questions need to be reconsidered in the light of the demise of what was once a consensus on the causes and sources of early Christian proselytizing. Since Adolf Harnack's thesis that a Jewish Hellenistic mission failed but nonetheless prepared the way for Christian expansion, it has generally been supposed that Jewish proselytizing was one of the sources that accounted for Christian missions.[59] Over several decades this view has

---

tasks, has been impressively shown by Ron Cameron in his essay, "Alternate Beginnings—Different Ends: Eusebius, Thomas, and the Construction of Christian Origins," in Bormann et al., *Religious Propaganda and Missionary Competition*, 512–15 nn. 55–63.

[57] See above, pp. 185–86 and n. 36; cf. Ascough, "Translocal Relationships," 237 n. 67.

[58] See Ascough, "Translocal Relationships," 232–33, 232 n. 44; cf. Martin Goodman, *Mission and Conversion*, 28. On commissions received in the course of apocalyptic heavenly journeys, see Taylor, *Paul, Antioch and Jerusalem*, 91 n. 6.

[59] Adolf Harnack, *The Mission and Expansion of Christianity in the First Three Centuries* (ed. and trans. James Moffatt; 2 vols.; 2nd ed.; Theological Translation Library 19–20; New York: Putnam's; London: Williams & Norgate, 1908).

been eroding, and the most recent treatment of the subject by Martin Goodman presents a major contribution continuing the trend.[60] Goodman's book is centered on issues of Jewish proselytizing (four of the eight chapters of the book are devoted to it), but it takes up a more general problem, arguing against the common view that proselytizing was characteristic of the religions of the Greco-Roman world and that it represents a normal religious impulse. Goodman thinks the evidence he surveys points rather to an absence of such an impulse in the religions of the Greco-Roman world, including its absence to a considerable extent in Christianity. Christianity did not triumph over its proselytizing competitors, but according to Goodman it did initiate a proselytizing mission whose impulse and rationale have not yet been adequately explained.

Crucial to the delimiting of the study is a typology of missions in which Goodman distinguishes informative, educational, and apologetic missions from a proselytizing mission. An informative mission involves the conviction that one has a message to impart to others. In Goodman's words, "Its aim was to tell people something, rather than to change their behaviour or status." The educative mission is designed to change the behavior of the auditors but did not require the auditors to acknowledge the novel behavior and attitudes "as part of the belief system espoused by the missionary." The apologetic mission seeks "recognition by others of the power of a particular divinity without expecting their audience to devote themselves to his or her worship." A proselytizing mission can be distinguished from the other types in that it aims not only to change behavior but also to incorporate outsiders into the group. Goodman qualifies his definition of proselytizing mission further. Recruiting into the membership of a group relatives, friends, or household slaves with whom one already had social relations would not qualify because such recruiting does not signify in

---

[60] Goodman's *Mission and Conversion* is the published form of the Wilde Lectures in Natural and Comparative Religion, presented at Oxford in 1992; see also his earlier essay, "Jewish Proselytizing in the First Century," in *The Jews among Pagans and Christians in the Roman Empire* (ed. Judith Lieu et al.; London: Routledge, 1992), 53–78. See also Scot McKnight, *A Light among the Gentiles: Jewish Missionary Activity in the Second Temple Period* (Minneapolis: Fortress, 1991); and Edouard Will and Claude Orrieux, *"Prosélytisme juif"? Histoire d'une erreur* (Paris: Les Belles Lettres, 1992). The rejection of a movement of extensive Jewish proselytizing in the Greco-Roman world is also found in Shaye J. D. Cohen, "Respect for Judaism"; idem, "Crossing the Boundary"; idem, "Adolf Harnack's 'The Mission and Expansion of Judaism': Christianity Succeeds Where Judaism Fails," in *The Future of Early Christianity: Essays in Honor of Helmut Koester* (ed. Birger A. Pearson et al.; Minneapolis: Fortress, 1991), 163–69; A. T. Kraabel, "The Disappearance of the 'God-Fearers,'" *Numen* 28 (1981): 113–26; idem, "The Roman Diaspora: Six Questionable Assumptions," *JJS* 33 (1982): 445–64; and Paula Fredriksen, "Judaism, the Circumcision of Gentiles, and Apocalyptic Hope: Another Look at Galatians 1 and 2," *JTS* 42 (1991): 532–64.

itself "a missionary impulse towards total outsiders."[61] It is likely on these grounds that recruitment in early Christianity, as much as in "pagan" or Jewish communities, would not constitute a proselytizing mission because of the tendency to recruit through already established networks.[62] The concern for communal solidarity within a society, what one might call inward, targeted mission for the sake of social order, is also to be distinguished from a mission that is "outward-looking in its scope and inclusive in its intent."[63]

For all of Goodman's efforts carefully to distinguish proselytizing mission from other types, he may end up with a category that is either too narrow to be usefully applied (or worse, with a category that, despite his desire to study the subject free of the usual Christian assumptions on the matter, is in fact defined so that only early Christianity will fit) or is one that overlaps so much with the other categories in respect to available evidence that it cannot differentiate the phenomena adequately. But if his view can be sustained that most evidence of the spread of Hellenistic cults, the existence of philosophical schools, and the evidence of Jewish sympathizers in diaspora synagogues is attributable to the activities of those engaged in apologetic and educative missions, there is perhaps justification in distinguishing among first-century diaspora Jews some who engaged in an effort to change the behavior of non-Jews, specifically to bring them to renounce their gods and to integrate them as equal members of a new association of believers in Christ.[64] In Goodman's estimate:

> Such a proselytizing mission was a shocking novelty in the ancient world. The amazed reactions of Jews to the policy of making gentiles

---

[61] Goodman, *Mission and Conversion*, 3, 4, 5.

[62] See *Semeia* 56 (1992), edited by L. Michael White and titled *Social Networks in the Early Christian Environment: Issues and Methods for Social History*; cf. Rodney Stark, *The Rise of Christianity: A Sociologist Reconsiders History* (Princeton: Princeton University Press, 1996), 73–94.

[63] Goodman, *Mission and Conversion*, 6.

[64] Goodman's discussion of pagan cults and the philosophical schools is far briefer (ch. 2) and, in my judgment, less convincing than the argument he makes for the absence of any clear interest in a proselytizing mission among Jews prior to the talmudic era (chs. 3–4). A key factor in Goodman's discussion of Judaism prior to the second century C.E. is the generally tolerant attitude exhibited toward Gentile cults outside the Holy Land. Wisdom of Solomon 13–15 and *Sib. Or.* 3.545–49, 601–7 are viewed as exceptions that in any case emphasize the foolishness, not the moral wickedness, of idolatry (ibid., 55–56). The attitude is different in the rabbinic Noahide laws that prohibit idolatry to all Gentiles. Goodman attributes the change to the Roman policy in 96 C.E. that stated that only practicing Jews were liable to the *fiscus Iudaicus*. The positive attitude toward proselytizing found in some midrashic traditions about Abraham is thought by Goodman to be a response to the success of Christian proselytizing (chs. 6–7).

"members of the same body" (Eph. 2: 11–3: 21) show that Paul was not seen by them as simply continuing Jewish proselytizing in a special form. If he had been only the Christian inheritor of a Jewish concept of mission he would have had no call to speak so emotionally about his calling as the apostle to the gentiles. Only familiarity makes us fail to appreciate the extraordinary ambition of the single apostle who invented the whole idea of a systematic conversion of the world, area by geographical area.[65]

Despite this statement, Goodman does not think that a proselytizing mission to Gentiles in early Christianity can be fully explained on the basis of the usual appeals to a natural religious instinct, Jewish proselytizing, Jesus, the apostle's divine call, the threat of damnation without Christ, apocalyptic eschatology, Paul's peculiar personality and theology, or the need to rationalize delay of the parousia.

The additional factor, the determinative factor for Goodman, however tentatively suggested, was a response to the vehemence of debate over the terms of inclusion of Gentiles. What may initially have been granted as permissible, the full inclusion of Gentiles without becoming Jews, continued to be a source of conflict. Continued opposition not just in theory but in practice evoked a response that changed the terms of the argument. Not only was it permissible to include Gentiles as Gentiles, but it was desirable. The argument could be won by proving it. Thus, a proselytizing mission to Gentiles. Goodman points to examples of this "bloodymindedness" in Josephus and rabbinic sources in which the urge to win permission for some behavior led to the much stronger claim that it was desirable.[66] Goodman certainly does not intend this as a psychologism but as a

---

[65] Ibid., 105–6. It is not completely clear to me how Goodman reached this conclusion. In ch. 5 he presents a good bit of evidence from early Christian writings, including Paul's letters, for the presence of apologetic and educative missions: "To some extent, then, and despite the lack of such a clear-cut theological basis, some early Christian institutions mirrored those in contemporary Jewish society. From a very early date there existed self-aware Christian communities into which an outsider could be inducted. Conversely, it was in theory just as possible to be a sympathizer close to, but outside, a Christian *ecclesia* as it was to be a sympathizer on the fringes of Judaism. The story of the freelance exorcist in Mark 9:38–40 suggests that the notion was not always ruled out" (102). Moreover, one wonders whether anyone really would meet the criteria of a universal proselytizing mission before the prophet Mani, but for Goodman "the origins of Mani's attitude to mission can be firmly sited within the Church" (157). What is clearly in the foreground of Goodman's characterization of the Pauline mission is the vehement opposition to paganism (96–97, 105); but cf. Peder Borgen, "'Yes,' 'No,' 'How Far?': The Participation of Jews and Christians in Pagan Cults," in *Paul in His Hellenistic Context* (ed. Troels Engberg-Pedersen; Minneapolis: Fortress,1995), 30–59; and Ascough, "Translocal Relationships," 236 n. 62.

[66] Goodman, *Mission and Conversion*, 170–73.

reminder of the argumentative character of Judaism.⁶⁷ In Acts 26:19, Paul can tell King Agrippa that he was not disobedient to the heavenly vision and sound perhaps like a prophet of Yahweh or like a priest of Isis. But in Rom 11:13–14 he can tell Gentiles that, as apostle to the Gentiles, he magnifies his ministry to them in order to make his fellow Jews envious and thus save some of them. So evidently he does carry on a mission to Gentiles to make a point, and makes it, perhaps, with some of the bloody-mindedness that Goodman has in view.

Unlike Goodman, I am prepared to think that internal dispute over issues of who belongs and under what conditions may often have accompanied the expansion of Hellenistic cults. Since these were also religions with roots in ancestral lands, and religions with emerging diaspora forms of association that were constrained by Roman law and challenged in a cosmopolitan milieu, we might expect that opening the membership to those outside the ethnic group would not happen automatically and without debate about the propriety and the conditions. Nonetheless, when one reads Paul's letters, particularly Galatians and Romans, one is struck by the fact that even the language of concession and recognition makes use of pejorative labels, for the terms ἀκροβυστία and περιτομή referring to groups of people are not the self-reference of Jews or Gentiles, and used as a metonymy they can hardly be imagined otherwise than as intended slurs, at least initially (Rom 2:26–27; 3:30; 4:9; 15:8; Gal 2:7–9; Phil 3:3; Col 3:11; Eph 2:11; cf. Gal 5:12; Phil 3:2).⁶⁸ But however censorious the labels, what was at stake were the changing forms of collective identity under conditions in which the claims of the past and the situations of the present were not always easy to negotiate. The Jesus people in Antioch and elsewhere, like the followers of Jesus in Jerusalem and elsewhere, however differently situated, were among the emerging associations that looked to homeland and ancestral traditions, while adapting to the cosmopolitan environment of the empire in order to redefine traditional collective identities.

II

Let me begin with an observation of Taylor's on Gal 2 and Acts 15 that I think has an importance that is often overlooked: "There is no indication

---

⁶⁷ Ibid., 170–71: "It was a characteristic of Judaism, unlike other religions in antiquity, that devotees expected to discover the divine will about correct human behaviour by argument. In other cults, the wishes of the gods were either revealed by some special means such as an oracle or a dream or were taken as obvious."

⁶⁸ See Joel Marcus, "The Circumcision and the Uncircumcision in Rome," *NTS* 35 (1989): 67–81.

in either record of the gathering that the Jerusalem leadership knew the delegation from Antioch were coming before they arrived, and absolutely no evidence that they summoned them to Jerusalem."[69] In one sense this is not surprising. The controversy that brought Paul and Barnabas to Jerusalem was not occurring in Jerusalem and did not concern matters with which that *collegium* had to deal in its own affairs. Whether Gentiles were to be incorporated into the association in Jerusalem, let alone on what terms, was not in view. The most likely ways that such issues could have directly affected those followers of Jesus domiciled in Jerusalem are with respect to their standing and the perception of them in the city and with respect to the possibility of achieving some form of recognition and relations between associations. The situation to which Taylor points also suggests that there would have existed no legal mechanisms by which to issue a summons to appear before the Jerusalem leadership for the adjudication of an issue occurring elsewhere. The fact that the gathering appears to be ad hoc, as Taylor indicates,[70] at least leaves room to suppose that initially the Jerusalem group and leadership did not view as their own affair a situation occurring in Antioch and its environs. These considerations stand in sharp contrast to the kind of importance scholars generally attribute to the meeting and to the dominant role and superior authority of Jerusalem. When the importance of the meeting and the superior authority of Jerusalem are brought together and explained, the result is invariably one version or another of the dominant paradigm of Christian origins, as we have already seen in Taylor's account of the κοινωνία that existed between Antioch and Jerusalem.[71]

It is worth taking note of another contrast. As we have seen, the problems addressed in Gal 2 and Acts 15 are about matters that are occurring

---

[69] Taylor, *Paul, Antioch and Jerusalem*, 103.
[70] Ibid.
[71] See above, pp. 188–90. As I will argue later in the paper, it is reasonable to suppose that some kind of prior relationship did exist between the groups in Antioch and Jerusalem. It is another thing, however, when Taylor assumes the relationship included an acknowledgment on the part of Antioch of Jerusalem's right to regulate the behavior of Jesus people in Antioch. In my judgment, Taylor has taken the expression in Gal 2:9 (δεξιὰς ... κοινωνίας) and interpreted its significance from the perspective of the book of Acts (*Paul, Antioch and Jerusalem*, 103–10). In this way, Taylor can also argue that the subsequent incident in Antioch did not involve Cephas, James, or Barnabas in a violation of the agreements reached at Jerusalem. The request to remember the poor included an implicit right to regulate behavior in Antioch in consideration of the special position and circumstances of the Jerusalem group. According to Taylor, this right was exercised in view of persecution experienced by the Jerusalem group subsequent to the conference (128–31, 135). I find Taylor's evidence for the persecution faced by the Jerusalem group at the time of the Antioch incident to be completely unconvincing, particularly in the light of Taylor's estimate that the Antioch incident took place only several months after the Jerusalem meeting (124).

in diaspora settings, and yet they appear to be taken to Jerusalem for adjudication. Moreover, it also appears to be the case that those who have made the circumcision of Gentiles an issue are people who come from Judea and/or Jerusalem. In Acts 15:1 τινες κατελθόντες ἀπὸ τῆς Ἰουδαίας are teaching the brothers in Antioch that one cannot be saved unless one is circumcised according to the custom of Moses (cf. Acts 11:2; 15:5, 24). Paul refers to the παρεισάκτους ψευδαδέλφους who slipped in to spy out our freedom (Gal 2:4). This makes it clear that Paul wants his readers to see them as outsiders, but from where is not indicated. If Gal 2:3–5 is not parenthetical, referring back to the situation that led to the trip to Jerusalem, then we might suppose that they are Judeans who are outsiders to the Jerusalem group. In Gal 2:12 Paul refers to τινας ἀπὸ Ἰακώβου (cf. Acts 15:24) and to fearing those ἐκ περιτομῆς, though the latter reference may be very general and should not be equated with a specific faction, as they are in Acts 11:2–3. In contrast, we are never told in Acts of any dissension among the believers in Antioch, and in Antioch Paul contends with Cephas but not with Barnabas or the Jewish members of the Antioch church (nor, interestingly enough, with those from James). Although Paul's references are even less specific than those in Acts, the combination of the two sources has tended to give the impression that controversy about the circumcision of Gentiles has arisen among factions of the Jesus people in Judea and Jerusalem. On the contrary, I would submit that it is these very sources (Galatians and Acts) that give us reason to doubt the force of this impression and to suppose instead that the people engaged in controversy about the relationship of Gentiles to Judaic ethnic practices are to be found in diaspora loci. But this will come into view only as we are able to differentiate the position of Jerusalem and its leadership from the various versions of Paul's relationship with them that were in circulation in the diaspora.

In an article written some fifty years ago, Olof Linton showed that when we compare Paul's account of his relationship with Jerusalem in Gal 1–2 with passages in Acts 9, 11, and 15, we are confronted not with two accounts of this relationship but with at least three.[72] Clearly, Paul is writing the letter in order to respond to the circumstance of itinerant "teachers" who have entered churches in Galatia and are teaching what Paul regards as another gospel that includes the requirement of circumcision (Gal 1:6–9; 4:17; 5:10, 12; 6:12).[73] Since it is hard to imagine why Paul would focus on

---

[72] Olof Linton, "The Third Aspect: A Neglected Point of View. A Study in Gal. i–ii and Acts ix and xv," *ST* 3 (1949): 79–95.

[73] I have taken the term *teachers* from J. Louis Martyn, "A Law-Observant Mission to Gentiles: The Background of Galatians," *SJT* 38 (1985): 307–24. The term is preferable to *opponents, intruders,* or *troublers,* which express only Paul's point of view. My use of the

his relationship with Jerusalem in Gal 1–2 unless it was directly relevant to the situation in Galatia, one can be relatively certain that the new teachers have presented their own version of that relationship. Thus, as Linton pointed out, there is not only the description given by Paul in the letter and the description in the book of Acts, but there is also the version presented by the new teachers in Galatia that Paul seeks to contest and correct in the letter.[74] What is more important, there appear to be obvious similarities between certain features of the account in Acts and what Paul appears to be contesting in Gal 1–2.[75] Linton also noted that it was understandable that these similarities would tend to be overlooked by scholars because the writer of Acts is later and a venerator of Paul, whereas the Galatian teachers are contemporaries and appear to be disparaging Paul.[76]

Paul's autobiographical report in Gal 1:11–2:6 features a series of negations. Paul's gospel is not of human origin (οὐκ ἔστιν κατὰ ἄνθρωπον). He did not receive it from a human source, nor was he taught it (οὐδὲ ... παρὰ ἀνθρώπου ... οὔτε ἐδιδάχθην, 1:11–12). He received it through a revelation (1:12c), and when he had received it (1:16a) he did not immediately take counsel with flesh and blood, nor go up to Jerusalem, but went into Arabia (εὐθέως οὐ προσανεθέμην σαρκὶ καὶ αἵματι οὐδὲ ἀνῆλθον εἰς Ἱεροσόλυμα ... ἀλλὰ ἀπῆλθον εἰς Ἀραβίαν, 1:16b, 17ab). After three years he did go up to Jerusalem to get acquainted with Cephas, but he did not see any other apostle except James (ἕτερον δὲ τῶν ἀποστόλων οὐκ εἶδον, 1:19). On this matter he swears he is not lying. Then he went into the regions of Syria and Cilicia and still was not known personally in the churches of Judea (ἤμην δὲ ἀγνοούμενος τῷ προσώπῳ, 1:22). Then after fourteen years Paul went up again to Jerusalem with Barnabas, taking Titus along. But even Titus, who was a Greek, was not compelled to be circumcised (ἀλλ' οὐδὲ Τίτος ..., Ἕλλην ὤν, ἠναγκάσθη περιτμηθῆναι, 2:3). To the false brothers who slipped in to spy out their freedom, Paul and Barnabas did not yield submission even for a moment (οἷς οὐδὲ [the negative is lacking in Codex D, Irenaeus, Tertullian, and others] πρὸς ὥραν εἴξαμεν τῇ ὑποταγῇ, 2:5a). From those who seemed to be highly regarded—whatever they actually were is nothing to Paul; God shows no partiality—indeed to Paul [that is, with respect to the gospel he preaches] those of repute added nothing additional (ὁποῖοί ποτε ἦσαν οὐδέν μοι διαφέρει. πρόσωπον [ὁ] θεὸς ἀνθρώπου οὐ λαμβάνει—ἐμοὶ γὰρ οἱ δοκοῦντες οὐδὲν προσανέθεντο, 2:6).

---

term does not entail agreement with Martyn's notion of a law-observant mission to Gentiles in competition with Paul. Martyn's thesis is developed in his commentary, *Galatians* (AB 33A; New York: Doubleday, 1997).

[74] Linton, "Third Aspect," 80.
[75] Ibid.
[76] Ibid., 80–81.

While Linton may go too far in supposing that every denial by Paul is responding directly to an assertion of the teachers in Galatia, it seems to me that one can hardly avoid the observation that the tensions between Paul's denials and the account in Acts also reveal a similarity between the account in Acts and views circulating among the Galatians as a result of the presence of the teachers.[77] According to the account in Acts, Paul met Ananias after his conversion (9:17–19a, although there is no indication that Paul received instruction).[78] Then Paul was with the disciples in Damascus for some days (9:19b). After a narrow escape from Damascus (9:23–25; cf. 2 Cor 11:32–33), he came to Jerusalem and was brought to the apostles by Barnabas and went in and out among them in Jerusalem (9:26–28).[79] The writer of Acts has clearly subordinated Paul to the Jerusalem apostles, and nowhere more so than at the so-called Apostolic Council in Jerusalem. Moreover, the account in Acts hardly accords with Paul's denial (they "added nothing to me") that no indispensable requirements for Gentile members were promulgated by the Jerusalem leaders. In Acts, Paul

---

[77] On the pitfalls of mirror-reading a polemical letter, but also with very useful criteria for achieving valid results, see John M. G. Barclay, "Mirror-Reading a Polemical Letter: Galatians as a Test Case," *JSNT* 31 (1987): 73–93. Barclay's second pitfall is the danger of overinterpretation: "In a polemical letter like this we are inclined to imagine that every statement by Paul is a rebuttal of an equally vigorous counter-statement by his opponents" (79). In a section on a possible methodology Barclay states, "If Paul makes a *denial*, we may assume that, *at least*, those whom he addresses may be prone to regard what he denies as true, and *at most*, someone has explicitly asserted it; ... between these two extremes there is a range of other possibilities" (84, emphasis original). In debate with the thesis of George Lyons, *Pauline Autobiography: Toward a New Understanding* (SBLDS 73; Atlanta: Scholars Press, 1985), that mirror-reading is a totally unworkable approach, Barclay responds, "I fail to see how Paul's detailed description of his movements in 1.17–24 can fit Lyons's conclusion that the only purpose of Paul's autobiography is 'as a paradigm of the gospel of Christian freedom which he seeks to persuade his readers to reaffirm in the face of the threat presented by the troublemakers.' ... Lyons has not taken sufficient account of Paul's repeated emphases in these chapters, or the fact that the troublemakers must have considered Paul's work in Galatia insufficient" ("Mirror-Reading," 93 n. 44, citing Lyons, *Pauline Autobiography,* 171). Among the matters that Barclay considers certain or virtually certain are the identity of the opponents as Christians, the fact that "they wanted the Galatians to be circumcised," and that "they brought into question the adequacy of Paul's gospel and his credentials as an apostle." Under highly probable conclusions Barclay lists the opponents' being "*Jewish* Christians" and their expecting "the Galatians to become circumcised proselytes and to observe the law, as the hallmark of the people of God" ("Mirror-Reading," 88, emphasis original).

[78] Linton, "Third Aspect," 84: "Such an instruction from 'men' the Galatian propagandists have evidently ascribed to Paul, whereas Paul himself energetically denies it (Gal. i, 12). To the author of Acts there is, however, evidently nothing disparaging in Paul's being instructed by Apostles or other good Christians."

[79] Paul of course denies all this. As Linton notes, "Paul did not, as the Galatian agitators said (and Acts confirms), go to Jerusalem to the Apostles at once, and he has not been in Jerusalem with the Apostles for many years" (ibid., 85).

(together with Silas) even delivers to his churches the decrees concerning appropriate Gentile behavior ordained by the apostles and elders in Jerusalem (16:4), decrees that clearly are related to the so-called Antioch incident in Gal 2:11–14, where Paul vehemently opposes what he describes as forcing Gentiles to live as Jews (2:14).[80] Hence, a view of the Jerusalem meeting similar in perspective on issues of authority and additional requirements to what is reasonably to be supposed for the teachers in Galatia is evident in Acts. But if there are similarities, they are clearly not the same account and are even opposed on the matter of the necessity of circumcision, for Acts agrees with Paul in Galatians that circumcision was not required (15:5, 6–21).[81]

For Linton, the difference between Acts and the Galatian teachers cannot be stated simply in terms of one who venerates Paul, on the one hand, and those who regard him as a false teacher, on the other. The author of Acts venerates Paul but nevertheless will correct him to make him better. The Galatian teachers have no intention of defaming Paul's credentials but charge him with inconsistency in order to please men.[82] However, while the relationship between Acts and the Galatian teachers is analogous in

---

[80] According to Acts, Judas and Silas, members of the Jerusalem church, were appointed to go back to Antioch with Paul and Barnabas to deliver the decisions to the Gentile believers in Antioch, Syria, and Cilicia (15:22–23). At the same time, it is acknowledged that persons coming from the Jerusalem church, but with no instructions from the apostles, were the source of the original agitation (15:24).

[81] I have left out of consideration the matter of the circumcision of Titus because of the textual variant in Gal 2:5. It seems to me unlikely that Paul would have referred to it at all if in fact he had submitted to the demand, even if he might still argue that there was no compulsion from the Jerusalem leadership to do so. If the shorter text were superior, there would be some interesting implications, as Linton has noted. Not only would we have to relate the Titus matter to the case of Timothy in Acts 16:4, and especially because "in both cases the circumcision was performed out of consideration to people whose opinion was in no sense authoritative to Paul" ("Third Aspect," 88), but we would also be able to relate both cases to Paul's statements about the "principled inconsistency" of his manner of life, all of which is "for the sake of the gospel" (1 Cor 9:19–23; cf. Gal 2:5b).

[82] Ibid., 86, 94–95. "There existed, however, also a mediatory view concerning Paul [and not only Paul's own self-conception, the view of the writer of Acts, and those who regarded Paul as a false apostle]. According to this [namely, the position of the Galatian teachers] he had received his insight into Christian faith from the Apostles and had thus got a good instruction, was in so far a true Evangelist. But he had not been steadfast in his faith. In order to 'please men' (Gal. i, 10; 1 Thess. ii, 4) he had made certain concessions and thus without any authorisation granted exemptions from indispensable divine commandments" (86); cf. Gal 5:11, and see the thesis of Peder Borgen, "Paul Preaches Circumcision and Pleases Men," in *Paul and Paulinism: Essays in Honour of C. K. Barrett* (ed. M. D. Hooker and S. G. Wilson; London: SPCK, 1982), 37–46. Borgen holds that Paul is not responding to an accusation in Gal 5:11 but rather to the fact that the teachers have cast themselves as allies of Paul; see also Barclay, "Mirror-Reading," 79–80.

some important respects, the similarities need not be accounted for on the basis of direct influence. When Linton supposes that the writer of Acts has adapted and edited traditions that were already circulating in Paul's lifetime, he is led to explain the relationship between Paul and Jerusalem on the basis of the narrative in Acts. According to Linton, despite Paul's own claim to equal or even superior apostolic credentials, "to the ordinary Christians it must have been evident that the immediate disciples of Christ who had been in the company of Jesus 'all the time that the Lord went in and out among us' (Acts i, 21) held a special position within the Church impossible to reach for any other Christian."[83] Once again, the foundation narrative of Acts provides the account that explains the discrepancies between Paul and Acts as well as the similarities between Acts and the Galatian teachers. In that case, the differences between Paul, the Galatian teachers, and the book of Acts on the conference in Jerusalem can also be understood as different interpretations that arose quite naturally almost the moment the conference ended: "If the negotiations and results of a conference are related by two concurring parties, the relations are seldom identical, not even the very day after the meeting. It is therefore very reasonable that the conference at Jerusalem immediately was reported in a very different way."[84]

It is quite possible, indeed likely, that the Jerusalem meeting left much in ambiguity and much in doubt and invited different interpretations. But if Paul is responding some four to eight years after the Jerusalem meeting to teachers who are promoting different practices and an alternative message, or at least what they think is an improved message to the one preached by Paul, why should we suppose that the source of this is something said and done in Jerusalem years earlier, rather than something said and done years later among groups in Antioch, or among itinerant teachers in the regions where they carry on their activities? That the writer of Acts has a perspective on Paul that he finds useful for the larger goals of his narrative, and that in some respects is analogous to the views of earlier Galatian teachers, does not require us to suppose that this perspective arises from individuals present at the meeting who have their own particular slant on what took place. Why should we take for granted that a similar attribution of superior status and authority ascribed to the Jerusalem leadership by the writer of Acts and by the Galatian teachers is to be accounted for by the narrative of Acts itself?[85]

---

[83] Linton, "Third Aspect," 86.
[84] Ibid., 91.
[85] The similarities first pointed out by Linton do make it much less likely that the Galatian teachers are "gnostics" who have *accused* Paul of dependence on Jerusalem; contra Walter Schmithals, *Paul and the Gnostics* (trans. John E. Steely; Nashville: Abingdon, 1972), 13–32.

The thesis of this essay depends on a different perspective. The status and authority of Jerusalem and its leadership, the conceptions of their role and the representations of their views, are largely constructions fabricated in the interest of making sense of and promoting behaviors and relations in groups such as those in and around Antioch that have become independent of synagogues and in the interest of the preaching of Christ in diaspora settings by itinerant teachers and "apostles." The Jerusalem "church," as they thought of it, serves as a link to a past and thus to identities that are in the process of change, although in different ways and to different degrees. In other words, the Jerusalem "church" is not the presupposition, or the precursor, or the final court of appeal concerning situations and issues arising in Damascus and in Antioch, in the Pauline "mission" and the "missions" of others. Rather, the Jerusalem reflected in our sources is in large part the result of these developments. Changing arrangements and alignments taking place in the first generation are likely to have encouraged differing discourses of homeland. In turn, particular constructions of homeland will have been related to issues of continuing synagogue affiliation and to contestation over the boundaries of interaction with the diverse populations of Hellenistic cities.

Attempting to construct a profile of a Jerusalem group and to clarify the role of the Jerusalem "pillars" in the affairs of the Antioch church by means of some critical combination of the evidence in Acts and Galatians, or even by means of a mirror-reading of Gal 1–2, will not take us very far. It is not that these methods shed no light but that what they illuminate are the contested practices and quests for legitimation going on elsewhere. This implies what in any case we should always have supposed: *the main parties to contested practices and differing quests for identity and legitimation are the parties engaged in the activities that occasion controversy in the locations in which the activities occur.* Nonetheless, in some way Jerusalem must have been involved. I would suggest that a better way to gain some footing is to do a second reading of Gal 1–2 that deliberately

---

There is no clear consensus on the identity of the Galatian teachers. Barclay writes, "The questions of the opponents' origin and motivation are even harder to answer. The prominence of Jerusalem in this letter (as well as Gal 1–2, see 4.25–26) probably indicates that they had some links with the Jerusalem church; but they could have come from Antioch or almost any other church which included Jewish Christians" ("Mirror-Reading," 87–88). If the teachers in Galatia did have some links with Jerusalem, we should not conclude as a matter of course that their views are derived from those contacts. As Barclay puts it, "Given Paul's ironic but not wholly negative attitude to 'those in repute' at Jerusalem, it is inconceivable that 'the pillars' had actually commissioned Paul's opponents" (88). It seems to me even more to the point to recognize that the teachers in Galatia are involved with a Gentile community and thus with an environment and with questions that are not part of the daily experience of those in Jerusalem.

brackets the insights gained by means of a mirror-reading. This is necessary because there is a difference between what Paul is responding to and how he has decided to respond. One can make some cautious judgments from Paul's highly selective curriculum vitae about the Galatian teachers' stress on being properly subject to the Jerusalem leaders and faithful to their practices. But this does not mean that Paul has chosen to answer in kind. It is obvious that he has not, and the difference between what Paul is responding to in the Galatian situation and how he has responded may open just enough space to notice the position of Jerusalem.

D. J. Verseput has correctly observed that Paul is "typically perceived to be defending the source of his gospel and the legitimacy of his apostleship in the first two chapters of the letter, before moving on to a theological defense of his message in chapters 3 and 4."[86] In that vein, Gal 1:13–24 defends the source of his gospel against the contention that he received instruction from men, specifically from those in Jerusalem, 2:1–10 supports his authority as an apostle by showing that it was acknowledged by the pillars, and 2:11–21 shows Paul's willingness to confront the premier apostle on the basis of the truth of his (i.e., Paul's) gospel.[87] Against this reading, Verseput argues that the narrative in Gal 1–2 is not a defense of his apostolic authority or the source of his gospel but a defense of the independence of his mission:

> His [Paul's] Gentile mission was an independent work of God, genetically unrelated to the Jewish Christian community (1.13–24), yet fully approved by them (2.1–10), and not to be troubled by "forcing the Gentiles to live like Jews" (2.11–21). That is to say, the historical roots of the Pauline churches did not extend back to the community of the Torah covenant.... In short, Paul employs the story of his own independent calling and career to defend neither his right to preach the gospel nor his authority over the Galatian church, but to support the validity of his converts' salvation without incorporation into the ranks of Jewish Christendom.[88]

In my judgment, the contrast suggested by Verseput is too sharply drawn, first by contending that οὐκ ... κατὰ ἄνθρωπον in 1:11 and οὐδὲ ... παρὰ ἀνθρώπου in 1:12 refer to very different matters, and then by claiming that the narrative is an exposition of the phrase in 1:11 and not the phrase in 1:12.[89] Nonetheless, I believe that Verseput's point can be sustained in a

---

[86] D. J. Verseput, "Paul's Gentile Mission and the Jewish Christian Community: A Study of the Narrative in Galatians 1 and 2," *NTS* 39 (1993): 36–37.
[87] Cf. ibid., 39.
[88] Ibid., 38.
[89] Ibid., 38–39.

different way. The central issue of the meeting in Jerusalem for Paul was not a personal claim, though his response to the Galatian situation has compelled him to respond with that in view. The way to see the difference is to note that, however puzzling in some ways the content and intention of Gal 2:7–9 may be, what appears to be the issue requiring mutual recognition by the parties is the validity of different "missions" or responsibilities, not the relative authority of those engaged in them. In both formulations (the one in 2:7, "I [Paul] ... just as Peter," and the other in 2:9, "we [Paul and Barnabas] ... they [James, Cephas, and John]"), the references to insight and to recognition (ἰδόντες, 2:7, and γνόντες, 2:9) are directed to the validity of the gospel of the uncircumcision (τὸ εὐαγγέλιον τῆς ἀκροβυστίας) entrusted to Paul and the gospel of the circumcision ([τὸ εὐαγγέλιον] τῆς περιτομῆς) entrusted to Peter (2:7), and to the division of responsibility to the Gentiles (εἰς τὰ ἔθνη) and to the circumcision (εἰς τὴν περιτομήν, 2:9).

On the difference in these formulations, Taylor writes, "There is no reason, other than Paul's polemical purpose in Galatians, to understand the apostolate in terms of anybody's particular status."[90] Taylor is obviously correct that the formulation in 2:7–8 cannot be a citation of the meeting's business protocol. Paul certainly had a hand in formulating it, but the use of the Greek nickname Peter only in these verses (otherwise, Paul always uses the Aramaic Cephas) suggests that it is not merely Paul's personal formulation but a usage current in Greek-speaking groups that had already linked the spread of the gospel with the names Paul and Peter.[91] Galatians 2:9 is the more difficult and more important formulation because the very sign of fellowship given by the Jerusalem leadership (δεξιὰς ... κοινωνίας), and therefore the very matter to which mutual recognition pertained, seem to have in view a division of responsibility between the parties directed to different groups and/or areas. But Taylor argues that neither an ethnic nor a geographical division could have been workable, for both are too grandiose and ignore the fact that relatively few were represented at this meeting, and both ignore the demographic realities of Gentiles in Palestine and of Jews dispersed throughout the eastern Roman Empire. Moreover, in Taylor's view, these interpretations also ignore the fact that Antioch was a mixed church, as well as the evidence that Paul did preach to Jews (1 Cor

---

[90] Taylor, *Paul, Antioch and Jerusalem*, 113.
[91] Cf. the analysis of these verses in Lüdemann, *Paul, Apostle to the Gentiles*, 64–71. While I agree with Lüdemann that 2:7–8 are not simply a personal formulation nor a protocol of the meeting, I am not convinced by his view that the formulation originates from Paul's first meeting with Cephas nor that the aorist participle (ἰδόντες) and the perfect passive (πεπίστευμαι) require that we imagine the formulation to have predated the Jerusalem meeting; cf. the aorist participle and aorist passive participle in 2:9a.

9:20).⁹² Rather than the delimitation of territory, or a racial division, Taylor argues "that the Jerusalem conference agreed that the two churches would adhere to the gospel as they understood it, and neither would attempt to impose its views on the other."⁹³ For Taylor this entails the following:

> Barnabas, Paul and the Antiochene church would continue to preach and practise their form of Christianity, in which Gentiles were not obliged to be circumcised, but they would not compel Jewish Christians to desist from observing the Law. The gospel of uncircumcision might apply only to Gentiles, but this did not mean that the Antiochene church ... would not preach to Jews. Similarly, the gospel of circumcision would apply only to Jews, and the Jerusalem church would not impose circumcision and legal observance on Gentile Christians.⁹⁴

Taylor's interpretation of Gal 2:9 is helpful in some respects, though I find his major point to be problematic. By way of agreement with Taylor, first, there is the fact that recognized leaders of the Jerusalem group are parties to the κοινωνία and that Barnabas is also a party with Paul, making it clear that the responsibilities entailed concern more than Paul and Peter. Whether or not Paul went to the meeting as a representative of the Antioch church, the presence of Barnabas and the pillars signifies that leaders of two associations are also in view. Second, Taylor's recognition that the agreement involves a very limited representation is important for understanding the scope of responsibility and jurisdiction intended. Further, if it is the case that the recognition of different interpretations of the gospel is implied, we have no reason to imagine that the scope of those differences was limited to practices of Torah. Indeed, how could one imagine that this would not entail quite different understandings of Jesus? However, in sharp contrast to Taylor, I would argue that the description of the conditions of mutual recognition certainly does imply, and in practical terms virtually requires, separation along ethnic lines, whereby Paul could say with justification that nothing additional was required of him in his preaching to Gentiles, while at the same time the Jerusalem leaders could maintain a proper concern for practices of ancestral piety as these pertained to Jews.⁹⁵

Behind the rhetoric of superior apostolic credentials and the issue of dependency on the Jerusalem group there is a line of negotiation and

---

⁹² Taylor, *Paul, Antioch and Jerusalem*, 113–15.
⁹³ Ibid., 115.
⁹⁴ Ibid.
⁹⁵ Contrary to Taylor (and to the book of Acts), it is unlikely that Paul directed his preaching of the gospel to Jews, despite 1 Cor 9:20 and 2 Cor 11:24; see the discussion in Martyn, *Galatians*, 213–16.

interest that makes sense in relation to the narrative of Gal 1–2. Paul could say what was obvious. He and Barnabas had brought Gentiles to the worship of the true God through Jesus whom they called Christ. As a result of this spreading of the word, groups whose constituency was largely Gentile had come into existence. The pillars and members of the Jerusalem group had absolutely nothing to do with any of this. Thus, in fact, they had no basis on which to claim jurisdiction. But could the pillars have failed to register any interest in these matters and simply have ignored them? So Paul notices their interest and curiosity ("when they saw that I had been entrusted ... when they recognized the grace that had been given to me," 2:7a, 9a). On the other hand, could the pillars have had either the means or the interest to impose on these groups now the requirement to live as Jews? How would this have been arranged and supported among largely Gentile populations? Moreover, this work was not conducted in Palestine and therefore did not entail the issue of geographical boundaries, which might have raised other questions. For their part, the pillars would not have been without contemporary cultural or religious resources to imagine how they might see themselves related to these new associations of Gentiles, since both the temple and the synagogues could have provided analogies. In any case, the sign of fellowship was extended directly to Paul and Barnabas, which could have left in some doubt how it might apply to the associations formed in connection with their labors. Furthermore, the pillars must have known that those Jewish followers of Jesus who, like Barnabas and Paul, go to the Gentiles are placed in a situation that necessarily tended to compromise and erode their Jewish practices. Given the attempt to establish a place and a work in Jerusalem and its environs, the Jesus people there would have need to clarify to those with whom they were entering into fellowship their concern for the Torah piety of Jews. In view of this concern, it would be important for the pillars, from their side, to establish and receive acknowledgment of their interest in and direct responsibility for the Torah piety of those who spread the teachings of Jesus to Jews. Thus, a sign of fellowship could be extended on the grounds of a mutual acknowledgment that included recognition of the different interests being served by the manner in which the "accord" was formulated. Paul hardly shared the concern of the pillars for the adherence of Jews "in Christ" to practices of Jewish piety, any more than the pillars were likely to agree with Paul on what was at stake in a movement of "Gentiles for Jesus."

Viewed in this perspective, the mutual recognition achieved in Jerusalem does indeed beg the question of what was thought and intended with respect to behaviors and arrangements in the meetings of mixed congregations. Admittedly, it seems very unlikely that the pillars would be ignorant of the constituency and practices of the Antioch groups, since at least Barnabas, if not Paul, was a member and probably a leader in the Antioch association. But we should not exaggerate the problem by requiring ourselves to imagine the participants' ignorance or naivete concerning the existence of many Jesus groups with mixed constituencies, as though the formulation of Gal 2:9 implied worldwide responsibilities. What would have been in immediate view was Antioch and its environs, and one would suppose that the situation there was already a matter for discussion at the Jerusalem meeting.

Gerd Lüdemann resolves this problem by linking the decision of the conference directly to the problem of the mixed constituency of the Antioch community. "As the decision of the conference is preserved by Paul (Gal. 2:9), it reads as if it is an undoing of church relationships as they existed in mixed congregations before the conference."[96] This reading contributes to his reconstruction of the chronology of events to which Paul's narrative refers. According to Lüdemann, the so-called Antioch incident should be understood to have preceded the Jerusalem conference and actually to have been the occasion and situation that brought about the conference.[97] But it is hardly the case that Gal 2:9 reads as a *directive* for the mixed congregation at Antioch. It would be easier to read the formulation with emphasis on the exclusive responsibility of the individuals named, and that would work nicely for Paul against the teachers who have come into the Galatian congregations. For these reasons, Lüdemann must make his own separation and addition to Paul's account:

> Despite this injunction for the *mixed* congregation in Antioch, the stipulation "we to the Gentiles—they to the Jews" still makes good sense, for the mission to the Gentiles was the prerogative of the Pauline and Antiochene mission. That is ... the valid form of the decision of the conference for the Pauline congregations. For the congregation in Antioch this stipulation will have been accompanied by an additional clause that was similar to the Apostolic Decree and that regulated the communal life of Jewish and Gentile Christians.[98]

---

[96] Lüdemann, *Paul, Apostle to the Gentiles*, 73.

[97] Ibid., 75–77.

[98] Ibid., 74, emphasis original. In his chronological study, Lüdemann argued that Paul had already founded churches in Asia Minor, Macedonia, and Achaia prior to the Jerusalem meeting. Thus, he did not go up as a delegate of the Antioch church and therefore, in contrast to Taylor and others, the Antioch incident did not create a crisis of apostolic consciousness in Paul's life. According to Lüdemann, Paul's emphatic ἐμοὶ γάρ (Gal 2:6c) reveals that no additional stipulations were placed on his mission but conceals the stipulations placed on Barnabas in his capacity as one of the leaders of the Antioch congregation. My reading is not committed to Lüdemann's chronology of the Pauline mission nor to his reversal of the chronology of the conference and the Antioch incident. On the other hand, I am also not

The relation of the meeting in Jerusalem to the Antioch incident might be a bit easier to unravel if, in the first place, we could exercise some warranted skepticism regarding a picture of things at Antioch that is normally taken for granted on the basis of the narrative in Acts. According to this picture, relations between Jews and Gentiles in the church at Antioch were not only well established but idyllic until some Judeans came to Antioch (Acts 15:1). This picture seems to be confirmed by Paul's own account. It was certain ones from James who caused a sudden reversal of the behavior of Cephas, Barnabas, and the rest of the Jewish members of the church of Antioch. However, here a number of considerations should be raised. First, Paul, who by his own account is hardly in awe of Cephas, never confronts the messengers or representatives from James. This is in contrast to Paul's direct confrontation of the "false brothers" (Gal 2:4–5). We might speculate that if Paul had confronted those arriving from Jerusalem, as he did those who "slipped in," the withdrawal and separation of the Jewish members of the Antioch church may have been avoided, just as Titus was not compelled to be circumcised. Though there are other ways to account for the "James people" not being mentioned again, one possibility would be that their visit was not accompanied by a set of demands, even if their visit did precipitate the action of Cephas to which Paul refers. One should not conclude that overt pressure was applied on the basis of the "fear" that Paul attributes to Cephas, since Paul clearly intends to disparage the behavior of Cephas.[99] Furthermore, the reference to "those from the circumcision" (2:12c) should not be taken as a reference to the people from James. If such a specific identification were intended, a simple αὐτούς would have served that purpose more clearly and efficiently.[100] Moreover, to refer to those who are circumcised or to those who are advocating the circumcision of Gentiles is not particularly what one would expect in a situation in which the focus is on table fellowship between Jews and Gentiles. The assumption that this was in fact the demand of the messengers from James depends very heavily on assimilating Paul's reference to those in

---

committed to the view that Paul went up to Jerusalem with Barnabas in the capacity of a representative of the Antioch church, though Gal 1:21 and 2:11–14 would seem to indicate that he had close relations with that church (the relationship is obviously much more firmly in place in Acts). This also entails that my reading is not dependent on the notion that the Antioch incident constituted a watershed in the development or the mode of rationalization of Paul's apostolic consciousness.

[99] Cf. Verseput, "Paul's Gentile Mission," 52 n. 32.

[100] On the identification of those from the circumcision, Verseput suggests that they "are to be broadly understood as the Jewish Christian community 'within' the Torah covenant from whom Paul has been at pains to distance his mission" (ibid.). The difficulty of identifying Paul's reference is clear from the number of different identifications that have been suggested; see, e.g., Taylor, *Paul, Antioch and Jerusalem*, 133.

Acts (see 11:2; 15:1, 5), whereas it would seem to be more appropriate to suppose that Paul has chosen a description that is easily assimilated to the teachers in Galatia. In addition to a motivation related to the Galatian situation, Paul may have made this reference not because of what was being demanded by the visitors, nor because of what was intended by the withdrawal, but simply because he also knew that there were Jewish members of the association in Antioch who did in fact advocate the adoption by Gentiles of Jewish practices, including circumcision.

Second, prescinding from the chronological rearrangement adopted by Lüdemann, two options are often taken as viable alternatives: (1) either the issues of table fellowship in the Antioch congregation never arose at the meeting, an option I find unlikely; or (2) James, or those supposed to be pressuring him, changed their minds and were exercising the prerogative of their superior authority to make demands they did not make at the meeting. This is perhaps the most usual solution to the problem. However, on my reading this option obviously assumes an authority that I think did not exist and ignores what the Jerusalem pillars sought most to establish at the meeting: their interest in the maintenance by Jews of appropriate forms of Jewish piety.

A third consideration concerns Paul's accusation that Cephas, though a Jew, is living not like a Jew but like a Gentile and yet wants to compel Gentiles to live as Jews (Gal 2:14). But this charge of hypocrisy is suspicious, because it works too well for Paul when he asserts that the Galatian teachers want to compel Gentiles to adopt Jewish practices, and only in order to make a good showing in the flesh, while they themselves do not keep the law (Gal 6:12–13). In both passages we are dealing with polemical statements, and therefore we have reason to question the motives attributed by Paul to the targets of his polemic and to exercise caution in assuming the accuracy of descriptions of his opponents' behavior.[101] For example, the Galatian teachers may have advocated circumcision impressively but without compulsion. At Antioch, the meal practice may already have included some consideration of Jewish dietary laws, and what was advocated was a stricter practice.[102] The withdrawal and separation may have been adopted temporarily in view of the stricter practice of the visitors or, what I think is more likely, as the best solution precisely to avoid compelling Gentiles to live as Jews, while advocating stricter adherence to Jewish dietary laws for the Jewish members.

I believe that the matter of meal practices in the Antioch groups was already discussed at the Jerusalem meeting as an issue that concerned the

---

[101] Cf. Barclay, "Mirror-Reading," 80–81, 86.
[102] See Dunn, "Incident at Antioch," 31–33.

implications of their mutual recognition for relations between two associations. Indeed, I would suggest that this issue must have arisen before the meeting. It would have been in the more protracted context of working out practical relations between two associations on matters pertaining to mutual hospitality and gifts that it had seemed important to some members of the Antioch church to bring to Jerusalem for consideration the question of their practices in recruiting Gentiles. At least one party at the Jerusalem meeting was a member of the Antioch church, where meal practices stood in tension with Jerusalem's interest in the adherence of Jews to practices of Judaic piety. The central problem was whether the language of division formulated at the meeting could nevertheless accommodate an extension of reciprocal rights and benefits, that is, what might be expected of hospitality to be shown to members of similar *collegia* located in different provinces. At least some in the Jerusalem group may have felt such an extension to be empty, first, because they did not feel free to visit the groups in Antioch, given the current practices there, and second, because they had no authority to intervene in these practices any more than they would expect Antioch to intervene in theirs. In view of what subsequently occurred, I assume the matter was left unresolved at the Jerusalem meeting, in part because Jerusalem people were divided on whether they could make an exception to their major concern because of an already established practice in Antioch. It also seems likely that, for many Jewish members of the Antioch church, the question whether they remained members of the larger Jewish community in Antioch continued to be a pressing one precisely because, as Jesus people, they had formed an independent association with a mixed ethnic constituency and had already begun to develop mythic rationales to account for what had emerged. That issue would surely have concerned the possibility of ongoing participation in Jewish trade associations and food markets. If these considerations are at all on target, I think we should also suppose that there was a continuing interest among members of the Antioch groups in experimenting with practices and rationales that could have an effect on relations between Jews and Gentiles in their own *collegia* and between themselves as Jesus people and the network of Jewish synagogues in Antioch. An interest in relations with synagogues would continue among the Jesus people of Antioch and in the course of time would be found among members of a largely Gentile church.

It is difficult to determine whether there is any particular connection between the presence of Cephas in Antioch and the arrival of envoys from James, because we cannot even be sure that James and those he sent knew of Cephas's presence at the time. Since a change of relations in the matter of common meals took place in the wake of the arrival of the guests from

Jerusalem, we can suppose that Cephas at that point was made aware of conditions that at least James and those who supported him in Jerusalem had concluded in the meantime would be necessary if they were to be in a position to participate in meals with the Jesus groups in Antioch. The ball was in Antioch's court. How to respond must have been left to the members of that community; Jerusalem had neither legal nor any operative jurisdiction. But it was clear that the rub was the failure of the Jewish members to adhere to a standard of Jewish dietary practices in their common meals. In that case, what was Cephas doing in coming to Antioch and sharing the group's meal practice? Having come to Antioch prior to a meeting of minds in Jerusalem on the matter, Cephas, I presume, was operating on his own view that the matter should be resolved by giving consideration to the established practice of the Antioch group and to any new arrangements that might be forthcoming as a consequence of conducting their own business, without establishing any precedent contrary to what was given recognition at the Jerusalem meeting.

Paul focuses the account of the situation in Antioch strictly on his confrontation with Cephas. Since it is unlikely that Barnabas and the rest of the Jewish members of the church were simply following the example of Cephas—he was not even a member but a guest in Antioch—we must inquire why it is Cephas who is represented by Paul as the prime mover in the situation. I suspect it is for the same reason that Gal 2:7 presents a form of the division of "mission" with Paul and Peter as the exclusive agents and that this formulation circulated in Pauline circles. The Galatians had heard about Cephas, and perhaps the Galatian teachers had intentionally drawn him into their circle of teaching. We have already tried to show that Paul's description of the incident at Antioch has the situation in Galatia clearly in view. One wonders how long Cephas remained in Antioch. While it is unlikely that Antioch became a home base for supporting the itinerant movements and activities of Cephas,[103] it is quite possible that later Antioch became a crossroads of traditions, some that linked Peter to Jesus as a prominent disciple, others that stressed his role as an "apostle" authorized by an "appearance" of Jesus.

The Jewish members of "the church" in Antioch withdrew from common meals with Gentiles, though we need not suppose this happened suddenly or all at once. Nor are we compelled to conclude that the situation was seen as the creation of two communities. Under the circumstances, some Gentile members may have preferred the separation to becoming dependent on Jewish markets, while other Gentile members

---

[103] See 1 Cor 9:4–6 and the discussion of Antioch's role in the support of itinerants in Taylor, *Paul, Antioch and Jerusalem*, 93–94.

may have thought that adopting Jewish food practices was the solution to be preferred. The Jewish members are likely to have been motivated by considerations focused on their relations with the larger community of Jews, but for some at least I would suggest that the primary consideration was compensatory and imaginative, that an arrangement of κοινωνία with the followers of Jesus in Jerusalem would give them a more tangible link with the homeland, a link in danger of being lost because of the organization and practices of the association in its Antioch setting to which they were certainly committed. This was by no means an entirely new consideration. Had not some Jesus people in Antioch recommended that the conditions of membership for Gentiles be taken under advisement with Jerusalem as an issue that required consideration of their perspective? Already it was possible not just to think about mutual hospitality but to imagine what the Jesus people in Jerusalem and their leaders could mean for the support and formation of a diaspora Jewish identity in a network of Jesus groups. As for others, I would guess—and this is no more than a guess—that Paul had forgotten that some Jewish members had supported his position, if not his sense of betrayal of the gospel, because membership in the Jesus groups of Antioch was to them an important resolution of their relations with non-Jews in the city and because they had already lost ties with the larger Jewish community. Paul may have forgotten this because it was not particularly pertinent to the occasion of writing the letter to the Galatians. What concerned Paul in the Galatian situation had nothing to do with dietary practices maintained by those "in Christ" (to use Paul's language) who were Jews. Nor was he now particularly concerned about whether James and company recognized the meal practice at Antioch. The issue for Paul in writing to the Galatians was the undermining of the Jerusalem "accord," which acknowledged the integrity of the gospel he preached to Gentiles and its freedom from the imposition of Jewish covenantal law. All of this appeared to be threatened by the teachers in Galatia who claimed to be improving Paul's message by introducing Jewish practices in conformity with the practices of the leading "apostles" in Jerusalem.

In writing to the Galatians, Paul was not dealing directly with James or with Cephas but with Jewish teachers from the diaspora who represented Jerusalem as the mother church (cf. Gal 4:26) and its leaders as the original "apostles" whose life of Jewish piety was to be imitated, to the extent possible, by those who shared their faith. Christ had fulfilled the covenant through his faithfulness and had opened righteousness as a possibility to Gentiles who come to know the true God. But can they have renounced their gods with all of the social uprooting that accompanies this renunciation without being adopted into another family or people? How can they acknowledge the God of Israel without incorporation into the family of

Abraham?[104] Whatever success the teachers have had, it has moved Paul to contemplate the prospect that he has labored in vain among the Galatians (φοβοῦμαι ὑμᾶς μή πως εἰκῇ κεκοπίακα εἰς ὑμᾶς, 4:11; cf. 3:4; 5:2). I believe this helps to explain why, having sought to demonstrate the divine source of his calling and the independence of his gospel from the influence of the "apostles" in Jerusalem (Gal 1:11–24), and having stated that he went up to Jerusalem by revelation (2:2a), that is, not under any human compulsion nor by way of establishing any precedent, Paul nonetheless seems to acknowledge that had he not received from the pillars approval of the gospel he preaches among the Gentiles, his labors would somehow have been in vain (μή πως εἰς κενὸν τρέχω ἢ ἔδραμον, 2:2bc). Paul is in doubt not about his authority to preach nor about what he preaches but about its outcome. Again, his formulation in Gal 2:2bc has in view the situation in Galatia. Through the instrumentality of the Galatian teachers, the pillars may turn out to have intervened and undermined Paul's work, quite apart from the fact that in Jerusalem they had acknowledged the autonomy of his labors.[105] Paul hopes that the outcome in Galatia will turn out as it did

---

[104] Cf. Martyn's mirror-reading of the teachers' sermons (*Galatians*, 345): "The covenant God made with the first proselyte Abraham is the same as the covenant God reaffirmed through Moses at Sinai, thus establishing in all its generations the ancient and venerable people of Israel, a people set apart from all the other peoples of the earth by being the people of the covenantal Law. What are you Gentiles to do, then? You are to follow in the steps of Abraham, the first proselyte. By undergoing circumcision, you are to make your way into the covenant people, the seed of Abraham, the true Israel, the church of God that has as its mother the congregation of the apostles in Jerusalem." Strictly speaking, what is at stake in the Galatian situation is not the conditions for entry into the ἐκκλησία but the identity of the community and the conditions required or not required for maintaining one's status in the community. For the teachers' part, they may see themselves conducting an educational rather than a proselytizing mission, to use Goodman's distinction (see above, pp. 193–94). The teachers are not denying the Galatian membership in the ἐκκλησία but are educating them in the behaviors appropriate to those who have become children of Abraham.

[105] I think this explanation for Gal 2:2bc has more justification than other attempts to account for it. For example, Martyn writes (*Galatians*, 192–93): "At stake in the meeting was the gospel being preached to Gentiles by a number of missionaries sponsored by the Antioch church. It follows that the anxiety which Paul emphatically personalizes ... was first of all an anxiety experienced by the Antioch church as a congregation"; cf. Taylor, *Paul, Antioch and Jerusalem*, 99. Martyn writes further that the danger lay in the possibility that Jerusalem would fail to perceive God's powerful work in Paul's preaching, and, even more, that failure to reach an accord "would have destroyed his assumption that the one 'truth of the gospel' is in fact bringing into being one church of God made up of former Jews and former Gentiles" (193). It seems to me that in writing Galatians Paul is principally concerned with the autonomy of his own churches and with establishing boundaries against the encroachment of those preaching a different gospel. For Paul, then, going up to Jerusalem had as its primary goal, not the unity of the people of God, but the establishment of agreed boundaries, so that his own preaching of the gospel might have a fair chance to bear fruit without interference.

in Jerusalem, not as it did in Antioch. That is also why Paul presents the Antioch incident as he does. Writing to the Galatians from Corinth or Macedonia, he fears that the outcome of the Antioch incident is being used as a precedent for Jerusalem's authority and intervention in his communities. He is certainly not in awe of the pillars themselves, not at least when he writes the letter. When he refers to their reputation in the Jerusalem community (which he does four times, 2:2, 6 [2x], 9), he is hardly deferential: "what sort of persons they were makes no difference to me" (2:6).[106]

But the immediate targets of Paul's polemic in Galatians are the teachers. In order to maintain that his gospel was in no way rooted in or determined by brothers and sisters of the same ἔθνος, he had to dissociate Christ from notions and forms of fictive kinship that sought to relate the novelty of his Christ associations to some sense of generational continuity. He does this by linking Christ directly with Abraham. In the process, he counters the notion that Gentiles establish themselves in the continuity of the descendants of Abraham by means of imitating the act that establishes the covenant with Abraham and his descendants and by following the practices of the mother community in Jerusalem. Paul begins in 3:8 with an identification of the true children of Abraham, and he concludes in 3:29 by assuring the Galatians that it is they who are the true kin of Abraham. But in between, Paul has dissociated the notion of covenant from circumcision and the law (3:15) and has identified it exclusively with the promises (3:17), the recipients of which are not the children of Abraham who receive the law but rather the single seed Christ (3:16). What Paul intends to negate depends on this identification. As Burton L. Mack has written, "Everything hinges on the Abraham-Christ connection. This is a marvelous example of mythmaking strategy, seeking a pristine point of contact with a foundational moment of the past and making a connection that brackets all the intervening and recent histories of failure to achieve that ideal."[107]

---

[106] Cf. Martyn's paraphrase of Gal 2:6, "remains a matter of indifference to me today, a fact I cite in the face of the Teachers, whom you constantly hear extolling the Jerusalem leaders" (*Galatians*, 199).

[107] Burton L. Mack, *Who Wrote the New Testament? The Making of the Christian Myth* (San Francisco: HarperSanFrancisco, 1995), 118. Cf. Martyn, *Galatians*, 347–48, 350: "We can see that Paul's interpretation of the seed to whom God made the covenantal promise is as polemically *punctiliar* as it is polemically *singular*.... That covenantal promise did not create its own epoch, calling into existence a corporate *sperma Abraam* that would extend generation after generation—in a linear fashion—through the centuries.... If, then, we had only Paul's letter to the Galatians, we would have no reason to credit the apostle with a belief in the divine election of the ancient people of Israel. Indeed, precisely the opposite" (emphasis original). I should point out that what for Martyn is a powerful example in Paul of "theology" over "religion" (349) is for Mack a particularly strained example of the normal logics of Hellenistic rhetoric: "In order to make his case, however, Paul had to press both the logic of the

As a consequence, however, Paul's Christ in Galatians is not only set in the role of recipient of the promise, the sole descendant, but must in some ways be imagined as also the ancestor whose children are those who have been initiated into the community by baptism (3:26–29).[108] The difficulty of such a notion is somewhat tempered by the fact that Paul then sets Christ in the role of divine agent whose redemptive death makes it possible for those who belong to Christ to be adopted as God's children (4:4–6).[109]

But Paul is not yet finished with the polemic against the teachers in Gal 4. The allegory of the slave woman and the free woman is essentially a countermyth designed to challenge the teachers' perception of the Jerusalem assembly and its leaders as the source from which Paul's churches in Galatia draw their life and upon which they are to depend, and to replace it with an image of the fruitfulness of Paul's own mission, with its multiple assemblies drawing sustenance from a displaced and therefore more transcendent Jerusalem. I am in agreement with much of the analysis provided by J. Louis Martyn in his commentary on the section 4:21–5:1.[110] It is hard to dismiss as fortuitous the opposition "present Jerusalem" in slavery with her children/"Jerusalem above" free and our mother (4:25–26) and the opposition Paul wishes to establish between the source and fruit of his own labors and the work and message of the teachers now in Galatia. This is especially obvious when what follows in 4:27 is a citation of Isa 54:1, where the opposition could hardly be applied in a general way to Christians and Jews but is rather easy to imagine as an oracle announcing the greater success Paul is claiming for his own work, which is carried on without the earthly sponsor to which the teachers appeal.[111] It is therefore also likely that Paul intends the citation of Gen 21:10 as a directive to the Galatians to expel the teachers (4:30).[112] Paul views the teachers as intruders, their work as bringing Gentiles into slavery, and therefore the activity in which they are engaged as persecution

---

Christ myth and the plain sense of the Abraham stories much too far" (*Who Wrote the New Testament*, 118); cf. Mack's rhetorical analysis of Galatians in idem, *Rhetoric and the New Testament* (GBS; Minneapolis: Fortress, 1990), 66–73.

[108] On the expression ἐν Χριστῷ in Galatians, see Mack, *Who Wrote the New Testament*, 119: "Paul found himself having to deal with the implicit suggestion that Christians were Christ's 'children.'"

[109] As Mack observes, "Christ in this conception [in Galatians] combines the notions of personal deity, tribal patriarch, genealogical agent, ethnic principle, cultural spirit, and cosmic power.... We can conclude only that the strange jumble of condensed imagery must have been impelled by a very serious challenge to Paul's gospel, a challenge that, in the last analysis, Paul was unable to counter" (ibid., 119, 120).

[110] Martyn, *Galatians*, 431–66.

[111] Ibid., 441–43.

[112] Ibid., 446.

(4:29).[113] All of this is confirmed by Paul's other references to Jerusalem, which refer either to the location of the "church" or to that "church" itself (1 Cor 16:3–4; Rom 15:19, 24–26, 30–31; Gal 1:17, 18; 2:1–2).[114]

Martyn argues throughout his commentary that the teachers represent something much more significant than merely intruders into Paul's churches in Galatia. They are Jewish Christians engaged in a law-observant mission to Gentiles. In this effort, he believes they are at least encouraged and perhaps sponsored by the false brothers, who are now leaders of the circumcision party in the Jerusalem church and are having an increasingly strong voice in the church and influence on its leaders. In response, Paul has created an allegory that represents Sarah and Hagar and the two sons as two covenants, an identification that finds no basis in scripture nor in Paul's earlier argument. According to Martyn, the two covenants have in view two different missions to Gentiles, and the Jerusalem church is implicated in the covenant that is bearing children for slavery (4:24). "Thus, *to the degree* that, under the sway of the False Brothers, the Jerusalem church is offering support to the Teachers' work—thus reaching into the life of his churches as it earlier reached into the life of the Antioch church—Paul is sure that the Jerusalem congregation is itself producing Gentile churches that are enslaved."[115]

Paul's reference to the Jerusalem above that is free and that is our mother is therefore intended to counter a similar description attributed by the teachers to those whom they regard as the leading "apostles" in Jerusalem. But whereas Martyn takes as a context for the teachers' estimate of the Jerusalem "church" a law-observant Gentile mission sponsored, at least in part, by the "apostles" in Jerusalem, I have been arguing all along that the boundary-crossing that produced the mixed church of Antioch and the "missions" of Paul and Barnabas among Gentiles, and the issues raised by these efforts and accomplishments, are the issues of the boundary-crossing people involved, namely, diaspora Jews. That there were teachers who had taken upon themselves the task of urging Gentiles who had formed Christ assemblies to live among Gentiles as Jews is possible to imagine only for people aware of the novelty and strangeness of the territory they had entered and who were now looking for maps to reveal more familiar bridges for crossing back. Their teachings may have already included an incipient narrative of origins in the homeland; in any case, they authorized their appeal with reference to "the mother church" in Jerusalem. In order to do this, all they really had to know was the Jewish

---

[113] Ibid., 444–45.
[114] Ibid., 457–59.
[115] Ibid., 464–65, emphasis original; see also 454–57, 459–66.

piety of the Jesus people in Jerusalem. On the other hand, the Jerusalem group does not consist of Jews who are boundary crossers. They did not conceive of directing their own efforts to Gentiles, nor does a reading of Gal 1–2 convince me that they were likely to encourage or support those in their midst who might be inclined to do so. It is easier to imagine on their part a reticence toward the very efforts that were aimed at Gentile populations in the diaspora (cf. Matt 10:5–6). It is an important consideration that they did not reject the Antioch project. To have taken responsibility to direct such a project, even if through the agency of others, would have been in fact too deep an involvement. It seems to me this can be seen from the Antioch incident itself, where the issue for Jerusalem was not Gentile adherence to Torah but Jewish adherence.

For Paul's part, responding to the situation in Galatia included the displacement of the Jerusalem community from the role attributed to it by the teachers. In displacing the Jerusalem community, Paul has substituted a utopian myth of origins for a locative myth. The true mother is nowhere on earth (cf. Phil 3:20), but one can catch a glimpse of her many offspring in Paul's labors (Gal 4:19), including those among the Galatians, that is, if they will heed Paul's warning (Gal 5:2). It may not have escaped Paul's notice that Isa 54:1 has in view an earthly Jerusalem, one that is about to be visited from on high. However pointed his reference to the present Jerusalem bearing children for slavery, it is not Paul's last word about the saints in Jerusalem. Indeed, despite Gal 4:21–26, Paul can reverse himself in another context and bring to bear his own mythic version of origins in Jerusalem. It is well known that Paul expresses himself more carefully in Romans and softens, or even drops, some of the harsher statements of Galatians. However, in Rom 15:27 one seems to be reading a statement drawn from a speech of Paul in the book of Acts. Never mind Gal 4:25. If Paul went to Jerusalem earlier armed with an argument that the gospel he preached among the Gentiles was in no way dependent on Jerusalem, how can he say what he says in Rom 15:27 in anticipation of another visit? This raises a matter thus far left out of account: the collection for the saints in Jerusalem.

III

A collection for the poor among the Jesus people in Jerusalem is found as a request that concludes the statements acknowledging a division of responsibility at the Jerusalem meeting: μόνον τῶν πτωχῶν ἵνα μνημονεύωμεν, "[the] only [other thing agreed was] that we should remember the poor," ὃ καὶ ἐσπούδασα αὐτὸ τοῦτο ποιῆσαι, "which very thing I was eager to do" (Gal 2:10). In his monograph on Paul's collection for Jerusalem, Dieter Georgi argues that the term "the poor" does not refer primarily to an indigent group among the Jesus people in Jerusalem, nor does the verb "remember" in the present subjunctive refer primarily to material aid.[116] Instead, he concludes, "The absolute use of this appellation in Galatians 2:10 and the fact that it does not need any explanation show that it must have been a title commonly bestowed upon that congregation."[117] The title signified that the Jerusalem Jesus congregation had a privileged place in the eschatological drama of the redemption of Zion and Israel that according to biblical promises would also bring the pilgrimage of the nations to Jerusalem. The Jerusalem Jesus people were the eschatological vanguard, the remnant, and that essential dignity was continually to be kept in mind. The remembering was therefore not an annual subvention, a tax. It did not have to do primarily with monetary aid, and the present tense of the verb is therefore not a problem.[118] The scenario presented by Georgi is surely a familiar one:

> The post-resurrection appearances of Jesus in Galilee ... prompted them [the disciples] to form communities, and one of them, around Peter and the Twelve, had returned to Jerusalem. This second anabasis to the Holy City where Jesus' crucifixion had occurred in the meantime can only be explained by the new christological certainty and eschatological awareness they had gained. In this expectation Jerusalem must have received an important place—an importance that city had never been credited with by Jesus himself. This shift in understanding explains why Peter, the Twelve, and those around them went back to Jerusalem and remained there in spite of the extreme hardships and pressures they had to face, adversities that were undoubtedly intensified further by the dangerous claim of representing the chosen people of God in possession of the promise of the impending eschatological completion.[119]

---

[116] Dieter Georgi, *Remembering the Poor: The History of Paul's Collection for Jerusalem* (Nashville: Abingdon, 1992), 21–42.

[117] Ibid., 34.

[118] Ibid., 41–42: "The primary meaning of the expression 'to remember' was not one of financial assistance to be given to the Jerusalem congregation. Such succor was certainly implied as well, but something more comprehensive was in view: the situation the congregation at Jerusalem found itself in. Its significance and achievements were to be brought into memory to the Antiochene and Gentile churches continuously. In other words, the 'remembering' meant primarily an inner attitude—an attitude that was to be expressed through recognition, gratefulness, intercession by prayers, and, finally, financial aid as well."

[119] Ibid., 36. Compare this statement on Christian origins with Georgi's perspicacious judgments about the deleterious effects on the enterprise of comparison of an "eschatological" imagination operative in New Testament scholarship (idem, "Rudolf Bultmann's *Theology of the New Testament* Revisited," in *Bultmann, Retrospect and Prospect: The Centenary Symposium at Wellesley* [ed. Edward C. Hobbs; HTS 35; Philadelphia: Fortress, 1985], 82). It appears to me that Georgi's judgments in the Bultmann volume would implicate his own description quoted above; see further, Ron Cameron, "The Anatomy of a Discourse: On 'Eschatology' as

While the scenario is familiar, it is a rather large construction to erect on the use of πτωχοί in Gal 2:10, as though it were the origin of the designation of the later Ebionites. For one thing, it is difficult to determine that a titular usage is intended. On what basis would we distinguish the usage in Luke 6:20? How else would a specifically economic sense be indicated in the Galatians passage?[120] Moreover, in Rom 15:26 it is quite clear that Paul is referring to a monetary contribution to help meet the material needs of the poor among the saints in Jerusalem.[121] In other ways, too, Georgi's judgment regarding Gal 2:10 seems difficult to sustain. He states that the Jerusalem group could not have survived in Jerusalem without financial aid, yet financial aid was only a secondary consideration.[122] He would also have us believe that a claim of eschatological priority on the part of the Jerusalem congregation, which is for Georgi the very meaning of the designation in 2:10a, would carry with it no special judicial claims, a distinction I find hard to accept.[123] This is not to say that eschatological ideas could have played no role in the thinking of the parties at the Jerusalem meeting. If we take eschatology to refer to mythic scenarios of final resolutions, such ideas sometimes provide a framework for achieving new arrangements that are workable precisely because they allow one to bracket what can neither be abandoned nor resolved. Thus, at the meeting, the parties may have been able to acknowledge each other because they recognized that in some way both Jerusalem and Antioch were engaged in a redefinition of *Israel* and that what appeared to be irreconcilable differences concerning the entailments of their distinctive engagements could be

---

a Category for Explaining Christian Origins," *MTSR* 8 (1996): 231–45, citing Georgi's article in the Bultmann volume on p. 240 n. 17.

[120] See Lüdemann, *Paul, Apostle to the Gentiles*, 79.

[121] Georgi does not deny this: "Contrary to the terminology used in the Jerusalem agreement, the term 'the poor' in this particular context is no longer used in an absolute sense as in Galatians 2:10 and, therefore, does not constitute an eschatological title, but rather a sociological designation.... The economic perspective had been included in the venture since the beginning, but originally these economic considerations were treated as almost identical with the eschatological ones" (*Remembering the Poor*, 114). This only raises the question of the grounds for arguing that πτωχοί means anything different in the two passages.

[122] Ibid., 40: "Indeed, the congregation at Jerusalem could never have gone through with their exemplary task on behalf of the entire Jesus movement and would have had to abandon its eschatological outpost had it been denied financial support. Still, such economic assistance was only secondary to the clearly theological principle entailed in 'remembering.'"

[123] Ibid., 42: "The agreement on the necessity to 'remember the poor'—that is to say, to honor the demonstrative eschatological status of the congregation at Jerusalem ...—constituted a confession of unity of the community of Jesus Christ grounded in the hope of Christ's impending return. It did not imply the recognition of any kind of judicial authority held by the Jerusalem congregation or its leaders."

bracketed in different eschatological scenarios without being abandoned. But, true, not everything could be postponed.

I have already suggested that we view the Jerusalem meeting as a particular occasion in a more protracted attempt to work out a relationship between Jesus groups in Jerusalem and environs and those in Antioch and environs, but without reversing the chronology of the meeting in Jerusalem and the incident in Antioch. I have further supposed that what they accomplished at the meeting could neither effectively nor legally have involved a juridical or organizational tie between private associations in cities of different provinces and, therefore, that it is unlikely that the meeting took place on the basis of a recognition of Jerusalem's authority to hand down decisions concerning the arrangements or the affairs of the groups in Antioch. On this account, to ascribe some sort of superior, not to say unique, status to the Jesus people in Jerusalem would be rather empty, at least with respect to any effective relationship with Antioch, and could only be a provocation to the real powers in Jerusalem. It would be one thing for teachers in Galatia to paint such a picture of the "apostles" in Jerusalem before the eyes of the credulous in Galatia (Paul's witchcraft accusation is understandable, since apparently he had put on his own demonstrations, Gal 3:1), quite another for the Jerusalem Jesus folk to want to carry around that banner in Jerusalem. On the other hand, I have emphasized that the effective ideological role of the Jerusalem group for Jesus people in Antioch is more likely to have concerned the past rather than the future, that is, the need to render intelligible the changes they themselves had brought about in relation to some sort of memory of the past. But what was at stake for Jerusalem in an arrangement with Antioch?

The agreement in Gal 2:9 necessarily entails some notion of separation.[124] The emphatic position of the poor in 2:10 represents the current link between the two associations.[125] The group in Jerusalem may therefore have recognized that a movement toward some form of translocal

---

[124] Martyn sees this clearly: "Here [in the formulation of the agreement in Gal 2:9] it is important to notice that something Paul came in time to regard as an antinomy characteristic of the Old Age was written right into the formula: the distinction between Jew and Gentile (see 3:28)" (*Galatians*, 221–22). Cf. Georgi, *Remembering the Poor*, 32, who acknowledges that a reading of Gal 2:9 "concedes the existence of different theologies, organizations, lifestyles, and missionary activities."

[125] I am taking up Georgi's important observation: "The reason for which the emphasis is put on 'the poor' here is rooted in the content of the preceding subordinate clause, which runs parallel to this statement. As it were, this subordinate clause does refer to separation. The emphasis on 'the poor' ... highlights the second half of the parallelism, which can be interpreted as meaning that the second final clause simply refers to the only visible link between the Gentiles and the Jews in the church" (*Remembering the Poor*, 33).

relationship with an established association in Syrian Antioch, a major city with a large Jewish population, was important to the viability of its own group in Jerusalem, many of whose members were probably not well established in the city. Remembering the poor was not a tax incumbent on Gentiles to be paid to the new temple of the last days, although some people from both groups may have viewed the activity in analogy with freewill offerings sent to the temple. It was requested as a tangible sign of κοινωνία that helped to ensure the continued existence of the Jerusalem group. In making the request a part of the agreement, Jerusalem was also acknowledging in a more direct way their relationship with Antioch and with the groups emerging in the wake of the activities of Paul and Barnabas. But surely Jerusalem, for its own part, would have to make tangible that the relationship ran both ways. I suggested earlier that the visit of Cephas took place on his own initiative, but perhaps it was undertaken as a sign of the existing κοινωνία between the two groups. If so, it turned out to be unsatisfactory to others in Jerusalem, who felt that conditions had to be attached with respect to the practices of the Jewish members in Antioch. This would also place the delegation from James in a somewhat different light. They came not in protest nor with demands but out of the increasing pressure that was felt in Jerusalem to acknowledge and reciprocate in an appropriate way the acceptance of gifts from Antioch and its satellite communities. The irony of making it depend on a separation may be more apparent to us than to them. In one way, the problems were simply those that would tend to arise at a juncture of interest and activity in forming some sort of translocal relationship between autonomous local associations engaged in different practices that bore a different relationship to ancestral traditions.

As has often been noted, Paul refers only to himself, and in the past tense, in expressing the response to the request: "which very thing I was eager to do" (Gal 2:10b). I think the better solution to the problem this poses is to suppose that Paul was not engaged in the activity of a collection when he wrote the letter and that the reason for this had to do with the incident at Antioch and a straining of his relations with that community as well as with Jerusalem.[126] However, when Paul did engage in a collection for the poor among the saints in Jerusalem in his own churches, it is clear from 1 Cor 16:1 that the churches in Galatia were included. If, as most scholars think, Gal 2:10b implies that arrangements for the collection were not yet underway in Galatia at the time of the writing the letter, we must suppose that Paul made the arrangement subsequently, either through a

---

[126] See Taylor, *Paul, Antioch and Jerusalem*, 197–98; Martyn, *Galatians*, 222–28. For a different reconstruction, see Lüdemann, *Paul, Apostle to the Gentiles*, 77–88.

visit or a letter that is lost.[127] After writing the polemical letter to the Galatians, it is certainly a matter of interest how Paul would have approached them with this project on behalf of those "bearing children for slavery." The fact that the Galatians are not included among the participants in Rom 15:26 may indicate that in the long run they rejected Paul's effort to associate them with a collection from his churches, which, of course, would be a likely indication of the success of the teachers.[128] In any case, I am more interested in the undertaking itself, how we might account for it, and what it might signify.

We can take note briefly of a few different views. Taylor believes that the collection was undertaken by Paul in the wake of a return trip to Antioch (Acts 18:22). The visit may have enabled Paul to improve relations with Antioch and to get some estimate of a project undertaken by his churches for Jerusalem. The intention would be to establish a relation of κοινωνία between his churches and Jerusalem similar to that established between Antioch and Jerusalem.[129] Martyn thinks that Paul conceived the idea as he reflected on what was likely to be the effect of the volatile letter sent off to the Galatians. However, the fundamental conviction was theological; despite the struggle with false brothers and their allies, it signified the bond that actually existed between all the "local outposts of God's redemptive invasion of the world in Jesus Christ."[130] Georgi notes that Paul introduced the project of the collection for Jerusalem in Galatia and in Corinth at a time that would appear inauspicious, for each community was undergoing serious internal problems that concerned Paul and with which he was deeply engaged. But Georgi thinks Paul intended to utilize the collection as a "pedagogical instrument for straightening out the confused minds of his converts."[131] In particular, preparations for the collection in Corinth follow Paul's discussion of Christ's resurrection. According to Georgi, "First Corinthians 15 is meant to instill the idea of historic indebtedness on the part of later Jesus-believing congregations to the first witnesses."[132]

---

[127] On the relationship between dispatching the letter to the Galatians and approaching the Galatians on participation in the collection, see the somewhat different views of Martyn, *Galatians*, 226 n. 79; and Georgi, *Remembering the Poor*, 49.

[128] This is the position of Martyn, *Galatians*, 227 n. 81; Georgi thinks that the representatives of the Galatian churches had not yet arrived in Corinth or that they had not made a final commitment when Romans was written (*Remembering the Poor*, 123).

[129] Taylor, *Paul, Antioch and Jerusalem*, 199.

[130] Martyn, *Galatians*, 226; cf. his nn. 76–77.

[131] Georgi, *Remembering the Poor*, 50.

[132] Ibid., 52, adding: "As far as those first witnesses themselves are concerned, it is not possible to refer to them without remembering the first Jesus-believing community as well (this being for Paul the community in Jerusalem). The emergence of a Jesus community in that city

For Francis Watson, Paul's collection for Jerusalem is undertaken neither from ecumenical motives designed to achieve or to express the unity of Jews and Gentiles in Christ nor as a pedagogical tool aimed at internal issues in his churches. Rather, Paul was convinced on the basis of his Galatian experience of the vulnerability of his churches to infiltration by emissaries of the Jerusalem church. Paul intended the collection "as a means of convincing the Jerusalem church of the legitimacy of the law-free congregations he had founded, so that they would stop trying to undermine them."[133] On this basis Watson is able to maintain that Rom 15:27 is not really in conflict with the polemical aims of Galatians. It is simply a different strategy for achieving the same goal but with a growing awareness of the power of the opposition:

> The stress in Rom. 15:27 on the indebtedness of Gentiles to Jerusalem is therefore not to be understood as an entirely guileless expression of Paul's real feelings, but as a continuation of the strategy of Rom. 11 (cf. also 15:8f): Paul attempts to secure recognition for his congregations by setting his own position in the context of Jewish Christian beliefs (in this case, belief in the supremacy of the Jerusalem church).[134]

It is difficult to see any close relationship between the request in Gal 2:10a and the collection initiated by Paul in his churches. For one thing, apart from Galatians, there are no other references in Paul's letters to the request from Jerusalem, and despite lengthy passages in the Corinthian correspondence that concern the collection, Paul never indicates that he is making good on a commitment he made in Jerusalem. Thus, there is at least no indication that Paul has explained the reason for this project in his churches by reference to a prior agreement. Moreover, Paul is organizing a one-time effort, in contrast to the formulation of the request in Galatians. We should also take account of a change of situation. If indeed Paul's

---

bore witness to the power inherent in the testimony of the appearances of the resurrected Jesus, a power capable of calling into existence the church.... Hence, the Jerusalem community acted as a constant reminder to every Jesus believer and to all Jesus-believing communities of their common origin: the resurrection of Jesus from the dead."

[133] Francis Watson, *Paul, Judaism and the Gentiles: A Sociological Approach* (SNTSMS 56; Cambridge: Cambridge University Press, 1986), 175.

[134] Ibid., 176. For Watson, 2 Cor 9:12–14 is an expression of what Paul hopes will be the outcome of the collection: a change of attitude on the part of the Jerusalem church toward his Gentile congregations. In view of Watson's estimate of the opposition to Paul, however, one would have to think that Paul is whistling in the dark. Cf. the explication of these verses in Georgi, *Remembering the Poor*, 102–7, who views the passage as Paul's transformation of a Hellenistic cult mystery into a worldwide spiritual worship in the drama of the concrete historical unity of the Christ community expressed as a material occurrence.

labors in Galatia, Asia Minor, Macedonia, and Greece took place subsequent to the Jerusalem meeting and his leaving Antioch, he has covered a much larger area in a considerably shorter time than in the work with Barnabas, and he has independently carried on a work among Gentiles whose assemblies are of sufficient stability for Paul to be able to undertake a collection for Jerusalem. While I would suppose that already at the Jerusalem meeting there was a sharing of mutual accomplishments among the representatives, it seems unlikely that members of Jerusalem and affiliated groups in Judea would have been able to imagine at the time what might confront them some seven or eight years later from more distant lands, especially if this were to be presented as a consequence of the preaching and community organization of this self-styled, Jeremiah-like apostle to the Gentiles (Gal 1:15; cf. Jer 1:5). Moreover, although we cannot say exactly what was known in Jerusalem about Paul's controversies with other Jewish teachers, his response in Antioch very likely was known in Jerusalem.

Nonetheless, I think there is a tendency to dramatize Paul's anxiety about the opposition he expects to meet when he reaches Jerusalem and about his concern for the acceptability of the gift for the saints (Rom 15:30–31). We think we know what happened, and Paul must have had good reason for the premonition. But in the context of the letter to the Romans, it would appear that Paul's intent is already to enlist the support of the addressees in his cause and in the cause of his churches through the labor of their earnest prayers and in anticipation of the support he hopes to receive from them in a mission to the west (Rom 15:22–24, 28–29). Given the extent, duration, and vicissitudes of the project and the way in which Paul has come to speak of the collection as the undertaking of his churches (1 Cor 8:1–5; 9:1–2; Rom 15:26), I do not imagine that he would have persisted to its completion without strong hopes of success in the delivery and reception of the gift. Thus, while I agree with Watson that the collection for Jerusalem has something to do with recognition of his churches, I see the matter in a significantly different light.[135] Had Paul been quite certain

---

[135] Watson himself recognizes that Paul does not go up to Jerusalem "with the sombre sense that the end of his apostolic labours was near" (*Paul, Judaism and the Gentiles*, 105). However, the degree of opposition that existed between Paul and the Jerusalem group, according to Watson, would appear to make Paul's prospects of success in Jerusalem very unlikely; indeed, it would make the undertaking dangerous. Watson's treatment of Romans argues that the letter is addressed primarily to Jewish Christians in Rome: "The letter itself was an essential part of these [Paul's future travel] plans ...: to persuade the Roman Jewish Christians to accept the Paulinists, in preparation for Paul's longer-term plans" (ibid.). The collection and the letter are therefore closely related: "This means that the collection was intended to accomplish in Jerusalem exactly what the letter to the Romans was intended to

that there was active opposition among Jesus people in Jerusalem who had intended all along to undermine his efforts among Gentiles, I do not think he would have undertaken the collection. Moreover, the manner in which the Jerusalem group and its leaders may have been represented by Jewish opponents of Paul in the areas of his activity does not constitute evidence to conclude that the Jerusalem leaders would be in a position to intervene effectively on Paul's behalf. If Paul actually thought they could intervene, why did he not travel to Jerusalem and remind James and others of the recognition his labors had received at the Jerusalem meeting, before he made efforts for a collection that clearly required much persistence and persuasion?

When we start from the view that early Jesus associations were principally local phenomena, formed and organized on a local basis, we put the significance of the collection into relief. The various maneuvers and persuasions Paul made in its behalf underline the significance that it had for Paul. Moreover, it seems that he did manage to persuade most churches in the areas of his activity to participate and made arrangements for representatives to accompany him to Jerusalem (1 Cor 16:3–4; cf. Acts 20:4). While we cannot know for sure how members of these churches regarded the matter, we can see from 2 Cor 8–9 and Rom 15 that there was indeed a pedagogical intent, though not, I think, one aimed at correcting "the confused minds of his converts,"[136] but rather one intended to instill Paul's own sense of "his" churches sharing a wider horizon of relationships by engaging them in a common enterprise for a group that was itself far away. However local the horizons of the churches may have remained, Paul's own horizons were not local. Where was home? Paul crossed and erased boundaries continually and then established his own boundaries that he most certainly wanted to defend (consider Galatians), while also insisting that he did not want to invade anyone else's turf (2 Cor 10:12–18). I am quite sure Paul had an extensive network both of Jews and Gentiles, but he was also an outsider everywhere he went. Was a third trip to Jerusalem a homecoming for Paul? No, it was clearly just a way station. For Paul, beyond Jerusalem were Rome and Spain. Nonetheless, if Paul had persisted in a collection for the poor among the saints in Jerusalem and was bringing to the Holy City representatives of the Gentile churches, Jerusalem could not be thought of by Paul as merely a way station for the representatives of these churches.

---

accomplish in Rome: recognition by Jewish Christians who observed the law of the legitimacy of Pauline Gentile Christians who did not" (176). For a reading of Romans that takes the letter's encoded audience of Gentiles as its methodological starting point and as a major consideration for achieving a coherent interpretation of the letter, see Stanley K. Stowers, *A Rereading of Romans: Justice, Jews, and Gentiles* (New Haven: Yale University Press, 1994).

[136] So Georgi, *Remembering the Poor*, 50.

The collection had pedagogical aims, but also an epic dimension. In Rom 9–11 Paul engages in a stunning revision of Israel's epic that is designed to show the implied audience the present priority of the Gentile mission in God's plan and at the same time to warn Gentiles against displacing Jews from the advantages that they still hold. I would suggest that Rom 15:26–27 does the same thing with respect to the collection. Gentiles have taken the initiative to establish a κοινωνία with Jews by bringing a gift for the poor among the saints in Jerusalem. They were glad to do it because they owed it to them. It is not they who support the root but the root that supports them (Rom 11:18). If then Paul was not coming home, he was bringing his churches home with the gift that was being conveyed. And what were the spiritual blessings of Jerusalem that Gentiles had come to share? The proclamation of Paul's gospel, of course. The pedagogical intent of the collection was not recognition of the Jerusalem "apostles" as first witnesses to the resurrection.[137] It was the recognition of Jerusalem as the place of origin of Paul's gospel (Rom 15:8–12, 18–21). However different the perspective and historical location of the writer of Acts from the perspective and circumstances of Paul, the later writer was not the first to conceive the idea that the gospel not only to Jew but also to Gentile had gone forth from Jerusalem. Paul's point in Gal 1–2 and his point in Rom 15 are therefore virtually opposites. In the former, the gospel he proclaimed among the Gentiles was not in the debt of Jerusalem. Now, in anticipation of Jerusalem's acceptance of the gift of his churches, it would be fitting to imagine that the gospel of the uncircumcision was coming home to the city of its origin. This is not to speak about what Paul expected to accomplish in Jerusalem or what he thought his companions would learn about the saints in Jerusalem, but about how he chose to represent the matter in Romans.

I would suggest a similar opposition between Gal 1–2 and 1 Cor 15:3b–11. In Galatians, Paul thematizes his own calling and gospel as a divine ordination while dismissing the local reputation of the pillars as a matter merely of human judgment (Gal 2:6). He does not refer to a kerygmatic tradition that he received and passed on, nor does he express his calling to be an apostle in the language of appearances of the risen Christ (Gal 1:16). He dissociates himself from Jerusalem in his preaching of the gospel to Gentiles. In 1 Cor 15, on the other hand, the essentials of the gospel he preached are said to constitute a received tradition, and the appearance of

---

[137] Contra Georgi, *Remembering the Poor*, 116: "The 'spiritual goods' in Romans 15:27 are not the Jewish tradition as understood in Jerusalem, nor are they the tradition of the historical Jesus, but are rather things belonging to the new creation ... rooted in Jesus' resurrection—that is to say, primarily the message of the resurrection as that which constitutes the church."

Christ to Paul links him to others in a chain of prior appearances, including those to Cephas and James. Just as in Rom 15 the gospel Paul preaches among the Gentiles can be imagined to have gone forth from Jerusalem, so in 1 Cor 15 Paul preaches as matters of first importance what others in Jerusalem also preach (15:11), presumably not only Cephas and James but also the Twelve and all the apostles (and perhaps also those among the "more than five hundred" brothers and sisters?). In 15:3b–11 Paul secures his own legitimation as an apostle by applying to himself a formula of legitimation (καὶ ὅτι ὤφθη Κηφᾷ ... ἔσχατον δὲ πάντων ... ὤφθη κἀμοί, 15:5a, 8). At the same time, he is appealing to tradition and the names of presumed authorities as attestation to the resurrection. Thus, he ensures that his preaching will not be viewed by the Corinthians as the only claim on which the kerygma is based (15:11).

Since Paul has obviously added himself to the list, there is no question of supposing that he has not made any contribution to the tradition he passes on. Moreover, while the issue Paul has to address makes it necessary for him to use the appearance formula (the formula of legitimation) as a tradition of multiple attestations of the resurrection, we should not assume that the attributions involved (which may indeed be intended to suggest a foundational role for Jerusalem) settle the question of the actual provenance or function of the list. In my judgment, a crucial question concerning the provenance of 15:5–7 is whether the appearance formula was originally linked to this particular form of the kerygma (15:3b–4), for if that is the case we have to suppose a similar provenance for both. Following Mack, who has shown that the kerygma of Jesus' saving death and vindication is a martyr myth related to the identity and social legitimation of the mixed congregations of Jews and Gentiles in Antioch, I would be inclined to propose a similar provenance for the appearance formula in 15:5–7.[138] However, it is not clear that the appearance formula was originally transmitted with the kerygma. Despite the variety of kerygmatic formulae in the

---

[138] Burton L. Mack, *A Myth of Innocence: Mark and Christian Origins* (Philadelphia: Fortress, 1988), 102–13; cf. Merrill P. Miller, "How Jesus Became Christ: Probing a Thesis," *Cont* 2/2–3 (1993): 251–57. The assumption that the appearance tradition must ultimately stem from Jerusalem is unwarranted. Thus, despite Gerd Lüdemann's confidence on this matter—*The Resurrection of Jesus: History, Experience, Theology* (trans. John Bowden; Minneapolis: Fortress, 1994), 36, "On the whole the alternative 'Jerusalem or Antioch' seems to be exaggerated. 'For even if the tradition came to Paul by way of the community in Antioch, it would only have reproduced what it too had received—from Jerusalem'" (citing Eduard Lohse, *Martyer und Gottesknecht: Untersuchungen zur urchristlichen Verkündigung vom Sühntod Jesu Christi* [2nd ed.; FRLANT 64; Göttingen: Vandenhoeck & Ruprecht,1963], 113)—Lüdemann can only refer to 1 Cor 15:11 as evidence. But 1 Cor 15:11 does not inevitably reveal the provenance of the tradition, but the reason that Paul cites it. And if the tradition originated in Jerusalem circles, why should we suppose that Antioch would "only have reproduced" the tradition?

Pauline corpus, only in this instance do we find the kerygma linked to a sequence of appearances. Indeed, there are no other instances of the appearance formula in Paul (cf. the language of Gal 1:16; see also 1 Tim 3:16). It is in Acts that one finds narrative statements in speeches referring to the death and resurrection of Jesus and to the function of the apostles as witnesses to the resurrection (Acts 2:32; 3:14–15; 5:30–32; and especially 10:39–41; 13:29–31; Acts 13:31 and Luke 24:34 are the only other instances of the formula).[139] Thus, whatever the provenance of 15:5–7, statements about appearances of Jesus that make use of a formula of legitimation could have arisen without any connection to the kerygma, while the kerygma does not seem to have been regularly transmitted with this formula.[140]

Questions also arise about the form of the tradition Paul received. Did Paul himself create the temporal sequence from discrete traditions or from a list originally linked by the conjunction καί? Was it only 15:5 that Paul found joined to the kerygma of 15:3b–4 (note that the ὅτι *recitativum* appears four times in 15:3–5)? Was Paul himself responsible for the list of appearances, while the tradition itself ended at καὶ ὅτι ὤφθη? This last possibility creates a formal parallel with καὶ ὅτι ἐτάφη and a material parallel emphasizing that Jesus really died and was really raised.[141] This view cannot be excluded on formal grounds. The kerygma in 15:3b–4 with the two references to scripture, the inclusion of the burial, and the temporal reference to the third day is already a more elaborate statement than other forms of the kerygma. On the other hand, it is typical of references to the saving death and vindication of Jesus that they are expressed without specifying the manner of death and without including a reference to the tyrant. Thus, here too burial and appearance do not require further qualification. But is Paul likely to have included himself in the way that he does if he was composing the list himself? This cannot be ruled out. In Gal 1:17 Paul refers to those in Jerusalem who were apostles before him, so obviously he would not have placed himself first in the list.[142] But would Paul have

---

[139] Whether the subject of the appearance formula was *christos* is not clear. *Christos* is the subject throughout 1 Cor 15 because of the firm place the term already holds in the kerygma. In 1 Cor 9:2 Paul refers to seeing Jesus our Lord; *kyrios* is also the subject of ὤφθη in Luke 24:34.

[140] It is for this reason that not just the provenance but the transmission of the tradition is important. For even if the appearance formula was first used in Jerusalem, the conclusion that the kerygma was also cultivated in Jerusalem circles does not follow. The formula does presuppose a change of status and destiny for Jesus, but this could have been entertained as a disappearance, ascension, translation, transfiguration, departure, or exaltation without any necessary link with the saving death and resurrection/vindication of a martyr.

[141] This view is argued by Mack, *Myth of Innocence,* 113 n. 11.

[142] In using the term *apostles* in reference to the time of his conversion, Paul is probably applying anachronistically to those of repute in Jerusalem a term that carried authority later

referred to all the apostles (15:7b), giving the impression that they formed a closed circle, and only then included himself? Perhaps, because it gives him an opportunity to turn the formula into a brief narrative elaboration that he urges as a paradigm of the special effectiveness of God's grace in him. In my judgment the major problem with supposing that Paul created the list is the formula itself using the aorist passive of ὁρᾶν plus the dative. For one thing, this is not Paul's language of visions of the Lord (2 Cor 3:18; 12:1), nor is it his way of referring to his calling in Gal 1:16. More important is Paul's use of the perfect active of ὁρᾶν in 1 Cor 9:1, which seems to me to presuppose the circulation of a formula that makes use of the same verb. Paul probably did not use the list in his earlier preaching to the Corinthians, since it seems pertinent in particular to the problem addressed in 1 Cor 15. Nonetheless, on the whole, it seems to me that Paul's strategy of calling special attention to the paradigmatic character of his calling and of widening the support for the truth of his gospel gains in rhetorical effect if we suppose that he is drawing on a formula with which the Corinthians are familiar.

Since Paul utilizes the same formula for all the appearances and clearly intends to legitimate his own apostolic claims by applying the formula to himself, it is likely that the aorist passive of ὁρᾶν plus dative functions in each case as a formula of legitimation.[143] In his recent book on the resurrection of Jesus, Lüdemann agrees with this view, but only with strong qualifications: "However, it should not be claimed that the legitimation formulae do not allow us to make any inferences about the process of legitimation ... [and] that the phrase 'he appeared' was only a literary form of expression of the authority of the one legitimated."[144] Throughout the discussion of 1 Cor 15:1–11, Lüdemann argues against the view that the resurrection is a sui generis event that is not amenable to historical investigation of the experiential process that stands behind the formulaic

---

in his own circles; alternatively, he may be using a term applied to the Jerusalem leaders by others.

[143] See Ulrich Wilckens, "Der Ursprung der Überlieferung der Erscheinungen des Auferstandenen: Zur traditionsgeschichtlichen Analyse von 1. Kor. 15,1–11," in *Dogma und Denkstrukturen* (ed. Wilfried Joest and Wolfhart Pannenberg; Göttingen: Vandenhoeck & Ruprecht, 1963), 56–95, repr. in *Zur neutestamentlichen Überlieferung von der Auferstehung Jesu* (ed. Paul Hoffmann; Wege der Forschung 522; Darmstadt: Wissenschaftliche Buchgesellschaft, 1988), 139–93; and Rudolf Pesch, "Zur Entstehung des Glaubens an die Auferstehung Jesu: Ein Vorschlag zur Diskussion," *TQ* 153 (1973): 201–28.

[144] Lüdemann, *Resurrection of Jesus*, 37; cf. 202 n. 160, in opposition to the earlier position of Pesch, "Zur Entstehung des Glaubens," esp. 214–15. For the later position of Pesch, see idem, "Zur Entstehung des Glaubens an die Auferstehung Jesu: Ein neuer Versuch," *FZPhTh* 30 (1983): 73–98, esp. 87, repr. in Hoffmann, *Zur neutestamentlichen Überlieferung von der Auferstehung Jesu*, 228–55, esp. 243–44.

language. Lüdemann concludes that the resurrection experience involved for both Peter and Paul subjective hallucinations accompanying the experience of personal forgiveness.[145] The appearances to others are secondary in that they are already influenced by the proclamation of the risen Christ.[146] It is symptomatic of the study of Christian origins that Lüdemann can formulate the historical problem of the resurrection only in terms of the alternatives of an irreducible mystery or a personal subjective experience of radical transformation. But in any case, Lüdemann fails to show that the formula is transparent to a particular kind of experience. He notes that many scholars have pointed to the LXX use of ὤφθη plus dative or preposition (corresponding to the Hebrew *nipʿal* formation of *rʾh*) in reports of an appearance of Yahweh or an angel to Abraham, Isaac, Jacob, and Moses, and have concluded that the theophany formula does not allow the scholar to arrive at an event lying behind it. "No wonder then that some exegetes could speak of a legitimation formula without any real background relating to experience."[147] Lüdemann counters by noting that in the LXX ὤφθη can have subjects other than God in which a visual aspect is present.[148] This is of course the case, but it has no pertinence for the issue. A formula that presupposes the special destiny of Jesus is obviously closer to the theophany formula than it is to the use of ὤφθη plus the dative with other subjects in the LXX. The same problem arises in connection with 1 Cor 9:1, where again Lüdemann appeals to the visual aspect of ὤφθη against the cogent arguments of Hans-Willi Winden, who states that the "polished rhetoric of this verse ... bears witness to the *self-legitimation of the apostle* as the sole aim of his argument." Thus, 1 Cor 9:1 according to Winden does not reflect "any revelation event ... and might have been formulated by Paul first of all on the basis of his knowledge of his traditional ὤφθη statements from 1 Cor. 15.5–7."[149] The historical question is not, as Lüdemann believes, the question of what sort of personal experience lies behind the legitimation formula, but rather the claims and social investments authorized by the formula and the historical consequences of its use.

What, then, does the formula authorize? If we can put together some clues, we might also get some purchase on the provenance of the formula.

---

[145] Lüdemann, *Resurrection of Jesus*, 96–100.
[146] Ibid., 100, 108–9.
[147] Ibid., 48.
[148] Ibid., 48–49.
[149] Hans-Willi Winden, *Wie kam und wie kommt es zum Osterglaube? Darstellung, Beurteilung und Weiterführung der durch Rudolf Pesch ausgelösten Diskussion* (Disputationes Theologicae 12; Frankfurt am Main: Lang, 1982), 104, emphasis original, cited in Lüdemann, *Resurrection of Jesus*, 51.

The authority being claimed is not merely within the context of the local community. This is especially clear in the case of Jerusalem, because as far as the authority of James, Cephas, and John is concerned, one gathers that Paul's references in Galatians to those of repute (οἱ δοκοῦντες) and to the pillars (οἱ στῦλοι) are the terms used locally for the principal leaders of the Jerusalem group. Since Paul refers to James as the brother of the Lord, it is likely that the authority of James in the community rests largely on a familial relationship to Jesus. The authority of Cephas and John was probably recognized on the basis of their role in the earliest formation of the group in Jerusalem and perhaps also on their claim to transmit teachings of Jesus. Paul's "put-down" of those held in repute (Gal 2:6) implies that their authority can be perceived to rest in human relationships. Moreover, Paul's contrary claim for himself in Galatians is not responding to similar claims made by the Jerusalem leaders but rather to claims of dependence upon them that he rejects. In Galatians Paul wants to distance his credentials from anything the pillars might claim as their own. Finally, and most important because it concerns translocal matters, the separate lines of responsibility for Jews and Gentiles found in Gal 2:7–9 are authorized only by the mutual recognition of existing interests and practices. There is no indication that the authority of the Jerusalem leaders presupposes, depends upon, or has in view claims that rest on the sort of formula of legitimation being considered here. On the contrary, the indications of authority that we have for the pillars suggest that it rests on other bases.

I have already indicated the reasons that we cannot be sure that the appearances of Jesus, formulated as a discourse of legitimation, arose in connection with the kerygma. But it can still be argued that linked to the particular kerygmatic form, 1 Cor 15:3b–4, it is pre-Pauline. In comparison with other kerygmatic formulae, 15:3b–4 gives evidence of an effort to encompass the saving death and vindication of Jesus in a biblical horizon. The double reference to κατὰ τὰς γραφάς at the end of 15:3–4 may have in view particular scripture, Isa 53:4, 5, 12 LXX in connection with "for our sins," and Hos 6:2 LXX in connection with "on the third day." This is suggested especially by the fact that κατὰ τὰς γραφάς follows these phrases. The biblical horizon is present even if particular scriptures are not in view. It is a question of the conformity of the kerygma to the divine purpose. On Mack's hypothesis, the martyr myth answered Jewish questions about the righteousness of Gentiles.[150] It would appear that the kerygma is formulated here also with a Jewish sensibility in view, a sensibility that may have become more urgent and insistent as the Jewish

---

[150] See above, p. 228 and n. 138.

constituency of the membership in most locales was overshadowed by success among Gentiles.

This Jewish sensibility in the formulation of the kerygma in 15:3b–4 has its counterpart in the appearance formula. Apart from the reference to the "more than five hundred" at one time, the list features Cephas and James and the circles that had come to be associated with their names, the Twelve and all the apostles, respectively. The names and circles specified are clearly intended to emphasize the special role of Jerusalem. But taking account of the provenance of the kerygma, as well as the different terminology and grounds of authority that seem to be internal to the Jerusalem group, I am led to conclude that the appearance formula did not arise in Jerusalem, but more likely in Antioch and its environs. The distinctive features of this form of the kerygma can be correlated with a concern for a continuing effort to attract Jews to Jesus groups in the environs and areas of mission of Antioch. According to Gal 2:9, James, Cephas, and John had acknowledged the responsibility of Barnabas and Paul, and thus very likely the Antioch association as well, for determining appropriate practices for Gentiles in their own groups and satellite communities and in connection with their own labors, while at the same time receiving from Paul and from Barnabas and Antioch acknowledgment of their own responsibility for the practices of Jews. Thus, for Antioch to authorize its own interest in attracting Jews to Christ, two considerations had to come into view. First, there had to be a connection with the kerygma, for it was already in vogue in Antioch and environs as a discourse of legitimation; second, it would be necessary for Antioch to conceal itself and stand in the shadow of Jerusalem's authority with respect to the responsibility toward Jews. Those in Antioch who shared an interest in renewing or continuing an effort to attract Jews would have taken the responsibility of the Jerusalem leaders not as an exclusion but as an invitation to link themselves to that responsibility. If Paul could come to imagine Jerusalem as the place of origin of the preaching of the gospel to the Gentiles, there is no reason why some in Antioch could not come to think of Jerusalem as the locus of authorization of the preaching of the gospel to diaspora Jews. It would not have been difficult for diaspora Jews to draw on a formula of legitimation from the LXX. Nor would people for whom Jesus had come to be thought of as vindicated by resurrection have had a problem with appearances, since representing such occasions is a ubiquitous form for the transmission of divinely authorized promises, the granting of authority, commissioning to special tasks, and presenting specially authorized, "pristine," yet hitherto "unknown" teaching. Early Christianity is especially indebted to the narrative representation of such occasions for its "pluralism," to say nothing of its internal rivalries. The bare formula, ὤφθη plus dative, could of course authorize almost anything, and as we see in 1 Cor 15 could also be used as attestations to the resurrection of Christ. I have therefore taken as an important clue to what is being authorized the fact that Paul adds himself to the list not in order to have one more attestation of Christ's resurrection but for the purpose of authorizing his calling to preach the gospel.

The legitimation formula may initially have represented rival claims. I do not think this possibility is excluded by my hypothesis of the formula's provenance or function. An interest in Antioch in attracting Jews to their association does not mean that those who shared this interest necessarily agreed on tactics or behaviors. Differences on these issues could have been expressed in terms of the different "authorities" to whom appeal was made. Nevertheless, 1 Cor 15 demonstrates a use of the list not to establish rival claims but to correlate claims. It also demonstrates, at least on this hypothesis, that what originated as an authorization directed to Jews was soon transmitted in an area of Paul's activity among Gentiles.[151] Finally, it is important to note that Paul's presentation of the appearances as a tradition and as a witness to the resurrection is another way in which a precursor of the apostolic tradition of Luke-Acts can be seen in the first generation.[152]

On the other hand, it has been the intention of this essay to demonstrate something quite different: why we have to imagine the interests that were served in establishing relationships between individuals and between local groups without assuming that these individuals and groups must have shared some "essential" elements of the gospel of Jesus Christ. How could the Jerusalem pillars have known about the gospel that Paul preached among the Gentiles and have acknowledged the autonomy of his labors, and not have shared with Paul some kerygmatic convictions regarding the significance of Jesus? Hermeneutical variations of a common kerygma,

---

[151] I would not exclude the possibility that the presence of Cephas in Antioch was a factor in giving his name pride of place in the sequence. Nor would I exclude the possibility of a connection, however indirect, between a Cephas faction or influence in Corinth and the transmission of 1 Cor 15:5–7 as a tradition in the sphere of Paul's activity among Gentiles. The versatility of Peter in early Christian writings and the different attempts both to place him and to displace him may have received some of its initial impetus from the duality of his placement in homeland and diaspora. This is not to say, however, that Cephas was in Corinth or that Cephas had a hand in formulating the tradition. It is clear from Paul's own usage that the sequence of appearances was created as a third-person account and that use of the first person comes most naturally from one who takes up the narration on his own behalf as someone who has not been named.

[152] I have not treated the appearance to the "more than five hundred" because I do not know what to do with it. At least part of the problem is that it may have originated as an independent tradition. It is obvious that Paul draws on it as evidence for the resurrection. His own gloss makes that clear (15:6b). So it may not have any connection with the hypothesis that I have put forward.

even some substantive ones, are possible to concede; everyone does. But no martyr's death, no resurrected Messiah, and no appearances of Jesus as common points of departure for shared interests and mutual recognition, for agreements or disagreements about conditions for membership and social behaviors? How is that possible? But we are in the same position when we try to imagine how Paul could have spent a fortnight with Cephas and heard all about the teachings of Jesus and yet have left very little evidence of being compelled by any such legacy. In both cases, we are trapped in the myth of origins we wish to explain. Instead, we need to be working with more fluid notions of social experiments driven by the broader currents of imperial policies and differentiated local responses, those of homelands and diasporas. In the case of Jesus people, these local responses will be inflected by the cultivation of "teachings" as a "legacy" authorized by Jesus and by emerging myths of origin focused on the legitimation of contested practices and the struggle to reinvent social boundaries and collective identities.

What Do We Really Know about the Jerusalem Church? Christian Origins in Jerusalem according to Acts and Paul

Dennis E. Smith

The idea that the "church" began in Jerusalem is based on a story found only in Luke-Acts. To be sure, Paul also discusses the importance of Jerusalem in the early years, and when Paul is read through the lens of Luke-Acts, one can easily assume that Paul supports the Luke-Acts picture. However, as Merrill P. Miller has reminded us, the thesis of Jerusalem origins no longer fits the evidence as neatly as once supposed. The purpose of this essay is to reexamine the issue of Christian origins in Jerusalem in the light of new perspectives on the data.[1]

The data derives from two sources, Paul and Luke-Acts. Although the Luke-Acts story has come to dominate all standard interpretations of Christian origins, it actually derives from a much later period than other evidence we have. To clarify this point, it is helpful to consult a standard chronology of the most likely dates for relevant events discussed in this essay:

✦ ca. 30–31 C.E.: Jesus of Nazareth is executed while in Jerusalem for the Passover festival.

---

[1] Merrill P. Miller, "'Beginning from Jerusalem...': Re-examining Canon and Consensus," *Journal of Higher Criticism* 2/1 (1995): 3–30. This essay was written as a response to Miller's article and owes much to the arguments developed there. The first draft of this essay was produced for the Ancient Myths and Modern Theories of Christian Origins Seminar at its meeting in Orlando in November 1998 and was originally written as a study of the Pauline data alone. The second draft, in which I extended the study to include the data from Acts, was prepared for the Acts Seminar of the Westar Institute, for which I serve as chair. Here I benefited greatly from Christopher R. Matthews's paper, "Acts and the History of the Earliest Jerusalem Church" (in this volume). That draft has now been published as "Was There a Jerusalem Church? Christian Origins according to Acts and Paul," *Foundations and Facets Forum* NS 3/1 (2000): 57–74. This is the third draft, prepared for inclusion in this collection of studies.

- ca. 32–35: Paul is "converted" and later (early 50s), when recounting that conversion, denies that he went to visit apostles in Jerusalem at that time (Gal 1:17).
- ca. 35–38: Paul visits Peter in Jerusalem and stays with him for fifteen days (Gal 1:18).
- ca. 48: Paul, Barnabas, and Titus visit Jerusalem to defend "the gospel that I proclaim among the Gentiles" in Antioch. Also present at that meeting are Cephas, James, and John, whom Paul refers to as "pillars." Paul is requested to "remember the poor," which seems to refer to Paul's gathering a collection in various of his mission churches to take back for the "poor among the saints at Jerusalem" (Gal 2:1–10; Rom 15:26).
- ca. 48/49: Cephas, and later a delegation from James, visit Paul and Barnabas in Antioch and create a controversy at the table, presumably over dietary laws (Gal 2:11–14).
- ca. 49–53: Jewish Christian missionaries oppose Paul in Galatia and claim special status for the Jerusalem church.
- ca. 56: Paul takes the collection to Jerusalem (Rom 15:25–28).
- ca. 60: Paul dies in Rome (most probable date).
- 70: The temple is destroyed and Jerusalem is razed as a result of the Jewish war with Rome. The temple and the Jerusalem Christian community (such as it was) are no more.
- ca. 70: "Mark" writes his Gospel in which he presupposes Christian origins not in Jerusalem but in Galilee (Mark 16:6–8).
- ca. 80: "Matthew" writes his Gospel, using Mark and Q as sources, and also presupposes Christian origins in Galilee (Matt 28:5–10, 16–20).
- ca. 90: "John" writes his Gospel, perhaps using Mark, and presupposes Galilee as the place where the disciples return after the death of Jesus (at least this is the presupposition of what might be a second or third edition of John, as represented in John 21).
- ca. 90–125: "Luke" writes his Gospel, which includes Acts, and, using Mark, Q, and other unknown sources, proposes for the first time in our literature that Jerusalem is the place where "Christianity" originates.

New Perspectives on Luke-Acts

It has increasingly been recognized in scholarship on Luke-Acts that Acts cannot simply be read as history, though there is a long-standing Christian tradition to do so (see, e.g., Eusebius, fourth century C.E.). There are two primary components of the more cautious scholarly reading of

Acts. One is that Luke has come to be recognized as an author with a theological agenda. Thus he constructs his work with a specifically theological, rather than specifically historical, goal in mind. Second, the genre of Acts, long assumed to be history, has been identified in more recent scholarship as clearly related to novelistic "romance" literature of the ancient world, literature characterized by adventure stories in which the heroes survive shipwrecks, imprisonment, and all manner of dangers before finally completing whatever task or quest the author has set up for them.[2] Today some scholars still propose that Acts can be defined under the genre of ancient history in some sense,[3] but the burden of proof has now shifted to those who would claim historicity for Acts.

Although this is the case, there is still no clear methodology for deriving history from Acts, particularly from Acts 1–14, since those chapters have no parallels in Paul or other canonical literature. Yet even though there is no clear methodology, there has still been a tendency to reconstruct early Christian history on the basis of Acts, to some extent simply because it has had no competition; that is, we have had no other sources for much of what Acts writes about. Now that situation has changed. One advantage we have over previous generations of scholars is a more richly developed data base defining multiple groups at the earliest levels of Christian origins. Now we must factor in the existence of very early groups behind the *Gospel of Thomas* and the Sayings Gospel Q that do not fit the pattern proposed in Acts, either in terms of their Christology (no passion story) or in terms of their proposed connection with Jerusalem.[4] This helps to mitigate the view that Acts is "the only story we have." Consequently, we are now in a position to challenge the fundamental theses of Christian origins proposed by Luke-Acts.

THREE THESES OF ACTS THAT I DISPUTE

Fundamental to the argument of Acts are the following three theses.

ACTS THESIS 1
Resurrection appearances in Jerusalem served as the foundation event for the faith of the first disciples. This thesis is indicated by the ending of Luke,

---

[2] See esp. Richard I. Pervo, *Profit with Delight: The Literary Genre of the Acts of the Apostles* (Philadelphia: Fortress, 1987).

[3] See the recent multivolume series, *The Book of Acts in Its First Century Setting* (ed. Bruce W. Winter; 6 vols.; Grand Rapids: Eerdmans; Carlisle: Paternoster, 1993–), a project designed to buttress the thesis that Acts is a reliable historical source.

[4] Miller, "Beginning from Jerusalem," 25; Burton L. Mack, *A Myth of Innocence: Mark and Christian Origins* (Philadelphia: Fortress, 1988).

which is interwoven with the beginning of Acts. Luke ends with a resurrection appearance in Jerusalem, instructions by the risen Lord to stay in Jerusalem, and an ascension (Luke 24:36–53). Acts opens with the Jerusalem appearance, instructions to remain in Jerusalem, and an ascension (Acts 1:1–11).

This thesis actually has two parts. Part one is the idea that the faith of the first disciples began with a resurrection event. This is a thesis shared by the other Gospels as well.[5] Luke's version has a resurrection discourse so specific to Luke's themes that it is hard to envision how one could claim historicity for it.[6] If it originates with Luke, as seems likely, one has clear evidence here that resurrection discourses were open to creative manipulation by any conscientious early Christian theologian or pious community. In any case, resurrection as an originating event is certainly a slippery issue. A case can be made that the resurrection stories began not as originating events but as pious legends arising in already-existing faith communities.[7] They may represent interpretations of experiences,[8] or they may simply represent the development of stories about early Christian heroes. After all, it is only the heroes about whom such stories develop. Moroever, of all of our stories, only Paul's reference in 1 Cor 15:8, and possibly by analogy Gal 1:15–16 and 2 Cor 12:2–4, qualify as first-person accounts. The other resurrection stories in the Gospels have the form of pious legends. Furthermore, the texts from Paul are tantalizingly limited in what they tell us about what a "resurrection appearance" experience might have been. Certainly Paul himself does not tell a resurrection "story."

The other component of this thesis of Luke-Acts is the idea that resurrection experiences, assuming they did constitute an originating event for the disciples, took place initially in Jerusalem. As noted above, this thesis contrasts with Luke's source, Mark, and, not incidentally, with Matthew as well. In addition, though John does have Jerusalem appearances (John 20:11–29), his story concludes with Galilee appearances (John 21). It is Luke, and only Luke, who combines a resurrection appearance in Jerusalem with instructions to remain there. This serves as the foundation for his story of Christian origins in Jerusalem.[9]

---

[5] See the review of these texts in Robert W. Funk, ed., and the Jesus Seminar, *The Acts of Jesus: What Did Jesus Really Do?* (San Francisco: HarperSanFrancisco, 1998), 449–95.

[6] E.g., Joseph A. Fitzmyer identifies it as Lukan (*The Acts of the Apostles* [AB 31; New York: Doubleday, 1998], 199).

[7] See, e.g., John Dominic Crossan, *Who Killed Jesus? Exploring the Roots of Anti-Semitism in the Gospel Story of the Death of Jesus* (San Francisco: HarperSanFrancisco, 1995), 209–10.

[8] Gerd Lüdemann, *Early Christianity according to the Traditions in Acts: A Commentary* (trans. John Bowden; Minneapolis: Fortress, 1989), 30.

[9] Lüdemann (ibid.) affirms resurrection appearances in Jerusalem as historical, but only after such appearances in Galilee.

A rebuttal. I would argue that the thesis that resurrection appearances in Jerusalem served as the foundation event for the faith of the first disciples is a Lukan fiction created to fit Luke's theological and literary program.

ACTS THESIS 2

The first church was founded in Jerusalem, and all of Christianity spread from there. Despite the claims made by Acts, the evidence suggests that the origin of the Christian community in Jerusalem is shrouded in mystery, just as is the origin of every other early Christian community, except perhaps for those whose origins are mentioned in Paul's letters. Even in the case of Paul's churches, however, what we know about actual origins is very sketchy.

The stories in Acts that describe Christian origins are embedded in Luke's overarching thesis of Jerusalem origins and so are brought under suspicion from the outset. When arguments are made for their historicity, it is often on the basis of a claim for "Palestinian traditions" or "Jerusalem traditions" as the sources for certain details of stories that are otherwise attributable to Luke. This is, of course, a scholarly guess.[10] I would propose the following methodological critique. While it might be possible exegetically to determine that Luke has used a source, identifying it as a Palestinian source is another matter altogether. And supposing that the identity of a Palestinian source was felt to be probable, it is still a leap to assume that it is therefore historical. It is especially the historical leap that should be given close attention.

The ways in which the Pentecost story (Acts 2:1–42) is handled are instructive. Joseph A. Fitzmyer, for example, argues that the datum "that [Peter] addressed Jews assembled in Jerusalem for the first feast after Jesus' death and burial [is] substantially historical." Yet he also points out that the story is found only in Luke, with no reference to such an event anywhere else in canonical literature, and he concludes that the story itself is "basically a Lucan composition." Yet even when he draws this conclusion, he still claims that Luke "makes use of Palestinian tradition, possibly oral, about events that transpired in Jerusalem and mixes it with his own reflection."[11] How he can have such confidence in such an assertion, and then conclude that therefore the event is historical, is not clear from his exposition. C. K. Barrett, though apparently more skeptical than Fitzmyer, would also presuppose that some sources, apparently historical, lie behind Luke's story. He concludes in regard to the Pentecost story that "Luke himself composed

---

[10] For a review of the classic theories, see Hans Conzelmann, *Acts of the Apostles* (Hermeneia; Philadelphia: Fortress, 1987), xxxvi–xl.

[11] Fitzmyer, *Acts of the Apostles,* 125, 232, 236, 236–37.

the whole on the basis of the convictions outlined above [i.e. Luke's theology] and various traditions of outstanding events distantly recollected from the earliest days of the church."[12] Hans Conzelmann discusses the issues for historicity with a tone of skepticism but refrains from providing a final conclusion.[13] Yet on such a shaky foundation scholars such as Fitzmyer would still wish to build a historical edifice.

The references to a possible Jerusalem *ekklesia* in Paul, especially in Galatians, are more substantial and deserve more detailed analysis, especially since Paul's is a first-person account. Yet the standard interpretations of Paul, as I argue below, are subject to critique and reconsideration.

Finally, one detail that has been missing from all discussions of the Jerusalem community that I am aware of is a realistic social analysis of its form and makeup. Given the general presupposition in our data that the earliest Christian communities met in homes, the question that arises is this: Whose home would have been available in Jerusalem, since all of the leaders (Peter, James, John) came not from Jerusalem but from Galilee (at least, if we accept Gospel tradition on this point)?[14] Furthermore, if Peter, James, and John are but simple fishermen (according to Gospel tradition) or, better yet, are peasants,[15] how do they travel so much, and how can they host the *ekklesia*? And how do we imagine that this *ekklesia* could have been constituted as one community or "congregation," when we have indications of factions within it in such sources as Paul in Gal 2, when he refers to a "James group" that is in opposition to Peter? To be sure, questions such as these must be addressed by any theory of the origins and existence of a Jerusalem *ekklesia,* but to this point in scholarship they have not received much attention.

A rebuttal. I would argue that the thesis that the first church was founded in Jerusalem and all of Christianity spread from there is a Lukan fiction created to fit Luke's theological and literary program.

---

[12] C. K. Barrett, *Acts* (2 vols.; ICC; Edinburgh: T&T Clark, 1994–98), 1:110.

[13] Conzelmann, *Acts of the Apostles,* 15–16.

[14] Of course, Paul does say in Gal 1:18 that he not only visited Peter in Jerusalem but stayed with him for fifteen days. Whether this indicates that Peter lived in Jerusalem (or was just visiting) and whose house he was staying in when Paul became his houseguest—these are open questions.

[15] See John Dominic Crossan, *The Historical Jesus: The Life of a Mediterranean Jewish Peasant* (San Francisco: HarperSanFrancisco, 1991), who argues that Jesus and the Jesus movement were peasant phenomena. In Crossan's *The Birth of Christianity: Discovering What Happened in the Years Immediately after the Execution of Jesus* (San Francisco: HarperSanFrancisco, 1998), 235, he argues that "Jesus' kingdom-of-God movement began as a movement of peasant resistance but broke out from localism and regionalism under scribal leadership" (emphasis omitted). The social realities of that transition are not fully accounted for by Crossan, in my opinion.

ACTS THESIS 3

Jerusalem had a claim of authority over other churches, especially the Gentile churches of Paul's mission. This thesis is derived from references in Luke to the prominence of Jerusalem (as in Acts 8:14–15; 11:1–18; 15:1–33). It is also a component of the argument of Paul's opponents in Galatia that he was required to submit to Jerusalem (as implied by Paul's defense in Gal 1:12, 16–18; 2:1, 6, 9–10) and can be proposed as a factor behind Paul's visits to Jerusalem (Gal 1:17–18; 2:1), though, as I argue below, I dispute this interpretation.

A rebuttal. I would argue that the Jerusalem "church" as a power broker in Christian origins was a mythological construct from the outset, first appearing among Paul's opponents in Galatia, then picked up and elaborated on by Luke in Acts. The actual *ekklesia* in Jerusalem, such as it was, most likely played a minor role in Christian origins. But the Jerusalem of myth was utilized to buttress a mythological Jerusalem "church" in order to gain advantage in the early debates among the Jesus movements.[16]

To further support my rebuttals of Luke-Acts, I will now review the evidence from Paul.

ANALYZING THE JERUSALEM CHURCH ACCORDING TO PAUL

As noted in the chronology given above, the data from Paul is earlier than that from Luke. Paul has some tantalizing references to Christianity in Jerusalem, and this data is often interpreted in correlation with the data in Acts. But if it is read as independent data separate from Acts, a different profile of the so-called Jerusalem "church" can emerge.

The primary data in Paul is found in the letter to the Galatians, dated to approximately 50 C.E.[17] It is here that we find Paul recounting his earlier trips to Jerusalem and his meetings with such important figures as Cephas, James, and John. However, it should be remembered that these references by Paul are written in response to a critique coming from his opponents in Galatia. They are apparently accusing Paul of reneging on his earlier allegiance to the authority of Jerusalem. It is for the purpose of self-defense that he writes as he does, and his rhetoric must be analyzed accordingly.[18]

---

[16] See also Miller, "Beginning from Jerusalem," 27, who argues that the idea of Jerusalem origins for Christianity based especially on resurrection appearances is "likely to reflect the internal disputes and competing claims for legitimating individuals and communities engaged in a mission to Gentiles beginning in the late forties and the decade of the fifties."

[17] J. Louis Martyn, *Galatians* (AB 33A; New York: Doubleday, 1997), 20 n. 20.

[18] For a discussion of Paul's rhetoric in Galatians, see Burton L. Mack, *Rhetoric and the New Testament* (GBS; Minneapolis: Fortress, 1990), 66–73.

That is to say, when he refers to the past, he does so from the perspective of his current concerns at the time when he writes the letter.

CHRISTIANITY IN JERUSALEM IN THE 30S AND EARLY 40S

I would propose the following theses as alternative interpretations of the earliest data we have on the presence of Jesus people in Jerusalem, namely, that from Paul.

Thesis 1. When Paul makes his first trip to Jerusalem, three years after his "conversion," thus roughly 35–38, there is no identifiable Jerusalem "church," though Paul does refer vaguely to "assemblies (ἐκκλησίαις) of Judea in Christ" (Gal 1:18, 22).

Thesis 2. Paul does not explicitly confirm that there *were* other apostles in Jerusalem in the early years. Rather, he simply denies the charge that he visited "other apostles before me in Jerusalem" at the time of his conversion (1:17) or saw "other apostles" in Jerusalem three years later when he visited Cephas (1:19).

Thesis 3. Contrary to traditional interpretations, the fact that Cephas was in Jerusalem for Paul to visit for fifteen days, and James was there for him to "see," does not necessarily mean that they both lived in Jerusalem and were leaders of the Jerusalem church. It could simply mean they were there during a festival season, for example, since it was quite common for Jews to make frequent pilgrimages to Jerusalem, as did both Jesus and Paul. This thesis is buttressed by thesis 1. It is notable that, in the context in which he refers to visiting Peter in Jerusalem for fifteen days, Paul mentions "*ekklesiai* of Judea in Christ" that had never seen him face to face but does not mention any contact with, or avoidance of, an *ekklesia* in Jerusalem, which would certainly have been one of the "*ekklesiai* of Judea." Consequently, if there was an *ekklesia* in Jerusalem at this time, it is remarkable that Paul was able to avoid all contact with it during the fifteen days he spent with Peter.

Further Comments. The phrase "churches [*ekklesiai* or assemblies] of Judea in Christ" (Gal 1:21–22) deserves further analysis. (1) "Assemblies" or *ekklesiai* (ἐκκλησίαι) certainly seems to carry a technical meaning in the later Paul of the 50s, but what the social phenomenon was that he was describing in 35–38 is not clear, nor is it clear that the term was in general use at that period as a reference to "Jesus people." (2) "Judea" for Paul is viewed as a region in contrast to Syria and Cilicia. What region might "Judea" refer to in Paul's mind? Might it also include "Galilee"? (3) "In Christ" is a problematic term, without a clear meaning at this early stage, though by the time Paul writes he has begun to give it content within his own theology. J. Louis Martyn suggests that Paul uses it as a term for the "theological location" of these churches, in contrast to their geographical location, thus by implication drawing them into his theological orbit.[19] But again it must be remarked that the technical term "in Christ" in the later Paul may be anachronistic at this early period. In fact, Paul obviously knew very little about these groups, since, as he says, he never visited them. By the time he wrote this letter, such groups may have become mythologized by the growing mythmaking that had developed in regard to the Jerusalem church. Of course, Paul does suggest in hindsight that he received general approval from them ("they glorified God in me," 1:24), but once again this is a statement made in an apologetic context years later. The reality in 35–38 C.E. is much more elusive.

In 1 Cor 15:1–8, when Paul refers to the tradition he received and then lists a succession of resurrection appearances, including Cephas and James, there is no specifically Jerusalem connection to any of the references. As for the date when this tradition would have taken shape, that also is unclear. Most scholars connect Paul's reference in 1 Cor 15:8 to his having seen the risen Lord with the reference in Gal 1:16 to the event where "God was pleased to reveal his Son in me." But even if that is the experience Paul is referring to in 1 Cor 15, it does not necessarily mean that the entire mythological construct of the tradition was already in place at that time. It is more likely that the "tradition" developed after the fact as a mythmaking activity to explain the new faith than that the "tradition" actually serves as a record of its origin. Whatever the contribution of a life-changing experience to Paul's change of direction, it is only later that he can fully interpret it according to a larger mythological structure.[20] One further note: it is highly unlikely that James would have called himself the brother "of the Lord" (1:19).[21] This is the language of the Paul of the 50s; it need not be pushed to reflect the language of either Paul or James in 35–38. It is further evidence that Paul anachronistically used perspectives of the 50s when referring to events of the 30s.

THE MEETING IN JERUSALEM (CA. 48) (GALATIANS 2:1–10)

Thesis 4. Though the meeting took place in Jerusalem, there is nothing in Paul's account to lead to the conclusion that it is a conference between the Antioch church and the Jerusalem church (contrary to the interpretation of most scholars).[22] That reading of the data is largely developed out of Acts. However, the Acts account is problematic in so many

---

[19] Martyn, *Galatians*, 176.

[20] See also Burton L. Mack's view that Paul's "experience" was simply a radical change of perspective, not an external event (*Who Wrote the New Testament? The Making of the Christian Myth* [San Francisco: HarperSanFrancisco, 1995], 102).

[21] Suggested by Ron Cameron in a critique of an earlier draft of this paper.

[22] Represented most recently by Martyn, *Galatians*, 189.

other respects, particularly in the conclusion claimed for the conference, that it must be read with great care in comparison with Paul. At this point, I prefer to bracket Acts from consideration and develop this thesis from Paul alone.[23]

Thesis 5. A primary purpose of the meeting was to compare evangelistic messages, as seen by the outcome dividing the mission field into two camps (2:9).

Thesis 6. The term "pillars" is best interpreted as a local Judean term, understood either as a local variant of "apostle" or perhaps as a rough equivalent to "founder." It therefore would not refer to local church leadership but to missionary leadership. See the discussion in thesis 18 on the idea that the self-identity of "Christians" tended to be in relation to their "patron" in the faith rather than to a geographical location. Martyn has some helpful data on the background to the term "pillars," noting that it is used in rabbinic literature to refer to the patriarchs, Abraham, Isaac, and Jacob. James, Cephas, and John could then be seen, he notes, as "the indispensable connecting link between Jesus of Nazareth and his church."[24] I am willing to grant that possibility as an aspect of their status in Judea, but I reject his view that "it was doubtless easy to think of these three men as the pillars of the eschatological temple that would shortly house the congregation made up of God's new people at the end of time."[25] The concept of "founder" that I am proposing would represent the claims of James, Cephas, and John to be the founding patrons of the Jesus communities in Judea. It is primarily their identity as founding patrons that gives them their status.

Thesis 7. Jerusalem may simply be the location for the meeting as a central location for representatives from "the *ekklesiai* of Judea in Christ" to meet with the representatives from the Gentile mission. Whether one of the *ekklesiai* was actually in Jerusalem then becomes a moot point. Judeans in general, including those of Galilee, might claim Jerusalem as their ancestral "home,"[26] but there is not yet a clear indication that anyone is claiming eschatological primacy for Jerusalem.

Thesis 8. Just as Paul, Barnabas, and Titus were there not as local church leaders but as representatives of a larger mission effort, so also James, Cephas, and John may be considered representatives of a larger mission effort rather than local church leaders. In fact, we know very little about "local church leaders" at this phase of early Christian history. Thus

---

[23] See Barrett, *Acts*, 2:xxxvi–xlii, for a review of historical problems with Acts 15, though I have even less confidence in the potential historical value of Acts 15 than Barrett.

[24] Martyn, *Galatians*, 205.

[25] Ibid.

[26] Suggested by Stanley K. Stowers in a critique of an earlier draft of this paper.

it is anachronistic to think of James as "authoritative leader of the Jerusalem mother-church," as Crossan states, for example.[27]

Thesis 9. The "false brothers" represent another faction at the meeting who, since Paul refers to them as having come "to spy out our freedom in Christ in order that they might enslave us" (2:4), may also represent another delegation of Judean Christian missionaries rather than Jerusalem church officials.

Thesis 10. Based on Paul's reference to the fact that Titus was not compelled to be circumcised (2:3) and the fact that Peter is conceded the mission field of the circumcised at the conclusion of the meeting (2:8), the theology of the pillars and "false brothers" seems to be much more embedded in traditional Jewish ritual law than is Paul's.

Thesis 11. Conversely, the "Christ cult" theology of Paul, since it has its rationale in his mission to Gentiles, does not seem likely to have been shared by the pillars and false brothers.[28]

Thesis 12. The agreement that Paul is to "remember the poor" may simply represent a compromise regarding Paul's radical view of "justification by faith not by works of law" (2:16). In effect, the pillars could have been saying to Paul, "You may have thrown out circumcision and dietary laws, but are you going to throw out almsgiving too?" After all, almsgiving would have formed the financial base for the movement. Later, when Paul had gathered the collection specifically for "the poor among the saints at Jerusalem" (Rom 15:26), it would represent a diplomatic move on his part to maintain good relations with the Jewish Christian wing of the movement, analogous with his policy of "becoming a Jew to Jews" (1 Cor 9:20; see further discussion in thesis 21 below). It may also be his way of continuing to deal with the ideology that first surfaced among his opponents in Galatia, that Jerusalem should in fact be considered the "mother church" of Christianity (see thesis 20 below).

Thesis 13. The "false brothers" would evidently not have concurred with the decision. Their legacy may, in fact, be traced in such groups as Paul's opponents at Galatia, as has often been suggested.[29]

THE INCIDENT AT ANTIOCH (CA. 48/49)

Thesis 14. The agreement in Jerusalem did not anticipate what would happen when observant Jewish Christians and nonobservant Gentile Christians attempted to participate in a community meal together.

---

[27] Crossan, *Birth of Christianity*, 467.
[28] Mack provides a review of Paul's theology as a "Christ cult" theology in *Who Wrote the New Testament*, 75–121.
[29] Martyn, *Galatians*, 219.

Thesis 15. Paul sees the separate tables as undermining the universality of the gospel as he understands it. It is this event that most likely radicalized Paul's theology into the form that we find represented in Galatians and Romans.[30]

Thesis 16. Since Paul, Peter, and Barnabas can freely eat at a Gentile table, they provide evidence for the view that there was great variety in Judaism at this time regarding dietary laws. This is further evidence for the view suggested by Alan Segal that "we do not know exactly how ordinary Jews, as opposed to strict Pharisees, observed the dietary laws in the first century."[31] I would argue, therefore, that, outside of the Pharisees, dietary laws were not universally followed in everyday life among otherwise law-abiding Jews. However, in cases where Jewish self-identity was especially at stake, such as had been the case in the Maccabean period and such as was perhaps the case with the Judean Jesus group when it found itself among Gentiles in Antioch, the function of "boundary maintenance" that was so clearly connected with the dietary laws kicked in,[32] and suddenly it became imperative to be punctilious about observance.

Thesis 17. The group "from James" is not specifically identified with Jerusalem but is identified as representing the position of observant Jewish Christians as represented at the Jerusalem meeting. This may simply be one among many positions among "the *ekklesiai* of Judea in Christ." Peter is from this same church tradition, yet he is not "observant" in the same way that the group from James is. Consequently, the group from James represents a more conservative approach to dietary laws and may actually represent a different *ekklesia* than Peter's.

Thesis 18. The terminology "from James" would represent the fact that they are converts of James, related in the patron-client sense, rather than the idea that they were official emissaries. Their self-identity is related to their spiritual patron rather than to their local "church." This follows the pattern Norman R. Petersen elaborates in Paul, whereby Paul refers to Philemon as one who "owes me even your own self" and Onesimus as one to whom he became a "father."[33] A similar pattern is used by Paul in referring to his relationship to his churches in other letters; for example, he commonly refers to church members as well as entire churches as his

---

[30] As suggested by J. D. G. Dunn, "The Incident at Antioch (Gal 2:11–18)," in *Jesus, Paul and the Law: Studies in Mark and Galatians* (Louisville: Westminster John Knox, 1990), 162.

[31] Alan Segal, "Romans 7 and Jewish Dietary Laws," in *The Other Judaisms of Late Antiquity* (BJS 127; Atlanta: Scholars Press, 1987), 175.

[32] See, e.g., Mary Douglas, "Deciphering a Meal," *Daedalus* 101 (1972): 61–81.

[33] Norman R. Petersen, *Rediscovering Paul: Philemon and the Sociology of Paul's Narrative World* (Philadelphia: Fortress, 1985), 66, 128.

children, as in 1 Cor 4:14, 17; 2 Cor 6:13; 12:14–15; Gal 4:19; 1 Thess 2:7, 11.[34] Thus the terminology "from James" could represent a distinct "patron-client" relationship and most likely a different *ekklesia* as well.

Paul's Debate with Jerusalem Mythmakers

Thesis 19. The "opponents" of Paul in Galatia are best understood as a group of Jewish Christian missionaries who promote their authority via their credentials as representatives of Jerusalem.[35] Behind Paul's defense that he was never beholden to Jerusalem may be found the critique that he should have been. These opponents would then be our first clear promoters of the myth of the primacy of Jerusalem.

Thesis 20. The mythological nature of their critique of Paul may be seen in the form that Paul's response takes in Gal 4:21–5:1, the allegory of Hagar and Sarah. Against the view likely promoted by his opponents, that Jerusalem is the "mother church,"[36] Paul proposes that "the present Jerusalem is in slavery with her children ... but the Jerusalem above ... is our mother" (4:25–26). For Paul, then, "Jerusalem," as the symbol of Jewish Christian theology, can never be given primacy. For Paul, it is the symbol of "slavery to the law," which can be seen as his term for the theology of the Judean churches. This correlates with theses 10 and 11 above. It also suggests either that Paul does not know or does not put credence in a tradition that Christianity began in Jerusalem.

Thesis 21. When Paul, in Rom 15:25–27, refers to the collection from the Gentile churches for "the poor among the saints at Jerusalem," he couches it in terms of a debt that is "owed" by the Gentile churches to "the saints at Jerusalem" because they "have come to share in their spiritual blessings." The language of owing a debt comes from the patron-client system.[37] This is usually interpreted as Paul's acknowledging Jerusalem as the "mother church" in some sense.[38] However, Paul may simply be acknowledging Jerusalem as representative in a general sense of the origins of Gentile Christianity in Judaism (as in Rom 9–11). The "saints" in Jerusalem, or the Judean Christians, then become so closely identified with the Jewish heritage that they become stand-ins for the nation of Israel as a whole as debtee. This indicates how far Paul now sees that his theology is from

---

[34] Ibid., 124–51, esp. 128.

[35] See, e.g., Hans Dieter Betz, *Galatians* (Hermeneia; Philadelphia: Fortress, 1979); Martyn, *Galatians*.

[36] Martyn, *Galatians*, 462–63.

[37] As in Phlm 18–19; see Petersen, *Rediscovering Paul*, esp. 75–77, on "the metaphor of debt."

[38] E.g., Dieter Georgi, *Remembering the Poor: The History of Paul's Collection for Jerusalem* (Nashville: Abingdon, 1992).

Judean theology, as also indicated in his Hagar and Sarah allegory in Galatians (see thesis 20 above).

The Jerusalem Myth According to Luke-Acts

Thesis 22. When Luke-Acts was written, the actual Jerusalem church was but a distant memory, but the mythological Jerusalem church had grown in stature. Luke took that myth and restructured it to fit his own needs.

Thesis 23. Here I would suggest a somewhat sketchy summary of the Lukan myth of the Jerusalem church, as follows: Luke's goal is to provide a connection between the Gentile churches in the diaspora and the Jerusalem church. This is important for apologetic purposes, primarily to provide justification for Gentile Christian origins. He does this by recounting a story that moves from "Jerusalem, [to] all Judea and Samaria, and to the ends of the earth," a pattern commanded by the risen Lord (Luke 24:47; Acts 1:8) and followed precisely by the plot of Acts. That this is God's will is further confirmed by the roles of the Holy Spirit and angels in Acts. Throughout Acts major developments in the plot are provoked by the Holy Spirit, the voice of God presented through a vision, or an angelic visitor. This includes the origin of the church in Jerusalem at Pentecost (2:1–4), the spread beyond Jerusalem (8:26), the choice of Paul as an apostle (9:4–5), the official conversion of the first Gentile (10:3, 9–23, 44), the commissioning of Barnabas and Saul for a mission to the Gentile lands (13:2), and the decision by Paul to go to Macedonia (16:9). Beginning the story at Jerusalem serves to provide a historical and theological pedigree, foreshadowed in Luke 4:16–30, which certifies the theological legitimacy of the Gentiles.

Conclusion:
Rethinking the Canonical Story of Christian Origins in Jerusalem

It is now clear that the generally accepted version of Christian origins in Jerusalem derives almost entirely from Acts and, furthermore, depends on a historical reading of Acts. But because the genre of Acts is not just history, but also clearly romance as well, if not exclusively so,[39] and because Acts is so clearly organized around a theological agenda, a historical reading of Acts can no longer be taken for granted. Given the weight attached to the Jerusalem church in Luke's overall theological

---

[39] Pervo, *Profit with Delight,* esp. 115–38. For Acts, Pervo prefers the subcategory of the ancient novel that he dubs the "historical novel."

scheme, it is appropriate that we question the entire hypothesis of Christian origins in Jerusalem.

A reconsideration of the evidence from Paul, read in isolation from Acts, shows that the evidence for the existence of a Jerusalem "church" at the earliest phase of Christian origins, much less a "church" with strong regional leadership, is much thinner than we once thought. Indeed, it is not even clear that there was such a community in Jerusalem at the time of the so-called Jerusalem "conference."

I would therefore propose that a radical rethinking of the Jerusalem "church" must take place. When can we affirm that a community existed there? What can we say about its form? And what can we justifiably say about its influence in the period prior to the destruction of the temple? Any such attempt to reconstruct the origin and importance of the Jerusalem Christian community or communities would need, at minimum, to take into account issues such as the following:

- sources for Acts: The story in Acts is only as good as its sources, and there has been much romanticizing in scholarship about the sources of Acts and their reliability. This is now a wide-open question and must be approached in light of new perspectives on Acts, its genre, and its place in Christian history.
- chronology of the data: The very fact that the Jerusalem origin of the church, in a "big bang" form, is a thesis known only to Luke, who is one of the latest of the canonical writers, and not to any of the earlier Christian writers, casts doubt on the Luke-Acts reconstruction of Christian origins.
- the Jerusalem myth: In any historical reconstruction, it is essential that we give proper weight to the mythological/metaphorical dimension given to Jerusalem in early Christian theology.
- sociological realities: The sociological realities of an early group identified as a "Christian *ekklesia*," or according to some other category of group formation, needs to be defined in more precise terms than we have done to this point.
- Pauline rhetoric: Since our earliest, and to my mind only, reliable data is found in the letters of Paul, we need to pay close attention to the rhetorical context in which that data is found in order to interpret it properly.
- evidence for other early Jesus communities: Finally, whatever reconstruction we propose must be coordinated with the new evidence that has developed in recent scholarship for other early Jesus communities, particularly since they can be seen to

be quite early and quite distinct from the "norm" suggested either by Paul or by Luke-Acts.

A Jewish Jesus School in Jerusalem?

Burton L. Mack

My assignment has been to suggest a reconstruction of the Jesus people in Jerusalem, controlled by a reflection on the methods proposed for the work of the Seminar and supported by a bit of social theory implicit in the proposal. The responses to Merrill P. Miller's paper,[1] as well as his response to the responses,[2] have been eagerly read with great interest and profit. Three major approaches to a redescription of the Jesus people in Jerusalem have been taken. (1) The dominant paradigm has been problematized by means of a critical analysis of its logic and its underlying assumptions. We can be thankful to E. P. Sanders for his thorough argumentation in support of the Gospel stories as historical[3] and to Miller for his careful analysis of the implausibility of Sanders's conclusions. (2) The texts that have served as data base for the dominant paradigm have been recognized as highly imaginative, rhetorical constructions that call for their own analyses as early Christian mythmaking at particular junctures of separate social histories and formations. Special attention has been paid to Paul's report in Gal 1–2 as the most important text, but reference has also been made to the Lukan "history," the Markan "passion narrative," Paul's report of the "tradition" of the kerygma, and a few other "themes" (from the literature as a whole), such as characterizations of James and various attitudes toward the temple and Jerusalem. All of these have been looked at critically with the question in mind of finding hard evidence for a group of Jesus people or early Christians in Jerusalem. (3) The goal has been to ask whether a reconstruction of a Jerusalem group is possible at all, and if so, what its place and role may have been in relation to other groups of Jesus people and early Christians.

---

[1] Merrill P. Miller, "'Beginning from Jerusalem ...': Re-examining Canon and Consensus," *Journal of Higher Criticism* 2/1 (1995): 3–30.

[2] Merrill P. Miller, "Antioch, Paul, and Jerusalem: Diaspora Myths of Origins in the Homeland" (in this volume).

[3] E. P. Sanders, *Jesus and Judaism* (Philadelphia: Fortress, 1985).

I would like to draw some conclusions from these discussions. The first is that the critical analyses of texts, assumptions, and argumentations traditionally used to support the dominant paradigm have made it impossible to continue thinking of Christian beginnings that way. This should mark a turning point in the way we talk about the Jerusalem group and Christian origins. Beginning with a few bits of hard evidence, the social orientations, interests, activities, and ideologies of this group will need to be reconstructed with great care in order to imagine historically plausible alternatives to the traditional view. This reconstruction will have to be argued by drawing upon analogies from other Jesus movements, contemporary Jewish groups and practices, and similar Greco-Roman social formations in response to the times conditioned by similar situations of social and cultural moment.

The traditional model, a combination of the Lukan story and Paul's pictures of the congregations of the Christ, can no longer be used as the source of analogies for comparison. It is that model which has been shown to be problematic. Note therefore that a number of assumptions about Christian origins that belong to that model can no longer be used as matters of course in the reconstruction of the Jerusalem group. These include the belief in Jesus as Messiah, the cult of presence based on appearances of the resurrected Jesus, the notion of (starting) "missions" to both Jews and Gentiles in the interest of a global program of conversions to the Christian "church," eschatological ideology, anti-Jewish identity markers and/or reformist programs (whether the target be "law," "temple," "Pharisees," "Judaizers," or whatever), claims to authority based on the notion of (twelve) "disciples" or "apostles," and so forth. Our challenge is to imagine a Jerusalem group with some connection to the Jesus movements (rather than assuming connections only to the congregations of the Christ, as has been customary), of interest to Paul for some reason (intentionally leaving that reason open for argument and reconstruction), with an interest in (at least) listening to Paul explain his "gospel" and (subsequently?) becoming involved in questions about the social formation of the Jesus people as a mixture of Jews and Gentiles in Antioch.

The challenge is great because such an imagination will have to be achieved without appeal to the Lukan or Christ-cult models and with very little hard evidence. The temptation will be to suggest that, since there is not enough evidence to construct scenarios other than the traditional Lukan portrayals, must we not allow this or that feature of the regnant model to remain in play, at least as a possibility? My response to that temptation is that all features of the regnant model are themselves in need of explanation wherever they pop up in our literature and thus cannot be used as explanatory for any group, much less for a group where they are not at all in evidence. Thus, any feature taken from the Lukan-Pauline models, such as the notion of Jesus as Messiah, would have to be argued for the Jerusalem group without benefit of hard textual evidence to ascribe it to the Jerusalem group and without assuming the Lukan-Pauline models as the social formations that could provide an appropriate (socio-)logical context for the mythology of Jesus as Messiah. Such an argumentation would have to be laborious and enormously complicated with layers of hypotheses required both for the extra-Christian, comparative data on the term—reminding ourselves of studies in the volumes on the topic edited by Jacob Neusner et al. and James H. Charlesworth, which have not been able to track down a single, contemporary Jewish notion of "the messiah"[4]—and for the reasons why a Jesus movement would have come upon the notion in the first place. Since such a labor makes no sense for clusters of data where the term does not appear, we should not be led astray by that ghost from the canonical past.

In any case, to attempt an explanation for any feature of the dominant paradigm, whether in regard to the Jerusalem group or wherever it may occur in our literature, much less to consider any feature explanatory of other features, will become increasingly more difficult. That is because the projects proposed for this Seminar are based on an anthropological perspective that differs fundamentally from that assumed by the dominant paradigm of Christian origins. We are exploring the possibility that the Jesus people and early Christians were engaged in making sense of their social and cultural worlds just as others were doing during the Greco-Roman age, and just as all other peoples have been doing since the dawn of human history. All items of the dominant paradigm traditionally regarded as given, descriptive, and explanatory are thus in need of explanation themselves. They need to be explained as notions that might make (mythmaking) sense for groups in the process of working out particular social experiments grounded in understandable social interests. We can no longer treat early Christians as a special breed of humans, whether because of unusual enlightenments, unique mystifications, or novel spiritual experiences. Thus we need to account for their notions, activities, and social constructions in other terms. I would like to suggest that we are already far along in thinking of those early Christians as normal human beings with interests common to the human enterprise of social formation, even though those interests may have taken particular forms of expression during the Greco-Roman period and not be recognized as variants of human

---

[4] Jacob Neusner et al., eds., *Judaisms and Their Messiahs at the Turn of the Christian Era* (Cambridge: Cambridge University Press, 1987); James H. Charlesworth, ed., *The Messiah: Developments in Earliest Judaism and Christianity* (The First Princeton Symposium on Judaism and Christian Origins; Minneapolis: Fortress, 1992).

interests in general. But some such anthropology based on a conception of human interests in general is surely implicit in our attempts to argue for this or that historical-ideological reconstruction as more or less plausible (or implausible) than other reconstructions. We now take for granted both the sense-making interests and the rhetorical interests that produced early Christian persuasions and literature. That means that we are trying to imagine early Christians engaged in human activities that combined social and rational features. If so, it might be helpful to use the concept of interests to set our work in relation to more general theories of social formation and mythmaking. We have already used the term *attraction* to rephrase questions about the spread of early Jesus groups. Now we are trying to ascertain the *interests* shared by a group for which the usual markers thought to account for the attraction and success of Christianity are not in evidence. What may those interests have been?

I would like to begin by referring to my earlier response (in my letter of 12 March 1998) to Miller's paper, "Beginning from Jerusalem." I find that I have not had to change my mind about much of the strategy I suggested for dealing with the "hard evidence" for the Jerusalem group. But I do need to take back a few of my assumptions and notions in light of considerations made by others in the course of our summer's cogitations. I am no longer thinking of the Jerusalem group as a composition only of *Galileans* who had decided to *move* to Jerusalem because of some intentional plan with respect to *Jerusalem* called for by some conception of the Jesus *movement* that included a sense of *mission* there (taking "mission" in the sense of program, purpose, or teaching, not in the traditional sense of seeking expansion via conversions). I also no longer assume that notions of *authority* for a *network* of groups were in anyone's mind except, perhaps, Paul's.

This leaves me with the following profile of features with which to work. There were people in Jerusalem with some knowledge about or relationship to what we might call Jesus groups. From Paul's reports, this Jerusalem group was together from the late 30s through the 40s. Lore from a much later period about the death of James and the flight to Pella could extend the time of its existence to the 60s. One of the known figures of this group was a brother of Jesus by the name of James. Paul called the leaders of this group "pillars," a metaphor indicating some measure of organization, although the only glimpses we have of group activity focus on gathering for the discussion of social issues. That would not have required a great deal of special self-definition or organization. And even the practice of gathering may not have been formalized, as Paul's account of his first visit there indicates, namely, that he did not meet any others except James while staying with Cephas for fifteen days (Gal 1:18–19). One wonders about the circumstances of this visit and whether

Cephas may have been a long-time resident of Jerusalem. In any case, the group that gathered to talk to Paul on his second visit (Gal 2:1–10) consisted mainly of Jewish males (Judeans or of Judean extraction). The issues in evidence revolved around the implication of Jewish practices for Jewish self-definition and Jewish-Gentile relations, one of which (the circumcision of Gentiles) involved questions of ethnic identity, the other of which (meal practice) involved etiquettes of cross-ethnic association and may well have included considerations of purity codes with respect to foods. Since we have evidence that such questions were being discussed by Jews in general as issues of concern for determining Jewish ethnic identity and practice during the Greco-Roman age, not all the participants in these discussions need have been Jesus people, much less (Pauline-type) Christians. Paul does mention "gatherings" (*ekklesiai*) of what I am calling Jesus groups in Judea (whom Paul wanted to think of as "in Christ," the term he used most often to conceptualize the incorporation of disparate Jesus and Christ groups into a single, singular, and universal entity), whom he said had heard about him. The group in Jerusalem did gather to hear what he had to say when told that he had arrived. So there was mutual recognition of some kind based on some common interests with regard to social issues where the Jesus legacy overlapped with Jewish concerns with Jewish-Gentile questions.

If we now consider the range of locations referred to in which these issues were being discussed, from Jerusalem and Judea to Antioch and Galatia, it does appear that different kinds of groups had emerged in which the overlap of Jewish practice and the Jesus legacy produced rather vociferous debates about the Jewish-Gentile question. Whether all of that social formation was a direct result of a Jesus movement spreading out from Galilee or a Christ cult spinning off from the ethnically mixed diaspora synagogues in Syria is no longer clear. I am afraid we have allowed Paul's personal missionary passions to color the question of the spread of the Jesus legacy and the reasons for it. The only things of which we can be sure from Paul's reports are (1) that Jews were taking note of the Jesus legacy, whether that legacy was an impulse to social formation, an ideology for a social program, or a way of thinking cultivated as a school of thought; (2) that the issues raised for Jews by the Jesus legacy had much to do with Jewish identity (I was tempted to say "belonging to Israel"), little with loyalties or markers pertinent to self-definition as a Jesus school or Christ cult; and (3) that, however, Jews from Jerusalem to Galatia were acting as if Jewishness (or whatever they had in mind for Jewishness as a social concept) had a stake in the outcome of these debates. Thus, having set aside the Lukan-Pauline scenario, the picture of Christian origins changes markedly in the direction of ad hoc social formations and wide-open ideological debate where and when people interjected the Jesus legacy into the situation of Jewish response to the Roman world. I am not sure what to make of the "right hand of fellowship" except to say that it need not have meant an "official" recognition of anything other than mutual respect among fellow Jews engaged in debating critical social issues. I am even less clear about the request to "remember the poor" except to say that, however one understands it, the request and Paul's agreement to it tell us more about Jewish interests in the new diaspora developments than about the distinctive features of those developments. Thus we are left with a set of indicators that suggests a social formation in Jerusalem quite different from the pictures we have had of the "church" or the congregations of the Christ. Do these indicators make a set, and can they be elaborated to produce a coherent profile of real people engaged in the pursuit of interests known to be important for the times? The answer seems to be yes.

This is hardly the place to rehearse what we have learned about *Palestinian Parties and Politics* from Morton Smith and others or to review the major themes in common throughout the huge volume of literature produced by Jewish intellectuals during the Greco-Roman period.[5] It is enough to remind ourselves that a sizable number of experimental social formations entered the picture, that differing schools of thought were widely recognized and debated as a matter of course, and that the ideological issues under debate in all social locations had to do with reconceptualizing the shape and place of collective Jewish presence in a world that had called the current incarnation of the ancient temple-state model into question. The recurrent genres are familiar. They include epic revisions; patriarchal testaments; stories of prophets, teachers, and kings; priestly genealogies; temple description and design; instructions in righteousness; warnings against ungodliness; laments over the fate of Jerusalem in the hands of foreign rulers; visions of restoration; and polished examples of wisdom textbooks and exegetical commentaries to be used for educational purposes in diaspora "schools." Not much interest in personal romances there. Even the highly imaginative portrayals that give these fictions color, images of fantastic figures and events of the past and wild projections into the future, were obviously generated by social interests and serious thought. It is not difficult to see that the recurrent themes are rooted in social interests. These include interests in the land, the city, the temple, leadership roles, rituals, special occasions, genealogies, social codes, the marks of ethnic identity, place among the nations, and so forth. What if we said that these themes, while distinctively Jewish in their particularity, are

---

[5] Morton Smith, *Palestinian Parties and Politics That Shaped the Old Testament* (2nd ed.; London: SCM, 1987).

nevertheless variants of interests common to all peoples and that such apparently disparate interests can be reduced to a single basic interest that humans take in creating social structures and maintaining social existence? Then the entire field of ethnography and cultural anthropology would be available for testing our theories and marveling at the creativity of particular social formations.

A sustained argument to this effect cannot be spelled out here. Some of you know that I have been toying with a social theory of religion in which human interest in the social enterprise is struggling for conceptualization and articulation.[6] But note that many of the cognitive systems and social structures commonly observed by ethnographers and used by cultural anthropologists to describe and theorize human societies are concepts into which the Jewish interests just mentioned can easily be translated. Why not try your hand at correlating the above (or your own) list of themes and interests characteristic for Jewish intellectuals and authors in Late Antiquity with the following list of social structures, cognitive systems, and patterns of activity commonly used by cultural anthropologists: kinship and kingship as ways to structure a society; language for communication; dual classification systems for organizing knowledge of flora, fauna, and subsocial family units; maps and tracks by which terrain becomes habitat; stories of forebears (heroes and gods) as ways to imagine the legacy of the past; technologies of construction and production with accompanying modes of tuition and the assignment of roles; calendrical and ritual modes of keeping times and tracing histories, preparing for seasons, and performing rites of passage; and marking each other with various insignia to assure distinction in the face of other peoples.

Now that we know that these ways of organizing knowledge and situating people in their worlds are not "given" in the "natural" orders of the world but that all of them are products of the interface where cognitive capacities, environmental manipulation, and social patterning create and foster human interests, an exception need not be made for religion as if it alone were the way in which humans traffic with the "supernatural," an order of reality that transcends the empirical. All cognitive systems and social constructs are "supernatural" in the sense that their generation and maintenance take place at the level of human interests that lodge in conceptual systems that transcend the natural world; they have not and cannot be derived from natural processes without the interest and conceptual

---

[6] Burton L. Mack, "Social Formation," in *Guide to the Study of Religion* (ed. Willi Braun and Russell T. McCutcheon; London: Cassell, 2000), 283–96; idem, "A Radically Social Theory of Religion," in *Secular Theories on Religion: Current Perspectives* (ed. Tim Jensen and Mikael Rothstein; Copenhagen: Museum Tusculanum Press, 2000), 123–36; idem, *The Christian Myth: Origins, Logic, and Legacy* (New York: Continuum, 2001), 81–99, 101–25, 201–16.

manipulation that humans bring to them. Religion also is a human construct intertwined with other human constructs in the interest of social formation and maintenance. Note the variations of conceptual abstractions across the range of the cognitive and structural systems typical for human societies. They include several levels of abstraction, rules of logical inference, mathematical operations, memory and imagination, and so forth. Myths and rituals can be given their place within this family of intellectual procedures as modes of manipulating the coordinates of times and places in the interest of reflecting upon human activity apart from any given actual performance of an everyday action (which action, of course, would not even be noticeable for humans without some form of consciousness that transcends the moment). If, for instance, social formation involves taking an interest in maintenance over time, and maintenance over time is thought of as generational continuity, and making generational continuity possible is imagined on the model of tuition, the human capacity for myth-making is not at all surprising. Myth is a way of shifting the cognitive systems integral to the present social structure into the past. It is a way of accounting for the fact that the social patterns are already there when any given generation comes along. Myths help imagine the past as the arena of precedent-setting activities. And since those activities and those who perform them are highly condensed abstractions of collective interests and social constructions, it is no wonder that their depictions take on extravagant proportions. But enough—this is not the place to elaborate on theories of myth and ritual. The point should be clear about the social interests involved in the range of topics and issues under debate in Jewish circles during the Greco-Roman world. Does debate about the right way to think about the land, Jerusalem, temple, history, heroes, Israel, Gentiles, wars, codes, rituals, and what it would take to set things right indicate unsettling social circumstances? Yes. Can the claims wont to be made in the face of actual circumstances to the contrary be regarded as mythmaking? Of course.

What, then, can be said about the interests of the Jerusalem group of Jesus people? We have seen that they overlap with a number of interests shared by Jews in general: location in Jerusalem, family connections, ethnic purity, meal-practice etiquette, and interest in gathering for debate on the issue of social relations with non-Jews. In one respect, this is not much to go on. It is certainly not a large enough list of interests to paint a plausible picture of an independently active group. However the interests do match a portion of those typical for Jewish intellectuals of the day in general, and it is not unreasonable to think that this group may have shared many more of those interests. If we note that the debate as reported focused only upon the Gentile question and that this question was introduced by Paul because of events taking place in the diaspora, we have no reason to believe that the Jerusalem group had previously been particularly exercised by the problem. That suggests a fairly thorough Jewish sensibility and leaves us with the question of their own particular configuration of interests to be meeting as a group in Jerusalem. The problem is not with the notion of a group of Jewish intellectuals who may have held distinctive views or wanted to debate social issues in the shadow of the Roman threat to the temple-state. Our problem is to recognize that Jewishness and then find ways to account for (1) Paul's interest in them, (2) their interest in discussing the Gentile question with Paul, and (3) their relationship to the Jesus movement in general and other Jesus groups in particular.

As for Paul's interest in the Jerusalem group, several of us have suggested ways to start the discussion, and Miller's brilliant application of Jonathan Z. Smith's point about diaspora perspectives on the homeland provides us with a remarkably firm theoretical foundation upon which to proceed. So I need not say more, except to note (a) that the "perspectives" outlined by Smith and Miller fit readily into a general theory of social "interests" and (b) that the interests in common that made mutual recognitions possible among the Jerusalem group, Paul, and the diaspora congregations must have been those we now associate with the Jesus movements, not those traditionally associated with Paul's depiction of the Christ cults.

As for the interest on the part of the Jerusalem group in talking to Paul, Paul's vignettes are not enough to convince me that the questions about circumcision and table fellowship were burning, practical issues for the Jerusalem people. Their responses, in any case, are much more plausible as the expressions of theoretical positions, the kind of position taking that any Jew could have exercised whether or not confronted by an actual social situation of immediate and personal experience and concern. Thus their reception of Paul could have been motivated by mutual concerns of self-definition made problematic by the inclusion of Gentiles into the congregations of the Christ in Antioch. But it certainly need not have been. The important question is whether the Jerusalem group saw themselves as part of a movement that included the Christ congregations and got exercised about the acceptance of Gentiles within that movement, or whether their interest in Paul's question was more academic, that is, a question of importance for Jews and Jewish institutions in general. It is possible that their discussion of the question was more a matter of interest in the constituency and identity of the Antioch *synagogue* than in the definition of the new social formation Paul was calling the *church*. Paul's reference to the "false brothers" who were "brought in" to the discussion seems to support this supposition. They need not have been "Christians" at all.

As for finding a place within the Jesus movements for the Jerusalem group, that may not be as difficult as it once seemed. Now that we can identify several streams within the movement, all of which felt free to go their own way, developing strikingly different views of the founder, interpretations of his teachings, ways of linking up with Jewish epic mythologies, and attitudes toward other social configurations, both within the family of Judaisms and without, it is no more difficult to account for the Jesus movement taking a turn toward Jerusalem than toward Antioch. As a matter of fact, the emergence of the Christ cults is much more surprising when thought of as a consequence of the Jesus movement than is the picture of a group of Jews in Jerusalem who got interested in talking about the significance of Jesus, his teachings, and the various groups forming in his name, for Jewish institutions and self-definition. On the basis of Q, the pre-Markan Jesus materials, and the *Gospel of Thomas,* overlaid by the traditional assumptions of an anti-Jewish bias of some kind at the beginning of the Christian persuasion, it has been difficult to think that anyone would have, could have merged the teachings and legacy of Jesus with plain old Jewish interests in the Jewish institutions of the time. But we do have evidence in the cases of Matthew, the *Didache, 1 Clement,* and other texts that accommodations of that kind—if indeed it was really necessary to make "accommodations"—were easily worked out at a later time. This does not answer the question we will have to ask about the interests that must have been held in common by what appears to be widely divergent social formations and mythologies among the early Jesus groups. However, since that question gets us to the heart of the matter, both the matter of my theory of social formation and mythmaking and the matter of the project of this Seminar, I would say we were very close to setting a significant agenda for discussion.

HISTORY, HISTORIOGRAPHY, AND CHRISTIAN ORIGINS: THE JERUSALEM COMMUNITY*

Luther H. Martin

There can be no "proper history" which is not at the same time "philosophy of history."
— Hayden White[1]

Contemporary historiography finds itself lodged between two theoretical extremes: positivism (i.e., the vestiges of modernism), on the one hand, whereby the evidence—primarily textual—is considered to speak more or less for itself if we can only get it right, and postmodernism, on the other, whereby historiographical narratives might be creatively imagined (or reimagined) regardless of the question about whether there is sufficient (or, indeed, any) evidence to support the integrity of that narrative. Finding historiographical balance between these theoretical extremes has often been compared to the work of a detective who must reconstruct a crime that has occurred at some point in the past on the basis of the evidence that survives in the present. The task of the detective is to decide what constitutes relevant evidence in the first place and to establish an explanatory relationship between that evidence collected in order to construct a viable case. The reconstruction of the crime that is so convincing to the detective may, however, prove less so to others. Rather, the relevance of the evidence presented may be challenged along with the investigative methods whereby the evidence was gathered; further evidence may be

---

* I prepared these remarks for discussion by participants of the Ancient Myths and Modern Theories of Christian Origins Seminar at its meeting in Orlando in November 1998; although I have revised it for clarity and format, it is printed here essentially as originally presented. I expanded on many of the ideas presented here in a paper entitled "History, Historiography and Christian Origins," which I prepared for a Research Conference on Historical Theories, Methods, and Knowledges in the Study of Ancient Religions, organized by Per Bilde and Jeppe Sinding Jensen at the University of Aarhus, Denmark, in September 1999. That paper was subsequently published in *SR* 29 (2000): 69–89.

[1] Hayden White, *Metahistory: The Historical Imagination in Nineteenth-Century Europe* (Baltimore: Johns Hopkins University Press, 1973), xi; cf. 428.

discovered; the theoretical assumptions upon which the case has been constructed may be questioned and an alternative case suggested. The "truth of the matter" is determined finally only by a consensus of jurors as that which is "beyond reasonable doubt" and is, of course, subject to appeal.

I have been invited to think about historiographical questions as they might apply to Christian origins and especially to the "Jerusalem community," the topic of our discussion this year. At the outset, I have formulated, for the sake of efficiency, some "theses" that are central to any historical investigation. I do not suppose that any one will find much new in these theoretical formulations; I rehearse them here to emphasize that a critical historiography is a theoretically informed practice, the principles of which even seasoned "professional" historians often find themselves unintentionally in violation. In a second section, I shall venture to comment on the work of the Seminar in light of these theses. My comments in neither section are intended to be in any way exhaustive but solely evocative of our continuing discussions.

1. Historiographical Theses

[ἡ] ἱστορίη [... ἐς] τὰ γενόμενα ἐξ ἀνθρώπων
τῷ χρόνῳ ... [ἐστὶν] ἱστορίης λόγο[ς]
— Herodotus 1.1; 7.96

1.1. The subject matter of historiography is "human doings" in the past (τὰ γενόμενα ἐξ ἀνθρώπων τῷ χρόνῳ or *res gestae*).

1.1.1. The ontology of the past is beyond the grasp of historiography. Although the "past is by definition, a datum that nothing in the future will change,"[2] any direct access to it remains, since the 1895 publication of H. G. Wells's *Time Machine*, only the fantasy of science-fiction imagination.

1.1.2. *Res gestae* must be distinguished from *historia rerum gestarum*, "the narration of human doings" in the past based upon historical remains.[3] Since both are signified in English—as in Greek—by the single word "history,"[4] accounts of human doings in the past are often taken to represent accurately the "reality" of historical occurrences.

---

[2] Marc Bloch, *The Historian's Craft* (trans. Peter Putnam; New York: Random House, Vintage Books, 1953), 58.

[3] Georg Wilhelm Friedrich Hegel, *The Philosophy of History* (trans. J. Sibree; New York: Dover, 1956), 60.

[4] Whereas ἱστορίη in Herodotus is usually to be translated in its lexical sense of "inquiry," it is used in Herodotus 7.96 in the sense of "written account of one's inquiries." See LSJ s.v. II (842a); W. W. How and J. Wells, *A Commentary on Herodotus* (2 vols.; Oxford: Clarendon, 1912), 2:163.

1.2. Historical remains may be characterized as either intentional or unintentional.[5]

1.2.1. Intentional historical remains may be characterized as "propaganda" in the sociological sense of materials produced and/or preserved by the ideological convictions of special-interest groups.[6] Largely literary, these products are those consciously intended to persuade readers, whether contemporaneous or future.

Cautioning against what he termed a "fetishism of documents," Edward Hallett Carr has warned against confusing historical texts with "factual" accounts. "No document," he concludes, "can tell us more than what the author of the document thought—what he thought had happened, what he thought ought to happen or would happen, or perhaps only what he wanted others to think he thought, or even only what he himself thought he thought."[7] Similarly, M. I. Finley has concluded that "the first questions to be asked of any written source are, why was it written? why was it 'published'?"[8]

1.2.2. Unintentional historical remains may be classified as the products of everyday social life. Largely archaeological documents (discarded refuse, funerary ornamentations, coins, etc.), though including inscriptions and certain kinds of texts, they are not designed to influence others but are intended for socially internal uses.

1.2.3. There is often a discrepancy between the two, that is, between historiographical interpretations of literary and material cultures, that must be explained.

1.3. Historiography attempts an *explanation* for human actions based upon historical remains. As Marc Bloch argues:

> The only sciences which ... [the human intellect] admits to be authentic are those which succeed in establishing explanatory relationships between phenomena.... History will rightfully claim its place among those sciences truly worthy of endeavor only in proportion as it promises us, not simply a disjointed and, you might say, a nearly infinite enumeration, but a rational classification and progressive intelligibility.[9]

1.3.1. Historical data may be explained in different ways.

---

[5] Bloch, *Historian's Craft*, 60–69.
[6] Robert K. Merton, *Social Theory and Social Structure* (enl. ed.; New York: Free Press; London: Collier-Macmillan, 1968), 160, 563.
[7] Edward Hallett Carr, *What Is History?* (New York: Knopf, 1961), 15, 16.
[8] M. I. Finley, *Ancient History: Evidence and Models* (New York: Viking, 1986), 105.
[9] Bloch, *Historian's Craft*, 10.

1.3.1.1. Theories of history determine the theoretical object of historiography, such as political history, intellectual history, social history, economic history, religious history, and so on. These different historical "objects of study" may determine different periodizations, catchments of data, and so forth.

1.3.1.2. Cognitive theories. Since all historical data have already been processed by human minds—including the minds of prior and present historians—historical data may be explained, first of all, in terms of how human minds process and transmit any data.[10]

1.3.1.2.1. In contrast to individual psychology, cognitive psychology is the attempt to identify mental processes that operate to constrain human activities in common, such as processes of social formation and maintenance.

1.3.1.2.2. The theoretical premise animating the significance of contemporary cognitive research for historiography was already anticipated by Giambattista Vico in the eighteenth century and Georg Simmel in the nineteenth century. According to Vico, "There must in the nature of human institutions be a mental language common to all nations, which uniformly grasps the substance of things feasible in human social life and expresses it with as many diverse modifications as these same things may have diverse aspects."[11] In the view of Simmel, "Mind is the material of history.... If history is not a mere puppet show, then it must be the history of mental processes.... Those matters which come first in the rational order of things—the cognitive functions of the mind—come last from the standpoint of our awareness and our observation."[12] As François Hartog concludes in his study of Herodotus, "Between the narrator and his addressee there exists, as a precondition for communication, a whole collection of semantic, encyclopedic, and symbolic knowledge common to both sides."[13]

1.3.1.3. Social theories. Whether or not social categories may be explained as domain-specific cognitive competence[14] or as cultural formations in the

---

[10] See, e.g., Dan Sperber, *Explaining Culture: A Naturalistic Approach* (Oxford: Blackwell, 1996); Pascal Boyer, "Cognitive Tracks of Cultural Inheritance: How Evolved Intuitive Ontology Governs Cultural Transmission," *American Anthropologist* NS 100 (1998): 876–89.

[11] Giambattista Vico, *The New Science of Giambattista Vico* (trans. Thomas Goddard Bergin and Max Harold Fisch; Ithaca, N.Y.: Cornell University Press, 1968), §161.

[12] Georg Simmel, *The Problems of the Philosophy of History: An Epistemological Essay* (trans. Guy Oakes; New York: Free Press, 1977), vii, 39, 43.

[13] François Hartog, *The Mirror of Herodotus: The Representation of the Other in the Writing of History* (The New Historicism: Studies in Cultural Poetics 5; trans. Janet Lloyd; Berkeley and Los Angeles: University of California Press, 1988), 7.

[14] Lawrence A. Hirschfeld, "Is the Acquisition of Social Categories Based on Domain-Specific Competence or on Knowledge Transfer?" in *Mapping the Mind: Domain Specificity in Cognition and Culture* (ed. Lawrence A. Hirschfeld and Susan A. Gelman; Cambridge: Cambridge University Press, 1994), 201–33.

tracks of biology,[15] sociology shares with historiography the subject matter of *res gestae,* the *common* doings of human beings.

1.3.1.4. Sociology and historiography. To clarify the theoretical relationships between sociology and historiography is to increase theoretical issues exponentially while nevertheless constraining and clarifying their possibilities. Various theoretical relationships between sociology and historiography have been proposed.[16]

1.3.1.4.1. Max Weber's model of "ideal types" proposes a methodological strategy whereby historical deviations from a formally-structured general sociological concept might be charted.[17]

1.3.1.4.2. Weber's distinction between the general and the particular exemplifies the theoretical problem of the relationship between sociology and historiography, such as between a "synchronous whole" and a "chronological series";[18] between "statics" and "dynamics" (A. Comte); between "equilibrium" and "innovation" (F. Gottl); between the interests of human beings and "the forms in which these [interests] embody themselves" and between occurrences "taking place between two definite dates in two different dimensions of time (past and present)";[19] and between society as the subject matter of sociology and society as the only empirically detectable factor in the historical process (Marx).

1.3.2. The historical shaping of the historian remains a significant problem not addressed here apart from the observation that the data *selected* as relevant for historical reconstruction depends upon the explanatory theory (whether implicit or explicit) employed by the historian.[20]

1.4. Historiography is a type of generalization about what has been selected as historical data.

1.4.1. To situate data is to compare them,[21] either with selected data prior to and following upon the selected datum (i.e., chronologically), or with selected data from the same time frame as the selected datum (i.e., synchronously), or with both.[22]

---

[15] Walter Burkert, *Creation of the Sacred: Tracks of Biology in Early Religions* (Cambridge: Harvard University Press, 1996).

[16] Nathan Rotenstreich, *Between Past and Present: An Essay on History* (New Haven: Yale University Press, 1958), 169–91.

[17] See Max Weber, *The Theory of Social and Economic Organization* (trans. A. M. Henderson and Talcott Parsons; New York: Oxford University Press, 1947), 92.

[18] Bloch, *Historian's Craft,* 110.

[19] Rotenstreich, *Between Past and Present,* 186.

[20] [Luther H. Martin], "Historicism," in *The HarperCollins Dictionary of Religion* (ed. Jonathan Z. Smith; San Francisco: HarperSanFrancisco, 1995), 454–55.

[21] Bloch, *Historian's Craft,* 110.

[22] Rather than "reconstituting *chains of inference,*" Michel Foucault, for example, proposes to describe successive discursive formations or *"systems of dispersion"* (*The Archaeology of*

1.4.2. To compare data is to categorize those which have been selected as being, in some sense, similar. In contradiction, then, to theorists who would relegate historiography to a concern with particulars (following Aristotle, who first so characterized history [*Poet.* 9]), history is a type of generalization. In the conclusion of Carr, "Those who reject generalization and insist that history is concerned exclusively with the unique are, logically enough, those who deny that anything can be learned from history."[23]

1.4.3. If historiographical generalizations are to be explanatory (in contrast to "commonsensical," collectively learned, and uncritically assumed generalizations; or propagandistic, ideological generalizations produced by special-interest groups), they must be formulated as theoretical constructs that "try to find in [the] subject matter a basis for comparison, classification, interpretation, or generalization," and their validity must, in some sense, be testable; that is, they must conform "at least ... to all the known facts" and "to certain general standards and tests—of human behavior, of logical antecedents and consequences, of statistical or mass trends."[24]

1.5. Theory and historiography

Historiography is not a positivistic method for arriving at a factual content but, like any kind of generalizing, is a theoretical activity that stipulates a theoretical "object" or body of data and offers a probable explanation for that data. As such, it provides an intellectual framework for critical discussion, investigation, and refinement.[25]

Knowledge and the Discourse on Language [trans. A. M. Sheridan Smith; World of Man; New York: Pantheon, 1972], 37, emphasis original; see idem, *The Order of Things: An Archaeology of the Human Sciences* [World of Man; New York: Pantheon, 1970]). Jonathan Z. Smith argues for a history of "analogous" processes and settings (*Drudgery Divine: On the Comparison of Early Christianities and the Religions of Late Antiquity* [Jordan Lectures in Comparative Religion 14; London: School of Oriental and African Studies, University of London; Chicago: University of Chicago Press, 1990], esp. 112–21).

[23] Carr, *What Is History*, 84–85.

[24] Louis Gottschalk, foreword, in *Generalization in the Writing of History: A Report of the Committee on Historical Analysis of the Social Science Research Council* (ed. Louis Gottschalk; Chicago: University of Chicago Press, 1963), v, vi. In the case of Christian origins, Merrill P. Miller has argued against the canonical paradigm precisely on the basis of evaluating "logical antecedents and consequences" ("'Beginning from Jerusalem ...': Re-examining Canon and Consensus," *Journal of Higher Criticism* 2/1 [1995]: 3–30). Rodney Stark has presented arguments against the same paradigm on the basis of his plausible reconstruction of "statistical ... trends" (*The Rise of Christianity: A Sociologist Reconsiders History* [Princeton: Princeton University Press, 1996]). Perhaps historiographical standards of conformity to "human behavior" might also be a consequence of the empirical researches of cognitive psychologists?

[25] Luther H. Martin, "Rationalism and Relativity in History of Religions Research," in *Rationality and the Study of Religion* (ed. Jeppe S. Jensen and Luther H. Martin; Acta Jutlandica 72/1; Aarhus: Aarhus University Press, 1997), 145–56.

2. Historiography and Christian Origins: The Jerusalem Community

> More than any other special field of historical study, New Testament research has always suffered from a curious inability to be thoroughly historical in method and in aim.... [It has been a historical science only] in so far as it has produced scientifically valid results.... It has a future only if this fact will at long last be fully recognized and consistently acted upon.
> — Paul Schubert[26]

A critical history of Christian origins must in no way privilege its object of study but must employ the same theoretical concerns and methodological procedures as the study of anything. Like that of historiography generally, the subject matter of a critical historiography is *res gestae* (see §1.1 above) and not τὰ γενόμενα ἐκ θεῶν τῷ χρόνῳ or *gestae dei*, which are properly the subject matter of theologically constructed *Heilsgeschichten*.[27] Rather, it is as objects of the human imagination that the gods, like anything "in the life of men and societies," are "a suitable subject for history."[28]

It is the working hypothesis of the Seminar on Ancient Myths and Modern Theories of Christian Origins that the historical texts produced by the early Christianities are not historiographical but are propagandistic; that is to say, these texts are produced out of the self-interested theological/ideological/mythological imagination of various early Christian groups (see §§1.1.1; 1.2.1 above).[29] As such, these sources are better viewed, in the formulation of Merrill P. Miller, as "social artifact[s]" of a "mythmaking" process at a "particular juncture of ... social history."[30] If the texts produced by early Christians are to be understood as the products of their mythmaking, they cannot then count as historiographical documentation in

---

[26] Paul Schubert, "Urgent Tasks for New Testament Research," in *The Study of the Bible Today and Tomorrow* (ed. Harold R. Willoughby; Chicago: University of Chicago Press, 1947), 214, 212.

[27] R. G. Collingwood, *The Idea of History* (New York: Oxford University Press, 1956), 9; see Willi Braun, "Amnesia in the Production of (Christian) History," *BCSSR* 28/1 (1999): 3–8.

[28] Jacques Le Goff, *The Medieval Imagination* (trans. Arthur Goldhammer; Chicago: University of Chicago Press, 1988), 5. Karen Armstrong's book, *A History of God: The 4000-Year Quest of Judaism, Christianity and Islam* (New York: Knopf, 1993), illustrates how god(s) can, indeed, be "a suitable subject for history," when understood as "objects of the human imagination."

[29] On the Hellenistic period as "the propaganda age," see A. Haire Forster, "Propaganda Analysis Applied to Alexandrian-Jewish Apologetic," in Willoughby, *Study of the Bible,* 269.

[30] Miller, "Beginning from Jerusalem," 24, 28. Miller's position here is similar to that of Maurice Godelier, who proposes viewing the influence of ideas, ideologies, and myths as themselves a type of material cause (*The Mental and the Material: Thought Economy and Society* [trans. Martin Thom; London: Verso, 1986], 4, 5, 29).

support of events portrayed in their production. Even though these Christian myths might employ categories drawn from their setting in the wider world (places, persons, powers, whether political or cosmic, etc.), this does not mean that they convey information *about* that world; in fact, it is characteristic of myths to distort historical events in service to their own propagandistic/ideological/mythological work. If, for example, references to "Jerusalem" in Acts and Galatians belong to instances of Christian mythmaking, as Miller argues, we must question the extent to which it is possible to use this mythographic data for any historiographical description of a "Christian" group in Jerusalem. The case of the Jerusalem community, in other words, is quite unlike the problematic of "imagining" a profile for those social groups that produced the Sayings Gospel Q, for example, or the *Gospel of Thomas*. Although there seems no good reason to doubt the existence of an early Jerusalem community of "Jesus people,"[31] the historical "fact" remains that this community "made no myths" of its own (or, at least, none that survived). Rather, the "Jerusalem community" survives solely as a datum in the "mythmaking" formations of others, namely, the Pauline and the Lukan theological projects.[32]

My impression is that a number of the responses to Miller's paper, "'Beginning from Jerusalem ...': Re-examining Canon and Consensus," retain vestiges of the exegetical tradition of liberal biblical scholarship,

---

[31] Merrill P. Miller, "Antioch, Paul, and Jerusalem: Diaspora Myths of Origins in the Homeland" (in this volume).

[32] Lukan references to a Christian group in Jerusalem are suspect as historigraphical data for two reasons. (1) Hans Conzelmann, whatever his own "kerygmatic" convictions (cf. Ron Cameron's letter of 21 December 1998), has nevertheless established that the author of Luke "employs geographical factors for the purpose of setting out his fundamental conception" and that this *Heilsgeographie* structures events in his life of Jesus as a persistent movement toward Jerusalem, culminating with the arrival of Jesus in that city (Hans Conzelmann, *The Theology of St Luke* [trans. Geoffrey Buswell; New York: Harper & Row, 1961], 27). This structure is "not determined by the source material employed, but by the work of arrangement carried out by the author" (ibid., 72). In other words, Conzelmann has demonstrated that geographical references in Luke-Acts are subordinate to Lukan "mythmaking" and cannot be accorded historical status. (2) The theological (mythological) orientation of the author of Luke is derivative from Paul (or from sources about Paul), including, perhaps, the *heilsgeschichtliche/ heilsgeographische* place of Jerusalem in Paul's own theological (mythological) scheme. Paul's references to Jerusalem raise the questions of (a) what we can know about the Christian group in Jerusalem with any historical probability, apart from the likelihood that there was one; and (b) the place of Jerusalem in the mythmaking activities of non-Christian communities. Apart from the early Christianities, Jerusalem is obviously a central mytheme for Judaism generally in which the mythic character of the city may, however, have far exceeded its historical significance (see Niels Peter Lemche, *The Israelites in History and Tradition* [Library of Ancient Israel; London: SPCK; Louisville: Westminster John Knox, 1998]). What is the place of Jerusalem in the mythmaking activities of the various Jewish groups contemporary with the early Christianities?

namely, the view that the New Testament documents contain kernels of historical content from which extraneous (mythological/theological/rhetorical/strategic) chaff may, by careful textual exegesis, be separated. The primary difference between these responses and earlier biblical scholarship is that, previously, a relatively larger amount of detritus was produced.[33] More appropriately historiographical questions (of the sort suggested by Miller's view of texts as social artifacts) that might be posed of the "Jerusalem" data include the following: What is the place given to "Jerusalem" in the myth-making activities of the Pauline and the Lukan communities (keeping in mind the question of the dependency of the latter on the former) and in the subsequent environment of Christian mythic formations? How did "Jerusalem" come to be the widely accepted "root metaphor of the imagination of Christian origins"?[34]

If the sources for the early Christianities are understood to be myths produced as a consequence of social formation, then we must clearly stipulate not only our historiographical theory (or theories) but also our theory (or theories) of social groups and their formation. To rely upon implicitly held or privately employed theory (or theories) in our historiographical work is to revert to assumptions about data alone as the public arbiter of historiographical validity—hardly an advance over nineteenth-century models of historical positivism upon which classicists (and biblical scholars) have traditionally relied in their textual studies and which tacitly assume that historical (textual) evidence, carefully gathered and accurately presented, speaks convincingly for itself. We must, in other words, clearly state our view of the theoretical connection between mythmaking and social formation in historiographical research.[35]

---

[33] Many of the concerns of the Seminar seem to be rooted in the sociohistoriographical interests of form criticism. Rudolf Bultmann attributed such interests to the nineteenth-century historian Jakob Burckhardt (*The History of the Synoptic Tradition* [rev. ed.; trans. John Marsh; New York: Harper & Row, 1963], 4 n. 2). See Jakob Burckhardt, "Zur geschichtlichen Betrachtung der Poesie," in *Weltgeschichtliche Betrachtungen* (3rd ed.; Stuttgart: Spemann, 1918), 69–80; ET: "On the Historical Consideration of Poetry," in *Reflections on History* (Indianapolis: Liberty Classics, 1979), 107–19. We might also mention in this connection the "sociohistorical" method associated with the "Chicago School" of biblical exegesis (see William J. Hynes, *Shirley Jackson Case and the Chicago School: The Socio-historical Method* [SBLBSNA 5; Chico, Calif.: Scholars Press, 1981]).

[34] Miller, "Beginning from Jerusalem," 3.

[35] The relationship between religious practices and sociology is, of course, one of the foundations of the modern social sciences, from Karl Marx's critical view that religious productions represent "false consciousness," to Émile Durkheim's positive view that religious productions reflect and reenforce social structure, to Max Weber's analytic view that religious productions are correlate with political and economic structures. With the exception of some work in the neo-Marxist tradition, however, the differing structures built upon this foundation have been little remodeled since their original construction.

The fascinating but theoretically contested relationship between mythology and sociology and the consequent methodological deduction of the latter from the former remains a theoretically open question (see §1.3.1.4 above).[36] Burton L. Mack, for example, is attempting to elaborate and to employ a "social theory of religion" in which historical variants of social formation and maintenance might be a characteristic of "a single basic interest that humans take in creating social structures and maintaining social existence."[37] This implicit allusion to human universals ("human interests in general")[38] is a theoretical matter that requires explanation.[39] Might the researches of contemporary cognitive psychologists into the mental constraints common to all humans be of help here (see §§1.3.1.2; 1.4.3 above)?[40] If, after all, social interests affect and are expressed in such cultural processes as mythmaking, they affect and are expressed through human minds.[41]

Finally, we might consider whether the "social artifacts" of later (second- and third-century) Christian material culture[42] might offer some insight into the social history of those early "Christian" groups, such as the Jerusalem community, that either did not produce any literary/mythic materials or for which such materials have not been documented or preserved (see §1.2.3 above).[43] The remains of a (later) Christian material culture seem, after all,

---

[36] Henry A. Green's study on Gnosticism with respect to these questions includes his summary and critique of previous attempts by E. Michael Mendelson, Hans Kippenberg, and Kurt Rudolph to describe social context on the basis of surviving myths (*The Economic and Social Origins of Gnosticism* [SBLDS 77; Atlanta: Scholars Press, 1985], 1–4). See also E. Michael Mendelson, "Some Notes on a Sociological Approach to Gnosticism," in *Le Origini dello gnosticismo: Colloquio di Messina, 13–18 Aprile 1966* (ed. Ugo Bianchi; SHR 12; Leiden: Brill, 1967), 668–74; Hans G. Kippenberg, "Versuch einer soziologischen Verortung des antiken Gnostizismus," *Numen* 17 (1970): 211–31; Kurt Rudolph, "Das Problem einer Soziologie und 'sozialen Verortung' der Gnosis," *Kairos* NS 19 (1977): 35–44.

[37] Burton L. Mack, "A Jewish Jesus School in Jerusalem?" 259 (in this volume).

[38] Ibid., 255–56.

[39] Donald E. Brown, *Human Universals* (New York: McGraw-Hill, 1991); see Luther H. Martin, "Comparativism and Sociobiological Theory," *Numen* 48 (2001): 290–308.

[40] Luther H. Martin, "Biology, Sociology and the Study of Religion: Two Lectures," *Religio: Revue pro Religionistiku* 5 (1997): 21–35. For a more recent model of the relationship between cognitive constraints, i.e., modes of memory, and sociopolitical patterns, see now Harvey Whitehouse, *Inside the Cult: Religious Innovation and Transmission in Papua New Guinea* (Oxford Studies in Social and Cultural Anthropology; Oxford: Clarendon, 1995); idem, *Arguments and Icons: Divergent Modes of Religiosity* (Oxford: Oxford University Press, 2000).

[41] Dan Sperber, "Anthropology and Psychology: Towards an Epidemiology of Representations," *Man* NS 20 (1985): 78–79.

[42] Graydon F. Snyder, *Ante Pacem: Archaeological Evidence of Church Life before Constantine* (Macon, Ga.: Mercer University Press, 1985).

[43] We might well consider what "types" of social groups are even possible in the Hellenistic world. Toward this end, see my proposal for a kinship/kingship model of sociopolitical

to accord more with the interests of those communities that produced Q and *Thomas* than with the theological schemas of either Paul or Luke.

Like criminal investigation, no historical description (or redescription) can ever be made with certainty. Rather, the goal of even the most positivistic of historians is about probability in the face of historical possibility.[44] Consequently, the historian of religion must concede, for example, the *possibility* of the canonical account concerning the role of the Jerusalem "church" in the origins of Christianity. Nevertheless, this same historian of religion must conclude, based upon available data, that this interpretation is most improbable. The basis for this conclusion, however, cannot be based upon details gleaned from the text by historical-critical research—more data, in other words, for the incessant and inexhaustible mills of possibility that produced the Lukan scenario of Jerusalem as the site of Christian origins in the first place. Rather, this conclusion is based on historiographical generalizations about the various early Christian groups, how these groups represented themselves (or how they were represented), and how these representations were transmitted.

---

organization in the Hellenistic world (Luther H. Martin, "Akin to the Gods or Simply One to Another? Comparison with Respect to Religions in Antiquity," in *Vergleichen und Verstehen in der Religionswissenschaft: Vorträge der Jahrestagung der DVRG vom 4. bis 6. Oktober 1995 in Bonn* [ed. Hans-Joachim Klimkeit; StOR 41;Wiesbaden: Harrassowitz, 1997], 147–59).

[44] Bloch, *Historian's Craft*, 124. Categories such as chance, possibility, and probability are mathematical categories rarely considered by historians. For interesting discussions of these categories, see William Kruskal, "Miracles and Statistics: The Casual Assumption of Independence," *Journal of the American Statistical Association* 83 (1988): 929–40; Persi Diaconis and Frederick Mosteller, "Methods for Studying Coincidences," *Journal of the American Statistical Association* 84 (1989): 853–61.

AGENDA FOR THE ANNUAL MEETING, DISCUSSION, AND REFLECTIONS

Ron Cameron

An agenda for the first year of the Seminar, held in Orlando in 1998, was prepared from issues raised in the papers, from points on which the papers appeared to converge, and from preliminary responses to the papers in letters and e-mail. Three principal questions were on the agenda:

1. Did we have any usable, hard evidence—any data—that we could agree gave us some historical features for a profile of a Jerusalem group in the 30s and 40s? This issue is all the more urgent since we have identified in our sources no surviving myths that derive from a Jerusalem group from that early period. As Martin remarked in his paper, "although there seems no good reason to doubt the existence of an early Jerusalem community of 'Jesus people,' the historical 'fact' remains that this community 'made no myths' of its own (or, at least, none that survived). Rather, the 'Jerusalem community' survives solely as a datum in the 'mythmaking' formations of others."[1] Indeed, in his review of recent scholarship on Acts, Matthews observed that even though "Luke's understanding of Jerusalem participates in an intertexture of other symbolic cartographies that place Jerusalem at the center of the world," nevertheless, "when Luke wants to illustrate a 'breakthrough moment' in the spread of Christianity, he ends up using stories that have no necessary association with Jerusalem."[2] Accordingly, in discussing this question, our goal was to control the reimagination of "Jerusalem" by (1) assessing the scholarly arguments and historical scenarios that have been proposed in the papers; (2) recognizing which early Christian constructions of the past were made in the interest of mythmaking claims specific to their own situations; (3) determining what is left that

---

[1] Luther H. Martin, "History, Historiography, and Christian Origins: The Jerusalem Community," 270 (in this volume).

[2] Christopher R. Matthews, "Acts and the History of the Earliest Jerusalem Church," 172, 174 (in this volume).

would count as data for Jerusalem; and (4) constructing a profile of features that would constitute a coherent set.

2. Could we adjudicate on the basis of plausibility between different constructions that could be put on the isolated data? This issue is important because, in their papers, Miller and Dennis Smith agreed that the Jerusalem church of our canonical texts existed from the beginning in the mythmaking of diaspora communities, but they differed in their assessments of the role of the "pillars" as historical agents and of the nature of the conflicts and agreements between and among Paul, Antioch, and Jerusalem, all of which had a bearing on constructing a profile of a Jerusalem group. For Miller, "any historical reconstruction of the Jerusalem group and its leaders to be won from the data of Paul's letters ... must be wrested from competing mythic imaginations of 'Jerusalem' of diaspora Jews engaged in projects of teaching, recruitment, and community formation among Jews and Gentiles in Hellenistic cities outside Palestine."[3] For Smith, "the Jerusalem 'church' as a power broker in Christian origins was a mythological construct from the outset, first appearing among Paul's opponents in Galatia, then picked up and elaborated on by Luke in Acts.... [And so,] given the weight attached to the Jerusalem church in Luke's overall theological scheme, it is appropriate that we question the entire hypothesis of Christian origins in Jerusalem."[4] Accordingly, in discussing this question, our goal was to construct a scenario of plausibility of one or another configuration of features of a Jerusalem group by (1) analyzing how "Jerusalem" survives in the mythmaking formulations of others; (2) situating a locus or loci for early Christian imaginings of Jerusalem; (3) determining what was the basis for mutual recognition between Paul and a Jerusalem group; and (4) correlating the data used to construct a historical profile of a Jerusalem group with alternative readings of the texts as rhetorical and ideological constructions.

3. On the basis of a developing profile, what analogues from the cultures of context seemed appropriate, and how would we position a Jerusalem group if we compared its features to those of other Jesus and Christ groups? This issue is critical in order to render our profile historically plausible by providing a comparative analysis of an early Jesus group in Jerusalem. In his paper Mack argued that "the interests in common that made mutual recognitions possible among the Jerusalem group, Paul, and

---

[3] Merrill P. Miller, "Antioch, Paul, and Jerusalem: Diaspora Myths of Origins in the Homeland," 181, emphasis omitted (in this volume).

[4] Dennis E. Smith, "What Do We Really Know about the Jerusalem Church? Christian Origins in Jerusalem according to Acts and Paul," 243, 250–51 (in this volume).

Agenda for the Annual Meeting, Discussion, and Reflections 277

the diaspora congregations must have been those we now associate with the Jesus movements, not those traditionally associated with Paul's depiction of the Christ cults."[5] Accordingly, in discussing this question, our goal was to compare the Jerusalem group with other early Jewish and Christian social formations by (1) noting the similarities and differences between the Jerusalem group, according to the profile that was emerging, and the Jesus schools and Christ cults; (2) working out the problems of sequence, recognition, and connection between and among those groups; (3) constructing a profile of common interests and attractions that produced early Christian social formations; and (4) assessing what difference all this would make for the scholarly imagination of Jerusalem and Christian beginnings.

The agenda was intended to help us move from a discussion of a plausible profile for a Jerusalem group to considerations of appropriate analogies, noticing the effect of our profile for the expansion of the new map we were constructing, and taking stock of a discourse that could explain mutual recognition and common interests among the diverse social formations that were beginning to come into view. What we found out was that our discussions at the annual meeting in Orlando could hardly have been expected to meet such an ambitious agenda. We could not start from an already established discourse when our sessions were an occasion of face-to-face discussion in a limited time frame. But, more important, the degree to which the papers converged on the problematizing of the dominant paradigm made the task of constructing a profile of a Jerusalem group seem unattainable and, indeed, unimportant to some, while to others it seemed to require much more time evaluating the detailed proposals of Miller's paper and debating the differences between Miller and Dennis Smith. In addition, a few members thought that a much fuller description was needed in order to achieve a convincing alternative to the various pictures scholars have constructed by harmonizing Luke and Paul, or by correcting Luke and paraphrasing Paul, or by correcting Paul and paraphrasing Luke.

The scholarly assurance of the reliability of "Jerusalem" as a datum of "Christian origins" lies at the heart of replicating the myth of Christian origins as the hermeneutical embellishment of a historical event. Nevertheless, the papers by Matthews, Miller, Smith, Mack, and Martin—in their various ways—did succeed in putting the assumption of Christian origins in Jerusalem to the test. This should be recognized as a signal achievement. As Mack noted in his debriefing (in a letter of 30 November 1998), no one argued for any of the features of the traditional view of the "Jerusalem church" or against the conclusion that Luke's achievement in the book of

---

[5] Burton L. Mack, "A Jewish Jesus School in Jerusalem?" 261 (in this volume).

Acts is mythmaking in the service of an agenda in Luke's own time, not the preservation of written sources or historical traditions that can be used as data for a "Jerusalem group in the 30s and 40s that comes into view in Galatians 1–2." Moreover, Mack remarked, no one was troubled by the arguments for the reconstruction that Miller put forth in his paper on Paul or with a number of his conclusions:

- the "message" under review [in Gal 2:1–10] was not the kerygma ... but the principle (or declaration) that gentiles need not be circumcised in order to belong to *Israel* or the people of God
- Paul's interest in meeting with the Jerusalem people was not in establishing his credentials or authority but in working out an agreement vis-à-vis the gentile-circumcision issue
- the gentile-circumcision issue was generated in [a] diaspora situation, not initiated by the Jerusalem group
- the basis for the mutual recognition between Paul and the Jerusalem group must have included acknowledgment of common interests in Jewish identity questions as well as interests in the formation of groups that appealed to the legacy of Jesus
- the Jerusalem group had no capacity or desire to control the activities or thinking of Jesus groups in other locations
- the Jerusalem group was drawn into the debate about gentile circumcision because of diaspora issues and initiatives, not because the question had been of practical importance for the Jerusalem group
- the Jerusalem people apparently agreed that gentiles need not be circumcised, but requested in return that their own interests in Jewish pieties and practices be recognized as legitimate by the diaspora Jesus people
- the real rub in establishing mutual hospitalities between the two kinds of Jesus group[s] was not different "christologies" or incompatible views on the circumcision question, but the practice of meal etiquette (compounded perhaps by different views on dietary purity)

The implications of the Seminar's successful problematization of Jerusalem origins were summed up at our meeting by Jonathan Z. Smith, who concluded that we did not simply reject in general the dominant (essentially Lukan) paradigm of Christian origins. Rather, he stated, what we argued means that we can now draw the following specific conclusions: (1) we have been able to describe, on the basis of our earliest evidence, a nonmessianic, nonkerygmatic characterization—whether for Jesus' own speech or for that of his earliest followers; (2) we have problematized Jerusalem as a historical datum in such a way that "Jerusalem" is no longer a helpful category; and (3) from now on we may imagine Christian origins without Jerusalem—as "an historical datum" and as "the locus of what Christianity is [all] about and how it got started."[6] The all-pervasive notion of Christian apocalyptic, messianic origins in Jerusalem, a frame of reference in which almost all New Testament scholarship—despite many differences in detail—continues to situate itself, no longer can be presumed or taken as self-evident. The assumption that an essential bond existed and a continuous development led from the historical Jesus to the Gospel story of his appearance, death, and resurrection, and from there to the Jerusalem church in Acts and the apostle Paul and his mission, has been decisively overturned by our redescription. That these conclusions are not the way scholars have usually understood the matter may be illustrated by the remarks of Hans Conzelmann and Andreas Lindemann, who begin their treatment of "the Rise of the Christian Church" (in one of Conzelmann's last discussions of the "History of Early Christianity") by stating:

> The decisive primary source for the rise of the church is the early Christian credo in the form of 1 Cor 15:3ff. Peter is the first recipient of an appearance of the Risen One (likewise Lk 24:34); in other words, *historically* Peter is the founder of the church, which presupposes that faith considers this founding to be the deed of the resurrected Jesus.... Thus the rise of the church probably has to be explained via Peter's vision, which stands at the beginning. It was Peter who concluded from the appearance "to him" that he was to constitute God's eschatological people, through the twelve as representatives of the church. And this decision would then have been confirmed explicitly by the appearance to this new circle. In any case, it is clear that the appearances at once constituted a community. All of the recipients of a revelation of the Risen One immediately understand it as a mandate to missions. The self-understanding of the new Christian community expresses itself, among other things, by establishing itself in Jerusalem (without detriment to the existence of further communities in Galilee) and immediately begins with the mission among the Jews.... [Therefore,] one may, with all reservations, consider it to be probable that the first appearances occurred in Jerusalem. The rise of the Christian church which was constituted on account of these appearances is clearly bound up with this city.[7]

---

[6] Merrill P. Miller, "'Beginning from Jerusalem ...': Re-examining Canon and Consensus," *Journal of Higher Criticism* 2/1 (1995): 3.

[7] Hans Conzelmann and Andreas Lindemann, *Interpreting the New Testament: An Introduction to the Principles and Methods of N.T. Exegesis* (trans. Siegfried S. Schatzmann; Peabody, Mass.: Hendrickson, 1988), 341, 342, 343, emphasis original.

In addition to our problematization of the dominant paradigm of Christian origins, our repositioning of Luke's account of origins and redescription of the place and subsequent influence of the book of Acts, and our profiles of a Jesus group in Jerusalem, two major issues emerged from a discussion of the papers at our sessions. First, though no one called into question Miller's reading of Galatians or his thesis of diaspora myths of origin in the homeland (based on a model of homeland and diaspora which scholarship has identified as a persistent feature of Hellenistic religions in general), a number of questions were raised about the applicability and use of the model. In particular, there was some concern about the limits of being able to test the model on the basis of the kind of data that we have. In his working paper on "Churches as Voluntary Associations," Stephen G. Wilson, acknowledging that all we require of the model is a disciplined and imaginative use of it, asked if the homeland/diaspora schema breaks down when applied in detail to this particular example.[8] He noted, for example, that inscriptional evidence may suggest that, in certain situations, an association in a homeland may exercise control over its diaspora outpost. Comparison is complicated, as Miller has observed (in an e-mail of 25 May 1999), by the different kinds of data we are dealing with, as well as by the different situations that must be imagined for a movement that was in its earliest stages in both diaspora and homeland locales. Familiarity with a pattern of homeland control may thus be important at the ideological level, the level of the rationalizing of practices, rather than being indicative of actual social relations between Judean and diaspora Jesus groups. The problem with the applicability and use of the model, therefore, may actually be one of not having the evidence to test it, or of the disparate temporal frameworks involved. On the other hand, the problem may be a matter of using a category that is not native to the Christian religion, which was, of course, precisely the strategy that Miller intended in the interest of redescription.

Second, Miller argued not only that Galatians can be read as mythmaking, but also that there is still data in the text that can be read historically and from which one may be able to describe the issues that were under debate. The question that emerged from this reading involved more than the matter of data available for constructing a profile of a possible Jesus group in Jerusalem. The serious problem was whether a profile would have any importance for the categories we were testing. How could we identify an intersection of mythmaking and social formation for a Jerusalem group if we agreed that the locus of such an intersection was to

---

[8] Stephen G. Wilson, "Churches as Voluntary Associations" (paper presented at the Annual Meeting of the Society of Biblical Literature, Boston, Mass., November 1999).

be seen in diaspora situations, concerns, and congregations? This question was raised in Martin's paper on theories of history and historiography, which challenged the Seminar to clarify its theories of mythmaking and social formation and to recognize the complicated issues pertaining to their relationship, and their consequences for historiographical work. Emphasizing that "critical historiography is a theoretically informed practice,"[9] Martin's concern is that we are, in effect, aware that our texts are mythographic but, nevertheless, are drawing "kernels of historical content" from them. In Martin's view, "more appropriately historiographical questions ... that might be posed of the 'Jerusalem' data include ... the place given to 'Jerusalem' in the mythmaking activities of the Pauline and the Lukan communities," and how "'Jerusalem' [came] to be the widely accepted 'root metaphor of the imagination of Christian origins.'"[10] We should indeed be asking about just such diaspora groups, for our real site is not Jerusalem but has been relocated to the diaspora. However, the fact that a text makes better sense when much of its rhetoric is interpreted as a mythic construction does not mean, necessarily, that it does not—or cannot—have any historical content at all relative to its narrative time. This is why Miller proposed a second reading of Galatians, with questions of mutual recognition, forms of relationship, and common or competing social interests in view. The "Jerusalem" of our canonical texts is no longer helpful as a category for a critical historiography of the beginnings of the Jesus movements, but it does have a position of great import as an object of mythmaking. Since Jerusalem has occupied and continues to possess a privileged place among the data that bear on the beginnings of Christianity, we thought it important to attempt some kind of profile of a Jerusalem group, in order to reposition a privileged site of the canonical paradigm of Christian origins.

Miller's paper is designed to problematize the bases upon which we can make any historiographical reconstructions, but to do so from the perspective of mythmaking. We are thus operating, at least tacitly, with a theory of history and historiography. We are suggesting, in effect, that historical continuity and change can be grasped best, albeit artificially, through the analytic category of social formation, and that our notion of intersections or junctures of mythmaking and social formation has much to commend it as a focus for constructing historical accounts. We are arguing

---

[9] Martin, "History, Historiography, and Christian Origins," 264.

[10] Ibid., 271, citing Miller, "Beginning from Jerusalem," 3. For a critique of the use of Acts as the main source and model for writing the history of early Christianities, beginning with Jerusalem, see Ron Cameron, "Alternate Beginnings—Different Ends: Eusebius, Thomas, and the Construction of Christian Origins," in *Religious Propaganda and Missionary Competition in the New Testament World: Essays Honoring Dieter Georgi* (ed. Lukas Bormann et al.; NovTSup 74; Leiden: Brill, 1994), 501–25.

that we have some material with which to work, in terms of social interests and by analogy with other groups. For if we can reconstruct analogies on the basis of social interests, then we can infer the social logic of a mythmaking that would be appropriate. By knowing something about a group's mythmaking, therefore, we can infer something about Jerusalem. The problem of whether a profile of a Jerusalem group would have any importance for testing our categories of mythmaking and social formation was not resolved at our sessions. However, Mack's paper did suggest that there is enough comparative data from later developments within the Jesus movements, from the way our profile of Jerusalem differs from those of other early Jesus groups, and, more broadly, from analogies in the Judaisms of the times—Pharisees, in particular, were mentioned—to have some idea of the social interests being generated and, thus, to posit hypothetically the sort of myths that would make sense in relation to those interests. What we could plausibly infer and assume seemed to cohere and present a certain profile, a "picture of a group of Jews in Jerusalem who got interested in talking about the significance of Jesus, his teachings, and the various groups forming in his name, for Jewish institutions and self-definition."[11] Such a profile, suggesting that a Jesus legacy and a concern for Jewish piety and identity had come together for a group forming in Jerusalem, indicates that we could do something historiographically with Jerusalem, and that it would make a difference redescriptively, in terms of expanding our understanding of the Jesus groups. As Mack put it in his debriefing (of 30 November 1998), "Let us place the Jerusalem group on the map of early Jesus and Christ groups, note that its features challenge us to broaden the scope of interests that may have been involved, and use it to ask ourselves whether our erstwhile views of the Jesus groups à la Q and the *Gospel of Thomas* need correction."

---

[11] Mack, "A Jewish Jesus School in Jerusalem?" 262.

PART 3
A PRE-PAULINE *CHRISTOS* ASSOCIATION

Proposal for the Second Year of the Seminar
Ron Cameron

"Paul," says Burton L. Mack, "was converted to a Hellenized form of some Jesus movement that had already developed into a Christ cult."[1] By the adjective "Hellenized," Mack is referring essentially to features that would be typical of the Hellenistic cults of the time and especially to a characteristic not found in the early Jesus movements, namely, the divinization of Jesus as a patron deity and the claim to have been exalted to sovereign Lord of the cosmos. It may be misleading, in some respects, to locate this phenomenon at a temporal point prior to Paul's conversion. We surely need to think of something that takes place over a longer stretch of time, as Mack's subsequent analysis makes clear. It is important to remember that the term "pre-Pauline" does not refer principally to what was in place before Paul's "change of mind" but to discursive formations and patterns of practices that existed independent of Paul and, perhaps, in some cases, in conjunction with Paul, that is, a context in which Paul was embedded and active over the course of his career. Of the six characteristics listed by Mack that invite cultic description,[2] only two, the kerygma of

---

[1] Burton L. Mack, *A Myth of Innocence: Mark and Christian Origins* (Philadelphia: Fortress, 1988), 98.

[2] Ibid., 100 n. 2: "The term Christ cult is used in a general sense to distinguish the congregations of the Christ from the Jesus movements. The characteristics that invite cultic description are (1) the kerygma of the death and resurrection of the Christ, (2) the production of a myth of cosmic destiny, (3) the mythic ritualization of the meal, (4) the rite of baptism with its symbolic associations derived from the kerygma, (5) the notion of spiritual 'presence,' and (6) the creation of liturgical materials, including acclamations, doxologies, confessions of faith, and hymns." Elaborating on the distinction between the congregations of the Christ and the Jesus movements, Mack notes that "the Christ cult differed from the Jesus movements in two major respects. One was a focus upon the significance of Jesus' death and destiny.... [This] had the result of shifting attention away from the teachings of Jesus and away from a sense of belonging to his school. It engendered instead an elaborate preoccupation with notions of martyrdom, resurrection, and the transformation of Jesus into a divine, spiritual presence. The other major difference was the forming of a cult oriented to that spiritual presence" (idem, *Who Wrote the New Testament? The Making of the Christian Myth* [San Francisco: HarperSanFrancisco, 1995], 75–76).

the death and resurrection of Christ and the rite of baptism, received any attention in the Seminar's work on this site, and even these did not constitute our main focus.

Having initially labeled our site the "Hellenistic Christ Cult," we soon realized in planning our work that we would have to give attention to several issues that might have the effect of preventing us from addressing pertinent features of the Hellenistic (pre-Pauline) congregations that would come under the general rubric of the Christ cult. First, we did not want to take for granted that we knew what counted as data for pre-Pauline Christianity. Thus, we would need some review of the history of scholarship that had argued for, or had taken for granted, the category of Hellenistic Christianity as the locus for a pre-Pauline cult of Christ. These were issues for which we hoped to solicit contributions from members of the Seminar. The second issue, which proved to be the continuing focus of the year's work, was the introduction of the term *christos* as a designation for Jesus. The co-chairs sent out a cover letter (on 21 December 1998) asking Seminar members to respond to two papers written by Merrill P. Miller on *christos:* one recently published,[3] which reviews, engages, revises, and extends Mack's thesis on the origins of the Christ cult, the other an unpublished essay on "The Problem of the Origins of a Messianic Conception of Jesus" (included in this volume). We also asked the Seminar to address other issues concerned with tasks that could be taken up in the interest of a redescription of the Christ cult:

- How did Jesus become Christ?
- What is the logic of the Christ myth?
- Where and among whom was Jesus' death imagined as a saving event?
- How would the Christ myth have made (social) sense to Gentiles?
- What is the relation of the Christ cult to the Jesus-school traditions?
- Are there stages in the social history of the Christ cult?
- What is the relation of Paul and his gospel to the Christ myth?
- What analogies from the cultures of context are most helpful in understanding the Christ cult?
- Can we construct a profile of the Christ cult?
- How is one to understand the categories "messiah," "Christ," "kerygma," "apostle," and "mission"?

---

[3] Merrill P. Miller, "How Jesus Became Christ: Probing a Thesis," *Cont* 2/2–3 (1993): 243–70.

♦ Did the term *christos* originate as a term of authorization, in which Jesus' characterization, authority, and status were mythically enhanced?

The reason for circulating Miller's essays should be seen, first of all, in their relation to Mack's argumentation in *A Myth of Innocence*. With respect to his fundamental distinction between the Jesus movements and the congregations of the Christ (the "Christ cult"), Mack's work is often assumed to be based on the framework and assumptions of an earlier *religionsgeschichtliche Schule,* with its distinction between Palestinian Judaism, on the one hand, and Hellenistic Judaism and Gentile Christianity, on the other. This genealogy is fundamentally mistaken; to understand the distinction and his arguments, one should look rather to Mack's scholarship on Hellenistic Judaism, to his wide reading in ethnographic studies and the history of religions, and to the influence of the cognitive and social anthropology that underlies the program that Jonathan Z. Smith has laid out for the academic study of religion. In the history of modern New Testament scholarship, no one prior to Mack has located the introduction of the kerygma and the Christ term *exclusively* in the pre-Pauline Hellenistic congregations, on the grounds that they are sociomythic inventions that did not have to appeal to beliefs or reports about appearances of the risen Jesus. Similarly, Mack is the only scholar who has presented a sustained and reasoned account of the Markan passion narrative that rests its case entirely on the Evangelist's own literary creation (and not on earlier formative narrative traditions of the arrest and execution of Jesus), and that appeals solely to factors in the Evangelist's own milieu that bear on an intersection of mythmaking and social formation (and not to memories of the historical Jesus).

Miller's essays on *christos* make the case for a similar distinction of time, place, and sociomythic junctures on the basis of the strikingly different usages of the term in the earlier Pauline writings, on the one hand, and the later canonical Gospels and Acts, on the other. Just as on Mack's account the pre-Pauline martyr myth (the "kerygma") did not presuppose memories of Jesus embedded in a narrative of Jesus' arrest and execution in Jerusalem, so on Miller's account what could be inferred on the basis of Paul's letters about pre-Pauline usages of *christos* did not presuppose the usages of the term in the Gospels and Acts to designate Jesus as a messianic figure of general expectation. This meant that Miller had reversed the usual assumptions about the provenance and significance of the term in its earliest usage and, thus, the reasons for its introduction. The work of the Seminar on the Jesus schools in Galilee and southern Syria, based on early sayings-of-Jesus collections in which the term *christos* does not appear, together with its work on Jerusalem, was consistent with a reading of the data on *christos* that argues against the common assumption of the emergence of Christianity as a messianic sect. Instead, Miller proposes to read the data as evidence of distinctive sociomythic moments in the history of the Jesus groups, highlighting the cognitive and social interests registered at different junctures in the social formations of early Christianities. The characteristic Pauline references suggest that the term took hold as a cognomen, or byname, for Jesus in pre-Pauline groups, in order to support features of the ethos and collective identity of associations as they distinguished themselves from local synagogues. In contrast, the use of *christos* to designate the messianic status of the earthly Jesus and to characterize him as a figure of general expectation came to expression only later in the narrative tradition of the canonical Gospels. The social anthropology of this latter discursive formation responded to issues of mutual recognition between Jesus and Christ groups, addressed situations of the Jesus groups in the wake of the Roman-Jewish war, and resolved cognitive problems related to the construction of biographies of Jesus.

The sayings-of-Jesus tradition associated with the Jesus movements in Galilee and southern Syria never use the designation *christos* for Jesus. Moreover, there is nothing in Paul's letters of his usage of *christos* that would suggest that he was the one who introduced the term, even though *christos* clearly has a place in traditions that Paul cites. The extraordinary number of instances of the term *christos* in Paul must mean that he knew a usage that had already taken hold among people whose discourse influenced him. But what that usage was cannot be derived from what is to be found in the Gospels and Acts. The influence lies in the other direction. The possibility of using the term as an exclusive title of honor for Jesus in the Gospels and Acts is not a simple appropriation of biblical or early Jewish uses of the term but is rather an adaptation of an earlier exclusive connection of the term with Jesus as his byname, though this should not be taken as anything like a full explanation for its use in composing a biography of Jesus. If, as Miller has shown, the kerygma is also not the likely locus of the introduction of *christos,* we must imagine the social logic and interests that could account for the introduction of the term to have constituted the situation of a Jesus movement known to Paul, and we must distinguish this moment from a series of subsequent moments that would become definitive for what we had been calling the pre-Pauline Hellenistic Christ cult. Miller's essays, then, indicate how he conceives of the problem and is trying to resolve it. He argues that the markedly different usages of the term *christos* in the (earlier) Pauline writings and the (later) Gospels and Acts—together with the absence of the term from the sayings-of-Jesus tradition—show that there was no messianic conception of Jesus until the Gospels' narrative portrayal of Jesus as a figure of expectation. The emergence of such a conception of Jesus is therefore seen to be largely an affair of composing a *bios* of Jesus in a post-destruction situation among the heirs of the earliest Jesus movements. Accordingly, one can neither appeal to a messianic conception of Jesus to explain Paul's own use of *christos* nor move back from a Pauline (or pre-Pauline) usage of the term to a Palestinian or Jerusalem milieu, either for a messianic sect or a messianic conception of Jesus.

In his paper on "How Jesus Became Christ," Miller differed from Mack on the introduction of *christos* in one respect that proved to be significant for redefining the social locus of our site. Miller argued that the Christ term would not have easily come to mind in conjunction with the vindication of a martyr and was probably already in place for other reasons. Thus, Miller's claim was that the term was not indigenous to the Christ myth (Mack's label for pre-Pauline kerygmatic formulae of Jesus' death and resurrection, which characterize Jesus as a vindicated martyr) but could be imagined as a distinguishing feature of a Jesus movement that had formed in one of the urban centers of northern Syria, most likely Antioch. It would be the first Jesus movement, Miller considered at the time, to think of Jesus in royal terms in order to support a collective kingdom ethos. It would be what one might imagine as a pre-Pauline *christos* association. The prospect of having a site that differed from the Pauline congregations and that could not really be described as a pre-Pauline cult of Christ, yet one that also differed from the Jesus movements of Galilee and southern Syria, would be an important and appropriate finding for a model of distribution and difference, of expanding the creative moments of beginnings for writing a critical history of Christian origins. Indeed, one might insist that to have problematized the whole imagination of the messianic origins of Christianity on the data of the usage of the term *christos* was, itself, to have changed the picture dramatically. But would members of the Seminar agree? And beyond that, would we be able to imagine the sort of mythmaking and social interests entailed in this one feature of our hypothetical site?

The Seminar was asked to evaluate Miller's arguments and their implications, in light of the issues he raised and the questions we have listed above. All of the responses acknowledged that Miller's care with sources and attention to the distribution and types of usage of the term *christos* were seriously damaging to the usual kinds of solutions that scholars have proposed to explain how Jesus became Christ. Several agreed that his grounds for arguing an early nonmessianic usage were sufficiently persuasive to attempt to clarify and test them. Thus, while doubts were raised about Miller's notion of *christos* as a byname, Barry S. Crawford (in his e-mail of 29 January 1999) took the matter as a crucial element of Miller's argumentation and proposed his own project on nicknames in a school context to test Miller's thesis. Christopher R. Matthews (in his e-mails of 25 and 27 February 1999) found parts of Miller's argument convincing but considered the overall thesis to have been presented as too much of an all-or-nothing proposition. He noted that Miller's description of the significance and provenance of the term in its pre-Pauline context was not entirely consistent—and became confusing, in that Miller's attempts to identify and describe changes in the use of the term, as well as to locate shifts in the social situations in which the term was used, mean that he expressed himself somewhat differently in his two papers. In addition, Matthews wondered how Miller could sustain the notion that there were no messianic connotations in view in the introduction of the *christos* term, considering the weight of current scholarship on Jewish messianism that does not posit a singular figure or uniform messianic tradition.

In his response (of 11 February 1999), Mack agreed with the critique of his own earlier attempt to account for the emergence of the *christos* term,[4] though he noticed a number of social concepts, triggered by the term, that were used in Miller's essays and that need clarification and more solid argumentation in order to say more about the social attractions of a Christ association for Jews and Gentiles. Moreover, Mack not only noted that Miller has demonstrated that "the messianic status of Jesus can [best] be ... understood as a later development of early Christian mythmaking." He also observed that even though "the messianic concept" seems to have "played no role at the beginning of the Christian experiment," that did not curtail its importance, since "the term *christos* finally settle[d] into place as the single, most important mythic cipher held in common, though invested with decidedly different symbolic constructions, by the many forms of social experimentation that came to share the designation and thus, presumably found in it a vehicle for mutual recognition." Therefore, in making his argument Miller has proposed a "hypothesis that isolates [at a discrete juncture of social history] several social and ideological factors that must have pertained on the occasion of a shift from a Jesus movement to a 'Christ cult.'" This is significant, Mack explains, for it "expands the data base to include what we have from the Jesus movements, even while paring down the features of each set of data (from pre-Pauline materials and materials from the Jesus movements) that may have relevance for explaining such a shift." What Mack has taken note of in Miller's argumentation is really quite important. Since *christos* is a term of consequence for a number of different groups, a careful assessment of its usage socially will enable us first to identify and describe various differences between groups and then to ask about the import and meaning of those differences. Thus, Miller's papers not only exemplify the critical tasks of problematization and redescription;

---

[4] Ibid., 246, 251–57, 262–65.

they also deal with the issue of comparison, right in the midst of a historiographical discussion. Focusing on the uses of the term *christos,* in the context of a shift from a Jesus movement to a Christ cult, lets us assess issues of recognition and difference, of distinctive mythologies and distinct groups, between the Jesus movements and the Christ cults, at one and the same time.

INTRODUCTION TO THE PAPERS FROM
THE SECOND YEAR OF THE SEMINAR

Ron Cameron

Miller's paper on "The Problem of the Origins of a Messianic Conception of Jesus" represents a first attempt to reinvent *christos* as a category for understanding Christian origins. The appropriateness of the term most frequently applied to Jesus in the New Testament has always been a puzzle in modern critical scholarship. Scholars have sought to resolve the problem in two different ways: by maintaining that (1) Jesus was, in fact, a political revolutionary who failed, though his failure was concealed in the later Christian movement; or that (2) Christianity, as a movement that emerged out of Judaism, defined its own uniqueness precisely by means of a stunning reinterpretation and transfiguration of Jewish messianic hopes. Various forms of this second solution, in particular, have dominated modern scholarship. The debate has been about where to locate the dramatic revision of Jewish messianism. What is most striking about this solution is the way in which it recapitulates the canonical paradigm of Christian origins: Judaism is presupposed and transcended in the inaugural moment of Christian origins. Miller's paper exposes the problem of *christos* in New Testament scholarship as a problem in the enterprise of comparison. As pursued all too typically in this scholarship, the comparative moment invariably yields a thoroughly Christian Messiah at the beginning. Instead of occasioning an intellectual debate concerned with features of similarity and difference in the interest of taxonomy, the apparent anomaly of *christos* as a designation for Jesus is resolved in ways that secure its place as an expression of the unique ground of Christian self-definition. For Miller, the term does not answer to some inaugural transformative experience but responds to social and conceptual challenges that were confronted at different times and places in early Christianities. And so, in Miller's revision of the comparative project, the comparative moment gives special notice to the construction of social identity in pre-Pauline associations and to the cognitive task of constructing an ideal figure of expectation in Jesus movements after the Roman-Jewish war. It is suggested that the important analogues might come not from descriptions of eschatological figures in particular but from the use of bynames, honorifics, and other descriptive epithets in school settings, at first, and from the conceptual challenges of composing the *bios* of an ideal figure, at a later time.

Crawford's paper on "*Christos* as Nickname" is an effort to put Miller's thesis to the test. He sees clearly that Miller is able to provide explanations for the introduction of the term and for its later usage that are related to collective interests, rather than to dramatic events or overwhelming personal encounters, because Miller has reversed the usual sequence in accounting for the different usages of the term. In Crawford's assessment, this makes Miller's argument that *christos* was initially used as a byname for Jesus, rather than as an eschatological title, "the linchpin"[1] of his thesis. Crawford turns to Diogenes Laertius's *Lives of Eminent Philosophers* with Miller's suggestion about appropriate analogues in view, concluding that the evidence of Diogenes's *Lives* generally supports the view "that *christos* was originally Jesus' nickname as founder of a movement based on his teaching."[2] In addition, Crawford calls attention to the usual view of the term as having explosive political, social, and religious significance and counters that this is more likely the consequence of apologetics operating in New Testament studies than a measured assessment of the incidence and use of the term in ancient Jewish literatures. Nevertheless, caution is advised, for there are two findings that require further attention because they do not fit the picture that Miller has drawn. First, while nicknames are commonly associated with the discipline of philosophy in Diogenes's *Lives,* they appear to be given for characterizing personal traits rather than to exhibit the collective interests of a group. Second, nicknames do not appear to be awarded posthumously.

Matthews's paper, "From Messiahs to Christ: The Pre-Pauline Christ Cult in Scholarship," investigates the history of scholarship. How did the existence of a pre-Pauline Hellenistic cult of Christ come to be accepted or taken for granted as a datum of early Christianity? On the basis of the evidence Matthews reviews, the existence of this type of social formation was not a conclusion drawn primarily from pre-Pauline traditions identified on literary and form-critical grounds, though the texts cited by Paul as "traditions" in 1 Cor 11:23–25 and 15:3–5 have always figured prominently as evidence. Rather, such a phenomenon had to be presupposed if the differences between Jesus and Paul, or between the primitive Palestinian community and Paul's own congregations, were to be explained as developments emerging from the single trunk of Christian origins. Fundamentally,

---

[1] Barry S. Crawford, *"Christos as Nickname,"* 340 (in this volume).
[2] Ibid., 346.

then, pre-Pauline Hellenistic Christianity was conceived as a bridge, rather than a new departure. For Matthews shows that without assuming either Jesus' own messianic consciousness or the existence of an apocalyptic Messiah/Son of Man Christology (or both), and without presupposing Jesus' own meal practice or the existence of cultic meals in the primitive Palestinian community (or both), scholars could not account for the cult of Jesus as *kyrios* and as Son of God in the Pauline congregations. In the history of scholarship, therefore, the pre-Pauline Hellenistic Christ cult is the conduit through which memories of the historical Jesus and the primitive Palestinian tradition are transmitted and transformed. Of the scholars surveyed by Matthews, only Mack has departed from this consensus, because for Mack the kerygma is not the hermeneutical consequence of Jesus' death and resurrection appearances but the intellectual labor of mythmaking in the interest of legitimating a social experiment. In Mack's case, a pre-Pauline Hellenistic Christ cult is not a stage in a hermeneutical trajectory but a particular phase in the social history and mythmaking activity of social experiments, the investments in which give rise to different myths of Jesus and of Christ. However, Matthews also concludes that locating *christos* in a pre-Pauline Hellenistic context does not call into question the original titular significance of the term as a translation of "Messiah."

In his paper on "The Anointed Jesus," Miller takes a broader look at scholarship on messianism, clarifies his position on a number of critical issues raised in e-mail responses to his two earlier papers, and revises his discussion of the connotations of *christos*. The paper is divided into four parts. The first part presents some critical reflections on "messianism" and "messiahs" as analytical and comparative categories, showing by way of examples what Miller thinks these categories obscure in the study of early Judaisms and Christian origins, and why the broader category of "ideal figures" is to be preferred for a social anthropology concerned with such matters as the ordering of social practices, marking of temporal boundaries, authorizing of political structures, and ranking of leadership roles.

In the second part of his paper Miller gives his attention to reviewing his earlier papers and to clarifying matters of definition and strategy, while also addressing specific questions raised by members of the Seminar. Miller was attempting to address the impasse in scholarship on the question of how to account for the most common way of referring to Jesus in the New Testament—namely, as Christ—by reconceptualizing the problem along lines that would demonstrate "another instance of constructing exemplary figures."[3] Indeed, his thesis depends on giving full weight to different usages of the *christos* term and especially on recognizing that the appeal

---

[3] Merrill P. Miller, "The Anointed Jesus," 384 (in this volume).

of the term, as well as the provenance and reasons for its introduction, must be inferred from our earliest source, the letters of Paul, rather than from the narrative traditions of the Gospels and the speeches in Acts, as has been the common practice in biblical scholarship. What hangs in the balance, in distinguishing where different uses of the *christos* term signify social formation, is a more plausible reading of beginnings, an understanding of the Jesus movements as alternative points of departure for the description of Christian origins, rather than as branches (e.g., the Sayings Gospel Q) or fallen limbs (e.g., the *Gospel of Thomas*) from the trunk of a messianic tree, or as text traditions encompassed by the wider movement of messianic beginnings. For if messianic beginnings are a point of departure, then the Jesus movements as we have understood and redescribed them will be lost, absorbed by the dominant (canonical) paradigm of Christian origins. Accordingly, Miller reviews the reasons for retaining "messiah figures" as a category and for defining the category as having in view "figures of expectation," and he returns to the evidence for his contention that *christos* in Paul is not a term that signifies such a figure, as it is in the Gospels and Acts.

Miller maintains that the easiest way to account for the evidence in Paul is to suppose that *christos* first took hold as a byname for Jesus, and not as the kind of absolute title of honor to be found in the Gospels and Acts. He argues that this latter usage is not a locution already available in the literatures of early Judaisms but is, in fact, the creation of the Evangelists. However, Miller's case does not rest on a simple opposition between a second name for Jesus and a full title of dignity. Obviously, the term *christos* could only become a byname by being used as such. It is equally clear that the term did come to be used that way. Miller's argument that such a usage is early is based, in part, on the fact that there is nothing in biblical or early Jewish use of *christos* that would make attaching it directly to a personal name an obvious way to use the term, rather than associating it with any one of a number of roles and offices—yet employing the term this way, by attaching it to a personal name, is the particular usage that all early Christian literatures have in common. Attaching *christos* directly to "Jesus" virtually guaranteed that it would be taken as a byname, though this is not to deny that Pauline usage also provides evidence that the term retains an honorific or titular sense. What cannot be said, on the basis of evidence in Paul's letters, is that the term must already have signified for followers of Jesus a title for a figure of general expectation, or have been taken up and applied as a technical term for a specific office or role. Neither the biblical and early Jewish evidence nor the evidence of Paul's own letters gives any reason to make either one of these inferences. They must depend upon the evidence of the canonical Gospels and Acts. On the other hand, the term is often used to refer to figures of the past. There is no reason to suppose that appeal to the anointed status of a figure of the past could not suggest the importance of a continuing legacy.

In both of his earlier papers ("How Jesus Became Christ" and "The Problem of the Origins of a Messianic Conception of Jesus"), Miller emphasized the royal connotations of *christos*. The third part of "The Anointed Jesus" is the longest section because here Miller reconsiders the connotations of the term by means of a survey and comparison of biblical and postbiblical usages to the end of the first century C.E. There are three reasons for focusing a survey on the incidence of the term *christos* rather than more broadly on so-called messianic figures. First, the most striking datum requiring explanation is why a term whose incidence in Jewish literatures is relatively infrequent suddenly has such a prolific incidence in a small corpus of Pauline texts. Second, Miller considers the different usages of *christos* in the New Testament to be a more important datum for the redescription of Christian origins than the relationship of this term to other titles for Jesus. Third, the most important reason to confine a survey to the term itself is that the very attention given to "messianic figures" is what has tended to distort the significance of the term, by putting far more emphasis on expectations of a future royal figure exercising judicial and military roles than is warranted by the variety of applications of the term. Miller finds that "outside biblical literature there is no evidence to suggest that the term was especially associated with the role and actions of a royal figure."[4] This is not to conclude, however, that the survey is unhelpful with respect to the reasons that can be suggested for the introduction of the term in pre-Pauline circles.

To refer to an "anointed" or "anointed one(s)" is one way of highlighting that a particular role or office is represented by those who are divinely authorized. Thus, Israel has legitimate leadership whether one is speaking of the past, the present, or the future, or referring to prophets, priests, or kings. In general, the use of the term is intended as an expression of the theocratic grounding of the central institutions responsible for the establishment of Torah in Israel. Where there is an anointed leadership, there is an authentic Israel. Miller is suggesting that the principal attraction of the term for a pre-Pauline situation is that it exudes divine initiative and approval of the status and empowerment of representatives of Israel in circumstances in which an independent association is being formed and, thus, in conditions one can imagine would give priority to the grounds of claiming, for this association, identity and status as an "Israel" and authorizing a particular legacy and set of practices. What such a Jesus group may have appeared to lack with respect to any link to a traditional institutional

---

[4] Ibid., 406.

heritage and to symbols, practices, and constituency with an obvious Torah orientation was compensated for by the novelty of linking the term to their founder-teacher, thereby suggesting as well that the connotations of divine initiative and approval applied especially, if not exclusively, to the one to whom they appealed.

Drawing on the work of Louis Dumont[5] and Jonathan Z. Smith[6] in the fourth part of his paper, Miller offers some reflections on purity and power as dual ideological systems of hierarchy in order to underline his thesis that *christos* took hold as a byname for Jesus for reasons that had to do more with the identity and status of the association than with invoking claims on royal power and judicial authority. He suggests that terms such as "holiness" and "righteousness" have different significance depending on the system of discourse to which they belong. In an effort to account for why the *christos* identification struck roots in particular in the kerygmatic formulae of the martyr myth, Mack has stressed the importance of the epic anchor that *christos* provided.[7] Miller calls attention to the possibility that both the *christos* identification and the notion of righteousness in the martyr myth exhibit parallel rhetorical strategies of invoking the character and perspective of God, once one begins to think of "righteousness" within a discourse of purity that brings to focus a "corporate ethos marked by recognition of appropriate standards, arrangements, and practices."[8]

In his paper "Why *Christos*? The Social Reasons," Mack has undertaken to answer, at least in a preliminary way, the question of how to imagine the social situation and underlying social interests that can be inferred when the term *christos* first took hold as a designation for Jesus. In presenting his reflections, Mack operates within two constraints that emerge from Miller's work: (1) "the first usage [of *christos*] was not titular, not royal, not eschatological, and not martyrological";[9] and (2) the locus of the introduction of *christos* must be a social situation that marks a transition from one Jesus movement to another. Both types of social formation provide evidence for locating *christos* as an open-ended byname signifying some

---

[5] Louis Dumont, *Homo Hierarchicus: The Caste System and Its Implications* (rev. ed.; trans. Mark Sainsbury et al.; Chicago: University of Chicago Press, 1980).

[6] Jonathan Z. Smith, *To Take Place: Toward Theory in Ritual* (CSHJ; Chicago: University of Chicago Press, 1987).

[7] Burton L. Mack, "Why *Christos*? The Social Reasons," 366–68, 370–72 (in this volume).

[8] Miller, "Anointed Jesus," 414.

[9] Mack, "Why *Christos*?" 365. The conclusion that the connotations of the term *christos* were (1) not martyrological is based on Miller's arguments in "How Jesus Became Christ," (2) not titular and (3) not eschatological is based on Miller's arguments in "The Problem of the Origins of a Messianic Conception of Jesus," and (4) not royal is based on Miller's arguments in "The Anointed Jesus."

special (but deliberately unspecified) role as "God's choice ('anointed') for the task and times."[10] Like the Jesus movements, the hypothetical Jesus-*christos* group thinks of itself as having a stake in Israel's epic traditions, but now not by thinking of Jesus as being like Moses or Elijah, or a prophet or sage, but by designating him an anointed one and thus making a direct claim to an important place in the purposes of the God of Israel. Like the Christ cults, the *christos* group is more an independent association than a school, differentiating itself from urban synagogues of the diaspora, probably at first in Syrian Antioch, but without the social issues for which a martyr myth and its later elaboration as a Christ myth were cultivated, or those circumstances to which a mythology of the cosmic rule of Christ or the presence of the spirit of Christ would answer. Among the many "systems of signs and patterns of practices"[11] found in the ethnographic record that are fundamental to social formation and maintenance, and which can be shown to be present in the subcultural groups of the Greco-Roman world, though with important transformations, Mack finds the "social interest of group identification" to be the most obvious and pervasive. And so, since "collective identity was a very important consideration, problem, and issue for everyone during this period," the "trajectory of social formation and identity quest from Galilee to Antioch can easily be understood on the basis of a common interest in the teachings of Jesus as the basis for a kind of 'school' that formed a kind of association in the shadow of the synagogue."[12] Thus, it is the contribution that the *christos* attributive or byname makes to the quest for identity as a legitimate and competitive form of Israel that best explains the introduction of the term.

Mack underlines the attraction of diaspora synagogues for Jews and Gentiles as one of the more successful among the many kinds of subcultural groups in preserving ethnic, national, and cultural traditions, while adapting to the fragmentation and mixtures of peoples created by centuries of imperial policies. Hence, the anointed Jesus, while marking a group's claim to be an "Israel" precisely by means of its difference in cultivating a Jesus legacy, also bears witness to the attraction of Jewish social institutions supported by an epic heritage that was cultivated, debated, and continually reinvented. In a similar way, the collective motivations for constructing a myth of Jesus as martyr may be as much an indication of the attraction of a Maccabean martyr tradition cultivated in Antioch synagogues as evidence of conflict and contestation. Mack takes the Christ myth to be the last window through which we may catch a glimpse of this pre-Pauline

---

[10] Mack, "Why *Christos*?" 365.
[11] Ibid., 369.
[12] Ibid., 373, 372–73.

association. The martyr myth is elaborated with a view to justifying the social boundaries of the Jesus-*christos* association by appealing to God's vindication of Jesus by raising him from the dead, and to securing a stronger epic anchor by taking Christ as the subject and correlating his death and resurrection with scripture. Mack recognizes that focusing on this reconstructed *christos* site does not yet bring to account the kind of social formation, or at least the stage of social history, that is in view when reference is made to the pre-Pauline Christ cults—but that is another locus.

The Problem of the Origins of a Messianic Conception of Jesus*

Merrill P. Miller

The Princeton Symposium: Central Issue and Review of Data

In the preface to the volume from the first Princeton Symposium on Judaism and Christian Origins, the editor, James H. Charlesworth, presents several agreements reached by members of the symposium on the concept of the Messiah in earliest Judaism and Christianity. One of these agreements states, "*Christos* is the title or term most frequently applied to Jesus in the New Testament. Scholars agreed that the crucial question is the following: How did this happen, since 'the Messiah' is rarely found, and the functions or attributes of 'the Messiah' are even less explained, in extant pre-70 Jewish documents?"[1] The problem is not only from the side of the Jewish provenance of the term but just as much from the side of early Christianity. Charlesworth's assessment is hardly idiosyncratic: "No other title would have been so difficult to align with the life and thought of Jesus of Nazareth."[2]

---

* By "messianic conception of Jesus" in the title of this essay, I refer strictly to the use of the term *māšîaḥ/mǝšîḥā'/christos* to designate (1) a figure of expectation (whether priest, prophet, or king) who will come in order to execute in some way or to accompany a decisive change of the status quo for some existing Israel, or (2) an individual who has appropriated the term in order to enhance a claim currently being made by or for him that he is authorized to hold office as ruler or leader of some Jewish community. It should be recalled that in biblical usage the term never refers to an eschatological figure of expectation.

[1] James H. Charlesworth, ed., *The Messiah: Developments in Earliest Judaism and Christianity* (The First Princeton Symposium on Judaism and Christian Origins; Minneapolis: Fortress, 1992), xv. In his own essay in this volume, "From Messianology to Christology: Problems and Prospects," Charlesworth concludes with the same question: "Why did Jesus' followers claim above all that he was the Messiah?" (35).

[2] Charlesworth, "From Messianology to Christology," 34. Cf. Nils Alstrup Dahl, "The Crucified Messiah," in *Jesus the Christ: The Historical Origins of Christological Doctrine* (ed. Donald H. Juel; Minneapolis: Fortress, 1991), 39: "Rarely has it been made clear how strange it is that precisely the title 'Messiah' was applied to Jesus and became his name."

The prevalence of the association of *christos* with Jesus may also give a false impression about the significance of messianic conceptions in the development and varieties of Christology in early Christianity. In an earlier volume on the same theme, Charlesworth noted the variety of kerygmata and titles for Jesus and the fluidity of creedal formulations: "There was no set creed ... no pontificated title that was binding. Many early Christians may well have denied that Jesus had been the Messiah; some may have expected him to return as the Messiah (cf. Acts 3:20); others may have believed that 'Lord,' 'Servant,' 'Prophet,' 'Son of Man,' 'the Righteous One,' 'the Lamb,' or 'Wisdom' were more representative titles."[3] This is also not an isolated judgment. In the same volume George MacRae concluded, "Given the developments in Christianity after the New Testament period and the common understandings of it that are still prevalent, one may be surprised to observe, not how central the messianic idea is to the gospel, but how it is in a sense peripheral."[4] Donald Juel, while arguing that Christian appropriation of scripture has its starting point in the confession of Jesus as Messiah, also acknowledges that this confession is the presupposition not the content of New Testament theology: "the title Messiah is not subject to further development in the way 'Son of God' is—as, for example, in Johannine tradition. 'Christ' becomes a virtual second name."[5]

If the Jewish sources and the christological developments make the characteristic identification of Jesus with *christos* seem anomalous, the distribution of the term in the New Testament and other early Christian writings is also puzzling. More than half the instances of *christos* appear in the genuine letters of Paul, our earliest New Testament literature, but the status of Jesus as Messiah is never argued nor at issue in that corpus.[6] This

---

[3] J. H. Charlesworth, "From Jewish Messianology to Christian Christology: Some Caveats and Perspectives," in *Judaisms and Their Messiahs at the Turn of the Christian Era* (ed. Jacob Neusner et al.; Cambridge: Cambridge University Press, 1987), 253.

[4] George MacRae, "Messiah and Gospel," in Neusner et al., *Judaisms and Their Messiahs*, 184.

[5] Donald Juel, *Messianic Exegesis: Christological Interpretation of the Old Testament in Early Christianity* (Philadelphia: Fortress, 1988), 81.

[6] For a discussion of *christos* in Paul, see esp. Nils Alstrup Dahl, "The Messiahship of Jesus in Paul," in *Jesus the Christ*, 15–25; cf. M. de Jonge, "The Earliest Christian Use of *Christos*: Some Suggestions," *NTS* 32 (1986): 321–24; D. E. Aune, "Christian Prophecy and the Messianic Status of Jesus," in Charlesworth, *Messiah*, 405; and Martin Hengel, "'Christos' in Paul," in *Between Jesus and Paul: Studies in the Earliest History of Christianity* (trans. John Bowden; London: SCM, 1983), 65–77, 179–88. Dahl ("Messiahship of Jesus in Paul," 15, 17, 24 nn. 11–12) observes that in Paul's letters *christos* is never a general term (as it is in Acts 17:3; 26:23) but always refers to Jesus, nor is it used as a predication of Jesus (as in Acts 18:5, 28), nor does Paul add a genitive (as in Luke 2:26; 9:20; Acts 3:18). However, Dahl also maintains that messianic connotations with or without the definite article may be detected in Rom 1:1–2; 9:5; 15:8; 1 Cor 1:23; 10:4; 15:22; 2 Cor 5:10; 11:2–3; Gal 3:16; Phil 1:15, 17; 3:7. "But in no case in Paul can *Christos* be translated 'Messiah'" (24 n. 11).

is also the case in the other epistolary literature with the exception of 1 John 2:22 and 5:1.[7] The predominant use of *christos* in this literature is as a second name, even though it is evident also that it is taken as a byname or honorific.[8] Romans 9:5 may signal a titular use, but it is not a general reference but, as always in Paul, a reference to Jesus.[9] N. A. Dahl argues from the fact that *christos* has not entirely lost its titular significance in Paul, and his use of messianic testimonies from scripture, to the conclusion that the messianic identity of Jesus must have retained importance for Paul, though his own letters attest that the content of *christos* is rooted in the person and work of Jesus and not significantly in a Jewish matrix of messianic expectations.[10] MacRae's judgment is different. Paul does not consider the messianic identity of Jesus to be central to the gospel, although Christ fulfills the function for Paul of an agent of eschatological salvation, and he is aware of the claim that Jesus is the Messiah (Rom 1:2–4; 1 Cor 15:23–28).[11]

On the other hand, while the term is much less frequent in the Gospels and Acts, the status of Jesus as Messiah is clearly a matter that is at issue or requires interpretation or is to be demonstrated in the course of the narrative.[12] As a result, a situation arises in which a term that can only have its source in Jewish culture and religion is applied to Jesus frequently in our earliest Christian literature without strong interest in the messianic status of Jesus, while that interest is clearly evident in later Christian literature, though the term itself is used less frequently. As D. E. Aune has asked, "Why do the Gospels and Acts, written ca. 70–100 C.E.,

---

[7] Aune, "Christian Prophecy," 405.
[8] de Jonge, "Earliest Christian Use of *Christos*," 321.
[9] Ibid.
[10] N. A. Dahl (rev. D. H. Juel), "Messianic Ideas and the Crucifixion of Jesus," in Charlesworth, *Messiah,* 391, 392: "His own understanding of Christ is shaped by the Christian faith much more than by messianic ideas which he may have had before his conversion.... Relative to the rest of the NT, in Pauline letters the messiahship of Jesus is seldom clearly visible at the surface but is present at a deeper level and shapes the entire theology." Dahl ("Messiahship of Jesus in Paul," 22) has pointed especially to Rom 9–11 for evidence of the importance of Jesus' messiahship for Paul: "Paul apparently attached little importance to teaching pagans the meaning of the name 'Christ.' But his entire work as an apostle is conditioned by the messiahship of Jesus." Cf. Hengel, "'Christos' in Paul," 73–74, who argues largely on the basis of Acts that the messianic status of Jesus was part of Paul's missionary preaching and that a passage such as 1 Cor 10:1–11 presupposes that the congregation in Corinth is aware of the real meaning of *christos.*
[11] MacRae, "Messiah and Gospel," 170–73. MacRae points to a writer such as Luke, who, despite a largely Gentile audience, emphasizes the messiahship of Jesus, and to Paul's own detailed references to scripture to call into question the notion that a largely Gentile audience accounts for the absence of any attempt in his letters to demonstrate the messianic status of Jesus.
[12] See the survey in Marinus de Jonge, "Christ," *ABD* 1:917–19; and the summary statement in Aune, "Christian Prophecy," 405–6.

exhibit a seemingly anachronistic concern with the problem of Jesus' messianic status?"[13]

A further issue concerning the distribution of the term in the Gospel literature must also be noted. The term is virtually absent from the sayings of Jesus and from collections of such sayings.[14] On this matter Dahl has commented appropriately, "The problem of the relationship between the Jesus-tradition and the gospel of the crucified and risen Christ is a problem within the early church and not simply to be subsumed under the question 'the historical Jesus and the kerygmatic Christ' or, in the earlier and more popular formulation, 'Jesus and Paul.'"[15]

A TYPOLOGY OF ALTERNATIVE PROPOSALS TOWARD A SOLUTION

In general, one can point to four directions in which a solution has been sought to the question of how it came about that a designation of biblical and Jewish provenance with seemingly little appropriateness for the characterization of Jesus and limited possibilities of christological development is the most frequent term applied to Jesus in the New Testament, keeping in view as well that it is in the genuine letters of Paul to predominantly Gentile congregations that the term is found with greatest frequency. One way has been to argue from evidence in the Gospel of Mark that Jesus viewed himself in the role of Israel's Messiah but sought to reinterpret how that role was to be fulfilled. This would account for the frequency of the term as well as for its seeming lack of appropriateness as a designation for Jesus.[16] However, this sort of solution presupposes the existence of a well-defined role for a figure designated Messiah in early Judaism, which has been shown to be extremely tenuous in recent

---

[13] Aune, "Christian Prophecy," 406.

[14] See the evidence in Dahl, "Messianic Ideas," 396–98.

[15] Ibid., 398, adding: "The distinction between the ongoing tradition (i.e., teaching and preaching of sayings of Jesus) and the proclamation of the crucified Christ cuts across the distinction between 'orthodoxy' and heresy. The first type is attested by 'Q,' the Gospel of Thomas, and other writings, while Valentinian doctrines about Christ (or several 'Christs') to a much higher degree presuppose and transform a more 'Pauline' proclamation of the crucified and vindicated Christ."

[16] T. W. Manson, *The Servant-Messiah: A Study of the Public Ministry of Jesus* (Cambridge: Cambridge University Press, 1953); Oscar Cullmann, *The Christology of the New Testament* (trans. Shirley C. Guthrie and Charles A. M. Hall; 2nd ed.; Philadelphia: Westminster, 1963); C. F. D. Moule, *The Origin of Christology* (Cambridge: Cambridge University Press, 1977); Joachim Jeremias, *The Eucharistic Words of Jesus* (trans. Norman Perrin; New York: Scribner's, 1966); and Marinus de Jonge, *Jesus, The Servant-Messiah* (New Haven: Yale University Press, 1991). The opposite of this position is found in S. G. F. Brandon, *Jesus and the Zealots: A Study of the Political Factor in Primitive Christianity* (New York: Scribner's, 1967), who builds on the political aspects of Jesus' messiahship in the earlier work of Reimarus and Eisler.

discussion.[17] Moreover, scholars have differed on whether the four central Markan passages (8:27–30; 12:35–37; 13:21–22; 14:61–62) point to a qualified acceptance of the designation by Jesus or his rejection of it.[18] Why would Jesus use or acknowledge a designation that required significant reinterpretation, if in the first place its political implications were problematical and dangerous? Moreover, if he rejected an attempt to apply the term to his teaching and activity, how did it subsequently come to be applied to him by his followers?

A different direction has been taken by scholars who emphasize the fluidity of terminology and conceptions that express ideals and hopes in the contemporary forms of Judaism. They point to the variety of types to whom the designation *anointed one* might be applied. Thus, it is argued that the designation was applied to Jesus during his ministry not as a royal and nationalist figure but as an anointed prophet and messenger of good news and wisdom who suffers the common fate of the prophet. The conception is not a reinterpretation or christianizing of Jewish messianic political language but the appropriation of a Davidic messianic tradition that was already reinterpreted in Hellenistic Jewish wisdom tradition and applied to a number of types: the martyred and vindicated prophet-sage; the royal sage who is initiated into wisdom as the son, child, or servant of God; and Solomon, the son of David, as a type of the sage who heals.[19]

---

[17] The two recent volumes on the subject—Neusner et al., eds., *Judaisms and Their Messiahs;* and Charlesworth, ed., *Messiah*—have scored this point repeatedly. For earlier treatments of the question, see M. de Jonge, "The Use of the Word 'Anointed' in the Time of Jesus," *NovT* 8 (1966): 132–48; and Morton Smith, "What Is Implied by the Variety of Messianic Figures?" *JBL* 78 (1959): 66–72.

[18] See Reginald H. Fuller, *The Foundations of New Testament Christology* (New York: Scribner's, 1965), 109. Cf. the treatment of the question in MacRae, "Messiah and Gospel," 174–76, with the treatment presented by D. H. Juel, "The Origin of Mark's Christology," in Charlesworth, *Messiah*, 449–60.

[19] This position has been developed in several major articles by Klaus Berger and has been drawn on extensively in the work of A. E. Harvey and Edward Schillebeeckx. See Klaus Berger, "Zum traditionsgeschichtlichen Hintergrund christologischer Hoheitstitel," *NTS* 17 (1970–71): 391–425; idem, "Die königlichen Messiastraditionen des Neuen Testaments," *NTS* 20 (1973): 1–44; idem, "Zum Problem der Messianität Jesu," *ZTK* 71 (1974): 1–30; A. E. Harvey, *Jesus and the Constraints of History* (Philadelphia: Westminster, 1982), 120–53; and Edward Schillebeeckx, *Jesus: An Experiment in Christology* (trans. Hubert Hoskins; New York: Seabury, 1979). The work of de Jonge has also been influenced by Berger's studies. See de Jonge, "Christ," 921; idem, "The Use of Ο ΧΡΙΣΤΟΣ in the Passion Narratives," in *Jésus aux origines de la christologie* (ed. J. Dupont; 2nd ed.; BETL 40; Leuven: Peeters and Leuven University Press, 1989), 170–71, 190–91; idem, "The Christological Significance of Jesus' Preaching of the Kingdom of God," in *Christology: Essays in Honor of Leander E. Keck* (ed. Abraham J. Malherbe and Wayne A. Meeks; Minneapolis: Fortress, 1993), 12–14; see also idem, *Jesus, The Servant-Messiah*. Many of de Jonge's earlier essays can now be found in H. J. de Jonge, ed., *Jewish Eschatology, Early Christian Christology*

While this view attempts to show how the term *christos* could be appropriately applied to the activity and fate of Jesus, it is precisely the absence of the term that is striking in this prophetic-sapiential conception of the king. Moreover, it appears to be a particular Lukan emphasis in connection with Jesus' healing and teaching (Luke 4:16–19; Acts 10:38), whereas the passion narrative in Mark, on the contrary, underscores popular and Davidic royal traditions in the use of the term *christos* and in the confrontation of Jesus with his accusers and persecutors.[20]

A third direction moves away from the influence of antecedent Jewish traditions or the teaching and healing activities of Jesus in Galilee and stresses instead the event of Jesus' execution in Jerusalem as "king of the Jews." On this view, had Jesus not been put to death as a messianic pretender, the designation *christos* would never have been closely associated with Jesus let alone become a second name. The appropriation of the term by his followers is therefore ironic and is the basis for subsequent christianization of the term.[21] Thus, the origins of its use by followers of Jesus cannot be accounted for either in terms of Jewish categories for understanding Jesus' activity or teaching or by recourse to traditions of a martyred and resurrected sage/son of God. The solution is as problematic as it is trenchant. While the irony of the Markan passion narrative can be argued, it could only work in that way for those for whom the Christian significance of the term was already in place.[22] As an explanation of how the term came to be used by followers of Jesus, it would seem altogether improbable. If a charge of blasphemy or sedition were trumped up, his followers in Jerusalem would only be claiming that

---

and the Testaments of the Twelve Patriarchs: Collected Essays of Marinus de Jonge (NovTSup 63; Leiden: Brill, 1991).

[20] See Burton L. Mack, *A Myth of Innocence: Mark and Christian Origins* (Philadelphia: Fortress, 1988), 281–83, 289–90; and Juel, *Messianic Exegesis,* 89–117, esp. 102–3; cf. R. A. Horsley, "'Messianic' Figures and Movements in First-Century Palestine," in Charlesworth, *Messiah,* 276–95. On Matthew's Son of David, see below, pp. 319–20.

[21] The principal proponent of this view is Dahl, "Crucified Messiah," 37: "That the title 'Messiah' was inextricably bound up with the name of Jesus can be explained only by presupposing that Jesus was actually crucified as the Messiah. Otherwise one falls into great difficulties and cannot make historically understandable the title's Christian meaning and its wide use as another name of Jesus." Dahl maintains that even though Jesus never made a messianic claim, he did not deny the role when it was raised against him (ibid., 44); cf. Fuller, *Foundations of New Testament Christology,* 108–11, 158–62. MacRae has also expressed this as a possibility: "Whether Jesus himself accepted or, more probably, rejected the title, it is possible that the inscription on the cross lies at the root of the Christian preoccupation with the title" ("Messiah and Gospel," 175). Juel presents his book *Messianic Exegesis* as a testing of Dahl's thesis by attempting to demonstrate that the confession of Jesus as Messiah is the focal point of the development of early Christian exegetical traditions.

[22] See Juel, "Origin of Mark's Christology."

the false charge was true.[23] If Jesus had done something to make the charges plausible, those same followers in Jerusalem would have set themselves more directly than Jesus on a collision course with the authorities by publicly proclaiming the vindicated Jesus as Messiah. As it is, however, a movement of his followers managed to establish itself in Jerusalem and maintain a continuous existence at least until the outbreak of the Roman-Jewish war.[24]

The most common solution to the problem associates Jesus' messianic status with early Christian belief in his resurrection. Since the confession that God raised Jesus from the dead is generally thought to be the foundation of all early Christian groups, one is able to account for how *christos* comes to be so closely associated with Jesus without having to argue that there must have been some sort of messianic claim by Jesus or his disciples during Jesus' ministry. The messianic status of Jesus is linked to a postmortem divine destiny. However, there are major differences among scholars regarding the way in which this is to be viewed.

One position has argued that the resurrection was interpreted in the earliest period to mean that Jesus was *Messias designatus* and would exercise his messianic status in his expected imminent return.[25] Yet there are relatively few texts that link *christos* with the parousia (Phil 1:10; 2:16), and the strength of the position has depended upon associating a messianic

---

[23] Cf. the view of Ferdinand Hahn, *The Titles of Jesus in Christology: Their History in Early Christianity* (trans. Harold Knight and George Ogg; Lutterworth Library; New York: World, 1969), 161–62: "In the very earliest times the concept and the title of Messiah were not applied to Jesus. This indeed contradicts the widespread opinion that the messianic faith of the early church was centred on the risen Christ and came into use on the basis of the Easter event.... 'Messiah' as a title of dignity, and equally the messianically understood titles of exaltation such as 'Son of David' and 'Son of God' can thus not be assumed for the very earliest period. Both the attitude of Jesus Himself as well as the fact of the false accusation will have caused the church to avoid in the first place the messianic conception."

[24] I have discussed the problem of trying to hold Jesus' death as a messianic pretender (i.e., on a charge of sedition) together with the existence in Jerusalem of followers who are described in Acts as publicly proclaiming his divinely attested messianic status while directly condemning the Jewish authorities for his crucifixion (Merrill P. Miller, "'Beginning from Jerusalem...': Re-examining Canon and Consensus," *Journal of Higher Criticism* 2/1 [1995]: 3–30). If the confession "Jesus is the Messiah" constitutes the foundation and public stance of followers of Jesus in Jerusalem and is understood as the consequence of his execution as "king of the Jews," one must be prepared to explain the political nonconsequences of this for the community that formed there in his name.

[25] Thus Hahn, *Titles of Jesus in Christology*, 168: "The whole hope of salvation in the earliest days of Christianity was focused on the imminent eschatological event; the earthly work and the resurrection of Jesus were conceived only as a prelude to this." On this view, the messianic status of Jesus is obviously more closely associated with the parousia than with the resurrection.

figure with a Palestinian apocalyptic Son of Man figure, a construction that is strongly contested today.[26]

Alternatively, Jesus' messianic status is thought to have its point of departure in the use of Ps 110 to signify the resurrection as Jesus' exaltation to messianic power and authority. This position depends upon taking the argumentation in Peter's Pentecost speech in Acts 2 as evidence of the earliest Palestinian preaching and use of scripture.[27] It is hardly likely that Ps 110:1 could be used at the outset to establish Jesus' messianic status; rather, it presupposes that status and provides royal imagery with which to interpret the resurrection. The citation of this same Psalm text in Mark 12:36 and the allusion to it in Mark 14:62 also presuppose a developed stage of argumentation bringing together "Son of David" and "Lord"; "Christ," "Son of God," and "Son of Man."[28] Moreover, a better case can be made for early tradition in the pre-Pauline confessional formula of Rom 1:2–4 and the hymn in Phil 2, which speak of resurrection and exaltation without reference to Ps 110:1.[29]

A third variant of the position that links *christos* with the resurrection takes its point of departure from texts in the corpus of Paul's genuine letters. In our earliest corpus of New Testament writings, *christos* is associated most frequently with Jesus' death as a saving death (Χριστὸς ἀπέθανεν ὑπὲρ ἡμῶν/ὑμῶν: Rom 5:6, 8; 14:15; [1 Cor 8:11]; 2 Cor 5:14–15; 1 Thess 5:9–10; cf. 1 Cor 1:13; Gal 2:21; 3:13) but also frequently with the double formula of Christ's death and resurrection (1 Cor 15:3–5; 2 Cor 5:15; Rom

---

[26] Dahl, "Messianic Ideas," 395, has shown that the more detailed descriptions of Christ's glorious coming are derived from theological not messianic language. Dahl further notes, "Modern critics have often, and with many variations, reconstructed the earliest history according to a model which to a large extent depended upon the agreement of A. Schweitzer and W. Bousset that the point of departure was the identification of Jesus as the coming 'Son-of-Man-Messiah' in earliest Palestinian Christianity. This construction ... proceeds on the assumption that there was an apocalyptic Son of Man figure who was identified with Jesus and was supposed to come from heaven to earth" (ibid., 396).

[27] This general position is held by many scholars, but it has been worked out in detail in relation to early Christian use of scripture by Barnabas Lindars, *New Testament Apologetic* (London: SCM, 1961). On the use of Ps 110 in the New Testament, see David M. Hay, *Glory at the Right Hand: Psalm 110 in Early Christianity* (SBLMS 18; Nashville: Abingdon, 1973). For a critique of Lindars's view, see Juel, *Messianic Exegesis*, 139–41. See also Martin Rese, "Die Aussagen über Jesu Tod und Auferstehung in der Apostelgeschichte—ältestes Kerygma oder lukanische Theologumena?" *NTS* 30 (1984): 335–53; cf. Ulrich Wilckens, *Die Missionsreden der Apostelgeschichte: Form- und traditionsgeschichtliche Untersuchungen* (3rd ed.; WMANT 5; Neukirchen-Vluyn: Neukirchener Verlag, 1974).

[28] Juel, *Messianic Exegesis*, 141–46.

[29] See Philipp Vielhauer, "Ein Weg zur neutestamentlichen Christologie? Prüfung der Thesen Ferdinand Hahns," in *Aufsätze zum Neuen Testament* (TB 31; Munich: Kaiser, 1965), 141–98.

8:34; 14:9; 1 Thess 4:14).[30] If traditional formulas relating to Jesus' death are seen to have a different provenance than statements attesting the resurrection, the question remains how *christos* has come to be closely associated with the saving death of Jesus. Werner Kramer has recourse to a primitive Aramaic-speaking Jerusalem church for the confessions "God raised Jesus from the dead" and "Jesus is the Messiah" (or perhaps the order should be reversed); subsequently, both confessions were transmitted to the Hellenistic churches of the pre-Pauline Gentile mission and linked with formulations of Jesus' saving death.[31] On the other hand, it is argued that both formulas (of death and of resurrection) arose in the same pre-Pauline Hellenistic Christian milieu; thus, one can suppose that the term *christos* was first associated with Jesus in connection with his resurrection as an expression of the vindication of the martyr without assuming the provenance of the term in the earliest Palestinian communities.[32] However, since *christos* is not an obvious designation to associate with a martyr's vindication, one suspects that other factors were involved.[33]

The Problem of the Sources

The foregoing review serves to underline the difficulty of solution and thus the appropriateness of what the members of the Princeton Symposium regarded as the crucial question of how it came about that *christos* is the most frequent term applied to Jesus in the New Testament. What is clear is that each type of solution must depend on texts that already mark a considerable Christian development and that, therefore, a solution must depend on inferences about earlier stages that are largely hidden from view. MacRae has put most succinctly the issue of the New Testament sources that provide our most direct documentation: "What we can document most directly are the reflections of either Hellenistic Jewish authors such as Paul or gentile Christian writers such as Luke."[34] Since it is generally thought that Christianity began as a Palestinian Jewish sect, the problem of what sources might provide access to this earliest milieu becomes acute.

However, the earliest sources we have are not very promising. As already noted, Paul's genuine letters provide us with more than half of the

---

[30] Werner Kramer, *Christ, Lord, Son of God* (trans. Brian Hardy; SBT 50; Naperville, Ill.: Allenson, 1966), 19–44.

[31] Ibid., 33–41.

[32] See Mack, *Myth of Innocence*, 111.

[33] See my discussion of Mack and Kramer on this issue in Merrill P. Miller, "How Jesus Became Christ: Probing a Thesis," *Cont* 2/2–3 (1993): 259–62.

[34] MacRae, "Messiah and Gospel," 169.

instances of *christos* in the New Testament, yet even pre-Pauline traditions (e.g., Rom 1:4; 1 Cor 15:3; Phil 2:11) do not require the assumption that the term is more than a name. If we turn to Q as an early collection of the sayings of Jesus, we find no instances of *christos*. Our earliest canonical Gospel, Mark, makes sparing use of the term as a title, but, more importantly, all instances are found in the second half of the Gospel and are focused on Jerusalem and the passion narrative. Peter's confession in 8:29 clearly looks ahead to the passion. On the other hand, usage similar to what we find in Paul is found in the incipit in 1:1 ("the gospel of Jesus Christ") and in 9:41 ("because you bear the name of Christ": ὅτι Χριστοῦ ἐστε; cf. 9:37 and 1 Cor 1:12; 3:23; 2 Cor 10:7).[35] When we take account of the fact that *christos* is absent not only from Q and the *Gospel of Thomas* but with few exceptions from the entire tradition of Jesus' sayings until the time of Justin Martyr, it becomes clear that *christos* as a messianic title belongs to the Gospel narrative tradition.[36] Among the Gospel narratives, the occurrences of *christos* in connection with Jesus' miracles also appear to be secondary (Matt 11:2; Luke 4:41; John 7:31; 9:22; 11:27). Excluding the genealogies and birth narratives would leave the passion narrative as the only Gospel tradition that might provide material for an early stage of the use of *christos*.[37]

The problem of whether we have sources for documenting a messianic use of *christos* in the earliest Palestinian communities has had no real effect on how the use of the term is thought to have developed, nor on our ways of conceptualizing Christian beginnings. The reason for this can be attributed to the common notion that Christianity began as a Jewish messianic sect. Since the term *christos* is a translation of Hebrew *māšîaḥ* or Aramaic *mašîḥāʾ* and could only have arisen in a Jewish context, one cannot really imagine how *christos* could become a name without assuming knowledge of its titular significance. Thus, while Paul does not demonstrate the messianic status of Jesus, he must certainly recognize it. For this reason, when scholars turn to Paul's letters as our earliest source, they presuppose that his letters constitute not a point close to the earliest uses of *christos* but a point that marks the end of what must have preceded. The conclusion seems to follow that the conceptual labor of establishing and interpreting the messianic status of Jesus must have taken place between 30 and 50 C.E. The starting point would

---

[35] In fact, all New Testament authors use the double name Jesus Christ.

[36] Mark 9:41; 12:35; John 17:3; Matt 23:10 are clearly secondary additions of the Evangelists; see Dahl, "Messianic Ideas," 397.

[37] Ibid., 398: "My aim has simply been to show that the absence of *Christos* in sayings collections confirms that the crucifixion and the messiahship of Jesus belong inseparably together in the early Christian tradition."

necessarily have been the confession that Jesus is the Messiah. Thus, Dahl has stated:

> Paul's letters represent a strikingly advanced stage in the evolution that transformed *Christos* from a messianic designation to Jesus' second proper name.... Paul's unemphatic use of *Christos* presupposes that it is part of the standard Christian vocabulary. His usage can be explained only by assuming that the confessions and proclamation of the Aramaic-speaking church were summarized in the affirmation: "Jesus is the Messiah."[38]

The problem is that our sources hardly permit us to trace this evolution from confession of Jesus' messianic status to *christos* as little more than a surname. Dahl himself acknowledges the probability that from the earliest period "Christ" was understood as a proper name by many Gentile Christians and supposes that only later were they taught its significance.[39] However, the more serious problem is (1) that Dahl has shown that even without any specific messianic emphasis, *christos* in Paul is not a colorless name but still an honorific, and (2) that the texts that directly confess or proclaim Jesus as the Messiah do not depend on Jewish messianic conceptions or expectations, diverse as these were, but on distinctly Christian conceptions that show signs of later theologizing.[40] But this is also the point of Dahl's explanation of the origins of *christos*. It is not the confession "Jesus is the Messiah" that initially expresses faith in Jesus but, emphatically, "the crucified Jesus is the Messiah." Jewish messianic conceptions are radically transformed from the very start.[41] The confession takes up and transforms the accusation on which Jesus was crucified, just as God reverses the judgment of Jesus' persecutors by raising him from the dead. Christianity indeed begins with the use of the term *christos* as a

---

[38] Dahl, "Messiahship of Jesus in Paul," 18–19.
[39] Ibid.
[40] Dahl, "Crucified Messiah," 37: "[In Paul] it [*christos*] is not a colorless proper name, however, but an honorific designation, whose content is supplied by the person and work of Jesus Christ. Where *Christos* appears as a more general term for the Messiah announced in the Old Testament, there are often signs of later theologizing, which is also to be seen in patristic literature. For example, in Luke, as in Justin, the primitive kerygma 'Christ died ... according to the scriptures' has developed into two statements: 'the Anointed One must suffer,' and 'Jesus is the Anointed One.' Actually, what these writers and many after them present as the Old Testament doctrine of the Messiah has been conformed to their image of Jesus the Christ."
[41] Ibid., 38: "If he was crucified as an alleged Messiah, then—but only then—does faith in his resurrection necessarily become faith in the resurrection of the crucified Messiah. In this way the distinctiveness of the Christian idea of the Messiah, in contrast to the Jewish, was given from the outset. Whether it is said that God will send the foreordained Messiah, Jesus (Acts 3:20f.), or that Jesus is enthroned as Messiah (Acts 2:36), or that Christ died for our sins (1 Cor. 15:3) is a matter of minor importance in this context."

response to dramatic events of reversal. "But this means that the application of the title 'Messiah' to Jesus cannot have had its origin in the study of Scripture and in the discussion of the first Christians with Jews. Both are only secondary factors. The messiahship of the crucified Jesus is rather the presupposition that lies at the root of all the scriptural evidence *de Christo*."[42]

Juel has sought to demonstrate the fruitfulness of this last statement by showing that early Christian reflection on scripture has its starting point in "the recognition that Jesus was the expected Messiah *and* that he did not fit the picture."[43] The textual starting point for Juel's study is the traditional formula cited by Paul in 1 Cor 15:3–7, but again it presupposes a rich exegetical history behind the phrases (15:3b–4) that "Christ died for our sins in accordance with the scriptures ... and that he was raised on the third day in accordance with the scriptures." That history is virtually complete by the writing of Paul's first letter.[44] What Juel wants to show in the study is that the earliest Christian use of scripture is motivated by the need to reflect on and interpret the significance of the confession that Jesus is the crucified and risen Messiah. This is something quite different and far more innovative than the use of scripture and Hellenistic Jewish traditions to express the vindication of the righteous martyr.[45] It stands not only at the beginning but at the center of the Christology: "The exegetical history behind 1 Cor. 15:3–7 involves the whole of NT christological tradition and brings us close to the heart of the religious enterprise."[46]

From the historical starting point of the execution of Jesus as a messianic pretender one can go even further. Martin Hengel also holds that the historical roots of the confession "that the *Messiah* died for our sins" is the execution of Jesus as "King of the Jews": "After the resurrection event upon which the Church was founded, the early Christian proclamation could not do otherwise than concentrate on this point which so radically contradicted the prevailing Jewish hope."[47] However, this means that the scandal of the cross is not the execution of a Jewish martyr: "A crucified Jewish martyr, a martyred innocent, a second Socrates could have appealed to Jews and Greeks as an edifying example; a crucified

---

[42] Ibid., 39–40.

[43] Juel, *Messianic Exegesis*, 26, emphasis original.

[44] Ibid., 17: "The exegetical traditions that provide a foundation for the NT writings were largely completed prior to the writing of Paul's first letter and certainly prior to Mark's Gospel."

[45] Ibid., 12, 102, referring first to the use of *christos* in 1 Cor 15:3, then to the royal imagery and motifs in the Markan passion narrative.

[46] Ibid., 13.

[47] M. Hengel, "Christological Titles in Early Christianity," in Charlesworth, *Messiah*, 445–46, emphasis original.

The Problem of the Origins of a Messianic Conception of Jesus 313

God was for every educated person in antiquity a shameless impertinence, indeed, an absurdity."[48] For Hengel, the whole christological development of the New Testament is essentially in place within less than twenty years after the death of Jesus. That development leaves Jewish messianic hopes and "every possible form of pagan–polytheistic apotheosis far behind."[49]

What the foregoing shows is that the very attempt to resolve the problem identified at the outset of this essay can result in the sort of historical solution that is itself an expression of the drama, novelty, and dialectic of Christian faith. What are considered to be contingent circumstances of the death of Jesus are transformed in the inaugural miracle of resurrection and generate in a brief span of some twenty years a history of reflection whose creative period is virtually complete. The time is so short and the inaugural events so generative that one hardly has to ask how—let alone where, what, and to whom—any of this reflection might be related to anything that is happening in this period. It is enough to deduce from the "late" usage of Paul that the messianic status of Jesus must have been the inaugural confession of the primitive church, must have gained wide currency in Palestinian and Hellenistic Christian communities, and must have been a stunning claim that left behind at the very outset every form of Jewish messianic hope. Thus, the Jewish messianic hope is presupposed and transcended in the inaugural moment of Christian origins—truly a miracle, and yet one that is presumably rooted in a particular historical circumstance. However, can it be chance circumstance that this is exactly what the canonical narratives of the Gospels and Acts say?

Against this tendency to root *christos* as a title for Jesus in inaugural and dramatic events in Jerusalem, to collapse into the first fifteen to twenty years the creative period of development in the use of the term, and to imagine that pre-Pauline christological formulas must somehow be dependent upon oral traditions that lie behind the Markan passion narrative, I would argue that the Pauline usage does not presuppose the messianic status of Jesus as a figure of expectation or the use of *christos* as an absolute and titular designation as we find it in a range of contexts in the Gospels and Acts. On the contrary, prior to the writing of the Gospel of Mark, those who cultivated and transmitted Jesus traditions had not thought of Jesus in messianic terms, at least not in any way that can be documented on the basis of the earliest sources and that does not require an explanation of the programmatic canonical narratives on the basis of these narratives themselves.

---

[48] Ibid., 443, emphasis original.
[49] Ibid.

Instead of the assumption that Paul's letters mark an endpoint in the development of a messianic conception of Jesus, I would maintain that we should attend to the significant differences of usage of *christos* that are documented in the two major sources to which MacRae has referred (see above, p. 309). Paul's letters and Luke-Acts stand approximately two generations apart. Both sets of writings emerge in a context of interest in defining the place of Gentiles in relation to revisionary readings of Israel's epic. All of the distinctive uses of *christos* in Paul's letters are determined by Christian conceptions—the death and resurrection of Christ as saving events; association with the nouns πίστις, κήρυγμα, εὐαγγέλιον and related verbs; identification as an apostle/servant of Christ; corporate belonging to Christ; baptism into Christ; Christ as model in parenesis—and do not argue nor require for their intelligibility the messianic status or messianic conceptions of Jesus. In contrast to this, Luke-Acts has a variety of applications of *christos* that include genitive constructions for specification typical of biblical and early Jewish usage with *māšîaḥ* (Luke 2:26; 9:20; Acts 3:18; cf. 4:26); many instances of a titular use, sometimes in the predicate position, referring to Jesus in an absolute and exclusive sense (Luke 4:41; 22:67; 23:35, 39; 24:26, 46; Acts 3:20; 5:42; 8:5; 9:22; 17:3; 18:5); general references to *christos* as a well-known figure of expectation and destiny (Acts 17:3; 26:23); and a use of *christos* joined directly to *kyrios* (Luke 2:11;[50] cf. Acts 2:36), along with many instances of its use as a name in Acts (2:38; 3:6; 4:10; 8:12; 9:34; 10:36; 11:17; 15:26; 16:18; 28:31).

In Luke-Acts Jesus' messianic status is an integral part of the whole counsel of God that is set forth in the course of a narrative that in its very appeal to biblical and Jewish heritage tells the Christian story. Jesus is the Messiah of biblical promise by virtue of descent and birth; by divine announcement, recognition, and approbation; in the necessity of his suffering and humiliation; through his resurrection/exaltation and the outpouring of the Holy Spirit; and in view of his future sending by God. It is presupposed that the Christ is an acknowledged figure of ancestral promise and current expectation of the people of Israel. While there is evidence among some groups in Roman Palestine of expectation of an anointed one of the house of David, what is assumed in the Lukan narrative as common ground concerning the Messiah and concerning the referent of scriptural texts is not the consequence of prior Jewish tradition

---

[50] The form Χριστὸς κύριος is probably influenced by Hellenistic practice in which a title such as κύριος βασιλεύς was common. The designation σωτήρ in the same verse makes this the more likely; see *Ps. Sol.* 17.32 and the discussion in Robert R. Hann, "Christos Kyrios in PsSol 17.32: 'The Lord's Anointed' Reconsidered," *NTS* 31 (1985): 620–27. Hann argues that the reading of the manuscripts is correct and that *christos* has been combined with a political honorific used as an appositional modifier.

The Problem of the Origins of a Messianic Conception of Jesus 315

concerning a royal figure of expectation but the byproduct of the writer's effort to establish Jesus' exclusive claim to messianic status. It is the Lukan appropriation of Israel's epic that creates the impression of a common Jewish expectation.

Some two generations after Paul, a writer who is generally thought to be writing in some area of the earlier Pauline mission attempts to do what Paul does not do in his letters: establish the proclamation of salvation in Jesus Christ by telling the story in such a way that the name that belongs exclusively to Jesus and by which he is already commonly known in the writer's circles will be recognized as having its origin in Jesus' rightful claim to the office of the Messiah. In chronological terms, to move from Paul to Luke is to see that Jesus Christ is the precursor and presupposition of Jesus the Christ. In narrative terms, the author of Luke-Acts can place the name of Jesus Christ of Nazareth in the mouth of the leading apostle in Jerusalem (Acts 3:6) because his narrative has already established the exclusive right of Jesus to messianic rank. Paul sought confirmation of the place of his Gentile churches of Christ in the purposes of the God of Israel not by appeal to Jesus as the long-awaited Messiah of Israel but by a revisionary reading of Israel's epic (Rom 9–11), by appeal to a catena of scripture such as the one found in Rom 15:9–12, and by imagining his apostolate as beginning from Jerusalem (Rom 15:19b). The writer of Luke-Acts extended the myth of origins to include the first generation, so that a network of predominantly Gentile churches would take its place in the purposes of the biblical God. The more the writer sought to achieve an institutional history for this network of congregations, the more important the story of Israel for the story of the church, and the more central the messianic status of Jesus in appropriating the one story for the other.

To take as one corpus the authentic letters of Paul and to set it next to the Lukan writings about two generations later is to be able to document significant differences in the register of the term *christos*. Given the fact that Luke-Acts also presupposes the familiarity of its readers with the double name, Jesus Christ, we might suppose that these differences constitute a history of the use of the term *christos* between roughly 50 and 100 C.E. The importance of this is that it is the opposite of what is usually assumed.

CHRISTOS AS BYNAME

A. E. Harvey has pointed to the "hesitancy of the Jewish writings immediately previous to or contemporary with the New Testament to make use of 'Messiah' as a self-explanatory term" and has contrasted this to the tendency of the Gospels and Acts, where "'the Christ' (meaning the Messiah and not simply a reference to Jesus) is used without any further qualification or description."⁵¹ This contrast might actually help to explain the origins of the use of *christos* for Jesus. Harvey suggests that it arose as a byname similar to Simon "who is called Peter" (Matt 10:2), Thomas "who is called Twin" (John 20:24; 21:2), and Jesus "who is called Justus" (Col 4:11).⁵² Although he notes that there are instances in the Gospels and Acts that suggest that *christos* requires explanation or qualification (Matt 1:16; 16:16; 27:17, 22; Mark 14:61; Luke 2:26; 9:20; 23:35; Acts 3:18), he recognizes that the assumption in Christian writings of a Jewish expectation of *the* Messiah is the result of Christian identification of the term with Jesus:

> It is possible, therefore, that they had learnt to use the specific title "Messiah," or "Christ," first for Jesus himself, and then for that figure of popular expectation with whom they identified Jesus. In other words, instead of assuming ... that the title existed already in popular speech and was simply claimed by or assigned to Jesus, we should perhaps allow for the possibility that there was something about Jesus which caused him to be distinguished from other men called Jesus by this additional name, and that this name then became the determinative title both for Jesus himself and for that person of Jewish expectation whom his followers believed him to be.⁵³

While Harvey's interest is to show that the byname was applied to Jesus during his lifetime, I would contend that the evidence that is best explained by his suggestion can be found in Paul's letters. Initial use as a byname would explain why we have many instances in Paul's letters where it is difficult to determine whether it carries connotations of an honorific or a title or is merely a proper name. Clearly, we have evidence in Paul that shows that it cannot be taken merely as a proper name. Yet such evidence never requires the messianic status of Jesus to be argued, nor is it ever the point on which Paul's argument rests. It is easy enough to imagine that the characterization intended in the byname can be lost with constant repetition; at the same time, the name can continue to be used in ways that highlight the honorific, thus providing a basis for reflection on

---

⁵¹ Harvey, *Jesus and the Constraints of History*, 79.

⁵² Ibid., 80–81.

⁵³ Ibid., 82. Cf. de Jonge, "Earliest Christian Use of *Christos*," 321: "For Paul and his readers the term χριστός is intimately connected with Jesus. Christ has become a *cognomen* which can be used together with the proper name Jesus—like Peter for the disciple Simon or Augustus for Octavian and his successors." On the parallel between Paul's ceremonial usage, ὁ κύριος Ἰησοῦς Χριστός, and the Roman usage, *Imperator Caesar Augustus*, see Hengel, "'Christos' in Paul," 68: "Jesus was the real proper name, 'Christos' the cognomen and 'Kyrios' the title." Hengel also notes the common transformation of titles into names in Semitic parlance (75).

the term as a title. What is most important to underscore is that both tendencies have the same effect of identifying the term exclusively with Jesus. Accordingly, I would maintain that the use of *christos* as a proper name has little to do with a growing Gentile constituency in the church and that the absolute titular use, the Messiah, has equally little to do with appropriating contemporary Jewish expectations of an eschatological deliverer. However, as I will try to show, these tendencies have taken hold at different times and relate to different circles and circumstances among the followers of Jesus.

Christos in Context: The Canonical Gospels and Acts

John's Gospel provides us with the clearest and strongest examples of the use of *christos* as a title in public debate with "the Jews" and with the Jewish rulers. It is only used twice in John as a name (1:17; 17:3). In contrast with Mark, it is found mostly in the public ministry of Jesus in the first half of the Gospel rather than being closely linked with the passion narrative (7:26, 27, 31, 41–42; 10:24; 12:34).[54] Again, unlike Mark, recognition of Jesus as the Messiah is the basis for taking up the path of discipleship at the outset, rather than a confession or revelation at the midpoint of the narrative (1:41). The Baptist explicitly denies the title as a self-reference (1:20; 3:28), and the Samaritan woman and her townsfolk are able to ascertain, though perhaps without full understanding, that Jesus is the Messiah (4:25, 29). Martha's confession of Jesus gives climactic significance to the identification of Jesus as the Messiah in John (11:25–27; cf. 20:31), bringing the titles Son of God and Messiah in apposition in connection with Jesus' life-giving power.

Most importantly, Jesus' followers are cast out of the synagogue on the basis of confessing him to be the Christ (9:22; cf. 12:42–43). However, as a confession that separates the community of Jesus' followers from "the Jews" and expresses the purpose for which the Gospel was written (20:31), *christos* does not have a content that Jewish expectations could anticipate or affirm. Public debate on the matter in John is inconclusive, if not downright wrongheaded. In any case, such questions and debate could not actually have constituted the terms of debate between the Johannine community and a wider public. Who would care about the credentials of someone who was not present in any case to make such claims or to act upon them? And who would think that such claims could be made for a figure of the recent past? Obviously, only followers of Jesus. For this reason questions and public debate about the identity of Jesus in the Gospels

---

[54] See MacRae, "Messiah and Gospel," 176–78.

must be understood as mythmaking in the interest of authorizing the investment of individuals in the charter of a particular social formation. The wider public could not have cared directly about the credentials of Jesus, but only about groups that had formed in his name. Moreover, in the Gospel of John it is not the identification of Jesus with the Messiah but the content given to the term that marks out the distinctiveness of Jesus' followers, and precisely as a definition of separation from the ethnic communities of the Jews. There is of course no question of the Gospel writer's rejecting the appropriateness of the title for Jesus.[55] On the contrary, its use is enhanced as a title and confession of Jesus' divinity in a manner related to the community's social experience.[56] It is another expression of the divine mission and status of Jesus reflecting the exclusive authority of Jesus for the Johannine community in its separation from the assemblies of Jews in a period subsequent to the first Roman-Jewish war.

I have already suggested that in Luke-Acts the title *christos* serves to anchor the story of the church in the story of Israel, thereby enabling a network of Gentile congregations to find its place in the world-encompassing purposes of the biblical God.[57] The Evangelist can look back from his own time and view Jesus as a Jewish culture hero, anointed with the Holy Spirit and power, who went about doing good (Acts 10:38) and who, by being first to rise from the dead (Acts 26:23), establishes the light of a new worldwide culture through the witness of his apostles who testify that Jesus

---

[55] MacRae maintains that *Messiah* is not only reinterpreted in debate with Jews but reflects inner-Christian debates respecting the adequacy of the miracles for faith in relation to the self-revealing discourses of Jesus. There may be inner-Christian debates that relate to the titular use of Messiah for Jesus, but as MacRae notes, the Evangelist has affirmed the title in emphatic ways (ibid., 178). There can be no question of suggesting its inadequacy; rather, it must be shown to be a fully adequate expression of Johannine Christian faith. Different uses of the term are different ways, appropriate to different communities and circumstances, of assuring that Jesus has exclusive right to the title. That is best achieved by assuring that it will have little in common with public expectations or the expectations of marginal followers.

[56] See P. M. Casey, *From Jewish Prophet to Gentile God: The Origins and Development of New Testament Christology* (Cambridge: Clarke; Louisville: Westminster John Knox, 1991), 23–40, 156–59, 161.

[57] For differing positions on the Christology of the missionary speeches in Acts, see Wilckens, *Missionsreden der Apostelgeschichte;* and Rese, "Aussagen über Jesu Tod." On the function of Old Testament citations in Luke, see Paul Schubert, "The Structure and Significance of Luke 24," in *Neutestamentliche Studien für Rudolf Bultmann zu seinem 70. Geburtstag am 20. August 1954* (ed. Walther Eltester; BZNW 21; Berlin: Töpelmann, 1954), 165–86; and Martin Rese, *Alttestamentliche Motive in der Christologie des Lukas* (SNT 1; Gütersloh: Mohn, 1969). Juel has argued that "Luke's exegesis is neither typical nor primitive" (*Messianic Exegesis*, 19). For a recent introduction to the speeches in Acts, see Marion L. Soards, *The Speeches in Acts: Their Content, Context, and Concerns* (Louisville: Westminster John Knox, 1994), 1–17.

Christ is Lord of all (Acts 10:36) and is ordained by God to be the judge of the living and the dead (Acts 10:42).

The Evangelist Matthew also looks back to Jesus as a Jewish culture hero, specifically, to a Messiah of royal Davidic lineage. For the Evangelist, this culture hero is also Jesus Christ (1:1), the revealed Son of the living God (16:16), who is given all authority in heaven and on earth to commission a worldwide mission of discipleship and to promise his divine presence throughout the age (28:18–20; cf. 16:19; 18:18). Matthew's portrait of an ideal ruler is to be seen against the backdrop of the failure of Herodian princes, temple priesthood, and popular messiahs remembered from the Roman-Jewish war and against the current competition of Pharisaic leaders, whose teachers cannot possibly compete with the authority of the Messiah.[58]

Since Matthew establishes Jesus' credentials as the Davidic Messiah from birth, he can portray Jesus' earthly activity in messianic terms.[59] Nevertheless, Jesus' messianic identity is not self-evident, but a divine revelation (16:17). In his activity, Jesus' messianic status is portrayed especially in his role as the "therapeutic Son of David."[60] Matthew has expanded the use of the title Son of David beyond his Markan source (see Mark 10:47–48 // Matt 20:30–31; Mark 12:35–37a // Matt 22:41–46; Matt 1:1, 20; 9:27; 12:23; 15:22; 21:9, 15). This development should not be associated with a later Jewish magical tradition of Solomon as exorcist, since Matthew has in any case toned down the Markan emphasis on exorcisms and on manipulative techniques in the healings.[61] The title should also be distinguished from an

---

[58] Far from being a dominant and continuous tradition from biblical times, the expectation of an anointed ruler of Davidic lineage appears to be limited to the Roman period and to function as a critique of Roman and Herodian rule. See Kenneth E. Pomykala, *The Davidic Dynasty Tradition in Early Judaism: Its History and Significance for Messianism* (SBLEJL 7; Atlanta: Scholars Press, 1995), 159–70 (on *Ps. Sol.* 17), 180–217 (on the Davidic messiah at Qumran). It should also be noted that apart from later rabbinic texts, the titular use of the term *māšîaḥ* in an absolute sense (without further qualification) is found in Jewish literature only in the postdestruction apocalypses of Ezra and Baruch, referring to an eschatological ruler descended from David (*4 Ezra* 12.32; *2 Bar.* 29.3; 30.1; 72.2).

[59] MacRae, "Messiah and Gospel," 180: "Since Jesus is established by virtue of his birth or even conception as the Messiah, Matthew can go on to write his Gospel as a description of the Messianic Age in which the deeds of the Messiah are visibly present."

[60] See Dennis C. Duling, "The Therapeutic Son of David: An Element in Matthew's Christological Apologetic," *NTS* 24 (1977–78): 392–410; and more recently, idem, "Matthew's Plurisignificant 'Son of David' in Social Science Perspective: Kinship, Kingship, Magic, and Miracle," *BTB* 22 (1992): 99–116.

[61] See Dennis C. Duling, "Solomon, Exorcism, and the Son of David," *HTR* 68 (1975): 235–52, in debate with Loren R. Fisher, "'Can This Be the Son of David?'" in *Jesus and the Historian: Written in Honor of Ernest Cadman Colwell* (ed. F. Thomas Trotter; Philadelphia: Westminster, 1968), 82–97; cf. Evald Lövestam, "Jésus Fils de David chez les Synoptiques," *ST*

earlier Davidic descent tradition linked with the resurrection of Jesus that makes use of imagery and metaphors drawn from the Old Testament and does not utilize the title Son of David.[62]

Matthew has created his therapeutic Son of David not only by expanding his Markan source but by identifying Jesus' healing activity as the deeds of the Christ (Matt 11:2–6) rather than the deeds of prophets such as Elijah and Elisha, as the summary of the deeds drawn from texts of Isaiah might suggest (Isa 61:1–2 LXX; 42:6–7; 35:5; 29:18–19).[63] As Dennis C. Duling points out, "In Matthew Jesus' twofold function is more like the twofold function preserved in Q rather than that represented in Mark [preaching and casting out demons]. Not only does Matthew cite the Q section, but it is generally considered to refer back to his miracle section in chs. viii–ix (e.g. 'the *deeds* of the Christ ... ')."[64] The sage-prophet of Q has become a royal figure. As such, he is addressed as Lord and Son of David (9:27–28; 15:22; 20:31). The man of authority in Mark has become the Davidic Messiah. As such, he does not exact taxes but heals. In Jerusalem, he enters as king to the cries of "Hosanna to the Son of David" (21:9), but he does not drive out the Romans; he heals the lame and the blind (21:14). In contrast to the Pharisees, the disciples of Jesus have one teacher, the Christ (23:10), who has already climactically defeated the Pharisees by citing Ps 110:1 as a conundrum that silences all opponents in the temple and by asking what only Christians will grasp: How can David call him Lord, and how then can the Christ be David's son?

Q's rejected prophet and Mark's martyred Messiah have become in Matthew the Messiah of deed, a royal figure in both his teaching and his healing. Jesus' absolute right to the royal dignity in his birth, his ministry, and his entry into Jerusalem is a recasting of the byname *christos* in terms appropriate to a Jesus movement, part of which may once have been linked with the Q people but which by the time of the Evangelist has come to be identified as the ἐκκλησία of the Christ, the Son of God, in the absence of any possible claimant to royal dignity among the heirs of client

---

28 (1974): 97–109; and Berger, "Die königlichen Messiastraditionen"; and see Duling, "Therapeutic Son of David," 393–99.

[62] See Dennis C. Duling, "The Promises to David and Their Entrance into Christianity—Nailing Down a Likely Hypothesis," *NTS* 20 (1973–74): 55–77.

[63] See John S. Kloppenborg, *The Formation of Q: Trajectories in Ancient Wisdom Collections* (SAC; Philadelphia: Fortress, 1987), 107–8, with reference to Rudolf Pesch (*Jesu ureigene Taten? Ein Beitrag zur Wunderfrage* [QD 52; Freiburg: Herder, 1970], 36–44, who "draws attention to the prophetic character of not only restoration of sight and evangelization of the poor (Isa 61:1–2) but also the raising of the dead and the healing of lepers (1 Kgs 17:17–24; 2 Kgs 4:18–37; 5:1–27)" (*Formation of Q*, 108 n. 25).

[64] Duling, "Therapeutic Son of David," 394.

kings, priestly elites, or their retainers.[65] By way of contrast to those who have failed in their rule, Jesus is the ideal earthly king of Davidic promise whose teaching retains its authority for the "discipling" of the Gentiles, as the expression and exercise of his transcendent power and presence to the end of the age.

All the Evangelists are aware of the use of *christos* as a byname for Jesus. At the same time, each Evangelist has made use of the term to express in particular ways the messianic status of Jesus as a figure of expectation in his earthly life. Matthew, having shown how Jesus becomes the child of Joseph, son of David, virtually creates the Davidic Messiah in the image of Jesus. Luke creates a Jewish culture hero who fulfills the deliberate counsel of God for the benefit ultimately of Gentiles. For neither Evangelist is the messianic status of Jesus a matter that is seriously challenged. It is conveyed by linking the story of Jesus in different ways with images, figures, themes, and texts from biblical tradition. In the case of John, it appears to be the messianic claim of Jesus that is the source of challenge and division. However, the relationship between Jesus' healings and signs, the public debate about his status, and expulsion from the synagogue are only rightly grasped through the discourses of Jesus, which show that his messianic status is in fact a claim to divine status. All appeal to the authenticity of prior tradition must be tested in the light of that claim, which is of course the real matter that separates the Johannine community from its earlier environment.

Mark, our earliest canonical Gospel, uses *christos* as a title more sparingly than the others. Unlike John, the messianic status of Jesus is not a matter of public debate during Jesus' ministry in Mark but a matter of Peter's recognition, followed by teaching on the theme of discipleship and Jesus' fate in Jerusalem. Jesus' command to the disciples not to tell anyone about him (8:30) is understandable in the light of his trial in Jerusalem. Once his messianic status is public knowledge, he will go to his death.[66] The title *christos* is not rejected by Jesus in Mark, nor is the point of the problematic that it requires reinterpretation. While the self-designation Son of Man is important both in the Fourth Gospel and in Mark, in the former it expresses the divine origin and destiny of the Christ, while in the latter it expresses the vindication of Jesus' royal status. The problematic in Mark is that the exercise of Jesus' royal office is delayed and requires an

---

[65] On the relationship between Q and Matthew, see James M. Robinson, "The Q Trajectory: Between John and Matthew via Jesus," in *The Future of Early Christianity: Essays in Honor of Helmut Koester* (ed. Birger A. Pearson et al.; Minneapolis: Fortress, 1991), 173–94; and Burton L. Mack, *The Lost Gospel: The Book of Q and Christian Origins* (San Francisco: HarperSanFrancisco, 1993), 183–85.

[66] Mack, *Myth of Innocence*, 282.

apocalyptic resolution. Thus, in 14:61–62 Jesus' affirmative response to the high priest's question does not entail a reinterpretation of the titles "the Christ, the Son of God" in terms of another title of dignity, "the Son of Man"; rather, Jesus follows with a prophecy of the apocalyptic vindication of his royal status drawing on Ps 110 and Dan 7.[67]

Mark's references to the Son of David can be seen in the same light. Blind Bartimaeus's repeated call for mercy to Jesus, Son of David, in Jericho (10:47–48) contrasts what the blind man sees with what the disciples do not yet see in anticipation of Jesus' royal entry into Jerusalem. If the title is Mark's own addition to the story, it may be the earliest evidence of the attempt to link the healing miracles of Jesus with his characterization as a royal figure, although given its position in the Markan text that may be more than what is intended.[68] Jesus' question concerning the scribes' view of the Messiah as David's son (12:35–37) only poses a puzzle to those who may not know that Ps 110:1 refers to the postmortem vindication of the Messiah.[69] Thus, it is not a question of rejecting the scribal expectation of the Messiah but of appropriating that expectation exclusively for Jesus in the assurance of his ultimate vindication.[70]

It has been argued by Hengel that the Markan passion narrative does not present Jesus in the role of the righteous sufferer: "The pattern of the humiliation and exaltation of the righteous is far too general and imprecise to interpret the event which Mark narrates so skilfully and with such deep theological conviction. He is concerned with the utterly unique event of the passion and crucifixion of the Messiah of Israel which is without any parallel in the history of religion."[71] The foregoing statement is cited in a fuller form by Juel in his chapter on the influence of the psalms of lament (Pss 22; 31; 69) in the composition of Mark 15.[72] The chapter is entitled "Christ the Crucified," and Juel wants to show that these particular psalms

---

[67] See Juel, "Origin of Mark's Christology," 452.

[68] See Christoph Burger, *Jesus als Davidssohn: Eine traditionsgeschichtliche Untersuchung* (FRLANT 98; Göttingen: Vandenhoeck & Ruprecht, 1970), 62; Vernon K. Robbins, "The Healing of Blind Bartimaeus (Mark 10:46–52) in the Marcan Theology," *JBL* 92 (1973): 242; and Duling, "Solomon, Exorcism, and the Son of David," 249–52.

[69] Cf. Juel, "Origin of Mark's Christology," 453–55, who refers to Evald Lövestam, "Die Davidssohnsfrage," *SEÅ* 27 (1962): 72–82. Juel maintains that the pericope presupposes 2 Sam 7:12–14 and reflects the category of alleged scriptural contradictions.

[70] Contra Werner H. Kelber, *The Kingdom in Mark: A New Place and a New Time* (Philadelphia: Fortress, 1974), 96, who argues that Jesus is disclaiming Davidic sonship; cf. Bruce Chilton, "Jesus ben David: Reflections on the *Davidssohnfrage*," *JSNT* 14 (1982): 102: "The best explanation for the *Davidssohnfrage* ... is that Jesus said pretty much what is attributed to him, and that he intended to deflect the growing suspicion that he claimed to be messiah."

[71] Martin Hengel, *The Atonement: The Origins of the Doctrine in the New Testament* (trans. John Bowden; Philadelphia: Fortress, 1981), 41.

[72] Juel, *Messianic Exegesis,* 89–117; the citation from Hengel is found on p. 103.

belong to the composition of the passion narrative not because they are appropriate for describing the persecution of the righteous sufferer but because they were understood to be laments spoken by the Lord's anointed. The argument is based on verbal links between the passion psalms and Ps 89, where the speaker of the lament (89:38–51) is the Lord's anointed who is clearly a king of the Davidic dynasty. Words of insult and mocking from Ps 89 appear in Heb 11:26 and 1 Pet 4:14, and these same words are cited from Pss 31 and 69 in Mark 15. Verbal links with messianic tradition are more difficult to establish in Ps 22. However, Juel concludes:

> From Psalm 89 Christians learned that one could speak of the scorn and humiliation endured by the Messiah in scriptural terms. They learned from the psalm that the Messiah, as well as David, could speak in psalms. They encountered a fairly specific vocabulary with which to speak of that suffering. Perhaps that is a sufficient explanation for the identification of Psalm 22 as a "royal" psalm.[73]

One does not have to be convinced of Juel's analysis of the speaker of Ps 22 in order to agree with the contention of both Juel and Hengel that Jesus suffers as a royal figure in the Markan passion narrative. However, this in no way excludes the influence of traditions of the wisdom story of the suffering righteous one.[74] Burton L. Mack has shown that the composition of the Markan passion narrative weaves together the characterizations of a messianic figure with those of the wisdom tale of the righteous one and of the martyr. Though Mack appeals more to the influence of recent popular messiahs than to Christian scribal tradition for the messianic characterization, he also shows the importance of the warrior martyr motif for depicting the death of a king.[75]

The issue of a pre-Markan passion narrative also arises in Juel's discussion. Though he believes the persistence of source analyses of Mark 14–15 indicates that "there is justification for viewing Mark as an author who composed by working with traditional material,"[76] he concludes that "source criticism provides an insubstantial basis upon which to construct theories about the development of the passion tradition."[77] While the use of scriptural material may provide a more promising foundation, what he

---

[73] Ibid., 113.

[74] Juel's argument is responding specifically to Harvey, *Jesus and the Constraints of History*; Berger, "Die königlichen Messiastraditionen"; and Lothar Ruppert, *Jesus als der leidende Gerechte? Der Weg Jesu im Lichte eines alt- und zwischentestamentlichen Motivs* (SBS 59; Stuttgart: Katholisches Bibelwerk, 1972).

[75] Mack, *Myth of Innocence*, 281–83, 306–8.

[76] Juel, *Messianic Exegesis*, 97.

[77] Ibid., 98.

is able to show is that the passion psalms must always have been integral to the narrative.⁷⁸ In my judgment, the passion narrative is a Markan composition. But there is hardly any question that Mark intends to depict the martyrdom of Jesus as the death of the king Messiah. It is the appropriation of *christos* to signify the long-awaited figure of expectation and its use as an exclusive title for Jesus that prevents the death of Jesus from being simply the execution of a pious sage. Indeed, it is this construction of *christos* and its exclusive appropriation for Jesus that also prevents the Son of God from being simply another cultic deity and the resurrection of Jesus from being simply the apotheosis of a culture hero.

Paul, the Early Jesus Movements, and the Origins of the Use of *Christos*

Andrew Chester reminds us again of the problem of relating Pauline Christology to contemporary Jewish messianic expectations:

> We are confronted with a curious phenomenon: this title (or term) Messiah/Χριστός, for which we have struggled to find more than a handful of instances in the plethora of Jewish texts over the course of three centuries (many of them directly concerned with the final age and events, and hence where one could naturally expect them to include some reference to a messianic scenario), now occurs more than 200 times in the (not especially extensive) writings of a Jew of the mid-first century AD, but it turns out to be mainly bland and apparently insignificant in the way it is used.⁷⁹

Chester's solution is to argue for a deliberate attempt to neutralize and transcendentalize messianic concepts that were at home in Jewish millenarian movements, including earliest Palestinian Christianity. Thus, according to Chester, it is probable that:

> Paul undertakes this "neutralizing" of the tradition both because the messianic kingdom has not manifested itself ... and also because the radical implications of this messianic hope would present problems for him, especially as he and the Christian movement moved more and more into the main centres of the Roman Empire. Thus to retain or develop an emphasis of this kind would mean, for Paul and his churches...,

---

⁷⁸ Ibid., 113: "If there is a pre-Markan passion tradition that can be isolated, the psalms surely form the basis of the tradition. It is unlikely that Jesus' story was ever told as a recitation of facts."

⁷⁹ Andrew Chester, "Jewish Messianic Expectations and Mediatorial Figures and Pauline Christology," in *Paulus und das antike Judentum* (ed. Martin Hengel and Ulrich Heckel; WUNT 58; Tübingen: Mohr Siebeck, 1991), 66.

focussing on something that was in practice incapable of being realised within society, and also potentially politically embarrassing.[80]

The main point of this paper has been to suggest that the Pauline phenomenon is curious because of the common notion that Christianity began as a Jewish messianic sect and that therefore the earliest Christian uses of *christos* would have to be related to or in confrontation with some standard or combination of existing Jewish messianic conceptions or must have resulted from specific historical circumstances related to the life and death of Jesus. I would submit that there are a range of problems with this scenario. First, if anything has emerged from recent exploration of Jewish messianic conceptions of the function and range of ideal figures, eschatological hopes, heavenly mediatorial figures, and the relatively rare references to (an) anointed one(s), it is that we are dealing with particular attempts of particular Jewish groups and constellations to make sense of their time and place, not with widely diffused expectations and traditions.[81] Second, it is difficult to understand the transcendentalizing of messianic hopes because of their potential political ramifications in the context of Paul's mission and to imagine at the same time that no such considerations would be in play in Jerusalem, the place of Jesus' execution, and that a messianic sect could successfully establish its center there and continue until the outbreak of the Roman-Jewish war.[82] Third, none of the narrative materials of the canonical Gospels and Acts surveyed in the preceding section are evidence of the earliest stages of Jesus movements in Palestine and Syria, nor can their features be correlated with pre-Pauline traditions. The titular, absolute, and general uses of *christos,* the royal characterizations of Jesus the Messiah in the passion narratives and in the genealogies and birth narratives in Matthew and Luke, the Son of David in the Matthean tradition of Jesus as healer, and the confessions of Jesus as the Christ in the Johannine literature are better understood as various attempts to construct an impressive focal figure for a biographical tradition of a Jesus already known in these circles by the cognomen *christos* in the wake of the collapse of recent popular movements and the destruction of the Jewish national religious center.

---

[80] Ibid., 68.

[81] In addition to the recent studies in Neusner et al., eds., *Judaisms and Their Messiahs;* and Charlesworth, ed., *Messiah,* see also John J. Collins and George W. E. Nickelsburg, eds., *Ideal Figures in Ancient Judaism: Profiles and Paradigms* (SBLSCS 12; Chico, Calif.: Scholars Press, 1980); and Pomykala, *Davidic Dynasty Tradition.* For a response to the Neusner and Charlesworth volumes that does not, in my judgment, significantly alter the picture, see John J. Collins, *The Scepter and the Star: The Messiahs of the Dead Sea Scrolls and the Other Ancient Literature* (ABRL; New York: Doubleday, 1995).

[82] See Miller, "Beginning From Jerusalem."

As a consequence of the devastation of the war, Jesus movements had to account for a changing situation, confront and distinguish themselves from emerging Jewish leaderships in Palestine and southern Syria, take note of the existence of associations in the name of *christos* with their increasingly Gentile constituencies in cities of the western diaspora, and develop their own stories, charters, and rituals in order to engage and compete with local town and village synagogues. Royal characterization of Jesus as a figure of transcendent power and destiny, whether as Christ, Lord, or Son of God, could already be found as an expression of the distinctiveness and ambition of some Jesus Christ associations in Greco-Roman cities. Who could really argue with the royal characterization of the human figure of Jesus of the past, since such characterization depended for its cogency not on actual memories of Jesus but on the possibility of constructing the *bios* of an ideal figure to explain the debacle of the war and to authorize the new situation confronting the Jesus movements.

Finally, I see no way to sharply distinguish the use of *christos* as a second name from its use as an honorific in Paul's letters.[83] I certainly do not believe one can reconstruct discrete stages in the history of early Christianity on the basis of this distinction. Instead, I am suggesting that the term *christos* first took hold as a byname among Jewish followers of Jesus, perhaps in Damascus or Antioch, as a way of characterizing the founder of a community of mixed ethnic origin that was in the process of establishing itself as an independent association in interaction with but self-consciously distinguished from a network of Jewish synagogues. Since all the titles of Jesus in the Pauline corpus carry royal status, I assume that the connotations of the byname were royal, but I would also suggest that this was intended to say as much about the community as about the founder figure. It signified that followers constituted a royal realm that Jesus was divinely authorized to establish and over which he would come to be viewed as the one installed as ruler. The byname did not make Jesus an eschatological deliverer or the expected king of Israel or a cosmic ruler but the anointed (and thus divinely approved) founder of a very self-conscious alternative community.[84]

---

[83] Perhaps the most illuminating example is 1 Cor 1:12–13. Paul refers to Christ in a series of names. Then he asks rhetorically, "Is Christ divided?" using the definite article. While the article does not signify that *christos* is a title to be translated "the Christ," it would seem in context to suggest that the name is recognized as carrying special meaning. One is not baptized into the name of Paul; one can belong only to *christos*. Paul certainly knows that *christos* means anointed one, as one can see in 2 Cor 1:21, where it is said that "it is God who establishes us with you in Christ and has anointed us."

[84] See above, p. 301, the introductory note.

In the course of time, the attempt to legitimate the movement, especially to its Jewish members, to articulate its place in relation to Jewish and Greco-Roman polities, and to account for its spread gave broad social circumstance to intellectual efforts to attribute to Christ the role of martyr-Savior, to celebrate his authority and power as cosmic Lord, to imagine his divine mission as Son of God, and to appropriate scripture in order to set the new communities in an epic context. However, *christos* as the byname of the founder figure continued to identify the community and its distinctiveness more than any other designation. In my judgment, it is this circumstance, along with the fact that it is the term most appealed to for personal authorization, that most directly accounts for its prolific use in Paul. Almost all of the characteristic Pauline uses of *christos* trade on its significance as a term of personal authorization and corporate identification. One belongs to Christ, is empowered by Christ, and has the faith of Christ. The churches are the assemblies of Christ and those for whom Christ died. *Christos* takes hold as a byname because that usage more than the titular lends itself to authorizing and characterizing those who meet, act, and speak in his name, rather than serving primarily as a designation of Jesus' office and rank. The typical Pauline terms for Jesus' office and rank are Son/Son of God and Lord. The appropriate analogues for thinking about *christos* as a byname may not be found in figures of expectation, nor in popular royal claimants, but in schools where teachers and disciples are compared and values and authority are sorted out by means of nicknames and honorifics.

While this view of the origin of the use of *christos* is hypothetical, I would maintain that it accounts better for the evidence because it resolves the problem of the distribution of the term without requiring a tenuous reconstruction of a history of traditions, drawn from literature of different genres spanning several generations, which claims the entire range of usages of *christos* within the first fifteen to twenty years of the death of Jesus. Instead, it becomes possible to account for the strikingly different ways in which the term is used in Paul's letters from what we find in the Gospels and Acts and to relate this evidence to different communities, times, and circumstances.

Christos in Context: Pre-Pauline Traditions

We have tried to account for the origins of *christos* as a byname and for its prolific use in Paul's letters. However, we have not treated the particular association of the term with the kerygma, nor with the use of scripture, nor yet with the notion of resurrection as exaltation to cosmic rule in pre-Pauline contexts. By doing this, we can move beyond the question of how and why the term was first introduced and attempt to locate and situate several uses of *christos* that belong, in my judgment, to the spread and changing constituency of Jesus Christ associations prior to Paul's mission in the Aegean area or perhaps even contemporaneous with the earliest period of Paul's activity in that area. A central mythic construction supporting the legitimation of such groups is the conception of Christ as vindicated martyr. Beyond this, there is the formation of a discourse that imagines the worldwide spread of the movement. Two features are prominent: (1) the cosmicizing of Jesus' rule as the resurrected Christ, and (2) the beginnings of a *heilsgeschichtlich* conception of the place of communities of mixed ethnic constituencies in the scheme of the biblical God.

The traditional kerygmatic formula that Paul cites beginning in 1 Cor 15:3b has long been debated on matters of provenance, composition, and history of tradition. Though some have taken the traditional formula to extend through 15:7, others argue that it ended with 15:5.[85] For our purposes, discussion can focus on 15:3b–4. While the list of resurrection appearances (conveyed by means of a formula of legitimation) is crucial to Paul's argument in 1 Cor 15, this is the only place outside the book of Acts in which reference to appearances of the risen Christ are linked to a kerygmatic formula referring to his death and resurrection.[86] The case for a translation of our verses from a Semitic original and for a Palestinian provenance of the formula as we have it in these verses has been shown to be quite weak.[87]

Although a Jewish-Hellenistic milieu is evident in such features as κατὰ τὰς γραφάς and in allusions to Isa 53 LXX, a Palestinian provenance for some recension of the formula cannot be completely excluded, if for no other reason than the evidence of the great variety of ways in which the death and resurrection of Christ have been formulated in early Christian literature.[88] But I consider an appeal to Paul's contacts with Jerusalem to be irrelevant to the issue of the source from which Paul received the tradition. If the formula itself suggests a Jewish-Hellenistic milieu, there is no

---

[85] See the discussion in John Kloppenborg, "An Analysis of the Pre-Pauline Formula 1 Cor 15:3b-5 in Light of Some Recent Literature," *CBQ* 40 (1978): 351–52, 357–60. Ernst Bammel, "Herkunft und Funktion der Traditionselemente in 1. Kor. 15,1–11," *TZ* 11 (1955): 402, has argued on formal grounds that the tradition Paul cites ended with καὶ ὅτι ὤφθη and excluded Κηφᾷ εἶτα τοῖς δώδεκα. Mack, *Myth of Innocence,* 113 n. 11, has argued on formal and substantive grounds for the elimination of the list of resurrection appearances from the original formula.

[86] See Acts 1:22; 2:32; 3:15; 4:33; 5:32; 10:41; 13:31; cf. Luke 24:34. The apostolic witness (the circle of the Twelve) to the resurrection is programmatic in Acts.

[87] See Hans Conzelmann, "On the Analysis of the Confessional Formula in I Corinthians 15:3–5," *Int* 20 (1965): 18–20; Kloppenborg, "Analysis of the Pre-Pauline Formula," 352–57.

[88] Cf. Kloppenborg, "Analysis of the Pre-Pauline Formula," 357, who believes it likely that an earlier recension originated in the Palestinian church.

problem of the source of transmission to Paul. An appeal to Paul's statement in 1 Cor 15:11 is also problematical. In context, Paul's assertion in 15:11 is clearly aimed at establishing a broader attestation for the proclamation that Jesus has been raised from the dead. It should be clear that defense of his apostolic credentials and the issue of attestation of the resurrection can hardly be separated in this context. It is not simply a matter of Paul including himself in the line of those whose apostolic credentials are legitimated on the same grounds. It is as much a question of showing that his claim to have received a revelation of Christ is not the only basis for the claim that Christ is raised from the dead. In a different context (Gal 1–2), Paul makes no appeal to a common kerygmatic tradition in his meeting with the Jerusalem pillars but only to their recognition of the independence of his mission to Gentiles.

While the thesis that Paul or the pre-Pauline tradition combined four independent formulas has largely been rejected, the view that the pre-Pauline tradition is composite and goes back to a more compact formulation of the kerygma has been widely held.[89] However, different suggestions have been made. Kramer believes two independent formulas were combined in the Jewish-Hellenistic milieu, one referring to the saving death of Christ, the other to Jesus' resurrection from the dead—"Christ died for us and was raised from the dead" (cf. 2 Cor 5:15b)—and was expanded to include ἐτάφη, κατὰ τὰς γραφάς, and ὤφθη Κηφᾷ.[90] John Kloppenborg argues for the simple antithesis found in 1 Thess 4:14, "died and rose/was raised," which was expanded by a soteriological interpretation of the death, ὑπὲρ τῶν ἁμαρτιῶν ἡμῶν, and by the phrases ἐτάφη, τῇ ἡμέρᾳ τῇ τρίτῃ, and κατὰ τὰς γραφάς.[91]

Kramer's reconstruction of the earliest form can be interpreted as confession of a martyr's vicarious death and vindication. Mack has given a social-historical account of the origins of this confession in its function as a legitimation of the Gentile constituency of a mixed community. Thus, it serves as a rationalization, a myth of origins, for mixed congregations in cities such as Antioch and reflects especially the concerns of the Jewish constituency of such communities.[92] The attractiveness of Mack's proposal is that it allows us to see the kerygma not merely as a variety of traditional formulas, each with its particular *Sitz im Leben*, but as intellectual labor related to issues of social experimentation and identity

---

[89] The thesis of four independent traditions was based on the repetition of ὅτι; see Wilckens, *Missionsreden der Apostelgeschichte*, 76 n.1; and Reginald H. Fuller, *The Formation of the Resurrection Narratives* (New York: Macmillan, 1971), 13–14.

[90] Kramer, *Christ, Lord, Son of God*, 32–38.

[91] Kloppenborg, "Analysis of the Pre-Pauline Formula," 362–65.

[92] Mack, *Myth of Innocence*, 108–11.

formation that we know were seminal at particular junctures among groups with which Paul was in touch for a considerable period prior to his activities in the Aegean world.

On the other hand, it is obvious that Kloppenborg's argument for a simple antithesis relates much less to the formation or legitimation of community and focuses instead on the destiny of Christ. In my judgment, Kloppenborg's appeal to the wide distribution of this form in early Christian preaching is somewhat misleading. Is the antithetical formulation that we have in the preaching in Acts (3:15; 4:10; 5:30–32; 10:40–41; 13:30–31; 17:3; cf. Luke 24:26) derived from the same formula that appears in some variety in the Pauline corpus (1 Thess 4:14; Rom 8:17, 34; 14:9; Gal 2:19b–20a)? The preaching in Acts presupposes the narrative of the trial of Jesus in which the suffering and endurance of the martyr are highlighted and the vindication of the martyr is at the same time the threat of judgment on tyrannical rulers. As Mack has pointed out, it is precisely the trial of Jesus with its naming of the tyrant that is not present in the Pauline corpus.[93] The significance of the antithesis in the Pauline corpus depends entirely on the specific context. Indeed, it suggests that Paul himself has formulated the simple antithesis in view of the particular point he is making. Thus, the formulation in 1 Thess 4:14 is intended to give assurance to those who have already died. The antithesis relates to the issue of those who have already died, whose deaths are of course not vicarious. It is Christ's function as Lord of the dead and the living that conditions the kerygmatic formulation in Rom 14:9, and his role as model does the same in Rom 8:17. On the other hand, the formulas in Rom 8:34 and Gal 2:19b–20a actually presuppose the saving death of Jesus.

The anarthrous *christos* is clearly a Pauline usage in statements about the death and resurrection of Jesus. Since it is typical of Paul, but by no means the only designation in such statements, one cannot be certain that *christos* stood in the formula Paul received or that it was necessarily the designation used in earlier forms of the kerygma.[94] However, on my own hypothesis, Paul's usage is not surprising. If *christos* was first used as a byname to express the royal ethos of a community established independently of local synagogues, it is quite natural to suppose that under pressure

---

[93] Ibid., 111. Paul twice refers to those who put Jesus to death, once in reference to cosmic powers (1 Cor 2:8) and once with reference to the Jews in a context that links the death of Jesus with the death of the prophets (1 Thess 2:14–16). The context is clearly one of rejection and interference by Jews in Paul's mission; in this respect, it can be compared to the accusations in Q concerning responsibility for the death of the prophets as a response to rejection. The passage in 1 Thessalonians is regarded by some scholars as inauthentic.

[94] Kloppenborg discusses the evidence in "Analysis of the Pre-Pauline Formula," 356 nn. 37–38.

The Problem of the Origins of a Messianic Conception of Jesus 331

to give further definition to the righteousness of the community, *christos* would also designate the one who holds title to his community by virtue of his dying for its cause and the one who guarantees the righteousness of his realm by his resurrection from the dead. This accounts for how a royal designation comes to be associated with a martyr figure without recourse to Mark's story of martyrdom or appeal to particular historical circumstances of Jesus' death, and without having to imagine both the execution of Jesus on a charge of sedition and the existence of a group of Jesus' followers in Jerusalem successfully establishing and perpetuating itself as a messianic sect.

The double reference to κατὰ τὰς γραφάς at the end of 1 Cor 15:3–4 may have in view particular scripture: Isa 53:4, 5, 12 LXX ("for our sins") and Hos 6:2 LXX ("on the third day"). This is particularly suggested by the fact that κατὰ τὰς γραφάς follows on these phrases. On the other hand, the double reference to scriptural congruity may indicate a more general conception of the conformity of Christ's death and resurrection with the divine purpose. These possibilities do not exclude each other.[95] On Mack's hypothesis, the martyr myth answered Jewish questions. It is understandable that in the interests of a Jewish sensibility, the death and resurrection of Christ would be given expression in conformity with the purposes of the biblical God and in language that alluded to particular scriptures. In my judgment, the composite formula of 1 Cor 15:3b–5 testifies to the likelihood that this sensibility intensified the more the Jewish constituency of these groups was overshadowed by success among Gentiles.

I would suggest a similar sort of sensibility and social situation for the quite different pre-Pauline formula found in Rom 1:3b–4. Paul has bracketed the confession (and anticipated it) by reference to the "gospel of God that he promised beforehand through his prophets in the holy scriptures, [the gospel] concerning his son" and by identifying the one confessed as "Jesus Christ our Lord." Here we do not find the term *christos* itself in the confession, nor does the confession speak directly of its significance for the community but refers only to the status of Jesus. Thus, we are concerned with what it expresses of a messianic conception of Jesus.

Minimally, the earliest form of the confession included the words τοῦ γενομένου ἐκ σπέρματος Δαυὶδ τοῦ ὁρισθέντος υἱοῦ Θεοῦ ἐξ ἀναστάσεως

---

[95] See the discussion in ibid., 364. Precisely on the basis of a text such as 1 Cor 15:3b–5, I find it doubtful that formulation of a *heilsgeschichtlich* aspect of Jesus' death and resurrection should be seen as an earlier technique than allusion to scripture. Although a *heilsgeschichtlich* aspect can be expressed without allusion to scripture, it should not be used as a criterion of early tradition, for example, in the case of the Markan passion predictions or the references to divine necessity in Luke-Acts.

νεκρῶν.⁹⁶ It seems likely that it also included the phrases κατὰ σάρκα and κατὰ πνεῦμα ἁγιωσύνης.⁹⁷ These phrases should not be understood here on the pattern humiliation/exaltation as we have in the hymn in Phil 2, though the addition of ἐν δυνάμει by Paul, or earlier, does move in that direction. As Kramer has maintained, these phrases do not have a competitive or polemical relationship, though they do establish a contrast.⁹⁸ Descent from David marks the beginning of the earthly existence of Jesus; resurrection from the dead inaugurates the heavenly rule of the Son of God.⁹⁹ The phrases introduced by κατά are temporal and spatial.¹⁰⁰ Nevertheless, I do not find the notion of a *Zweistufenchristologie* to be helpful as a description of this confession.¹⁰¹ Descent from David does not signify the messianic status of the earthly Jesus in Rom 1:3–4. Rather, it roots the confession of the inauguration of the cosmic rule of the Son of God in the earthly Jesus. It is not that Jesus was once the Messiah of Israel and is now cosmic ruler but rather that the claim to be the Son of God is legitimated in relation to the genealogical descent of the earthly Jesus. Thus, his appointment to rule is transcendental, belonging to the sphere of the spirit and holiness, entered upon out of the resurrection from the dead. But the

---

⁹⁶ See Robert Jewett, "The Redaction and Use of an Early Christian Confession in Romans 1:3–4," in *The Living Text: Essays in Honor of Ernest W. Saunders* (ed. Dennis E. Groh and Robert Jewett; Lanham, Md.: University Press of America, 1985), 113; and Duling, "Promises to David," 72.

⁹⁷ Contra Jewett, "Redaction and Use," 103–17, who argues that the latter phrase cannot be from Paul because "spirit of holiness" is not a Pauline locution. Nor can either phrase have been part of the original confession because the words "according to the flesh/according to the spirit" establish an antithesis that stands in tension with the formula "descended from David/designated Son of God by resurrection from the dead." But the problem is created in the first place by Jewett's interpretation of the antithesis as well as his interpretation of the original formula. Moreover, having pointed out that "spirit of holiness" cannot be from Paul, Jewett (117) nevertheless attributes the modifying terms ἁγιωσύνης and ἐν δυνάμει to Paul.

⁹⁸ Kramer, *Christ, Lord, Son God*, 108–11.

⁹⁹ Cf. Hahn, *Titles of Jesus in Christology*, 247–51. Hahn's view that the idea of exaltation here is a "de-eschatologization of the messianic office of Jesus" (251) depends on his arguments for a purely apocalyptic framework of the earliest messianic conception of Jesus. The reference to resurrection from the dead can be taken as an eschatological notion, but the very fact that this confession is concerned with the status of Jesus and not with the general resurrection of the dead shows that one should be cautious in attributing mythic ideas of present heavenly rule and future consummation to different provenance and stages of Christology. The distinctions are often matters of emphasis in different literary contexts. Thus, the author of Mark 14:61–62 has no difficulty drawing on images of exaltation from Ps 110, while stressing final vindication in allusion to Dan 7.

¹⁰⁰ Duling, "Promises to David," 72 n. 1.

¹⁰¹ I also do not find it helpful in describing hymnic materials such as 1 Tim 3:16 and 1 Pet 3:18–19, 22.

one to whom this cosmic dignity already belongs is the earthly Jesus who claims the dignity as a birthright.

Duling has shown that references to Davidic descent in the New Testament are associated mostly with the resurrection/exaltation of Jesus and do not make use of the title Son of David:[102]

> If one gathers up the *non*-synoptic references to the Davidic descendant, what one immediately has are metaphorical, non-titular references derived from the promise tradition. Thus, *apart* from the synoptic Son of David sayings, the phenomena of early Christianity look very much like the phenomena discussed so far, i.e. references to metaphors and conflations of texts, but now in reference to Jesus, especially in his resurrected and exalted state.[103]

Duling concludes that Rom 1:3–4 "provides what is most probably the earliest point of entry of the promise tradition into early Christianity."[104] It makes reference especially to the "seed of David" and the language of "raising up" from 2 Sam 7, and also to Ps 2:7 for appointment to the office of Son of God.

I would suggest that a Davidic descent tradition developed in the context of the spread and increasing attraction of Gentiles to Jesus Christ associations. The object was to prevent the heavenly status of Jesus as the Son of God from floating completely in the air uprooted from the earthly Jesus. The claim of Davidic descent gave to Jewish sensibility an appropriate etiology of the resurrected Son of God, making it possible to find a place within a Judaic imagination for a network of communities that engaged an increasingly Gentile constituency by thinking of the heavenly appointment of the founder figure as a Davidic heritage. It was especially the language of 2 Sam 7 and related texts that was called upon to prevent this dissociation of the heavenly Christ from the earthly Jesus.[105] In Pauline texts the present rule of Christ drew especially on the language

---

[102] Cf. 2 Tim 2:8; Luke 1:32–34, 69; Acts 2:30; 13:23; Rev 22:16; John 7:42. In John, the expectation of the Davidic descent of the Messiah can reflect the ignorance of the crowd and point at the same time to the believer's knowledge of the transcendent origin and destiny of Jesus. Qumran references to a Davidic Messiah also make use of scriptural metaphors and images but do not refer to the Son of David; cf. *Ps. Sol.* 17.21; and see Pomykala, *Davidic Dynasty Tradition,* 180–216.

[103] Duling, "Promises to David," 68, emphasis original.

[104] Ibid., 77.

[105] On the importance of 2 Sam 7 in the project of Christian domestication of scripture, see, in addition to Duling's article on "Promises to David," the chapter on "Christ the King" in Juel, *Messianic Exegesis,* 59–88.

of Pss 110:1 and 2:7 (1 Cor 15:25; Rom 8:34),[106] but it is not messianic prophecies that Paul excavates. As Richard B. Hays has shown, Paul's hermeneutical strategies are not christocentric, but ecclesiocentric.[107] It is therefore consonant with his own labors that the Hellenistic Jew, Paul, should draw on this same Davidic etiology at the conclusion of the catena of scripture in Rom 15:12 in order to imagine how God's faithfulness to the patriarchs finds fulfillment in the risen Christ's rule over the Gentiles: "The root of Jesse shall come, the one who rises to rule the Gentiles" (Isa 11:10 LXX).

Conclusion

It is the achievement of the canonical Gospels to have conceived of Jesus as an ideal figure of the past by imagining his life as the coming of a figure of expectation. The achievement was adumbrated in several distinctive ways in the Jesus Christ associations. As a figure of the heavenly realm, *christos* came into the world at the opportune time according to a divine plan of salvation. Or, from a different perspective, Jesus Christ, appointed Son of God by virtue of his resurrection, is the earthly Jesus born of the seed of David. The former pattern mirrors the descent of divine messengers; the latter provides an etiology for the rule of the heavenly Christ in language associated with the promises to David. But it is only in the redactional stages of certain Jesus traditions that we begin to see the efforts to portray the earthly Jesus as a figure of expectation. In the later stages of Q we have the query whether Jesus is the one who is to come. The catenae of feeding and healing miracles in Mark and John portray Jesus as a type of Moses or Elijah. The redaction of earlier chreiai in Mark associates Jesus with David.

The writing of a *bios* is an attempt to portray an ideal figure. However, the reputation of Jesus was neither sufficiently widespread nor sufficiently removed from the time of the Gospel writers to make it either easy or natural to construct an ideal portrait. What compensates for this lack is the characteristic perspective of the Gospels to portray Jesus as a figure of ancestral expectation. With a few strokes of the pen, the writer of the Gospel of Mark has set John and Jesus in the context of prophetic

---

[106] On the use of Ps 110 in the development of Christology, see, in addition to Hay, *Glory at the Right Hand*, the chapter on "Christ at the Right Hand" in Juel, *Messianic Exegesis*, 135–50; and W. R. G. Loader, "Christ at the Right Hand—Ps. CX. 1 in the New Testament," *NTS* 24 (1977–78): 199–217.

[107] See Richard B. Hays, *Echoes of Scripture in the Letters of Paul* (New Haven: Yale University Press, 1989).

expectation. But given the pre-Markan traditions noted above, one suspects that much experimentation went on in an effort to find the right characterization for the writing of a biography of Jesus. It may finally have been the already well-established use of *christos* as a byname for Jesus that was decisive in this effort. The term had several advantages. It carried the sense of a royal figure who acted with divine authority and thus could serve as a critique of the recently failed collaboration of Roman and Judean rule, a critique that the use of the term occasionally conveys in Jewish writings of the Roman period. By taking a term that had epic precedence and applying it to the characterization of Jesus as a title for a well-known figure of expectation, the Gospel writers were able to forge a link with the authority of a past epoch and to create the aura of novelty demanded by a change in the status quo. This was a quite remarkable achievement, considering that Jesus was a person of marginal reputation from the recent past.

CHRISTOS AS NICKNAME

Barry S. Crawford

How did Jesus become Christ? The usual answer is that this happened in two stages.[1] In the first stage, the term *christos* (χριστός, the Greek translation of the Hebrew *māšîaḥ* = Aramaic *məšîḥāʾ*, "anointed one") was applied to Jesus (probably in its original Hebrew or Aramaic form) by the earliest Palestinian Christian community in Jerusalem as a title of majesty designating Jesus as the expected Davidic hero who would restore the fortunes of Israel and bring salvation to the Gentiles.[2] Opinion is divided on how Jesus came to be thought of in such terms. Some think it was because he was crucified as a messianic pretender, though he made no such claims himself.[3] On this view, it was Jesus' opponents who introduced the idea of Jesus' messiahship, which his first followers then embraced as a fitting expression of his status as founder of their movement. Others believe it was through reflection on key scriptural texts, such as Ps 110:1 or Isa 61:1, that Christians came to think of Jesus as Messiah.[4] Perhaps the most common explanation is that it was Jesus' resurrection that gave him his messianic credentials, or at least singled him out as the one destined to be revealed as Messiah in the future.[5] Whatever the actual process, most

---

[1] For a helpful summary of the issues involved in describing these stages and tracing their development, see George MacRae, "Messiah and Gospel," in *Judaisms and Their Messiahs at the Turn of the Christian Era* (ed. Jacob Neusner et al.; Cambridge: Cambridge University Press, 1987), 169–85.

[2] Modern students of the historical Jesus find little warrant for tracing the use of the term *māšîaḥ/christos* back to Jesus himself. See, e.g., John Dominic Crossan, *The Historical Jesus: The Life of a Mediterranean Jewish Peasant* (San Francisco: HarperSanFrancisco, 1991); E. P. Sanders, *Jesus and Judaism* (Philadelphia: Fortress, 1985).

[3] See, e.g., Nils Alstrup Dahl, "The Crucified Messiah," in *Jesus the Christ: The Historical Origins of Christological Doctrine* (ed. Donald H. Juel; Minneapolis: Fortress, 1991), 27–47.

[4] On Ps 110:1, see David M. Hay, *Glory at the Right Hand: Psalm 110 in Early Christianity* (SBLMS 18; Nashville: Abingdon, 1973). On Isa 61:1, see A. E. Harvey, *Jesus and the Constraints of History* (Philadelphia: Westminster, 1982), 136–53. Barnabas Lindars, *New Testament Apologetic* (London: SCM, 1961), remains basic to the study of early Christian use of scripture.

[5] Typical is Rudolf Bultmann's remark, made a half-century ago, on the original meaning of faith in Jesus' resurrection: "Indeed, that is the real content of the Easter faith: God has

scholars think that the term *christos* (or, more likely, *māšîaḥ*) was originally applied to Jesus as a title, which early Christians used to invoke the constellation of ideas and images surrounding the Jewish hope for the coming of a righteous king from David's house.

In the second stage of the standard view of the route that led from Jesus to Christ, the original titular sense of *christos/māšîaḥ* was no longer retained, and the designation became simply a proper name. Exactly how or why this happened is not entirely clear. The spread of the Christian movement into predominantly Gentile territory in Northern Syria, Asia Minor, and Greece, where Hebrew and Aramaic were alien tongues and converts might not have been as interested in Jesus' messianic status, has been offered as a possible reason for this shift.[6] At any rate, this transformation must have taken place very soon, because already in Paul's letters (composed in the 50s) *christos,* with only one or two possible exceptions, always appears as a proper name, either by itself or in some combination with "Jesus" ("Jesus Christ," "Christ Jesus," "Jesus Christ our Lord"), not as a title identifying Jesus as the Messiah of Jewish expectation.[7]

All this has recently been called into question. In a series of provocative studies, Merrill P. Miller has proposed that the usual explanation of how Jesus became Christ has everything backwards.[8] According to Miller, *christos* was originally applied to Jesus not as a title conjuring up the image of the long-awaited Davidic savior but simply as a second name, a byname or nickname, describing Jesus as the "anointed" founder of a movement formed in his memory.[9] Used this way, the term had little to

---

made the prophet and teacher Jesus of Nazareth Messiah!" (*Theology of the New Testament* [trans. Kendrick Grobel; 2 vols.; London: SCM, 1952–55], 1:43).

[6] Though acknowledging the plausibility of this suggestion, MacRae cautions that Jesus' messiahship can indeed be a major concern in New Testament writings addressed primarily to Gentiles, the Gospel of Luke being a striking example ("Messiah and Gospel," 170).

[7] The possible exceptions are Rom 9:5 and 1 Cor 10:4, but in neither case does the context demand that *christos* be anything other than a proper name. It should also be noted that the presence of the definite article before *christos* in these passages is no indication that the term is to be understood as a title. The presence or absence of the article before *christos* has no bearing whatsoever on whether the term is to be read as a title or a name. As Werner Kramer has shown in his study of Paul's use of *christos,* "it is not permissible to confuse the question of the article with the question of titles" (*Christ, Lord, Son of God* [trans. Brian Hardy; SBT 50; Naperville, Ill.: Allenson, 1966], 211). For more on Paul's use of *christos,* see Nils Alstrup Dahl, "The Messiahship of Jesus in Paul," in *Jesus the Christ,* 15–25; Walter Grundmann, "χρίω κτλ.," *TDNT* 9:540–62.

[8] See Merrill P. Miller, "How Jesus Became Christ: Probing a Thesis," *Cont* 2/2–3 (1993): 243–70. Especially important are two of Miller's working papers for the Seminar, "The Problem of the Origins of a Messianic Conception of Jesus" (in this volume); idem, "The Anointed Jesus" (in this volume).

[9] Miller, "How Jesus Became Christ," 262–64; idem, "Problem of the Origins," 316–17, 325–27.

do with traditional Jewish eschatological expectations. Its chief function, rather, was to express the distinctive ethos and self-consciousness of a community seeking divine authorization for its novel social experiment.[10] Simply put, the group asserted the validity of its new way of life by claiming descent from a divinely anointed (in the sense of "appointed" or "chosen") leader. In Miller's view, it was the Greek form *christos* that was probably used at first, most likely in a mixed Jewish-Gentile community in Syrian Antioch.[11] With the name *christos* firmly in place, Christian groups in Antioch, in growing conflict with local synagogues and utilizing both Jewish and Greek martyrological traditions, then developed the distinctive kerygma of the death and resurrection of *christos* and the cult that surrounded it.[12] This new understanding of *christos* as martyr provided legitimacy for the peculiar Jewish-Gentile mix of a community not wishing to be fully Torah-observant yet still wanting to be identified as an "Israel": the group had God's approval because a divinely sanctioned hero gave his life to establish it. According to Miller, *christos* finally became a full-blown messianic title in still other circles of early Christianity, principally those interested in linking up their stories of Christian beginnings with the Jewish national epic.[13]

Miller's conception of how Jesus became Christ represents yet another bold contribution to the Seminar's project of redescribing Christian origins.[14] For the first time, a compelling case is offered for taking the evidence *as we have it*. After all, Paul's use of *christos* as a proper name comes about a generation before the appearance of the term in the Gospels as a messianic title. Equally important, however, Miller is able to explain the way *christos* was used among various Christian groups in terms that do not require explosions of the numinous from heaven or shattering personal experiences here on earth. Critical moments in Christian beginnings are accounted for without wrapping them in time-worn mystifications insulating them from critical scrutiny.[15] Instead, the process by which Jesus became Christ is seen

---

[10] Miller, "How Jesus Became Christ," 263; idem, "Problem of the Origins," 326–27.

[11] Miller, "How Jesus Became Christ," 262–63; idem, "Problem of the Origins," 326.

[12] Miller, "How Jesus Became Christ," 251–57; idem, "Problem of the Origins," 327–31.

[13] Miller, "Problem of the Origins," 317–24.

[14] See the critical reexamination of the myth of Christianity's origins in Jerusalem in Merrill P. Miller, "'Beginning from Jerusalem...': Re-examining Canon and Consensus," *Journal of Higher Criticism* 2/1 (1995): 3–30; see also idem, "Antioch, Paul, and Jerusalem: Diaspora Myths of Origins in the Homeland" (in this volume).

[15] Typical of these would be claims to the effect that Jesus was somehow "revealed" to his followers as *christos/māšîaḥ* in a dramatic series of postmortem appearances or in mystical experiences of his continued presence at the community's common meals or in radical personal transformations undergone during the conversion process. Far from inviting scholarly study, such claims bring further inquiry to a halt.

to have occurred at particular junctures of social formation and mythmaking in early Christianity, as real people struggled to forge a new sense of meaning and identity in the real world.

The linchpin of Miller's thesis on how Jesus became Christ is his assertion that *christos* was originally a second name for Jesus, not a title designating Jesus as the expected Jewish Messiah. It is important to be clear about what Miller means by this. He is not suggesting that *christos* was merely an ordinary byname or nickname for Jesus, as "Jack" is for John or "Bill" is for William today. Nor is he arguing that by referring to Jesus as *christos,* early Christians were doing no more than what people do today when they call an employer "boss" or a ship's captain "skipper." Miller is well aware that *christos* was more than a colorless appellative substituting for, or attached to, Jesus' real name, that it was instead a term of honor, brimming with Jewish connotations of a divinely appointed leader.[16] The point Miller wants to drive home is that however exalted or luminous a term *christos* might have been, it was not originally applied to Jesus for the purpose of invoking the full panoply of Jewish messianic expectations.[17] According to Miller, those seeking the origins of the term *christos* as a designation for Jesus will find proper analogues "*not* ... in figures of expectation, nor in popular royal claimants, but in *schools* where teachers and disciples are compared and values and authority are sorted out by means of nicknames and honorifics."[18]

This appeal to the practice in antiquity of conferring nicknames on teachers and leaders of philosophical schools requires a closer look. How prevalent was this practice? Under what circumstances would a nickname be given to a teacher—or to anyone, for that matter? Can we reasonably expect this to have happened to Jesus, not only during his lifetime, but, especially, afterward? These questions are crucial to Miller's thesis. If one assumes, along with the majority of scholars, that *christos* was originally a messianic title for Jesus and that over time the title degenerated into a simple proper name, then one has thereby already advanced at least the beginnings of a credible explanation for how Jesus became Jesus Christ. This is, presumably, how Octavian "the August One" became simply "Augustus." However, if one claims, with Miller, that *christos* was originally a nonmessianic nickname for Jesus, given to him after his death by his followers, perhaps in Antioch, then one must be able to demonstrate, not just how *christos* matched the interests of early Antiochene Christians, but that such a thing was likely to have occurred at all.

---

[16] Miller, "Anointed Jesus," 383–409.
[17] Miller, "How Jesus Became Christ," 259.
[18] Miller, "Problem of the Origins," 327, emphasis added.

Nicknames seem to have been widespread in Greco-Roman antiquity.[19] In ancient Greece, where it was customary for both men and women to have only one name, nicknames were quite common. In Hellenistic times, people from all walks of life, from kings (e.g., Ptolemy II "Philadelphus," Antiochus IV "Epiphanes") to slaves (e.g., "Onesimus" ["Useful"]), were known by their nicknames. In ancient Rome, just about everyone (males, at least) had one. In early Roman times, adult males had two basic names: a *praenomen* (the personal name, e.g., Gaius, Lucius, Marcus) and the *nomen* or *nomen gentilicium* (the clan name; e.g., Aurelius, Julius, Lucretius). Hence, "Gaius Julius" and "Marcus Aurelius" were the "full" names of two of the most famous politicians in Roman history. Since the number of both the *praenomina* and the *nomina* was fixed (at about forty for the former and around a thousand for the latter), many people ended up with the same names. This is why many individuals had a *third* name, a cognomen, or nickname, added to the two they already had. These *cognomina* could represent a host of things about the person: from distinguishing physical features (Albinus, "White-haired"; Longus, "Tall One"; Naso, "Big-nosed"), to occupations and offices (Pictor, "Painter"; Censor, "Magistrate"), to geographical locations ("Africanus," "Asiaticus"), to qualities of a more abstract nature (Felix, "Happy"; Lepidus, "Elegant"; Tacitus, "Silent"). While many Romans gained notoriety under their clan names (e.g., Ovid, Horace, Virgil), a surprising number are known to us chiefly by their nicknames: e.g., Caesar ("Hairy"), Cato ("Wise One"), Cicero ("Chickpea").

Important figures in early Christianity were also given nicknames. Simon was called "Peter," the "Rock" (Mark 3:16); James and John Zebedee, the "Sons of Thunder" (Mark 3:17); Thomas, the "Twin" (John 20:24); and Joseph, Paul's traveling companion from Antioch, was better known as "Barnabas," a term Acts wants us to understand as "Son of Encouragement" (Acts 4:36). It is Miller's contention that Jesus had a nickname too, that it was *christos,* and that it was given to him in a way similar to how founders and leaders of philosophical schools in Mediterranean antiquity were given nicknames by their students or admirers. It is to the search for such analogues that we now turn.

Diogenes Laertius's *Lives of Eminent Philosophers* is a compendium of eighty-two biographies of ancient Greek philosophers, beginning with Thales of Miletus (ca. 580 B.C.E.) and ending with Epicurus (341–270 B.C.E.). Since Diogenes mentions philosophers who lived in the third century C.E.

---

[19] See *The New Century Classical Handbook* (ed. Catherine B. Avery; New York: Appleton-Century-Crofts, 1962), 755–56, s.v. "nomen"; Theodore John Cadoux, "Names, Personal," *The Oxford Classical Dictionary* (ed. N. G. L. Hammond and H. H. Scullard; 2nd ed.; Oxford: Clarendon, 1970), 720–21.

(Theodosius the Skeptic, Sextus Empiricus, and Saturninus), he is usually dated somewhere around 225–250 C.E. Diogenes' *Lives* is important not so much for the historical value of the information it provides, or because of its penetrating analyses of the views of the philosophers cataloged in its pages, but because it often turns out to be our only source on key figures and moments in ancient Greek philosophy.[20] For the most part, Diogenes' biographies are entertaining collections of anecdotes and aphorisms illustrating the character or temperament of his subjects, rather than serious presentations of their lives or philosophical ideas. In the process, however, we do learn something of importance for the question before us, namely, that a great many philosophers were given nicknames (at least Diogenes thinks so)—and in ways that appear to derive from their prowess as great thinkers or as founders or leaders of philosophical schools. Among the many cases in which a philosopher named by Diogenes is said to have had a nickname, the following may be mentioned.[21]

- Acron: known as the "Physician" (8.65).
- Aeschines: the philosopher Timon, whose biography is included in the *Lives* and whom Diogenes often cites, called Aeschines "the Might of Aeschines" (2.62). We also learn that Aeschines' only disciple, a certain Aristotle (not the famous one), was nicknamed "Mythos," or "Story" (2.63; cf. 5.35).
- Alexinus of Elis: called "Elenxinus" (Ἐλεγξῖνος), or "Wrangler," because of his love of controversy (2.109).
- Anaxagoras: nicknamed "Nous," or "Mind," according to Timon (2.6).
- Antisthenes: sometimes credited with founding the Cynic movement. Called a "'Hound' pure and simple" (6.13, 19). Socrates used to swear by "the Dog" (probably Antisthenes; (7.32).
- Apollodorus: the *Lives* includes three references to someone called Apollodorus, each time with a different nickname: the

---

[20] "Diogenes has acquired an importance out of all proportion to his merits because the loss of many primary sources and of the earlier secondary compilations has accidentally left him the chief continuous source for the history of Greek philosophy" (Herbert S. Long, "Introduction," in *Diogenes Laertius: Lives of Eminent Philosophers* [trans. R. D. Hicks; 2 vols.; LCL; Cambridge: Harvard University Press, 1972], 1:xix).

[21] References to the *Lives* are given by book and section number. Included are not only those philosophers given separate treatment in individual biographies bearing their names but figures Diogenes mentions only in passing. To keep things manageable, the list given here is limited to nicknames directly related to the philosopher's vocation as thinker, teacher, or founder-leader of a school of disciples.

"Calculator" (8.12), the "Grammarian" (8.52), and the "Tyrant of the Garden" (10.25). Is this one person with three nicknames or three different individuals?

+ Apollonius: known as "Cronus." His pupil Diodorus was also called "Cronus" (2.111, 112).
+ Archelaus: called the "Physicist" (2.16, 19).
+ Aristippus: called the "King's Poodle," or "Royal Cynic," by Diogenes of Sinope (2.66). Aristippus's grandson (also named Aristippus) was known as "Mother's Pupil" (2.83, 86).
+ Aristotle: Diogenes regards "Peripatetic" as a nickname for the philosopher himself, not just his school (5.2).
+ Bion of Borysthenes: known as the "Theodorean" from the school he joined (4.23).
+ Chrysippus: called "Crypsippus" (Κρύψιππος), or "Horse-hidden," by Carneades, because he was a small man and his statue was hidden by that of a horse (7.182).
+ Cleanthes: nicknamed "Phreantles" (Φρεάντλης), or "Well-lifter," because he supported himself by drawing water from a well (7.168). His industry also won him the name "Second Heracles" (7.170). He was something of a dullard, however, and his fellow-pupils called him the "Ass" (7.170).
+ Crates: called the "Cynic" (2.117; 6.93). Also known as the "Door-opener" (6.86).
+ Democritus: nicknamed "Wisdom" (Σοφία), according to Favorinus in his *Miscellaneous History* (9.50).
+ Diogenes of Sinope: with Antisthenes he was credited with founding the Cynic movement. Diogenes was widely known as the "Dog" or "the Cynic" (6.33, 40, 46, 55, 60, 61, 77).
+ Dionysius: pupil of Zeno of Citium. Dionysius was called the "Renegade," as well as the "Spark," because he defected to the "doctrine of pleasure" (5.92; 7.23, 37, 166).
+ Empedocles: called the "Wind-stayer" because he once cleverly checked the violent Etesian winds (8.60).
+ Epicurus: called the "Schoolmaster's Son" by Timon because he followed in his father's footsteps (10.3).[22]
+ Epimenides: gave himself the nickname "Aeacus," or "Wailer," probably because of dire predictions against Athenians and Lacedaemonians (1.114).

---

[22] Noting that the "Schoolmaster's Son" means "a schoolmaster like his father before him," R. D. Hicks points out that "patronymics were used of persons engaged in hereditary occupations" (*Diogenes Laertius*, 2:530–31 n. c).

- Eudoxus: known as "Endoxus" ("Ἔνδοξος), or "Illustrious," because of his brilliant reputation (8.91).
- Hegesias: pupil of Diogenes the Cynic; nicknamed "Dog-collar" (6.84).
- Heraclides: inscribed the name "Thespis," or "Inspired One," on tragedies he wrote (5.92).
- Heraclitus: called the "Physicist" (8.6).
- Lyco: some altered his name to "Glyco" (Γλύκων), or "Sweet One," because of the sweetness of his voice (5.66).
- Menedemus: called a "Cynic" and a "Humbug" by the Eretrians (2.140).
- Menippus: called a "Cretan hound" and a "Money-lender on daily interest" by Diogenes (6.99, 100).
- Metrocles: called the "Cynic" (2.102).
- Pausanius: called Ἡρακλειτιστής, or the "Imitator of Heraclitus" (9.15).
- Phocion: a hearer of Diogenes the Cynic; called Χρηστός, or "Excellent One" (6.76).
- Plato: this famous philosopher's real name was Aristocles. Diogenes reports that he was given the nickname "Plato" by Ariston, the Argive wrestler, on account of his robust figure. However, Diogenes also indicates that the name could refer to Plato's broad forehead or, more important for our purposes, to the breadth of Plato's hermeneutical style (διὰ τὴν πλατύτητα τῆς ἑρμηνείας οὕτως ὀνομασθῆναι; 3.4).
- Pythagoras: this too was probably a nickname. According to Diogenes, Aristippus of Cyrene stated that this philosopher was named "Pythagoras" (Πυθαγόρας) because "he uttered the truth as infallibly as did the Pythian oracle" (ὀνομασθῆναι ὅτι τὴν ἀλήθειαν ἠγόρευεν οὐχ ἧττον τοῦ Πυθίου; 8.21).
- Strato: known as the "Physicist" (5.58, 61).
- Thales: the first to receive the name of "Sage" (σοφός; 1.22, 39).
- Theodorus: known as the "Atheist" and subsequently as "God" (2.86, 100, 116; 4.52; 6.97).
- Theophrastus: a disciple of Aristotle, his real name was Tyrtamus. Aristotle renamed him "Theophrastus" (Θεόφραστος, "God-like speech") because of his graceful style (5.38).
- Xenophon: earned the name of the "Attic Muse" because of the sweetness of his narrative (2.57). Xenophon's two sons were called the "Dioscuri" ("Sons of Zeus"), after Zeus's twin sons Castor and Pollux (2.52).
- Zeno of Elea: Plato called him the "Eleatic Palamedes," after the name of a proverbially clever and cunning inventor (9.25).

From this list it would appear that Diogenes (whose own name "Laertius" may be a nickname derived from a Homeric formula for addressing Odysseus as "Son of Laertes") thought it the rule that Greek philosophers would come to have nicknames, many of them based on some trait or quality the philosopher exhibited during his career. It is impossible to know, however, whether each and every name listed above as a nickname actually was one, that is, a widely known and commonly used substitute for the philosopher's given name. For example, Diogenes tells us that Timon referred to Aeschines as the "Might of Aeschines," but did Timon do this on a regular basis, and did anyone else follow him in this? "Might of Aeschines" could have been strictly Timon's epithet for this philosopher and, moreover, one he seldom used.

On the other hand, it seems clear that most of the names listed above as nicknames can be safely taken as such; that is, they reflect more than merely one writer's way of referring to this or that philosopher but are instead alternate names that worked their way into common parlance. "Plato," "Theophrastus," and probably "Pythagoras," for example, were not only genuine nicknames in this sense, but they actually eclipsed the philosophers' real names. Mention could also be made of Diogenes of Sinope, who was often called simply the "Cynic," the "Dog," and who was apparently in the habit of referring to himself that way (*Lives* 6.33, 55, 60, 61).

The list also indicates that philosophers were commonly given nicknames stemming directly from their involvement in the discipline of philosophy.[23] Indeed, the name by which one of the most illustrious philosophers of all time is known—Plato—may have come from the way he went about his work. Diogenes himself may have been of the view that Plato's gymnastics coach gave him this name because of his powerful physique. Yet Diogenes' tantalizing reference to Plato's "breadth of hermeneutical style" as an alternative explanation for his nickname raises the very real possibility that "Plato" became this philosopher's name because of the range of skills he brought to bear in examining and interpreting important philosophical issues.[24]

---

[23] This was not always the case, however. Diogenes tells us that a certain Alcaeus gave the philosopher Pittacus (a portly man, apparently) several nicknames: "Clubfoot," "Chapped-foot," "Braggart," "Paunch," "Potbelly," "Diner-in-the-Dark" (a reference to sloppy table manners?), and "Slob" (*Lives* 1.81). None of these unflattering monikers seems to be related to the occupation of philosophy.

[24] It may be unrealistic to expect certainty with regard to the precise circumstances in which an individual first receives a nickname. Exactly how, for example, did Lawrence Peter Berra come to be known as "Yogi"? A recent PBS documentary on Yogi's life and career in baseball ("It's Déjà Vu All over Again," hosted by Bob Costas) offers competing versions of

Diogenes' report that Democritus was nicknamed "Wisdom" ("Sophia") may offer an important analogue to what transpired in some circles of early Christianity with regard to reflection on the person and work of Jesus. In the group (or groups) that produced the Sayings Gospel Q, for example, Jesus was thought to be the embodiment (or child) of Wisdom (e.g., Luke 7:35 // Matt 11:19). Q speaks of Jesus in such terms because of his message, his teaching, not because of his saving death and resurrection, which play no role in Q. Similarly, Democritus is given the name "Wisdom" because of his accomplishments as a deep thinker and teacher. One wonders what transformations Democritus's image would have undergone if those who named him "Wisdom" had been able to call upon Jewish wisdom theology, as the Q people did when contemplating the meaning of Jesus' teaching, to enhance the power and authority of their teacher's words.

The evidence of Diogenes' *Lives* would thus appear to be generally supportive of the view that Jesus may have become *christos* in the way Miller argues, that *christos* was originally Jesus' nickname as founder of a movement based on his teaching. As for why the particular designation *christos* was chosen rather than some other epithet, such as *basileus* ("King"), *kyrios* ("Lord"), or *sōtēr* ("Savior"), Miller suggests that it was because of the *novelty* of the term (especially if used in its Greek form), which matched the novelty of the group that was in the process of forming itself, a group that wanted to be an "Israel" without the traditional Jewish identity markers.[25]

Recent research on Jewish messianic expectations indicates that the term *christos* (or *māšîaḥ*) would indeed have been a novel choice. William Scott Green has shown that the so-called Jewish messianic hope—to say nothing of the messianic title itself—was simply not a widely attested or uniformly consistent category in early Jewish thought.[26] In Green's view,

---

how he acquired his name. Yogi's family and acquaintances in St. Louis say he got it from his supposed physical resemblance to a Hindu character in a movie he and his friends saw. Yogi himself believes that he was first called Yogi during a neighborhood sandlot baseball game as he sat cross-legged (i.e., in a lotuslike posture) on the bench, waiting his turn at bat.

[25] Miller, "How Jesus Became Christ," 263–64; see also idem, "Anointed Jesus," 385.

[26] William Scott Green, "Introduction: Messiah in Judaism: Rethinking the Question," in Neusner et al., *Judaisms and Their Messiahs,* 1–13. In the Hebrew Bible, the term "Messiah" always refers to a present or past historical figure, never to a future savior. In the few noncanonical texts that do use the expression to point to a future deliverer (e.g., *Psalms of Solomon, 1 Enoch, 4 Ezra, 2 Baruch,* the Dead Sea Scrolls), a homogeneous portrait does not emerge. See J. H. Charlesworth, "From Jewish Messianology to Christian Christology: Some Caveats and Perspectives," in Neusner et al., *Judaisms and Their Messiahs,* 225–64; idem, "From Messianology to Christology: Problems and Prospects," in *The Messiah: Developments in Earliest Judaism and Christianity* (ed. James H. Charlesworth;

"the primacy of 'the messiah' as a subject of academic study derives not from ancient Jewish preoccupation, but from early Christian word-choice, theology, and apologetics."[27] Thus, *christos/māšîaḥ*, though in origin a Jewish term, may have been a peculiarly Christian designation, rich in meaning to Jesus' followers but not especially significant to outsiders. Far from being the incendiary bomb—socially, politically, or religiously—it is often thought to have been, *christos* might have been a relatively innocuous nickname (or title) to bestow upon Jesus. The mere invocation of the term *christos* by early Christians might not have alarmed anyone about a dangerous threat in their midst to the social, political, or religious order.

The nickname *christos/māšîaḥ* could therefore have been applied to Jesus just about anywhere Christians thought of themselves as constituting a novel social formation whose legitimacy stemmed from a divinely appointed founder, teacher, or leader—even in Jerusalem. As to where this happened first, Miller offers a pretty compelling case for Syrian Antioch, and he may be right. After all, even the author of Luke-Acts, who wants to have everything originate from Jerusalem, acknowledges that it was in Antioch, not in the city he chose as center and source of the movement, where the disciples were (said to be) first called *christianoi* (Acts 11:26).

Some concluding words of caution are in order. Although Diogenes' testimony about how various philosophers got their nicknames offers intriguing analogues to the way Miller imagines Jesus became Christ, there do not appear to be any cases in which the match is exact. This absence of congruity is especially obvious in the following two areas. First, as we have seen, Miller is of the view that Jesus was called *christos* not so much because of what Jesus himself was or did or said, but because of forces at work in the social formation of the group gathered together in his name: the Jesus (or Christ) people called their founder *christos* as a way of securing divine authorization for their movement; the social experiment in which they were engaged was legitimate because God himself had "anointed" their leader expressly to get such a movement started. In Diogenes' *Lives*, on the other hand, nicknames are given to philosophers because of some trait or quality they themselves exhibited or were thought to possess. For example, Plato himself was (or was thought to be) in some sense "broad," Democritus "wise," Lyco "sweet-voiced," and so forth. Nowhere in Diogenes' *Lives* does there appear to be an instance in which a philosopher is given a nickname as an expression of the social

---

The First Princeton Symposium on Judaism and Christian Origins; Minneapolis: Fortress, 1992), 3–35.
[27] Green, "Introduction: Messiah in Judaism," 4.

dynamics of the school or group to which the philosopher's disciples belonged. Is this lack of fit of little consequence, or does this represent a serious problem for Miller's thesis?

Second, and perhaps more important, Miller maintains that the nickname *christos* was conferred upon Jesus after his death, most likely by a group of his followers in Syrian Antioch. With the possible exception of Chrysippus, who was called "Crypsippus" ("Horse-hidden") because his statue was hidden by that of a horse (I am assuming here that Chrysippus's statue was some type of memorial), and the note that Plato was called the "*divine* Aristocles" in an inscription on his tomb (*Lives* 3.43), every philosopher chronicled in Diogenes' *Lives* who was given a nickname apparently received it while still alive. How customary was it for a nickname to be given to a dead person from the recent past? Miller's case would be greatly strengthened if sufficient evidence of posthumously awarded nicknames could be found.

These two caveats highlight the need for more work to be done on nicknames in Greco-Roman antiquity. Who knows? There may be much to learn about how Jesus became Christ by probing further into the question of how he got his nickname.

From Messiahs to Christ:
The Pre-Pauline Christ Cult in Scholarship

Christopher R. Matthews

If Jesus never possessed a messianic consciousness of divine mission, nor spoke of the coming, or present, "Son of Man," nor was executed as a messianic pretender—as is maintained by radical criticism untroubled by historical arguments—then the emergence of Christology, indeed, the entire early history of primitive Christianity, is incomprehensible.[1]

Some advance the following reasoning as an argument from history: The Church's belief in the messiahship of Jesus is comprehensible only if Jesus was conscious of being the Messiah and actually represents himself as such—at least to the "disciples." But is this argument valid?[2]

This essay takes a selective look at how the pre-Pauline Hellenistic Christ cult came to be assumed in the history of scholarship. A cursory examination of opinion from the time of the Enlightenment suggests a rather straightforward answer. Virtually all researchers apart from certain Deists accept as a matter of course some type of messianic consciousness on the part of Jesus, frequently in connection with the Son of Man title, which is often taken to indicate the human nature of Jesus (or his action on the part of humanity). Although Jesus' own understanding of his messianic status is often said to have been badly misunderstood and consequently transformed by the disciples, nevertheless some form of messianism (even if not, e.g., the "original," spiritual messianism of Jesus) is thought to be available for mediation at the start via the first Christian community in Jerusalem. Thus, for example, such scholars as Hermann Samuel Reimarus, Georg Lorenz Bauer, Heinrich Eberhard Gottlob Paulus,

---

[1] Martin Hengel, "Jesus, the Messiah of Israel: The Debate about the 'Messianic Mission' of Jesus," in *Authenticating the Activities of Jesus* (ed. Bruce Chilton and Craig A. Evans; NTTS 28/2; Leiden: Brill, 1999), 327.
[2] Rudolf Bultmann, *Theology of the New Testament* (trans. Kendrick Grobel; 2 vols.; New York: Scribner's, 1951–55), 1:26.

Friedrich Schleiermacher, August Neander, Heinrich Ewald, David Friedrich Strauss, Johann Leonhard Hug, Ernest Renan, and Theodor Keim all presume some form of "messiahship" for Jesus.[3] Consequently, there was no impetus to raise the question of the origin of Christ devotion in pre-Pauline Hellenistic circles. William Wrede is apparently the first critical scholar to assert that the life of Jesus was "unmessianic."[4] A review of the thought of Wilhelm Bousset and Rudolf Bultmann on this topic may serve to typify the stance of historical-critical research during the first part of the twentieth century.

CHRIST AND SON OF MAN

To turn to Bousset's *Kyrios Christos* or Bultmann's *Theology of the New Testament* to gain an appreciation for how the Hellenistic Christ cult came to be assumed in scholarship is to encounter crucial presuppositions that remain essentially unexamined in their respective presentations. Although these scholars hardly can be labeled "uncritical" in their attempts to explicate the earliest beginnings of Christianity, their analyses are rooted in several key assumptions that determine the subsequent course of their reconstructions. Their casual acceptance of the "Jerusalem church" and confidence in their ability to delineate the intellectual history of the "Palestinian primitive community" (primarily on the basis of the Synoptic Gospels and Acts) allow ample space for a subsequent project of reimagination.

---

[3] I have relied on William Baird (*From Deism to Tübingen* [vol. 1 of *History of New Testament Research*; Minneapolis: Fortress, 1992]) for succinct presentations of the views of all these scholars (and more). Though Reimarus is certain Jesus identified himself as the Messiah (using Son of Man to indicate his humanity) who would inaugurate God's kingdom on earth, he supposed that after Jesus' death the disciples put forward a new conception of the Messiah borrowed from Jewish apocalyptic (171–72). Bauer traced Jesus' self-perception as Messiah to the Son of Man title in Dan 7 (190). Paulus identified Jesus' messianic consciousness in spiritual terms so that Jesus' adoption of Daniel's Son of Man title "represented the spiritual and rational aspects of a universal humanity" (203). For Neander, Jesus was conscious of his messianic calling by the outset of his public ministry and used Daniel's Son of Man title to designate the nature of his messianic status (237). Ewald connects Jesus' messiahship with the "idea of the celestial Messiah ... developed by Daniel and Enoch" (289). For Hug, "Jesus was unique, a Messiah different from Jewish expectation" (334). According to Keim, Jesus called himself the Son of Man, and the disciples recognized him as Messiah at Caesarea Philippi (386–87). Helpful summaries of opinion on this topic may also be found in Walter P. Weaver, *The Historical Jesus in the Twentieth Century: 1900–1950* (Harrisburg, Pa.: Trinity Press International, 1999).

[4] Werner Georg Kümmel, *Introduction to the New Testament* (trans. Howard Clark Kee; rev. ed.; Nashville: Abingdon, 1975), 89–90; John K. Riches, *A Century of New Testament Study* (Valley Forge, Pa.: Trinity Press International, 1993), 22–23.

BOUSSET

Already with his second sentence, Bousset reveals the controlling role that the Lukan conception of the Jerusalem church plays in and behind the scenes of his analysis:

> However disputed the questions about the so-called self-consciousness of Jesus may be, still it can be taken as fully assured that the community in Jerusalem from the very first was united on the basis of the conviction that Jesus of Nazareth was the Messiah who was to be expected by the Jewish people.[5]

Not noticing how much he has already taken over, Bousset immediately rules out Acts as a useful source to aid in the determination of the nature of the messianic conception (political or transcendent) applied by the primitive community to Jesus. Instead one must turn to the Synoptic tradition, where "especially in its older stratum" one may find the "work of the Palestinian primitive community":

> We shall have to assume a priori that the community of Jesus' disciples has deposited in the gospel tradition its faith and its view of the messianic meaning of the person of Jesus, even when it has frequently only repeated genuine material of its master's messianic self-expressions and has not created something. For the gospel tradition is sketched from the first from the standpoint of a community of messianic faith and for the purpose of bearing witness to this messianic faith.[6]

Bousset then proceeds to examine the messianic titles applied to Jesus in the Gospels to ascertain in what sense the early community identified Jesus as the Messiah. He assumes that the "most general and to Jewish messianology the most familiar title Χριστός" appears "in part in good historical tradition" (Mark 8:29; 14:61; 15:32),[7] to which Acts also bears witness (e.g., 2:31, 36; 3:18, 20; 4:26; 5:42; 8:5; 9:22). Yet "that Jesus was the Χριστός to his first disciples is indeed guaranteed quite apart from this."[8]

In accord with the majority of his predecessors, Bousset determines that it is particularly with the Son of Man sayings that "we have before us

---

[5] Wilhelm Bousset, *Kyrios Christos* (trans. John E. Steely; Nashville: Abingdon, 1970), 31.
[6] Ibid., 33.
[7] "We can hardly help conjecturing that the tendency of the messianic secret has also colored the scene at Caesarea Philippi. That does not mean that, as Wrede was inclined to assume, the whole scene is fabricated. The messianic confession of Peter will have to stand as historical. But unfortunately, through the retouching tendency of the evangelist, the answer of Jesus has been lost to us" (ibid., 108).
[8] Ibid., 34.

the deposit of the theology of the primitive community."[9] Moreover, "the Jewish transcendent Messiah picture of the Son of Man and the historical experience of Jesus' suffering and death, completely suffice in and by themselves to account for the messianic faith of the first Christian community in its genesis."[10] Well, not quite, since Bousset has already made it clear that appearances of Jesus as well as the latter's charismatic nature have had a decisive effect:

> The first community of the disciples of Jesus viewed him as the Messiah, in that they, half-consciously rejecting the Son-of-David ideal, adapted to him the Jewish apocalyptic figure of the Son of Man.... We may suspect that the Messiah–Son of Man idea was approximately as ancient in the primitive community as the belief in Christ itself. The messianic faith of the primitive community *could* be formed after the death of Jesus in no other form than that of the ideal of a transcendent Messiah.... Very soon, after the disciples of Jesus grasped the daring faith that in spite of his suffering and death Jesus was the promised Messiah, their messianic faith will have taken on the form of the expectation of the Son of Man.... The tradition as it is given in its purest form by Paul in I Cor 15 tells us that the disciples, particularly and first of all Peter, had a series of visions in which they saw Jesus and through which they came to the conviction that he was still alive.... The driving force was the incomparable, powerful, and indestructible impression which Jesus' personality had left behind on the souls of his disciples.... But then it was further of tremendous importance that in the contemporary apocalyptic a ready-made image of the Messiah had been created which appeared to hold the clue to the entire perplexing riddle which the disciples had experienced.... The first Christian community was gathered around the conviction that Jesus is the Messiah–Son of Man.[11]

Bousset obviously presupposes the "thoroughly eschatological character of the primitive Christian community,"[12] which is fixated on the coming of the Son of Man.

Even though it is the Fourth Gospel that contains the "Son-of-Man dogma of the primitive community in the clearest fashion,"[13] Bousset turns to the Synoptics to reconstruct the primitive community's picture of Jesus. Since the Markan passion narrative "represents the most ancient kernel of a coherent tradition of the 'life' of Jesus," and because "it is wholly dominated

---

[9] Ibid., 42.
[10] Ibid., 56.
[11] Ibid., 49–51, emphasis original.
[12] Ibid., 51.
[13] Ibid., 52.

by the messianic idea," it may be concluded that "it is a witness of faith of the first rank which the primitive community here gives."[14] While Bousset's analysis is critical insofar as he attempts to show "how the messianic thrust of the community tradition has rewritten history,"[15] it is naive to the extent that nearly the entire Gospel tradition can be called upon to illustrate the activities of the "primitive community." Diachronic considerations are almost completely submerged in his synchronic demonstration. Thus one can turn to Luke 22:67 (εἰ σὺ εἶ ὁ Χριστός, εἰπὲ ἡμῖν) under the assumption that "Luke stood somewhat nearer to the historical state of affairs with its account" than Mark.[16]

It is obvious that for Bousset the Christ cult was mediated to the Hellenistic church by the primitive community.[17] When one examines Paul's letters in order to reconstruct the basic convictions of the Hellenistic communities, one finds that

> the old titles which have dominated the community's faith in Christ almost completely disappear. In the Pauline era the title "Christ" is about to change from a title into a proper name. To be sure a sensitivity for the titular nature of the term still appears to hold sway in that Paul almost always says Χριστὸς Ἰησοῦς (the Christ-Jesus) and only rarely Ἰησοῦς Χριστός, and that where a second title appears, he places the name "Jesus" in the middle: κύριος Ἰησοῦς Χριστός, υἱὸς (Θεοῦ) Ἰ[ησοῦς] Χρ[ιστός]. But basically the title "Christ" in Paul no longer has an independent life.[18]

---

[14] Ibid., 70, 71.

[15] Ibid., 72.

[16] Ibid., 74, adding this supporting appeal to psychological criteria: "And the restrained way in which Jesus answers the (first) question about messiahship in Luke, and the way in which he refers to his identity with the Son of Man only in an oblique manner, may still best be understood psychologically."

[17] Without the "messianic faith of the primitive community" Paul's conversion "remains psychologically incomprehensible" (ibid., 119).

[18] Ibid., 121. This observation is later confirmed by Werner Kramer (*Christ, Lord, Son of God* [trans. Brian Hardy; SBT 50; Naperville, Ill.: Allenson, 1966], 214, emphasis original): "We find, however, within the Pauline corpus a particular linguistic tradition which is pre-Pauline and which could never have arisen without the awareness that *Christ* was originally a title. Paul speaks of *the Lord Jesus Christ*, of *our Lord Jesus Christ*, and of *the Lord Jesus*, but not of *the Lord Christ*. Similarly, Paul uses the formulae 'in the *Lord Jesus Christ*' and 'in *Christ Jesus our Lord*,' but not 'in *Christ the Lord*' (ἐν Χριστῷ κυρίῳ). In all these instances *Lord* and *Christ* never stand immediately side by side.... This can surely not be accidental. Moreover, if we take into consideration that *Lord* is a title and that *Christ*, as a translation of 'Messiah,' originally ranked as a title, it is natural that the two titles were not made to follow immediately upon one another. It remained customary to keep them apart, so much so that the custom was still followed, even when all awareness of the original significance of *Christ* as a title had disappeared. So the custom survives as a witness to something forgotten."

Of course, at this point in his investigation Bousset turns his full attention to the κύριος designation, which becomes dominant in the cultus of the Christians. "It is, in fact, the *Hellenistic* community in which this development so important for the history of religions took place, through which, out of the future Messiah Jesus, the present cult-hero as Kyrios of his community came into being."[19] Thus it is clear that the "personal Christ piety of the apostle Paul arose on this foundation of the Kyrios faith and the Kyrios cultus in the Hellenistic primitive Christian communities."[20]

BULTMANN

Unlike Bousset, Bultmann accepted Wrede's judgment on the post-Easter origin of the messiahship of Jesus.[21] Since Jesus' life and work in the Synoptic tradition were not shaped according to "traditional messianic ideas" and Paul did not understand it as messianic, Bultmann locates the origin of Jesus' messiahship in and with belief in the resurrection.[22] Moreover, it was *"Easter faith in Jesus' resurrection"* that enabled the church to recognize that "Jesus' coming itself was already eschatological occurrence. Indeed, that is the real content of the Easter faith: God has made the prophet and teacher Jesus of Nazareth Messiah!"[23] In Bultmann's existentialist analysis, Jesus' call or demand for decision implies a Christology that becomes "explicit in the earliest Church to the extent that they understood Jesus as the one whom God by the resurrection has made Messiah, and that they awaited him as the coming Son of Man."[24] Thus the earliest church "is conscious of being already the called and chosen Congregation of the end of days," and "the kerygma of Jesus as Messiah is the basic and primary thing which gives everything else—the ancient tradition and Jesus' message—its special character."[25] Bultmann's analysis is, therefore, determined by positing the "unique" orienting power of "Easter faith," which gives rise to the eschatological consciousness of the earliest church. The latter simply made explicit what was implied in Jesus' Christology-evoking call to decision.

---

[19] Bousset, *Kyrios Christos*, 136, emphasis original, adding: "The *Son of Man* of the primitive community stems from Jewish eschatology and remains an eschatological entity.... He is the future Messiah who is to come in glory, and the fundamental attitude of his disciples is the fervent expectation of his coming. But the *Kyrios* of the Hellenistic primitive community is a being who is *present* in the cult and in the worship" (151, emphasis original).

[20] Ibid., 153.

[21] Rudolf Bultmann, "Die Frage nach dem messianischen Bewusstsein Jesu und das Petrus-Bekenntnis," *ZNW* 19 (1919–20): 165–74; Peter's confession is from the perspective of Easter.

[22] Bultmann, *Theology of the New Testament*, 1:26–27.

[23] Ibid., 43, emphasis original.

[24] Ibid., 43–44.

[25] Ibid., 42.

The task of delineating more precisely the circumstances surrounding the application of the title Messiah to Jesus by the earliest church (i.e., the "Palestinian church") is not pursued by Bultmann as a discrete matter for investigation. Recourse to the title is taken for granted at an early stage as a logical deduction on the part of Easter faith. But when the term Χριστός enters the milieu of "Hellenistic Christianity," its significance recedes into obscurity, and so it continues solely as a proper name. Although it is clear that Paul inherited the title, he employs it almost exclusively as a proper name. "For Paul, 'Lord' and not 'Christ' is Jesus' title."[26] And so more broadly "in place of the titles 'Son of Man' and 'Christ' (= messianic king), which are dying out, there appears in the Hellenistic congregations the *title* '*Kyrios,' Lord*."[27]

Apart from dispensing with the idea of the messianic self-consciousness of Jesus, Bultmann's assessment is rather similar to that of Bousset. In line with the majority of their predecessors (and successors), the figure of the Messiah and that of the Son of Man are inextricably linked. Thus when Bultmann refers to "the messiahship of Jesus" (see the epigraph, above, with n. 2), he adds the clarifying note: "Disregarding the distinction between Messiah and Son of Man; after all, both mean the eschatological bringer of salvation."[28]

CHRIST AND JESUS

To illustrate the typical treatment of the topic currently, I turn now to the sixteenth and final chapter of Gerd Theissen and Annette Merz's *The Historical Jesus,* which treats "The Historical Jesus and the Beginnings of Christology."[29] After broaching the principal problems that arise in discussions of Christology and the historical Jesus (the Easter gulf, the break in the tradition, Jesus' consciousness of his authority), they first present a schematic review of scholarship on Jesus' messiahship since Reimarus.[30] This results in summary characterizations of "moderate historical criticism," which "assumes an explicit, evoked and implicit christology for Jesus himself (especially for the titles Messiah and Son of Man),"[31] and "more radical

---

[26] Ibid., 80; cf. 49, 64.
[27] Ibid., 124, emphasis original.
[28] Ibid., 26.
[29] Gerd Theissen and Annette Merz, *The Historical Jesus: A Comprehensive Guide* (trans. John Bowden; Minneapolis: Fortress, 1998), 512–67.
[30] Ibid., 514–20.
[31] Ibid., 523. The categories are defined as follows: "*Explicit christology*: possibly Jesus himself expressed his authority with a christological title.... *Evoked christology*: possibly Jesus already aroused christological expectations among others during his lifetime.... *Implicit*

historical criticism," which "denies Jesus all titles." In the latter case the titles Messiah and Son of Man are understood to have been transferred to Jesus in "Palestinian Jewish primitive Christianity."[32] Thus, according to this assessment all critics would seem to agree that the titles Messiah and Son of Man were current in the "primitive community," whether or not they had been utilized by Jesus. As was the case in previous scholarship, there is no reason to formulate the question of the origin of the Christ cult in Hellenistic Christianity; that is, there are no perceived gaps in the presumed historical scenario. Since the messianic identity of Jesus from the start is a datum of the primitive community—whether by inheritance or innovation—it is assumed to be readily available to all subsequent Christian groups.

Theissen and Merz use the next part of chapter 16[33] to expand on the christological possibilities for the historical Jesus by considering: Jesus the charismatic—implicit Christology in the historical Jesus (e.g., use of the "amen" formula, use of emphatic "I" as in Matthew's antitheses, forgiveness of sins); Jesus as Messiah—evoked Christology in the historical Jesus; and Jesus as Son of Man—the question of an explicit Christology in the historical Jesus. Under the rubric "Jesus as Messiah," they first locate the derivation of the term "Messiah" in connection with the anointed figures of the Old Testament (kings, high priests, and prophets), while its content originates from texts that do not use the term "Messiah" but refer to the "expectation of a saving king who will defend Israel against his enemies and bring peace (Isa. 8.23–9.6; 11.1ff.; Micah 5.1ff.; Zech. 9.9f.)."[34] Next they distinguish among "four forms of eschatological and messianic expectations":[35] eschatological expectation of messianic figures with the term "Messiah";[36] eschatological expectation of messianic figures without the term "Messiah";[37] the usurping of messianic expectations by political

---

christology: possibly Jesus expressed his status without a title, but in fact fulfilled the conditions of a 'Messiah'" (520–21, emphasis original).

[32] Ibid., 523, specifying that moderate historical criticism allows that the Kyrios and Son of God titles are "post-Easter transferences of Old Testament/Jewish traditions to Jesus," while more radical interpreters locate this transference in "Hellenistic-pagan primitive Christianity."

[33] Ibid., 523–53.

[34] Ibid., 532. They list (533) the following as texts interpreted secondarily in a messianic sense: Gen 49:10 (see LXX rendering; 4QCommGen A [4Q252] frg. 1 v 1–5); Num 24:17 (CD vii 19–21); 2 Sam 7:12–16 (4QFlor [4Q174] iii 10–13); Ps 2 (4QFlor [4Q174] iii 18–19; *Ps. Sol.* 17.23–24, 30); Amos 9:11–12 (4QFlor [4Q174] iii 11–13).

[35] Ibid., 533; cf. 533–37.

[36] Texts cited (ibid., 534–35) include: CD ii 12; xii 23; xiv 18–19; xix 10–11; xx 1; 1QS ix 9–11; 1QSa ii 11–12; 4QCommGen A (4Q252) frg. 1 v 1–5; 4QMessAp (4Q521) frg. 2 ii 1; 11QMelch (11Q13) ii 14–25; 1 Sam 2:10 (LXX); *Ps. Sol.* 17–18; *1 En.* 48.10; 52.4.

[37] Texts cited (ibid., 536) include: Dan 7:14; *1 En.* 90.9ff., 37–38; *Sib. Or.* 3.49–50, 286–87, 652–53; Philo, *Praem.* 95; *T. Levi* 18; *T. Judah* 24; Josephus, *Ant.* 20.9.1 §200.

rulers;[38] and eschatological expectations without a messianic figure.[39] Then after suggesting that "messianic hopes were alive among the people—probably more alive than appears from the sources"—they conclude that "it is historically probable that Jesus was confronted with them."[40] Moreover, on the basis of the sayings tradition, the narrative tradition, and the formula tradition in the letters of Paul,[41] they advance the following hypothesis:

> Jesus had a messianic consciousness, but did not use the title Messiah. He aroused messianic expectations among the people and among his followers, and because of that was executed as a royal pretender. After Easter his disciples attributed a new messianic dignity to him as the suffering Messiah whose death had saving significance.[42]

Yet at the same time they insist that:

> It is historically improbable that the title Messiah was transferred to Jesus only after Easter.... The title Messiah would have been unsuitable for interpreting a life which focussed on the cross and resurrection.... Therefore the title Messiah must already have been associated with Jesus if it was to live on after Easter: it could not have interpreted the cross

---

[38] Texts cited (ibid., 536–37) include: 1 Macc 14:4–15 on Simon; Josephus, *Ant.* 15.11.1 §§380–87 on Herod I.

[39] Texts cited (ibid., 537) include: *Jub.* 23; Bar 2:34–35; 4:36–37; 5:5–6; Tob 13:11–17; 14:4–7; *As. Mos.* 10:1–10.

[40] Ibid., 537, 538.

[41] Sayings tradition: Mark 9:41; Matt 16:20; Luke 4:41; Matt 23:10; Luke 24:26; narrative tradition: Mark 8:29 (cf. 10:46–52; 11:10); 14:51; 15:26 (cf. 15:32); formula tradition: Rom 5:6, 8; 1 Cor 15:3ff.; etc. (ibid., 538).

[42] Ibid. A selection of additional citations illuminates the thinking behind the hypothesis: "That historically Jesus confronted messianic expectations is suggested by the fact that very different circles express similar expectations or fears: on the one hand followers (Mark 8:29; 10:46f.; 11:10) and on the other opponents (Mark 14:61; 15:26)" (538–39). "In our view, the saying about the Twelve who will rule over Israel [Matt 19:28 par.] shows that Jesus took up messianic expectations but did not endorse them by using a messianic title.... Jesus is so terse about the 'messianic' title, not because he rejected it but because he was more than a Messiah: he gave the status and dignity of a Messiah to others. He reshaped the messianic expectation which was focussed on an individual into a 'group messianism'" (539–40). "Jesus must have been confronted with a messianic expectation above all in the trial before Pilate. For the *titulus* on the cross shows that he died as a Jewish royal pretender. Probably this messianic expectation also played a part in the deliberations of the Sanhedrin in which the charge against Jesus was prepared. If Jesus was executed as a royal pretender, one thing is certain: he did not distance himself from the messianic expectations of his followers (and the corresponding fears of his opponents) before his accusers and judges" (540).

and resurrection, but the cross and resurrection could have given it a deeper meaning.[43]

> From a post-Easter perspective the *title Messiah* was associated with Jesus even more closely than before. Now Jesus was not just confronted with messianic expectations; he became the Messiah. The messianic expectations had been fulfilled in him, albeit in a paradoxical way, through suffering and death.[44]

Moving on to Jesus as Son of Man, Theissen and Merz assume that Jesus "most likely" used the term self-referentially, even though it is unclear how it is to be understood.[45] They conclude, after covering the evidence for the various types of sayings, that it is "most probable [that] Jesus spoke of both the present and the future Son of Man.... An everyday expression which simply meant the human being or a human being was evaluated in 'messianic' terms by Jesus."[46]

In the next section and the conclusion to the chapter[47] the function of Easter faith in the analysis of Theissen and Merz is clearly expressed in a manner with ample precedent:

> The origin of christology can be understood only if already before Easter there was a debate over a claim to an exalted position (implicit, evoked or explicit) which was confirmed in the resurrection by God.[48]

If Messiah was a title attributed to Jesus by others prior to his death, "after Easter the title of Messiah ... was taken up as 'Son of God' and developed further to great effect," while Son of Man, which Jesus himself had invested with messianic connotations, receded.[49] The "acclamation of Jesus as 'Kyrios' was the most far-reaching innovation after Easter."[50]

In their "Retrospect: A Short Life of Jesus,"[51] Theissen and Merz affirm a quite traditional image of the culmination of Jesus' life. Jesus' disruption

---

[43] Ibid., 540. Theissen and Merz advert frequently to the "Emmaus disciples" (Luke 24:13–35; taken in rather realistic terms!) to explain the process of reinterpretation that the title Messiah undergoes in light of the death of Jesus (cf. 541, 553, 555).

[44] Ibid., 562, emphasis original.

[45] Ibid., 542.

[46] Ibid., 552–53.

[47] Ibid., 553–63.

[48] Ibid., 553.

[49] Ibid., 556. Of course, the Son of Man title also has to be accommodated to the suffering of Jesus, resulting in the passion predictions (557).

[50] Ibid., 560.

[51] Ibid., 569–72.

of the temple provoked the aristocracy to move against him with political charges, accusing him of seeking power as a royal pretender.

> In fact many among the people and his followers expected that he would become the royal Messiah who would lead Israel to new power. Jesus did not dissociate himself from this expectation before Pilate. He could not. For he was convinced that this God would bring about the great turning-point in favour of Israel and the world.... After his death Jesus appeared first either to Peter or to Mary Magdalene, then to several disciples together.... They recognized that he was the Messiah, but he was a suffering Messiah, and that they had not reckoned with.[52]

Christ and Cult

A more sophisticated approach to the topic without explicit focus on the Christ title nevertheless would place its origin at the very start of the history of the Jesus peoples. Here Christ comes in via a ritual meal imagined as a messianic banquet. Helmut Koester highlights the close association of story and cult in the emergence of the Roman Empire as well as in the history of Israel as crucial contexts for understanding the history of Christian beginnings.[53] Jesus, who carried on John the Baptist's announcement of the imminent reign of God, was crucified by Pilate as "the king of the Jews" on the day before Passover around 30 C.E. The earliest sources for what happened after this are the letters of Paul. Since Paul's "calling as an apostle must be dated no later than the year 35 CE, possibly earlier," he "clearly belongs to the first generation and is the sole surviving contemporary witness to the earliest developments." With this early date in hand, Koester concludes that such traditional formulae as appear in Paul's letters "may be dated to the very first years of the new Jesus communities."[54]

In 1 Cor 11:23–25 Paul traces the eucharistic "ritual of the community," with its reference to an archetypal last meal of Jesus with his disciples, to "the Lord." This coordination of the community's ritual meal and Jesus' last meal in fact stands as an element of continuity with the historical Jesus. Since there is "good evidence" that "Jesus celebrated common meals with his disciples and friends," Koester finds it likely that at some point "these common meals were understood as an anticipation of the messianic banquet."[55]

---

[52] Ibid., 571–72.
[53] Helmut Koester, "The Memory of Jesus' Death and the Worship of the Risen Lord," *HTR* 91 (1998): 335–50.
[54] Ibid., 343, 344.
[55] Ibid., 344, 345. That such an anticipation was possible is substantiated by the meal practice of the Essene community as well as the eschatological nature of the meal prayers in

He judges that the "eschatological component" of the eucharistic traditions preserved in the *Didache* as well as in 1 Cor 10–11 and Mark 14 "derives directly from Jesus himself." The "eucharistic prayers of the *Didache,* as well as the words of institution, belong to the earliest period of the formation of Christian communities and may well predate the first collections of Jesus' sayings."[56] Does this imply that no documentation can be found (e.g., Q¹) to overturn the portrait of the gathering of the earliest followers of Jesus as gatherings of messianists?

Koester locates the "fixed tradition" of the words of institution that Paul received in the "Hellenistic community of Antioch," while the *Didache* was "at home early in Syria and Palestine," perhaps even Jerusalem.[57] However, one may trace the tradition still further, behind the tradents of the putative "Palestinian community," for "there is no reason to doubt that all three elements" of the ritual tradition, "the eschatological outlook, the understanding of the bread as symbol of the community, and the cup as symbol of the new covenant have their origin in meals that Jesus celebrated, in particular in his last meal before his death."[58] This would seem to open the door to tracing the origin of the use of the Christ title directly to Jesus, whether explicitly or implicitly.

Paul also draws on a received tradition connected to the death of Jesus in 1 Cor 15:3–7. In both 11:23–25 and 15:3–7, "the formulations quoted by Paul as tradition already presuppose not only an institutionalized ritual but also larger contexts of narrative and interpretation."[59] Thus "close linguistic parallels" between the former texts and Isa 53 suggest that the latter "was part of the liturgy of the eucharist."[60] Further, "Paul's reference to 'the night in which he was handed over' also reveals that both the apostle and the Corinthian community knew an entire story about Jesus' death and suffering—otherwise, the mention of a specific time would not make sense."[61] All of this suggests that

---

Did. 9–10 (345 n. 28). The Last Supper "reports" (Mark 14:22–25 par.; 1 Cor 11:23–26) and the stories of miraculous feedings (Mark 6:30–44 par.; 8:1–10; John 6:1–14) confirm a "messianic banquet" interpretation (345 nn. 26–27).

[56] Ibid., 345.

[57] Ibid., adding: "The close connection of the *Didache*'s eucharistic prayers with Jewish meal prayers points to a Jewish Christian community in Jerusalem or Galilee" (345 n. 31).

[58] Ibid., 346.

[59] Ibid., 347.

[60] Ibid., 347, 348. Nearly thirty years ago in a dissertation directed by Koester, Sam K. Williams concluded with reference to Isa 53 (*Jesus' Death as Saving Event: The Background and Origin of a Concept* [HDR 2; Missoula, Mont.: Scholars Press, 1975], 229) that "it is not until Hebrews and I Peter that one finds an assured allusion to that chapter or an adoption of its phrases in connection with the meaning of Jesus' death for sinful men."

[61] Koester, "Memory of Jesus' Death," 348.

the earliest tangible presence of Jesus must therefore have been the story of his suffering and death. It utilized the tradition and language of the ancient scriptures of Israel in order to narrate an eschatological event in the context of a cultic action that was rooted in a ritual practice instituted by Jesus himself. It was in this ritual and story that the earliest Christian communities established their relationship to the history of Jesus.[62]

Koester concludes by identifying the pattern of story and ritual "with the establishment of a political community and the formation of its religious foundation":

> The new understanding of the significance of Jesus' celebration of common meals in anticipation of the "messianic banquet" and the story of his suffering and death provided the constitutive elements for the self-definition of the community as a new nation and of its claims to eschatological fulfillment of the hopes of all people.[63]

CHRIST AND COMMONWEALTH

Burton L. Mack shares a number of significant starting points with Koester and even certain conclusions. He agrees that Paul's letters are "precious" early evidence, "full of small bits of material that bear the marks of cultic formation"—notably 1 Cor 11:23–26 and 15:3–5.[64] Further, he accepts that the early Jesus movements continued Jesus' practice of eating together[65] and that "the primary symbols of the meal (wine and bread) became ritualized moments for remembering Christ's death."[66] Moreover, he suggests that "what happened, apparently, was the transformation of a Jesus movement into a religious association on the model of a mystery cult with political overtones."[67] However, he avoids any supposition that gatherings for common meals were construed as anticipations of a "messianic banquet." Rather, gathering for common meals is taken as an indication that "social formation ... on the association model" had taken place, and this in turn provides the key for understanding the supper text.[68]

---

[62] Ibid.
[63] Ibid., 348, 349.
[64] Burton L. Mack, *A Myth of Innocence: Mark and Christian Origins* (Philadelphia: Fortress, 1988), 98–100.
[65] Ibid., 82–83.
[66] Ibid., 100.
[67] Burton L. Mack, *Who Wrote the New Testament? The Making of the Christian Myth* (San Francisco: HarperSanFrancisco, 1995), 96.
[68] Ibid., 90.

Mack argues that the scene in 1 Cor 11:23–25 "assumes that the death of 'the Lord Jesus' was a martyrdom."[69] Instead of explaining community ritual by drawing various lines of continuity with the practice of Jesus, he focuses his attention on "a new social experiment under pressure to give an account of itself." It is here that he locates "a critical juncture in the social history of the Jesus Christ association."[70] "The need to justify the inclusion of gentiles called forth a venture in mythmaking that shifted attention away from Jesus the teacher and his teachings to focus on his death as a dramatic event that established the movement's claim to be the people of God."[71] Further development of such assumptions led to the conclusion that "Jesus' death was a 'sacrifice' that sealed a 'covenant' that founded the Christian community, and the Christian community acknowledged that foundation by making of their common meal a memorial of that sacrifice."[72] Instead of an almost immediate cultic formation after Jesus' death, Mack reconstructs a longer period of social formation and "intellectual labor."[73] If the martyr myth emerged as the earliest Christology[74] only as a result of that intellectual effort, and 1 Cor 11:23–26 is the resulting "etiological legend," then the Gospel accounts of the Last Supper represent the later historicizing of this etiology,[75] when the event "imagined" to have happened in history ("the night in which he was handed over") was fleshed out.[76]

In his analysis Mack endorses Sam K. Williams's demonstration that early Christian thinking about the death of Jesus was fundamentally connected with Hellenistic-Jewish martyrology along the lines of 4 Maccabees. Mack notes that "the distinction between 'sinners' and 'the righteous' was a common shorthand formula in some Jewish circles for Gentiles and observant Jews." Then he highlights Williams's treatment of Rom 3:25–26 and the latter's demonstration that "it was the distinction between sinners (Gentiles) and the righteous (Jews) that was addressed."[77] But since Williams does not "press the logic all the way," Mack goes on to sketch "the argument implicit in the application of the martyr myth to Jesus":

> The argument was that, if Jesus' death could be regarded by God as a demonstration of Jesus' *pistis,* and the God in question were the God of

---

[69] Ibid., 88.
[70] Mack, *Myth of Innocence,* 108, 109.
[71] Mack, *Who Wrote the New Testament,* 86.
[72] Ibid., 90.
[73] Ibid., 86.
[74] Mack, *Myth of Innocence,* 109 n. 8.
[75] Ibid., 120 with n. 15.
[76] Ibid., 121–22.
[77] Ibid., 109.

Israel and righteousness, then all those who shared Jesus' *pistis* also were justified. One sees that the event, thus theologized, points both ways—to Israel's God and history, as well as to the association of Jesus people.[78]

Unlike Williams, Mack insists that the early martyrology underlying Rom 3:25–26 is about Jesus, not Christ.[79] How, then, does the Christ title enter the picture? It may be an attempt to call upon traditional biblical language to designate Jesus as selected and approved by God.[80] Or, if Jesus had been "religious" and conversant with "ethical and theocratic ideals,"[81] perhaps it makes sense that the Christ title was introduced "by Jewish members in the course of trying out ideas about Jesus as the sovereign ('king') of the 'kingdom' he had founded."[82] In short order, however, "the title Christ became a personal name used mainly to refer to the one whose death and resurrection founded the community as a saving event."[83]

* * * * *

Although there is ample reason to conclude that Christ was taken by Gentiles in the Pauline period as a personal name, it would appear to be difficult to dispute that "*Christ* was originally the translation of 'Messiah' and as such must have had 'titular' significance."[84] That documentation exists for various messiahs in one of the cultures of context for the early Jesus peoples might suggest that the identification of Jesus as the Christ represents a moment of self-definition. How significant a moment and what the definition (or "spin") entails may be left as items for discussion.

---

[78] Ibid.

[79] Mack, *Who Wrote the New Testament*, 85. Compare the last sentence in Williams's book (*Jesus' Death as Saving Event*, 254), which reads: "Because God regarded Christ crucified as a means of expiation for all men (Rom. 3:25), Gentile as well as Jew could now confess: 'Christ died for our sins' (I Cor. 15:3)."

[80] Mack, *Who Wrote the New Testament*, 84.

[81] Mack, *Myth of Innocence*, 73–74.

[82] Ibid., 111.

[83] Ibid., 100.

[84] Kramer, *Christ, Lord, Son of God*, 212, emphasis original; see n. 18 above.

WHY *CHRISTOS*? THE SOCIAL REASONS
Burton L. Mack

As all of you know, I have been working on a social theory of religion to help me understand Christian beginnings. The concept of social interests has appealed to me as a way to talk about collective motivations that might be identified, and our co-chairs have asked me to see if I could bring any of that to bear upon the pre-Pauline groups within which the use of *christos* must first have occurred. Merrill P. Miller's paper is basic.[1] He not only spread out the range of connotations and uses for the term *christos* both within and without early Christian literature but also was able to argue that its function as a name in Paul's letters must mean that the term was used as a name (or cognomen) among those from whom Paul learned about the new movement. In his earlier paper,[2] Miller argued convincingly that my location of the emergence of the term in the process of working out the so-called Christ myth was wrong. I have agreed with him on that, which means that I can no longer assume the logic of the Christ myth or the social situation that logic addressed to imagine the social locus for thinking the thought of Jesus as an anointed one.

In my efforts to locate such a moment, I have taken seriously the two constraints that Miller's work has presented. One has to do with the connotations of the term *christos*. The first usage was not titular, not royal, not eschatological, and not martyrological. It was instead a byname drawing upon the attribution of a general connotation of a social leadership role (unspecified) as a way of asserting that Jesus was "okay" in God's view (something like "God's choice ['anointed'] for the task and times"). As a matter of fact, Miller has made it possible to think of the "messianic" connotation (the customary assumption that *christos* was the royal title for a figure of expectation in both early Jewish and early Christian literature and mentality) as the *end* result of a series of moves in early *Christian* mythmaking. One can easily imagine several discrete moments in this

---

[1] Merrill P. Miller, "The Problem of the Origins of a Messianic Conception of Jesus" (in this volume).
[2] Merrill P. Miller, "How Jesus Became Christ: Probing a Thesis," *Cont* 2/2-3 (1993): 243-70.

elaboration: from the open-ended attribution involved in its use as a cognomen (the moment we are trying to locate); through attachment to a martyrology first imagined for Jesus (not thought of in relation to "the Christ" attribution); to Paul's cosmic and corporate expansions of the Christ figure; Mark's royal eschatology; and the cipher that *christos* became in the second century that packed it all into a dense symbol of generation. It would be possible, I think, and necessary for the longer-range goals of our project, to work out the social situation and mythic rationale for some of these moments. In keeping with Miller's arguments, I plan now to focus solely on the problem of locating the moment of the pre–Christ myth.

The second constraint has to do with the social situation. If the term *christos* was already in use before the Christ myth was created, one cannot assume that it was triggered by the need to "justify" a social group composed of Jews and Gentiles (the social situation addressed by the logic of the Christ myth). Neither can it be imagined as a group on the model of the Jesus movements within which the term was not used. This means, I think, that the location we seek must be a social formation somewhere between a Jesus movement and a Christ-myth group.

Making no apologies for trying to imagine such a locus without direct textual documentation, it seems to me that a very plausible junction of social formation and thinking can be described. Antioch will do as a location as long as we do not allow the more advanced connotations of the Christ myth (and/or "cult") to influence our construction of the social situation. In addition, the Jesus movements can provide us with a point of departure if only we are able to mark the difference indicated by the use of the term *christos* when it appears. This at least has been the way I have gone about my attempt to imagine the social situation in which the term *christos* was first used. My provisional observations are as follows.

I went back to my earlier musings on the ways in which the figure of Jesus was enhanced within the various Jesus movements. I have argued that these enhancements could all be explained as appropriate for the founder-teacher of a school-like movement in which the cultivation of his teachings was the main interest. Three characteristics of these movements seem to be important for our present considerations. One is that a certain kind of group formation did take place in which mutual recognition of belonging was possible and in which differences from other immediately contingent groups were marked as borders of distinction. Another is that all of the several enhancements of the importance of Jesus appear as suggestions for ways of thinking about him, not as overt claims accompanied by specific titles and designations. As such, it was enough for these several movements to attribute to him speech and to cast him in roles that reminded one of Moses, Elijah, a prophet, a teacher, a scribe, or a sage. A third feature common to these groups can be granted when it is seen that this form of mythmaking reveals a general familiarity with what I have been calling the epic of Israel. This means that all of these groups in the Jesus movements thought of themselves, wanted to think of themselves, or wanted to give an account of themselves to others as a formation with legitimate claim to being okay within the range of Jewish configurations of the time. I confess to not having given enough thought to this feature of the Jesus movements when pursuing the Cynic analogies to the earliest stages of the teachings traditions. I did acknowledge this feature in my *Continuum* article[3] as the most important observation for being more precise about the ethos and mentality of these groups. I cannot say that I have made much progress on this front, but a reconsideration of Galilean demography would certainly be the way to go. My pressing for a "Galilee of the Gentiles" was a justifiable strategy, I think, as a way to parry the traditional "critique from within" theories of Christian origins and the need for traditionalists to argue that Galilee was incorporated into the Maccabean kingdom and therefore "Jewish." However, Miller has helped me see that the better way to set the scene for the early Jesus movements in Galilee would be to work out the various ways in which peoples of the Levant and in the various Jewish (Judean) and Samaritan diaspora communities made their claims upon the heritage of "Israel." Since Galilee was on the border between "homeland" and "diaspora" locations, and since its "Jewishness" under the Hasmoneans must have suffered second-class status similar to that of the Idumeans, and since its mixed ethnicities must have been an important factor when regrouping as Jesus people, the implicit claim of the Jesus movements to being okay in the light of Israel's epic has to be seen as a very significant index of social formation in great need of more study. In such a demographic circumstance it need not have been at first a matter of claim, contention, apology, argument, precision, or defense. However, it could easily have become the term with which a Jesus school began to look at and think about itself, especially if challenged. I suggest that this redescription of the Jesus groups can help us to locate the moment and circumstance in which Jesus people in Antioch began to refer to Jesus as *christos*.

To refer to Jesus as *christos,* whether as cognomen or adjectively, is both similar to and different from the other ways in which the Jesus movements linked Jesus up with the epic of Israel. It is similar in that it would not be a claim for a specific social role called for in the present time by means of a particular reading of the epic tradition. It would, however, be different in that thinking of Jesus as having been "anointed" would be more than a suggestion of a way to think about him. It would be an

---

[3] Burton L. Mack, "A Myth of Innocence at Sea," *Cont* 1/2 (1991): 140–57.

explicit claim to the importance of his role as a figure of recent history whose appearance not only fit with but continued the sense of divine purpose (unspecified, but) implicit to the epic. As such, calling Jesus *christos* would be a claim that he was "God's choice" for the social role of founder-figure of the Jesus movements and an implicit claim that the Jesus-movement formation should be thought of as a way of being "Israel." I find such a reconstruction thoroughly plausible, given the way in which epic designations, readings, theologies, and ideal figures were being reconfigured at the time by Jewish intellectuals. I have argued that this kind of activity was the way in which contemporary social issues were being critically analyzed and new social arrangements proposed and justified. What might that say about the social situation of the Jesus people daring such a thought?

It would say that the Jesus people found themselves in a social setting where it was important to make explicit their claim to the heritage of Israel, that they were not only not to be counted out but that they should be recognized as a group with credentials. Being careful not to read in all of the subsequent history of identity contestation between the congregations of the Christ and the diaspora synagogues in Antioch and beyond, the questions that would have been raised in an urban setting of association with a diaspora synagogue can easily be understood. One need not think that the social circumstance included the kind of challenge and contestation that called for the Jesus martyrology or even that the ethnic mix of the Jesus association had become the critical social issue. Needing to give an account of oneself as a Jesus group in the process of forming an association would be enough. To draw upon the heritage, attraction, and resources of the synagogue while cultivating the teachings of Jesus as a separate association could well have created circumstances in which the thought of Jesus as *christos* was first suggested. Note, too, that the diaspora-homeland distinction with which Miller was able to mark different perspectives on Jerusalem would work as well to account for a heightened interest in the Israel question once a Jesus group formed in Antioch. And if all of this makes sense, investments in a social formation can be imagined that could easily account for the further enhancements indicated by the Jesus martyrology and the Christ myth when the issue of ethnic inclusion became critical.

I would like now to take up my assignment, asking whether my theory of social interests might help us understand the investments people obviously made in this new (Jesus-) *christos* association. In my outline paper[4] I

---

[4] Burton L. Mack, "The Christian Origins Project: A Description in Outline" (paper presented at a joint session of the Ancient Myths and Modern Theories of Christian Origins

referred to two different types of evidence for the concept of social interest. The major emphasis was upon the systems of signs and patterns of practices that cultural anthropologists have analyzed for traditional societies. The reasons for building upon this set of data should be obvious. I wanted to get outside the Western frame of reference in order to argue that myths and rituals ("religion") could also be understood as systems of signs and patterns of practices created collectively because of social interests. The second type of evidence was a brief appeal to the reader to call upon what we know from personal experience in our time, namely, that, although we have taken social interest for granted and not given it a name, our roster of terms for personal interests assumes social existence as the interest that underlies all personal manifestations. I should probably note the difference in the types of society from which these two sets of data are taken and acknowledge that neither matches the social configurations of the Greco-Roman age. In the outline paper I simply said that all of the traditional social interests were in evidence in the early Christian groups, even though these groups were subcultural formations and not fully orbed productive societies. The question that interests me now is whether these differences in society types threaten my concept of social interest and its application to Greco-Roman social formations. But I do not want to be misunderstood, as if the problem here is that personal interests are hampered in traditional societies and that the social interests structural to traditional societies no longer influence the way we relate. Neither is true. Yet the social shape and circumstance of a people do affect the way in which social interests are noticed, expressed, ranked, and cultivated. So what about the special circumstances of the Greco-Roman age?

I have always thought that a wide-angle lens on the Greco-Roman age would quickly highlight its distinctive features and that these features should be in mind as we attempt to understand what we are calling social experimentation. The age of the ancient Near Eastern empire was at an end. The Alexandrian conquests unleashed three hundred years of cultural imposition accompanied by unrelenting military activity in and among all the districts ruled by his so-called successors. Kingships were dismantled, societies fragmented, peoples displaced, and cultures that did not match were nevertheless poured together into a big mixing bowl. It thus became a setting for social experimentation.

Many of the marks of social and cultural interests taken by peoples during this period are familiar to us, though, to my knowledge, we have not treated them as data and evidence for social experimentation. Such

---

Seminar of the Society of Biblical Literature and the North American Association for the Study of Religion, Boston, Mass., November 1999).

would be the emergence of associations, the many ways in which diaspora institutions were constructed, the founding of *poleis* throughout the Levant, what we have called the "mystery cults," various kinds of enclaves such as the one at Qumran, social-modeling activity on the part of intellectuals and authors, creating networks of hospitality, taking interest in cultural differences and remarking both the concept of *ethnos* and its many applications. The list could easily be expanded, for many of the social forms and professional traditions customary for the old empires were revised in response to the new set of circumstances. Further, social relations of importance for the social structures of the Hellenistic age, such as "friendship," were conceptualized, defined, discussed, and taken up into larger systems of philosophic and ethical instruction. I spell this out for two reasons. One is that it takes the edge off the aura of the avant-garde that early Christian social formation has always had in Christian interpretation. The other is that it allows us nonetheless to recognize features of the social experimentation of the time that really do mark it as different from traditional societies. The most relevant of these for our attempt to describe early Christian social formation is, I think, the formation of clubs, associations, and other subcultural institutions. These were not fully orbed, productive societies but were nevertheless social units capable of maintaining fundamental loyalties to ethnic, national, and cultural traditions. The diaspora synagogue may be the prime example. If all of this is so, one cannot expect the list of social interests manifest in the several systems of signs and patterns of practices definitive for traditional societies to work the same way.

This means, I think, that a range of associations should be in mind as we try to isolate the interests at work in the formation of early Christian groups. As Stephen G. Wilson has laid it out for us, there were several kinds of common interests around which associations formed.[5] Since all of these may be seen as social interests, the point would be to notice that, given the circumstances, a given interest or cluster of interests was enough to provide for social formation, and an appropriate rationale was enough to sustain and cultivate the life of the group. As subcultural units, the members of these associations did not cease living in their larger social arenas, but they may well have been aware of the way in which their social loyalties and values were fragmented and ranked because of the several social orders they had to negotiate in the everyday. In my outline paper I got as far as suggesting that the early Christian lived in two worlds, cultivating mainly the social interests of belonging to a "family" with claim to the

---

[5] Stephen G. Wilson, "Churches as Voluntary Associations" (paper presented at the Annual Meeting of the Society of Biblical Literature, Boston, Mass., November 1999).

heritage of "Israel." The question has been whether such a social interest makes sense at all, and whether it is enough to account for all of the energies, activities, and mythic creations these societies produced.

My answer, of course, is yes. And I think it a remarkable coincidence that the lack of documentation for the first use of the *christos* epithet leaves me with social identity as the only social interest to surface at this reconstructed site. There is, of course, more to be said about the significance of social identity as an interest as soon as the change in setting from Galilee to Antioch is accepted, the epic anchor seen, and the Israel idea involved. If we now flesh out just a bit of the subsequent but still pre-Pauline developments at Antioch, the social-identity interest receives even greater specification and the social-interest thesis greater cogency.

A next step window into the mythmaking activity of these Jesus-Christ people would be their attribution of a martyrdom to Jesus. The evidence for this is the pre-Pauline material in Rom 3:25–26 as studied by Sam K. Williams[6] and David Seeley[7] and the fact that the martyrology of the Christ myth makes better sense as an elaboration of a Jesus myth than as an event ascribed to a *christos* of any kind. What may have triggered such a remarkable meditation? Well, if the synagogues in Antioch were the place where a diaspora perspective on the Hasmonean period produced the Maccabean martyrologies, as some scholars have argued, a martyrdom for Jesus to support the claims of the Jesus association would certainly be thinkable and not nearly as desperate and dramatic a move as it might otherwise appear. Here also features of the Jesus association that required identity justification become clear. The issue was clearly the "justification" of the group from God's point of view (the ultimate vantage point in mythmaking). Comparing Jesus to the Hasmoneans would have required a bit of chutzpah, to be sure, for at first the leadership roles that came to mind would not have matched well. But merely to suggest a martyrdom for Jesus (at the hands of the Romans?) would have triggered a much more interesting and inventive set of intellectual reflections about the Jesus association than the (somewhat later elaborated) Christ myth would have (with its unlikely assertions built in as rationale). In any case, "justification" may well have covered the inclusion of Gentiles, but that need not have been the only issue. Loyalty to a Jesus association based on teachings that did not expressly call for a Torah *ethos* or (priestly?) purity code would have created challenge enough. Thus, whether the issue was "Jesus people" in

---

[6] Sam K. Williams, *Jesus' Death as Saving Event: The Background and Origin of a Concept* (HDR 2; Missoula, Mont.: Scholars Press, 1975).

[7] David Seeley, *The Noble Death: Graeco-Roman Martyrology and Paul's Concept of Salvation* (JSNTSup 28; Sheffield: Sheffield Academic Press, 1990).

general or the inclusion of Gentiles in particular, forming an association with claims upon the heritage of "Israel," the martyrdom said they were okay. Thus this next window (a Jesus martyrology) supports our conclusions about the significance of the *christos* designation being a claim upon Israel's epic, and it illustrates just how important the social interest of identity as Israel was.

With the Christ myth, yet another moment in the social history and mythmaking activity of this association can be seen. This moment is also "pre-Pauline." The mythmaking elaborations on the Jesus martyrology are obvious. Now there is express claim to epic validation of some kind, the emphasis upon resurrection as a validation of the martyrdom, and a claim to divine involvement for authentication. It would therefore have been rather easy to start thinking of the Jesus martyrology in terms of his *christos* attributive. Paul makes it look as if the designation *christos* were in mind all along as the subject of the mythmaking and as if the point of the resurrection were to commission apostles to report on the martyrology. There is reason to be suspicious of both of these features, but it is true that the designation *christos* does appear to have gotten attached to the martyrology before Paul and that, in Paul, it took on titular and honorific connotations as well as sovereign, cosmic, and divine functions. So one might stay right here for a while and ponder the circumstances under which the attachment took place. Since the logic of the martyrdom makes no sense at all if the figure martyred were cast as the royal figure of expectation common to later "messianic" scenarios, the most reasonable solution would be to think that the first attachment happened simply because *christos* as epithet had gained currency and fit the epic argument better than the name Jesus.

This means that none of the indices for a transition from a Jesus movement to a Christ cult indicates the need to posit drastic social contestation or, heaven help us, dramatic personal "religious" experience in order to account for it all. That a cult of the Christ (or the continuing presence of Jesus, the spirit of the Christ, the Spirit of God, the "Lord," whether Jesus or God, etc.) did in fact eventually emerge is clear. But that is another story, hopefully to be unraveled next year when we take a look at the Corinthian Christians. For now, focusing on the transition from a Jesus movement to a Jesus *christos* association in Antioch, the social-interest theory should be enough to account for the social formation and the mythmaking. Collective identity was a very important consideration, problem, and issue for everyone during this period. I have already referred to Miller's helping me see that the social situation in Galilee, for instance, is best described as a confusion of ethnic identities (rather than emphasizing economic dis-ease, social critique, political resistance, or ideological debate, all of which also appear to have been factors). So the trajectory of social formation and identity quest from Galilee to Antioch can easily be understood on the basis of a common interest in the teachings of Jesus as the basis for a kind of "school" that formed a kind of association in the shadow of the synagogue. It does mean, however, that we allow the social interest of group identification to gather up many other interests, both social and intellectual, on the way to forming a replicable society, positioned politically, with grand mythic rationale. I am beginning to think that what we have called the "Jewish" roots of the Christian experiment need to be acknowledged in order to grasp fully the social interests involved in the claims to be the legitimate heirs of Israel on the part of early Christian groups. The synagogue may well have been the most interesting and attractive association for diaspora replication. After all, the Jews were able to put many more features of a fully orbed society into the diaspora synagogue than other peoples had done with their shrines, schools, and temples. The evidence seems now to be that all sorts of "Gentiles" (meaning not only Greeks, as our scholarly tradition has tacitly assumed) became interested in what the Jews had achieved and wanted to learn more. If the beginnings of Christianity cannot be explained except by tracing the history of relations with the diaspora synagogue, it means that all of the social interests under cultivation in the synagogue can be considered at work among the early Christians as well. That, I think, gives the identity interest we have been considering more than enough reason to account for the social formations and mythmaking of early Christians.

I would like to conclude by noting that, were we able as a Seminar to come to some agreements along this line, we would, in my estimation, have achieved a redescription of some importance for our project. Not only would we have succeeded in problematizing the customary views of a "messianic" persuasion at the beginnings of Christianity, but we would also have substituted a reasonable explanation for the emergence of the designation *christos* and the congregations of the Christ. We need do no more as long as we have not abused any of the data relevant to the social locations we seek to imagine. We will not be able fully to paint the picture of any of these way stations. But then, few of the locations imagined for Christian origins on the traditional model have ever been fully described. All are imaginations calculated to give the impression that some mythic event was in some sense historical. So our challenge is not to render fully and complete alternative descriptions of every social locus of significance for Christian origins but to offer better and more reasonable explanations of the relevant data. It is the explanatory power of the alternative explanation that counts as a redescription on the way to a consideration of social theory. The social locations we are now seeking to imagine for the emergence of the designation *christos* are certainly more believable than thinking of Peter drawing such a conclusion on the basis of Jesus' miracles, of Paul's claim that Peter saw the resurrected Jesus, or that he (Paul) saw the risen Lord. So I would say we are making progress.

THE ANOINTED JESUS
Merrill P. Miller

I

In his comprehensive survey of messianic expectations from the Maccabees to Bar Kokhba, Gerbern S. Oegema has set out the following conclusions: "We can speak of neither a messianic 'idea' in Judaism nor of a history of ideas in the development of messianic expectations. We can only locate its historical realizations, but not the idea itself."[1] Oegema continues, "Messianic expectations and the messiah concepts of the various traditions in Judaism of antiquity point much more to the decisive character of the political dimension of the culture in those days."[2] These statements reflect the major thesis of the book, which makes the following claim about the development of messiah concepts in early Judaism: "It seemed as if the messianic expectations were conceptualized in either a conserving or in a critical-polemic way, but always in analogy with the balances of power. Only thus can we explain, why certain messiah concepts are found only in certain periods."[3]

I do not intend to evaluate this thesis directly. Its validity depends on many sources whose dating is a matter of dispute, on the cogency of many

---

[1] Gerbern S. Oegema, *The Anointed and His People: Messianic Expectations from the Maccabees to Bar Kochba* (JSPSup 27; Sheffield: Sheffield Academic Press, 1998), 306. Given most recent discussions of messiahs and messianism in early Judaism, there is nothing particularly striking in the statement cited above. The only recent study of which I am aware that takes a contrary view is William Horbury, *Jewish Messianism and the Cult of Christ* (London: SCM, 1998). The first three chapters of Horbury's book develop the thesis that a widely diffused messianic myth existed in Judaism of the Second Temple period, whose origins can be traced in the royal ideology of biblical Israel and the ancient Near East. On this basis Horbury argues a second thesis in the fourth and concluding chapter of the book: Jewish messianism had much in common with contemporary Greek and Roman ruler cults and served as the primary conduit for adaptation of the discursive formations of contemporary ruler cults in the formation of a cult of the Christ. My thanks to Christopher R. Matthews for calling the Seminar's attention to the Horbury book in his e-mail of 2 March 1999.
[2] Oegema, *The Anointed and His People*, 306.
[3] Ibid., 305.

particular exegetical decisions, and on Oegema's definition of a messianic figure: "A Messiah is a priestly, royal or otherwise characterized figure, who will play a liberating role at the end of time."[4] But suppose our interest was not in cataloging features of an "end-time" liberator's role in particular but in the lively and long debate about political structures and roles in general that his own thesis must presuppose. In that case, there would be no particular reason to isolate eschatological or future figures, as though debate about the structures of a society or the roles of leadership could only be matters for reflection when projected on the future. As Burton L. Mack has shown in his careful comparison of the high priest in Sirach, the righteous sage in the Wisdom of Solomon, and the future anointed one of the Davidic line in the *Psalms of Solomon,* there are similar strategies of epic revision and of concern to make sense of society and its prospects cast in the very different characterizations of ideal figures.[5]

---

[4] Ibid., 26. I would call attention to the way in which Horbury has sought to tie his own thesis to the thesis of Oegema. First, he qualifies Oegema's main point: "This [Oegema's] proposal rings true in general, but external politics should probably be reckoned as just one important factor in the formation of messianic conceptions; they interacted with an existing myth, and, flexible as it was, it had its own coherence and impetus" (*Jewish Messianism,* 34). However, Horbury wants to use Oegema's thesis to support his own thesis of "messianism as a counterpart to contemporary ruler-cult and the ideas surrounding it" (69; see 182 n. 15). This seems to me to be disingenuous because Horbury's view of the influence of messianism on the formation of the Christ cult could not be sustained in the way he has argued without the prior thesis of the existence of a coherent and sustained messianic myth in Second Temple Judaism, a view that Oegema clearly rejects. Horbury's description in the introduction to the book states, "Messianism was then correspondingly influential in the Judaism of the Greek and Roman periods, and the biblical passages which expressed it were at the heart of a vigorously developing interpretative tradition, with vivid details which formed a ramified but not incoherent messianic myth and expectation" (2). This description should be compared with a series of statements by Oegema at the conclusion of his book: "Only a few biblical passages have been interpreted more than once.... For the rest, verses from almost all biblical books have received messianic interpretations.... Those verses that have been interpreted more than once do not present a uniform messianic idea.... One and the same biblical verse is generally interpreted in the most different ways.... Put in a thesis, it means that none of the biblical verses lead to specific and definite messianic interpretations" (*The Anointed and His People,* 302–3).

[5] Burton L. Mack, "Wisdom Makes a Difference: Alternatives to 'Messianic' Configurations," in *Judaisms and Their Messiahs at the Turn of the Christian Era* (ed. Jacob Neusner et al.; Cambridge: Cambridge University Press, 1987), 15–48. While Horbury, *Jewish Messianism,* 47, is certainly correct to note that *kingship* became a major topos of philosophers, historians, and poets in the Greek and early Roman periods and that the theme has left its imprint in many contemporary Jewish writings, his judgment that this is indicative of "an environment favourable to royal messianism, continuing throughout the period from Alexander the Great to the time of Christian origins," is surely subject to challenge given the considerable evidence for the subordinate role of the king in the ideal polity of Israel, and especially as this is seen to rest on the authority of the Torah as Israel's sacred constitution. On this, see below, pp.

The Qumran texts give clear evidence of reflection on theories of state and leadership roles cast in the functions of figures of expectation. The ideal royal figure of the future (variously identified as the anointed one of Israel, the branch of David, or the prince of the congregation) is subservient to the instruction of priests and the laws of Torah.⁶ For example, in 4Q161 (4QpIsaª) 8–10 III, 18–25, after citing Isa 11:1–4, the pesher follows:

> [Interpreted, this concerns the Branch] of David who shall arise at the end [of days].... God will uphold him with [the spirit of might, and will give him] a throne of glory and a crown of [holiness] and many-coloured garments.... [He will put a sceptre] in his hand and he shall rule over all the [nations]. And Magog ... and his sword shall judge [all] the peoples. And as for that which he said, *He shall not [judge by what his eyes see] or pass sentence by what his ears hear:* interpreted, this means that ... [the Priests] ... As they teach him, so will he judge; and as they order, [so will he pass sentence]. One of the Priests of renown shall go out, and garments of ... shall be in his hands.⁷

In 1QSa 2.11–21 (*Rule of the Congregation*) the anointed one of Israel is subordinate in rank to the priest who is the head of the whole congregation

---

377–78. Further, Horbury's contention that the Hebrew scriptures have been edited and collected in the Persian and Greek Empires around national aspirations connected with kingship should be compared with Mack's summary description of the Jewish scriptures as charter for the Judean temple-state in idem, *A Myth of Innocence: Mark and Christian Origins* (Philadelphia: Fortress, 1988), 27–31; idem, *Who Wrote the New Testament? The Making of the Christian Myth* (San Francisco: HarperSanFrancisco, 1995), 19–23, 35–36; see esp. Mack's remarks on the topos of the ideal king (33–34).

⁶ If these epithets are different ways of referring to an ideal royal figure, it does not seem appropriate to treat them as determinative or exclusive titles. For that reason I have preferred to render them in lowercase in English. However, since at times I am drawing on the translations, or citing the statements, of other scholars who do treat these epithets as titles, they are occasionally capitalized in this essay.

⁷ Translated in Geza Vermes, *The Complete Dead Sea Scrolls in English* (New York: Allen Lane/Penguin, 1997), 467; for the *editio princeps*, see John M. Allegro, "161. Commentary on Isaiah (A)," in *Qumrân Cave 4.I (4Q158–4Q186)* (DJD 5; Oxford: Clarendon, 1968), 14; cf. Florentino García Martínez and Eibert J. C. Tigchelaar, eds., *The Dead Sea Scrolls Study Edition* (2 vols.; Leiden: Brill, 1997–98), 1:316. On the law written for the king expanding on Deut 17 in a noneschatological context, see 11Q19 LVI–LIX, esp. LVIII, 18–21 (in Yigael Yadin, ed., *The Temple Scroll* [3 vols. in 4; Jerusalem: Israel Exploration Society, 1977–83], 2:250–70, esp. 264–65); cf. Josephus, *Ant.* 4.8.17 §§223–24. On the role of the priests and the high priest in war, see 1Q33 (1QM) 7.15–9.9; 15.4–6; 16.13; 18.5; 19.11 in Jean Duhaime, "War Scroll (1QM; 1Q33; 4Q491–496 = 4QM1–6; 4Q497)," in *Damascus Document, War Scroll, and Related Documents* (vol. 2 of *The Dead Sea Scrolls: Hebrew, Aramaic, and Greek Texts with English Translations;* ed. James H. Charlesworth et al.; The Princeton Theological Seminary Dead Sea Scrolls Project; Tübingen: Mohr Siebeck; Louisville: Westminster John Knox, 1995), 96–141 (hereinafter PTSDSSP 2).

at the meal of those called for the council of the community.⁸ The priority given to priestly functions in future contexts clearly relates to the priestly leadership of the sect.⁹ The duality of structure expressed in the phrase "the anointed one(s) of Aaron and of Israel," whether referring to one or two figures, seems to reflect the influence of Jer 33:19–26 and Zech 4:14; it may also be a response to the assumption of priestly and royal functions and titles by the Hasmoneans.

According to Johan Lust, there is a stinging rebuke and judgment on the assumption of royal powers by the Hasmoneans found in Ezek 21:30–32 LXX.¹⁰ In contrast to the judgment on the Judean king in the MT, reflected in part by references to removal of the turban and the crown, here the judgment is pronounced on "a profane, lawless leader of Israel" (βέβηλε ἄνομε ἀφηγούμενε τοῦ Ισραηλ), who is accused of having removed the turban (i.e., the high priest's headdress) and put on the crown ('Αφείλου τὴν κίδαριν καὶ ἐπέθου τὸν στέφανον). The text continues the accusation: "She [αὕτη, presumably referring to high priest's turban] shall not be the same. You have abased what is high and exalted what is low."¹¹ The situation will continue, and there will be further defilement "until he comes to whom it is fitting, and I will give it to him" (ἕως οὗ ἔλθῃ ᾧ καθήκει, καὶ παραδώσω αὐτῷ; MT: עַד־בֹּא אֲשֶׁר־לוֹ הַמִּשְׁפָּט וּנְתַתִּיו). Lust understands the final clause to refer to giving the turban to a priestly figure of expectation who will restore the high priesthood. In contrast, the MT either has in view a final judgment (presumably by Nebuchadnezzar) on the city of Jerusalem and its elite or might be announcing the advent of a future king, depending on the textual and literary judgments made in the analysis.¹²

---

⁸ See James H. Charlesworth and Loren T. Stuckenbruck, "Rule of the Congregation (1QSa)," in *Rule of the Community and Related Documents* (vol. 1 of *The Dead Sea Scrolls: Hebrew, Aramaic, and Greek Texts with English Translations;* ed. James H. Charlesworth et al.; The Princeton Theological Seminary Dead Sea Scrolls Project; Tübingen: Mohr Siebeck; Louisville: Westminster John Knox, 1994), 116–17 (hereinafter PTSDSSP 1).

⁹ Cf. *T. Jud.* 21.1–2 on the general priority of the priesthood to kingship: "And now, children, love Levi so that you may endure.... To me God has given the kingship and to him, the priesthood; and he has subjected the kingship to the priesthood" (trans. H. C. Kee, "Testaments of the Twelve Patriarchs," in *The Old Testament Pseudepigrapha* [ed. James H. Charlesworth; 2 vols.; Garden City, N.Y.: Doubleday, 1983–85], 1:800); cf. Philo, *Legat.* 278.

¹⁰ Cf. Josephus, *Ant.* 14.3.2 §§40–41.

¹¹ See Johan Lust, "Messianism and Septuagint," in *Congress Volume: Salamanca, 1983* (ed. J. A. Emerton; VTSup 36; Leiden: Brill, 1985), 174–91, esp. 180–90. Lust argues that the MT understands the turban and crown in a figurative sense and that therefore in this context they should be taken as synonymous (182–83); however, they cannot be taken in this sense in the LXX as the respective objects of the verbs (188). The Maccabean high priest Jonathan received the *stephanos* from Alexander Balas (1 Macc 10:20) as a symbol of royal authority, but as vassal of his Seleucid lord. Cf. Sir 45:12.

¹² Ibid., 190. Regarding claims that a more developed messianism can be found in the LXX, Lust gives his judgment at the conclusion of his survey: "In questions of theology such

The final temporal clause in Ezek 21:32 (27) is similar to the clause found in Gen 49:10, "until Shiloh comes" (or "until he comes to Shiloh," or with the Syriac, "until he comes to whom it belongs"). Genesis 49:10 is regarded as a classic "messianic" text, at least with respect to its later usage, but the phrase is a standard way of introducing a figure of expectation whose appearance marks a temporal boundary. I would suggest that this is a more compressed formulation of what Mack has noticed as one of the structural features of situating an ideal figure, "plac[ing] it in such a way as to bracket the recent past and the present between the image as ideal and the more remote traditions it claimed to articulate."[13] The *locus classicus* of the so-called two-messiah doctrine of the Dead Sea Scrolls appears in the *Rule of the Community* (1QS 9.10–11). The figures of expectation are introduced to mark a temporal boundary that situates the present time of the community. Those who enter the *Yahad* are to govern themselves by specific rules, to be guided by the sons of Aaron alone in judicial and financial matters, and are to separate themselves and their wealth from those who walk in perversity. "They shall be governed by the first regulations in which the men of the *Yahad* began to be instructed, doing so until the coming of a prophet and the anointed of Aaron and Israel" (עד בוא נביא ומשיחי אהרון וישראל).[14]

---

as messianism, one cannot treat the LXX as a unified entity. Each relevant text should be studied on its own. At the present stage of the investigation we may conclude that the LXX certainly does not display a uniform picture of a developing royal messianism" (191). Cf. the different judgment of Horbury, *Jewish Messianism*, 46–51.

[13] Mack, "Wisdom Makes a Difference," 43.

[14] Text in Elisha Qimron, "Rule of the Community (1QS; cf. 4QS MSS A-J, 5Q11)," in PTSDSSP 1:40. The usual translation of the Hebrew, "until the coming of the Prophet and the Messiahs of Aaron and Israel," tends to turn an expected prophetic role into a title and the expectation of legitimate representatives of restored priestly and royal institutions into eschatological savior figures. In this context, and in many others, those ideas are misleading. According to Philip S. Alexander, "The Redaction-History of *Serekh Ha-Yahad:* A Proposal," *RevQ* 17 (1996): 452–53, "It is not certain that *1QS* 9:11 involves messianism in any strong sense of that term. The words can be given a very minimalist reading: 'until the coming of a prophet, and until the priesthood (= the anointed of Aaron) and the kingship (= the anointed of Israel) are restored.'" Alexander is writing in the context of the currently much-discussed and disputed matter of the tradition and composition history of the *Rule of the Community* with possible implications for the history of Qumran messianism, but especially for questions of the role of the Zadokite priests in the history of the sect. Some scholars have argued that the fragments of the *Community Rule* from Cave 4 represent earlier recensions of the *Rule* than the text from Cave 1 and do not evidence messianism (1QS 9.10–11 is not found in MS E of the Cave 4 fragments) or the authority of the Zadokite priests. Alexander, on the other hand, argues that there was a loss of Zadokite influence in the history of the sect. For different evaluations of the significance of the Cave 4 fragments for the history of the *Rule of the Community*, in addition to Alexander, see Sarianna Metso, *The Textual Development of the Qumran Community Rule* (STDJ 21; Leiden: Brill, 1997); James H. Charlesworth and Brent A.

A similar structure is found in the *Damascus Document*. In times past, when God punished the misdeeds of Israel and those who had spoken rebellion against the commandments of God through Moses and against "the anointed ones of holiness" (במשיחו הקודש), he remembered the covenant of the forefathers, "and he raised up from Aaron men of discernment and from Israel wise men; and he allowed them to hear." There follows a midrash on Num 21:18:

> The "well" is the Torah and those who "dig" it are the penitents of Israel who depart from the land of Judah and dwell in the land of Damascus.... And the "ruler" [המחוקק] is the interpreter of the Torah [דורש התורה], of whom Isaiah said, "He takes out a tool for his work." And the "nobles of the people" are those who come to excavate the well with the statutes which were ordained by the ruler to walk in them in the entire time of evil, and (who) will obtain no others until the rise of one who will teach righteousness in the end of days [עד עמד יורה הצדק באחרית הימים].[15]

The same pattern can be seen a number of times in the *Damascus Document* with reference to the appearance of the anointed ones of Aaron and Israel: "And this (is) the rule for the settlers of [the] c[amps] who walk in accordance with these (rules) during the time of wickedness until the

---

Strawn, "Reflections on the Text of *Serek Ha-Yaḥad* Found in Cave IV," *RevQ* 17 (1996): 403–35; James H. Charlesworth, "Challenging the *Consensus Communis* Regarding Qumran Messianism (1QS, 4QS MSS)," in *Qumran-Messianism: Studies on the Messianic Expectations in the Dead Sea Scrolls* (ed. James H. Charlesworth et al.; Tübingen: Mohr Siebeck, 1998), 120–34; A. I. Baumgarten, "The Zadokite Priests at Qumran: A Reconsideration," *DSD* 4 (1997): 137–56; Markus Bockmuehl, "Redaction and Ideology in the *Rule of the Community* (1QS/4QS)," *RevQ* 18 (1998): 541–60. For a recent study of 1QSa and 1QSb and their relations to 1QS and the development of Qumran messianism, see Hartmut Stegemann, "Some Remarks to *1QSa*, to *1QSb*, and to Qumran Messianism," *RevQ* 17 (1996): 479–505.

[15] CD A 5.20–6.11 (text and trans., Daniel R. Schwartz, "Damascus Document [CD]," in PTSDSSP 2:22–23). I have translated משיחו הקודש as "the anointed ones of holiness" rather than Schwartz's "anointed holy ones." It is likely that משיחו is an error for the plural construct משיחי rather than a defective writing of משיחיו; cf. the reading of this text in 6Q15 3.4 (ibid., 78). In this passage, the interpreter of the Torah appears to be a figure of the past, but not necessarily to be identified with the righteous teacher. The teacher who will arise to teach righteousness may therefore be conceived as a latter-day interpreter of the Torah (see 4Q174 [4QFlor] 1.11), and not the righteous teacher redivivus. The interpreter of the Torah also appears in CD A 7.18–19 in a midrash linking Amos 5:27; 9:11 and Num 24:17. Here the one to arise in the future is the "prince of the whole congregation" (נשיא כל העדה). Like the interpreter of the Torah, the prince of the whole congregation also appears in some Qumran texts as a historical leader. Joseph A. Fitzmyer has remarked on this tendency to use the same epithets (or titles) for past and future figures in his recent essay on "Qumran Messianism," in *The Dead Sea Scrolls and Christian Origins* (Studies in the Dead Sea Scrolls and Related Literature; Grand Rapids: Eerdmans, 2000), 99 nn. 78–79.

arising of the anointed of Aaron and Israel" (עד עמוד משוח אהרן וישראל).[16] In the alternate version of the *Damascus Document* (MS B) the biblical citations and personnel have changed, but the paralleling of past and future times of punishment is found together with emphasis on the safety of the poor and of those who repent.[17] This version also shows that the present age of wickedness is a time of backsliding among the Covenanters:

> Thus all the men who entered the new covenant in the land of Damascus and returned and betrayed and departed from the well of living water will not be accounted among the council of the people; and when (the latter) are written, they will not be written from the day the unique Teacher [מורה היחיד] was gathered in until there arises the anointed from Aaron and from Israel [עד עמוד משיח מאהרן ומישראל]. And this (is) the judgment for all those who entered the congregation of the men of perfect holiness but recoiled from doing the regulations of the upright: He is the man "who is melted in the midst of a furnace" (Ezek 22:22).[18]

The temporal phrase in Gen 49:10 is applied to a future figure in column 5 of 4Q252 (*Commentary on Genesis A*, formerly *Patriarchal Blessings* or *Pesher Genesis*). The text appears to be a paraphrase and expansion in the manner of rewritten Bible and forms part of a set of commentaries on passages in Genesis, beginning with Noah in chapter 6. Column 5 reads:

> "*The sceptre shall* [n]*ot depart from the tribe of Judah*" (Gen 49:10a). When Israel rules [*there will not*] *be cut off one who occupies the throne for David* (Jer 33:17). For "*the staff*" [המחקק] (Gen 49:10a) is the covenant of the kingship; the [thousa]nds of Israel are "*the standards*" (Gen 49:10a) *vacat* until the coming of the anointed of righteousness, the branch of David [עד בוא משיח הצדק צמח דויד]. For to him and his seed has been given the covenant of the kingship of his people for everlasting

---

[16] CD A 12.23–13.1 (text and trans., Joseph M. Baumgarten, "Damascus Document [CD]," in PTSDSSP 2:52–53). The passive participle משוח is probably an error for משיח. Here, as in other instances, the singular may be intended in a distributive sense rather than referring to a single figure. But the matter remains under debate. In this passage as well as the others from CD below, I have translated "anointed" or "anointed one(s)" rather than "Messiah," which is the translation of these passages in CD by Schwartz and Baumgarten.

[17] Thus, we read in CD B 19.7–11: "when that happens of which it is written by Zechariah the prophet, 'Awake, O sword, upon my shepherd and upon the man (who is) close to me—God says—strike the shepherd so the sheep will be scattered and I will turn my hand to the little ones.' But those who guard it (the precept) are the poor of the sheep. These will escape at the time of the visitation. But those who remain will be handed over to the sword when the anointed of Aaron and Israel comes [בבוא משיח אהרן וישראל]. (And this will be) as it happened at the first time of visitation" (text and trans., Daniel R. Schwartz, "Damascus Document [CD]," PTSDSSP 2:30–31).

[18] CD B 19.33–20.3 (text and trans., ibid., PTSDSSP 2:32–35).

generations, which he kept ... [   ] the Law with the men of the community, for [   ]....¹⁹

It should be noted that Gen 49:10 is understood in this text to refer to a Davidic dynasty and not only to the expectation of a single figure. The establishment of the law proceeds not from the ruler alone but together with the congregation.²⁰ But how is the present time, the time of Israel's dominion, to be conceived? The intention may be to signal that it is a time of wrong rulers, Hasmoneans and Herodians, in which case the coming Davidic ruler/dynasty reestablishes what is promised in the blessing. However, the present may also be conceived as a royal military establishment embodied in the Qumran-Essene conception of its own military organizational structure, that is, the reference to "standards" in the rendering of the Genesis text being interpreted as the thousands of Israel.²¹ These are not mutually exclusive alternatives. Whether the present is characterized as an age of wickedness or as a time of perseverence and of apostasy, or as a period with its own particular forms of authority and legitimacy, it should be recognized that the marking of temporal boundaries by reference to figures of expectation serves as a quasi-legal formula of the sort similar to the proclamation legitimating and, at least implicitly, limiting the authority of the Hasmonean regime under Simon in 1 Macc 14:41: "The Jews and their priests have resolved that Simon should be their leader and high priest forever, until a trustworthy prophet should arise" (ἕως τοῦ ἀναστῆναι προφήτην πιστόν).²²

---

¹⁹ 4Q252 6 V, 1–6 (text and trans., George Brooke, "252. 4QCommentary on Genesis A," in *Qumrân Cave 4.XVII: Parabiblical Texts, Part 3* [ed. George Brooke et al.; DJD 22; Oxford: Clarendon, 1996], 205–6). Brooke translates משיח הצדק as "the messiah of righteousness" and צמח דויד as "the shoot of David."

²⁰ See Gerbern S. Oegema, "Messianic Expectations in the Qumran Writings: Theses on their Development," in Charlesworth et al., *Qumran-Messianism*, 73: "For the near future the keeping of the Torah is expected to be given not to one particular person, but to a hereditary 'kingship.' Although the 'Branch of David' is part of this tradition, he is not portrayed as the one and only 'latter-day liberator' or 'messiah.'"

²¹ I am again dependent on an observation of Oegema: "We are dealing here with a rewritten Bible on the several elements of the text from Genesis, whose interpretation is that Judah will possess a military (as we may undertand the 'clans [or thousands] of Israel') kingdom in Israel until the one who will take over his rule will come" (ibid.).

²² Cf. 1 Macc 4:46. It should not be supposed that the writer of 1 Maccabees is content to base the authority of Simon's office of leader, ethnarch, and high priest on the rehearsal of his numerous benefactions for his people. The biblicizing language of the eulogy (14:4–15) not only characterizes his actions as bringing to his people a time of salvation but is implicitly comparing his deeds to those of heroes of old. In all, the formula in 1 Macc 14:41 intends both authorization and reserve with respect to what may be seen to be unprecedented. For similar examples of the use of a final temporal clause, see Mic 5:2 (3); Dan 9:25; 4Q246 2.4; *L.A.B.* 51.6; *T. Reu.* 6.8; cf. Gal 3:23–25.

I am suggesting that *messianic expectations* and *messiahs* as categories for comparison and analysis may be quite problematic, especially when they tend to shift the focus away from what can be seen as more fundamental structures and issues. When a social anthropology is in view, there is very little to be gained in comparing the features of individual "eschatological" figures, taken as a differentiated set of future expectations, and there is always the suspicion that these categories have been generated primarily from christological interests. Different ways of casting and relating leadership roles entail the sort of intellectual effort concerned with how a society works, with determining what has gone wrong and imagining what would be better, and for whom, irrespective of the temporal placement of the figure. In the case of the particular temporal formula we have observed, I would maintain that these figures are not primarily intended to conjure hopes or give expression to longings for a hero-savior. Thus, to classify as messiahs the anointed one(s) of Aaron and Israel is to seriously misconstrue the significance of references to them in 1QS and CD. Their future roles are implied but not the focus of interest. They but serve to situate, problematize, adjust, and authorize the life-world (including its future horizon) of those addressed in the writing. The figure (or figures) of expectation authorizes a particular pattern of behavior in the absence of agreed precedents and in the face of radically different patterns in the wider milieu, or creates continuity with the time of established precedents, and registers the temporal and therefore limited range of agreement for social stability.[23]

II

In my earlier essay I wanted to show that the impasse in recent scholarship on the question of how to account for *christos* as the foremost term associated with Jesus was an indication that the problem itself required reconceptualizing.[24] The problem has generally been conceived as one of having to account for the shift from Jewish messianic conceptions to specifically Christian conceptions of Jesus as the Christ. The debate has been about where to locate the dramatic revision of Jewish messianism: in

---

[23] Another example of redescribing so-called messianic texts can be seen in John Lübbe, "A Reinterpretation of 4QTestimonia," *RevQ* 12 (1986): 187–97. Lübbe argues that what is usually described as a collection of messianic proof texts is better understood as a collection of warnings concerned with contemporary fidelity to the sect's teachings in the wake of an earlier apostasy of dissenters from the sect.

[24] Merrill P. Miller, "The Problem of the Origins of a Messianic Conception of Jesus" (in this volume).

the historical Jesus and his ministry, in the circumstances of his execution, in theological reflections on the resurrected Jesus, or in some combination of these factors, this last option retaining the dominant position in scholarship. However, this way of conceiving the problem always ends in variations of the canonical account in which Christianity, while dependent on supposedly deep-rooted Jewish expectations of an end-time deliverer, transcends them in the moment of origination. In order to construct an alternative conception, I have argued that the use of the term *christos* in early Christianity as a byname and as a title should be related to the process of social formation at different loci and should be viewed as another instance of constructing exemplary figures in the interest of establishing a horizon of authority for the articulation and legitimation of collective practices and identities. Reconceptualizing the problem was seen to be closely tied to the issue of how to relate the Pauline uses of *christos* to those found in the canonical Gospels and the book of Acts. My arguments led to conclusions that reverse the usual assumptions about pre-Pauline usage. However, I was not attempting to construct an alternative line of development or to trace a different trajectory but to disperse the moments of mythmaking and social formation along the lines set out in Mack's book, *A Myth of Innocence.*

Before the publication of that book no modern scholar of whom I am aware had ever imagined the locus of origin for the use of *christos* among Jesus people to be anywhere but in the earliest confession of faith ("Jesus is the Messiah") of the earliest community in Jerusalem, and usually in close connection with a supposed apocalyptic Son of Man Christology linked to apocalyptic conceptions of the resurrection of Jesus. The reason for Mack's "oversight" in this regard had nothing to do with the notion of a Hellenistic Christ cult characterized as groups cultivating the spiritual presence of Jesus in the community, since the operative title for that description was *kyrios,* as it had been for Wilhelm Bousset and other members of the history of religions school. The reason was that Mack had recognized a variety of mythmaking in early Jesus groups in Galilee and southern Syria that did not presuppose Jesus as the Christ and, further, because he had reconceptualized the locus and logic of the kerygma in which the Christ term was clearly present. This had crucial historical and theoretical implications, because some form of the kerygma was always thought to have originated in the earliest *Palestinian community* (as that community was usually labeled) and was always linked to the way Christian origins were imagined.

Although I took a different view on where to locate the pre-Pauline use of *christos,* it should be clear that I have presupposed Mack's analysis of mythmaking in Jesus groups prior to the composition of Mark and his social construction of the circumstances and sense-making of the kerygma.²⁵ Along more independent lines, I questioned the logic and historical plausibility of conceiving of the Jerusalem church as a messianic sect, exposing the dilemma of trying to make historical sense of the connection between the passion narrative and the opening chapters of Acts in Jerusalem.²⁶ And I found nothing at all compelling about Jerusalem as the locus of introduction of the term *christos* for Jesus in my essay on Galatians;²⁷ nor did any of the other papers in our work last year on Judean/Jerusalem groups.

Since I have been questioning the analytic usefulness of the categories *messiahs* and *messianic expectations* as these are usually conceived, I will certainly be queried about my own attempt to locate a portrayal of Jesus as a messianic figure and about the propriety of the expression "messianic conception" in the title of my essay. The shorthand response to this is to note that I have used these terms for strategic purposes, first, to highlight the difference in the usage of *christos* in Paul's letters from what is found in the canonical Gospels and Acts, and second, to show that portraying Jesus as the expected Messiah in the Gospels is itself a strategy for constructing the *bios* of one who was still a figure of minor reputation from the recent past. The consequence of this strategy was actually to create the category of *the Messiah,* the unique figure of expectation. The Jesus of Mark's Gospel is intended to be without peers. His role is to belong to a category he alone can exemplify, thereby enhancing the novelty but also attesting the precarious identity of the group by his own resistance to classification.²⁸ But along with this, Mark's Jesus is the fabrication of an alternative to the recently failed Roman-Jewish leadership that ended in the destruction of the temple, while the figure of the Son of Man establishes a future horizon designed to shed light on the conflicts and clarify the alternatives of those addressed by the Evangelist.

In my essay on "The Problem of the Origins of a Messianic Conception of Jesus," I was not applying the expression "messianic conception" to eschatological expectations in general but to those focused on a figure of expectation in particular. I also had in view current popular royal

---

²⁵ See Merrill P. Miller, "How Jesus Became Christ: Probing a Thesis," *Cont* 2/2–3 (1993): 243–70.

²⁶ Merrill P. Miller, "'Beginning from Jerusalem...': Re-examining Canon and Consensus," *Journal of Higher Criticism* 2/1 (1995): 3–30.

²⁷ Merrill P. Miller, "Antioch, Paul, and Jerusalem: Diaspora Myths of Origins in the Homeland" (in this volume).

²⁸ See Jonathan Z. Smith, "Good News Is No News: Aretalogy and Gospel," in *Christianity, Judaism and Other Greco-Roman Cults: Studies for Morton Smith at Sixty* (ed. Jacob Neusner; 4 vols.; SJLA 12; Leiden: Brill, 1975), 1:21–38, repr. in *Map Is Not Territory: Studies in the History of Religions* (SJLA 23; Leiden: Brill, 1978; repr., Chicago: University of Chicago Press, 1993), 190–207.

claimants. (With respect to the latter, however, our term is never attested with named figures, the later instance of Bar Kokhba being a possible exception.) On the other hand, I had no intention of limiting the term to royal figures, nor was I eliminating so-called apocalyptic messianic figures that come from the divine world. Nor did I insist strictly on eschatological as opposed to more vaguely conceived future figures. While these distinctions are important in some studies, I did not think that they were decisive for my own.

What I did want to eliminate was an equation that allows one to identify any expression of royal ideology with messianism. In that case, references to the anointed of the Lord in the royal psalms, usually thought to refer to the reigning Israelite king, or to the enthronement of an Israelite king, would belong to the category of messianic figures, or at least would be seen to adumbrate messianic expectations. While there are scholars who hold the view that messianism has its roots in ancient Israelite royal ideology, almost all scholars today would insist on a distinction between the ideology of the king as a sacral figure and the projection of an ideal king onto the future.[29] Messianism may have its roots in royal ideology, but the circumstances in which messianism is thought to actually make its appearance above ground are those in which the Davidic dynasty of Judah has come to an end, or even later in a post-Alexandrian colonial world. The irony of messianism in biblical literature is that the very texts which refer to the renewal of a Davidic dynasty or to the coming of an ideal ruler almost never make use of the term *anointed* or *anointed one*. (Zech 4:14 might be considered an exception, but the anointed ones [lit. "sons of oil"] are contemporaries of the writer, who has in view the project of rebuilding the temple.) Applied to royal figures, the term refers to a particular agent of the past or present or to the institution of the Davidic dynasty. The situation is not altogether different in nonbiblical or postbiblical Jewish literature. The majority of passages usually identified by scholars as messianic do not contain the term.

---

[29] I am aware, of course, that in part 1 of this paper I have questioned the categorical usefulness of this very distinction. I do maintain that the notion of *figures of expectation* has not served the interests of discerning social anthropologies. Nonetheless, in the current state of scholarship, to eliminate the distinction between royal ideology and messianism is only likely to return us to a more synthetic use of the category, as the recent work of Horbury seems to me to exemplify (see above, nn. 1, 4). It is necessary to retain the categories *messianism* and *messiah(s)* precisely in the study of Christian origins because it is the canonical presentation of Jesus the Messiah that has created these categories in biblical scholarship in the first place. Thus, the analytic usefulness of these categories concerns the need to distinguish between the canonical presentation of Christian origins and its continuing impact on scholarship, and our own project of redescription.

My limiting of the data to texts in which the term *māšiaḥ/mašîḥāʾ/ christos* appears was bound to cause confusion because I did not sufficiently clarify what was intended.³⁰ The limitation is one that I imposed because of the issues I wanted to address in that essay, and even then I did not apply it with complete consistency, since the study does take up references to son of David and Davidic origin passages. However, the limitation was not intended as a recommendation for the study of Jewish messianism in general, although the case for considering only passages in which the term appears has been made by some scholars and with good reason, given the synthetic portraits of the Messiah produced in earlier scholarship as a consequence of combining and reducing to a common denominator the disparate features of many texts.³¹ Nor did I intend to suggest that there are no other titles that come into play to refer to Jesus as a figure of expectation. It is obvious that the designation Son of Man is sometimes used in that way, but I was not comparing titles of honor attributed to Jesus and their contribution to Christology, and I did not focus on different ways in which Jesus could be represented as a figure of expectation. I was interested in the different uses of the term *christos* itself, since it is the most common designation of Jesus, and yet is virtually absent from the sayings tradition. What was the earliest locus of the term, and what were its connotations and the reasons for its introduction? In that study, *figure of expectation* was intended to distinguish between uses of the term in the canonical Gospels and Acts in contrast to Pauline

---

³⁰ See the introductory note in Miller, "Problem of the Origins," 301.

³¹ I doubt that the rectification of the categories *messianism* and *messiah(s)* could actually be achieved without taking account of a wider range of texts than those in which the term appears, if the central issue is the anthropology implied in the construction of ideal figures. What is important about focusing on the term itself in the Jewish literature prior to and contemporary with Christian origins is to note the range and contexts of its use (in addition to the discussion in part 1 of this essay, see part 3 below). There is also the crucial issue of translation. Should every instance in which *māšiaḥ/mašîḥāʾ/christos* is applied to a future figure (or to future figures) be translated Messiah(s), signifying the one who brings redemption, rather than Anointed One(s), signifying the theocratic legitimation of an office or role of leadership? Should the term be understood as a sufficiently determinate title of a particular office and role and thus be capitalized in translation or rendered as a general honorific or qualification with the lowercase? See Johann Maier, "Messias oder Gesalbter? Zu einem Übersetzungs- und Deutungsproblem in den Qumrantexten," *RevQ* 17 (1996): 585–612, who has argued that there are no instances in the Qumran texts in which our term in the singular or plural should be translated "messiah(s)" rather than "anointed one(s)," precisely because of the conceptual confusion thereby created with issues focused on Christology. In my judgment, Maier's contention should also be applied to the translation of the term in the study of Christian origins. For Maier's view is correct, in my judgment, and the issues he raises are important, not least for the task of redescribing the introduction and significance of the term as a qualification for Jesus.

uses of the term. My attempt to show that *christos* bears on the way in which the beginnings of Christianity are imagined and on different junctures of mythmaking and social formation depends on the way I have argued for the significance of different uses of the term. In the Gospels and Acts *christos* is used as both a title and a name, but one does not encounter there the characteristic that is so typical of the letters of Paul, where we are clearly dealing with a name but not only or merely with a second name for Jesus. In the Gospels and Acts Jesus is identified with a figure of general expectation, the Messiah, but this is not the case in Paul. In the Gospels and Acts Jesus is recognized and confessed as the Christ, and his identity as the Christ is a focus of argumentation; this is never the case in Paul. I have argued that Paul's *christos* does not presuppose the Christ of the Gospel narrative traditions or of the speeches in Acts; in sum, the letters do not associate the term *christos* in particular with a figure of general expectation.

I am not proposing that Paul never has a figure of expectation in view. He clearly has such a figure in view in Rom 11:26–27: "Out of Zion will come the Deliverer" (ἥξει ἐκ Σιὼν ὁ ῥυόμενος), citing in part Isa 59:20–21. As is obvious in this case, the issue is whether our term is the one in particular that Paul associates with the notion. In 1 Thess 1:10 it is the Son who is awaited from heaven, Jesus who delivers from the wrath to come. In Phil 3:20 Paul speaks of expecting a Savior from heaven, the Lord Jesus Christ. In some instances Paul's use of identifying terms is determined by having started with a particular designation. That seems to be the case in 1 Cor 15, which is remarkably uniform in referring to Christ. In 15:23b Paul speaks of Christ as the "firstfruits" (of those who die) and then refers to the parousia of Christ—but not quite. In a typical Pauline locution he says, "Then, at his coming, those who belong to Christ" (ἔπειτα οἱ τοῦ Χριστοῦ ἐν τῇ παρουσίᾳ αὐτοῦ). Again, Paul can give a temporal duration in Gal 3:24 for the law's function as παιδαγωγός until Christ (εἰς Χριστόν), but in Gal 4:4 he refers to God sending his Son when the fullness of time had come. Since the whole argument is about who belongs to God's family—who are the heirs, the children of Abraham promised blessing, who are the sons, and on what basis—it would appear that Jesus as God's Son is the operative designation for the argument as a whole (cf. Rom 1:2–3a). The only clear exceptions to my point are the references to the day of Christ in Phil 1:10 and 2:16 (εἰς ἡμέραν Χριστοῦ). However, this locution is unusual (cf. 1 Thess 1:10; Rom 2:5, 15–16; 1 Cor 1:8; 2 Cor 1:14).

It was probably inevitable that the central argument of the essay would appear to depend on the suggestion that *christos* was first used as a byname or cognomen. That consequence is not quite what I had in mind. I did want to think about connotations the term might have carried among those groups in Damascus and Antioch that Paul first came to know without having to suppose immediately that it would have been available and attractive only as a technical term for an expected Davidic ruler or for some other kind of savior figure who would make all things right at the end. But neither was I assuming that it was available as a byname in some locus of Jewish culture and society. That was the point. It would have required reflection on the connotations of the term to settle on using it that way. It would not have been a divine revelation (Matt 16:17) but a construction put on the term, perhaps after much debate and taking into consideration whatever intertextual exchange may have been circulating. Given the evidence of early Christian texts, the term was perhaps not considered by some, perhaps rejected outright by others, but was definitely a winner in some circles and eventually became established more widely as a term of recognition among different groups.

In the main, the suggestion was intended to account for the ubiquity of the term and the variety of locutions in Paul's letters. It may seem simpler to suppose, as most have, that a title has been reduced in the course of repeated use to a mere name in communication with groups unfamiliar with the titular significance of the term. Yet even in such a scenario there is no reason to suppose that the significance of the term was self-evident and that there was no flexibility and experimentation with respect to its use. But I still do not think the usual view accounts for the Pauline data. The fact that the term is never explained, that in no instance is there compelling reason to translate it "Messiah," and, more important, that no argument or point Paul wishes to register is dependent on some particular significance of the term—all give the impression of its use merely as a second name.

However, that is only one side of the equation. What must also be taken into account are distinctions that can be made with respect to typical locutions and contexts in the various terms Paul uses for Jesus.[32] It is equally important to consider that Paul reverses the order and refers to Christ Jesus far more often than to Jesus Christ. This cannot be accounted for on the basis of grammatical considerations alone, since the most common form of this reversed order is with a preposition that takes the dative case and thus clarifies the case of Ἰησοῦ. The reversal is therefore not demanded on grammatical grounds. Even if one surmises that grammatical considerations are nevertheless in play, it is doubtful that the extent to which Paul's letters show this order can be explained without supposing that *christos* is recognized as something more than a second name for Jesus. Some would argue that only on the grounds of its use as a title can

---

[32] Werner Kramer's *Christ, Lord, Son of God* (trans. Brian Hardy; SBT 50; Naperville, Ill.: Allenson, 1966) is still the major work on these matters.

this phenomenon be explained,[33] but if this is so it is surprising that Paul never brings out the titular significance of the term. A byname does not require us to imagine that Paul's communities had received the term merely as an alternative name for Jesus and were innocent of any honorific associations carried by the term (the reverse order in Paul's letters suggests otherwise). But it does make understandable why it is never identified by Paul as the determinative title for grounding some important aspect of his gospel.

Since our term is almost always thought to have originated among Aramaic-speaking Jews it is sometimes suggested that Ἰησοῦς Χριστός is a direct translation of *yəšûaʿ məšîḥāʾ* and in its Aramaic form constituted a confession of faith: "Jesus is the Messiah."[34] But even if we suppose an Aramaic usage at first, one need not assume that the direct juxtaposition of the two terms constitutes a sentence of proclamation or confession. As far as I know, one will not find our term (with or without the article) directly following a proper name in biblical or postbiblical literature.[35] The

---

[33] See S. Vernon McCasland, "Christ Jesus," *JBL* 65 (1946): 377–83. Cf. the discussion in Martin Karrer, *Der Gesalbte: Die Grundlagen des Christustitels* (FRLANT 151; Göttingen: Vandenhoeck & Ruprecht, 1991), 48–52. Karrer notes that it was not only common in the Greco-Roman world for titles to become names but that *cognomina* could come to be used as titles (59 n. 52).

[34] Martin Hengel, "Jesus, the Messiah of Israel," in *Studies in Early Christology* (Edinburgh: T&T Clark, 1995), 8, emphasis original: "Presumably, the confession formula 'Jesus is the Messiah' (ישוע משיחא; Ἰησοῦς [ὁ] Χριστός), by virtue of constant use, gave rise (automatically, as it were) to a permanent name both among Christians, who thereby emphasized that only *one* could bear this name, and their Gentile auditors, who were not particularly conversant with the language of Jewish piety." Cf. Nils Alstrup Dahl, "The Messiahship of Jesus in Paul," in *Jesus the Christ: The Historical Origins of Christological Doctrine* (ed. Donald H. Juel; Minneapolis: Fortress, 1991), 18–19: "His [Paul's] usage can be explained only by assuming that the confessions and proclamation of the Aramaic-speaking church were summarized in the affirmation: 'Jesus is the Messiah.'"

[35] There is the instance of apposition in Isa 45:1: "Thus says the Lord to his anointed, to Cyrus" (MT: לִמְשִׁיחוֹ לְכוֹרֶשׁ; LXX: τῷ χριστῷ μου Κύρῳ). However, the term is used with the typical pronominal suffix referring to the anointed of the Lord. Cf. the Qumran text 4Q377 (4QapocrPentB) 2 II, 4–5: "Cursed be the man who fails to preserve and car[ry out] all the command[ments of the L]ord as spoken by Moses His anointed" (בפי מושה משיחו; trans. Michael Wise, in Michael Wise, Martin Abegg Jr., and Edward Cook, *The Dead Sea Scrolls: A New Translation* [San Francisco: HarperSanFrancisco, 1996], 338). For the text, see García Martínez and Tigchelaar, *Dead Sea Scrolls Study Edition*, 2:742–45; and Martin G. Abegg and Craig A. Evans, "Messianic Passages in the Dead Sea Scrolls," in Charlesworth et al., *Qumran-Messianism*, 193. While Moses is never described as the Lord's anointed in the Bible, he appears to be described in this text not only as the paradigmatic prophet but also in lines 11–12 as the preeminent herald of glad tidings (cf. Isa 61:1–5; see Abegg and Evans, "Messianic Passages," 201). According to the statement found in *y. Taʿan.* 4.5 (68d), R. Akiba is reputed to have said of Bar Kokhba, "This is the anointed King" (דין הוא מלכא משיחא). (For the translation and usage, see the discussion below, pp. 400–401.) There is no indication from

combination could be taken in apposition and rendered "Jesus, the anointed one." However, the combination could also be taken adjectivally, as in "the anointed [high] priest" (*hakkōhēn hammašîaḥ*).[36] On grammatical grounds, there is no reason to exclude an adjectival rendering of *yəšûaʿ məšîḥāʾ*, that is, "the anointed Jesus." Again, the suggestion that the term was initially used as a byname was prompted by considering the possible adjectival connotations of the term. However, I did tend to emphasize royal connotations in my earlier papers.[37] I am no longer convinced that this emphasis is the most appropriate one for explaining why the term was introduced and why it took hold as a byname for Jesus.

III

Let me return briefly to the study of Oegema as a way to initiate a reconsideration. In order to include a treatment of New Testament writings in a survey of Jewish messianic expectations defined as expectations of a figure "who will play a liberating role at the end of time," Oegema felt it necessary to confine this part of his study almost exclusively to passages related to the parousia of Jesus.[38] He noted that, according to his working definition, references to Christ did not necessarily have such a figure in view[39] and concluded a summary of the results of his analysis with this observation:

> When we look at the whole of the development of messiah concepts and its connection with Jesus within the New Testament canon asking whether a Jewish messianic expectation has been "Hellenized" might be the wrong

---

the coins or documents from the Judean desert that Bar Kokhba received or adopted this designation. We should, of course, distinguish between possible support for Bar Kokhba and his military activities among some rabbis and the affirmation and repudiation of his messianic identity in later rabbinic traditions. Even R. Akiba seems to have been given both views in *y. Taʿan.* 4.5 (68d). For a different view of the significance of this text and messianic traditions attributed to Akiba, see Craig A. Evans, "Was Simon ben Kosiba Recognized as Messiah?" in *Jesus and His Contemporaries: Comparative Studies* (AGJU 25; Leiden: Brill, 1995), 183–211. Given the grounds on which Evans argues for authentic messianic traditions attributed to Akiba, it hardly matters, or at least is not decisive, whether Akiba actually made this statement or used the term *māšîaḥ* directly in reference to Bar Kokhba. In any case, we find no form that matches the construction *yəšûaʿ məšîḥāʾ*.

[36] Lev 4:3, 5, 16; 6:15; cf. Exod 28:41; 30:30; 40:15; Num 3:3; 35:25; cf. 4Q375.
[37] Miller, "How Jesus Became Christ"; idem, "Problem of the Origins."
[38] Oegema, *The Anointed and His People*, 26. Cf. 149: "Only those texts will be studied which explicitly mention the coming of Jesus as an eschatological liberation figure—that is, those mostly (but not always) concerned with his Parousia." For his survey and analysis, see 150–84.
[39] Ibid., 148.

question. Instead we should perhaps ask whether the expression "Christ," originating from a Hellenistic-Jewish community, ... has been used as the name and title of someone sanctified by God, namely Jesus, especially after his death and resurrection and whether the expression "Christ" has afterwards been reinterpreted in the Synoptic Apocalypses in a discussion with contemporary Jewish messianic expectations and messianic epithets within a specific political situation.[40]

Oegema's reference to Christ as someone sanctified by God is alluding to the work of Martin Karrer, who argued that the name and title were deduced from an understanding of the term more deeply associated with the sanctity of the cultus than with the power of royal dominion.[41]

As far as I have been able to check the matter, Karrer's *Habilitationsschrift* has not received much notice, which is unfortunate, since he has inquired into the bases for the significance of the term *christos* in early Christianity from a perspective that has not been seriously explored, namely, the range of cultural uses of anointing in the Mediterranean world.[42] What is particularly distinctive of biblical, Jewish, and Christian semantic formations for the theme of anointing is the derivation of a substantive from the verb "to anoint" to refer to the object or person receiving the action.[43] While there is evidence of the anointing of vassals and other high officials in the ancient Near East, no expression corresponding to the Hebrew *mašîaḥ YHWH* (the anointed of the Lord) has been found.[44] Karrer finds nothing surprising in the fact that in postbiblical Jewish literature our term refers in the singular and the plural only to figures of the past or to figures of the future but not to figures of the period of the composition. He takes this to be the result of the cessation of the ritual anointing of

---

[40] Ibid., 193.

[41] Karrer, *Der Gesalbte*, esp. 88–91, 211–12. Oegema has encapsulated the connotations of the term as it is used by Karrer in the words "holy for God" (*The Anointed and His People*, 148 n. 156).

[42] "Die anders als Königs- und Hohepriestersalbung nicht abgestorbenen, sondern höchst lebendigen kultischen und halbkultischen Salbungsvollzüge des Judentums um die Zeitenwende bilden keinen religionsgeschichtlichen Sonderbereich Israels, sondern zeigen dieses in den übergreifenden mittelmeerischen Religionsraum eingebettet. Denn durchweg begegnen—auf der gemeinsamen Basis sakraler Salbungswertung gemäss den jeweiligen Religionseigentümlichkeiten verschoben—pagane Äquivalente" (Karrer, *Der Gesalbte*, 209–10).

[43] Ibid., 211. In Gk. usage outside the New Testament, Septuagint, and dependent writings, χριστός, χριστή, χριστόν is a verbal adjective and means "spreadable," "smeared on," "anointed"; as a noun it is attested with the meaning "ointment." See Walter Grundmann, "χρίω κτλ.," *TDNT* 9:495.

[44] See Franz Hesse, "χρίω κτλ.," *TDNT* 9:497; K. Seybold, "מָשַׁח, *māšaḥ* I; מָשִׁיחַ, *māšîaḥ*," *TDOT* 9:49: "To date, no ancient Near Eastern parallel has been found to *mᵉšîaḥ YHWH* as a title of theological provenience."

kings, at least by the fifth century B.C.E., and of priests, including the high priests, at least by the Hasmonean period, rituals which were not renewed during Hasmonean or Herodian rule.[45] Nonetheless, during these latter periods cult objects and objects offered to God continued to be anointed with oil, while the innermost part of the sanctuary, the holy of holies, was designated "the anointed place."[46]

Karrer stresses a commonality of experience with respect to acts of anointing in the Hellenistic and Roman periods, whether it be in the spheres of cult and burial rites, of magic and apotropaic rites, in the practices of medicine and cosmetics, or those of sports and the military.[47] In the sphere of the cult, what everyone knew is that whatever was anointed was thereby brought close to and set apart for divinity. Thus, while the term *christos* may at first have sounded strange to non-Jewish ears, the significance of being anointed was not. Karrer believes that the general sensibility about the anointing of objects and persons in conjunction with the singularity of the name would have made *christos* as a designation for Jesus particularly attractive to Gentiles:

> In unschätzbarer Weise sicherte sie auf der Basis der gemeinantiken Sprachgebrauchs, "wer/was gesalbt ist, ist heilig, Gott nah, Gott übergeben" der christlichen Verkündigung des Gesalbten (Christos) schlechthin an die Völker (ἔθνη) ihre Einzigartigkeit, bewahrte sie vor einem Abgleiten in die Vielfalt mittelmeerisch-halbmagischen Volks- und Aberglaubens. Anders gesagt: Bei aller Einbettung in ein breites, positiv gewertetes religiöses Erfahrungsfeld klang "der Gesalbte" paganen Ohren zur Zeit der Entstehung des Christentums als singuläre, den eigenen Erfahrungsbemühungen

---

[45] On the cessation of the anointing of kings, see Karrer, *Der Gesalbte*, 95–147, esp. 128–47; on the cessation of the anointing of priests, see 147–72. While Karrer is correct about the absence of the term to refer to a present figure in Jewish writings of the Hasmonean and Herodian periods, this may have little to do with the cessation of anointing cultic or political leaders. With respect to the royal figure, the anointed of the Lord may always have referred to the king as a sacral figure rather than to any actual anointing as a legal act by representatives of the people. See Jonathan Z. Smith, "Wisdom and Apocalyptic," in *Religious Syncretism in Antiquity: Essays in Conversation with Geo Widengren* (ed. Birger A. Pearson; Missoula, Mont.: Scholars Press, 1975), 146, repr. in *Map Is Not Territory*, 79: "The major discovery of archaic Wisdom was the paradigmatic figure of the sacred king."

[46] See Exod 30:22–33; 29:36; 40:9–15; Num 7:1, 10, 84, 88; Lev 8:10–12. Karrer views these texts as evidence of continued anointing of high priests until the Seleucid period. He reads the text of Dan 9:26 LXX as a reference to the holy of holies as the anointed place. What is cut off after the sixty-two weeks is not "an anointed one" (MT, probably referring to Onias III) but "the anointing" (χρῖσμα), and what is destroyed is not only the city and the sanctuary (MT) but the city and the sanctuary with its anointed place (καὶ τὸ ἅγιον μετὰ τοῦ χριστοῦ; *Der Gesalbte*, 174–76, with n. 15). On the continued practice of anointing the offerings for sacrifice to the end of the Second Temple period, see Josephus, *War* 5.13.6 §565.

[47] Ibid., 172–209.

vermittel- und doch durch sie nicht nivellierbare religiöse Würdebezeichnung. Religiöse Konnotationsfähigkeit und Singularität verbanden sich in einer Weise, die "Christos" zum idealen Missionsbegriff machte.[48]

Without endorsing Karrer's notion of *christos* as a designation of singular religious value and as an ideal concept for mission, it is easy enough to imagine that among people of various cultural and ethnic backgrounds the connotations of anointing are more likely to have been those of sanctity, consecration, purity, health, blessing, and well-being in general than those of royal power and judicial authority in particular.[49] If that is the case, it is equally clear that the term itself is drawn from the sphere of biblical and Judaic discourses. Assuming its quite deliberate appeal to issues of identity and legitimation related to some collective notion of Israel, it does not follow that the term could only have been appropriated as a royal title, let alone as a technical term for an eschatological figure. A survey and comparison of biblical and postbiblical usage focused on texts that can be dated prior to the destruction of the Herodian temple will confirm this.

If we exclude the postdestruction apocalypses of *4 Ezra* and *2 Baruch*, the Targumim, and postmishnaic rabbinic literature, the application of our term to a royal figure is less pronounced in texts outside the Bible than what we find in the Bible. The term is used most often in the Bible in reference to a named king—Saul, David, Solomon, or Zedekiah—or as a surrogate for an unnamed king of the Davidic dynasty, using the nominal expression *mašîaḥ YHWH/christos kyriou,* or with the pronominal suffix referring to the deity ("his, my, your anointed one").[50] Outside the Bible, these forms are rarely attested in reference to a royal figure.[51] The plural,

---

[48] Ibid., 211.

[49] Purification is clearly one of the major functions of ritual anointing in the ancient Near East. See the detailed discussions of functions of anointing in ancient Near Eastern records in Ernst Kutsch, *Salbung als Rechtsakt im Alten Testament und im alten Orient* (BZAW 87; Berlin: Töpelmann, 1963).

[50] 1 Sam 24:7, 11; 26:9, 11, 16, 23; 2 Sam 1:14, 16; 19:22; Lam 4:20; cf. 2 Sam 23:1; using the pronominal suffix: 1 Sam 2:10, 35; 12:3, 5; 16:6; 2 Sam 22:51; Isa 45:1; Hab 3:13; Pss 2:2; 18:51; 20:7; 28:8; 84:10; 89:39, 52; 132:10, 17; 2 Chr 6:42. The reference is always to a native king with the exception of Isa 45:1, where it refers to the Persian king, Cyrus.

[51] The longer construct form, "the anointed of the Lord," is attested in *L.A.B.* 59.2, where the biblical text is closely followed. The original reading of *Ps. Sol.* 17.32 is disputed, though most commentators have emended the text to χριστὸς κυρίου, probably without sufficient justification; see the discussion below, pp. 400–401. The two other instances that probably reflect the construct form are found in *Ps. Sol.* 18, in the superscription and in 18.7. In both instances, the Gk. is χριστοῦ κυρίου, making it grammatically unclear whether it should be read χριστὸς κύριος, as in the Greek manuscripts of *Ps. Sol.* 17.32, or χριστὸς κυρίου, reflecting the Hebrew construct form. However, the reference to χριστοῦ αὐτοῦ in 18:5, reflecting the shorter pronominal-suffix form *mašîḥô* (his, i.e., the Lord's anointed), makes the latter the

"anointed ones," with the first-person singular pronominal suffix appears in Ps 105:15 (= 1 Chr 16:22), where it parallels "my prophets," referring to the protected status of Israel's patriarchs in their wanderings.

In the Dead Sea Scrolls (DSS) our term is found as a surrogate not for a royal figure or dynasty but for prophets in a collective sense. What is stressed in this identification is the status of holiness and the divine sanction that attaches to prophetic guidance. For example, in all of the appointed times, God has called people by name and "informed them by the hand of the anointed ones of his holy spirit."[52] In time past, the land of Israel was devastated, "for they had spoken rebellion against the commandments of God (given) by the hand of Moses and also by the hand of the anointed ones of holiness."[53] "And by the hand of your anointed ones, seers of fixed decrees, you have declared to us the ti[mes of] the wars of your hands."[54] Among those whom God has decreed to remove is the one who speaks "rebellion against the anointed ones of the holy spirit."[55]

Another Qumran text that may provide a further example of a collective use of our term with reference to prophets is 4Q521. Fragments 2 and 4 of this text in particular have elicited the special interest of New Testament scholars, and the fragments have already been the subject of intense debate. The text was published by Émile Puech under the title, "Une apocalypse messianique."[56] It is highly questionable whether either term in the title is appropriate. In his analysis of the text and review of current discussion, Michael Becker maintains that the text should be understood in a prophetic horizon closely related to other Qumran references to prophets as anointed ones. It does not provide pre-Christian evidence of a (Davidic) Messiah cast

---

more likely reading of the Greek genitive forms in *Ps. Sol.* 18. Besides *Ps. Sol.* 18.5, the shorter form using the pronominal is found in *1 En.* 48.10; 52.4. The few clear instances in the Dead Sea Scrolls refer to a prophet or prophets (1QM 11.7–8; 4Q521 1 II, 1; 4Q377 2 II, 5).

[52] CD A 2.12: ויודיעם ביד משיחו רוח קדשו (text in Daniel R. Schwartz, PTSDSSP 2:14). משיחו is probably an error for the construct plural משיחי.

[53] CD A 5.21–6.1, reading משיחי הקודש for משיחו הקודש; see above, p. 380 n. 15. A parallel to this text is found in 4Q267, which has the construct plural form; see Joseph M. Baumgarten, "267. 4QDamascus Document[b]," in *Qumran Cave 4.XIII: The Damascus Document (4Q266–273)* (DJD 18; Oxford: Clarendon, 1996), 97; cf. 1Q30 1.2, מ]שיח הקודש, in J. T. Milik, "30–31. Textes liturgiques (?)," in *Qumran Cave 1* (ed. D. Barthélemy and J. T. Milik; DJD 1; Oxford: Clarendon, 1955), 132.

[54] 1QM 11.7–8: ביד משיחיכה חוזי תעודות (text in Jean Duhaime, PTSDSSP 2:118).

[55] 4Q270 2 II, 13–14: ידבר] סרה על משיחי רוח הקדש (text in Joseph M. Baumgarten, "270. 4QDamascus Document[e]," in *Qumran Cave 4.XIII: The Damascus Document [4Q266–273]*, 144). This text has no counterpart to the medieval CD. It also seems more likely to be related to the present than to the past.

[56] Émile Puech, "Une apocalypse messianique *(4Q521),*" *RevQ* 15 (1992): 475–522. For the *editio princeps*, see idem, "521. 4QApocalypse messianique," in *Qumrân Grotte 4.XVIII: Textes Hébreux (4Q521–4Q528, 4Q576–4Q579)* (DJD 25; Oxford: Clarendon, 1998), 1–38.

as a miracle worker.⁵⁷ Becker argues that, on balance, the reference to "his anointed" (2 II, 1) in the phrase, "[for the hea]vens and the earth shall listen to his anointed" (כי הש[מ]ים והארץ ישמעו למשיחו]) should be read as a defective plural and taken as a parallel to "holy ones" in the next line.⁵⁸ Actions attributed to the herald of Isa 61:1–2 are reflected in fragments 2 and 4, although the influence of Ps 146:6–9 is stronger.⁵⁹ The actions include reviving the dead, which is not found in either biblical text but is included in Jesus' response to the disciples of John in Q 7:22. However, in the Qumran text, especially in lines 10–13, these actions are attributed directly to God.⁶⁰

While *anointed ones* is clearly used as a surrogate for prophets in the DSS, it is not a title for an eschatological prophet but a descriptive term intended to underline the authority of the prophetic office and the authenticity of the prophetic word whether delivered in the past, present, or future. When the coming of a prophet in the future is clearly in view (as in 1QS 9.11), it can be stated without any other way of marking the special stature or authority of the prophet (cf. 1 Macc 14:41).

---

⁵⁷ Michael Becker, "*4Q521* und die Gesalbten," *RevQ* 18 (1997): 73–96. A similar position is held by Hartmut Stegemann, *The Library of Qumran: On the Essenes, Qumran, John the Baptist, and Jesus* (Grand Rapids: Eerdmans; Leiden: Brill, 1998), 206.

⁵⁸ Becker, "*4Q521* und die Gesalbten," 74–78; bibliography on the range of positions and current debate can be found in the notes in ibid., esp. 79 n. 34. John J. Collins has tentatively identified the figure (understood as singular) with the expectation of a returning Elijah-type figure as forerunner of the Messiah; see idem, "The Works of the Messiah," *DSD* 1 (1994): 98–112; idem, "Teacher, Priest and Prophet," in *The Scepter and the Star: The Messiahs of the Dead Sea Scrolls and Other Ancient Literature* (ABRL; New York: Doubleday, 1995), 102–35; idem, "Jesus, Messianism and the Dead Sea Scrolls," in Charlesworth et al., *Qumran-Messianism*, 112–19. For Becker's critique of this identification, see idem, "*4Q521* und die Gesalbten," 89, with n. 76. There is a clear instance of the plural form of our term with a feminine suffix in 4Q521 8.9 (וכל משיחיה). In context, the reference here may be to priests or to anointed cultic objects; cf. 9.3.

⁵⁹ The "herald of glad tidings" of Isa 61 is also featured in 11Q13 (11QMelch) 2.18, where he is described as "the anointed of the spirit" (משיח הרו[ח]). The role of the anointed of the spirit is not to be equated with Melchizedek in the same text but seems to have a connection with the prophecy in Dan 9:25 of an anointed prince. The herald is said to comfort the afflicted (interpreting Isa 61:2) "to make them understand all the ages of t[ime" (2.18–21). Text in Florentino García Martínez, Eibert J. C. Tigchelaar, and Adam S. van der Woude, "13. 11QMelchizedek," in *Qumran Cave 11.II: 11Q2–18, 11Q20–31* (DJD 23; Oxford: Clarendon, 1998), 225.

⁶⁰ Becker, "*4Q521* und die Gesalbten," 92: "Es steht jedoch fest, dass es immer Gott ist, der dies Heil wirkt, und keinesfalls der Messias oder eine ähnliche Gestalt." The phrase in line 1, "[for the hea]vens and the earth shall listen to his anointed," calls to mind in particular Deut 32:1 (and perhaps also Isa 1:2). The Mosaic cast of prophets as revealers of torah in the DSS may perhaps account for the description of Moses as the paradigmatic anointed prophet and herald of glad tidings in 4Q377; see above, n. 35.

The only certain instance in the Bible of a collective application of our term in the nominal form is Ps 105:15 (a reference to the patriarchs as prophets). However, there are cases in which the context suggests that "Yahweh's anointed" refers to the people of Israel.[61] The LXX of Hab 3:13 is most often noted in this connection, especially since most of the witnesses have the plural form: "You went forth for the salvation of your people, to save your anointed ones" (τοὺς χριστούς σου). Even the variant reading with the singular (as in the MT) may be taken in context as a heightened reference to "your people." There are a number of similar instances in the MT and LXX, for example, Ps 84:10a (83:10a LXX) and Ps 28:8 (27:8 LXX). Psalm 89:39–52 is held by some to require a collective application of Yahweh's anointed.[62] This is supported in the LXX version by the terms "holy place" (89:40) and "purification/cleanness" (89:45), where the MT has "crown" and "scepter," respectively. Karrer has argued that collective application of our term is stronger in the LXX than in the MT and relates this to the situation of Alexandrian Judaism. In *Sib. Or.* 5.68 the doom of Egypt is threatened "because you raged against my God-anointed children" (ἐμοὺς παῖδας θεοχρίστους).[63]

The Hebrew Bible never refers to a particular priest or group of priests as the anointed of Yahweh. Instead of a nominal form, we find an adjectival construction, "the anointed priest" (הַכֹּהֵן הַמָּשִׁיחַ, Lev. 4:3, 5, 16; 6:15), and the passive participle in the plural (הַכֹּהֲנִים הַמְּשֻׁחִים, Num 3:3). Since the anointing of priests and of cultic objects with holy oil is emphasized in the Pentateuch,[64] it is likely that the adjectival or participial formation is intended to stress the act of anointing as consecration to engage in cultic service. In Exod 40:13–15 not only are Aaron and his sons anointed and

---

[61] The broader issue of the collective interpretation of many prophetic oracles announcing the coming of a savior-king and many of the so-called royal psalms is argued by Joachim Becker, *Messianic Expectation in the Old Testament* (trans. David E. Green, Philadelphia: Fortress, 1980), 68–78; for the LXX, see Lust, "Messianism and Septuagint," 175–77. For a recent discussion of a collective interpretation of the "promise to David" in Deutero-Isaiah and in the Temple Scroll, see William M. Schniedewind, *Society and the Promise to David: The Reception History of 2 Samuel 7:1–17* (New York: Oxford University Press, 1999), 115–17, 161–63, 195, 204–5. On passages in the DSS referring to the exercise of royal dominion by the people of Israel, see the studies of Stegemann, "Some Remarks," 501–5. Stegemann (502) calls attention to the collective application to Israel of the "star ... from Jacob" and "the staff from Israel" (Num 24:17) in 1QM 11.6–9. See also Annette Steudel, "The Eternal Reign of the People of God—Collective Expectations in Qumran Texts (*4Q246* and *1QM*)," *RevQ* 17 (1996): 507–19. Cf. the discussion of 4Q252 above, pp. 381–82.

[62] See Becker, *Messianic Expectation*, 76.

[63] Karrer, *Der Gesalbte*, 228–31; for the text, see Joh[annes] Geffcken, *Die Oracula sibyllina* (GCS; Leipzig: Hinrichs, 1902). The text probably dates from the late first or early second century C.E.

[64] See esp. Exod 30:22–33; cf. 1 Chr 29:22b; Sir 45:15.

consecrated that they may serve Yahweh as priests, but their anointing is said to establish the Aaronides as a permanent institution of priesthood.[65] Since it is hardly likely that all serving priests were actually anointed in any period,[66] the references in Leviticus and Numbers to the anointed priest are often taken to refer to the high priest as the successor of Aaron in distinction from all other priests.[67] If the qualification of anointing for all Aaronides is a later generalization, it would seem to signify the priestly office itself, or perhaps it is intended to serve as a claim distinguishing qualified priestly families. In 2 Macc 1, the letter purported to be from Judas is addressed to Aristobulus, teacher of King Ptolemy VI (180–145 B.C.E.). He is described as belonging to the family of anointed priests (ὄντι δὲ ἀπὸ τοῦ τῶν χριστῶν ἱερέων γένους, 1:10b). The adjective would seem to denote a claim of legitimation or qualification for cultic service (in Jerusalem?).

The tendency to exalt the place of the priesthood at the expense of the royal office in some of the literature of early Judaism does not carry with it an increase in the use of our term in conjunction with the status or function of priests. The exalted description of the high priest in *T. Levi* 18 does not refer to anointing. Nor is anointing mentioned in *T. Jud.* 21. The only text in the *Testaments of the Twelve Patriarchs* that makes use of the biblical form in connection with the figure of the high priest stresses the teaching as well as the cultic function of Levi and his descendants. In *T. Reu.* 6.8 we read, "It is for this reason that I command you to give heed to Levi, because he will know the law of God and will give instructions concerning justice and concerning sacrifice for Israel until the consummation of times; he is the anointed priest [ἀρχιερέως χριστοῦ] of whom the Lord spoke."[68]

The DSS refer mostly to the sons of Aaron or the sons of Zadok. In 1QSb 3.22–4.28 (*Rule of the Blessings*), the Instructor addresses the sons of

---

[65] See Maier, "Messias oder Gesalbter?" 590: "Qumrans angeblicher 'Priestermessias' ist also nichts als eine bekannte jüdischen Institution im Zusammenhang mit dem Tempelkult."

[66] The qualification for all the sons of Aaron is found in Exod 28:41; 30:30; 40:15; Num 3:3; see J. J. M. Roberts, "The Old Testament's Contribution to Messianic Expectations," in *The Messiah: Developments in Earliest Judaism and Christianity* (ed. James H. Charlesworth; The First Princeton Symposium on Judaism and Christian Origins; Minneapolis: Fortress, 1992), 39; Seybold, "מָשַׁח, *māšaḥ* I," 9:53; Hesse, "χρίω κτλ.," 9:500–501.

[67] See esp. Lev 6:15 (22); 21:10; Num 35:25. Lev 21:10a is explicit: "The priest who is exalted above his fellows, on whose head the anointing oil has been poured."

[68] Trans. Kee, "Testaments of the Twelve Patriarchs," in Charlesworth, *Old Testament Pseudepigrapha*, 1:784–85; cf. the translation in H. W. Hollander and M. de Jonge, *The Testaments of the Twelve Patriarchs: A Commentary* (SVTP 8; Leiden: Brill, 1985), 105. For Hollander and de Jonge, who hold to the Christian provenance of the *Testaments*, "the anointed high priest" comes at the consummation of times and refers to Christ. For the Greek text, see M. de Jonge, *The Testaments of the Twelve Patriarchs: A Critical Edition of the Greek Text* (PVTG 1/2; Leiden: Brill, 1978), 12.

Zadok, blessing them with God's election and covenant of eternal priesthood among the holy ones, with whom they are to order destiny as they serve in the temple of the kingdom, but no reference is made to them as anointed ones. In 1QSa (*Rule of the Congregation*), the anointed one of Israel is clearly outranked at the feast of the congregation by the priest who enters at the head of the congregation. Yet the priest is not referred to with any special honorific. This is striking. Since 1QSa 2.11–22 is referring to a meal in which the anointed one of Israel is present, we would have expected an explicit reference to the anointed one of Aaron.[69] The exalted status of the institution of priesthood does not require a reference to our term. It is not a determinative title for the present or future exercise of priestly prerogatives, although it continues to be used to refer to the office of high priest.

---

[69] Stegemann, "Some Remarks," 503, has argued that 1QSa and 1QSb represent a second stage in the development of Qumran messianism (ca. 150–110 B.C.E.), when only a "Royal Messiah" was expected. According to Stegemann, the regulations for the meal pertain to the author's present and to any cultic meal of any assembly of Israel and are not regulations for a messianic banquet of the whole congregation of Israel at some future point in time. The "end of days" is understood as the last period of history in which the author already stands. What is envisioned is a circumstance in which the Royal Messiah (whose expectation is imminent and therefore whose presence is anticipated) might be present at any cultic assembly. In such a circumstance, any priest who presides takes precedence over the Royal Messiah at the meal (1QSa 2.19–20). In Stegemann's view, the expectation of a Priestly Messiah has not yet developed at this stage, and therefore one should not identify the officiating priest in 1QSa with this figure. It is important to recognize that Stegemann's interpretation of this text depends not only on an assessment of the divisions of the text, the filling of lacunas, the solution to several palaeographical problems, and the interpretation of key phrases, but on a developmental hypothesis related to the currently debated question of the composition history of these texts and their relation to 1QS and to the Cave 4 manuscripts of the *Community Rule*. Not least of the problems of interpretation of this text is the reconstruction of col. II, lines 11–12 (cf. the transcriptions and translations in ibid., 491; Émile Puech, "Préséance sacerdotale et Messie-Roi dans la Règle de la Congrégation [*1QSa* ii 11–22]," *RevQ* 16 [1994]: 358; and Charlesworth and Stuckenbruck, PTSDSSP 1:116–17, with n. 64). Most readings of the text accept the presence of an absolute use of our term in line 12, המשיח, and identify the figure with "the anointed of Israel" in lines 14 and 20. If this is correct, it would constitute the only instance of an absolute use of our term with the definite article in Jewish texts prior to the postdestruction apocalypses of *4 Ezra* and *2 Baruch*. This reading has not gone uncontested. Puech reconstructs הנשיא המשיח, "le Prince Messie" ("Préséance sacerdotale et Messie-Roi," 359–60). Maier proposes the reading הכוהן המשיח, "der gesalbte Priester" ("Messias oder Gesalbter?" 605). This locution appears in 4Q375 1 I, 9 in the interesting context of a study undertaken and a ritual of ordeal performed by "[the] anointed priest upon whose h[e]ad the oil of anointing has been poured" on the occasion of an accusation made against a prophet whose tribe has attested that the accused is a faithful prophet. For the *editio princeps* of this text as well as 4Q376, which also refers to "the anointed priest," see J. Strugnell, "375. 4QApocryphon of Moses[a]" and "376. 4QApocryphon of Moses[b]?" in *Qumran Cave 4.XIV: Parabiblical Texts, Part 2* (ed. Magen Broshi et al.; DJD 19; Oxford: Clarendon, 1995), 111–36.

The other biblical instances of our term appear in Dan 9:25–26. They are of particular interest because it is only in these verses that the nominal form is used in the absolute state. In 9:25 the term is followed directly by the political designation "prince" (*māšîaḥ nāgîd*), whereas in 9:26 "an anointed one" (*māšîaḥ*) appears without further determination. The anarthrous doubling of political honorifics is a common Hellenistic practice and may account for the anarthrous form in Dan 9:25. The same influence has been seen in *Ps. Sol.* 17.32. *Christos kyrios* is found in all available manuscripts and should not be taken as an error for a Semitic *Vorlage* that read *māšîaḥ YHWH*, nor as a Christian scribal alteration of *christos kyriou* (as is clearly the case in Lam 4:20 LXX), but as an instance of Hellenistic influence on the Hebrew form, *māšîaḥ ʾādôn*. Similarly, *christos kyrios* in Luke 2:11 is not to be viewed as an exclusively Christian usage but reflects the same Hellenistic pattern. Finally, the anarthrous forms found in later rabbinic and targumic texts, such as *Tg. Neof.* Gen 49:10 (*malkāʾ mǝšîḥaʾ*) and *Midr. Gen. Rab.* Gen 49:10 (*melek māšîaḥ*), and the reference to Bar Kokhba as *malkāʾ mǝšîḥaʾ* in the Palestinian Talmud (*y. Taʿan.* 4.5 [68d]) also reflect the Hellenistic usage for royal figures.

However, the likelihood that these instances reflect the Hellenistic practice of combining honorifics for rulers does not make a case for concluding that *māšîaḥ/christos* has become a technical title for an eschatological royal figure. Daniel 9:25–26 refers to figures in the past, probably to Zerubbabel or Joshua in the distant past (9:25), and to the more recent deposition and murder of the priest, Onias III (9:26). The anarthrous linking of *christos* and *kyrios* in reference to an ideal royal figure of the future does not establish *christos* in *Ps. Sol.* 17.32 as a titular usage but serves to intensify the claim to legitimacy. Unlike the biblical construct form *māšîaḥ YHWH*, the anarthrous *māšîaḥ nāgîd* and *christos kyrios* have not become surrogate terms for a ruler.[70] *Māšîaḥ* and *christos* are intended as qualifying terms, in the Daniel text as an allusion to Zerubbabel or Joshua, who were characterized by Zechariah as "the two sons of oil who stand before the Lord of the whole earth" (Zech 4:14), and in *Ps.*

---

[70] Note that the older biblical form is present in the superscription of *Ps. Sol.* 18, as well as in 18:7 in the genitive construction, *christou kyriou*. The translation "anointed of the Lord" is very likely correct in view of 18:5, where *christou autou* is the Greek rendering of *mǝšîḥô* (contra R. B. Wright, "Psalms of Solomon," in Charlesworth, *Old Testament Pseudepigrapha*, 2:669 n. f; cf. Robert R. Hann, "Christos Kyrios in PsSol 17.32: 'The Lord's Anointed' Reconsidered," *NTS* 31 [1985]: 625–26; and see above, n. 51). The anarthrous *māšîaḥ* in Dan 9:26, "an anointed one," is not at all an indication that the term has come to have a technical sense and therefore can be used without further qualification or determination. It is rather that we are dealing with the deliberate indefiniteness of apocalyptic writing where the referent is well known to those being addressed.

Sol. 17 in order to establish the contrast between legitimate rule and the present Hasmonean and Roman rulers. The expected ruler of *Ps. Sol.* 17.32 is "an anointed lord," a truly qualified king.[71] The Lukan text cited above can be translated in the same way.[72] As Johann Maier has noted, the anarthrous *melek māšîaḥ* in later Jewish writings can also be translated "anointed king" rather than the more usual "King Messiah," while the articular form (*ham*)*melek hammāšîaḥ* is probably patterned on the adjectival form for the high priest, *hakkōhēn hammāšîaḥ*.[73]

From the beginning of the eighth century B.C.E., Assyria dominated the Fertile Crescent, eventually to be displaced by far larger empires from the East and later from the West. In this imperial world, it is unsurprising that native scribes would include a king figure in imagining the restoration of native institutions.[74] Nor is it remarkable to find this royal figure depicted as the god's agent for defeating the enemies of his people and exercising judicial authority to execute the final representative of imperial power.[75]

---

[71] Cf. Marinus de Jonge, "Messiah," *ABD* 4:783: "the expression is used in *Ps. Sol.* 17:32 as a qualification rather than a title." Hann, "Christos Kyrios," 625, has commented, "Psalm of Solomon 17 ... stressed the legitimacy of the coming messianic king by applying to him the political title 'lord,' and thereby ... denied such legitimacy to the established authorities." Wright, "Psalms of Solomon," 668 n. z, makes the same point: "Since the adjectival use of *kurios* had as well the connotation 'legitimate,' it is not inconceivable that a group of religious and political dissidents such as the authors of the PssSol would have described the anticipated righteous king by that adjective with the phrase *christos kurios* and so denied the implication of legitimacy to the present, corrupt rulers." However, I would suggest that the adjectival connotations are carried by *christos* and that it is only Wright's assumption that the term is employed as a technical title that causes him to focus these connotations on *kyrios*. If *māšîaḥ nāgîd* in Daniel is appropriately translated "an anointed prince," I see no problem in translating *christos kyrios* "an anointed lord." Cf. Maier, "Messias oder Gesalbter?" 594: "könnte *kyrios* hier [*Ps. Sol.* 17.32] (ebenso wie in der jüdischen Vorlage von *Lk* 2,11) im Sinne einer hellenistischen Herrscherappellation verwendet worden sein und der Ausdruck folglich nichts anderes besagen als 'gesalbter König.' ... Wenn man in *Ps Sal* 17,32 also 'the Lord Messiah' übersetzt, ist das in jedem Fall nur auf Grund eines bestimmten christologischen Vorverständnisses nachvollziehbar, denn falls eine 'normale' Herrscherbezeichnung zugrunde liegt, dürfte in der Übersetzung eines jüdischen Textes weder 'Lord' noch 'Messiah' gross geschrieben sein und letzteres sollte überhaupt nicht verwendet werden."

[72] If one supposes a Jewish *Vorlage* behind Luke 2:11, there is no reason to give a different translation for this text (see n. 71). It is only the Christian context that makes "Christ, the Lord" or "the Messiah, the Lord" appropriate renderings.

[73] Maier, "Messias oder Gesalbter?" 594, 590.

[74] Smith, "Wisdom and Apocalyptic"; idem, "A Pearl of Great Price and a Cargo of Yams: A Study in Situational Incongruity," *HR* 16 (1976): 1–19, esp. 7–11, repr., with revisions, in *Imagining Religion: From Babylon to Jonestown* (CSHJ; Chicago: University of Chicago Press, 1982), 90–101, 156–62, esp. 94–96.

[75] 4Q285 7.3–4 (referring to Isa 11:1): "the Branch of David, and they will enter into judgement with [ ] and the Prince of the Congregation, the Bran[ch of David,] shall put him (the chief of the enemies) to death." For the text and translation, see P. Alexander and G. Vermes,

Nonetheless, it is the ideal of righteousness ascribed to the Davidic royal figure that is especially marked in Jewish writings of our period. Isaiah 11:1–5 is a familiar source for the characterization. *Psalm of Solomon* 17 describes an expected son of David as a "righteous king taught by God" (17:32a), for "the Lord himself will be his king" (17:34a); *T. Jud.* 24 characterizes the ruler who will arise as "the branch of God Most High" (24:4), "a rod of righteousness" (24:6); and 4Q252 refers to "the anointed one of righteousness, the branch of David" (משיח הצדק צמח דויד; cf. Jer 23:5; 33:15). The Davidic ascription in this last instance appears four other times in the DSS,[76] but only in 4Q252 is that ascription linked with our term. It is important to underline this observation. While it is true that an expected ruler is sometimes represented as a Davidic figure in the DSS, there is no clear tendency to use *māšîaḥ* to designate this figure. The preference is for the metaphor "branch of David," adapting the phrase in Jer 23:5, "I will raise up for David a righteous branch" (צֶמַח צַדִּיק). In my judgment, the statement of Marinus de Jonge concerning both priest and prince in the DSS holds true: "The people at Qumran looked forward to the times when the meaning of the Law would be fully clear and when God's will would be obeyed completely. Then, a duly appointed high priest and a Davidic prince would discharge their respective functions properly.... In a number of texts—but by no means everywhere—the anointed status of high priest and prince is mentioned, so that it is advisable to avoid the translation 'messiah,' which suggests titular use."[77]

Moreover, the branch of David is hardly a dominating figure in the DSS, any more than the figure designated the anointed one of Israel. Like the latter, he does not appear alone, and his role is legitimated by his adherence to the torah of the *Yaḥad* as interpreted and taught by the prominent priests.[78] The subordination of the royal figure is not surprising,

---

"285. 4QSefer ha-Milḥamah," in *Qumran Cave 4.XXVI: Cryptic Texts and Miscellanea, Part 1* (ed. Stephen J. Pfann et al.; DJD 36; Oxford: Clarendon, 2000), 238–39. For bibliography and an earlier discussion of this text, see Martin G. Abegg Jr., "Messianic Hope and 4Q285: A Reassessment," *JBL* 113 (1994): 81–91. For this same motif, see *2 Bar.* 40.1; *4 Ezra* 12.31–33.

[76] 4Q161; 4Q174; 4Q285 (2x).

[77] de Jonge, "Messiah," 4:783. Maier's position on the same issue is even more pointed; see above, n. 31.

[78] See above, pp. 377 on 4Q161 and 381–82 with nn. 20–21 on 4Q252. In 4Q174 1.11–13 "the branch of David" is said to arise with "the interpreter of the law." The branch of David is identified with the "fallen booth of David" (Amos 9:11) and is raised up by God to deliver Israel. The section that follows interprets Pss 1:1; 2:1, the latter passage referring to the nations conspiring against the Lord and his anointed. "The in[ter]pretation [is that the rulers of the na]tions [shall set themselves] and con[spire in vain against] the chosen ones of Israel in the last days" (1.19; for the *editio princeps*, see John M. Allegro, "174. Florilegium," in *Qumrân Cave 4.I [4Q158–4Q186]*, 53; cf. García Martínez and Tigchelaar, *Dead Sea Scrolls Study Edition*, 1:352, 354). The text goes on to explain that these chosen ones are a remnant

but it may cause us to lose sight of the fact that a royal figure must still be in the picture for the *Yahad,* when it is a matter of imagining the ideal functioning of the society. This may have less to do with reflection on the actual structures of political power, as Oegema has hypothesized, than with reflection on the ideal relations of the hierarchies of purity and power.[79]

Two instances of our term are found in the Similitudes of Enoch (*1 En.* 37–71).[80] In 48.10 its use is clearly triggered by the language of Ps 2:1–2, which is appropriated for the particular context. "In those days, the kings of the earth and the mighty landowners [who have oppressed the righteous and chosen ones] shall be humiliated on account of the deeds of their hands" (48.8a). They shall find no refuge and shall not be restored, "for they have denied the Lord of the Spirits and his anointed" (48.10c).[81] The usage is similar in 52.4. When Enoch asks the angel about the secrets of the mountains he has seen in the vision, he is told that they serve the authority (or dominion) of his anointed. The scene concludes with the assurance that in those days gold and silver and all the materials of war will not avail the powerful oppressors but will be "denied"[82] and destroyed when the chosen one appears before the Lord of Spirits.

As has often been observed, of the four epithets used to designate the figure depicted in the visions, "righteous one" as a substantive appears with certainty only once (53.6), "anointed one" is found twice, while "son of man" and "chosen one" each appear some sixteen times in

---

predestined to perform all of the law of God commanded through Moses. Here, God's anointed in Ps 2 has been interpreted collectively in relation to the establishing of torah. For a similar tendency in the rabbinic Eighteen Benedictions (the Amidah), see Reuven Kimelman, "The Messiah of the Amidah: A Study in Comparative Messianism," *JBL* 116 (1997): 318: "The Amidah thus corresponds to a tendency of rabbinic literature as well as of Qumran literature of downplaying the significance of Davidic rule."

[79] See Jonathan Z. Smith's reflections on, and adaptation of, the work of Louis Dumont (*Homo Hierarchicus: The Caste System and Its Implications* [rev. ed.; trans. Mark Sainsbury et al.; Chicago: University of Chicago Press, 1980]) in *To Take Place: Toward Theory in Ritual* (CSHJ; Chicago: University of Chicago Press, 1987), 54–56, 150–51; and see below, pp. 412–14.

[80] There is a growing scholarly consensus to date the Similitudes to the late first century B.C.E. or the first half of the first century C.E., despite the fact that, unlike other sections of *1 Enoch,* they have not turned up in the library of Qumran and are extant only in Ethiopic. See James H. Charlesworth, *The Old Testament Pseudepigrapha and the New Testament: Prolegomena for the Study of Christian Origins* (SNTSMS 54; Cambridge: Cambridge University Press, 1985), 102–19, 183–86; Jonas C. Greenfield and Michael E. Stone, "The Enochic Pentateuch and the Date of the Similitudes," *HTR* 70 (1977): 51–65; M. A. Knibb, "The Date of the Parables of Enoch: A Critical Review," *NTS* 25 (1979): 345–59.

[81] Trans. E. Isaac, "1 (Ethiopic Apocalypse of) Enoch," in Charlesworth, *Old Testament Pseudepigrapha,* 1:35–36; Isaac translates "his Messiah," rather than "his anointed."

[82] Ibid., 37 n. p.

the Similitudes.[83] Concerning the anointed one, J. C. VanderKam has observed, "As these are the only two uses of the title in the Similitudes, it is clear that it plays a modest role in the author's thinking and that little can be gleaned about the meaning which he attached to it."[84] James H. Charlesworth has commented in a similar vein:

> The references are strikingly terse and opaque, especially so in light of the rich pictorial descriptions of "the Son of Man," "the Righteous One," and "the Elect One" found also in *1 Enoch* 37–71. In an apocalyptic work so full of details regarding the future ... the references to and the descriptions of "the Messiah," or its derivatives, are impressively brief. The "Messiah" does not inaugurate a messianic kingdom. Surprisingly, the author has attributed to him no functions. There is no interest in or association with a descent from David.[85]

Recent studies have shown that the four epithets (or titles, as some scholars maintain) refer to the same exalted figure.[86] The composite portrait has been drawn mainly by combining features from Deutero-Isaiah and Dan 7. However, since the figure is cast in an exalted judicial role, and since some descriptions appear to draw on Isa 11 and Pss 2, 132, and 110, it is in fact noteworthy that our term is not found more often as an epithet for the figure who will sit on the throne of glory at the final assize.[87] On the other hand, it seems to me misleading to conclude that the composite portrait has been achieved by identifying the "Servant" of Isaiah, the Davidic "Messiah," and the Danielic "Son of Man," as though these labels

---

[83] See J. C. VanderKam, "Righteous One, Messiah, Chosen One, and Son of Man in 1 Enoch 37–71," in Charlesworth, *Messiah*, 169–91, esp. 169–76.

[84] Ibid., 171–72. It is possible that the two passages referring to "his anointed one" have been added in the transmission of the Similitudes; see Johannes Theisohn, *Der auserwählte Richter: Untersuchungen zum traditionsgeschichtlichen Ort der Menschensohngestalt der Bilderreden des Äthiopischen Henoch* (SUNT 12; Göttingen: Vandenhoeck & Ruprecht, 1975), 55–56.

[85] James H. Charlesworth, "Messianology in the Biblical Pseudepigrapha," in Charlesworth et al., *Qumran-Messianism*, 39. This article (21–52) is a revised version of Charlesworth's essay on "The Concept of the Messiah in the Pseudepigrapha," *ANRW* 19.1:188–218.

[86] This is what VanderKam seeks to establish in his essay, "Righteous One." His analysis is partly dependent (see 186, 188, 190) on Theisohn, *Der auserwählte Richter*. VanderKam also argues that the exaltation of the earthly Enoch to the role of the heavenly Son of Man in chs. 70–71 belonged to the original form of the Similitudes (177–85). James H. Charlesworth has also reached the conclusion that it is the same exalted figure that is in view in the Similitudes; see idem, "From Jewish Messianology to Christian Christology: Some Caveats and Perspectives," in Neusner et al., *Judaisms and Their Messiahs*, 237–41; cf. idem, "From Messianology to Christology: Problems and Prospects," in Charlesworth, *Messiah*, 31.

[87] *1 En.* 51.3; 55.4; 61.8; 62.2. For the influence of these biblical passages, see Theisohn, *Der auserwählte Richter*, 53–68, 89–91, 94–98, 137–39.

represented in the first century widely recognized titles and roles for figures of expectation that could be appropriated and reworked in different ways for Jesus by early Christians and for the antediluvian scribe of righteousness and his heavenly double by those who composed and transmitted the Similitudes.[88] The more obvious feature shared by the Similitudes and early Christian writings is the concentration of power and authority in a single figure. As ideological discourse, the relations of the hierarchies of purity and power tend to collapse in figures portrayed as sharing in divine power to the extent of appropriating the roles of the supreme deity. By comparison, the literature composed at Qumran, however separatist in orientation, expresses the distinction of roles and rankings with respect to the future that is characteristic of elite classes concerned with legitimate institutional representation and authorization.[89] However, in the instances with which

---

[88] Charlesworth, "From Jewish Messianology to Christian Christology," 241, writes: "Before C.E. 70, two groups in Early Judaism held messianic beliefs in which the Messiah was identified with the Servant and one like a Son of Man. One group portrayed the Elect One with terms, functions, and attributes derived from the traditions associated with the Isaianic Suffering Servant, the Davidic Messiah, and the Danielic Son of Man figure; the other group depicted Jesus of Nazareth in the same manner." Cf. this statement with Charlesworth's cautionary remark on the preceding page of his article: "This conclusion [that the four titles refer to the same figure] does not warrant the appealing corollary, that the functions and descriptions given to these other titles can readily be transferred to the Messiah" (240). In fact, much of the evidence for concluding that the Similitudes have in view a single figure is that the two common epithets, chosen (or elect) one and son of man, are used in connection with the same roles and attributes. Occasionally, as VanderKam ("Righteous One," 186) has noted, what is said of the servant in the biblical sources, e.g., that the servant will be a "light to the nations" (Isa 42:6; 49:6), is said of the son of man in the Similitudes (48.4), and what is said in Dan 7 about the son of man appearing with the "Head of Days" (7:13) is said of the chosen one in the Similitudes (55.1–4). At the same time, the figure depicted in the Similitudes is hardly the humiliated servant of Deutero-Isaiah whose fortunes are about to be reversed. While the motif of reversal is certainly applied in the Similitudes collectively to the chosen and righteous ones, it is not applied to the chosen one, the exalted judge of the end time. The same is true of the reversal of fortune of the collective son of man of Dan 7. It is not a feature of the individualized or hypostatized son of man who sits on the glorious throne in the Similitudes. In this same vein, I would suggest that "his anointed one" in the Similitudes has been drawn from Ps 2 because the term is closely linked in that biblical context with divinity and with the futility of resistance to, and thus denial of, the authority of the Lord's anointed by the nations and their rulers. The Similitudes have applied the motif to the judgment that will be rendered in favor of its own constituency and sympathizers against the powerful kings and wealthy landowners. This hardly constitutes a depiction of a figure of expectation called the Davidic Messiah about whom we might ask whether he has drawn to himself the roles of the Suffering Servant of Deutero-Isaiah and the Danielic Son of Man.

[89] By way of contrast, I would call attention to the choice of epithets for the figure depicted in the Similitudes. With the exception of "his anointed," they are not linked to leadership roles and offices of the central civic and sacral institutions of Israel. Rather, they tend to be associated with some collective representation of the people of Israel.

we are concerned, the concentration of power and authority in a single figure is not the consequence of reflection on the term whose usage we have surveyed. Not only is this obvious in the case of the Similitudes, which hardly make use of the term; it is equally true of *christos* as it appears in the earliest Christian literature, the letters of Paul. There is no indication in the Pauline writings that reflection on the term *christos* in distinction from the person of Christ accounts for the figure of Jesus as cosmic *kyrios* or as divine Son of God. But here, in contrast to the Similitudes, there is a problem, for our term seems clearly to have been established in some circles known to Paul prior to the writing of his letters and demands some account of why it was introduced and took hold.

Nothing in this survey thus far directly accounts for the most common uses of our term in the New Testament: on the one hand, as a term directly attached to a proper name, and on the other, as the determinate title for the figure of expectation par excellence. Indeed, I have intended to show that outside biblical literature there is no evidence to suggest that the term was especially associated with the role and actions of a royal figure.[90] It is not simply that the canonical Gospels and the book of Acts use the term in a titular way but that the implied reader is led to suppose that ὁ χριστός is the title of a figure of expectation known to everyone. We have not yet come across such an absolute usage. However, it can be found in the apocalypses of *4 Ezra* and *2 Baruch* in the generation following the destruction of the temple. Is this usage to be connected in particular with apocalyptic scenarios? We have an obvious instance in Mark 13:21 (cf. Acts 3:20). Karrer has proposed that the conditions that gave rise to this usage were in fact those of the Roman-Jewish war and refers to the long passage in Josephus concerning signs and portents that led many of the uninitiated astray.[91] The expectation of *the Messiah* is fixed when the term comes to refer to one of the standard tokens of salvation in a time of crisis.[92]

Whether Karrer is correct about the *Sitz im Leben* of this usage, the clear apocalyptic literary pattern associated with the absolute *hammāšîaḥ/ ho christos* is impressive. It differs from the pattern considered earlier in this essay in which certain conditions are to prevail until the coming of

---

[90] The instances are limited to *Pss. Sol.* 17–18, 4Q252, and the several passages in CD (4x), 1QS (1x), and 1QSa (2x, perhaps 3x); cf. 4Q458 2 II, 6, משיח בשמן מלכות ("anointed with the oil of kingship"), in E. Larson, "458. 4QNarrative A," in *Qumran Cave 4.XXVI: Cryptic Texts and Miscellanea, Part 1*, 358. This enumeration itself stretches the evidence, since we would have to take account of royal figures not so designated. Moreover, in most of these instances the royal figure is subordinated to some other source of authority or does not act in any capacity expressive of royal power and authority.

[91] Josephus, *War* 6.5.2–4 §§285–315; cf. Mark 13:22 and see Karrer, *Der Gesalbte*, 298–99.

[92] Cf. *m. Soṭah* 9:9–15.

some designated figure(s). In the apocalyptic pattern, what is important is that the figure, often conceived as being hidden with God, appears or is revealed at the foreordained moment in the context of a sequence of signs. Of course, this temporal pattern is typical of apocalyptic writing and clearly predates the destruction of the temple. It is found throughout the visions of the Similitudes, but in the Similitudes the interest focuses much more on the revealing and recognition of the judge who sits on the glorious throne. In contrast, *2 Baruch* and *4 Ezra* present an already recognized figure of expectation under the title "the Messiah"/"my servant, the Messiah"/"my son, the Messiah." The Messiah serves as one of the signals of recognition among the circles addressed by the writing. Although the period of judgment and dominion of the Messiah is clearly delimited in these texts, the key temporal term is not "until" but "when" or "after this." The pattern is more pronounced in *2 Baruch* but is evident also in *4 Ezra*.[93]

The identification of the absolute *ho christos* with the appearance of standard apocalyptic signs can be seen in Mark 13:21–22. However, I would not conclude that the use of this literary topos accounts for the broader tendency of the Gospels and Acts to present Jesus as the Messiah of general Jewish expectation. In my view, this tendency is a consequence of having appropriated the term exclusively for Jesus, while presenting his life in the context of revisionary readings of Israel's epic traditions. Such exclusive appropriation and absolute titular usage presuppose that *christos* was already a term of mutual recognition among a variety of Jesus and Christ groups, having first been linked with Jesus as a byname that carried honorific associations.

The results of the foregoing survey are consistent with the argument that our term was not initially linked to Jesus as an absolute royal title, the Messiah. *Māšîaḥ*/*christos* was not the title of a particular office or role, nor was it applied only to a single type of figure. Accordingly, it is not the biblical or Jewish uses of the term that justify creating an analytical category encompassing all figures who exercise, or might be thought to exercise, military and judicial roles in future or eschatological contexts, certainly not merely on the basis of the occasional application of our term to such a figure. Nor is there warrant for ascribing a titular significance when the term is applied to a future priest or king.[94] As far as I can see, there is no

---

[93] *2 Bar.* 29.3–30.5; 39.7–40.3; 70.2–72.6; *4 Ezra* 7.26–30; 11.37–12.34; cf. the man from the sea in *4 Ezra* 13.3–14.9. In Mark 13 there is also a sequential arrangement of signs, but the role of the Messiah in the Jewish apocalypses is paralleled in Mark by the Son of Man. Jesus does not return as the Messiah in Mark but rather warns of false messiahs whose signs and omens lead astray.

[94] Thus, I do not agree with Fitzmyer's conclusion in his recent essay, "Qumran Messianism," 104, when he says, "Although some writers have thought it better to speak only of an

difference in the *general* significance of the term itself whether it is applied to king(s), priest(s), or prophet(s), or whether it is used with reference to figure(s) of the past, present, or future. In the Qumran library (apart from biblical manuscripts) the most striking difference in application of our term, as compared to biblical literature, is not so much its several uses in future contexts but its surrogate function for prophets of the past rather than for kings of the Davidic dynasty. The term is also applied to a prophetic role in the future in 11Q13 (11QMelch) 2.18 and in 4Q521 1, II, 1, and continues to be used with reference to the office of high priest, as well as in connection with the future establishment of the Aaronide priesthood. However, none of these uses are titular in any exclusive or definitive way.

The general significance of the use of *māšîaḥ/christos* in Jewish literatures outside the Bible, at least until the latter part of the first century C.E., is to give theocratic grounding to each of the institutions considered essential to the proper functioning of the life of the people. In the DSS, the permanent establishment of torah in the life of the people receives emphasis by referring to the anointed status of the representatives of the prophetic, priestly, and royal institutions who bear chief responsibility for the interpretation, teaching, enactment, and maintenance of torah. That these representatives have been and will be "anointed ones" means that they are fully authorized by God for leadership roles and therefore that the institutions they represent are theocratically grounded.[95]

In my earlier essays I have argued that the most compelling way to account for the prolific use of *christos* in Paul's letters is to suppose that the Jesus people with whom Paul would have been most closely associated before his travels to Asia Minor, Macedonia, and Greece were people who called Jesus "*christos*."[96] My position in this essay is that the broad connotations of the term would have been those conveying divine authorization for a role of leadership. However, if we no longer need to equate the term with the expectation of an eschatological royal figure, it will also be clear that Jesus people would not have been able to compete with diaspora synagogues or with a network of communities such as the Essenes at the level of theocratic grounding of traditional institutional roles claimed for some conception of what God's people were or should be. The reason it is so difficult to identify the messianic role of Jesus in Paul's use of *christos* is not because Paul was addressing Gentiles who did

---

'Anointed One,' in my opinion the Qumran texts show that the term had already become titular in Judaism, referring to an expected or eschatological anointed agent of God."

[95] Maier's emphasis is the same ("Messias oder Gesalbter?" 590–94).

[96] Miller, "How Jesus Became Christ," 257–70; idem, "Problem of the Origins."

not understand the significance of the term but, first, because there was no such exclusive role, and second, because followers of Jesus applied the term to a particular person of the recent past rather than to past or future representatives of a particular institution or office. In the environs of Galilee, Jesus' status as founder-teacher was enhanced by comparison and analogy with figures of Israel's past.[97] In urban environs of Syria, the anointed Jesus, or Jesus as an anointed one, eventually settled in as the byname *christos* in order to lay claim to the perspective of the God of Israel in thinking about the role of Jesus as founder. The focus would not have been on Jesus as savior—at least not at first—but on what might be claimed of the heritage of Israel for the followers of Jesus, the kingdom-of-God people, in conversation with and differentiation from the synagogue people; and what might be said about the boundaries they were crossing and redrawing in the interests of an ongoing transactional enterprise of collective identity formation and maintenance.[98] As the expression of a quest for prestigious origins, the anointed Jesus belongs to the same category as most biblical myths, to ethnographic rather than to messianic myths.[99] It is concerned to define a society, rather than to save it. It reflects one attempt among others in the Greco-Roman world to redefine Israel—in this instance, by appeal to the anointed status of the founder; hence, by appeal to the God of Israel without invoking authority grounded in the institutions that embodied the practices of civic and national religion.

---

[97] See Mack, *Myth of Innocence*, 78–97; idem, *The Lost Gospel: The Book of Q and Christian Origins* (San Francisco: HarperSanFrancisco, 1993), 105–88; idem, *Who Wrote the New Testament*, 43–73.

[98] See Philip F. Esler, "Group Boundaries and Intergroup Conflict in Galatians: A New Reading of Galatians 5:13–6:10," in *Ethnicity and the Bible* (ed. Mark G. Brett; BibInt 19; Leiden: Brill, 1996), 215–40; Fredrik Barth, ed., *Ethnic Groups and Boundaries: The Social Organization of Culture Difference* (Boston: Little, Brown, 1969); Shaye J. D. Cohen, *The Beginnings of Jewishness: Boundaries, Varieties, Uncertainties* (Hellenistic Culture and Society 31; Berkeley and Los Angeles: University of California Press, 1999); Jonathan M. Hall, *Ethnic Identity in Greek Antiquity* (Cambridge: Cambridge University Press, 1997); Denise Kimber Buell, "Ethnicity and Religion in Mediterranean Antiquity and Beyond," *RelSRev* 26 (2000): 243–49.

[99] Cf., on a related issue, Thomas L. Thompson, *The Mythic Past: Biblical Archaeology and the Myth of Israel* (New York: Basic Books, 1999), 234, emphasis original: "Quite clearly, the goal of the biblical narrative is to present Israel as a people. One could say that the story is ethnographic rather than historiographic in intention. That is to say, it is not writing a history, but rather *defining* a contemporary society as a people." See also E. Theodore Mullen Jr., *Ethnic Myths and Pentateuchal Foundations: A New Approach to the Formation of the Pentateuch* (SemeiaSt 35; Atlanta: Scholars Press, 1997).

IV

Although it is the institutional interests that come to the fore in the use of our term in the DSS and in other contemporary Jewish writings, the term itself does not distinguish a particular role or office. Does the term carry implications of dignity and status or convey ideas of power and authority? As a substantive, adjective, or participle, *anointed/anointed one* can certainly be used in contexts that would appear to signify the legitimate exercise of judicial authority, command, and power. However, it is equally clear that our term can be used to distinguish the dignity and prestige of a particular identity based on lineage or function.

In his book on anointing as a legal act in the Old Testament and the ancient Near East, Ernst Kutsch begins by distinguishing two principal meanings of anointing with oil in everyday life: anointing with a view to its healing and therefore strengthening properties, and anointing for the purpose of cleansing and purification.[100] Occasions for which anointing is viewed as a legal act are grouped into two categories corresponding to the conceptions of purifying and strengthening. As a legal act, purifying is closely linked to making one free from claims upon the person, as in the instance of anointing when freeing a slave.[101] The other category involves ceremonies in which anointing is a legal act conveying power, might, and honor.[102] The anointing of kings, vassals, and high officials belongs to this category.[103] One of the more controversial proposals that Kutsch has made concerns the anointing of the high priest, which he has placed in the first category. Scholars have generally maintained that our postexilic sources for the anointing of priests reflect the transference of a ceremony originally conducted for the king and signal a recognition of the authority of the high priest in postexilic Judean life. Kutsch contends that the sources emphasize consecration, and thus the category of purity, and do not support a notion that anointing the high priest conveys power and authority.[104] In a review of the book, J. A. Emerton agrees that the anointing of the high priest, like the anointing of the stone at Bethel (Gen 28:18; 31:13; 35:14) and the anointing of the tent of meeting (Exod 29:28), confers holiness and thus a sacral status on the person or object anointed, but he follows S. Mowinckel in suggesting that the anointing of the king has the same purpose of conveying a sacred status. As Yahweh's anointed, the king is sacrosanct (1 Sam

---

[100] Kutsch, *Salbung als Rechtsakt*, 1–6.
[101] Ibid., 16–18.
[102] Ibid., 33–34.
[103] Ibid., 34–39.
[104] Ibid., 22–27.

24:6; 26:11). Emerton never disputes the idea that the anointing of the king conveys power and authority, only Kutsch's insistence that representatives of the people and not Yahweh were the source of the transference of authority.[105] It would seem, therefore, that for Emerton conferring holiness (i.e., sacral status) by means of anointing does not carry with it any conceptual distinction between power and purity.

If Emerton objects to the distinction Kutsch draws between the anointing of kings by representatives of the people and the anointing of a king by a prophet on Yahweh's behalf, Z. Weisman thinks that Kutsch has not given sufficient attention to the difference. In Weisman's view the prophetic-pattern anointing cannot be simply a theological projection of the actual ceremony of anointing in which representatives of the people are the subject of the action. "The differences between the two patterns, both in structure and in function, make it impossible to regard the first as a later projection of the second."[106] Weisman wants to show that the prophetic-pattern anointing of kings is a rite of nomination in contrast to a rite of installation, but he can find an analogy to the structure and purpose of the prophetic pattern only in the letter of Pharaoh Amen-hotep III to the king of Arzawa (1411–1375 B.C.E.), in which the pharaoh writes that he is sending a messenger to see the king's daughter, whom he intends to take as wife, and to anoint her head with oil. Kutsch had discussed this example in the category of purification, the anointing having constituted an act of consecration.[107] Weisman sees the anointing as nomination, that is, as bethrothal. However, Weisman acknowledges that none of the ancient records bearing on the anointing of kings has the implication that the ceremony is a rite of nomination. He therefore turns to phenomenological rather than historical comparisons in an attempt to clarify the context of the prophetic-pattern anointing.[108]

He turns to the art of Mesopotamia to find evidence of anointing as a mythical and ritual motif in the divine nomination of kings. His description

---

[105] J. A. Emerton, review of Ernst Kutsch, *Salbung als Rechtsakt im Alten Testament und im alten Orient*, *JSS* 12 (1967): 122–28, stating: "It is much more natural to suppose that Yahweh was thought to be responsible for their anointing.... Is it not possible that Yahweh was thought to act through the anointing, even if it was carried out by the people and even if a prophet was not involved?" (127). The reference to S. Mowinckel is to *He That Cometh* (trans. G. W. Anderson; Oxford: Blackwell, 1956), 5–7.

[106] Z. Weisman, "Anointing as a Motif in the Making of the Charismatic King," *Bib* 57 (1976): 386, adding: "The first is concerned mainly with the teleological aspects of kingship, the king as the one who was chosen by God to function as his agent and who was summoned to fulfil a definite historical mission.... The second is mainly concerned with the legal aspect of kingship; the king *vis-à-vis* the people, his citizens" (ibid., 383).

[107] Kutsch, *Salbung als Rechtsakt*, 28–29.

[108] Weisman, "Anointing as a Motif," 385–87.

of one of the Assyrian reliefs in Nimrud that decorated the palace of Ashur-naṣir-pal II (883–859 B.C.E.) follows:

> In a great relief, before which the throne was placed (B.M. No. 124531; cf. Budge, Pl. XI), the king is represented twice, standing on either side of the "sacred tree" between "winged figures" who touch his head with a "cone," while holding in their left hand a small bucket ("pail"). Above the "sacred tree" hovers the "winged disc," probably the high god (Ashur, or Shamash).[109]

Weisman has endorsed especially the interpretation of R. D. Barnett, who denoted the rite as anointing.[110] He also calls attention to the fact that this is the only scene he has encountered "where the king is represented in duplication and without any of his courtiers or his 'earthly' weapons (bow, sword etc.)"[111] and ventures the view that "the scene reflects the idea of the divine nomination of the king."[112] The king receives his anointing from the gods. "There are no other human attendants in this rite except the anointed and his anointers."[113] But if the prophetic pattern is clearly related to a mythological context, it has been historicized, and finally the significance of the parallels gives way to two different typologies, the mythological divine kingship of ancient Mesopotamia and charismatic kingship in ancient Israel:

> The first conceives the king as "šamšu kiššat nišē" (*sun* of the totality of mankind), a title which was used by the late Assyrian kings...—the "king of the universe," whose authority originates directly from the deities. The second views the king as a charismatic personality, who is chosen, as occasion required, by God to function among His people in the political arena. This is underlined by the sudden appearance of the Spirit of Yahweh upon the anointed which follows this rite.[114]

I have continued at some length with this discussion because I want to suggest that Weisman's categories (mythological divine kingship and charismatic kingship) could easily be redescribed in terms of the contrasting

---

[109] Ibid., 388. Weisman takes note of the great variety of views respecting the identity and function of the symbols and has therefore sought "the cue to the interpretation of this scene ... from the functional relations between the components of this composition as a whole" (ibid., 389).

[110] Ibid., 388–90, following R. D. Barnett, *Assyrian Palace Reliefs in the British Museum* (London: British Museum, 1970), 13–14.

[111] Weisman, "Anointing as a Motif," 391.

[112] Ibid., 392.

[113] Ibid.

[114] Ibid., 394, emphasis original.

hierarchies of purity and power: that is, the hierarchies of status and prestige, on the one hand, and of authority and command, on the other. The prophetic stories clearly underline the act of anointing not only as evidence of divine election but as ritual occasion for empowerment by the spirit of God. Insofar as this anointing is directed to a particular historical task, it is not replicable. Anointing with a view to status, on the other hand, can be replicated as long as the conditions necessary for belonging are maintained.

In light of the work of Louis Dumont on the ideological dimensions of systems of hierarchy, one tends to associate the hierarchy of purity with priestly functions and the hierarchy of power with royal functions.[115] However, it should be clear that the king is not always depicted in terms of political or military functions, nor, for that matter, can the priest be considered only from the perspective of sacerdotal functions. What is important is to see the oppositional and complementary relation between the two systems at the level of meaning. Jonathan Z. Smith summarizes this relation in the following way:

> Status is founded on the absolute dichotomy of the pure and the impure, and is expressed as a relative hierarchy of degrees of purity and impurity, with the priest at its summit. It is, essentially, a sacerdotal system. Power is dominance—a hierarchy of degrees of legitimate force, with the king at its summit. It is, essentially, a juridical system. The two systems exhibit a necessary complementarity. The king will always be impure with respect to the priest ... but the priest will be inferior to the king with respect to authority.[116]

In a stunning resignification, Smith gives further clarity to this formulation by identifying the distinction sacred/profane with the hierarchy of power and the royal function. In discursive terms, the hierarchy of status is "the language of vulnerability to degradation"; the hierarchy of power is "a language of dangerous access."[117] It would seem to be an implication of this formulation that *holiness* should be associated with a discourse of power.[118] Perhaps it is justified, however, to conclude that the term is ambiguous. From the perspective of power, holiness does indeed signify dangerous access, but when priests are said to be anointed for the purpose of consecrating themselves, they are understood to be qualified to approach and serve God. The danger for them is contact with sources of impurity

---

[115] Dumont, *Homo Hierarchicus*.
[116] Smith, *To Take Place*, 54–55.
[117] Ibid., 56.
[118] See, e.g., ibid., 68.

resulting in a degradation of status. Within the hierarchy of purity, people of lower status are not themselves in a state of defilement from contact with those of higher status. Terms such as *holiness* and *righteousness* seem to have different significance within different systems of discourse.

I have turned to notions of purity and power as ideological formations with the intention of underlining my thesis that the honorific *christos* took hold as a byname for Jesus in order to make a claim for the status of Jesus groups by labeling the founder with a term that carried traditional associations of divine nomination and recognition. I have maintained that initially the interests were those of collective identity and status rather than claims of royal power attributed to Jesus. A parallel can be drawn between appeal to Jesus as *christos* and appeal to God's righteousness in early formulations of the kerygma.[119] It should not be surprising that both can be located in the same circles. But I have also argued that *christos* is not indigenous to the martyr myth, though it must have come into use quite early as the preferred designation in kerygmatic formulae.[120] Accounting for this is not as simple a matter as I once thought.[121] Moreover, my suggestion that we think of *christos* as belonging to a discourse of status would seem to be at odds with a martyr myth that necessarily brings to mind power and its resistance. God's righteousness as the exercise of ultimate judicial authority reinforces the discourse of power. Nonetheless, Mack has noted the absence of any reference to tyrant and trial in formulations of the kerygma and has stressed the characterization of the group as the matter that is also at stake.[122] If we think of Jesus' *pistis* as referring not only to endurance in the face of power but also to the character of his life and teaching, we can remind ourselves that *dikaiosynē* is also a quality of God and a term of corporate ethos marked by recognition of appropriate standards, arrangements, and practices. I would therefore conclude that one reason *christos* became the preferred term in formulae of the kerygma is because the use of the honorific as a byname and the formulation of the kerygma constituted parallel rhetorical strategies of invoking the character and perspective of God in order to establish a legitimate place and characterization for kingdom-of-God people who were negotiating new boundaries without cultivating a torah ethos.

The ascription to Jesus of supreme power and authority in the cosmos as *kyrios* and Son of God does not stand in immediate connection with or in organic relation to thinking of Jesus as anointed. The anointed

---

[119] See Mack, *Myth of Innocence*, 105–11, esp. 110 n. 9; idem, *Who Wrote the New Testament*, 85–86.
[120] Miller, "How Jesus Became Christ," 262–63.
[121] Ibid.; cf. idem, "Problem of the Origins," 330–31.
[122] Mack, *Myth of Innocence*, 110–11; idem, *Who Wrote the New Testament*, 86–87.

Jesus represents a stage in the transition from Jesus movements and schools to Christ associations and cults only to the extent that interest in the status enhancement of the group may be correlated with a move to establish associations independent of its members' affiliation or nonaffiliation with local synagogues in urban environs of northern Syria. The Jesus who was first called "anointed" by some followers was now the divinely recognized teacher-founder of associations staking claims to redefine the constituency and practices of Israel in their own way, surely in part by appealing to the anointed status of Jesus. However, a different set of practices, circumstances and locations, and different constituencies must be taken into account in order to explain the Christ myths of Pauline and pre-Pauline associations (i.e., Jesus as exalted Christ, the divine Son of God come to earth, and the unique *kyrios* of the cosmos). The Gospel writers, for their part, collapsed power and purity in a single figure in their own ways when they undertook the task of drawing earlier Jesus traditions and the name *christos* as exclusively his own into the creation of a unique figure of expectation, the Messiah.

Agenda for the Annual Meeting, Discussion, and Reflections

Ron Cameron

An agenda for the second year of the Seminar, held in Boston in 1999, was prepared primarily from issues raised in the papers by Miller and Mack and from preliminary responses to their papers in letters and e-mail. Miller, in particular, had concluded that data for usages of an "anointed" or "anointed one(s)" in biblical and early Jewish literature, as well as usages of *christos* in the New Testament, supported the inference of a pre-Pauline diaspora locus for the introduction of the term among Jesus people. If, as Miller has argued, the kerygma was not the likely locus of the introduction of *christos,* then we must imagine the social logic and interests that could account for the introduction of the term to have constituted the situation of a Jesus movement known to Paul, and we must distinguish this moment from a series of subsequent moments that would become definitive for what we had been calling the pre-Pauline Hellenistic Christ cults.

Our plan was to focus the first session of the Seminar on *christos* as mythmaking. We wanted to explore its (social) locus, its connotations, and the rationale for the introduction of this term as a designation of Jesus. For if we can understand and redescribe *christos* as mythmaking, then we would eliminate from consideration the standard assumptions and usual scenarios put forth as explanations for the introduction of this term in early Christian discourse: the historical Jesus, recourse to his death, an appeal to the resurrection, apocalyptic eschatology, and the first church in Jerusalem. The first session included, as well, some discussion of all the papers written for the year's site, not just the papers published in this volume. To facilitate the discussion, each paper writer was assigned the task of formulating a question (or two) about one of the other papers, keeping in mind the issues that were (to be) the focus of the session. The questions that were addressed to the papers published in this volume relate mostly to what was described as the "underdetermined" *christos* designation in the papers of Miller and Mack. There was general agreement in the Seminar that a relatively underdetermined *christos* was, at the very least, a convincing formulation of what had been deconstructed of the usual scenarios of grand mythic design and full royal messianic panoply associated with canonical and scholarly imaginations of Christian origins. But could an underdetermined *christos* be grasped in a manner that would tell us what the introduction of the term was all about as mythmaking, and could the mythmaking be understood in connection with a plausible set of social issues and interests? It is not surprising that the questions addressed to the work of Miller and Mack conveyed the need to bring the term into some closer relationship with one or another of the more determinate uses found in biblical and early Jewish literatures. Responding to those questions, however, did not make the problems that others had with the absence of documentation for the site we wanted to reconstruct any easier to resolve.

We planned to focus the second session of the Seminar on *christos* and social formation. We wanted to explore what considerations were most persuasive in redescribing the social formation of the group(s) in which the term was first used. But if the tendency in the first session was to lose a bit of the hold we thought we had in specifying *christos* as a mythmaking moment, we had more difficulty in the second session working through issues of plausibility with respect to the location of the site, the shape of the group, and the circumstances and social interests to which the introduction of the *christos* attributive or byname could be conceived as a response. The task of problematizing the dominant paradigm was accomplished and did make a difference, but our efforts to turn the data into evidence for a significant juncture of mythmaking and social formation, or to test our conceptualizations of mythmaking and social formation as categories for the redescription of Christian beginnings, fell short. This was understandable. The thesis was so new, the redescription so startling, that to come to grips with it required a major rethinking of the dominant paradigm of Christian origins, with which all members of the Seminar were wrestling. To be able to nail down what we wanted to know, both theoretically and evidentially, and to figure out how we could talk about it in social terms, proved to be a difficult and demanding task. Ironically, the very success of our problematization made the task that much harder, both for determining the social significance of *christos* as myth and for appreciating the importance of distributing the junctures of mythmaking and social formation in such a way as to make social-historical sense of the sites we were seeking to redescribe in terms of a social logic.

Our model of distribution and difference, of expanding the moments of mythmaking and social formation, is not intended to demonstrate some inevitable narrative logic operating in the history of early Christianities. Although one may be left with a sense of incremental development in Mack's account, the strategy has a different intent. Our findings mean that "none of the indices for a transition from a Jesus movement to a Christ cult indicates the need to posit drastic social contestation or ... dramatic personal 'religious' experience in order to account for it all."[1] There are three separate judgments that surface in this statement. First, no grand moment has been posited to account for the emergence of the Christian religion. Second, the picture of messianic beginnings has been successfully problematized. This is an extraordinary accomplishment, all the more so in view of the fact that behind nearly every other reconceptualization of the drama and liberating power of Christian origins stands the Messiah as the personal emblem of utopian longings. Third, a more reasonable explanation for the emergence of the designation *christos* has been achieved. The notion of a *christos* association belongs to a redefinition of "pre-Pauline" as something that looks like, and has links with, the Jesus movements, which is not the conventional scholarly understanding of "pre-Pauline Hellenistic Christianity." We began by thinking that the Christ cults would prove to be more of a new departure than a bridge between the Jesus movements and the Pauline congregations, as they have always been in New Testament scholarship. What is different in our redescriptions is what has been conveyed. As we have demonstrated in our scholarship on Q and the *Gospel of Thomas,* the Jesus movements are hardly what is meant by "primitive Palestinian tradition." Moreover, in our redescriptions of a possible Jesus school in Jerusalem and of the Jesus-*christos* association, both "Jerusalem" and "Christ" turn out to be pre-Pauline, diaspora issues and constructions, not what has been imagined as either "the kerygma of the earliest Church" or "the Hellenistic Church aside from Paul."[2] All this is the consequence of our having begun to extend the reconstructed Jesus movements into the pre-Pauline sphere.

The responses that followed the Boston sessions were occasioned, in part, by the fact that the steering committee was not able to decide on the focus of the ensuing year's work at its meeting in Boston. Mack responded to this situation with a lengthy debriefing (in a letter of 30 November 1999), which argued for the cogency of addressing pre-Pauline Christ myths before moving on to Corinth. But Mack's response addresses more than the issue of the Seminar's next site. It constitutes a set of reflections on what he saw coming to issue in the three years of papers published in this volume and over the course of a number of exchanges that took place during that period. Mack received an important response from Willi Braun, written in the form of a letter (of 6 January 2000) to Mack following several conversations between them. Both Mack's debriefing (originally sent

---

[1] Burton L. Mack, "Why *Christos*? The Social Reasons," 372 (in this volume).
[2] So Rudolf Bultmann, *Theology of the New Testament* (trans. Kendrick Grobel; 2 vols.; London: SCM, 1952–55), 1:33, 63.

to the co-chairs of the Seminar) and Braun's letter were shared with the members of the Seminar. The editors have asked for permission to publish these materials essentially in their original form, thus retaining the informal styles and moods of each piece, but with our own caveat that the appeals addressed to the reader about how to take what is being written do not make less substantive the differences of opinion that surface. Mack's debriefing ("Backbay Jazz and Blues") and Braun's response ("Smoke Signals from the North: A Reply to Burton Mack's 'Backbay Jazz and Blues'") are followed by the editors' reflections on the substantive issues that have arisen over the course of three years' work, and which constitute, in part, a commentary on and evaluation of the issues raised by Mack and Braun.

Backbay Jazz and Blues

Burton L. Mack

Strictly Speaking Out of School

The members of the Seminar should probably know that the steering committee, meeting for luncheon on Tuesday after the sessions in Boston, was not able to decide on a site or strategy for next year's focus. We agreed to let things perk while we gave the problem more thought, and I, having perked for several days, am ready to switch from perking to sniffing where the blue Pacific wafts its airborne signals ashore in San Pedro. So for what it is worth, here is my report of the memories, dreams, and revelations that have occurred to me over the past few days, both while sleeping and awake, disturbing other trains of thought, and apparently generated by energies stimulated in Boston and still at work, thus much in need of being tranquilized. I'm hoping this memo will do it for me, at least for the time being. Whether it does anything for the committee or for the Seminar (supposing the co-chairs want to share this around) is another matter altogether. I'll try to start with a little soft jazz and hope to end with some Dixieland in the distance. Dixieland says that everything will be okay. But in the meantime there surely must be a bit of the blues.

The Jazz

In one respect, it was a most gratifying set of sessions, for discussions began that combine both theoretical and historiographic issues of direct relevance to our project in redescribing Christian beginnings. We began to see how each other thinks and what each wants to learn. That's progress for a group of scholars initially unacquainted with one another's works and ways. My toes were often tapping, as you know.

The Bumps

Unaccustomed as we all are to dancing with one another, however, it probably should not be thought surprising that we sometimes stepped on one another's toes. No one was actually hurt, to be sure, and everyone seems to be ready for the calling of the next tune. But the papers by Merrill P. Miller and me had set the stage for a very precise site-focus, and then we learned that, as a Seminar, we were really not able to get very far with its discussion. We had hoped to have all elbows swinging and the floor bouncing with Lindy Hoppers as we explored and debated the social logic of the un(der)determined *christos*. For some reason we couldn't do that. And we did not express much interest in refocusing on any configuration of what used to be called the "pre-Pauline Christ-cult," the site(s) that got postponed as the year's work progressed. Then, when the suggestion was made that we keep to our schedule by moving "on to Corinth" (where both social formation and mythmaking indices are all over the Pauline-Corinthian correspondence), differences of opinion quickly surfaced all around about exegetical method and where to start in a first attempt to focus on this site. I even wondered whether it would be possible to learn what I wanted to learn by moving to Corinth before working out the social logic of the Jesus *christos* mythologies. So I've been trying to figure out what all the interests may be that Seminar members have brought to the project and what all the reasons may have been for our getting bogged down at this point. That brings me to the blues.

THE BLUES

(1) There was restiveness with the idea of working with hypothetical social sites, trying to imagine social groups for which we do not have adequate data or documentation, social situations we have to "make up."

(2) There was concern that our project not let the privileged sites of the conventional grand narrative set the agenda for us, that we do not inadvertently produce a paraphrase of that grand narrative by tracing the links between the same old sites and thinking we have dispensed with it by noting the social formation/mythmaking equation at each turn.

(3) There were cautionary reminders that our interest in and assumptions about matters of sequence and connection among the several sites we project could trip us up by allowing us to continue thinking that there was a "continuity" to the "development" of "early Christian" something (myth, social formation, persuasion, interests, and so forth). This, of course, would take us back to the worst of the ills associated with the grand-narrative problem.

(4) It made some members of the Seminar uncomfortable that we always seemed to be starting with myths instead of social situations, trying to reconstruct the social situation from the myth instead of asking about the interests of a given social configuration that may have evoked or called for a certain kind of myth or that might be used to analyze the social logic

of a given early Christian mythology. Why not turn the equation around and look first for social issues and experiments that may have contributed to the generation of Christian mythmaking and the like?

(5) The desire to go "on to Corinth," similar to last year's desire to go "on to Antioch," seemed to have something to do with the desire to work with more direct documentary data as well as a more "complete" picture of a situation. If so, it may mean that we haven't yet found a way to translate bits of data into evidence for a redescription of a site. And that, perhaps, is making us nervous.

(6) There was strong resistance to the task of redescribing a "pre-Pauline, Hellenistic Christ cult," a notion no longer acceptable now that the agenda associated with Rudolf Bultmann (Jesus and Paul) and the older pattern of early Christian development (Palestinian to Hellenistic) have been discredited.

(7) There was some discomfort with the thought that, even if we found a way to "deBultmannize" the notion of "pre-Pauline," the need to isolate textual material from Paul's letters would quickly take us into the quicksand of unresolvable exegetical issues.

Taking a Break

It is obvious that the reasons for being uncertain about the next best move stem from very real theoretical and practical considerations. But the way it was left at the last session hardly resolves the dilemma, the suggestion namely that we find some way to move to Corinth on schedule, thinking to work out the social logics of the "Christ myths and rituals" on the side or as we come across them in the Pauline letters. You already know that I can't imagine moving to Corinth without redescribing the (hypothetical) social situations and the social logics of the several Jesus myths and rituals that Paul's letters document but that Paul did not make up. I can't jump from the Jesus movements to Paul's spin on these myths and rituals without asking about the changes in social formation, issues, and thinking that must have occurred to generate them. I do think I understand why the Corinthian correspondence seems more attractive and manageable than the Jesus-movement sites we have been exploring. Paul's Corinth is a richly documented site, and it does lend itself to comparative studies with Greco-Roman associations and cults as no other early Christian location. It is also the case that the rhetorical disjunctions between Paul and the Corinthians are obvious, and that would give us a chance to analyze the logic of the Christ-*kyrios* myths and rituals as Paul understood them and sought to apply them to the Corinthian situation. But before we rush on to Corinth, I would surely like to know why we have had such a difficult time with the *christos* site and what the Seminar is thinking about the project's rationale. If what we want to learn is not clear or agreeable to all of us, it's time to find that out. Otherwise, I'm afraid we'll be wallowing in our own blather in Corinth. I want therefore to share with you my response to the concerns listed above from the perspective of my own understanding of the project and its rationale. This is in the interest of stimulating a focused discussion of theory and method relevant to our need to reset the agenda. Please humor me as we both look for an appropriate tune for the next time around the table or floor.

I'VE NOT HAD BLUES IN MIND (OR: WHAT I'D RATHER LIKE TO KNOW)

Before engaging the considerations listed above directly, let me say that I'd like to understand the attraction that early Jesus and Christ groups had for all kinds of people during the first century. I do not need to have a complete picture of any, much less every, site. But I do need to imagine real people, the most plausible demographic configuration per site, something of their mutual interests and activities, and what they gained by entertaining the mythic claims they seemed to hold. As you know, I'd like to establish several such sites on a new map as a way of understanding Christian beginnings that does not need any appeal to the missions, miracles, divine interventions, and religious experiences customary for the traditional view. Insofar as I have been working with a theory of religion that differs markedly from that implicit to the traditional view, the project also presents me with a chance to test my theory and see how far I might be able actually to explain Christian beginnings as a human, social experiment or construction. However, since theories always need refinement in the course of testing and application, I'm not as concerned about the theory always matching as I am about a new map of data being charted. Thus the bottom line in my case is that the traditional scenario for Christian origins does not make sense and thus requires redescription. That the redescription requires making a switch from an individualistic psychology to a social anthropology is also basic for me. But after that, it's the data that counts together with the constraints data place upon us as we decide how to approach them. For me, constructing hypothetical sites is not an undisciplined product of a speculative imagination; it is a thoroughly rigorous and responsible scholarly labor, amenable to challenge and debate governed by historical knowledge and theoretical propositions.

SO, ALTHOUGH I'M NOT GOOD AT SINGING THE BLUES, HERE GOES

Re (1): It is not as if historians ever have the luxury of not using their imaginations. And in the case of the dominant paradigm, which of the sacred sites is not already purely a matter of (the Christian) imagination? If we want to redescribe these sites, data collection and its analysis will have to be used, not only to problematize the customary imagination but also to offer a more plausible picture. We surely do not want to overstep the constraints of the data, for those constraints will frequently be the basis for calling into question the traditional imagination of a site, and in any case we can't stop being scholars. But where the careful analysis of the data suggests a range of reconstructions more plausible than others, we should discuss them, debate them, and spell them out. In my estimation, we did do a respectable scholarly analysis of the data and a critique of the dominant paradigm with respect to the Jerusalem group, and Miller's suggestions for imagining an alternative social-mythic situation, though constrained by meager and incomplete data and thus insufficient for imagining a "complete" picture of the site, were enough to imagine a new place for this group on the new map we want to chart. It is true that we did not find a way to discuss Miller's reconstructions to the satisfaction of all, but I thought that was because we were just in the process of learning to talk to each other in ways not customary for our field. When, then, in Boston, we did not find it possible or interesting to explore the social logic of the "undeterminate *christos*" upon which it seemed we agreed (for no one argued against it), it became clear that more was at issue among us. Insofar as part of the problem appears to be a hesitation to imagine a setting for which we do not have direct documentation, I confess to some frustration. After all, the data in this case includes the incidence or lack of incidence of the term *christos* in all of the New Testament writings plus all of the literatures of cultural context with special focus on a detailed analysis of Jewish and early rabbinic writings. Only if one wants to argue that (1) the Jesus materials do not put us in touch with or tell us enough about Jesus movements, and that (2) the use of the term in either the "Christ myths" or the Pauline corpus makes sense only if the first usage of the term was definitely determined, would we have a different situation on our hands. Since neither of those options hardly makes sense when compared with the hypothetical situation we imagined, I fail to understand the reticence to discuss the range of connotations and the social logic implicit to the term and whether any of it might fit a plausible social situation of some Jesus movement on the way to becoming a *christos* association. Because we did not thrash that one out, we are left with an intellectual blank right where the usual mystifications have been located. None of the other connotations or uses of the term for which we have any textual evidence make sense as the way in which thoughtful persons may have come to think of Jesus as *christos*. But of course, the traditional scenario is not at all interested in attributing the thought of Jesus as *christos* to thoughtful persons and so has a number of other mystifying suggestions. I for one am not willing to leave it there, being persuaded that early Christians were not at all unthoughtful persons. I do need better to understand why we as a Seminar could not engage this question.

Re (2) and (3): I do understand the cautionary observations about letting the traditional account set the agenda with the fear that we would only succeed in paraphrasing the grand narrative by tracing a continuity of development from site to site called intersections of "social formation" and "mythmaking." I also realize that my training and history of battles with the guild of New Testament scholarship cannot be jockied into an argument for starting with a problematization of the traditional account, especially not in the context of postmodernist mentality, where the answer to the realization that the dominant paradigm is wrong is simply "to change the subject." The question then is always, What subject? I and others have toyed with the idea that a new map might be possible by starting with the range of plural Christianities that come into view in the late first and early second centuries and accounting for them as social and mythic constructions based on social interests and experimentation. It would certainly be easier to work in the second century than in the first, and the map would surely be more colorful. But goodness, to address the question of beginnings from that vantage point and hope to render a critique of the traditional notion of Christian origins would never do what I would like to do. Scholars have known about the diversity of Christianities in the second century for a very long time, and that has never called the gospel story into question. I have absolutely no interest in leaving the gospel story (or the mystery at its "core") in place while bouncing yet another hermeneutical ball off its pages as if they are the primary source for all of the hidden wisdom that only Christians are privileged to know. It is the gospel story that needs to be recognized and accounted for as first-century mythmaking, and I see no way to do that except to identify its component parts and their precursors and explain them and it as intertextual creations in the interest of social experiments. Diversity at the level of social and historical description; explanation at the level of generalization and anthropological theory. You will remember that, in order to account for the Gospel of Mark as mythmaking, I had to create a foil by describing its precursors as having contrastive histories and mythologies, including the "historical Jesus," several "Jesus movements," the "Christ myth and ritual," and the Pauline gospel. I refer to this, not only to illustrate the need to know something about the history of the precursor components of a mythmaking moment in order to identify the shifts in imagery that may have rhetorical significance in a given "performance," but also and mostly to mark the differences among the many moments of mythmaking and social formation "on the way" to Mark. To acknowledge connections with precursor moments in a myth's history of reconfigurations is not only honest but necessary. It does not mean that one has to think of the "development" as a continuous unfolding of the implicit significance of an originary moment. (Mark cannot possibly be thought of as the explication of the implicit significance of the appearance of the historical Jesus.) The link to previous configurations is always only one of the many factors in social interest, social formation, cultural context, and ideological position taking that impinge upon a new moment of mythmaking. So I do not see how "continuity" and "grand narrative" are the problem with our project or schedule. But leaving unexplored the intertextual factors of a mythmaking moment and its social logic, such as in the case of the designation Jesus *christos,* surely is a problem. Paul's usage will not help. And if Miller's critique of me is on target, my analysis of the social logic of the "Christ myth" won't help either. And if the other Jesus and Christ mythologies of martyrdom and cosmic enthronement, as well as the ritual meal texts, won't help as well, the sky is the limit all over again. I for one am not willing to leave Jesus *christos* cavorting in the sky with Lucy. What was wrong with Miller's and my suggestion that we limit the range of plausible constructions by closing the gap between "Jesus movements" and the congregations of the Christ documented in the Pauline letters? Why couldn't we think through the social implications of the social logic of just that mythmaking thought at some point in the social history of some Jesus movement? Why couldn't we?

Re (4) and (5): I surely wish we could turn the equation around. People are social beings, as Willi Braun says. No one was "unmixed" already, as Jonathan Z. Smith reminded us. And no one was without some location in a class, group, or social unit before experimenting with social formations and ideologies stemming from the Jesus movements, as William E. Arnal has insisted. It would surely be nice to start with social locations and practices, identify social issues of concern, then see what difference either the generation or the introduction of Jesus myths and rituals might make. It is surely the case that myths and rituals should be thought of as generated by social experimentation and formation, and not the other way around. But if we want to bring the three together (myths, rituals, social formations) in the case of Christian beginnings, we have to start with early Christian texts. We know these texts are weighted, not only on the side of mythmaking but also on the side of the views of a scribal class of authors. But use them we must, and that means finding ways to move from the rhetoric of mythmaking to social situations even while having to work very hard to catch sight of the social formation. That's one of the reasons, of course, why the search for social analogues in the Greco-Roman world is so very important to the project. It can provide us with material for fleshing out social descriptions as well as comparisons for social redescriptions. But the critical exchanges we seek to identify between social formations and mythmaking will always be found in these early texts. So I think we have to find a way to turn them into project data, not set them aside because they are not the kind of data we might prefer. But having said all of that, it is also my view that myth is a very big deal and that social formation and its demographics cannot be explained without also accounting for the cultural ideologies (myths) both old and new that problematize and authorize any social experimentation. What's wrong with asking about the social logic of a mythologoumenon?

Re (6) and (7): Yes, we were not wise to call our projected site the "pre-Pauline, Hellenistic Christ cult." No one among us thinks in those terms, at least not with the set of connotations that belonged to the older scholarly usage. Several of us have long since worked with very different pictures of the peoples, places, cultures, and early Christian groups than those implied by the language we used in this site designation. But you know what we had in mind. We have taken seriously the fact that the Jesus materials available to us not only do not use *christos* to attribute importance to Jesus; they also do not document, much less focus upon the significance of those events assumed by Paul to be central for his "gospel": crucifixion, resurrection, ascension, and cosmic lordship. Unless one is willing to think that it all came to Paul in a moment of revelation or that the Jesus movements knew of these events but overlooked them, the focus has to fall on myth*making* moments in social formations prior to Paul, known to Paul, and from which he learned about their myths. One need not assume a single "Hellenistic Christ cult" within which all of these myths were generated, nor that Paul's indebtedness to them documents the "kerygma of the earliest church," as Bultmann had it. But if we want to account for them as mythmaking in the interest of some social formation, we have to ask about the social logic they must have had "before" Paul put his own spin upon them. That is because, without Paul's spin (and to be sure, even with Paul's spin), these myths and rituals hardly address the Corinthian situation. Of course, the tradition of scholarly attempts to isolate pre-Pauline material is laborious and rife with disputes, a labor we shouldn't want to have to repeat. But if we can't say anything at all about the social logic of these myths and rituals except what Paul says about them, the game is up as far as I can see. That's because we won't have any purchase on the relation of mythmaking to social formation either in the case of the myths and rituals Paul himself says he got from "tradition," or in the case of the constructions Paul puts upon them in his address to the Corinthians, or in what looks to be a new social situation altogether, namely, the Corinthian situation itself.

How about a Foxtrot?

It should be clear that I personally would very much like to have another round on the social logic of the prewar myths produced by Jesus people apart from Paul before we take on the Corinthian correspondence. We just do not know what everyone in the Seminar thinks about the mythmaking and social formation reflected in Q, *Thomas*, the pronouncement stories, and the miracle chains, much less the social situations plausibly indicated by the attribution of a martyrdom to Jesus. And now everyone seems eager to get to Paul. I am trying to figure out why Paul seems to make more sense as a venue for redescribing Christian origins (testing our social formation/mythmaking thesis) than the sites from the Jesus movements we have already looked at. I am wondering whether the critical shift introduced by Q and *Thomas* has not fully registered among us, or what. It's clear to me that Bultmann's view of Jesus as the "presupposition" for Paul's kerygmatic theology is not the only way many American scholars have worked out the Jesus/Paul problem. One thinks automatically of the many New Testament scholars who find it very difficult to explore the logic of anything prior to Paul and of the ease with which many New Testament scholars say they "don't believe in Q," as if that takes care of it. So since we have had three sessions focused on the Jesus movements without much success in discussing their mythmaking moments, I do worry about taking Paul at his word and again leaving the "Christ myths" unexplored. That would be to let Bultmann win, as Christopher R. Matthews reminded us. Quite frankly, I had been hoping for some rough and rigorous battles to the mat on what we might understand the various myths of the various Jesus movements to have had as their social logics before getting to Paul. Since that has not happened, I am not sure what to suggest as a way to keep some focus on the "Christ myths" as we proceed. I'd still like to have a focused discussion of those pre-Pauline (or non-Pauline) mythmaking moments, but I don't know how to set it up any better than we have done for the Jesus-movement moments. Just think of the Jesus mythologies we have not taken up for discussion! And now, what about such things as a crucifixion, resurrection, ascension, and cosmic lordship as *christos* or *kyrios* mythologoumena before hitting Paul's *en christō* head on? And what will we be able to make of the Corinthians' fascination with *pneuma* unless we know how shaky its connection with the *christos* myth actually is? But I can't think of a way to guarantee a serious engagement of these sites, so I do not have any concrete suggestions for setting the agenda. Are we stymied? Don't we need some clarity as to why the *christos* and "Christ myth" questions have not created a spirited discussion among us before projecting another year's work? Oh, for a little banjo!

Is That Dixieland I'm Starting to Hear?

It is certainly true that there are several Seminar members who could bring marvelous leverage to bear upon the question of mythmaking and social formation in Corinth. We have people who could provide the grist for discussions of patterns of association, the supper, Paul's program and rhetoric, the Christ myth according to Paul, the political and social setting in Corinth, and questions about resurrection, spirit, a cosmic Christ, and a final apocalypse. And as Miller mentioned just before we left the luncheon, summing up what we thought we had heard at the second Seminar session, everyone seemed to agree that the Corinthian situation would have to be handled as a "double disjunction" site: Christ myths versus Paul's spin on them on the one hand; Paul's gospel versus the Corinthians' fascination with *pneuma* on the other. If we could find a way to order the topics and agenda for discussion, it seems to me that we might well set aside a year or two to redescribe the Corinthian situation even while working on the social logic of the Christ myths (as Arnal suggested). There might even be a way to order the sequence of discussions in such a way that we would have a chance to keep the project on track. I hope so.

In the meantime, I do want to cast my vote for the suggestion made at the meeting of the steering committee that Ron Cameron and Miller consider putting our Seminar papers together for a volume or two on sites from the Jesus movements. If they were able to use the work of the last three years, perhaps by means of rather complete introductions to the rationales for a year's work represented by the papers it produced, in order to problematize the conventional view of "pre-Pauline" Christianity, start charting a new map of Christian beginnings, and make some suggestions about the circumstances most probable for the emergence of the *christos* myths, we would have an example of what redescription can look like and how its consequences might be spelled out for both the old gospel story and the new map we envisage. It might even be that sharing with all of us a prospectus for such a set of volumes, perhaps with brief summaries of what they thought we accomplished, would trigger some of the critical discussion we need to have. (As you can see, I am looking for ways to keep the redescription goals of the Seminar in focus as we go along. In this case, it seems to me that it would help if we could find some way to make sure that what we have already accomplished not be sidetracked or postponed but kept before us as a reminder, guide, and emerging chart for continual reference and discussion.)

It is obvious that we have an excellent roster of first-rate scholars taking an interest in the Seminar and that we all want to contribute to the project as each understands it. The trick for the committee will be to bring work to the table in such a way that we can discuss its significance for and contribution to the shaping of common goals for our redescription project. There must be some way to call the tune for taking the next steps, to propose an agenda for dealing with Paul, the Christ myth, and the Corinthians. Let's work it out. With any luck, if only I can stop singing the blues, even

I might be able to think more clearly again. As a matter of fact, having gotten this memo off my desk, I do think I can hear a trumpet in the distance. Of course. And there's the banjo, the piano, the bass, the trombone, and the clarinet. Why, it's the happy sound of the Chicago Six. If you have not heard them, let me tell you, Country and Western cannot compete. Dixieland jazz à la the Chicago Six can drown out all that down and dirty Nashville that the Society plans to overwhelm us with. Wouldn't that be something? We'd be dancing to jazz. We wouldn't need a marquee with blinking lights, either. Soirées from the Jesus movements in Galilee to the twitchers in Corinth will be our vicarious venues. And if that's what's in the offing, why am I worried?

Please let me know if it's true. I'd like to repolish my dancing shoes.

Smoke Signals from the North: A Reply to Burton Mack's "Backbay Jazz and Blues"*

Willi Braun

As a way of sorting through the rich and complicated few days of discussions in Boston (November 1999), I thought it would be good to jot some things down while the mind is still tuned to the Boston channel. So, here they are—somewhat disjointed in order. To set you up for what follows, Professor Mack, I would like it if you would consider "thoughts" not in the strongest sense, for my ideas are not firmly fixed, and even when I appear to be yammering loudly, noise should not be mistaken for conclusive convictions. Indeed, if you imagine a question mark at the end of every sentence, you will have tuned into the mood on which these jottings float.

I

Merrill P. Miller's assiduous "archaeological" work, supplemented by the work of others,[1] then clarified and sharpened by the subsequent queries

---

* This is a slightly revised version of a letter written to Burton L. Mack (6 January 2000), leaving features of original epistolary style intact. Subsequently, at his urging, it was circulated to the members of the Seminar on Ancient Myths and Modern Theories of Christian Origins. Thanks to the persuasion of Ron Cameron and Merrill P. Miller of the Seminar's steering committee, I elbowed aside my sheepishness over making the private public in this volume. The revisions consist in removal of the most egregious infelicities of expression, taking up some lengthy asides, originally in footnotes, into the body of the letter, and adding a few clarifications and bibliographic items to specify the allusive references in the original.

[1] Merrill P. Miller, "How Jesus Became Christ: Probing a Thesis," *Cont* 2/2–3 (1993): 243–70; and the following papers presented at the 1999 Seminar sessions: Barry S. Crawford, "*Christos* as Nickname" (in this volume); Arthur J. Dewey, "*Christos*—An Appealing Name: An Investigation into the Pre-Pauline Christ Cult"; Burton L. Mack, "Why *Christos*? The Social Reasons" (in this volume); Christopher R. Matthews, "From Messiahs to Christ: The Pre-Pauline Christ Cult in Scholarship" (in this volume); Merrill P. Miller, "The Problem of the Origins of a Messianic Conception of Jesus" (in this volume); idem, "The Anointed Jesus" (in this volume); Hal Taussig, "The Pre-Pauline (Con)text of Galatians 3:26–28: An Exploration of Baptism and *Christos*"; Stephen G. Wilson, "Churches as Voluntary Associations."

and discussion during the Seminar's meetings in Boston, allows us to assume as probable that some Christians somewhere launched *christos* as a premythic brand name (1) without thick and grand connotations of and couplings to royal, martyrological, messianic, or other traditional-mythic complexes, and (2) without a *necessary* (though obviously possible) entailment of a specific *christos* myth such as we see sketched out in Phil 2. I can surely go with (2) as a datum; Miller's work is persuasive on this. But I hold on to some reservation with respect to (1), that is, the all-too-lightly connotative *christos* that Miller offers. Given the highly contestatory mood of the formational activities of early Christians everywhere, I tend to think that brand names, especially *christos,* were chosen precisely because they were already heavily greased with allusionary and connotative oil, to abuse Jonathan Z. Smith's oil-spill metaphor that he leaked at the Seminar table in Boston. What good is a brand name that does not evoke anything, that is blank enough so as to be hardly even able to carry the claim that "our Mr. *Christos,* he da man ... he's cool and because he's *our* man, we are cool too"? At least, I like to assume that as soon as *christos* was uttered by someone as the label for a group, the next breath must have begun with "because" (elaboration, rationalization),[2] where the follow-up to "because" must have been a kind of mythmaking in a recursive key, that is, by using and reforming the cultural givens with respect to the significance of *christos,* whether as king, priest, patron, hero, or some mishmash of these cooked in a cosmically flavored Hellenistic marinade.

What to do with this, though? I can't think of any answer that is all that interesting in a constructive sense. The chief value, I think, is that we can use Miller's conclusion sort of like a spray can of deodorant: the discovery of a rather naked *christos* allows us to defumigate sui generis full-blown christological complexes and much of the guild's "occult" inclination toward suppositions of supernatural causations. That is, the un(der)determined *christos* provides us first of all with the leverage to argue that the mythic elaboration of *christos* is a process of human doing, a process you have increasingly clearly and cogently described.[3] While this is in itself a

---

[2] In my ears still rings the ending to the provocative paper that you gave at the 1993 sessions of the Canadian Society of Biblical Studies in Ottawa: "It is not the clever insight or the dramatic moment of vision [or the selection of social-mythic brand names?] that counts. It is the elaboration" (Burton L. Mack, "Q and a Cynic-like Jesus," in *Whose Historical Jesus?* [ed. William E. Arnal and Michel Desjardins; Studies in Christianity and Judaism 7; Waterloo, Ont.: Wilfrid Laurier University Press, 1997], 36).

[3] I am thinking here of your sequence of papers on social formation, such as your programmatic inauguration of the Seminar, in Burton L. Mack, "On Redescribing Christian Origins," *MTSR* 8 (1996): 247–69; repr., with revisions, in *The Christian Myth: Origins, Logic, and Legacy* (New York: Continuum, 2001), 59–80; idem, "Explaining Religion: A Theory of Social Interests" (included in *Christian Myth,* 83–99) and "Explaining Christian Origins:

wonderful breath of fresh air, to go much further in trying to chase down the when, where, who, and why of the "Mr. Christ" utterance is not something for which I have map and compass. And so I was reluctant to try to go there. I recall my asking (or perhaps it was someone else) Miller to lead me to the Mr. Christ site as a way of testing if I missed something in his and your desire to imagine the social location and scenario where *christos*-as-cognomen could have been used as the rally cry for a group coming to think of itself as a group. Miller responded about as well as could be responded, but the response—a mixed group, perhaps in a synagogue, perhaps in Antioch, where one party contested its sectoral (sectarian?) interests—was strikingly unremarkable, I thought. There is not enough ethnographic data *in situ* to help us further articulate and specify social formation and mythmaking. The ethnographic reality is that we are unable to find the address of the group-in-becoming that labeled itself somehow with reference to *christos*. We can suppose (and very plausibly) Antioch, but to increase our chances of stumbling on the group we must deeply survey the social mixes, the problematics pertaining thereto, the spatial and social landscapes, the economic conditions, and so forth, on the basis of which we could then cogently speculate the emergence of a grouping from whom the nontitular, nonmessianic *christos* would compel itself (to the exclusion of other possible heroic or godly cognomina) as brand name for the start of something "novel" in terms of social regrouping and identification. Even if we would invest labors on these issues, I fail to be optimistic that we would uncover enough stuff further to develop and tinker with our conceptual instruments: social formation and mythmaking. *That,* I think, we must do elsewhere. So, not that Miller's scenario sounded implausible, just that it is so vague as to be able to stand as a supposed scenario for almost anything. If this is on the right track, I further thought, let's leave well enough alone. Miller's work is a mighty antidote to any "big bang" view of the rise of *christos*. I do not need any more. Sometimes a methodical deconstruction of regnant "goes without saying" assumptions is better than a shaky construction, I whispered to myself.

To go on about the same point: perhaps it would be possible by means of defensible historical imagination to come up with a more detailed picture that we could then stare at for traces of *christos* mythologizing and its "social logic" at some point prior to the (re)appearance of the *christos* myth

---

A Theory of Social Formations" (The Larkin-Stuart Lectures; Trinity College, Toronto, Ont., October 1999); idem, "Social Formation," in *Guide to the Study of Religion* (ed. Willi Braun and Russell T. McCutcheon; London: Cassell, 2000), 283–96; idem, "A Radically Social Theory of Religion," in *Secular Theories on Religion: Current Perspectives* (ed. Tim Jensen and Mikael Rothstein; Copenhagen: Museum Tusculanum Press, 2000), 123–36.

in the (pre-)Pauline traditions. Perhaps we could "make up" a hypothetical social site, as you suggest in point 1 of your "Blues."[4] Surely we could. And perhaps we can find "a way to translate bits of data into evidence for a redescription of a site."[5] I think that we could indeed. My nervousness, however, is not about making up social situations or describing social situations on the basis of tidbits of evidence.[6] Rather, it is about doing so before we know what we are doing—actually, just to make sure that I do not insinuate anything about you, the "we" should be read as "I." I have always thought that the success or failure of the Seminar's redescription project will turn not on our daring ethnographic work and social reconstructions, nor on exegetical busyness, but in concept formation and instrument construction.[7] To imagine the social situation and logic of the first use of Mr. *Christos* from the appellation itself (since we do not have much else)—well, Professor Mack, you will have to teach me how to do that.

And so I ask myself, Why risk crash-landing our conceptual craft on hardly visible, at least fragmentary runways before we know how to fly and land the damn thing smoothly even where there *are* relatively visible runways? One of the invisible runways was in Jerusalem last year (Orlando, 1998); this year (Boston, 1999) we seemed to want to land at another spot we cannot well spot on the ground. Why not, I ask myself, test our instruments on runways where we can actually land and take from our landings on existing runways the increased confidence in our instruments to say to ourselves that we could land anywhere there is a runway even on a cloudy or foggy day? Or, switching metaphors, why not portage our canoe around spots where the river runs dry and we can't practice our strokes anyway? That is, for example, if we can make sense of Q or *Thomas* in terms of social theories, surely we can by a process of analogous reasoning postulate social reasons for a *christos* use anywhere or somewhere, even if the

---

[4] Burton L. Mack, "Backbay Jazz and Blues," 422 (in this volume).

[5] Ibid., 423 ("Blues" point 5).

[6] I agree with Ron Cameron's comment (in his letter of 23 December 1999), referring to your "Backbay Jazz and Blues" debriefing, that focusing on "the social logic of an identified moment of mythmaking" is a "critical issue." I do not feel myself described, however, by his phrase "lack of interest"—though I take his point on "inability." My concern is over how to get at the social logic when the social facts are not available. It seems to me we have to go at these obscure social moments indirectly, by means of analogy. Until we are in a position do to that, I am for passing these socially obscure moments by and going on to moments that are less obscure. The matter is more a matter of difference on strategy than on theoretical interests, I think.

[7] I think I flagged this somewhat, though perhaps not elaborately enough, in my paper on schools and Q. See Willi Braun, "The Schooling of a Galilean Jesus Association (The Sayings Gospel Q)" (in this volume).

"somewhere" is obscure and even if we are unable to specify the particular social facts and interests that make up "somewhere." Mythologoumena do indeed have a social logic, as you say,[8] but the logic is not internal to the mythologoumenon; it becomes visible only in its use, in actual social *situ,* I am inclined to think. When the social *situ* is not possible to determine, nor necessary to determine for the sake of our project, then to pursue the quest for the social logic of the mythologoumenon (*christos,* say) looks almost indistinguishable from a quest for origination, which is itself a mythic desire rather than a requirement of social accounting. On this I am in total agreement with William E. Arnal, who remarked at the Seminar table in Boston on the historical irrelevance of the site of the first use of *christos.* While it is regrettable that we don't have the address of the original (first) use of *christos,* it is only so in a trivial sense, in the sense that it would be nice to have. As for our theorizing, it does not make any difference, for we can examine its use elsewhere. And it will be its visible use that can tell us something about social formation and mythmaking. Paul, Mark, Matthew, wherever: theologoumena do not elaborate themselves organically out of their internal *Geist* anyway, so finding first, second, or any sequential station stops on the way to elaborated myths is not necessary to get at the relationship between mythmaking and social formation. Is it?

To finish this comment with a strategic thought: if we are going to say something on the social logic of the use of an undetermined *christos* label and the beginnings of mythifying the same beyond what you have already said,[9] fine, I suppose, but I still think the most productive way to go is to make our case *that* there indeed was a social logic at work, a "that" for which the case is perhaps best made by analogy and comparison. Still strategically speaking, I am quite happy to leave the *christos* site for now and harbor the hope that we might return to it at a later time—even if only as a published retrospect by you or another member of the Seminar after our SBL-allotted time for discussion has expired—once we have gained increased clarity, if not agreement, on issues of social formation and mythmaking by working on more visible sites.

II

Some other things lurk around in the memory about our talks, both the public ones around the Seminar table and our chat over beer. You take

---

[8] Mack, "Backbay Jazz and Blues," 428.

[9] E.g., Burton L. Mack, *Who Wrote the New Testament? The Making of the Christian Myth* (San Francisco: HarperSanFrancisco, 1995); idem, "Why *Christos?*"

some of these up in your "Backbay Jazz" tune. One concerns issues of "continuity," "generation," and "development." You rightly note that some of us are antsy about these things, especially in combination with the itinerary of moments and sites that the Seminar's steering committee have set up as the agenda. (In my most mischievous moments I can hear Luke say "Gotcha" as he watches us retrace a recognizably Lukan itinerary, though of course our "social formation" and "mythmaking" have replaced Luke's holy ghost!) Now, I know you have before bristled at me for wondering if we have sufficiently purged ourselves of desires for origins, origination, genealogies, understanding later moments of mythmaking as spin-offs generated by earlier moments, that is, of desires to produce an alternate grand narrative. I don't want to antagonize you with mistaken insinuations, but I am still trying to understand why it is so important to find bridges or linkages from the Jesus movements to the Christ groups. Why can't you "jump"?[10] Why assume that there is any continuity between the two, whether conceived of tradition respun or some transmissional vehicle of contact, influence, or whatever? Why not try out coincidence of a somewhat shared name, a coincidence that is explainable in all sorts of ways that fall short of anything I would call development, generation, continuity, and other such terms that imply necessary, perhaps even sufficient, causation? Why not blast any presumption of monogenesis out of the water and go with what Daniel C. Dennett calls "convergent" developments that are not linked by causal transmitters of ideas (myths, theologoumena)?[11] Why not assault the monogenetic foundations of the traditional "story of Christianity" radically by proceeding with a thoroughly polygenetic starting assumption, an assumption that I take to be operative in a thorough social

---

[10] Mack, "Backbay Jazz and Blues," 423. Cf. the similar "leaping" language by Arthur J. Dewey, "*Christos*—An Appealing Name," 1: "Mack has ... rightly seen that there exists a quantum leap from the Jesus movements to the Christ cult." How curious! If early Christians apparently could perform quantum jumping jacks, why can't we do some jumping ourselves? Of course, our leap will have to be of a different kind—a conceptual one, which, if we take it, might just permit us to re-vision the supposed quantum leap from the Galilee to Philippi as a mere hop. *Our* leap will have to be from the train to the plane, so to speak, from wanting to travel along tracks of transmission (the myth of continuity) and a train powered by implicit homological comparative desire, to committing ourselves, as I thought we had done, to the plane you launched, namely, processes of mythmaking in the service of social interests, a craft powered by analogical comparative discipline. This is a leap we *must* do, *can* do, and, I assumed, had *done*. If Paul apparently didn't need the stuff of the Jesus movements to articulate his Christ stuff, why do *we* want to explain "Christ" by somehow zipping him to "Jesus"?

[11] Daniel C. Dennett, "Appraising Grace: What Evolutionary Good is God?" *The Sciences* 37 (1997): 39–44; idem, "The Evolution of Religious Memes: Who—or What—Benefits?" *MTSR* 10 (1998): 115–28.

theory of religion?[12] Why not assume that different groups came upon the Jesus or Christ label as a good idea independently, then fashioned it socially and mythically in particular social situations as a way of responding to social challenges? Why was it a good idea, and why was the good idea articulated just so by different Jesus groups and just so by the Christ groups and Paul, and so forth? Well, that is what we have to explain, and I have been attracted to the social categories you've introduced and insisted on in large part because they do not *require* us to posit any more continuity than a shared name or "meme," to use Richard Dawkins's language.[13] It is, rather, the shared, though not entirely identical, features of the challenge to pursue desirable social being and material well-being[14] in a generally shared imperial-colonial cultural situation that may be the "link" between the various Jesus and Christ groups.

To clarify and elaborate, let me here insert some excerpts from my comments to you (Professor Mack) and Russell T. McCutcheon at the NAASR session in Boston.[15] Here they are in quotes, to which I add a sentence or two: "I like the fact that Burton Mack ends his paper with the suggestion that one control on describing early Christianity in social terms is to keep one eye glued to 'a wide-angle lens focused upon the many ways in which people responded to the Greco-Roman age.' I would like to underscore that sharply. Presumably the social interests that get acted

---

[12] By way of analogy, by effect of my "tribal" heritage I am interested in the history and historiography of Anabaptist origins in the sixteenth century. Recent work has shown that Anabaptisms popped up in various modes in various locales as convergent though without evident generative relationships to each other—a convergent polygenesis that can be explained without recourse to what Dennett calls a "pathway of transmission," but rather by means of an argument that analogous, family-resemblance types of social emergences are generated by sociomaterial environmental conditions. My monogenesis versus polygenesis terminology (using "genesis" as "beginning" rather than "origin") is borrowed from James M. Stayer et al., "From Monogenesis to Polygenesis: The Historical Discussion of Anabaptist Origins," *Mennonite Quarterly Review* 49 (1975): 83–121, an article that launched a revisionist historiography of Anabaptist beginnings.

[13] Richard Dawkins, *The Selfish Gene* (New York: Oxford University Press, 1976).

[14] I am assuming here a notion of well-being pared to the basics, that is, to the two fundamental facticities of human being: corporeality and sociality.

[15] The reference is to a joint session of the Ancient Myths and Modern Theories of Christian Origins Seminar and the North American Association for the Study of Religion, held in Boston in 1999, and devoted to discussion of Russell T. McCutcheon, "Redescribing 'Religion' as Social Formation: Toward a Social Theory of Religion," in *What Is Religion? Origins, Definitions, and Explanations* (ed. Thomas A. Idinopulos and Brian C. Wilson; SHR 81; Leiden: Brill, 1998), 51–71; repr. in *Critics Not Caretakers: Redescribing the Public Study of Religion* (SUNY series, Issues in the Study of Religion; Albany: State University of New York Press, 2001), 21–39; and Burton L. Mack, "The Christian Origins Project: A Description in Outline." The quotation from Mack may be found, now, in his "The Christian Origins Project," in *Christian Myth*, 216.

on and mystified and mythologized by Christian groups were not interests unique to Christians. While Christians are getting all exercised about their new imaginaries that allow for rethinking self and society, there is this incredible similar energy spent in diverse forms: the height of popularity of a wide range of technologies related to the 'care of the self' (Foucault); the age of the writing of romance literature replete with desires of a social and corporeal kind; Aristides is meditating in the Asclepeion and relinquishing his power over himself to the gods; Stoics and Cynics are going around talking about mastering themselves. All this we know, of course, but I wonder if we ought not to make our general knowledge about this much more focalized and effective, guided by our questions concerning Christian social formations. It seems to me that if we will satisfactorily describe early Christian initiatives (both social and mythic) we will have to do so with reference to a wide, comparative archaeology of social challenges and interests. Does all this buzz of activity, so much of it focused on solving problems of social location and identity, make for a set?"

If this is okay, and if "similarity" here is on the level of analogy rather than homology, and if the shared stuff is at the level of the particulars of the cultural-social-political-economic hard surface rather than on the level of the content and vocabulary of the mythmaking and forms of social experimentation, why not assume a similar similarity between the varieties of Christianities? Is this not entailed in a thoroughly social theorizing? You know all this, of course. For me this kind of "similarity" suggests that we ought not to be too troubled about connecting all the dots on the "Christian" map. The connection may be not between them as much as around and underneath them: the realities of the Greco-Roman age. This is a lingering thought left over from my paper on Q, where I toyed with the notion that the Greek magical papyri, the Epicurean fraternities, and the creation of the early rabbinic corpus may be among the most useful analogies for understanding the Q project. A considerable strength of the "deracination" thesis, which Arnal contributed to our Seminar table,[16] is that it can account for "similarity" without requiring a chain of causation at the superstructural level.

It is from the ground of this kind of thinking that I am a bit baffled why some of us around the table want to chart the generative pathways leading from Galilee to Jerusalem to Antioch. Maybe my own fear of the grand narrative caused me to misunderstand and beat up on things that do not exist around the table. But then I can't think of any other good reason

---

[16] William E. Arnal, "Why Q Failed: From Ideological Project to Group Formation" (in this volume). For the long version, see idem, *Jesus and the Village Scribes: Galilean Conflicts and the Setting of Q* (Minneapolis: Fortress, 2001).

for the desire to jot linkages between Galilee, Jerusalem, Antioch, pre-Pauline Christ-myth groups, and Paul, except for the quest for continuous, linear causality at the idea level. Even if they could be located, we would still need to explain the Galilean experiments on their grounds in our terms, just as we would have to explain the Pauline experiments on his ground in our terms. Knowing the social logic of the pre-Pauline Christ endeavors thus is not an urgent requirement for our project, it seems to me. I am quite content to jump around from here to yonder, preferring, though, to jump where the social location is least foggy.

Seguing to a tangent on this: your rather autobiographical presentation at the NAASR session was most intriguing to me. I was reminded of your approach when I read your "Jazz and Blues" paper and noted there several references that suggest that you are playing your gig on a stage designed by our forefathers (a few mothers too, maybe) in our field. That is, you seem to want to whisper correctives to the ghosts of the fathers even as you are trying to do something radically different. Perhaps this social theorizing with a good tinge of polemical intent is what is confusing to me. Personally, I think the desire to "rectify the categories" of the fathers and contemporary brothers and sisters on *their* sites is doomed to failure anyway—if that is a desired outcome of our project. They have too many offspring who are singing the same song too loudly, and there are too many for whom this song is sweet music. My view is that we move our broadcast to the opposite end of the frequency dial so that our tune will not get confused with the overlay and static of the Christian superstation. Thus, just because they wanted continuity does not mean we have to entertain the same thing; just because they liked to camp in Jerusalem or Antioch does not mean we have to. Rather, it is precisely by trivializing (insofar as our historiographical assumptions and historical reconstructions guided by social theories permit) those sites that are especially sacred in the old, old story that we will clarify what we are up to. The fact that *they* (our predecessors in the field) have set the itinerary for our project is unfortunate and more driven by our polemical desires to mute our fathers than required by *our* emerging social theories. I would just as soon focus sharply on the latter and derive agenda and select station stops for examining social formations that make sense in relation to the terms of our theories.

I must end this epistle, but before I do, I doubly underline your comments in the "Foxtrot" section of your paper.[17] I, too, would like to have another round on the "prewar myths produced by Jesus people apart from Paul." I agree with all you say there. Things we did on Q and *Thomas* have

---

[17] Mack, "Backbay Jazz and Blues," 428–29.

indeed not fully registered even on those of us who were sent off on forays to these sites of mythmaking and social formation. Neither Arnal nor I, nor Cameron (if I can speak for him), received a critical once-over with a view toward clarifying what we are up to, if we understand each other, and so forth—never mind the question if the Q and *Thomas* projects could have been clarified by casting the net wider, to include both other Jesus groups (as you describe them in *A Myth of Innocence,* for example)[18] and non-Jesuanic social formations. But our traveling speed seems set by predetermined cruise control, alas.

Happy sailing!

---

[18] Burton L. Mack, *A Myth of Innocence: Mark and Christian Origins* (Philadelphia: Fortress, 1988), 78–97.

ISSUES AND COMMENTARY

Ron Cameron and Merrill P. Miller

Looking at the matter in retrospect at the end of the first two years of the Seminar, and following Mack's debriefing paper and Braun's response, we could surely revisit the papers on the Sayings Gospel Q by William E. Arnal and Braun from the third year of the Consultation with a sharper awareness of the issues of importance they raise for our discourse-in-the-making and for ways of thinking about the project that were not sufficiently clarified or discussed at the time, and which perhaps had not fully registered. Arnal not only presented an analysis in support of a particular thesis about Q and its tradents; he also deliberated on the categories of *social formation* and *mythmaking* and questioned what he understood to be the operative definitions of these categories and their relationship in the work of Mack. Moreover, in light of several of Braun's suspicions and queries in his "Smoke Signals from the North," one notices in his paper on Q, in particular, Braun's emphasis on the discontinuity of discursive formations, as well as his observation that the most interesting analogies to Q are not self-evident but the product of redescription in recent scholarship.[1] In short, these papers can be read as proposals about the matters to be given priority in a project of redescription. Instead of attending, as we did, to the sites that are central to the picture of Christian beginnings that scholars have always had in mind, we might have given priority to the clarification, fuller definition, and relationship of our theoretical terms—*mythmaking* and *social formation*—preparing to select and settle on whatever social-textual sites would best contribute to that end. Admittedly, there has been some lag in addressing theoretical issues. However, there is also some advantage in being able to entertain theoretical options in the context of a project now well under way, and one which the general introduction to this volume sets out in the context of a body of theoretical work.

---

[1] Willi Braun, "The Schooling of a Galilean Jesus Association (The Sayings Gospel Q)," 61–63, 65 (in this volume).

The significance of what has been achieved in the first two years of the Seminar needs to be highlighted as well as given critical scrutiny. It is appropriate to remind ourselves that the difficulties encountered at hypothetical sites are an index of our success in translating data, typically taken to signify divine interventions, momentous events, and transforming religious experience, into the data of mythmaking, from which we have sought, by means of a concept of social logic, to deduce social locations and social interests. Problematizing and defamiliarizing the data of a dominant paradigm are essential tasks for projects that aim at redescription.

There is thus an important matter of theory at stake in this project. The data of the dominant paradigm are what sustain a view of religion as an independent variable. Indeed, it is precisely at the guild's favorite, privileged sites that this view of religion is most easily and effectively taken for granted, and thus where it is most difficult to address, but also where it most needs to be called into question. The history of modern scholarship on Christian origins shows that one does not have to be committed to any particular first-order religious conviction in order to assume the adequacy of a presumption of the autonomy of religion as a second-order explanation. It is striking how easily this is swept under the table. Whereas there are many recent and important scholarly agendas that give occasion to repeated exhortations that our scholarship exhibit greater reflexivity with respect to our own historical location, politics, class, ethnicity, gender, culture, and sexuality, it is as if the exercise of such reflexivity somehow obviates the need to engage in an equally forthright reflexivity regarding assumptions about religion as an object of academic study when practicing biblical exegesis, making comparisons, and imagining the beginnings of Christianity.[2]

We need to review briefly the calculations that were made in the decision to spend the first two years of the Seminar focused on the strong texts of the canonical story of Christian origins. First, there was the matter of constructing a discourse on beginnings that did not continue to assume the normative picture while imagining that we were not beholden to it. Our

---

[2] See Jonathan Z. Smith, "Religion, Religions, Religious," in *Critical Terms for Religious Studies* (ed. Mark C. Taylor; Chicago: University of Chicago Press, 1998), 269, 281–82, whose review of "the use and understanding of the term 'religion'" since the sixteenth century demonstrates that "'religion' is not a native category ... no[r] a first person term of self-characterization ... [but] is a category imposed from the outside on some aspect of native culture.... 'Religion' is [thus] an anthropological not a theological category ... describ[ing] human thought and action.... 'Religion' is ... a term created by scholars for their intellectual purposes and therefore is theirs to define. It is a second-order, generic concept that plays the same role in establishing a disciplinary horizon that a concept such as 'language' plays in linguistics or 'culture' plays in anthropology. There can be no disciplined study of religion without such a horizon."

calculation was that this picture had to be addressed directly, before it could effectively be set aside in constructing our own discourse. The irony, of course, is that this calculation creates its own suspicion by remaining tied to loci that are central to the gospel story. However, we hope to show that our attention to these loci has not misfired but rather has occasioned a debate about the definition and relationship of our theoretical categories.

A second calculation was made about the importance of testing the notion of alternate beginnings. We had started with texts which we could demonstrate do not fit the usual assumption of apocalyptic-kerygmatic origins and which we could show also require a different way of accounting for the variety of social and discursive formations that appealed to Jesus or Christ as founder. We could justify starting with the Sayings Gospel Q and the *Gospel of Thomas* on the grounds of these texts' difference from the normative Gospel story, thereby gaining a cognitive advantage for the tasks of redescription. But could we justify the privileging of these texts, and could we sustain that privilege for constructing an alternative account of beginnings and for challenging an implicit theory of religion and its theistic view of history, without having directly argued the case that the data of the dominant paradigm made more sense as evidence of a generative process of social formation and mythmaking? We did not think that we could afford to leave aside the texts that were still considered to provide adequate grounds to account for that literature and for the imagination of origins that it sustained. For despite the fact that Q and *Thomas,* as well as the pre-Markan pronouncement stories, parable collections, and miracle catenae, neither fit the scenario of beginnings in Jerusalem narrated in the Gospels and Acts nor make sense as evidence of sects that took their rise from a belief that Jesus was the long-awaited Messiah of Israel, the difference these texts make for imagining beginnings will not—and cannot—be adequately registered until the canonical axis of Christian origins is, itself, relocated in the scholarly imagination and historiography of beginnings.

In the last century, the concept of pre-Pauline tradition, in particular, is what has sustained the complex of apocalyptic-kerygmatic beginnings and the privileged place of Jerusalem as the *fons et origo* of a messianic sect. This was because the bridge between "Jesus and Paul," and between the "primitive Palestinian tradition" and the "Hellenistic cult of Christ," was worked out by means of this concept, and in such a way that differences from one end of the trajectory to the other could be registered while maintaining, at the same time, a trunk-and-branches model of origins. No matter how discredited the terms "Palestinian" and "Hellenistic" have become as descriptive generalizations, and in spite of changing interests that have caused many scholars to move away from the theological concerns of Bultmannian and post-Bultmannian scholarship, the canonical picture of beginnings has never been seriously challenged. It is still sustained by imagining the impact of Jesus on his disciples and the events in Jerusalem as the generative factors that gave rise to a Jewish messianic sect and to a theological deposit that was subsequently transplanted and transformed in the wider Greco-Roman world.

It was this notion of pre-Pauline tradition that triggered a third calculation. The pre-Pauline concept was, in fact, the Gospel story. In modern scholarship, it was the kerygma of the early church. Its cogency depended upon ignoring or, more often, embracing three anomalies: (1) the pre-Pauline kerygma which had been reconstructed from Paul's letters did not presuppose, and did not fit, the Markan passion narrative or the speeches of the apostles in Acts; (2) Jesus did not fit the expectation of a Messiah; and (3) the picture of the Jerusalem church and its leaders did not fit what could easily be imagined as the consequences of the execution of Jesus in Jerusalem, supposedly on charges tantamount to insurrection. Our calculation was that it was possible to resolve these anomalies, whereas much of the history of scholarship could be read as an attempt to retain them. Thus, modern scholarship has allowed to stand as history a messianic drama in Jerusalem which is, in fact, a myth of origins. What calls for explanation, then, is the necessity of retaining—as a datum of history capable of accounting for beginnings—the anomaly of Jesus as crucified Messiah. On the one hand, it is the very improbability of such an anomaly that seems to guarantee its status as a historical datum. On the other, as an anomaly, it correlates well with conceptions of unique religious experience and dramatic reversal, of death and resurrection, where intelligibility is an altogether subsidiary matter and analogies need not apply. In the planning of the Seminar, we took into account the fact that some members of the Seminar had already begun to address these issues, which could then serve as a point of departure.

It is not unfair, we think, nor a real point of contention, to suggest that the agendas of the meetings in Orlando and Boston presupposed that we would try to "land ... our conceptual craft on hardly visible ... runways."[3] Nor do Mack and Braun disagree that we were not altogether successful. But whereas Mack thinks we should have been able to do more to clear a path in the jungle to make the runways visible, Braun responds that taking the risk is not worth what is to be gained for testing and improving our conceptual instruments. We do not find it necessary to choose between these judgments. Both are correct, though with different issues in view. The issue for Mack is leaving data unexplained precisely where the usual mystifications occur, especially when we could say more because

---

[3] Willi Braun, "Smoke Signals from the North: A Reply to Burton Mack's 'Backbay Jazz and Blues,'" 436 (in this volume).

analogies do exist, where data is fuller, to make our redescriptions thicker. For Braun the issue is the conceptual apparatus itself, not merely applying it but asking what we want to learn from it and choosing the strategies and sites that are optimal for achieving that end. But we need to remind ourselves that the runways were hardly visible to begin with, because we had been shortening, if not actually obliterating them, and rebuilding elsewhere. That is, the hardly visible runways of both years of the Seminar were the consequence of our resignifying and relocating the data of Jerusalem and the Messiah, which consisted of most of the work of the Seminar for those two years. And if we got ourselves into a predicament, we did so fully aware of what we were doing; indeed, we did it with the help of our conceptual instruments—together with the contributions of many scholars—though to say this is not to contradict Braun's point that we have not done much to sharpen those instruments themselves.

We think it important to linger for a moment over the suspicion that the Seminar itinerary and the attempt to find bridges from the Jesus movements to the Christ groups bespeak a continuing concern with continuity, generation, and development that could suggest that we are engaged in constructing some kind of alternative grand narrative with its own quest for absolute origination. Even though it is clear that Braun has used this suspicion to introduce a proposal about polygenesis, and that the particular charge is about attempting to establish continuity at the level of the transmission of ideas, we need to respond to what does not hit the mark, in our estimation, at least for the sake of clarifying what the issue might be. We are not following the Lukan itinerary. We segued to Jerusalem from Q and *Thomas,* and precisely because those texts were our point of departure. We have sought to determine whether the terrain occupied by earlier notions of pre-Pauline tradition and by groups thought of as pre-Pauline churches might turn out to look more like the Jesus movements we have envisaged than like the first church of Jerusalem of the book of Acts or like the Pauline congregations themselves. And so, while some of us have argued that the Jerusalem "pillars" and our hypothetical *christos* association make it possible for us to imagine a still greater variety of Jesus movements, we have not been concerned to establish any genealogy between, or relative chronology among, these movements. Thus far, at least, we have been able to imagine these movements and to entertain the question of mutual recognition from a synchronic perspective. And if, in our pursuit of Jesus movements, we have wanted to give attention to questions of mutual recognition, it has not been in quest of ideational continuity but in assessing comparability at the level of social interests.

Mack's question about why the members of the Seminar should want to rush to Corinth before taking up the Christ myths could appear to be a concern with tracing the sequence of stages of a developing myth. But just as Braun's counterquestion, "Why can't you 'jump'?"[4] is aimed at the more theoretical issue of the model of historical imagination with which we are operating, so Mack's question is directed to the issue of what is intended by the term *redescription*. In wanting to give some concentrated attention to the myths of martyrdom and of resurrection as cosmic enthronement, to Christ imagined as cosmic *kyrios* and divine son of God, Mack's immediate concern is that ignoring these myths makes it too easy to presuppose their attraction without having accounted for them. A redescription entails our being able to account for these myths on the grounds of our own social theories. We have not (yet) done that. As discursive formations, the Christ myths are not genetically linked to the myth of the *anointed Jesus*. They do not elaborate the social logic of the term *christos* as attributive and byname. Therefore, some other kinds of social conditions, factors, and interests will also have to come into the picture. It was this realization, together with the fact that *christos* is taken for granted as a cognomen in Paul's letters and is not found in the data from which the Jesus movements have been reconstructed, that strongly suggested something like a *christos* association in the first place. And the ways in which the Christ myths figure in Paul's letters—Paul's own theological spin—also do not answer the question of how these myths got into place but rather challenge us to ask that question.

Leaving data which have played a generative role in the traditional imagination of Christian origins unexplained, in our terms, is the problem Mack has in view, we suggest, not a quest for a developmental sequence in the formation of full-blown myths. Nevertheless, Mack's understanding of intertextual moments[5] also makes it clear that the sites selected for redescription are not intelligible as completely isolated moments. What is at issue here needs to be stated with some care, because we presuppose that Mack has no quarrel in general with Braun's appeal to polygenetic assumptions and coincidence, if what is meant is the emergence of similar (though not identical) types of response (none of which needs to be the cause of the other) occasioned by a set of conditions and challenges characteristic of the Greco-Roman world. However, since it does not seem at all likely that the term *christos* popped up as a cognomen here and there coincidentally as a response to similar conditions, we must suppose that the spread of this usage is much more likely to be an index of mutual recognition among different groups. *Christos* has to be in place as a sign of mutual recognition because the Christ myths, while not explicable as

---

[4] Ibid., 438, citing Burton L. Mack, "Backbay Jazz and Blues," 423 (in this volume).

[5] See the discussion of mythmaking and intertextuality in Burton L. Mack, *A Myth of Innocence: Mark and Christian Origins* (Philadelphia: Fortress, 1988), 15–24, 321–24.

elaborations of a *christos* myth or the ways of accounting for it, are nonetheless myths about Jesus Christ. Thus, to imagine the groups that fabricated Christ myths and to compare them with our hypothetical *christos* association would present our first interesting case of trying to account for historical continuity and change among groups that, at the very least, shared the cognomen. Signs of mutual recognition may be indicative of influences that are formative, if not determinative, for a particular discursive formation. Mack has argued this point in detail in the case of the Markan passion narrative,[6] and Miller has made the same point regarding the myth of Jesus the Messiah in the Gospel narratives.

While we remain convinced of the strategic importance of our sites for the task of redescribing the beginnings of Christianity as religion, we differ with Braun in his assessment of their relative significance for testing our social theories and sharpening our conceptual instruments only to the extent that we think his important queries and contentions are too dismissive of the ways in which the project has been guided by the program of category formation, comparison, redescription, and rectification available to us in the work of Jonathan Z. Smith. In fact, some of the points that Braun himself has highlighted are exactly the ones we would make. For example, we have introduced as second-level generalizations the terms *homeland* and *diaspora, ethnicity, social experimentation,* and *reflexivity*. The choice of these terms is informed precisely by considerations of the general conditions and challenges of the Greco-Roman world, that is, by "keep[ing] one eye glued to 'a wide-angle lens focused upon the many ways in which people responded to the Greco-Roman age.'"[7] Moreover, they are terms that are sufficiently distanced from those internal to early Christian literature, and to scholarship on Christian beginnings, to hold promise as analytical categories for a project of redescription.

The same considerations have been in play where a few deductions about *social interests* have been attempted and where questions of comparability among the Jesus movements have been entertained. Early Christian social experimentation belongs to the broader context of response to the social and cultural fragmentation of the times, in a world dominated by the political institutions of empire. Particular features of commonality such as fictive collective identities, appeal to Jesus as founder, and selective

---

[6] Ibid., 247–312, 315–49.

[7] Braun, "Smoke Signals from the North," 439, citing his own remarks to Mack at a joint session of the Ancient Myths and Modern Theories of Christian Origins Seminar and the North American Association for the Study of Religion, held in Boston in 1999. In his remarks, Braun quoted a critical comment of Mack, which may now be found in Burton L. Mack, "The Christian Origins Project," in *The Christian Myth: Origins, Logic, and Legacy* (New York: Continuum, 2001), 216.

appropriation and critique of elements from the cultures of context—all of these are expressions of legitimation and continuity invented out of, and because of, experiences of actual disruption and discontinuity in the social world. We think that the papers, discussions, and debriefings on both Jerusalem and *christos* have contributed to making these common features among the Jesus movements understandable as responses to conditions that were shared by many peoples of the Levant in the Greco-Roman period, rather than continuing to account for them by appealing to a shared experience of Jesus, a continuous historical development, or a common set of beliefs. Most of all, the work of the first two years of the Seminar, together with the contributions on the Sayings Gospel Q and the *Gospel of Thomas* from the third year of our Consultation, makes Braun's own query understandable as well as important: "Does all this buzz of activity, so much of it focused on solving problems of social location and identity, make for a set?"[8]

Mack had reduced to a set of social indicators what could be said of common interests generating different Jesus groups in the wake of our readings of Gal 2. He summarized this by stating: "Thus, having set aside the Lukan-Pauline scenario, the picture of Christian origins changes markedly in the direction of ad hoc social formations and wide-open ideological debate where and when people interjected the Jesus legacy into the situation of Jewish response to the Roman world." It could even be said that "the issues raised for Jews by the Jesus legacy had much to do with Jewish identity ... little with loyalties or markers pertinent to self-definition as a Jesus school or Christ cult." This seemed to be the case in particular for "the picture of a group of Jews in Jerusalem who got interested in talking about the significance of Jesus, his teachings, and the various groups forming in his name, for Jewish institutions and self-definition." Mack had set these indicators in the broader context of recurrent themes debated by Jewish intellectuals and suggested that they were all "variants of [social] interests common to all peoples." In addition, he noted that it would be possible to find "a place within the Jesus movements for [a] Jerusalem group," since the few indicators that we had could be compared with data from other Jesus groups, with later responses found in Q^3, Matthew, the *Didache,* and *1 Clement,* and with analogues from interest groups like the Pharisees.[9] This, surely, is not an interest in homologies,[10] in establishing

---

[8] Braun, "Smoke Signals from the North," 440.

[9] Burton L. Mack, "A Jewish Jesus School in Jerusalem?" 257–58, 257, 262, 259, 261 (in this volume).

[10] For a discussion of the distinction between "analogies" and "genealogies" (i.e., homologies), see Jonathan Z. Smith, *Drudgery Divine: On the Comparison of Early Christianities and the Religions of Late Antiquity* (Jordan Lectures in Comparative Religion 14; London: School

genealogical relations or "connecting all the dots"[11] between and among the Jesus groups. It is a question of difference and redescription, as Mack indicated in an earlier debriefing paper (of 30 November 1998): "Let us place the Jerusalem group on the map of early Jesus and Christ groups, note that its features challenge us to broaden the scope of interests that may have been involved, and use it to ask ourselves whether our erstwhile views of the Jesus groups à la Q and the *Gospel of Thomas* need correction." The prospect of being able to say more than we have about Jesus people in Jerusalem as an intersecting of a Jesus legacy with issues of Judaic practice would seem, finally, to depend in large part on a redescription of the Pharisees, itself a substantial undertaking, but an obvious desideratum in light of the redescription of the rabbinic guild and its literature in the work of Jack N. Lightstone.[12]

In addition, Mack has addressed programmatically the issues of social location and identity in a series of papers. In discussing "the social reasons" for using the term *christos,* Mack observed that one of the characteristics of the Jesus movements is a "form of mythmaking" shared by all these groups: an appeal to "the epic of Israel":

> This means that all of these groups in the Jesus movements thought of themselves, wanted to think of themselves, or wanted to give an account of themselves to others as a formation with legitimate claim to being okay within the range of Jewish configurations of the time.... As such, calling Jesus *christos* would be a claim that he was "God's choice" for the social role of founder-figure of the Jesus movements and [thus] an implicit claim that the Jesus-movement formation should be thought of as a way of being "Israel." ... What we have called the "Jewish" roots of the Christian experiment need to be acknowledged in order to grasp fully the social interests involved in the claims to be the legitimate heirs of Israel on the part of early Christian groups.... [And so,] if the beginnings of Christianity cannot be explained except by tracing the history of relations with the diaspora synagogue, it means that all of the social interests under cultivation in the synagogue can be considered at work among the

---

of Oriental and African Studies, University of London; Chicago: University of Chicago Press, 1990), 47–51; cf. 110, 112–14. On the use of "analogies" to account for "polygenesis," diversity, and difference, see idem, "Close Encounters of Diverse Kinds," in *Religion and Cultural Studies* (ed. Susan L. Mizruchi; Princeton: Princeton University Press, 2001), 3–21, esp. 14–15.

[11] So Braun, "Smoke Signals from the North," 440.

[12] Jack N. Lightstone, "Whence the Rabbis? From Coherent Description to Fragmented Reconstructions," *SR* 26 (1997): 275–95; idem, *Mishnah and the Social Formation of the Early Rabbinic Guild: A Socio-rhetorical Approach* (Studies in Christianity and Judaism 11; Waterloo, Ont.: Wilfrid Laurier University Press, 2002). Lightstone's work was called to the attention of Seminar members and discussed in Braun's paper on Q, "The Schooling of a Galilean Jesus Association," 63–65.

> early Christians as well. That ... gives the identity interest we have been considering more than enough reason to account for the social formations and mythmaking of early Christians.[13]

Therefore, in reviewing the plan and findings of "the Christian origins project," Mack concluded that "the social project [driving early Christian experiments] must have been both reflexive and cross-cultural by design. The project was to reimagine and reinvent the collective (in this case, 'Israel') in a form appropriate for the larger human horizon of the Greco-Roman age."[14] This observation can be underscored by recognizing that early Christian literature, like the literature of the Hebrew Bible, is largely ethnographic in intent, concerned with defining a society.[15] Such a recognition, we suggest, can help clarify what is at issue in trying "to imagine the social situation and logic of the first use of Mr. *Christos* from the appellation itself."[16]

The appellative *christos* needs to be seen in light of other uses of the term. In relation to a wider usage, the appellation is too novel to make it likely that it popped up coincidentally, as we have already noted. But the novelty makes social sense, once it is seen that our lack of more specific and detailed ethnographic data *in situ* is at least partially compensated by conceiving the attributive *christos* linked to the name Jesus as emblematic of an ethnographic myth. It claims that "we," that is, those who call Jesus "*christos*," are a resignified Israel. Indeed, as Arnal reminds us in his paper on Q that social identity is always already constituted within a larger totality,[17] the anointed Jesus should be taken as evidence of an intervention in the larger totality of Israel for the sake of a particular social program. In addition, the claim to represent an ancestral heritage by way of the anointed Jesus works as effectively by what it excludes as by what it names. It excludes the institutions with which the term is associated everywhere else. The *christos* association conceived of itself either as a displacement of these institutions or as a different way of imagining their representation. In fact, the alternative is easily imagined as a matter of internal debate. In either case, the appellation itself is an attestation of experimentation and reflexivity.

We have to locate this intervention where it is most likely to have been known to Paul: prior to the writing of his extant letters and the activities

---

[13] Burton L. Mack, "Why *Christos*? The Social Reasons," 367, 368, 373 (in this volume).
[14] Mack, "Christian Origins Project," 211.
[15] See Merrill P. Miller, "The Anointed Jesus," 409 with n. 99 (in this volume).
[16] Braun, "Smoke Signals from the North," 436.
[17] William E. Arnal, "Why Q Failed: From Ideological Project to Group Formation," 74 (in this volume).

that constituted their occasions, of course, and not among those Jesus groups for whom we have no evidence that they ever used the term. The choice of the term as an attribute of Jesus is an instance of mythmaking, since it establishes claims of status and identity on the basis of divine initiative and approval. What others would attribute to kings, priests, and prophets, past and future—and mostly for the sake of authenticating the current practices of particular social formations in contexts of debate and struggle over the institutions the writers imagined or sought to represent—was claimed by Jesus people known to Paul for their own constituencies and practices. In light of the evidence we have for usage of this term, it makes sense to suppose that this sort of attribution of status to Jesus was an exercise in legitimation and self-definition of associations in debate with but, increasingly, independent of the institutional practices and boundaries of synagogues of a major urban center in northern Syria. Only because it is used with reference to kings, priests, and prophets does the term carry royal, sacerdotal, and prophetic connotations and connect with these roles in particular. What is most clear about the earliest literary evidence we have from Christian sources is that the term was linked to the name Jesus without specifying that this Jesus was a king or a priest or a prophet. Since there is no problem articulating these role specifications, we ought to suppose that those who began to use the term with reference to Jesus were surely aware of its linkage to roles but did not find it attractive in particular as a claim that Jesus was an anointed king, priest, or prophet. If we wanted to connect the particular myth of the anointed Jesus with other early Christian mythmaking, we could simply say, on the one hand, that it is a pointed example of attribution to Jesus calculated at once to provide novelty and instant aging and, on the other, that its vagueness hints at a tendency to collapse all kinds of attributions, roles, and forms of authority in a single figure.

Thus, we are also invited to inquire about the particular attraction of the anointed Jesus. The main clue is that the term is always a cognomen in Paul's letters, but never a term of reflexivity. No argument in Paul's letters depends upon identifying Jesus as the Messiah. What is presupposed is that the cognomen is an easily transmitted form of mutual recognition. There is no need to rehearse, again, that Mack and Miller have tried to track down what that recognition may have been all about and how it might initially have taken hold, in order to present a more plausible account of beginnings than the appearance of the Messiah narrated in the Gospels and Acts. But this should not become an occasion for debate about the relative historical importance of first usages as compared with their later elaborations. First, *christos* as a cognomen is not merely a first usage. It is a common denominator. All early Christian sources that use the term use it (also) in this way. Second, the elaboration of a myth has to be located and identified. In the case of *christos* one cannot go just anywhere the term is used to find an elaboration. As we have already stated, Paul's letters do not present us with an elaboration of the myth of the anointed Jesus. The Christ myths that he takes up, that is, the myths formed around the cosmic role of Christ, are not elaborations of the ethnographic myth *christos* and do not amplify its social logic. They are attached to the cognomen because of its use among different groups. Moreover, it would be a serious misunderstanding of the arguments Miller has presented in his papers to suppose that they are driven primarily—or solely—by a concern with a first usage. Miller set out to locate and redescribe a messianic conception of Jesus. In order to do that, he had (1) to attend to all the data that bear on the uses of the term; (2) to redescribe the significance of the *term,* in contrast to messianic *figures,* in Jewish literatures to the end of the first century C.E.; (3) to reverse the consensus of scholarship on the relative chronology of appellative and titular uses of the term in early Christian literature; and (4) to rectify the category *messianic* with respect to the introduction and earlier use of the term, by suggesting that the category *ethnographic* is more appropriate. In other words, attention to an earlier usage, made possible in part by comparison with Jewish uses of the term, serves as a foil for the redescription of the Messiah of the Gospels and Acts. This work is not yet complete, but enough has been shown to see that Miller is arguing that *the Messiah* is an invention of the Gospel writers, who were addressing issues of the composition of a *bios* of Jesus and issues of the direction of Jesus movements in the wake of the Roman-Jewish war. The term is certainly not created out of whole cloth. It takes up apocalyptic ideas of the restoration of native kingship and makes use of what is, by now, a widely recognized cognomen (among Christ people), which also served as a precedent for linking the term exclusively with Jesus. But the term is not simply an elaboration of this earlier Christian usage, nor is it the application of a Jewish category. In that sense, too, Miller has in view the rectification of categories, as well as a reconsideration of the reasons for the fascination with messianism in Western cultures and histories.

What has not yet been addressed in this commentary is the core issue that we think can be stated, initially, as a question of privileged data. For a number of reasons, we have attended largely to the data of mythmaking. First, that is the data closest to hand in the literature. Second, translating the data presented as singular events, unique encounters with divinity, and incremental traditions, into evidence of mythmaking as a generative discursive practice, seemed to us a prerequisite for establishing a more analytic frame of reference and historical imagination wherein the permutations, revaluations, and reconfigurations of patterns of human practices, established by our own acts of comparison, might be accounted for by means of a theory of social interests. There is, finally, a third reason, which is more problematic, as we have come to see. We have presumed that social formations, programs, and agendas exist in some clearly discernible relation to mythmaking and that the latter can provide adequate clues of social situations and collective motivations. Social interests could thus be thought of as mediating the categories of social formation and mythmaking. But it might be argued, to the contrary, that mythmaking does not provide adequate—to say nothing of the best—clues for what is driving a social program or for what it is all about. Rather than having any determinative force as the causal factors or generative elements of a social formation, mythmaking might be thought of principally—or entirely—as the secondary effects of other factors, material and social. In that case, it could be charged that privileging the data of mythmaking misunderstands the relation between discursive and nondiscursive elements of a social formation, resulting in an obscuring or ignoring of other kinds of evidence of material and social factors capable of putting us in touch with the determinative forces that account for processes of historical continuity and change. Accordingly, we might attempt to summarize the theoretical issue at stake in the Mack-Braun correspondence with the following question: Are ideas and discourse constituted in their entirety by the material framework in which they operate, or are social formations and practices linguistic phenomena, the product of human intellectual labor? Whether this way of formulating the matter exaggerates the alternatives, or whether these alternatives can be mediated and their differences be reduced or resolved in other theoretical proposals, will have to be determined in the course of a project that remains tied to the tasks of redescribing particular loci of Christian beginnings. To keep that in view is not (meant as) a reminder of the project to which we are committed. It is intended as a matter of reflexivity, as Smith has persistently reminded us: "A methodological or theoretical position is not some magic wand that makes problems disappear. Each position assumed entails costs and consequences. The question is not one of deciding on solutions, but of choosing what set of costs one is willing to bear."[18] The issue, then, is not one of which data to choose and what strategy to use to redescribe it. For as Thomas S. Kuhn has observed, discussing the relationship of theory to argumentation, "in the absence of a paradigm or some candidate for paradigm, all of the facts that could possibly pertain to the development of a given science are likely to seem equally relevant."[19] The issue, rather, is theoretical and comparative.

---

[18] Jonathan Z. Smith, "Acknowledgments: Morphology and History in Mircea Eliade's *Patterns in Comparative Religion* (1949–1999), Part 2: The Texture of the Work," *HR* 39 (2000): 351.

[19] Thomas S. Kuhn, *The Structure of Scientific Revolutions* (2nd ed.; International Encyclopedia of Unified Science 2/2; Chicago: University of Chicago Press, 1970), 15.

"Contestation arises over competing claims to comprehend the *same* data, an argument that, therefore, can never be settled at the level of data."[20] As Smith, himself, has remarked:

> We're not going to solve today the problem of Plato's upward and downward path. We're not going to solve [here and now] the issue of induction and deduction, whether one moves from what's thick and attempts to achieve some clarity, or whether one starts with where one's relatively clear and complicates it. I take it that's actually what comparison is all about and why ... comparison becomes [such] an important object of attention. What we want is the revisionary juxtaposition of both: on the one hand, let's formulate a theory and then go and get evidence for it; on the other hand, let's be as thick as possible in the description of the evidence on which we base the theory we use.[21]

Thus, in our efforts to create a discourse among us, we need "to practice speaking and arguing with each other about such matters [of consequence for a redescription of Christian origins], in a way that, shunning univocality, aims, nevertheless, at displaying and clarifying informed choices."[22]

---

[20] Jonathan Z. Smith, "Connections," *JAAR* 58 (1990): 10, emphasis original, citing, in addition, the passage quoted above from Kuhn (ibid., 9).

[21] Jonathan Z. Smith, "Discussion" of idem, "The Domestication of Sacrifice," in *Violent Origins: Walter Burkert, René Girard, and Jonathan Z. Smith on Ritual Killing and Cultural Formation* (ed. Robert G. Hamerton-Kelly; Stanford, Calif.: Stanford University Press, 1987), 211.

[22] Smith, "Connections," 13.

PART 4
METAREFLECTIONS

Social Formation and Mythmaking: Theses on Key Terms

William E. Arnal and Willi Braun

I. Preamble

The theses below are the result of our decision, at some point prior to the third year of the Seminar, held in Nashville in 2000, to attempt to raise as pointedly as we were able our concerns over what we thought to be methodological and theoretical unclarities and uncertainties—meta-issues, in short—around the Seminar table. These uncertainties had already come to the fore, perhaps only implicitly and not sharply, on the occasion of our first formal presentations to the Seminar, in San Francisco in 1997, on Q and *Thomas*.[1] During the sessions in Nashville we decided to take advantage of a hiatus in the Seminar's forward momentum, following what was for us a baffling and ultimately stymied discussion of the "Christ" label in 1999, to attempt to address as clearly as possible the theoretical underpinnings of our collective project. We offer them as our reflections on the Seminar's deliberations, which, and this must be said without reservation, have successfully disrupted, perhaps even displaced, the standard "Lukan-Eusebian" model of Christianity's historical beginnings.

The thetic format was inspired primarily by Bruce Lincoln, whose "Theses on Method"[2] we admire for their acuity of thought and the bluntness of their expression. In light of the controversial discussion of our theses around the Seminar table, it should also be noted that the focus on such

---

[1] See William E. Arnal, "Why Q Failed: From Ideological Project to Group Formation" (in this volume); Willi Braun, "The Schooling of a Galilean Jesus Association (The Sayings Gospel Q)" (in this volume).

[2] Bruce Lincoln, "Theses on Method," *MTSR* 8 (1996): 225–27; repr. in *The Insider/Outsider Problem in the Study of Religion: A Reader* (ed. Russell T. McCutcheon; Controversies in the Study of Religion; London: Cassell, 1999), 395–98. For additional commentary, see idem, "Reflections on 'Theses on Method,'" in *Secular Theories on Religion: Current Perspectives* (ed. Tim Jensen and Mikael Rothstein; Copenhagen: Museum Tusculanum Press, 2000), 117–21.

keys terms as *mythmaking* and *social formation* is an acknowledgment of the extent to which this Seminar is indebted to Burton L. Mack's immensely productive formulation of the historical and historiographical problematic. The focus of the theses on Mack's key categories thus is not to be taken as our lack of commitment to "social formation" and "mythmaking" as elemental categories in the Seminar's project, much less as a shot across the bow of Mack's groundbreaking undertaking to place the study of early Christianities on new intellectual foundations. Rather, an effort is made here to clarify, to expand, and to sharpen our understanding and application of these terms and other linked concepts, in order to defog *our own* sense on how to move forward along the path that the steering committee had mapped for the Seminar.

The point of the theses, in spite of their positive and even aggressive formulation, was not—and this should be stressed—was not to articulate, then to cajole the Seminar into accepting a single theory about "social formation" and "mythmaking" and the nexus between them. This Seminar is not the place for such a grand project, and it is to be doubted—doubted very much—whether those of us seated around this table once a year ever could come to agreement on such weighty and complex matters. Rather, we sought to bring into the open the evident differences in the assumptions at work among us about this nexus by articulating as sharply as possible our own assumptions. In this way, we hoped, not only could our theoretical differences be clarified, but some progress might also be made in energizing our larger redescriptive project or, at the very least, in turning up the level of self-critical vigilance over our labors. For, in addition to a lack of theoretical clarity that has characterized some of our discussions, we have also felt a measure of suspicion that as a group we have been, in our substantive work on key "sites" of ancient Christian formations, quite unintentionally constructing simply an alternative narrative of Christian origins and thus simply engaging in—and falling under the spell of—mythmaking ourselves. On this point we must be adamant: if the task of redescription is the clarification of categories—minding Jonathan Z. Smith's repeated reminder—and, on the basis of such clarification, ultimately to work out a more cogent understanding of the historical phenomena in question, then writing a new story or, as is almost ineluctably the case, a new version of the old story will avail us nothing. We will, indeed, be engaging in the very project we are attempting to understand and thus will have made our "theories" practically interchangeable with our eponymous "myths."

To some degree, it seems to us, our efforts have already borne fruit. The theoretical problem facing us has been, we think, "foregrounded" much more, and the members of the Seminar have become even more self-conscious about certain types of theoretical assumptions and their problems than before. In addition, both of us have benefited from the effort to articulate these theses as well as from the discussion that they have generated. As a result, *our* ideas on the nexus of social formation and mythmaking are that much clearer, and the fact *that* this nexus is among the most crucial meta-issues facing the Seminar is all the more apparent to us.

The question, though, of where to go from here, remains open. As already noted, trying to come to a definitive agreement as a group on the theoretical relationship between social formation and mythmaking is not the best direction to pursue as the Seminar's focus. What is to be hoped for, however, is a more rigorous explication of the social theories underpinning individual Seminar members' varying uses of these concepts when they are applied to our subject matter.

In particular, we wish to draw the attention of the Seminar's members to the social half of our working concepts, "social formation and mythmaking." One might conceive of this formula as a juxtaposition of the social (power, material factors, collective structures and the pressures and antagonisms that they generate) with the cultural (rationalizations, ideals, ethics, and, of course, myths). If so, the key problematic may be less helpfully conceptualized as one of idealism over against materialism as one in which an investigation into social formation has been, at times, subordinated to an investigation into cultural formation.[3] That is, our disagreements may have more to do with a greater interest than we think is necessary in the cultural artifacts on their own terms, rather than in the social processes and the way they relate to cultural artifacts.

The extent to which these domains may or may not be conceived as independent of each other is an open question and a matter for further theoretical thought. But in the meantime, it seems that it would behoove us to remember the social element of this juxtaposition, and to guard against a too-exclusive focus on the merely cultural, which, as Mack has reminded us and as we also maintain, cannot be understood exclusively on its own terms but only in terms of, against the backdrop of, and with reference to the social. Until and unless we as a group can agree on a theoretical formulation establishing the relationship between these two domains, we cannot risk subsuming the social into the cultural and must work rigorously to address both facets of ancient Christianity. Otherwise, we may, like Luke or like Hegel, end up constructing little more than the story of the progress of Spirit.

---

[3] This was pointed out to us by Johannes Wolfart, a colleague at the University of Manitoba.

II. Theses

A. Social Formation

We regard all discourse, a collective term for verbal and nonverbal communicative forms, to be an irreducibly social phenomenon. As a result, analysis of the social world in which such discourse is generated, embedded, and efficacious should be theoretically and methodologically prior to examination of discourse itself—which, of course, includes all "mythmaking." Some social processes may be nondiscursive; no discursive practice is nonsocial.

1. *The social is not an interest but a basic fact of human being.* The term "social interests," which Mack has introduced as a weighty explanatory category, does not indicate an interest in sociality per se: humans are social beings who, as a matter of species-being, are constituted in groups. There is no presocial moment in which individuals choose to constitute themselves in groups, nor is there humanity without sociality. Therefore, "social interest" designates not a desire to form groups but a desire to pursue ends and agenda shared with and relative to others within the same social body. The practice of forming subgroups is not an end in itself but is a particular type of intervention in the larger social body of which the subgroup forms a part.

2. *Human interests are radically social.* That is to say, the ends pursued by human beings are pursued within and with a view to the social totality that forms the network and body of human being. Even apparently basic and conceptually individualistic goals, such as the provision of food or shelter, are undertaken in a social fashion and within a social body and thus have a social character. It is our contention—though it need not be accepted for this point to be taken—that social interests are differential and conflictual and hence organize themselves along class lines. It may be granted, with Althusser, that these class-based differential social interests refer *ultimately* to material well-being and that class identity therefore is a function of economic conditions and interests, without thereby depriving ideas and other social phenomena of a *relative* autonomy. Ideas representing similar social interests may take divergent forms (see further theses 3–5), so it is clear that they are not generated mechanically out of socioeconomic conditions. However, "in the final instance" they are constrained by, shaped by, and refer to those conditions.

3. *Morphologically divergent socialities may show themselves to be similarly motivated social formations in a shared totality.* "The social interests that get acted on and mystified and mythologized by Christian groups were not

interests unique to Christians.... The connection [between early Christian socialities] may be not between them as much as around and underneath them: the realities [totality] of the Greco-Roman age."[4] Or, to sharpen the point with a counterfactual question, can we imagine that Jesus-group X or Christ-group Y would have popped up on more or less similar motives and in more or less similar form without reference to "Jesus" or "Christ"? If the answer is yes, our point has been taken.[5]

4. *Relative to each other, early Christian groups are genetically independent.* Thus our understanding of Christian "polygenesis"—or, perhaps better, "concomitant variation"—should be understood as a sequitur to thesis 3.[6] This does mean drastically lowering the stress on Christian-group X providing generative motive and causal force for the popping up of Christian-group Y. It does not mean that there is no overlap or convergence between group X and group Y, only that this convergence, however specified, ought in the first place not to imply a genetic relationship, especially not if this genetic relationship is located in the realm of ideas (myths, mythmaking). This also does not mean that group X and group Y did not "mutually recognize" (Mack) each other (for surely they did), nor that this recognition did not have important impacts on a specified group's self-perception, self-representation, and perhaps even its social morphology.

5. *Social formations are overlapping, convergent in some respects, divergent in others. They are never self-contained or pure.* This does not mean that we should eschew abstracting types for the purpose of analyzing and explaining motives, organizational morphology, and patterns of self-representation and rationalization for any given sociality. It does mean, however, that the types are our heuristic constructions for the purpose of our understanding of the dynamics of social formation and mythmaking, rather than historical descriptions, although the types should of course be as historically plausibly described and located as possible, precisely as the Seminar has assiduously attempted to do with reference to various social forms (schools, voluntary associations of various kinds) in the Greco-Roman world.

---

[4] Willi Braun, "Smoke Signals from the North: A Reply to Burton Mack's 'Backbay Jazz and Blues,'" 439–40 (in this volume).

[5] We recognize that a full description of the totality of the Greco-Roman age is a desideratum that lies outside the explicit purview of this Seminar, but this should not erase the consequentiality of the theoretical point.

[6] "Polygenesis" was introduced in Braun, "Smoke Signals from the North," 438–39 with n. 12. Jonathan Z. Smith suggested a less-aggressive term, "concomitant variation," which conveys a less simplistic over-againstness of continuity and discontinuity.

B. MYTHMAKING

Mythmaking is a social intellectual activity whereby certain key terms, images, motifs, and idea complexes are elevated to a "self-evidently" authoritative status. These items may then be manipulated as a kind of discursive shorthand for the social body as a whole or the larger social units being addressed. Such manipulation allows intrasocial affiliations and differential (i.e., conflictual) claims to be (rhetorically) identified with or differentiated from the "culture" as a whole by the exercise of various affiliational or "differential equations."[7]

6. *Ideas, including more or less elaborated myths, do not have motive force except they are given motive force in specific and immediate context.* Ideas have no transformative power of their own; they are developed and used in specific ways by people, much in the fashion of a tool. Even when the ideas do have motive force in some specific and immediate context, they only do so through social vehicles and do not have that force in themselves. Moreover, the usual motive force ideas have is in the generation of new ideas, not in the generation of new social behaviors or structures. An idea (or rather, its prior social reception) may have a considerable impact on the identity and shape of subsequent ideas, but without thereby directly altering the shape of the social structure it reflects.

7. *Similarity of ideas, even when this similarity is the result of dispersal by some mechanism of transmission, is not automatically convertible to similarity or identity of motive force.* Similarity or identicality of ideas in different locales may, but need not, bespeak a genetic relationship. Thus, if we see *christos* language used by two groups, it may or may not mean that its use here is genetically attributable to its use there. But even if we can demonstrate genealogy at the idea level, this does not necessarily mean that the term has the same generative or representational value here and there. Two "christs" are not like two peas from the same pod that will generate identical pea plants no matter how remotely from each other the peas are planted.

8. *Mythologoumena do not elaborate themselves organically out of their internal force, so finding first, second, or any sequential station stops on the way to elaborated myths is not necessary to get at the relationship between mythmaking and social formation.* From the foregoing thesis follows: ideas do not develop on their own; people develop them. This implies that

---

[7] See Jonathan Z. Smith, "Differential Equations: On Constructing the 'Other'" (The University Lecture in Religion 13, Arizona State University, Tempe, Ariz., 5 March 1992).

Traditionsgeschichte, as it is understood and practiced in our field, while intrinsically of no less general interest, is in need of suspicious scrutiny regarding its utility for explaining social formation.

9. *Myths and mythmaking are ultimately effects, not causes, of socialities.* This statement may be regarded as a "useful distortion" (to use a Smithian phrase), not an either/or ultimatum. It is probably an idealist fallacy to regard ideas and discourse as something other than a component (analytically speaking) of the material framework in which they operate. In other words, there need not be anything idealist about ideas, in which case any dichotomy between ideas and material forces is itself idealist! But for our purposes here, and as a corrective, it is worth viewing those material social manifestations that present themselves as nonmaterial to be effects, if only for the sake of conceptual clarity.

10. *Linearity need not be eschewed in historical hypotheses but should not refer to ideas, concepts, or rhetorical constructions exclusively and primarily.* This point follows from and expands upon theses 8 and 9, that ideas and theologoumena do not elaborate out of an internal *Geist* and are best conceived as effects of social processes rather than the causes thereof. If these assertions are valid, then tracing the (supposed) linear progression of ideas will not yield a useful sequence of the historical causes and effects of social processes. It is worth underscoring, however, that our objections to *this* sort of linearity are objections to idealism, not to linearity as such. We are not insisting that all historical phenomena can only be conceived as isolated and unrelated moments. We assume that hypotheses concerning historical processes are not only possible but necessary. The point, rather, is simply that the kinds of causality and continuity that allow us to understand these processes are unlikely to be found at the level of ideas.

11. *Ultimately, ideas do not require an idealist analysis.* That is to say, even when one's focus of interest is on discourse (e.g., emphasizing the processes behind "mythmaking" more than "social formation"), this in itself need not require that our approach diminish the analytical priority of social phenomena. Ideas stubbornly present themselves as lacking context, but, as Ron Cameron and Merrill P. Miller note in their general introduction to this volume and as is underscored by their reference to Jack N. Lightstone's insightful article on the formation of the Mishnah,[8] it is improper to allow

---

[8] Jack N. Lightstone, "Whence the Rabbis? From Coherent Description to Fragmented Reconstructions," *SR* 26 (1997): 275–95.

discursive self-description to control the analysis of the phenomena in question. We should regard discourse's own presentation of the explicit or camouflaged motives for its self-presentation with as much suspicion as we regard the self-presentation of the source or character of any particular discourse, such as, for example, the writings of the New Testament or those of the Mishnah.

C. CONJUNCTIONS

The relationship between social formation and mythmaking—and, likely, differences among Seminar members on this relationship—is contained and concealed in the innocuous three-letter word "and." Although our view on the nature of the nexus between social formation and mythmaking is strongly implied, if not stated, in the previous points, two additional statements should be made.

12. *The "and" in "social formation and mythmaking" conveys a synchronic import.* It sets up our primary task as the need to deduce the generative and representational links between particular socialities and their ideas. This does not mean that issues of origin, development, evolution, and continuity—diachronic questions, that is—have no place in historical hypotheses, nor does it mean that there is not a relationship between synchronic analyses (the situational complexities between groups and their ideational ciphers; morphology or types of sociomythic inventions) and diachronic analyses (the evolution of the Christian myth; the evolution of Christian social formation), nor, finally, that the relationship is not an important question to consider. It does mean, however, recognizing the difference and to guard against importing notions of influence and causality that belong more to an idealist intellectual and narrational discourse than to the world of historical events into our effort to (re)describe discrete, particular "moments" of social formation and mythmaking.

13. *Mutual recognition is an effect rather than a cause of the proliferation of Christian groups.* The fact of "mutual recognition" (Mack) among Jesus associations and Christ groups does not, in our view, contradict anything stated above. We regard mutual recognition as a secondary moment—heuristically, not chronologically speaking. It is an effect rather than a cause of the proliferation of Christian groups. If Willi Braun's offer of the analogy of the polygenetic proliferation and mutual recognition of various Anabaptisms in the sixteenth century is not credible,[9] one should consider

---

[9] Braun, "Smoke Signals from the North," 438–39 with n. 12.

the analogous case of the polygenetic proliferation and mutual recognition of the mystery cults.[10] The key text follows:

> Behold Lucius I am come, thy weeping and prayers has moved me to succor thee. I am she that is the natural mother of all things, mistress and governess of all the elements, the initial progeny of worlds, chief of powers divine, queen of heaven, the principal of the gods celestial, the light of the goddesses: at my will the planets of the air, the wholesome winds of the seas, and the silences of hell be disposed; my name, my divinity is adored throughout all the world in diverse manners, in variable customs and in many names, for the Phrygians call me Pessinuntica, the mother of the gods; the Athenians call me Cecropian Artemis; the Cyprians, Paphian Aphrodite; the Candians, Dictyanna; the Sicilians, Stygian Proserpine; and the Eleusians call me Mother of Ceres. Some call me Juno, others Bellona of the Battles, and still others Hecate. Principally the Ethiopians, who dwell in the Orient, and the Egyptians, who are excellent in all kind of ancient doctrine and by their proper ceremonies accustomed to worship me, do call me Queen Isis.[11]

---

[10] Again, one might prefer the language of "concomitant variation" to that of "polygenetic proliferation," but the basic idea is conveyed by both turns of phrase.

[11] Apuleius, *Metam.* 11.5, adapted from Lucius Apuleius, *The Golden Ass* (ed. Harry C. Schnur; trans. William Adlington; New York: Collier; London: Collier-Macmillan, 1962), 261–62.

Remarkable

Burton L. Mack

This book documents a remarkable five years of intellectual endeavor. We gathered at the invitation of Ron Cameron and Merrill P. Miller to consider an ambitious undertaking. The traditional account of Christian origins did not make sense, they said, and the time had come to explain Christian beginnings some other way. Why not try a two-pronged approach, they suggested. One prong, the "Ancient Myths" part of the proposal, would be to acknowledge the largely mythic content of the early texts, mark their differences from one another, assign them to their own times and places, and note their fit in relation to the social situations in which they appeared. The other prong, the "Modern Theories" part of the proposal, would be to recognize the need for theoretical discussion, if in fact we wanted a better explanation of Christian beginnings than the traditional account offered.

Not surprisingly, a large number of scholars responded to the Consultations on this proposal. Many agreed that the grand narrative account was in trouble and that the time had come to do some remapping. Jonathan Z. Smith cautioned us about settling for a "paraphrase" of the Lukan model, a move customary with New Testament scholars that offers a new perspective on this or that feature of the traditonal scenario but without changing the gospel pattern. He warned us that a paraphrase would not, could not, provide a different explanation and that only a no-nonsense explanation could render a better account.[1] Hearing this cautionary consideration did not dampen our spirits, for a number of us thought that we could already catch sight of the new map we wanted to draw. After all, we now had Q, *Thomas,* and the "Jesus movements" to put in place of the traditional view of the "first church in Jerusalem." The historical Jesus hoopla was running out of banners, and, in any case, not one of the scholarly reconstructions of "the" historical Jesus could explain Christian origins any better

---

[1] Jonathan Z. Smith, "Social Formations of Early Christianities: A Response to Ron Cameron and Burton Mack," *MTSR* 8 (1996): 271–78.

than the traditional mystique of the gospel's son of god. Besides, hadn't the guild of New Testament scholars come to accept the plurification of early Christian texts, groups, "theologies," and "Christologies"? And were we not all fully committed to situating our early Christian groups and texts in their particular social and cultural contexts as defined by the Greco-Roman world?

So some of us said yes to the redescription project and formed a Seminar. My notion of finding the intersections for social formations and mythmaking was enough to lay out some "sites" for testing, and Smith's program of comparison and redescription was enough to point us toward rendering alternative explanations. The sites for Q, *Thomas,* the "pillars," and *christos* have been visited. And what an amazing generation of papers, exegeses, comparisons, theses, memos, demurrers, discussions, debates, and turn-abouts we've had. We haven't been able to settle on the contours of a new map with all its ways and byways, but we have succeeded in charting the terrain differently than it looked before. The terrain now coming into view is even more interesting, colorful, bouncy, experimental, mutable, vigorous, and feisty than anything we may have imagined. So because of our careful handling of texts under the rubric of facts-turned-into-data for comparisons and reconstructions, and by using the tools and skills customary for scholars trained in the discipline of New Testament studies, we have been able to problematize sites and notions fundamental for the canonical account, read some texts without any reference to "religious experiences," and see a few of the earliest peoples and places in the light of human activity typical for the Greco-Roman age. Clearly, we have made some progress on the redescription front. And a wonderful discourse is in the making, for we have learned to listen to each other with great care as attempts are made to talk about Christian beginnings without recourse to the usual mystifications.

But what about the map? What about explanation? What about finding some reasons for the particular attractions that these early groups and their teachings may have had? Here we have had a much more difficult time. A certain restiveness developed among us, indicating that many of us were eager to shift from the descriptive into the explanatory mode. That, of course, was a good sign. It meant that the aims of the project had been grasped. Simply describing our sites as intersections of social formation and mythmaking, whether in more detail or with greater attention to features now recognized as significant because of comparative work with analogous social phenomena from the Greco-Roman world, would not necessarily offer explanations for the emergence of these groups. We soon had before us some rather impressive essays on the comparison of this or that early Christian group with various schools, associations, and scribal classes, but we could not say that either the similarities or the differences noted in the comparisons could account for the Christian groups. It was becoming clear that we were having a problem with the "description" and "redescription" of our sites.

The first suggestions for proceeding were hardly radical departures from moves we already knew how to make. Some wanted to stay longer at a site to flesh out more fully the "profile" of a particular group, thinking that we may not have turned all of the "facts" at our disposal into "data" and that, had we more data, we might find among them the clues we needed to better account for the group. While there was nothing inherently wrong with such a proposal, it soon became clear that more detailed description was not at all what Smith's program had in mind under the rubrics of "description," "comparison," and "redescription." We had not yet found a way to sort through first-level features of a historical datum to ask which ones might be important at a second-level generalization for purposes of comparison and explanation.

Others wanted to move immediately to other sites where we could be sure to have more data, especially more data for constructing social settings. But along the way it began to dawn on us that what we needed most of all was some discussion of theory. The problems we were having were not simply due to a lack of data or a bad choice of sites. After all, we had a pretty good idea of what data there was for most of the sites we might consider. Most of the material indices were textual, and we had pored over them time and again. What we needed was some clarity among ourselves about explaining them. We needed to know how to think Christian origins differently, why looking for social formations was so important, what we might learn from being able to reconstruct or imagine the profile of a particular group, and what kinds of observations about such a group might count as clues to their own social interests and collective identity.

Questions thus began to be raised about the project's assumptions with regard to theories of history, social formation, and mythmaking as well as about whether the connection between social formation and mythmaking had been sufficiently explored. In retrospect, we discovered that these questions were already being raised in our third Consultation (on Q and the *Gospel of Thomas*). After that a rump group got together in the summer of 1999, piggy-backing on a conference at the University of Vermont, to ask whether a focused discussion of theory could be integrated with our more exegetical and descriptive project. The answer was most unclear. Later that year, however, the North American Association for the Study of Religion (NAASR) invited the Seminar to a special session on theory and Christian origins. I had been asked to think about spelling out in more detail my concepts of social formation and mythmaking, and Russell T. McCutcheon had just published an article on the topic.[2] These papers received a fine critical response from colleagues in the Seminar and in NAASR, and the responses made it clear that more theoretical work had to be done. Then, subsequent to the 1999 session on the *christos* question, Willi Braun initiated a focused discussion on the problems we were having with both of our aims: (1) the redescription of sites and (2) the explanation for attractions. The responses to Braun's debriefing paper[3] indicate that a discourse on theory has finally surfaced within the Seminar, a discussion that bodes extremely well for the future of our work together.

It is clear that the notions of "social formation" and "mythmaking" have been helpful in some ways, especially as a shorthand for defining a moment of "intersection" for historical analysis. If we take them as attempts to be a bit more specific about the (social) setting for a (mythic) text, there is nothing about either term that should startle the New Testament scholar. Locating a text in its specific social setting is standard practice. However, since "mythmaking" is a gerund, and "social formation" has been intended and used as such, the intersection of the two has suggested a moment of social and discursive activity that is generative. That alone makes it possible to begin to catch sight of the human investments responsible for the construction of these early Christian social groupings. And that shift in initiative from the traditional assumptions of "divine," extrahuman generation to normal human social interests and activities is the difference that makes a difference in our approach to New Testament texts. It is the human construction of social formations that the Seminar wants to establish and explain.

The problems arise when, after having determined a set of social and mythic indices for the description of a historical moment, some explanations are in order. Here is where, both at the first level of historiography and at the second level of theoretical control, our categories need to be taken up into larger systems of theory. We have no agreement about the relationship between social formation and mythmaking. We have not discussed the issues of initiative, sequence, or function as each category may relate to the other. What mythic datum may count for which change of social practice, or which social practice may call for which mythic rationale, are questions we have hardly been able to formulate, much less discuss.

---

[2] Russell T. McCutcheon, "Redescribing 'Religion' as Social Formation: Toward a Social Theory of Religion," in *What Is Religion? Origins, Definitions, and Explanations* (ed. Thomas A. Idinopulos and Brian C. Wilson; SHR 81; Leiden: Brill, 1998), 51–71; repr. in *Critics Not Caretakers: Redescribing the Public Study of Religion* (SUNY series, Issues in the Study of Religion; Albany: State University of New York Press, 2001), 21–39.

[3] Willi Braun, "Smoke Signals from the North: A Reply to Burton Mack's 'Backbay Jazz and Blues'" (in this volume).

And we have had no agreement on a theoretical frame of reference for understanding either social formation or mythmaking that is current in the disciplines of cultural and social anthropology.

I have assumed that the anthropology implicit in Smith's work would be enough for all of us, at least as a point of agreement and departure for more refined nuances. That is because it is not only radically "social" but also thoroughly rational (or intellectualist). Because that is so, I have had no trouble thinking that social formations and practices are human intellectualist (linguistic) products, just as mythmaking and discursive practices are; thus my attempts to conceptualize the notion of "social interests" as the mediating term. However, that has not satisfied everyone, nor has it answered the questions posed to me at the NAASR meeting about the social-intellectual mechanism (or practice) that functions to link social formations and myths in actual practice. This means that, "simply" by setting out to remap Christian origins, this Seminar has succeeded in introducing theoretical issues fundamental for the humanities into the discipline of New Testament studies. No matter how we end up negotiating this set of issues, surfacing them in this way has to be considered a very big academic win. We are talking about the impulse that makes humans tick, and we are not making an exception for mythmaking and "religion," as though they were human responses to the divine. We would like to draw some pictures of these early Christians at their most energetic moments of constructing associations, practices, and rationales that can be explained and understood as human productions that made sense for their times. I'd say bravo.

As we proceed, it might well be that abstract discussions of mythmaking and social formation will not be the best or only way to engage the theoretical issues we have encountered. A more direct approach might be to focus on the question of "attraction." We have used the term to mark and hold the place for the explanations we seek as alternatives to the customary and traditional notions of "religious" motivations implicit in the standard scenarios. If we are not able to suggest plausible and convincing reasons for the attractions of these groups that are grounded in humanistic theories of social formation and mythmaking, we should not be surprised to find the old "desire for religious experience," "epiphany of the sacred," or "contact with the divine" slipping into place. But as a matter of fact, a number of attractions have already been suggested that could set some kind of agenda for us. For instance, we have used the term "experimental." The term is both descriptive and potentially explanatory. At first it can be taken to describe the creative and generative aspects of these early Christian groups in contrast to the view that leaves them passive receptors of generative "traditions." But because it also automatically thrusts these groups into the larger context of the post-Alexandrian social and cultural arena, "reasons" are immediately suggested for these experiments as responses to the circumstances of that arena, reasons that put the early Christian experiments on a par with the many other "social experiments" that were generated within that world of changing cultures.

A more narrowly focused explanation lurks among our many references to "mixed constituencies" when coupled with "appeals to the epic of Israel" and "ethnic identity" issues. Some of us have begun to think that much early mythmaking was in the interest of laying claim to (fictional) collective ethnicity linked to the Judaisms of the time. We have not been able to grasp the "attraction" that such a claim may have had, but as a form of what I have been calling "social interest," ethnic identity is basic. Other myths indicate that various models of traditional and current social-political configurations were in mind. Images and practices reminiscent of landed estates, petty kingdoms, empires, and temple-states suggest various ways in which these early Christian social formations were thinking of themselves. These images need to be studied as possible clues to the rationales and ideologies that may have been involved in the "attractions" of these early movements and associations. But all of that starts with the myths we happen to have and then requires social constructions for which we have little other hard evidence. Moreover, the myths have the marks of an intellectual elite, so the other approach has been to look for social indices that suggest other kinds of interests that might be imagined for a less-elite people. The case has been made for the deracination of a scribal class in the Galilee, the attraction of a "school" and its teachings, the benefits of belonging to an "association," and the reasons for continuing a homeland "cult" in the diaspora.

Thus we have a lovely double disjunction on our hands. The one is the gap between facts and theories (or how to explain the facts); the other is between social formations and discursive practices (or which generates the other). Neither of these tensions is reason to conclude that our project is wrongheaded. The fact that both have surfaced together is evidence that we are on the right track. Together they have actually set the stage for thinking critically about Christian beginnings. And look what is coming into view! A set of human interests as rich and complex as one might expect for the times in which these early Christians lived. We are giving these early Christians their due, and we are enjoying watching some of their many moves, as those whose thoughts and practices made human sense for their times. However the Seminar finds it possible to rank and talk more frankly about them, one thing is already certain. This is a remarkable accomplishment for a group of New Testament scholars.

REDESCRIBING CHRISTIAN ORIGINS: HISTORIOGRAPHY OR EXEGESIS?

Luther H. Martin

[A critical thinker] compels the witnesses to answer questions which he has himself formulated.
— Immanuel Kant[1]

In a letter to Ron Cameron and Merrill P. Miller, sent shortly after the meeting of the Seminar in Boston (and dated 11 January 2000), Willi Braun characterized two different "voices" that seem to have emerged over the course of our Seminar meetings. In Braun's view, there are those Seminar participants who are "in the first place interested in category/theory development" and who, consequently, view the "specific early Christian sites" the Seminar has examined as "testing grounds, workshops in historical social *situ* for working out a social theory of social development and mythmaking. In this view, the choice sites are those that offer the best potential for the theoretical project." On the other hand, some Seminar participants "seem to be primarily interested in redescribing the sites themselves, using 'social formation' and 'mythmaking' as an analytic of sorts but more or less content to leave the terms relatively untheorized." In thinking about plans for the current publication of the Seminar proceedings, Braun suggested that these "different interests and orientations" might be noted and reflected upon in several "metareflections."

As should be clear from my earlier contribution to the Seminar,[2] I would consider myself to be among those who are less interested in redescribing the various sites of Christian origins per se than in viewing these sites as problematics for developing a theory (or theories) of religious formation that might have broader validity. Since I have been invited to contribute one

---

[1] Immanuel Kant, "Preface to the Second Edition [B xiii]," in *Critique of Pure Reason* (trans. Norman Kemp Smith; London: Macmillan, 1963), 20.
[2] Luther H. Martin, "History, Historiography, and Christian Origins: The Jerusalem Community" (in this volume).

of the metareflections on the Seminar's continuing work, I should like briefly to offer my views on why I think theorizing should take priority over "relatively untheorized" attempts at a redescription of Christian origins.

The object of critical redescription is, of course, previous description(s). There are two possible attitudes toward such previous descriptions: uncritical acceptance and critical evaluation. The latter may result either in an acceptance or a rejection of previous descriptions or perhaps in some sort of compromise. However, if one of these results—a rejection of previous descriptions, say—is an a priori assumption, then the critical question has been begged. While members of the Seminar are, by definition I should think, motivated by a critical attitude toward previous descriptions of Christian beginnings, this attitude should properly result in the formulation of a new theory (or theories) to solve those problems that, it has been determined, previous descriptions have not solved. Redescription then becomes the task of testing the robustness of the new theory over the old.[3]

The theme of the Seminar on Ancient Myths and Modern Theories of Christian Origins promises just such a new theoretical approach to the problems with previous descriptions. The premise of this Seminar, I take it, is that the story of Christian origins has been shaped, both for ecclesiastical circles and in scholarly investigation, by "ancient myths," that is, by the very accounts with which early Christians represented themselves and that were subsequently "authorized" by an emerging "orthodoxy" for transmission in a collection of texts known as the New Testament. The intersection of these early Christian mythmaking efforts with the respective self-interests of the various new (Christian) social formations might, it was hypothesized, form a critical basis for redescribing the earlier accounts of Christian origins. The problem, it seems to me, is that while members of the Seminar have critically and accurately identified the problems with previous descriptions of Christian origins, they have not fully addressed the problem of formulating a new theory (or theories) to address these problems. While concerns about the theoretical clarification of such categories as mythmaking, social formation, or social interests have been raised throughout the Seminar discussions and pursued to some extent by Seminar participants, no consensus concerning the definition and interaction of these categories has yet been determined.[4] For example, does a given early

---

[3] I have adapted this view of the "project of redescription" from Karl R. Popper's classic 1948 lecture, "Towards a Rational Theory of Tradition," *The Rationalist Annual for the Year 1949* (ed. Frederick Watts; London: Watts, 1949), 36–55; repr. in idem, *Conjectures and Refutations: The Growth of Scientific Knowledge* (New York: Basic Books, 1962), 120–35.

[4] These questions were addressed forthrightly only during the third year of the Seminar, held in Nashville in 2000, in the theses presented by William E. Arnal and Willi Braun on "Social Formation and Mythmaking: Theses on Key Terms" (in this volume).

Christian text in some way represent an actual (i.e., historically manifest) social interest, or does it, as a mythic (or ideological or propagandistic, i.e., self-interested) production of a particular group, project an (ahistorical, utopian) ideal held by that community (or by its literate leadership)?[5] Moving from an "ought" to an "is" begs, in other words, any number of historically possible antecedents. And does the "intersection" of social formation with mythmaking suggest that myths in some manner *reflect* a certain social situation, or are they in fact *constitutive* of that social situation? In other words, observations of correlations (or intersections) apart from the establishment of causality (i.e., of historical precedence and antecedence) tell us little that we do not already know.

The consequence of not clearly formulating a theoretically grounded set of questions to guide the project of redescription is, I would suggest, that the work of the Seminar has proceeded largely by rejecting previous descriptions of early Christianity as themselves mythic and by assuming that it might be possible to arrive at a historically sound redescription simply by acknowledging the mythic character of the early Christian textual remains that previous descriptions mistook as, in some sense, preserving historical data. However, the question remains of what constitutes sound historiography and what constitutes historical "soundness," for the historical redescription proposed by the Seminar remains as undertheorized as does that of the "analytical" categories employed. Moreover, by not offering a clearly formulated theory for the project of redescription, the work of the Seminar has tended to relapse into the familiar methodology appropriate to previous description (i.e., exegesis), even while overtly rejecting the allegedly "theoretical" (i.e., theological) orientation in terms of which that method has developed. Some of our discussions have reminded me of the plight of those characters in the recent spate of cyberfilms who become lost in the virtual reality of a computer-generated world—an ordinary place where extraordinary events occur—and have trouble differentiating this "virtual reality" from "reality," despite their avowed recognition of that difference.[6] Such is the power of "myth" (like the performance of ritual, a narration of an idealized and thus wondrous world of the "ought" vis-à-vis the ordinary world of the "is")[7] when that myth is

---

[5] Harry Y. Gamble, e.g., has noted that the question of literacy among the early Christians "has rarely been raised and has never been explored by historians of early Christianity" (*Books and Readers in the Early Church: A History of Early Christian Texts* [New Haven: Yale University Press, 1995], 2).

[6] E.g., Thomas Anderson (whose second or computer name is "Neo"), in the 1999 Warner Brothers movie *The Matrix*.

[7] See Jonathan Z. Smith, *To Take Place: Toward Theory in Ritual* (CSHJ; Chicago: University of Chicago Press, 1987), 109.

"effective"—and the Christian myth has demonstrated its effectiveness for some two thousand years.

The difference between exegesis and historiography, as I see it, is that in exegesis one begins with the givenness of a text (or set of texts)—that is, with the givenness of a previous description—and then seeks redescription primarily on the basis of that same text (or set of texts). However critically one might read the text(s), the text or texts selected have nevertheless established the framework for inquiry and thus for any redescriptive project.

The Seminar seems to assume that a quest for "social facts" in mythic texts is what elevates exegesis to historiography. In the view of Miller with respect to the work of the Seminar, texts are "social artifact[s]" of a "myth-making" process at a "particular juncture of ... social history."[8] Such an understanding of mythic texts as social facts assumes, however, that constituents of the community associated with a particular text collectively agree with and support the intentions and desires expressed in that text. It is this assumption of commonality as a collectively articulated and represented social coherence that has been taken by anthropologists (and others) to be an interpretable social fact—an assumption about early Christianity that is at least problematized by the contradictory evidence of its surviving material culture.[9] This assumption about commonality seems to be born from principles of literary criticism (to which the tradition of biblical exegesis gave birth) and from the singular or stipulated authorship it assumes, without paying attention to whether the historical conditions exist that would make such criticism of myth a valid endeavor.[10] Of course, Christian beginnings had no structures of power by which such commonality might have been authorized; in fact, it is the emergence of such authorization by texts that thematizes much of the history of Christian beginnings. Furthermore, it is precisely the counterfactual claims of myth and not some demythologized (social) meaning that define myth as mythic.[11] Since we may assume that a literate people have other means of expression available to them than the mythic—and this is clearly the case

---

[8] Merrill P. Miller, "'Beginning from Jerusalem...': Re-examining Canon and Consensus," *Journal of Higher Criticism* 2/1 (1995): 24, 28.

[9] See Graydon F. Snyder, *Ante Pacem: Archaeological Evidence of Church Life before Constantine* (Macon, Ga.: Mercer University Press, 1985).

[10] See Caroline Humphrey and James Laidlaw, *The Archetypal Actions of Ritual: A Theory of Ritual Illustrated by the Jain Rite of Worship* (Oxford Studies in Social and Cultural Anthropology; Oxford: Clarendon, 1994), 263.

[11] In this regard, I must confess my bewilderment at efforts by some members of the Seminar to demythologize (in contrast to resituate) the wonderously myth-laden category *christos* as it had been applied to Jesus.

in the Hellenistic world—the question remains about the significance of their selecting precisely this genre of representation.

In contrast to exegesis that assumes and works out of the givenness of a particular mythic text or set of texts, historiography situates the myth itself as an object of study. Maurice Godelier even proposes considering myths as a type of material cause—an alternative way of construing the understanding of "mythic text" as "social artifact."[12] Rather than seeking to demythologize mythic texts in order to discover some sort of meaning encoded in them, in other words, a critical historical approach to Christian origins might ask, first, about the significance of early Christian groups representing themselves with textual materials at all.[13]

Although a great deal of scholarship exists on the differences between groups that represent themselves in a written rather than an oral tradition,[14] a literate culture seems to be taken for granted for the Hellenistic period, a reasonable assumption given that even nonliterary groups tend to function within a literary universe of discourse once writing has been introduced.[15] Rather than orality as the alternative to textual traditions, however, the anthropologist Harvey Whitehouse has proposed "an imagistic mode of religiosity." In this theoretical model, the "imagistic mode of religiosity" is associated with small-scale, localized, face-to-face groups mobilized by emotionally intense but infrequently performed rituals and maintained by trenchant memories of these singular episodes; they are characterized by a figurehead leadership, periodic episodes of transmission, ideas only loosely linked by connotation, and variable beliefs and practices. Whitehouse contrasts this "imagistic mode of religiosity" with a "doctrinal mode" that is associated with large-scale, centralized, "imagined" communities (having a widespread but, consequently, largely anonymous membership). Such universalistic communities are mobilized by a dynamic but enduring leadership that deemphasizes the importance of ritual fervor in favor of a widely transmitted doctrinal uniformity. This uniformity of doctrine invokes, and is maintained in, "encyclopedic" memory by means

---

[12] Maurice Godelier, *The Mental and the Material: Thought Economy and Society* (trans. Martin Thom; London: Verso, 1986), 4, 5, 29.

[13] Luther H. Martin, "History, Historiography and Christian Origins," *SR* 29 (2000): 80–81. On textual communities, see Brian Stock, *The Implications of Literacy: Written Language and Models of Interpretation in the Eleventh and Twelfth Centuries* (Princeton: Princeton University Press, 1983), 12–87.

[14] E.g., Walter J. Ong, *Orality and Literacy: The Technologizing of the Word* (London: Methuen, 1982); see also Jack Goody, ed., *Literacy in Traditional Societies* (Cambridge: Cambridge University Press, 1968); idem, *The Power of the Written Tradition* (Smithsonian Series in Ethnographic Inquiry; Washington, D.C.: Smithsonian Institution Press, 2000).

[15] Stock, *Implications of Literacy*, 3.

of frequent repetition, orally or in writing[16]—just those traits typically associated with the transmissive advantages of such proselytizing communities as those associated with the Pauline and Lukan traditions.

Nondoctrinal, imagistic groups seem to have flourished during the Hellenistic period alongside the textual communities. For example, the widespread Mithraic cells may have been united solely by the harshness of their initiatory practices and the commonality of their imagery but, apart from local exegesis, may have operated without any "standardized" mythic narrative.[17] Other "imagistic" groups, while influenced by the Hellenistic universe of literary discourse, may nevertheless have largely retained their earlier mode of representation by adopting texts into their practices as iconic objects rather than media for the transmission of doctrine, such as the "books written with unknown characters" that were displayed during Isiac initiation rites (Apuleius, *Metam.* 11.22) or the Greco-Roman magical texts with their nonsensical but visually patterned incantations. In contrast to such doctrinal (kerygmatic) traditions as the Pauline and the Lukan, might the imagistic character of third- and fourth-century Christian material culture conform more to the imagistic mode of religiosity described by Whitehouse? Might the "charismatic" practices of the Christian community in Corinth that were opposed by Paul? Or the vividly imagistic but seemingly nondoctrinal character of "gnostic" myth (Irenaeus, *Haer.* 1.18.1)? Or even the "aphorisms" and "picturesque images" ascribed to Jesus that make up the Sayings Gospel Q?[18] Might the successes of "orthodox" Christianity rest more on its mode of representation and transmission than on the content of its message(s)? Might a redevelopment of the early Christianities be traced in terms of the incorporation and consolidation (or the rejection) of those who represented and transmitted their social interests in terms of an imagistic mode of religiosity by those who represented and transmitted their social interests doctrinally? Such groups as the Mithraic, the Isiaic, the

---

[16] Harvey Whitehouse, *Inside the Cult: Religious Innovation and Transmission in Papua New Guinea* (Oxford Studies in Social and Cultural Anthropology; Oxford: Clarendon, 1995); idem, *Arguments and Icons: Divergent Modes of Religiosity* (Oxford: Oxford University Press, 2000). Apart from Whitehouse's cognitive explanation for these two modes of religiosity on the basis of two types of human memory, his model is comparable to Jonathan Z. Smith's typology of "locative/utopian" communities (*Map Is Not Territory: Studies in the History of Religions* [SJLA 23; Leiden: Brill, 1978; repr., Chicago: University of Chicago Press, 1993], 100–103, 130–42, 147–51, 160–71, 185–89, 291–94, 308–9; idem, *Imagining Religion: From Babylon to Jonestown* [CSHJ; Chicago: University of Chicago Press, 1982], 112–17, 162).

[17] Luther H. Martin, "Reflections on the Mithraic Tauroctony as Cult Scene," in *Studies in Mithraism* (ed. John R. Hinnells; Storia delle religioni 9; Rome: "L'Erma" di Bretschneider, 1994), 217–24.

[18] Burton L. Mack, *The Lost Gospel: The Book of Q and Christian Origins* (San Francisco: HarperSanFrancisco, 1993), 105.

magical, the charismatic, and the "gnostic" provide comparative alternatives to the doctrinal representation, widespread textual transmission, and subsequent political selection by a particular Christian trajectory. From this perspective, the significance of the emergence of "Christian" textual communities must take precedence over any evaluation of the contents of their texts—should those contents prove, in light of conclusions about the previous questions, of any historiographical interest at all.[19]

My point is that the process of redescription must be a project in which our conclusions about the particulars of Christian origins derive from problems that have been critically identified in previous descriptions and for which theoretical alternatives have been clearly formulated in ways that can be "tested" against comparative data.[20] Otherwise, our redescriptions are likely to remain essentially a variation of previous descriptions, rather than interesting redescription.

Let me conclude by affirming that the Seminar on Ancient Myths and Modern Theories of Christian Origins has, in my judgment, succeeded in eliciting some of the most exciting scholarship in the area of biblical studies in recent years. This excitement is somewhat diminished, however, by a lack of theoretical coherence in the collective work of the Seminar. Rather, the theoretical sophistication in this scholarship remains the wanton characteristic of individual scholars. A collective realization by members of the Seminar of a theoretically grounded and, thus, generalizable redescription of Christian origins would not only make a significant contribution to the guild of biblical scholarship but also provide an exemplary case for the study of religions generally.

---

[19] As I have previously suggested, with reference to the work of Stock: "What such groups as the early Christianities shared in common, 'besides proximity in time,' had little or nothing to do with their 'social origins ... nor their doctrinal orientations,' but rather with the emergence of more literate societies themselves. Their texts did not represent, in other words, randomly fabricated representations of reality, but are better viewed as themselves a social reality" (Martin, "History, Historiography and Christian Origins," 80–81, citing Stock, *Implications of Literacy*, 99).

[20] Such a scientific approach to human history, analogous to other historical sciences (e.g., epidemiology, evolutionary biology, paleontology), has been proposed by Jared Diamond, *Guns, Germs, and Steel: The Fates of Human Societies* (New York: Norton, 1997), 420–25.

DAYYEINU

Jonathan Z. Smith

One must be obedient to the strictures imposed by Thomas S. Kuhn, that his well-known model of progress in the sciences does not apply to the social sciences, let alone the broader reaches of the human sciences. Nevertheless, one can note an analogy between Kuhn's model and the processes of discovery memorialized in this volume. A reigning paradigm—given the shorthand designation, the Lukan-Eusebian model—has been the framework for the "normal science" of the study of early Christianities for centuries, proving extraordinarily resilient in its capacity to absorb both new and revised data, new and revised methodological and theoretical perspectives. It is, therefore, significant that the work of the Consultation and its successor Seminar began with a catalogue of aporiae which the "standard" paradigm was unable to cover as well as a set of "unexamined assumptions" largely deployed to shore up the old model. At a more general level, the implicit theory of religion assumed in the standard paradigm was likewise inadequate when compared with developments in cognate fields such as history of religions and cultural anthropology.[1]

At this more general level, the project of the Consultation and Seminar places the study of earliest Christianities within the dialectic of the "near" and the "far" that is central to the practice of the human sciences. If one aspect of the work of the scholar is to reduce surprise in that which first appears "strange" by enterprises of familiarization (ranging from analogy and translation to explanation), the opposite and equally important impulse must be to introduce surprise into that which one is accustomed by means of enterprises of defamiliarization (most commonly through exercises in comparison). It is this latter imperative that prohibits the study of religion from being a mechanism for transmission, be it of identity or tradition. It is this same imperative that forbids "allowing the gospel paradigm to

---

[1] See Burton L. Mack, "On Redescribing Christian Origins," *MTSR* 8 (1996): 247–53; repr., with revisions, in *The Christian Myth: Origins, Logic, and Legacy* (New York: Continuum, 2001), 59–67.

define Christian origins."² For some members of the Seminar, one form of this defamiliarizing endeavor, in one sense of its original, literary-critical usage as a radical alteration of the habitual terms of description, is part of an exercise in "redescription."

Let us be clear. Even when limited to this sense, redescription has to be consequential; it can be neither an essay in substitution nor of synonymy.³ For a simple example of the latter, think of the recent convention of replacing B.C. and A.D. with B.C.E. and C.E., as if the problem was with the Greek and Latin titularies and not with the Arabic numerals which continue to affirm as self-evident the incarnational myth as an adequate means for organizing world history. (No wonder the majority of my students believe the abbreviations stand for "before the Christian era" and the "Christian era.") All remains familiar—or, to use the contemporary English equivalent of the Russian Formalist term, all is naturalized.

To the various particular redescriptions of specific texts and "sites," in this first sense, that have been proposed in the ongoing work of the Consultation and Seminar and ably summarized in the introductions in this volume, I am tempted to respond with a slightly revised version of the ninth-century Jewish liturgical formula: "If they had accomplished this and had not gone on to accomplish that, *dayyeinu,* it would have been sufficient." The topography of earliest Christianities has been decisively altered, dis-placed, re-placed. But ... there is more to be done.

There is a second sense of defamiliarization as redescription, implied already in Victor Shklovsky's initial formulation of the procedure as a description which "avoids the accepted names of [an object's] parts and instead names corresponding parts of other objects."⁴ This is redescription

---

² Mack, "Redescribing Christian Origins," 250; repr. in *Christian Myth,* 63.

³ This is another instance of my persistent concern for "insufficient difference" between a scholarly construction and its stipulated data, be it at the level of paraphrase or model. See, e.g., Jonathan Z. Smith, "Bible and Religion," *BCSSR* 29/4 (2000): 91, emphasis original: "Indeed, the cognitive power of any translation, model, map, or redescription ... is ... a result of its difference from the phenomena in question and not its congruence.... For this reason, a paraphrase, perhaps the commonest sort of weak translation in the human sciences, nowhere more so than in biblical studies, will usually be *insufficiently different* for purposes of thought. To summarize: a theory, a model, a conceptual category, *cannot be simply the data writ large."*

⁴ Victor Shklovsky, "Art as Technique," in *Russian Formalist Criticism: Four Essays* (ed. and trans. Lee T. Lemon and Marion J. Reis; Regents Critics Series; Lincoln: University of Nebraska Press, 1965), 13; cf. the French trans. in *Théorie de la littérature: Textes des formalistes russes réunis, présentés et traduits* (ed. Tzvetan Todorov; Paris: Éditions du Seuil, 1965), 84. The full quotation (in English) reads: "[Tolstoy] describes an object as if he were seeing it for the first time, an event as if it were happening for the first time. In describing something he avoids the accepted names of its parts and instead names corresponding parts of other objects." I take the first sentence to refer to what I have here termed the "first sense" of redescription,

as a result of comparison. By and large, the group has been more wary of this process, a caution which has led, in turn, to insufficient attention to the critical goal of rectifying generalizing categories that both result from and further enable strong comparative investigations.[5]

It is precisely at this level of middle-range, generic conceptualization and generalization, however, that consensual progress is most likely. Take, for example, the question of "ethnic identity," which has been deployed, at several junctures, as a proximate explanans for a diversity of phenomena. One cannot escape the sense that this term is being understood in too self-evident a fashion and therefore requires little discussion. I miss debate over whether it is a given, relatively stable category or is better understood as a constructed and mobile one;[6] nor am I confident that the sort of distinction, along with its theoretical implications, between "ethnic boundary" and "cultural stuff," made famous more than twenty-five years ago by Fredrik Barth, has been sufficiently problematized in our discussions.[7] Nor,

---

a "radical alteration of the habitual terms of description." I take the second sentence to refer to the "second sense" of redescription, that which is a "result of comparison." For an important example of the latter, which comes close to an exact reproduction of Shklovsky's characterization, consider the famous plate of structural correspondences between a bird and a human skeleton in Pierre Belon, *L'Histoire de la nature des oyseaux* (Paris: Cavellat, 1555; repr., ed. Philippe Glardon; Travaux d'Humanisme et Renaissance 306; Geneva: Librairie Droz, 1997), 40–41, a founding document in comparative anatomy. As Olivier Rieppel describes the illustration: "To depict this correspondence, Belon ... had to abstract from both form (shape) and function of the compared structures. He pictured bird and human as suspended from the skull, the limbs dangling down—a highly unnatural position and at the same time an artistic trick, forcing the reader to look at a bird skeleton in an unusual way. Once Belon had taught his readers this new 'way of seeing,' he conceptually cut the bird into pieces. He labelled individual bones with letters, and used the same letter to indicate structural equivalence of bones in the skeleton of the bird and human. He did not look at the skeleton as an integrated whole, but as a composition of parts, and he compared these parts neither in terms of shape, nor in terms of function, but in terms of another criterion of similarity: topology" ("Homology, Topology, and Typology: The History of Modern Debates," in *Homology: The Hierarchical Basis of Comparative Biology* [ed. Brian K. Hall; San Diego: Academic Press, 1994], 64).

[5] I have in mind here our discussions of categories such as "schools" or "associations" in which, at times, the overarching question appeared to be that of the degree of fit/no fit between the model and the early Christian data, rather than the possibility of rectifying the model in the light of the data. While not an element in these discussions, I should note that so limiting the question has, in the past, served as a stratagem for maintaining Christian uniqueness.

[6] See, e.g., George M. Scott Jr., "A Resynthesis of the Primordial and Circumstantial Approaches to Ethnic Group Solidarity: Towards an Explanatory Model," *Ethnic and Racial Studies* 13 (1990): 147–71.

[7] Fredrik Barth, ed., *Ethnic Groups and Boundaries: The Social Organization of Culture Difference* (Boston: Little, Brown, 1969), 9–38, esp. 13–15. See, further, the commemorative volume honoring this work: Hans Vermeulen and Cora Govers, eds., *The Anthropology of Ethnicity: Beyond 'Ethnic Groups and Boundaries'* (Amsterdam: Het Spinhuis, 1994).

in our appeals to the relations of "epic traditions" to identity formation and practical legitimation, have we asked the sort of anthropological questions that have energized contemporary discussions of these topics: "Why is such importance attached to finding the rules of the present embodied in the past?" "Why [should] legitimation reside in duration"? Why should "time [be] a measure of value"?[8] Rather, we have at times seemed impatient to move directly from a mode of redescription that "rectifies the names" to an overarching cultural theory at the expense of clarifying this middle range. Nevertheless, within the context of the study of earliest Christianities, a sense of urgency with respect to theory, and a concomitant willingness to see the Christian data not as ends in themselves but rather as exempla of broader theoretical and methodological issues in the imagination of culture and religion, are to be affirmed and applauded.

Within the Seminar, the dominant metaquestion which has emerged as inviting such inquiry is that of specifying the nexus between mythmaking and social formation. The challenge, here, will be to avoid formulations which see the one as the dependent variable of the other, or which see the one as congruent to the other. Such formulations introduce insufficient difference. The task, as Marshall Sahlins has consistently reiterated, is to provide an adequate account of myth both as "reproduction" and as "transformation,"[9] to provide both an adequate "sociological theory of symbolization" and an adequate "symbolic theory of society."[10] If these

---

[8] Michael Herzfeld, *Anthropology: Theoretical Practice in Culture and Society* (Oxford: Blackwell, 2001), 85, citing, for the first question, Valerio Valeri, "Constitutive History: Genealogy and Narrative in the Legitimation of Hawaiian Kingship," in *Culture through Time: Anthropological Approaches* (ed. Emiko Ohnuki-Tierney; Stanford, Calif.: Stanford University Press, 1990), 162, and for the last question, Michael Roberts, *Exploring Confrontation. Sri Lanka: Politics, Culture and History* (Studies in Anthropology and History 14; Chur, Switzerland: Harwood Academic Publishers, 1994), 202.

[9] This is the overarching theme of Marshall Sahlins, *Historical Metaphors and Mythical Realities: Structure in the Early History of the Sandwich Islands Kingdom* (Association for Social Anthropology in Oceania 1; Ann Arbor: University of Michigan Press, 1981). See, more recently, idem, "The Return of the Event, Again; With Reflections on the Beginnings of the Great Fijian War of 1843 to 1855 between the Kingdoms of Bau and Rewa," in *Clio in Oceania: Toward a Historical Anthropology* (ed. Aletta Biersack; Washington, D.C.: Smithsonian Institution Press, 1991), 37–99; repr. in idem, *Culture in Practice: Selected Essays* (New York: Zone Books, 2000), 293–351. Given the Seminar's discussions of the categories of "interest" and "attraction," a remark toward the end of Sahlins's *Historical Metaphors and Mythical Realities* is worth repeating: "'Interest' and 'sense' (or 'meaning') are two sides of the same thing, the sign, as related respectively to persons and to other signs. *Yet my interest in something is not the same as its sense*" (69, emphasis original).

[10] Marshall Sahlins, *Culture and Practical Reason* (Chicago: University of Chicago Press, 1976), 116. The context of this particular formulation is a critique of Émile Durkheim for having formulated the former while ignoring the latter.

challenges be addressed by the Seminar in a way that clarifies fundamental assumptions, that acknowledges and respects a given theory's intellectual costs and entailments, but results in reaching no final consensus—*dayyeinu*.

Mythmaking, Social Formation, and Varieties of Social Theory

Stanley K. Stowers

I wish first to make some broad observations about the work of the Seminar and point to some areas in which development and clarification might be helpful. Then I want to challenge the Seminar to think about some of the choices available in social theory and suggest how one choice might be used to address some of the historical and explanatory problems that the Seminar faces.

Many members of the guild will notice that the historical reconstruction being attempted by the Seminar depends upon a great deal of earlier work on Q and the *Gospel of Thomas*. The reconstruction furthermore depends upon extensive work by scholars on historically contextualizing the canonical Gospels and a commitment to doing that in a consistently critical way. The Seminar is quite well aware that its project will be controversial, but it is to be hoped that it will not be held as controversial for the wrong reasons. The members of the Seminar are doing what good historians anywhere do. In a professional environment in which scholars often invoke both the supposed bare facts and "the supernatural" or other conversation stoppers at the same time, the Seminar seeks to follow procedures deemed central to the natural, social, and human sciences that make its premises and inferences open, testable, and transparent to all. The earlier work mentioned above consists of a series of connected hypotheses that appear to have some consistency and coherency. These reconstructions open up a space for an account of "Christian origins" that does not depend upon taking the Christian church's own accounts of origins as authoritative for the work of historians. Instead, the Seminar seeks to advance social and historical hypotheses and theories that are constructed in order to be examined and modified when they prove unhelpful. One therefore does not have to agree with all of the reconstructions from earlier work or the hypotheses being developed by the Seminar in order to be sympathetic to the project. Unlike canonical interpretations, the Seminar must always be serious about making its theorizations, hypotheses, and reconstructions revisable.

In my estimation, the Seminar is at a point where it needs to sharpen its social theory with more detail and some choices about what kind of social theory it wants. Also, in my view, it is not the time to throw out some of the more promising, yet also problematic, hypotheses but to work on variations and refinements. One kind of refinement might develop from the intuition that the group has not fully escaped the grip of the "canonical" and Lukan picture of origins. Talking about the diversity of groups in the earliest period as opposed to the traditional account of monolinear development from an originary moment, I suggest, still implies too much teleology to allow for the most useful theorizing about social formation. It also might be useful to clarify just what is originating in the Seminar's talk of Christian origins. Is it Luke and Lukan Christianity? Is it "the Christian church"? Is it "Christianity"? Is it the diversity of "Christian groups" that clearly appear during the first half of the second century? By typical historical standards, the best answer might be the array of Christian groups in the second century that practice forms of mutual recognition and that have fairly clear historical connection with later Christian formations that will organize themselves using the mythmaking and social discourse found enshrined in the canonical Gospels, the supposed letters of Paul, and other writings. If the Seminar aims to construct a narrative, it cannot be much of a narrative of extinct Jesus groups or groups about which we know almost nothing. This does not mean that extinct and almost-invisible groups will not play a significant role in the larger narrative that tells a story of how something that we know as the Christian church came about. But since the Seminar seeks to explain origins, and the story and explanation will vary according to exactly how one defines what is originating, it is important to be clear about the latter.

The problem with the slightly modified versions of traditional Christian myths of origins espoused by New Testament scholars is not just that they are monolinear, but that they are linear. In support of ecumenism and pluralism, the guild has already committed itself to the "diversity of early Christianity." Concluding that there were several lines rather than one line in the earliest period of formation (going back to Jesus!) will not allow for an account that fully escapes the Christian myth. An advance will require social theorization that explains the continuity, lack thereof, and mutual recognition between, and among, individuals and groups. I find particularly troubling two conceptions that keep dogging the work of the Seminar: collective creativity and continuity of intentions. It is difficult to know what to make of language that suggests these conceptions, because participants have not made clear to what kinds of social theory they are committed. The exception may be William E. Arnal, who seems to hold, among other things, that social determination is always extradiscursive.

Most of the language about social processes used by the Seminar could lend itself either to nominalist and individualist social theories, including methodological individualism, or to one of the social structuralisms that are the successors to the nineteenth-century theories (and later functionalisms) that treated society as if it were an organism.[1] Individualist accounts explain social formations by reference to configurations of individuals and the determinations of their mental states and actions. Social structuralisms explain social formations by appealing to virtual abstract and substantial entities that are distinct from, yet formative of, individuals, their configurations, mental states, and actions. Weber and Schütz are classical individualists. Lévi-Strauss, Althusser, and Foucault in *The Order of Things* are social structuralists. Depending on how one understands his "social facts" and other proposals, Durkheim can be, and has been, interpreted either as an individualist or a structuralist. Social structuralisms have fallen on hard times because the abstract and substantial entities to which such theories appeal seem to have no more epistemological leverage than, say, appeal to angels and demons to explain social coexistence. Similarly, very few contemporary social theorists believe in an overall entity called society that has any explanatory value. My sympathies lie with theorists such as the later Foucault, Bourdieu, Dreyfus, Laclau and Mouffe, and Schatzki, who have developed theories of practice that hold together the basic intuitions of both individualism and structuralism but have more or less successfully dispensed with the abstract and substantial entities of the latter. The basic insight here is that individuals, their mental states, and their actions exist only within a context, site, or background of practices, or better, in my view, practices and arrangements of substances (artifacts, organisms, things) that prefigure human agency and constitute social formations. The approach agrees with social structuralism in holding to a determinative context that is more than configurations of individuals, their actions, and mental states, but finds this context only in practices and arrangements. For these theorists, practices (doings and sayings) are organized integral sets of actions that are open-ended and unfolding. Practices are the definitive units of social life passed down from generation to generation.

Individualists explain social formations as resulting from mental states of individuals sharing the same intentional objects including a certain "we-ness." Thus a group might be said to have resulted from a number of

---

[1] In what follows, I am indebted to many of the writings of Pierre Bourdieu and, above all, to Theodore R. Schatzki, who generously allowed me to read, prior to its publication, the manuscript of his book, *The Site of the Social: A Philosophical Account of the Constitution of Social Life and Change* (University Park: Pennsylvania State University Press, 2002).

individuals sharing the same myth and being conscious of that sharing. A group described as a conscious social experiment is easily explained in individualist terms. Most social structuralisms adopt individualist explanation of human agency to a point and then appeal to some abstract structure that supposedly governs agency. Social formation then is structure expressed in agency at a particular time and place. In the last thirty years or so, it has been popular to explain determination with the idea of a field of possibilities produced by structure. Mythmaking, in this view, might be explained as a cultural expression of the society's social structure that is involved in effecting a specific social formation. I do not find these social structural ideas at all helpful or persuasive. Practice theorists find the "structuring" within continuously unfolding and mutating, but interrelated and crisscrossing, practices that are the context or site (together with material arrangements) for agency and human coexistence. Explanations involve locating agency in an account of the organization of practices.

From the perspective of social theory, the central issue of the Seminar's work in the last few years might best be identified as an instance of the classical problem of social change. How does one explain the transition from a tiny school of a minor teacher in Galilee to the beginnings of the Christian church and the Christian religion in the wider Roman world? The Seminar has taken off from the critical realization that the very story suggesting the historical problem is the Christian myth itself. The conviction of the Seminar has been that mythmaking played a key role in the—and here the choice of metaphor becomes crucial—transition (or movement, contact, and so on) from one social formation to another on this trajectory. Traditional social theory has couched the problem in a series of oppositions: continuity/discontinuity, stability/change. Because the concept of structure is a reification, "social maintenance" has been readily explained in social theory that appealed to "society" and structure, but change and sociocultural diversification have been difficult for such theory. In light of practice theory, the oppositions themselves do not make sense because human action configured as practices is always evolving even as continuity is the norm. Practices typically come linked together with other practice so as to constitute larger social formations. Not only will the organization of individual practices change in new circumstances, but the bundle of practices in a particular formation will change. Practices can split and parts merge into other practices, become extinct, form as new practices from fragments around new techniques or cultural artifacts, and so on. The mental conditions and intentionality of individuals do not control and cannot explain this continuity and discontinuity, partly because these mental conditions are always already involved in what is constituted in practices. The idea of practices provides a radically contextual way of thinking about social life that also acknowledges the contingent nature of social change.

I also find one other advantage to this kind of social theory very important, for me even essential: in my estimation, only this kind of theorizing and certain kinds of (repugnant) individualisms can be reconciled with a neo-Darwinian account of human origins.[2]

The Seminar has identified eating practices and teaching/school practices as activities with which mythmaking practices may have been linked and as practices that may have evolved in ways that connect the social formations of the Jesus peoples and Paul. Over against the myth of Christian origins, however, strong elements of discontinuity are patent. I want to suggest one way of thinking about the question of continuity/discontinuity using the illustration of "Christ" and of appeals to Jesus followers in Jerusalem in Paul's mythmaking.

We need a notion that is the social equivalent of the neo-Darwinian idea of exaptation. An exaptation is a biological adaptation that had a different function or no function in an earlier environment and population. In several sorts of winged animals there was something winglike that had nothing to do with flying in an earlier environment or a different population, that became an organ of flight in a later environment and population. Exaptation, as evolutionary biologists know well, is a bit redundant and misleading as a concept because every adaptation at an earlier point developed out of structures that had a different or no function. But the term is useful precisely because biologists want to construct narratives that try to explain how later populations relate to earlier ones. In explaining the activity of human individuals, and more problematically, of social formations, we rightly use the mentalistic language of purposes, intentions, beliefs, and interests. We commonly use these to account for the continuity of identity or lack thereof between social groups or formations. But neglecting the aspects of human practices and behavior that do not rightly fall under mentalistic descriptions leads to the attribution of too much teleology to historical processes. The ideas of collective creativity and communal mind so beloved by all kinds of romantic social theory drip with excessive teleology. Another concept of the same pedigree is identity. I do not think that anyone in the Seminar wants to end up with a formulation such as "identity = myth in the collective mind of formation X," but much of our expression suggests such. Imagine one man building a house and using a large stone as a lintel for his door. The house eventually collapses, and a boat builder finds the stone and uses it as an anchor. In building practices the stone was a lintel, but in sailing, the same stone became an

---

[2] I do not think that we can any longer find credible the route of saying that the mechanisms of human evolution apply only up to the beginnings of culture and then autonomous social principles take over.

anchor. In practical terms, there was no continuity in the intentionality of the two people who made use of the stone.

A social exaptation would be a cultural artifact that in some sense originated in one social formation and environment but that came to serve a different use and function in another population, environment, and social formation. One can, I think, read the relation of "Pauline Christianity" to the "Jesus people of Jerusalem and Antioch" as one of social exaptations. In Gal 1–2 and 1 Cor 15, Paul tells stories to his readers about the relation of his "Christ enterprise" to those who came before him and who made claims on what he describes as a common legacy. Although Paul wants to lay claim to knowing people whom he calls apostles (a title of self-description for Paul), as well as a brother of Jesus, of being approved by them, and of sharing originary contact with Jesus, the risen Christ, he also acknowledges a distance from them and disapproval by them. I do not think it plausible, as has sometimes been suggested, that Paul invented the people and all the particulars. But this looks like a Pauline story told with Paul's distinctive ideas and categories that relates to these Jesus (or perhaps "Christ") people in Jerusalem and Antioch by social exaptation. It is not clear to me that he even understood quite what these people were about, but his story assimilates them to his own practices, project, and the originary myth of the social formations for which he claimed leadership. Perhaps we should stop looking for an original kerygma that Paul inherited and see these Pauline stories as, in a sense, the first myth of Christian origins. These texts catch Paul in moments of ongoing mythmaking. Paul's own accounts reveal that these Jerusalem people were interested in Jewish matters such as temple, food laws, poverty in Judea, and so on. They probably saw Jesus as a teacher and founder of a school. I can imagine some of them saying that Jesus had been the anointed one, but meaning only that Jesus had been a divinely approved teacher. What a radically novel appropriation for Paul and his early associates to say that Jesus had become a cosmic lord and judge in whose hands rested the fate of all the peoples! Testing the exaptation hypothesis would involve showing that the contexts of practices in which "Christ" made sense for some Jesus people and for Paul and company were analogous to the relation of house building and sailing in the earlier example.

The history of theorizing about the social in the West has left a fairly clear range of options that lead to different modes of explanation and that suppose different social ontologies. I do not think that one can simply work in some sort of neutral fashion or avoid the more basic theoretical and philosophical issues in the kind of work that the Seminar is doing. I am, however, far from advocating that people divide into dogmatic camps over social theory. This would be counterproductive, and social theory is far from being a subject for certainties. But by trying out hypotheses in a way that makes clear basic theoretical commitments, we can be much clearer about the costs and benefits of a particular type of theorizing. I hope that my comments have served in at least a suggestive way to illustrate how such clarification might be useful for the Seminar.

Conclusion: Redescribing Christian Origins
Ron Cameron and Merrill P. Miller

In his call paper for our first Consultation on Ancient Myths and Modern Theories of Christian Origins, Burton L. Mack argued that the most "serious obstacle to a redescription project," to "setting the gospel account aside," is "the theory of religion implicit in our scholarship and naively assumed as natural":

> The historian of religion would say that New Testament scholars work with a concept of religion that is thoroughly and distinctly Christian in its derivation and definition.... Familiarity with the Christian religion has taken the place of theoretical discussion, and Christianity has provided us with the categories we use to name and explain early Christian phenomena. The problem is that the understanding of religion implicit in our discipline is inadequate for the task of redescribing Christian origins.[1]

Two features of Mack's argumentation deserve special attention: (1) his recognition that the gospel story, largely Lukan, has been—and continues to provide—the frame of reference for the historical description of Christian beginnings; and (2) his demonstration that the theory of religion implicit in biblical scholarship, with its theistic view of history, can neither explain the emergence of Christianities nor enable us to redescribe Christian

---

[1] Burton L. Mack, "On Redescribing Christian Origins," *MTSR* 8 (1996): 251, 252, adding: "Interest in religion among New Testament scholars comes to focus on personal transformations, or what is sometimes called 'personal religious experience.' By this is meant some kind of contact with the divine, a contact that requires a breakthrough from both sides of a wall that inhibits clear vision, communication, and personal relations. The breakthrough from the divine side is imagined in terms of revelations, appearances, miracles, and dramatic events.... From the human side, the breakthroughs happen in terms of visions, conversions, and personal transformations that shatter older patterns of self-understanding and transfer persons into a new world order or relationship with the divine. [All] else in the myth-ritual package of Christianity ... are merely reflectors hung on the walls of the Christian sanctuary for the purpose of intensifying the focus of divine light upon the individual positioned at its centre" (ibid., 252; repr., with revisions, in *The Christian Myth: Origins, Logic, and Legacy* [New York: Continuum, 2001], 64, 63, 65, 66).

origins.² The significance of these observations is underscored by the critical response of Jonathan Z. Smith, who begins his metareflection by noting that:

> A reigning paradigm—given the shorthand designation, the Lukan-Eusebian model—has been the framework for the "normal science" of the study of early Christianities for centuries, proving extraordinarily resilient in its capacity to absorb both new and revised data, new and revised methodological and theoretical perspectives. It is, therefore, significant that the work of the Consultation and its successor Seminar began with a catalogue of aporiae which the "standard" paradigm was unable to cover as well as a set of "unexamined assumptions" largely deployed to shore up the old model. At a more general level, the implicit theory of religion assumed in the standard paradigm was likewise inadequate when compared with developments in cognate fields such as history of religions and cultural anthropology.³

In scholarship on Christian origins, Christianity has generally, and all too typically, been used as the model for what religion is—a model that Christianity alone can illustrate. The work of the Seminar marks an attempt to reverse that pattern and to turn the data of early Christianities into data for a different model of religion. Our aim is to redescribe the data of Christian origins in such a way as to contribute to the construction of another theoretical model: which is not focused on personal experience, transforming events, and dramatic breakthroughs; which does not imagine "religion" as a sui generis category, and thus, as an unfathomable mystery, nor regards "origins" as a cipher for unique encounters with divinity. To accomplish this goal, however, we have to turn that data—presented as singular events, regarded as incremental traditions, and assumed to reflect a human response to transcendence or the extraordinary "religious experience"⁴ of individuals—into *our* data, data for a different theory and

---

² "The customary 'explanations' for Christian origins," Burton L. Mack observes, "assume a certain view of human history (that it is open to divine interventions) and a certain anthropology (that mystifications and second-hand reports of revelations are automatic and sufficient modes of persuasion and belief)" ("The Christian Origins Project," in *Christian Myth*, 212).

³ Jonathan Z. Smith, "*Dayyeinu*," 483 (in this volume), with reference to Thomas S. Kuhn, *The Structure of Scientific Revolutions* (2nd ed.; International Encyclopedia of Unified Science 2/2; Chicago: University of Chicago Press, 1970); Mack, "Redescribing Christian Origins," 247–53; repr. in *Christian Myth*, 59–67.

⁴ For a critique of the category of "religious experience" and the authority of first-person discourse, see Wayne Proudfoot, *Religious Experience* (Berkeley and Los Angeles: University of California Press, 1985); Joan W. Scott, "The Evidence of Experience," *Critical Inquiry* 17 (1991): 773–97; Terry F. Godlove Jr., "Religious Discourse and First Person Authority," *MTSR*

Conclusion: Redescribing Christian Origins 499

understanding of religion. The three years of working papers, e-mail responses, and in-house discussion and debate, published for the first time in this volume, represent the Seminar's first step in the direction of using what has been the model for religion—Christianity—as data for an alternative model of religion. We have taken this step in terms of a redescription of the data of Christian origins, and that redescription has, itself, become the means by which we have begun to construct a new map of Christian beginnings.

Our efforts to redescribe the beginnings of Christianity as religion constitute what Smith has called the "'first sense' of redescription": a "radical alteration of the habitual terms of description."[5] We have undertaken our redescriptions of the data of Christian origins, in large part, by vocabulary displacements: taking a series of terms customary for the conventional description of Christian origins and replacing them with other terms that the Seminar has found useful, as descriptive generalizations, for the task of redescription. These new terms can then serve as the basis for a new set of categories with theoretical and explanatory power. Such vocabulary displacements are both the means by which we have redescribed the data of Christian beginnings and the consequence of that redescription, the result of our own analyses of the data of the dominant paradigm of Christian origins.

The possibility of a redescription of Christian origins is rooted in a different theory of religion. The displacement of one set of vocabulary with another is the way we have tried to put our theoretical model in place. Instead of understanding religion as a matter of private persuasion, we have introduced the notion of *attraction* to represent a different set of collective motivations. Instead of taking the history and development of early Christianities as variations or applications of a singular point of origin, we present a different sense of imaginative activity by employing the categories of *social experimentation* and *reflexivity,* expressive of the thoughtfulness, creativity, and intellectual labor involved in constructing and maintaining social formations in response to the opportunities and challenges of the Greco-Roman world. Instead of isolating individual traditions or charting a tradition history, we are engaged in a different kind of historiographical analysis: identifying *social locations,* our category for significant junctures of *mythmaking* and *social formation,* investigating their *social logics,* and deducing *social interests.* And so, as the means by

---

6 (1994): 147–61; Robert H. Sharf, "Experience," in *Critical Terms for Religious Studies* (ed. Mark C. Taylor; Chicago: University of Chicago Press, 1998), 94–116; Timothy Fitzgerald, "Experience," in *Guide to the Study of Religion* (ed. Willi Braun and Russell T. McCutcheon; London: Cassell, 2000), 125–39.

[5] Smith, *"Dayyeinu,"* 484–85 n. 4; cf. 483–84.

which we have been able to redescribe the data of Christian beginnings, vocabulary displacements have to do with our starting with an alternative theory of religion. Indeed, we have always had another theoretical model in mind to begin with—a social theory of religion—which informs our efforts to redescribe the dominant paradigm of Christian origins and, thus, to turn the data of Christian beginnings into data for a different social, cultural, and humanistic understanding of religion. For in the study of religion, as in any historical discipline, "the greatest impediment to scientific innovation is usually a conceptual lock, not a factual lack."[6]

Our efforts to use the data of early Christianities as data for an alternative model of religion are consistent with critical scholarship in cognate fields of study, including ancient Israel, early Judaism, the rabbis, and Islam. In all of these redescriptive efforts, what is shared is the critical issue of perspective: acknowledging the fact—together with its theoretical implications—that a religious community's narrative of its origins and (mythic) past cannot serve as the framework for a critical historiography. We are persuaded that the canonical narrative framework of Christian origins can, in fact, become our data and make sense, if problematized and redescribed in accordance with social theories of religion. But if we are to use the dominant paradigm as data, then we have to deal head-on with the issue, and the data, of "origins," since the theory of religion implicit in New Testament scholarship depends upon the canonical narrative framework of Christian origins. There is thus an important theoretical issue at stake in our choice of texts and terms to redescribe the data of Christian beginnings. Because the model for religion, in biblical scholarship, is always an appeal to (Christian) origins, the understanding of Christianity as a historical religion, according to this view, must also—invariably—appeal to origins. It follows that a redescription of the beginnings of Christianity as religion has to address forthrightly the data that furnish the basis, and establish the paradigm, for imagining Christianity as the model of origins. For the traditional picture of Christian beginnings has not changed—and will not change—unless we deal with the privileged data that provide both the gospel story of Christian origination and the model for understanding it; unless we take on the "canonical" texts of the dominant (gospel) paradigm, which supply the frame of reference for the theoretical model of understanding Christianity "as an otherwise inexplicable emergence of a brand new religion of unique conviction and singular faith."[7] Accordingly, the strong texts of the canonical paradigm have to be redescribed, or else the data of early

---

[6] Stephen Jay Gould, *Wonderful Life: The Burgess Shale and the Nature of History* (New York: Norton, 1989), 276.
[7] Mack, "Redescribing Christian Origins," 250; repr. in *Christian Myth*, 63.

Christianities cannot be used, as data, to construct an alternative theory and model of religion. Moreover, if we do not turn the data of the dominant paradigm into our own data, then any of our own redescriptions remain in danger of being co-opted by that very paradigm, which has "prov[ed so] extraordinarily resilient in its capacity to absorb both new and revised data, new and revised methodological and theoretical perspectives."[8]

The displacement of one set of vocabulary with another is not only the means by which we have redescribed the data of Christian beginnings but also the consequence of our redescriptions, the result of our efforts to resolve historical and exegetical anomalies by means of vocabulary displacements. Instead of paraphrasing the Lukan myth of (Christian) origins in Jerusalem as the single center for two great missions, first to the Jews and then to the Gentiles, we have expanded and distributed the creative moments of beginnings by introducing the categories of *homeland* and *diaspora*, based on locative factors characteristic of Hellenistic religions, in general, in both their native and foreign lands. Instead of assuming that Christianity was a messianic movement which emerged out of Judaism, we show that the term *christos* in the New Testament is used as an *ethnographic* category, to claim that Jesus was authorized as "'God's choice' for the social role of founder-figure of the Jesus movements."[9] Instead of perpetuating the view that early Christianities arose in response to the historical Jesus, we have employed the categories of *ethnicity* and *epic revision* to argue that early Jesus people were concerned with a sense of collective identity, searching the scriptures to claim to be part of the heritage of Israel. The historical and exegetical explanations we have offered are the product both of our changed theoretical vocabulary and starting point and of our redescriptions. We are persuaded that our vocabulary displacements provide a better way of explaining the data of Christian beginnings, as well as a better way of explaining aporiae or anomalies in the data, than the conventional way scholars have approached the matter.

Our theory of religion and theoretical vocabulary have thus had an important, critical effect on our choice of starting points. We launched our project by starting with the Sayings Gospel Q and the *Gospel of Thomas* because we thought that we could explain both of these texts in terms of our own theoretical perspective, and explain them better than by appeal to the canonical (gospel) paradigm. In fact, we are persuaded that we can explain the data of the dominant paradigm itself, better, by starting with the Jesus schools of Q and *Thomas* than the way New Testament scholars have traditionally approached the matter: (1) by presupposing at the

---

[8] Smith, "*Dayyeinu*," 483.
[9] Burton L. Mack, "Why *Christos*? The Social Reasons," 368 (in this volume).

inauguration of the Christian era a dramatic event, a kerygmatic conviction, and a linear development; and (2) by assuming that there was an essential bond that existed and a continuous development that led from the historical Jesus to the Gospel story of his appearance, death, and resurrection, and from there to the Jerusalem church in Acts and the apostle Paul and his mission. Indeed, we would argue that Q and *Thomas,* which provide two of the best examples of early Jesus groups whose patterns of mythmaking and social formation do not fit the canonical narrative framework of Christian origins, have not sufficiently performed their service for our redescription of Christian beginnings unless we show that the data of the dominant paradigm has to relate to them, not vice versa. For the whole utility of having alternate beginnings lies in not allowing these texts to be locked into the canonical (gospel) story of Christian origins, shoehorned into conventional categories of explanation and interpretation. Thus, we break with the dominant paradigm of Christian origins as a means, strategically, of reinterpreting it. The Sayings Gospel Q and the *Gospel of Thomas* demonstrate that we do not have to start with the historical Jesus, the crucified Christ, an eschatological event, or apocalyptic expectations to account for the beginnings of Christianity. The advantage of such alternate beginnings is not in having an alternative point of absolute origination, but in having a cognitive advantage and, thus, the possibility of new knowledge. Whether we actually gain new knowledge about Christian beginnings, however, depends on whether different points of departure contribute to a rethinking of other data, especially of data that have been crucial for maintaining scholarship in the grip of the dominant paradigm.

Redescribing Christian origins is thus an urgent exercise in "defamiliarization," in "making the familiar seem strange *in order to enhance our perception of the familiar.*"[10] It is this "imperative that prohibits the study of religion from being a mechanism for transmission, be it of [religious] identity or tradition. It is this same imperative that forbids 'allowing the gospel paradigm to define Christian origins.'"[11] Defamiliarizing the familiar story of Christian beginnings, not allowing that story to define the terms and frame of reference of New Testament studies, permits us to test our contention that the cognitive advantage of alternate beginnings is enormous, in giving us the possibility of new knowledge. It also means that we

---

[10] Jonathan Z. Smith, "Introduction," in *Imagining Religion: From Babylon to Jonestown* (CSHJ; Chicago: University of Chicago Press, 1982), xiii, emphasis original, citing Victor Shklovsky, "Art as Technique," in *Russian Formalist Criticism: Four Essays* (ed. and trans. Lee T. Lemon and Marion J. Reis; Regents Critics Series; Lincoln: University of Nebraska Press, 1965), 13; cf. 13–22.

[11] Smith, "*Dayyeinu,*" 483–84, citing Mack, "Redescribing Christian Origins," 250; repr. in *Christian Myth,* 63.

Conclusion: Redescribing Christian Origins

can test our working hypothesis that early Jesus groups were reflexive social experiments, engaged in and responsive to the challenges and opportunities presented by the social histories and diversities of cultures in the Greco-Roman world.

In our choice of vocabulary to redescribe the beginnings of Christianity, we have used three different sets of terms to serve as middle-range categories, displacing the traditional theological nomenclature of Christian origins. First, there is a set of technical terms that pertain to method and theory and bear on the relationship of theory and historiography:

+ *attraction* instead of "belief"
+ *social interest* instead of "individual transformation"
+ *social experimentation* instead of "religious experience"
+ *social logic* instead of "tradition history"
+ *social location* instead of "Sitz im Leben"
+ *reflexivity* instead of "hermeneutic"

As a means and result of redescription, we intend these vocabulary displacements to be consequential. Displacing one series of terms with another is not saying the same thing an alternative way, nor is it substituting one set of vocabulary for another. It is to change the terms of discourse and debate, using new categories to take the place of habitual terms of description. We have introduced these items as categories in the interest of an alternative theory and understanding of religion. The traditional theological vocabulary of New Testament scholarship, which these terms of redescription have displaced, is insufficiently critical as an instrument of explanation and analysis. Instead, the language of "belief," "individual transformation," and "religious experience" is mystifying, an appeal to an understanding of religion as a matter of private persuasion, a usage that persists and is kept in place to invoke the notion of origins. Our category of *attraction,* for example, displaces "belief" (in divine interventions) as an explanation of social formation. Attraction is our placeholder for a different set of collective motivations. By employing this category, we are attempting an explanation of early Christianity that can be understood anthropologically, in terms of *social interests* and *social experimentation.* With this first set of terms, therefore, we intend to show why we have insisted on redescribing the data of the dominant paradigm. Only by displacing the (Christian) language of origins can we get at the implicit theory and assumptions which are, in fact, the very reason that Christianity has been used as the model for religion. Only by making the data of Christian beginnings amenable to a different explanation—and we cannot do that without redescribing the gospel story of Christian origination, on which that theory and model rest—can we use the data of early

Christianities for an alternative social, cultural, and humanistic understanding of religion.

Instead of maintaining a trunk-and-branches model of origins, and taking the history and development of early Christianities as "hermeneutical" variations or univocal applications of a singular point of origin (be it the historical Jesus, the crucified Christ, or an eschatological event), we mean to convey a different sense of imaginative activity by employing the critical category of *reflexivity*. Along with the concept of *social experimentation*, reflexivity expresses thoughtfulness and creativity in response to the conditions, constraints, and challenges of the Greco-Roman world. Whereas early Christian social formations were "*experimental* in that the marks of novelty, discussion, debate, and changing configurations ... are features shared by all," they were also

> *reflexive* in relation to their social and cultural contexts. "Reflexive" means that they positioned themselves within and over against the larger social and cultural worlds by rendering critical judgments about their cultures of context and their relationships to them, and by seeking liaison with other groups and social institutions. This resulted in the critique, borrowing, rearrangement, and resignification of various practices and ideas from that larger world context.[12]

Accordingly, the commonality between and among the various Jesus movements is not a consequence of passing on a cultural deposit of tradition, however defined. It is, rather, the consequence of social experimentation which other groups, besides early Christians, were also involved in, with the result that one can find both commonalities between the various Jesus movements and analogies with other groups in the Greco-Roman world. Indeed, the Jesus movements may have as many differences among themselves as between them and other groups.

Our understanding of diversity is, therefore, no longer tied to notions of "trajectories"—from "the most embracing movement" to "more specific streams" of tradition, whether at "one stage of a movement" or "as a variant or eddy within a broader religious or cultural current," each branching off or flowing from a common point of departure[13]—but is connected to the wider environment by means of a model of distribution and difference.[14] As

---

[12] Mack, "Christian Origins Project," 211, emphasis original.

[13] James M. Robinson, "Introduction: The Dismantling and Reassembling of the Categories of New Testament Scholarship," in *Trajectories through Early Christianity* (ed. James M. Robinson and Helmut Koester; Philadelphia: Fortress, 1971), 13, 16, 14.

[14] "The traditional scholarly approach to intertextual relationships among early Christian literatures," Burton L. Mack observes, "has been to trace single line dependencies starting from

Conclusion: Redescribing Christian Origins 505

such, we are not concerned with isolating individual "traditions" (by means of a thin or static image of "Sitz im Leben") or charting a "tradition history," by tracing the history of the transmission of traditions, incrementally, back to Jesus or his first followers. Rather, we are engaged in a different kind of historiography: (1) identifying *social locations,* our category for significant junctures of mythmaking and social formation, and (2) investigating their *social logics,* our category for the relationship of a given myth to the processes of social formation. From the data of mythmaking, we have sought, by means of a concept of social logic, to deduce *social interests* (as "a way to talk about collective motivations")[15] and *social locations.* And so, the very method by which we talk about specific social-textual sites, in terms of placing our texts at particular moments or junctures of a lived social history, means that we are trying to avoid the notion that early Jesus groups were "passive receptors of generative 'traditions'"[16] or that the location of a tradition is tantamount to the location of a historical moment. Only when a tradition can be related to a locus of social history and formation can it be considered a significant historical moment or site of mythmaking and social formation. To locate such junctures in our texts is to represent historical continuity and change; by redescribing these loci, we can "turn [our] texts into sites on a new map of Christian origins."[17]

The metareflections are in general agreement that the Seminar has accomplished the critical task of problematizing the dominant paradigm of Christian origins. Having "successfully disrupted ... the standard 'Lukan-Eusebian' model of Christianity's historical beginnings,"[18] and having "succeeded in charting the terrain differently than ... before,"[19] the "topography of earliest Christianities has been decisively altered, dis-placed,

---

discrete (and preferably single) points of origin. This results in a 'stemma' or family tree arrangement. The desire has been to see junctures in the history of a textual tradition as interpretive developments of the essential ideas, insights, or implicit structures at the core of a tradition. All traditions eventually converge at the point of origin. The single trunk, naturally, has been imagined rooted in Jesus, or stemming from very early reminiscences about him." The approach taken in this volume differs in that, "since social history and experience have been emphasized as the human situation within which literature is generated, novelty is to be expected at every turn.... Thus 'creativity' or 'originality' has not been located solely at the beginning of a 'trajectory,' but dispersed and distributed among the many moments [or junctures of mythmaking and social formation]" (*A Myth of Innocence: Mark and Christian Origins* [Philadelphia: Fortress, 1988], 321–22 n. 3).

[15] Mack, "Why *Christos?*" 365.
[16] Burton L. Mack, "Remarkable," 473 (in this volume).
[17] Mack, "Christian Origins Project," 207.
[18] William E. Arnal and Willi Braun, "Social Formation and Mythmaking: Theses on Key Terms," 459 (in this volume).
[19] Mack, "Remarkable," 470.

re-placed."[20] We need to acknowledge, however, that the Seminar does not yet have a set of behavioral terms that we agree are explanations. Our vocabulary displacements have been introduced in quest of a different explanation of Christian beginnings and in the interest of a different theory of religion. We have used the term *attraction,* for example, as a category "to mark and hold the place for the explanations we seek as alternatives to the customary and traditional notions of 'religious' motivations implicit in the standard scenarios."[21] Nevertheless, the metareflections make it abundantly clear that there is no consensus among ourselves that the terms we have employed as middle-range categories offer explanations for the emergence of the groups that make up the early Jesus movements. There is, instead, a noticeable lack of agreement about how best to account for the attraction of, and interest in, the human construction of early Christian social formation and mythmaking. But it should be clear that our vocabulary displacements have been made for the sake of achieving such an explanation. And so, though our terms are intended as descriptive generalizations, as categories, to provide the basis for a genuinely critical discourse in support of the Seminar's efforts in historiography, we are aware that these terms are theoretically insufficient and in need, themselves, of rectification. We acknowledge that, in learning "how to think Christian origins differently,"[22] there is more work to do and that, in our theoretical formulations in particular, we need to introduce even more difference between our redescriptions and the data of the dominant paradigm.

The second set of terms that we have employed is derived from, and actually represents, our redescriptions of the data of Christian beginnings:

- *homeland* and *diaspora* instead of "origins" and "mission"
- *ethnographic* instead of "messianic"
- *christos* instead of "the Messiah"
- *ethnicity* instead of "personal salvation"
- *epic* and *epic revision* instead of "eschatology" and "eschatological persuasion"

We have introduced these terms as a consequence of having alternate beginnings. All of these categories are, in fact, the direct product of our redescriptions themselves, the result of our efforts to resolve historical and exegetical anomalies, heuristically, by means of vocabulary displacements. The traditional theological vocabulary of "origins" and "mission," of the

---

[20] Smith, "*Dayyeinu,*" 484.
[21] Mack, "Remarkable," 473.
[22] Ibid., 471.

"messianic" and the "eschatological," is thoroughly Christian language. "Origins," for example, is a quintessentially mythic notion, evocative of the gospel story, and invoked to appeal to the uniqueness of Christian origins and the incomparability of the Christian religion.[23] By displacing these notions with a new set of categories, we have tried to redescribe the issues in terms that are reflective of the cultures of context and applicable to most people in the Greco-Roman world: self-definition, social identity, belonging, and boundaries. The categories of *homeland* and *diaspora,* which displace "origins" and "mission," offer an explanation of difference based on a taxonomy of locative factors that are characteristic of Mediterranean religions, in general, in their Hellenistic and Late Antique phases. The homeland/diaspora distinction enables us "to mark different perspectives on Jerusalem"[24] and, thus, to redescribe four different sites—Jerusalem, Antioch, Galatia, and Paul's own situation itself—in terms of competing imaginative constructions of diaspora myths of origins in the homeland. This change of categories and perspectives means that we can resolve the anomaly created by the book of Acts—and by the letters of Paul when read in light of Acts—which makes it appear as if Jerusalem is acting as the initiator of issues in Antioch (and Galatia), and thus is (for Paul) the main problem, whereas in fact those issues would not have been part of an agenda of Jesus people in Jerusalem.

The category of *christos,* which displaces "the Messiah" of Christian imagination, is an *ethnographic*—not a "messianic"—term that is both mythic (in that it has to do with an ethnographic myth of origins for a Jesus-*christos* association) and descriptive (in that it signifies social formation, being used as a term of mutual recognition among different groups). Traditionally, "messianic" presuppositions have to do with some heroic notion of salvation and a unique figure who can execute that task. New Testament scholars have, accordingly, assumed that Christianity was a movement which emerged out of Judaism and defined its own uniqueness precisely by means of a stunning reinterpretation and transfiguration of Jewish messianic hopes. With the category of *christos* we are trying to resolve what scholarship has presumed and allowed to stand as history: the anomaly of a messianic drama in Jerusalem which is, in fact, a myth of origins.[25] It is

---

[23] See Jonathan Z. Smith, *Drudgery Divine: On the Comparison of Early Christianities and the Religions of Late Antiquity* (Jordan Lectures in Comparative Religion 14; London: School of Oriental and African Studies, University of London; Chicago: University of Chicago Press, 1990), esp. 1–35, 36–53, 79, 116–17.

[24] Mack, "Why *Christos?*" 368.

[25] All of "the locations imagined for Christian origins on the traditional model," Mack observes, "are imaginations calculated to give the impression that some mythic event was in some sense historical" (ibid., 373).

essential to note that this scenario not only recapitulates the dominant (gospel) paradigm of Christian origins but is also self-serving and convenient, in that the very notion of a crucified Messiah is an anomaly that is played with, precisely, to be expressive of paradox, dramatic reversal, and death and resurrection, as if the problem were really the solution. Such a scenario is, moreover, especially insidious in that it does double duty, serving as an emblem both of the uniqueness of Christianity and of its historical origins.[26] The actual usage of the term *christos* in the New Testament argues against the assumption of the emergence of Christianity as a messianic sect. Indeed, careful analysis of the uses of the term in early Jewish and Christian literature demonstrates that a "messianic" connotation, "the customary assumption that *christos* was the royal title for a figure of expectation in both early Jewish and early Christian literature and mentality," is actually "the *end* result of a series of moves in early *Christian* mythmaking."[27]

The import of *christos* as an epithet, *ethnographically,* is that it signifies an attempt by a Jesus-*christos* association to construct a collective, social identity in terms, and at the point, of a Jesus legacy intersecting with issues of Jewish identity and practice. To call Jesus *christos* conveys "divine authorization for a role of leadership" and, thus, is a way of enhancing "Jesus' status as founder-teacher … by comparison and analogy with figures of Israel's past … in order to lay claim to the perspective of the God of Israel in thinking about the role of Jesus as founder."[28] To refer to Jesus

---

[26] "The very attempt to resolve the problem [of the origins of a messianic conception of Jesus]," Merrill P. Miller observes, "can result [all too typically] in the sort of historical solution that is itself an expression of the drama, novelty, and dialectic of Christian faith. What are considered to be contingent circumstances of the death of Jesus are transformed in the inaugural miracle of resurrection and generate in a brief span of some twenty years a history of reflection whose creative period is virtually complete…. It is enough to deduce from the 'late' usage of Paul that the messianic status of Jesus must have been the inaugural confession of the primitive church, must have gained wide currency in Palestinian and Hellenistic Christian communities, and must have been a stunning claim that left behind at the very outset every form of Jewish messianic hope. Thus, the Jewish messianic hope is presupposed and transcended in the inaugural moment of Christian origins" ("The Problem of the Origins of a Messianic Conception of Jesus," 313 [in this volume]).

[27] Mack, "Why *Christos*?" 365, emphasis original.

[28] Merrill P. Miller, "The Anointed Jesus," 408, 409 (in this volume), adding: "The focus would not have been on Jesus as savior—at least not at first—but on what might be claimed of the heritage of Israel for the followers of Jesus, the kingdom-of-God people, in conversation with and differentiation from the synagogue people; and what might be said about the boundaries they were crossing and redrawing in the interests of an ongoing transactional enterprise of collective identity formation and maintenance. [And so,] as the expression of a quest for prestigious origins, the anointed Jesus belongs to the same category as most biblical myths, to ethnographic rather than to messianic myths. It is concerned to define a society, rather than to save it. It reflects one attempt among others in the Greco-Roman world to redefine Israel—in this instance, by appeal to the anointed status of the founder; hence, by appeal

as *christos* "would be an explicit claim to the importance of his role as a figure of recent history whose appearance not only fit with but [also] continued the sense of divine purpose ... implicit to the [Hebrew] epic.... Calling Jesus *christos* would be a claim that he was 'God's choice' for the social role of founder-figure of the Jesus movements and [thus] an implicit claim that the Jesus-movement formation should be thought of as a way of being 'Israel.'" Accordingly, an appeal to "the epic of Israel" has to be seen as both "a very significant index of social formation"[29] and a major "mythmaking strategy" of the Jesus movements, designed "to reimagine and reinvent the collective (in this case, 'Israel') in a form appropriate for the larger human horizon of the Greco-Roman age."[30] The struggle to appropriate the past by means of *epic revision* is a common scribal mentality and technique. *Epic,* understood as "myth in the genre of history," is an account or "rehearsal of the past that puts the present in its light. Setting the present in the light of an illustrious past makes it honorable, legitimate, right, and reasonable.... Revising the epic in light of present circumstances from a particular point of view to support a critical judgment about the present state of affairs," on the other hand, is a "form of mythmaking that can be called epic revision."[31] With our category of *epic* (and *epic revision*), then, we are displacing the theological nomenclature of "eschatology" (and "eschatological persuasion"), which scholarly usage has, all too typically, "dislodged from real apocalyptic settings in the Greco-Roman world ... [and] 'transformed into an indicator of absolute (ontological) uniqueness.'"[32]

The categories of ethnography, ethnicity, and epic revision are concerned with well-attested, ordinary issues—not claims of (Christian) uniqueness—that reflect the social interests and central elements characteristic of a

---

to the God of Israel without invoking authority grounded in the institutions that embodied the practices of civic and national religion" (ibid., 409).

[29] Mack, "Why *Christos*?" 367–68, 367.

[30] Mack, "Christian Origins Project," 211.

[31] Burton L. Mack, *Who Wrote the New Testament? The Making of the Christian Myth* (San Francisco: HarperSanFrancisco, 1995), 14, 36, 71.

[32] Ron Cameron, "The Anatomy of a Discourse: On 'Eschatology' as a Category for Explaining Christian Origins," *MTSR* 8 (1996): 240, adding: "In such a displaced usage, eschatology has come to be understood as 'a locus of uniqueness': the '"unique" becomes an ontological rather than a taxonomic category; an assertion of a radical difference so absolute that it becomes "Wholly Other," and the act of comparison is perceived as both an impossibility and an impiety'" (ibid., citing Smith, *Drudgery Divine,* 41, 38). Jonathan Z. Smith himself notes that "the term 'eschatological,' [which had been] intended to make the teachings of Jesus a typical example of a distant, alien worldview, has been converted into that which renders these teachings unique and accessible.... This has been accomplished by evacuating eschatology of any meaningful temporal (or spatial) content" ("Social Formations of Early Christianities: A Response to Ron Cameron and Burton Mack," *MTSR* 8 [1996]: 271).

variety of social formations in the ancient Mediterranean world: creating a collective, social identity; making and marking boundaries; identifying group membership; interacting with others; inventing and maintaining tradition (by means and in spite of change); and imagining cultural difference. Concern for *ethnicity*, which displaces the romantic notion of "personal salvation" (as a quest), is a product of the social fragmentation and confusion of identity in the Greco-Roman world. We have employed this category strategically, with a sense of its constructed and constructive character, as both an index of social identity and a mythmaking technique. While its definition remains disputed, for us *ethnicity* is a discursive formation with theoretical and analytical power, being used, for instance, as a *social interest* category to signify the *social logic* of *christos* as an *ethnic* claim with appeal to the Hebrew *epic*. Our redescriptions suggest, therefore, that the literature of early Christianity is largely ethnographic in intent. Its social interests are organized and driven by a quest to establish a collective, group identity. And the intellectual labor which accompanies that pursuit has to compensate, by way of mythmaking, for the absence or breakdown of stable features associated with ethnicity, as well as maintain a semblance of continuity in the context of a social and cultural mix.

There is no consensus among the members of the Seminar that this second set of terms, derived from our redescriptions of the data of Christian origins, provides us with behavioral indices or a description of social-textual sites that could be redescribed more fully in terms of social formation, not just as mythmaking. In fact, the metareflections question whether the identification of the self-referential character of a group provides an explanation for social formation and behavior, such as the emergence of a group or its social agenda. These questions raise the issue of the definition, clarification, and meaning of our terms of redescription. They also raise the question of behavioral description and explanation: whether, and to what extent, our categories contribute to the kinds of explanations that can account for the social formation and discursive practices of a particular group or groups. We acknowledge that the Seminar does not yet have a set of behavioral terms that we agree are explanations. Our vocabulary displacements have been introduced in the interest of resolving historical and exegetical anomalies, heuristically, in quest of a redescription of a select series of specific, constructed, social-textual sites. Not only have we used these categories heuristically; we have also employed them argumentatively—recognizing that these terms are intended as descriptive generalizations, lend themselves to critical reflection on the need to change perspectives on the social history and imaginative labor documented by our texts, and yet can have rather different implications, and thus are in need of more sustained attention to critical theory. Nevertheless, what we have accomplished through the use of these categories is a revisionary juxtaposition: on the one hand, we have redescribed the data of the dominant paradigm of Christian origins and data that does not fit that paradigm; and on the other, we have redescribed both sets of data by means of another theory and understanding of religion, instead of the old paradigm and (canonical) model of Christian origins.

Finally, there is a set of technical terms that make up the chief operating categories being used and tested by the Seminar:

- *mythmaking* instead of "the kerygma"
- *social formation* instead of "the church"

We have introduced these categories in the interest of changing perspectives on the object and definition of our study. New Testament scholars have traditionally resorted to notions of "the kerygma" and "the church" to give a theological account of the origins of Christianity. In the classic formulation of Rudolf Bultmann, "Christian faith did not exist until there was a Christian kerygma; i.e., a kerygma proclaiming Jesus Christ—specifically Jesus Christ the Crucified and Risen One—to be God's eschatological act of salvation. He was first so proclaimed in the kerygma of the earliest Church.... Thus, theological thinking—the theology of the New Testament—begins with the *kerygma* of the earliest Church."[33] Nevertheless, the theological vocabulary of "the kerygma" and "the church" is too parochial to serve, historiographically or comparatively, as descriptive generalizations. With the categories of *mythmaking* and *social formation,* we mean to convey a different sense of the social dynamics, discursive processes, and imaginative labor at work in the systems of signs and patterns of practices of early Christianities. And so, we introduced another set of terms—*schools* and then *associations,* for instance, as analogies exemplary of many common types of social formation, replacing the traditional theological nomenclature of "the church," which tends to signify a singular type of

---

[33] Rudolf Bultmann, *Theology of the New Testament* (trans. Kendrick Grobel; 2 vols.; London: SCM, 1952–55), 1:3, emphasis original. Whereas, technically, the "kerygma" refers to creedal formulae about the death and resurrection of Christ (see Rudolf Bultmann, *Die Geschichte der synoptischen Tradition* [9th ed.; FRLANT 29; Göttingen: Vandenhoeck & Ruprecht, 1979], 297–98; Helmut Koester, *History and Literature of Early Christianity* [vol. 2 of *Introduction to the New Testament*; Hermeneia: Foundations and Facets; Philadelphia: Fortress; Berlin: de Gruyter, 1982], 65; Mack, *Myth of Innocence,* 100 n. 2, 103, 104 n. 5; cf. 139, 253), for Bultmann the kerygma is the center of all theology and thus has come to refer, quintessentially, to the Christian proclamation of the gospel. As he states in the epilogue to his *Theology of the New Testament,* "In the New Testament, faith ... is man's response to God's word which encounters him in the proclamation of Jesus Christ. It is *faith in the kerygma,* which tells of God's dealing in the man Jesus of Nazareth" (*Theology,* 2:239, emphasis original).

origination, especially where "Jerusalem" and Paul are concerned. Both *mythmaking* and *social formation* are to be understood as gerunds,[34] indicative of dynamic processes, signifying the many different kinds of constructive and critical practices characteristic of reflexive social experiments. Whereas biblical scholars have taken "the kerygma" to be expressive of singularity, paradox, and mystery—representative of a dialectic of death and resurrection—the work of the Seminar has shown that the kerygma is but "one among many ways in which early Jesus movements and Christian groups imagined their beginnings."[35] The kerygma is neither the common core nor the theological center of early Christianities, neither the source nor the standard of what is generative, or definitive, in the Christian religion. It serves, instead, as the mythic rationale for a particular group—a myth formulated in the interest of its social logic[36]—to justify a group of Jews and Gentiles as the cause for which Jesus died. The imaginative labor of mythmaking, then, no less than the behavioral activities of social formation, is a social practice. *Mythmaking* describes the way in which people make the world work, place themselves in relation to their historical past and social present, negotiate structures of purity and power, produce conviction and schemes of meaning, define the boundaries of shared codes and conventions, and meditate on the differences between symbolic and social worlds. *Social formation* "defines the human enterprise"[37] in terms of "a concept of society as a collective human construct," emphasizing in particular "the complex interplay of many human interests that develop systems of signs and patterns of practice, as well as institutions for their communication, maintenance and reproduction." As such, the term refers to both "the process by which various configurations of these systems of practice are created and relate to one another in the formation of a given society" and "the resulting structure of a society formed by such a process." Since "religious practice" is also "a human construction in the interest of social formation,"[38] the discourse and practice of

---

[34] Mack, "Christian Origins Project," 214; idem, "Remarkable," 472; Russell T. McCutcheon, "Redescribing 'Religion' as Social Formation: Toward a Social Theory of Religion," in *What Is Religion? Origins, Definitions, and Explanations* (ed. Thomas A. Idinopulos and Brian C. Wilson; SHR 81; Leiden: Brill, 1998), 61; repr. in idem, *Critics Not Caretakers: Redescribing the Public Study of Religion* (SUNY series, Issues in the Study of Religion; Albany: State University of New York Press, 2001), 27.

[35] Burton L. Mack, review of Gary R. Habermas and Antony G. N. Flew, ed. Terry L. Miethe, *Did Jesus Rise from the Dead? The Resurrection Debate, History and Theory* 28 (1989): 219.

[36] See Mack, *Myth of Innocence*, 98–123; idem, *Who Wrote the New Testament*, 75–96; idem, "Explaining Christian Mythmaking: A Theory of Social Logic," in *Christian Myth*, 109–14.

[37] Mack, "Redescribing Christian Origins," 255; repr. in *Christian Myth*, 68.

[38] Burton L. Mack, "Social Formation," in *Guide to the Study of Religion* (ed. Willi Braun and Russell T. McCutcheon; London: Cassell, 2000), 283, 290.

religion—redescribed as mythmaking and social formation—may be said to reflect thoughtful, though ordinary, modes of ingenuity and labor. Understood theoretically within such a framework, a redescription of the beginnings of Christianity as religion is concerned with the human quest for intelligibility, with taking interest in the world and making social sense, without recourse to mystification or special pleading.

Our concept of social logic has led us to assume a correlation between mythmaking and social formation. Indeed, we have formulated our whole notion of intersections or junctures of mythmaking and social formation by means of such a logic. From the data of mythmaking, we have sought, by means of a concept of social logic (our category for the relationship of a given myth to the processes of social formation), to deduce social interests and social locations (our category for significant junctures of mythmaking and social formation). The plan for the Seminar has been to identify critical moments or junctures of mythmaking and social formation that make a difference in our understanding of the beginnings of Christianity and to subject them to a thick description and analysis. Such junctures would then become specific examples or loci in a redescription of Christian origins. Our primary strategy for the choice of data to be submitted for redescription has been to notice the way a text, or set of texts, might be relocated at a juncture of discursive activities such as epic revision, the formulation of codes, or rhetorical elaboration, and be related plausibly to a locus of social interests and attractions. In this way, an intersection of mythmaking and social formation can be identified and redescribed. Since a notion of social logic is presupposed in a linkage of mythmaking and social formation, our method has been to make inferences and deductions of social locations on the basis of the social logic of our myths.

The correlation we have made between mythmaking and social formation has produced an alternative picture of Christian origins. By making such a correlation we have changed the topography, map, and frame of reference of Christian beginnings. What the metareflections acknowledge has been accomplished in our redescriptions, in terms of "decisively alter[ing], dis-plac[ing], re-plac[ing]" the "topography of earliest Christianities,"[39] has been achieved by using a concept of social logic "to situate" and correlate the "social processes of myth formation."[40] We have problematized the data of the dominant paradigm of Christian origins at the very points of its privileged, most significant sites, by demonstrating that the social logic of that data always points to mythmaking. Insofar as the Seminar agrees that we have succeeded in problematizing the dominant

---

[39] Smith, *"Dayyeinu,"* 484.
[40] Smith, "Social Formations of Early Christianities," 272.

paradigm, it must be recognized that this is how it has been done. We have been able to redescribe the beginnings of Christianity, even though the Seminar has not (yet) come to a consensus about (1) the relationship of mythmaking to social formation or (2) whether priority should be given to one or the other of these categories. We have presumed that social formations, programs, and agendas exist in some clearly discernible relation to mythmaking and that the latter can provide adequate clues of social situations and collective motivations. Thus, we have found it possible to move from mythmaking to social formation by asking about the social logic of a myth. We have focused our entire redescriptions on the way we have imagined the relationship of mythmaking to social formation, starting with the intellectual activity of mythmaking, not least because the data of mythmaking is closest to hand in our literature, but also because specific, detailed data—hard evidence—for thick descriptions of social settings and their comparison is, for the most part, lacking in earliest Christianities. Although much of what we have accomplished depends on our concept of social logic, the issue of the correlation of mythmaking and social formation remains unresolved, a matter of considerable disagreement and debate. Some members of the Seminar have understood mythmaking and social formation to be sufficiently related such that one can move from one to the other, regarding their intersection or juncture as "a moment of social and discursive activity that is generative."[41] Others have argued that since all discourse is social, "analysis of the social world in which such discourse is generated, embedded, and efficacious should be theoretically and methodologically prior to examination of [that] discourse itself."[42] Accordingly, the theoretical question that needs "specifying" is "the nexus between mythmaking and social formation." As Smith remarked in his metareflection, "the challenge, here, will be to avoid formulations which see the one as the dependent variable of the other, or which see the one as congruent to the other."[43]

There is thus a nexus or correlation, of some sort, between mythmaking and social formation, though we have come to realize that the relationship

---

[41] Mack, "Remarkable," 472. For a theory of religion that takes mythmaking to be a correlate of social formation, emphasizing "social experience as the occasion for imaginative activity and literary production" (Mack, *Myth of Innocence*, 15; cf. 8, 16, 19–20 with nn. 8–9, 21–22), see idem, *Who Wrote the New Testament*, 11–15; idem, "Redescribing Christian Origins," 254–56; repr. in *Christian Myth*, 67–70; idem, "Social Formation," 292–94; idem, "Explaining Religion: A Theory of Social Interests," in *Christian Myth*, esp. 91–95; idem, "Explaining Christian Mythmaking," 115; idem, "Christian Origins Project," 205, 210, 212, 214.

[42] Arnal and Braun, "Social Formation and Mythmaking," 462.

[43] Smith, *"Dayyeinu,"* 486, adding: "Such formulations introduce insufficient difference" (ibid.).

is more complicated than we originally had thought. Our notion of intersections or junctures needs to convey a more complex situation than what has been reflected in this volume. The question is whether, and how, we can specify the nexus between mythmaking and social formation without assuming a relationship of conformity, causality, or reciprocity. Our concept of intersections or junctures of mythmaking and social formation needs to include situations of incongruity or discrepancy, ways to describe gaps between myths and social circumstances. Since "myth is best conceived not as a primordium, but rather as a limited collection of elements with a fixed range of cultural meanings which are applied, thought with, worked with, experimented with in particular situations ... the power of myth depends upon the play between the applicability and inapplicability of a given element in the myth to a given experiential situation."[44] As with myth, so with mythmaking. Perceptions of incongruity between a given myth and a social situation furnish occasions for the strategic application of critical thought.

Specifying the nexus between mythmaking and social formation, examining their relationship in our own terms, are theoretical and historiographical issues. Whether we have assumed too close a correlation, in general, between the social dynamics and discursive processes of mythmaking and social formation, and whether we have been able to do enough with social and behavioral issues, or with social and material conditions, will have to be tested and contested in the context of redescribing particular loci of Christian beginnings. Indeed, all of these issues need to be addressed in terms of site redescriptions, not simply as theoretical questions. We are persuaded that we must not allow the theoretical problems that confront us to become an excuse for leaving unexplained, in our own terms, any privileged, significant data from the dominant paradigm of Christian origins. The social locations we have selected for redescription have been chosen with a view to engaging the theoretical issues that have emerged—and remain unresolved—in our discourse, and to explaining, in terms of a social, cultural, and humanistic understanding of religion, the privileged data of the canonical (gospel) story. Accordingly, in the context of our current and continuing work on the Corinthian group, we intend to take up for redescription mythmaking and social formation in the Christ cults—which have not (yet) been addressed in this volume—and to conclude the Seminar by attending to our final sociomythic site: redescribing mythmaking and social formation in the Gospel of Mark. Such a strategy

---

[44] Jonathan Z. Smith, "Map Is Not Territory," in *Map Is Not Territory: Studies in the History of Religions* (SJLA 23; Leiden: Brill, 1978; repr., Chicago: University of Chicago Press, 1993), 308; cf. 299–300.

should not be construed as repeating, reverting to, or "falling under the spell of"[45] some version of the dominant paradigm, but recognized as, in fact, a theoretical issue: whether data on which the canonical (gospel) story of Christian origins depends, data which has to do with the very conception of our project, will remain—and be allowed to remain—unaccounted-for, and thus mystifying, in the discourse and scholarly imagination of Christian beginnings.

The purpose of the Seminar on Ancient Myths and Modern Theories of Christian Origins is to contribute both historiographically to a redescription of Christian beginnings and imaginatively to the construction of a general theory of religion. A seminar devoted to redescribing Christian origins must do more than repeat the slogan about the diversity of early Christianities. We intend to change the picture. We have undertaken our redescriptions by problematizing and defamiliarizing the data of the dominant paradigm, not "allowing the gospel paradigm to define [the terms and frame of reference of] Christian origins."[46] By making the data of Christian beginnings amenable to a different explanation—in terms of mythmaking and social formation—we have turned the data of early Christianities into data for a different social, cultural, and humanistic understanding of religion. What difference has the work of the Seminar made for reimagining the beginnings of Christianity? The possibility of a redescription of Christian origins is rooted in a different theory of religion. We have introduced another frame of reference and set of categories and have begun to construct a new map of Christian beginnings. We have developed constructive proposals for reimagining the patterns of discourse and social practice of early Christianities, as well as for rethinking the methods and models employed in the making of New Testament studies as a discipline. Having challenged directly, and set aside, the controlling position of the canonical (gospel) account in standard descriptions of Christian origins, we have offered another theory and historical account of the emergence of Christianities, employing alternative terms as categories for conceptualizing the tasks that have been or still need to be done. And so, by "redescrib[ing] Christian origins as a history of human inventiveness,"[47] we have rectified the category of *Christian origins,* making a "beginning" and marking the "end" of a "project of describing biblical traditions as ordinary components of religion resulting from equally ordinary processes of social formation."[48]

---

[45] So Arnal and Braun, "Social Formation and Mythmaking," 460.
[46] Mack, "Redescribing Christian Origins," 250; repr. in *Christian Myth,* 63.
[47] Mack, "Redescribing Christian Origins," 264; repr. in *Christian Myth,* 80.
[48] Smith, "Social Formations of Early Christianities," 277.

Select Bibliography

Arnal, William E. *Jesus and the Village Scribes: Galilean Conflicts and the Setting of Q*. Minneapolis: Fortress, 2001.

———. "The Rhetoric of Marginality: Apocalypticism, Gnosticism, and Sayings Gospels." *HTR* 88 (1995): 471-94.

Ascough, Richard S. "Translocal Relationships among Voluntary Associations and Early Christianity." *JECS* 5 (1997): 223–41.

Barclay, John M. G. "Mirror-Reading a Polemical Letter: Galatians as a Test Case." *JSNT* 31 (1987): 73–93.

Bousset, Wilhelm. *Kyrios Christos*. Translated by John E. Steely. Nashville: Abingdon, 1970.

Cameron, Ron. "Alternate Beginnings—Different Ends: Eusebius, Thomas, and the Construction of Christian Origins." Pages 501–25 in *Religious Propaganda and Missionary Competition in the New Testament World: Essays Honoring Dieter Georgi*. Edited by Lukas Bormann, Kelly Del Tredici, and Angela Standhartinger. NovTSup 74. Leiden: Brill, 1994.

———. "The Anatomy of a Discourse: On 'Eschatology' as a Category for Explaining Christian Origins." *MTSR* 8 (1996): 231–45.

———. "The *Gospel of Thomas* and Christian Origins." Pages 381–92 in *The Future of Early Christianity: Essays in Honor of Helmut Koester*. Edited by Birger A. Pearson, A. Thomas Kraabel, George W. E. Nickelsburg, and Norman R. Petersen. Minneapolis: Fortress, 1991.

———. "Mythmaking and Intertextuality in Early Christianity." Pages 37–50 in *Reimagining Christian Origins: A Colloquium Honoring Burton L. Mack*. Edited by Elizabeth A. Castelli and Hal Taussig. Valley Forge, Pa.: Trinity Press International, 1996.

———. "'What Have You Come Out to See?' Characterizations of John and Jesus in the Gospels." *Semeia* 49 (1990): 35–69.

Charlesworth, James H., ed. *The Messiah: Developments in Earliest Judaism and Christianity*. The First Princeton Symposium on Judaism and Christian Origins. Minneapolis: Fortress, 1992.

Charlesworth, James H., Hermann Lichtenberger, and Gerbern S. Oegema, eds. *Qumran-Messianism: Studies on the Messianic Expectations in the Dead Sea Scrolls*. Tübingen: Mohr Siebeck, 1998.

Dahl, Nils Alstrup. *Jesus the Christ: The Historical Origins of Christological Doctrine*. Edited by Donald H. Juel. Minneapolis: Fortress, 1991.
Davies, Philip R. *In Search of 'Ancient Israel'*. 2nd ed. JSOTSup 148. Sheffield: Sheffield Academic Press, 1995.
Frischer, Bernard. *The Sculpted Word: Epicureanism and Philosophical Recruitment in Ancient Greece*. Berkeley and Los Angeles: University of California Press, 1982.
Georgi, Dieter. *Remembering the Poor: The History of Paul's Collection for Jerusalem*. Nashville: Abingdon, 1992.
Goodman, Martin. *Mission and Conversion: Proselytizing in the Religious History of the Roman Empire*. Oxford: Clarendon, 1994.
Grabbe, Lester L., ed. *Can A 'History of Israel' Be Written?* JSOTSup 245. Sheffield: Sheffield Academic Press, 1997.
Juel, Donald. *Messianic Exegesis: Christological Interpretation of the Old Testament in Early Christianity*. Philadelphia: Fortress, 1988.
Karrer, Martin. *Der Gesalbte: Die Grundlagen des Christustitels*. FRLANT 151. Göttingen: Vandenhoeck & Ruprecht, 1991.
Kaster, Robert A. *Guardians of Language: The Grammarian and Society in Late Antiquity*. The Transformation of the Classical Heritage 11. Berkeley and Los Angeles: University of California Press, 1988.
Kloppenborg, John S. "Critical Histories and Theories of Religion: A Response to Burton Mack and Ron Cameron." *MTSR* 8 (1996): 279–89.
―――. "'Easter Faith' and the Sayings Gospel Q." *Semeia* 49 (1990): 71–99.
―――. *The Formation of Q: Trajectories in Ancient Wisdom Collections*. SAC. Philadelphia: Fortress, 1987. Repr., Harrisburg, Pa.: Trinity Press International, 1999.
―――. "Literary Convention, Self-Evidence and the Social History of the Q People." *Semeia* 55 (1991): 77–102.
Kloppenborg, John S., and Stephen G. Wilson, eds. *Voluntary Associations in the Graeco-Roman World*. London: Routledge, 1996.
Kloppenborg Verbin, John S. *Excavating Q: The History and Setting of the Sayings Gospel*. Edinburgh: T&T Clark, 2000.
Kramer, Werner. *Christ, Lord, Son of God*. Translated by Brian Hardy. SBT 50. Naperville, Ill.: Allenson, 1966.
Kutsch, Ernst. *Salbung als Rechtsakt im Alten Testament und im alten Orient*. BZAW 87. Berlin: Töpelmann, 1963.
Lightstone, Jack N. *The Commerce of the Sacred: Mediation of the Divine among Jews in the Graeco-Roman Diaspora*. BJS 59. Chico, Calif.: Scholars Press, 1984.
―――. "Whence the Rabbis? From Coherent Description to Fragmented Reconstructions." *SR* 26 (1997): 275–95.
Linton, Olof. "The Third Aspect: A Neglected Point of View. A Study in Gal. i–ii and Acts ix and xv." *ST* 3 (1949): 79–95.

Lüdemann, Gerd. *Early Christianity according to the Traditions in Acts: A Commentary*. Translated by John Bowden. Minneapolis: Fortress, 1989.

———. *The Resurrection of Jesus: History, Experience, Theology*. Translated by John Bowden. Minneapolis: Fortress, 1994.

Mack, Burton L. *The Christian Myth: Origins, Logic, and Legacy*. New York: Continuum, 2001.

———. *The Lost Gospel: The Book of Q and Christian Origins*. San Francisco: HarperSanFrancisco, 1993.

———. *A Myth of Innocence: Mark and Christian Origins*. Philadelphia: Fortress, 1988.

———. "On Redescribing Christian Origins." *MTSR* 8 (1996): 247–69.

———. "Q and the Gospel of Mark: Revising Christian Origins." *Semeia* 55 (1991): 15–39.

———. "A Radically Social Theory of Religion." Pages 123–36 in *Secular Theories on Religion: Current Perspectives*. Edited by Tim Jensen and Mikael Rothstein. Copenhagen: Museum Tusculanum Press, 2000.

———. *Rhetoric and the New Testament*. GBS. Minneapolis: Fortress, 1990.

———. "Social Formation." Pages 283–96 in *Guide to the Study of Religion*. Edited by Willi Braun and Russell T. McCutcheon. London: Cassell, 2000.

———. *Who Wrote the New Testament? The Making of the Christian Myth*. San Francisco: HarperSanFrancisco, 1995.

———. *Wisdom and the Hebrew Epic: Ben Sira's Hymn in Praise of the Fathers*. CSHJ. Chicago: University of Chicago Press, 1985.

Maier, Johann. "Messias oder Gesalbter? Zu einem Übersetzungs- und Deutungsproblem in den Qumrantexten." *RevQ* 17 (1996): 585–612.

Martyn, J. Louis. *Galatians*. AB 33A. New York: Doubleday, 1997.

Miller, Merrill P. "'Beginning from Jerusalem...': Re-examining Canon and Consensus." *Journal of Higher Criticism* 2/1 (1995): 3–30.

———. "How Jesus Became Christ: Probing a Thesis." *Cont* 2/2–3 (1993): 243–70.

Neusner, Jacob, William Scott Green, and Ernest S. Frerichs, eds. *Judaisms and Their Messiahs at the Turn of the Christian Era*. Cambridge: Cambridge University Press, 1987.

Oegema, Gerbern S. *The Anointed and His People: Messianic Expectations from the Maccabees to Bar Kochba*. JSPSup 27. Sheffield: Sheffield Academic Press, 1998.

Seeley, David. *The Noble Death: Graeco-Roman Martyrology and Paul's Concept of Salvation*. JSNTSup 28. Sheffield: Sheffield Academic Press, 1990.

Smith, Jonathan Z. "Bible and Religion." *BCSSR* 29/4 (2000): 87–93.

———. *Drudgery Divine: On the Comparison of Early Christianities and the Religions of Late Antiquity*. Jordan Lectures in Comparative Religion

14. London: School of Oriental and African Studies, University of London; Chicago: University of Chicago Press, 1990.

———. "The 'End' of Comparison: Redescription and Rectification." Pages 237–41 in *A Magic Still Dwells: Comparative Religion in the Postmodern Age*. Edited by Kimberley C. Patton and Benjamin C. Ray. Berkeley and Los Angeles: University of California Press, 2000.

———. "Here, There, and Anywhere." Pages 21–36 in *Prayer, Magic, and the Stars in the Ancient and Late Antique World*. Edited by Scott Noegel, Joel Walker, and Brannon Wheeler. Magic in History Series. University Park: Pennsylvania State University Press, 2003.

———. *Imagining Religion: From Babylon to Jonestown*. CSHJ. Chicago: University of Chicago Press, 1982.

———. *Map Is Not Territory: Studies in the History of Religions*. SJLA 23. Leiden: Brill, 1978. Repr., Chicago: University of Chicago Press, 1993.

———. "Native Cults in the Hellenistic Period." *HR* 11 (1971): 236–49.

———. "Religion, Religions, Religious." Pages 269–84 in *Critical Terms for Religious Studies*. Edited by Mark C. Taylor. Chicago: University of Chicago Press, 1998.

———. "Social Formations of Early Christianities: A Response to Ron Cameron and Burton Mack." *MTSR* 8 (1996): 271–78.

———. *To Take Place: Toward Theory in Ritual*. CSHJ. Chicago: University of Chicago Press, 1987.

Taylor, Nicholas. *Paul, Antioch and Jerusalem: A Study in Relationships and Authority in Earliest Christianity*. JSNTSup 66. Sheffield: JSOT Press, 1992.

Vaage, Leif E. *Galilean Upstarts: Jesus' First Followers according to Q*. Valley Forge, Pa.: Trinity Press International, 1994.

Weisman, Z. "Anointing as a Motif in the Making of the Charismatic King." *Bib* 57 (1976): 378–98.

Index of Ancient Texts

Hebrew Bible

Genesis
10	172
21:10	216
28:18	410
31:13	410
35:14	410
49:10	356, 379, 381, 382

Exodus
28:41	391, 398
29:28	410
29:36	393
30:22–33	393, 397
30:30	391, 398
40:9–15	393
40:13–15	397
40:15	391, 398

Leviticus
4:3, 5, 16	391, 397
6:15	391, 397
6:15 (22)	398
8:10–12	393
21:10	398

Numbers
3:3	391, 397, 398
7:1	393
7:10	393
7:84	393
7:88	393
21:18	380
24:17	356, 380, 397
35:25	391, 398

Deuteronomy
5:8	119
17	377
21:22–23	170
30:12–14	119
32:1	396

1 Samuel
2:10	356, 394
2:35	394
12:3	394
12:5	394
16:6	394
24:6	410–11
24:7	394
24:11	394
26:9	394
26:11	394, 411
26:16	394
26:23	394

2 Samuel
1:14	394
1:16	394
7	333
7:12–14	322
7:12–16	356
19:22	394
22:51	394
23:1	394

1 Kings
17:17–24	320

2 Kings
4:18–37	320
5:1–27	320

1 Chronicles
16:22	395
29:22	397

2 Chronicles
6:42	394

Psalms
1:1	402
2	356, 403, 404, 405
2:1	402
2:1–2	403

Index of Ancient Texts

Psalms (*cont.*)
2:2	394
2:7	333, 334
18:51	394
20:7	394
22	322, 323
28:8	394, 397
31	322, 323
69	322, 323
84:10	394, 397
89	323
89:38–51	323
89:39	394
89:39–52	397
89:40	397
89:45	397
89:52	394
105:15	395, 397
110	166, 167, 308, 322, 332, 334, 404
110:1	308, 320, 322, 334, 337
132	404
132:10	394
132:17	394
146:6–9	396

Proverbs
9:1	96

Isaiah
1:2	396
8:23–9:6	356
11	404
11:1	401
11:1ff.	356
11:1–4	377
11:1–5	402
11:10	334
29:18–19	320
35:5	320
42:6	405
42:6–7	320
45:1	390, 394
49:6	405
53	328, 360
53:4, 5, 12	232, 331
54:1	216, 218
59:20–21	388
61:1	337
61:1–2	75, 320, 396
61:1–5	390
61:2	396

Jeremiah
1:5	225
23:5	402
33:15	402
33:17	381
33:19–26	378

Lamentations
4:20	394, 400

Ezekiel
21:30–32	378
21:32	379
22:22	381
38:10–12	172

Daniel
7	322, 332, 404, 405
7:13	405
7:14	356
9:25	382, 396, 400
9:25–26	400
9:26	393, 400

Hosea
6:2	232, 331

Joel
2:28–32	167
2:32	166, 167

Amos
5:27	380
9:11	380, 402
9:11–12	356

Micah
5:1ff.	356
5:2 (3)	382

Habakkuk
3:13	394, 397

Zechariah
4:14	378, 386, 400
9:9–10	356

Index of Ancient Texts

JEWISH APOCRYPHA AND PSEUDEPIGRAPHA

Assumption of Moses
10.1–10 — 357

Baruch
2:34–35 — 357
3:24 — 96
3:29–30 — 119
4:36–37 — 357
5:5–6 — 357

2 Baruch
29.3 — 319
29.3–30.5 — 407
30.1 — 319
39.7–40.3 — 407
40.1 — 402
70.2–72.6 — 407
72.2 — 319

1 Enoch
26.1 — 172
37–71 — 403, 404
48.4 — 405
48.8 — 403
48.10 — 356, 395, 403
51.3 — 404
52.4 — 356, 395, 403
53.6 — 403
55.1–4 — 405
55.4 — 404
61.8 — 404
62.2 — 404
70–71 — 404
90.9ff. — 356
90.37–38 — 356

4 Ezra
7.26–30 — 407
11.37–12.34 — 407
12.31–33 — 402
12.32 — 319
13.3–14.9 — 407

Jubilees
8–10 — 172
23 — 357

Liber antiquitatum biblicarum
51.6 — 382
59.2 — 394

1 Maccabees
4:46 — 382
10:20 — 378
14:4–15 — 357, 382
14:41 — 382, 396

2 Maccabees
1:10 — 398

Psalms of Solomon
11.1–3, 7 — 172
17 — 319, 401
17–18 — 356, 406
17.21 — 333
17.23–24 — 356
17.30 — 356
17.32 — 314, 394, 400, 401, 402
17.34 — 402
18 — 394–95
18.5 — 394–95, 400
18.7 — 394, 400

Sibylline Oracles
3.49–50 — 356
3.286–87 — 356
3.545–49 — 194
3.601–7 — 194
3.652–53 — 356
5.68 — 397
5.249–50 — 172

Sirach
14:24 — 96
26:1 — 81, 82
45:12 — 378
45:15 — 397
51:23 — 96
51:26–27 — 115

Testament of Judah
21 — 398
21.1–2 — 378
24 — 356, 402
24.4, 6 — 402

Testament of Levi
18 — 356, 398

Testament of Reuben
6.8 — 382, 398

Tobit
13:11–17 — 357

Tobit (*cont.*)
13:14	81
14:4–7	357

Wisdom of Solomon
13–15	194

QUMRAN LITERATURE

1Q30
1.2	395

4Q161
8–10 iii, 18–25	377

4Q174
1.11	380
1.11–13	402
1.19	402
3.10–13	356
3.11–13	356
3.18–19	356

4Q246
2.4	382

4Q252
1 v, 1–5	356
6 v, 1–6	381–82

4Q270
2 ii, 13–14	395

4Q285
7.3–4	401

4Q375
1 i, 9	399

4Q377
2 ii, 4–5	390
2 ii, 5	395
2 ii, 11–12	390

4Q458
2 ii, 6	406

4Q521
1 ii, 1	395, 408
2 ii, 1	356, 396
8.9	396
9.3	396

6Q15
3.4	380

11Q13
2.14–25	356
2.18	396, 408
2.18–21	396

11Q19
LVI–LIX	377
LVIII, 18–21	377

Cairo Genizah copy of the *Damascus Document*
2.12	356
2.12 (A)	395
5.20–6.11 (A)	380
5.21–6.1 (A)	395
7.18–19 (A)	380
7.19–21	356
12.23	356
12.23–13.1 (A)	380–81
14.18–19	356
19.7–11 (B)	381
19.10–11	356
19.33–20.1 (B)	381
20.1	356

Milḥamah
7.15–9.9	377
11.6–9	397
11.7–8	395
15.4–6	377
16.13	377
18.5	377
19.11	377

Rule of the Blessings
3.22–4.28	398

Rule of the Congregation
2.11–12	356, 399
2.11–21	377
2.11–22	399
2.14	399
2.19–20	399
2.20	399

Serek Hayaḥad
9.9–11	356
9.10–11	379
9.11	379, 396

Index of Ancient Texts

NEW TESTAMENT

Sayings Gospel Q	18, 19, 20, 33, 34–37, 43–65, 67–87, 100, 133–35, 137–38, 501–2	12:2–7	67
		12:5	67
		12:8–10	67
3:7–9	51, 55, 67	12:10–12	53
3:16–17	51, 55, 67	12:11–12	67
4:1–13	67	12:13–14	71
6:20–49	51	12:21b–31	67
6:20b	76, 79	12:33–34	67
6:20b–23b	67, 75	12:34	65
6:21	78	12:39–40	67
6:21–23	80	12:42–46	67
6:22	77	12:49	67
6:22–23	67, 71, 78	12:51–53	67
6:23	77, 78	12:54–56	67
6:23c	67, 75, 76, 77	12:56	116
6:27–36	78	12:57–59	67
6:27–49	67	13:24	67
6:43–44	121	13:25–30	67
6:43–45	114	13:34–35	67
6:46–49	71	13:35	96
7:1–10	67	14:16–24	67
7:18–23	67	14:26–27	67, 71, 101–2
7:22	396	14:34–35	67
7:24–28	67	15:4–5	106
7:31–35	67	15:7	106
9:57–60	65	16:16	67
9:57–62	67, 75, 79	16:17	67
10:2–11	67, 75	16:18	67
10:3	71	17:23	67
10:12–15	67	17:24	67
10:16	67, 75	17:26–30	67
10:21–22	52, 67	17:33	67
10:21–24	67	17:34	128
10:23–24	112–13	17:34–35	67
10:24	112, 121	17:37b	67
11:2–4	67	19:12–27	67
11:9	111, 117	19:26	121
11:9–10	117	22:28–30	67
11:9–13	67	**Matthew**	
11:14–26	67	1:1	319
11:27–28	67	1:16	316
11:29–36	67	1:20	319
11:39–52	67	5:3–9	76
11:42c	67	5:11–12	76
11:52	121	8–9	320

Matthew (cont.)

9:27	319
9:27–28	320
10:2	316
10:5–6	218
10:6	96
10:16	121
11:2	310
11:2–6	320
11:8	96
11:19	346
11:28–30	115
12:23	319
15:13	121
15:22	319, 320
15:24	96
16:16	319
16:17	319, 389
16:19	319
16:20	357
18:18	319
19:28	357
20:30–31	319
20:31	320
21:9	319, 320
21:14	320
21:15	319
22:41–46	319
23:10	310, 320, 357
27:17, 22	316
28:5–10	238
28:16–20	238
28:18–20	319

Mark

1:1	310
3:16	341
3:17	341
4:38	101
6:30–44	360
8:1–10	360
8:27–30	305
8:29	310, 351, 357
8:30	321
8:31–9:1	102
8:34	102
9:37	310
9:38–40	195
9:41	310, 357
10:46–47	357
10:46–52	357
10:47–48	319, 322
11:10	357
12:1–8	90
12:35	310
12:35–37	305, 319, 322
12:36	308
13	407
13:21	119, 406
13:21–22	305, 407
13:22	406
14	360
14–15	323
14:22–25	360
14:51	357
14:58	93
14:61	316, 351, 357
14:61–62	305, 322, 332
14:62	308
15	322, 323
15:26	357
15:32	351, 357
15:34	97
16:6–8	238

Luke

1:27	96
1:32–34	333
1:69	96, 333
2:11	314, 400, 401
2:26	302, 314, 316
4:16–19	306
4:16–30	169, 250
4:41	310, 314, 357
6:20	220
6:20–21	76
6:22	76
7:35	346
9:20	302, 314, 316
17:21	118, 119
20:1	160
21:37–38	160
22:67	314, 353
23:35	314, 316
23:39	314
24:13–35	358

Luke (cont.)		1–14	239
24:26	314, 330, 357	1:1–11	240
24:34	229, 279, 328	1:1–14	164–65
24:36–53	240	1:1–8:3	164
24:46	314	1:8	173, 250
24:47	167, 250	1:13–14	165
John		1:15–26	165–66
1:17	317	1:20–26	166
1:20	317	1:21	202
1:41	317	1:22	328
2:16	96	2	160, 167, 308
2:19	93	2:1–4	166, 250
2:21	94	2:1–13	166
2:22	94	2:1–42	241
2:23–25	95	2:14–41	161
3:28	317	2:14–47	166–68
4:25	317	2:21	167
4:29	317	2:30	333
4:48	95	2:31	351
6:1–14	360	2:32	229, 328
7:26	317	2:36	311, 314, 351
7:27	317	2:38	314
7:31	310, 317	2:40	161
7:41–42	317	2:41	161
7:42	333	2:42–47	160, 167, 168
9:22	310, 317	3:1–10	168
10:24	317	3:1–26	168
11:25–27	317	3:1–4:31	168, 169
11:27	310	3:6	314, 315
12:34	317	3:14–15	229
12:42–43	317	3:15	328, 330
14:5	113, 127	3:18	302, 314, 316, 351
16:5	116	3:19–21	168
16:12–15	111–12, 116	3:20	302, 314, 351, 406
16:25–28	111–12, 116	3:20–21	311
17:3	310, 317	4	167
20:11–29	240	4:1–31	168–69
20:24	316, 341	4:4	162
20:24–29	93, 94	4:10	314, 330
20:29	95	4:26	314, 351
20:31	317	4:32–35	160, 167
21	238, 240	4:32–37	169
21:2	316	4:32–5:11	168
Acts		4:33	328
1	165	4:36	341
1–5	164	5	167
1–8	163	5:1–11	169–70

Acts (cont.)

Reference	Pages
5:12–16	160, 167, 170
5:17–42	170
5:30–32	229, 330
5:32	328
5:42	314, 351
6–7	171
6:1–6	170
6:1–7	170
6:5	174
6:8–15	171–72
6:8–7:1	170
7:1–53	172
7:4	173
7:54–8:3	172
7:58	174
8:1	173
8:3	174
8:4	174
8:4–25	174
8:5	314, 351
8:5–13	174
8:12	314
8:14–15	243
8:14–25	174
8:26	250
8:26–39	174
8:40	174
9	198
9:1–30	174
9:4–5	250
9:17–19	200
9:19	200
9:22	314, 351
9:23–25	200
9:26–28	200
9:34	314
10:3	250
10:9–23	250
10:36	314, 319
10:38	306, 318
10:39–41	229
10:40–41	330
10:41	328
10:42	319
10:44	250
11	198
11:1–18	174, 243
11:2	198, 210
11:2–3	198
11:17	314
11:22–24	174
11:26	347
13:2	250
13:23	333
13:29–31	229
13:30–31	330
13:31	229, 328
15	149, 190, 196, 197, 198, 246
15:1	198, 209, 210
15:1–33	243
15:5	198, 201, 210
15:6–21	201
15:22–23	201
15:24	198, 201
15:26	314
16:4	201
16:9	250
16:18	314
17:3	302, 314, 330
18:5	302, 314
18:22	223
18:28	302
20:4	226
21:8	174
21:9	166
21:20	162
26:19	196
26:23	302, 314, 318
28:31	314

Romans

Reference	Pages
1:1–2	302
1:2–3	388
1:2–4	303, 308
1:3–4	331, 332, 333
1:4	310
1:8	187
2:5	388
2:15–16	388
2:26–27	196
3:25	177, 363
3:25–26	362, 363, 371
3:30	196
4:9	196

Romans (cont.)		5:1–13	169
4:25	177	8:1–5	225
5:6	308, 357	8:11	308
5:8	308, 357	9:1	230, 231
8:3	177	9:1–2	225
8:17	330	9:2	229
8:34	308–9, 330, 334	9:4–6	212
9–11	227, 249, 303, 315	9:19–23	201
9:5	302, 303, 338	9:20	150, 205–6, 247
10	119	10–11	360
10:6–8	119	10:1–11	303
10:13	167	10:4	302, 338
11	224	11:23–25	294, 359, 360, 362
11:13–14	150, 196	11:23–26	360, 361, 362
11:18	227	15	223, 227, 228, 229, 230, 233, 234, 245, 328, 352, 388, 494
11:26–27	388		
12:12–13	167	15:1ff.	191
14:9	309, 330	15:1–8	245
14:15	308	15:1–11	230
15	226, 227, 228	15:3	177, 310, 311, 312, 328, 363
15:8	196, 302	15:3ff.	279, 357
15:8–9	224	15:3–5a	103
15:8–12	227	15:3–5	229, 294, 308, 331, 361
15:9–12	315	15:3–7	312, 360
15:12	334	15:3b–4	228, 229, 232, 233, 312, 328, 331
15:18–21	227		
15:19	217, 315	15:3b–11	227, 228
15:22–24	225	15:5	228, 229, 328
15:24–26	217	15:5–7	228, 229, 231, 234
15:25–27	249	15:5–8	147
15:25–28	238	15:5b–8	103
15:26	220, 223, 225, 238, 247	15:6	166, 234
15:26–27	187, 227	15:7	101, 165, 230, 328
15:27	150, 178, 218, 224, 227	15:8	228, 240, 245
15:28–29	225	15:11	150, 178, 191, 228, 329
15:30–31	217, 225	15:22	302
1 Corinthians		15:23	388
1:2	167, 187	15:23–28	303
1:8	388	15:25	334
1:12	310	16	149
1:12–13	326	16:1	222
1:13	308	16:3–4	217, 226
1:23	302	**2 Corinthians**	
2:8	330	1:14	388
3:23	310	1:21	326
4:14	249	3:18	230
4:17	249	5:1	96

2 Corinthians (cont.)
- 5:10 — 302
- 5:14–15 — 308
- 5:15 — 308, 329
- 6:13 — 249
- 8–9 — 226
- 8:1–15 — 186
- 9:1–5 — 186
- 9:12–14 — 224
- 10:7 — 310
- 10:12–18 — 226
- 11:2–3 — 302
- 11:6 — 46
- 11:9 — 186
- 11:24 — 150, 206
- 11:32–33 — 200
- 12:1 — 230
- 12:2–4 — 240
- 12:2–7 — 147
- 12:14–15 — 249

Galatians
- 1–2 — 145, 153, 179, 181, 198, 199, 203, 204, 207, 218, 227, 253, 278, 329, 494
- 1:4 — 177
- 1:6–9 — 198
- 1:10 — 201
- 1:11 — 204
- 1:11–12 — 199
- 1:11–24 — 214
- 1:11–2:6 — 199
- 1:11–2:14 — 189
- 1:12 — 147, 199, 200, 204, 243
- 1:13 — 174
- 1:13–24 — 204
- 1:15 — 225
- 1:15–16 — 240
- 1:16 — 147, 199, 227, 229, 230, 245
- 1:16–17 — 148, 199
- 1:16–18 — 243
- 1:17 — 166, 217, 229, 238, 244
- 1:17–18 — 243
- 1:17–24 — 200
- 1:18 — 217, 238, 242, 244
- 1:18–19 — 256
- 1:19 — 148, 199, 244
- 1:21 — 209
- 1:21–22 — 244
- 1:22 — 148, 199, 244
- 1:24 — 245
- 2 — 190, 192, 196, 197, 242, 450
- 2:1 — 149, 243
- 2:1–2 — 217
- 2:1–10 — 156, 178, 204, 238, 245, 257, 278
- 2:2 — 148–49, 214, 215
- 2:3 — 199, 247
- 2:3–5 — 198
- 2:4 — 198, 247
- 2:4–5 — 209
- 2:5 — 199, 201
- 2:6 — 149, 199, 208, 215, 227, 232, 243
- 2:7 — 205, 212
- 2:7–8 — 149, 205
- 2:7–9 — 196, 205, 207, 232
- 2:8 — 247
- 2:9 — 197, 205, 206, 208, 215, 221, 233, 246
- 2:9–10 — 149, 243
- 2:10 — 218, 219, 220, 221, 222, 224
- 2:11–14 — 149, 150, 201, 209, 238
- 2:11–21 — 204
- 2:12 — 198, 209
- 2:14 — 201, 210
- 2:16 — 247
- 2:19–20 — 330
- 2:21 — 308
- 3–4 — 204
- 3:1 — 221
- 3:4 — 214
- 3:8 — 215
- 3:13 — 308
- 3:15 — 215
- 3:16 — 182, 215, 302
- 3:17 — 215
- 3:24 — 388
- 3:26–29 — 216
- 3:28 — 221
- 3:29 — 215
- 4 — 216
- 4:4 — 388
- 4:4–6 — 216
- 4:5 — 182
- 4:11 — 214

Index of Ancient Texts

Galatians (*cont.*)
4:17	198
4:19	218, 249
4:21–26	218
4:21–5:1	216, 249
4:24	217
4:25	218
4:25–26	203, 216, 249
4:26	213
4:27	216
4:29	217
4:30	216
5:2	214, 218
5:10	198
5:11	150, 201
5:12	196, 198
6:12	198
6:12–13	210
6:13	150

Ephesians
2:11	196
2:11–3:21	195

Philippians
1:10	307, 388
1:15	302
1:17	302
2	308, 332
2:11	310
2:16	307, 388
3:2	196
3:3	196
3:7	302
3:20	218, 388
4:14–16	186

Colossians
3:11	196
4:11	316

1 Thessalonians
1:10	388
2:4	201
2:7	249
2:11	249
2:14–16	330
4:14	309, 329, 330
5:9–10	308

1 Timothy
3:16	229, 332

2 Timothy
2:8	333

Philemon
18–19	249

Hebrews
1	122
11:26	323

1 Peter
3:18–19	332
3:22	332
4:14	323

1 John
2:22	303
5:1	303

Revelation
22:16	333

Early Christian Literature

Apocryphon of James
2.7–39	101

Cologne Mani Codex
92.15	96

Didache
9–10	360

Eusebius, *Historia ecclesiastica*
1.12.4–5	101
2.1.2–5	101

Exegesis of the Soul
128.36; 129.5; 132.21; 137.11	96

Gospel of the Hebrews
frg. 7	101

Gospel of Thomas   18, 19, 20, 33, 37–41, 43, 61, 89–108, 109–32, 135–38, 501–2
prologue	105, 118
1	105, 118, 119
2	39–40, 105–6, 111, 115, 117–18, 119, 120, 125, 126
3	96, 118–20, 125, 126
5	100, 106

Gospel of Thomas (cont.)

6	96	60	61
8	107	61	128–29
11	129	65	90
12	101, 122, 124	68	77
12–13	40–41, 122	69	77, 106
13	115, 122, 123, 124, 125, 126	71	93–94, 95–96
16	96, 129	76	107
18	125, 126	80	61, 117
18–19	126	86	114
19	126	88	122, 125
21	128	89	96
22	124, 129	90	115, 116
23	129	91	96, 116
24	113, 126, 127	91–94	116
25	113, 127	92	106, 111, 112, 116, 117
26	127	93	116
28	114	94	106, 111, 116, 117
37	127	96	107
38	111, 112, 113, 120, 121	97	127
38–43	120–21, 127	98	107
39	96, 120, 121	101	102
40	121	102	96, 121
41	121	106	129
42	61, 114, 121	107	106–7
42–43	113	108	110, 123
43	96, 114, 121, 122	111	116–17
46	125	113	96, 127, 128
48	96, 129	114	96, 128–29
49	124–25	**Gospel of Truth**	
50	124–25	25.23	96
51	127	**Irenaeus, *Adversus haereses***	
52	96	1.18.1	480
53	96	**Oxyrhynchus papyri**	
55	101	654.5–9	105, 117
56	61	654.9–21	118
58	106, 115, 123	654.31	100
59	115	**Shepherd of Hermas, *Similitudes***	
		9.14.1	96

RABBINIC LITERATURE

Mishnah *Soṭah*
9:9–15   406

Midrash *Genesis Rabbah*
49:10   400

Targum *Neofiti*
Gen 49:10   400

Jerusalem Talmud *Taʿanit*
4.5 (68d)   390–91, 400

Greek and Latin Texts

Apuleius, *Metamorphoses*
11.5	467
11.22	480

Aristophanes, *Plutus*
535–54	75–76

Aristotle, *De memoria et reminiscentia*
451b19–20	11

Aristotle, *Poetica*
9	268

Crates, *Epistula*
21	53

Diogenes Laertius
1.22	344
1.39	344
1.40	120
1.81	345
1.114	343
2.6	342
2.16	343
2.19	343
2.52	344
2.57	344
2.62	342
2.63	342
2.66	343
2.83	343
2.86	343, 344
2.100	344
2.102	344
2.109	342
2.111	343
2.112	343
2.116	344
2.117	343
2.140	344
3.4	344
3.43	348
4.23	343
4.52	344
5.2	343
5.35	342
5.38	344
5.58, 61	344
5.66	344
5.92	343, 344
6.11	53
6.13	342
6.19	342
6.33	343, 345
6.40	343
6.46	343
6.55	343, 345
6.60	343, 345
6.61	343, 345
6.76	344
6.77	343
6.84	344
6.86	343
6.93	343
6.97	344
6.99	344
6.100	344
7.23	343
7.32	342
7.37	343
7.166	343
7.168	343
7.170	343
7.182	343
8.6	344
8.12	343
8.21	344
8.52	343
8.60	343
8.65	342
8.91	344
9.15	344
9.25	344
9.50	343
10.3	343
10.25	343

Epictetus, *Dissertationes*
2.2.20	101
3.22.26	123
3.22.38	122

Herodotus
1.1; 7.96	264

Josephus, *Jewish Antiquities*
4.8.17	377

Josephus, *Jewish Antiquities* (cont.)
    14.3.2 — 378
    15.11.1 — 357
    20.9.1 — 356

Josephus, *Jewish War*
    5.13.6 — 393
    6.5.2 — 96
    6.5.2–4 — 406
    7.3.3 — 183

Libanius, *Orationes*
    1.12 — 115

Philo, *In Flaccum*
    46 — 183

Philo, *Legatio ad Gaium*
    276–329 — 182
    278 — 378
    281 — 182

Philo, *De praemiis et poenis*
    95 — 356

Plato, *Phaedo*
    73D–74A — 11

Plutarch, *Conjugalia Praecepta*
    145–46 — 123

Quintilian, *Institutio oratoria*
    1.4.2 — 115

Thessalos
    1.proem.22 — 60

Vita Eutychii
    8 — 52

Select Index of Modern Authors

Alexander, Philip S. 379
Arnal, William E. 36–37, 61, 62, 130, 134, 135, 137, 145–46, 505, 514, 516
Ascough, Richard S. 184–87
Aune, D. E. 303–4
Baird, William 350
Barclay, John M. G. 200, 203
Barrett, C. K. 241–42
Bartchy, S. Scott 167–68
Becker, Michael 396
Berlin, Isaiah 14
Betori, Giuseppe 167
Bloch, Marc 264–65
Borgen, Peder 172
Borges, Jorge Luis 15
Bousset, Wilhelm 351–54
Braun, Willi 34–35, 135, 137, 439–40, 446, 448–52, 462–63, 475, 505, 514, 516
Brown, Peter 45
Bultmann, Rudolf 76, 101, 337–38, 349, 354–55, 419, 511
Cameron, Ron 5–6, 37–39, 509
Carr, Edward Hallett 265, 268
Carruth, Shawn 80
Chance, J. Bradley 173
Charlesworth, James H. 301–2, 404–5
Chester, Andrew 324–25
Chilton, Bruce 322
Conzelmann, Hans 169, 270, 279
Crawford, Barry S. 294
Cross, Frank Moore 3–4
Crossan, John Dominic 75–76, 242, 247
Dahl, Nils Alstrup 301–4, 306, 308, 310–12, 390
Davies, Philip R. 3–4
de Jonge, Marinus 316, 401–2
Dewey, Arthur J. 39–41, 137, 438
Duling, Dennis C. 319–20, 333

Emerton, J. A. 411
Finley, M. I. 265
Fitzmyer, Joseph A. 241, 407–8
Foakes Jackson, F. J. 159
Foucault, Michel 267–68
Frischer, Bernard 60
Gaston, Lloyd 177–78
Geertz, Clifford 45
Georgi, Dieter 5–6, 218–21, 223–24, 226–27
Giddens, Anthony 62
Goodman, Martin 193–96
Gottschalk, Louis 268
Gould, Stephen Jay 500
Green, William Scott 346–47
Haenchen, Ernst 165–66, 168, 171
Hahn, Ferdinand 307, 332
Hann, Robert R. 401
Hartog, François 266
Harvey, A. E. 315–16
Heitmüller, Wilhelm 191
Hengel, Martin 312–13, 316, 322, 349, 390
Herzfeld, Michael 486
Hicks, R. D. 343
Hill, Craig C. 170–71
Hobsbawm, Eric 148
Holmberg, Bengt 188
Hopkins, Keith 162
Horbury, William 376
Jewett, Robert 332
Johnson, Luke Timothy 98–99
Judge, E. A. 46–47
Juel, Donald 302, 312, 318, 322–24
Kant, Immanuel 475
Karrer, Martin 392–94
Kaster, Robert A. 52, 57–59
Kautsky, Karl 47

535

Select Index of Modern Authors

Kelber, Werner H. 109
Kimelman, Reuven 403
Kloppenborg, John S. 6, 49–50, 57, 62, 75, 100–102, 105–6, 320
Koester, Helmut 104, 359–61
Kramer, Werner 338, 353, 363
Kuhn, Thomas S. 455
Lake, Kirsopp 159
La Piana, George 185
Le Goff, Jacques 269
Leipoldt, Johannes 97–98
Lévi-Strauss, Claude 15, 18
Lightstone, Jack N. 63–65, 182–84
Lincoln, Bruce 54–55, 62
Linton, Olof 198–202
Lodge, David 89
Lohse, Eduard 228
Long, Herbert S. 342
Lüdemann, Gerd 151, 163–72, 208, 228, 230–31
Lust, Johan 378–79
Lyons, George 200
McCutcheon, Russell T. 136
Mack, Burton L. 2–3, 5–9, 12–13, 17, 21, 22–23, 26–28, 29, 43, 63, 68–72, 78, 92, 100, 101, 103, 106, 144, 146–48, 149, 155–57, 159, 172, 215–16, 272, 276–78, 282, 285, 290, 298–99, 361–63, 379, 418–19, 434, 436, 438, 439, 448, 449, 450, 451–52, 483–84, 497–98, 500–502, 504–9, 512, 514, 516
MacRae, George 302, 306, 309, 319
Maier, Johann 398, 401
Malina, Bruce 63
Mann, Michael 54
Martin, Luther H. 148, 157–58, 181–82, 187, 275, 281, 481
Martyn, J. Louis 214–17, 221, 223, 246
Matthews, Christopher R. 145, 151–52, 160, 275
Meeks, Wayne A. 183
Merz, Annette 355–59
Miller, Merrill P. 91–92, 99, 141–45, 152–55, 163, 243, 269–71, 276, 279, 281, 295, 297–98, 340, 478, 508–9
Oegema, Gerbern S. 375–76, 382, 391–92
Ong, Walter J. 111, 114
Quispel, Gilles 90–91
Rancière, Jacques 109, 120, 124
Reinhardt, Wolfgang 161
Rieppel, Olivier 485
Riley, Gregory J. 93–95, 97, 103
Roberts, Michael 486
Robinson, James M. 504
Rotenstreich, Nathan 267
Sahlins, Marshall 486
Said, Edward W. 99
Sanders, E. P. 142–43
Schubert, Paul 269
Schwartz, Daniel R. 173
Scott, Bernard Brandon 110
Segal, Alan 248
Seybold, K. 392
Shklovsky, Victor 19, 484–85, 502
Simmel, Georg 266
Smith, Dennis E. 155, 276
Smith, Jonathan Z. 6, 9–15, 18–19, 23–25, 26, 35, 59–60, 91, 92, 136, 152, 180, 393, 413, 444, 455–56, 484, 498–99, 501–2, 505–6, 509, 513–16
Stark, Rodney 161–62
Stock, Brian 481
Taylor, Nicholas 189–90, 196–97, 205–6
Theissen, Gerd 355–59
Thompson, E. P. 43, 62
Thompson, Thomas L. 409
Tuckett, Christopher M. 75
Vaage, Leif E. 57, 79
Valantasis, Richard 96
Valeri, Valerio 486
VanderKam, J. C. 404
Verseput, D. J. 204, 209
Vico, Giambattista 266
Walker-Ramisch, Sandra 185–87
Watson, Francis 224–26
Weisman, Z. 411–12
White, Hayden 263
Wilken, Robert L. 183
Williams, Sam K. 360, 363
Winden, Hans-Willi 231
Witherington, Ben 160–61
Wright, Erik Olin 44
Wright, R. B. 401

INDEX OF SUBJECTS

attraction 4, 5, 7, 18, 33–34, 81, 85, 100, 104, 108, 143, 147, 157, 183, 233–34, 256, 277, 290, 297, 299, 333, 368, 373, 389, 393, 424, 448, 453, 470, 472–74, 486, 499, 503, 506, 513
christos 286–91, 293–300, 301–3, 306–11, 313–18, 320–21, 324–28, 330–31, 334–35, 337–41, 346–48, 365–68, 371–73, 383–89, 392–94, 400–401, 406–9, 414–15, 417–19, 425, 429, 434–37, 447–54, 501, 506–10
comparison 5–14, 19, 22, 34, 37–39, 43, 57, 60–62, 73, 91, 107, 137, 152, 157, 178, 182, 219, 254, 267–68, 276–77, 280, 282, 291, 293, 295, 383, 387, 409, 411, 427, 437–38, 449–50, 453–56, 470–71, 483, 485, 498, 508–9
defamiliarization 19, 137, 444, 483–84, 502, 516
diaspora 145, 152–54, 156, 171–72, 180–83, 185, 187, 192, 194, 196, 198, 203, 213, 217–18, 233–35, 250, 257–58, 260–61, 276–78, 280–81, 299, 326, 367–68, 370–71, 373, 408, 417, 419, 449, 451, 474, 501, 506–7
dominant paradigm of Christian origins 2–5, 15–16, 18, 21–22, 33, 38–39, 92, 107–8, 138, 145, 147, 151, 155–56, 197, 253–55, 268, 277–78, 280–81, 293, 296, 418, 424–26, 444–45, 483, 498–503, 505–6, 508, 511, 513–16
epic 17, 20, 55, 71–72, 74, 227, 258, 262, 298–300, 314–15, 327, 335, 339, 367–68, 371, 372, 376, 407, 451, 474, 486, 501, 506, 509–10, 513

ethnicity 103, 149, 156, 180–81, 196, 198, 205–6, 211, 216, 257–58, 260, 299, 318, 326, 328, 367–68, 370, 372, 394, 409, 449, 474, 485, 501, 506, 509–10
ethnography 10, 157, 259, 287, 299, 409, 435–36, 452, 454, 501, 506–10
historiography 13, 17, 30, 36, 54, 60, 63–64, 99, 141, 145, 148, 152, 157–58, 174, 263–73, 281–82, 291, 409, 421, 439, 441, 445, 460, 472, 475–81, 499–500, 503, 505–6, 511, 515–16
homeland and diaspora 145, 152–54, 180–81, 185, 196, 203, 213, 217, 234–35, 261, 280, 367–68, 449, 474, 501, 506–7
interest. *See* social interest
locus. *See* social location
logic. *See* social logic
mythmaking 1, 4, 6–8, 18–22, 26, 29, 34, 36, 43–44, 47, 56, 62, 65, 72–74, 86, 103, 134–35, 145, 147–48, 151, 153–54, 158, 215, 245, 253, 255–56, 260, 262, 269–72, 275–76, 278, 280–82, 287, 289–90, 295, 318, 340, 362, 365, 367, 371–73, 384, 388, 417–18, 422–23, 426–29, 434–38, 440, 442, 443–45, 448, 451–55, 460–66, 470–74, 475–78, 486, 490, 492–94, 499, 502, 505–6, 508–16
problematization 30, 33, 37, 145, 155, 253, 277–81, 289–90, 373, 418–19, 425–26, 428, 430, 444, 470, 485, 500, 505, 513, 516
rectification of categories 6, 9, 12–13, 387, 441, 449, 454, 485–86, 506, 516

537

redescription 1–22, 29, 33–36, 44, 54, 60, 65, 86, 92, 100, 107, 136–38, 144, 147–48, 150, 153, 157, 177, 253, 273, 279–80, 282, 286, 290, 296–97, 339, 367, 373, 383, 386–87, 412, 417–19, 421, 423–25, 427, 429–30, 436, 443–45, 447–49, 451, 454–56, 460, 470–72, 475–78, 481, 484–86, 497–516

reflexivity 17, 20–21, 22, 444, 449, 452–53, 455, 499, 503–4, 512

social experimentation 7, 8, 17, 20–21, 26, 29, 56, 68, 70, 103, 148, 154, 181, 211, 235, 255, 258, 290, 295, 329, 339, 347, 362, 369–70, 373, 423–24, 426–28, 440–41, 449, 451–52, 470, 473–74, 499, 503–4, 512, 515

social formation 1, 4, 6–8, 13, 18–22, 26, 34–36, 43–44, 46–47, 54–56, 59–65, 69–74, 78, 84, 97, 103–4, 133–35, 137, 148, 154, 156–58, 179, 184, 188, 253–62, 266, 271–72, 277, 280–82, 287–88, 294, 296, 298–300, 318, 329–30, 340, 347, 361–62, 366–70, 372–73, 384, 388, 418, 422–23, 426–30, 435, 437–38, 440–42, 443, 445, 450, 452–53, 455, 460–66, 470–74, 475–77, 486, 490–94, 499, 502–7, 509–16

social interest 4, 17–18, 20, 22, 33, 37, 46–47, 62, 83, 85–86, 100, 104, 108, 136, 148, 152–57, 207, 210–11, 222, 232–35, 254–62, 267, 272–73, 276–78, 281–82, 288–89, 294, 298–99, 340, 365–66, 368–73, 414, 417–18, 422, 424, 426–27, 435, 437–40, 444, 447–52, 454–55, 462–63, 471–74, 476–77, 480, 493, 499, 503, 505–6, 509–10, 512–13

social location 18, 20, 22, 35, 56–57, 59, 133, 148, 183, 257–58, 280–81, 288–89, 298, 365–67, 373, 384–85, 387, 415, 417–18, 427, 435, 440–41, 444, 450–51, 455, 499, 503, 505, 513, 515

social logic 26, 39, 100, 107, 282, 286, 288, 362, 365–66, 372, 384, 417–18, 422–23, 425, 427–30, 435–37, 441, 444, 448, 452, 454, 499, 503, 505, 510, 512–14

translation 13–15, 19, 22, 38, 92, 259, 387, 423, 436, 444, 454, 483–84

Contributors

William E. Arnal
University of Regina
Regina, Saskatchewan

Willi Braun
University of Alberta
Edmonton, Alberta

Ron Cameron
Wesleyan University
Middletown, Connecticut

Barry S. Crawford
Washburn University
Topeka, Kansas

Arthur J. Dewey
Xavier University
Cincinnati, Ohio

Burton L. Mack
Claremont Graduate University
Claremont, California

Luther H. Martin
University of Vermont
Burlington, Vermont

Christopher R. Matthews
Weston Jesuit School of Theology
Cambridge, Massachusetts

Merrill P. Miller
University of North Carolina at Pembroke
Pembroke, North Carolina

Dennis E. Smith
Phillips Theological Seminary
Tulsa, Oklahoma

Jonathan Z. Smith
University of Chicago
Chicago, Illinois

Stanley K. Stowers
Brown University
Providence, Rhode Island

www.ingramcontent.com/pod-product-compliance
Lightning Source LLC
Chambersburg PA
CBHW021349290426

44108CB00010B/163